LE MANS
'THE PORSCHE YEARS'
1975-1982

Compiled
by
R.M.Clarke
with annual race summaries
by
Anders Ditlev Clausager

ISBN 1 85520 3871

 BROOKLANDS BOOKS LTD.
P.O. BOX 146, COBHAM,
SURREY, KT11 1LG. UK

A -LEMR75

Printed in Hong Kong

Brooklands Books

MOTORING

BROOKLANDS ROAD TEST SERIES

Abarth Gold Portfolio 1950-1971
AC Ace & Aceca 1953-1983
Alfa Romeo Giulietta Gold Portfolio 1954-1965
Alfa Romeo Giulia Coupés 1963-1976
Alfa Romeo Giulia Coupés Gold Port. 1963-1976
Alfa Romeo Spider 1966-1990
Alfa Romeo Spider Gold Portfolio 1966-1991
Alfa Romeo Alfasud 1972-1984
Alfa Romeo Alfetta Gold Portfolio 1972-1987
Alfa Romeo Alfetta GTV6 1980-1986
Allard Gold Portfolio 1937-1959
Alvis Gold Portfolio 1919-1967
AMX & Javelin Muscle Portfolio 1968-1974
Armstrong Siddeley Gold Portfolio 1945-1960
Aston Martin Gold Portfolio 1948-1971
Aston Martin Gold Portfolio 1972-1985
Aston Martin Gold Portfolio 1985-1995
Audi Quattro Gold Portfolio 1980-1991
Austin A30 & A35 1951-1962
Austin Healey 100 & 100/6 Gold Port. 1952-1959
Austin Healey 3000 Gold Portfolio 1959-1967
Austin Healey Sprite Gold Portfolio 1958-1971
Barracuda Muscle Portfolio 1964-1974
BMW 1600 Collection No.1 1966-1981
BMW 2002 Gold Portfolio 1968-1976
BMW 316, 318, 320 (4 cyl.) Gold Port. 1975-1990
BMW 320, 323, 325 (6 cyl.) Gold Port. 1977-1990
BMW M Series Performance Portfolio 1976-1993
BMW 5 Series Gold Portfolio 1981-1987
BMW 6 Series Gold Portfolio 1976-1989
Bricklin Gold Portfolio 1974-1975
Bristol Cars Gold Portfolio 1946-1992
Buick Automobiles 1947-1960
Buick Muscle Cars 1965-1970
Cadillac Allanté 1986-1993
Cadillac Automobiles 1949-1959
Cadillac Automobiles 1960-1969
Caprice 1965-1976 ☆ Limited Edition
Charger Muscle Portfolio 1966-1974
Checker ☆ Limited Edition
Chevrolet 1955-1957
Impala & SS Muscle Portfolio 1958-1972
Chevrolet Corvair 1959-1969
Chevy II & Nova SS Muscle Portfolio 1962-1974
Chevy El Camino & SS 1959-1987
Chevelle & SS Muscle Portfolio 1964-1972
Chevrolet Muscle Cars 1966-1971
Chevy Blazer 1969-1981
Chevrolet Corvette Gold Portfolio 1953-1962
Chevrolet Corvette Sting Ray Gold Port. 1963-1967
Chevrolet Corvette Gold Portfolio 1968-1977
High Performance Corvettes 1983-1989
Camaro Muscle Portfolio 1967-1973
Chevrolet Camaro & Z28 1973-1981
High Performance Camaros 1982-1988
Chrysler 300 Gold Portfolio 1955-1970
Chrysler Valiant 1960-1962
Citroen Traction Avant Gold Portfolio 1934-1957
Citroen 2CV Gold Portfolio 1948-1989
Citroen DS & ID 1955-1975
Citroen DS & ID Gold Portfolio 1955-1975
Citroen SM 1970-1975
Cobras & Replicas 1962-1983
Shelby Cobra Gold Portfolio 1962-1969
Cobras & Cobra Replicas Gold Portfolio 1962-1989
Cunningham Automobiles 1951-1955
Daimler SP250 Sports & V-8 250 Saloon Gold P. 1959-1969
Datsun Roadsters 1962-1971
Datsun 240Z 1970-1973
Datsun 280Z & ZX 1975-1983
DeLorean Gold Portfolio 1977-1995
Dodge Muscle Cars 1967-1970
Dodge Viper on the Road
Edsel 1957-1960 ☆ Limited Edition
ERA Gold Portfolio 1934-1994
Excalibur Collection No.1 1952-1981
Facel Vega 1954-1964
Ferrari 1947-1957 ☆ Limited Edition
Ferrari 1958-1963 ☆ Limited Edition
Ferrari Dino 1965-1974
Ferrari Dino 308 & Mondial Gold Portfolio1974-1985
Ferrari 328 • 348 • Mondial Gold Portfolio 1986-1994
Fiat 500 Gold Portfolio 1936-1972
Fiat 600 & 850 Gold Portfolio 1955-1972
Fiat Pininfarina 124 & 2000 Spider 1968-1985
Fiat X1/9 Gold Portfolio1973-1989
Fiat Abarth Performance Portfolio 1972-1987
Ford Consul, Zephyr, Zodiac Mk.I & II 1950-1962
Ford Zephyr, Zodiac, Executive, Mk.III & Mk.IV 1962-1971
Ford Cortina 1600E & GT 1967-1970
High Performance Capris Gold Portfolio 1969-1987
Capri Muscle Portfolio 1974-1987
High Performance Fiestas 1979-1991
High Performance Escorts Mk.I 1968-1974
High Performance Escorts Mk.II 1975-1980
High Performance Escorts 1980-1985
High Performance Escorts 1985-1990
High Performance Sierras & Merkurs
Gold Portfolio 1983-1990
Ford Automobiles 1949-1959
Ford Fairlane 1955-1970
Ford Ranchero 1957-1959
Ford Thunderbird 1955-1957
Ford Thunderbird 1958-1963
Ford GT40 Gold Portfolio 1964-1987
Ford Bronco 1966-1977
Ford Bronco 1978-1988
Goggomobil ☆ Limited Edition
Holden 1948-1962
Honda CRX 1983-1987
Imperial 1955-1970 ☆ Limited Edition
International Scout Gold Portfolio 1961-1980
Isetta Gold Portfolio 1953-1964
Iso & Bizzarrini Gold Portfolio 1962-1974
Kaiser • Frazer 1946-1955 ☆ Limited Edition
Jaguar and SS Gold Portfolio 1931-1951
Jaguar XK120, 140, 150 Gold Port. 1948-1960
Jaguar Mk.VII, VIII, IX, X, 420 Gold Port. 1950-1970
Jaguar Mk.1 & Mk.2 Gold Portfolio 1959-1969
Jaguar E-Type Gold Portfolio 1961-1971
Jaguar E-Type V-12 1971-1975
Jaguar S-Type & 420 ☆ Limited Edition
Jaguar XJ12, XJ5.3, V12 Gold Portfolio 1972-1990
Jaguar XJ6 Series I & II Gold Portfolio 1968-1979
Jaguar XJ6 Series III Perf. Portfolio 1979-1986
Jaguar XJ6 Gold Portfolio 1986-1994
Jaguar XJS Gold Portfolio 1975-1988
Jaguar XJS Gold Portfolio 1988-1995
Jeep CJ5 & CJ6 1960-1976
Jeep CJ5 & CJ7 1976-1986
Jensen Interceptor Gold Portfolio 1966-1986
Jensen Healey 1972-1976
Lagonda Gold Portfolio 1919-1964
Lancia Aurelia & Flaminia Gold Portfolio 1950-1970
Lancia Fulvia Gold Portfolio 1963-1976
Lancia Beta Gold Portfolio 1972-1984
Lancia Delta Gold Portfolio 1979-1994
Lancia Stratos 1972-1985
Land Rover Series I 1948-1958
Land Rover Series II & IIa 1958-1971
Land Rover Series III 1971-1985
Land Rover 90 110 Defender Gold Portfolio 1983-1994
Land Rover Discovery 1989-1994
Land Rover Story Part One 1948-1971
Lincoln Gold Portfolio 1949-1960
Lincoln Continental 1961-1969
Lincoln Continental 1969-1976
Lotus Sports Racers Gold Portfolio 1953-1965
Lotus Seven Gold Portfolio 1957-1974
Lotus Caterham Seven Gold Portfolio 1974-1995
Lotus Elan Gold Portfolio 1962-1974
Lotus Elan Collection No. 2 1963-1972
Lotus Elan & SE 1989-1992
Lotus Europa Gold Portfolio 1966-1975
Lotus Elite & Eclat 1974-1982
Lotus Turbo Esprit 1980-1986
Maserati 1965-1970
Matra 1965-1983 ☆ Limited Edition
Mazda Miata MX-5 Performance Portfolio 1989-1996
Mazda RX-7 Gold Portfolio 1978-1991
Mercedes 190 & 300 SL 1954-1963
Mercedes G Wagen 1981-1994
Mercedes S & 600 1965-1972
Mercedes S Class 1972-1979
Mercedes 230 • 250 • 280SL Gold Portfolio 1963-1971
Mercedes SLs & SLCs Gold Portfolio 1971-1989
Mercedes SLs Performance Portfolio 1989-1994
Mercury Muscle Cars 1966-1971
Messerschmitt Gold Portfolio 1954-1964
MG Gold Portfolio 1929-1939
MG TA & TC Gold Portfolio 1936-1949
MG TD & TF Gold Portfolio 1949-1955
MGA & Twin Cam Gold Portfolio 1955-1962
MG Midget Gold Portfolio 1961-1979
MGB Roadsters 1962-1980
MGB MGC & V8 Gold Portfolio 1962-1980
MGB GT 1965-1980
MGC & MGB GT V8 ☆ Limited Edition
MG Y-Type & Magnette ZA/ZB ☆ Limited Edition
Mini Gold Portfolio 1959-1969
Mini Gold Portfolio 1969-1980
Mini Gold Portfolio 1981-1997
High Performance Minis Gold Portfolio 1960-1973
Mini Cooper Gold Portfolio 1961-1971
Mini Moke Gold Portfolio 1964-1994
Morgan Three-Wheeler Gold Portfolio 1910-1952
Morgan Plus 4 & Four 4 Gold Portfolio 1936-1967
Morgan Cars 1960-1970
Morgan Cars Gold Portfolio 1968-1989
Morris Minor Collection No. 1 1948-1980
Shelby Mustang Muscle Portfolio 1965-1970
High Performance Mustang IIs 1974-1978
High Performance Mustangs 1982-1988
Nash & Nash-Healey 1949-1957 ☆ Limited Edition
Nash-Austin Metropolitan Gold Portfolio 1954-1962
Oldsmobile Automobiles 1955-1963
Oldsmobile Toronado 1966-1978
Opel GT Gold Portfolio 1968-1973
Opel Manta 1970-1975 ☆ Limited Edition
Packard Gold Portfolio 1946-1958
Pantera Gold Portfolio 1970-1989
Panther Gold Portfolio 1972-1990
Pontiac Tempest & GTO 1961-1965
Firebird & Trans-Am Muscle Portfolio 1973-1981
High Performance Firebirds 1982-1988
Pontiac Fiero 1984-1988
Porsche 356 Gold Portfolio 1953-1965
Porsche 911 1965-1969
Porsche 911 1970-1972
Porsche 911 1973-1977
Porsche 911 SC & Turbo Gold Portfolio 1978-1983
Porsche 911 Carrera & Turbo Gold Port. 1984-1989
Porsche 924 Gold Portfolio 1975-1988
Porsche 928 Performance Portfolio 1977-1994
Porsche 944 Gold Portfolio 1981-1991
Porsche 968 ☆ Limited Edition
Range Rover Gold Portfolio 1970-1985
Range Rover Gold Portfolio 1986-1995
Reliant Scimitar 1964-1986
Renault Alpine Gold Portfolio 1958-1994
Riley Gold Portfolio 1924-1939
Rolls Royce Silver Cloud & Bentley 'S' Series
Gold Portfolio 1955-1965
Rolls Royce Silver Shadow Gold Port. 1965-1980
Rolls Royce & Bentley Gold Port. 1980-1989
Rover P4 1949-1959
Rover P4 1955-1964
Rover 3 & 3.5 Litre Gold Portfolio 1958-1973
Rover 2000 & 2200 1963-1977
Rover 3500 & Vitesse 1976-1986
Saab Sonett Collection No.1 1966-1974
Saab Turbo 1976-1983
Studebaker Gold Portfolio 1947-1966
Studebaker Hawks & Larks 1956-1963
Avanti 1962-1990
Sunbeam Tiger & Alpine Gold Portfolio 1959-1967
Triumph Dolomite Sprint ☆ Limited Edition
Triumph TR2 & TR3 Gold Portfolio 1952-1961
Triumph TR4, TR5, TR250 1961-1968
Triumph TR6 Gold Portfolio 1969-1976
Triumph TR7 & TR8 Gold Portfolio 1975-1982
Triumph Herald 1959-1971
Triumph Vitesse 1962-1971
Triumph Spitfire Gold Portfolio 1962-1980
Triumph 2000, 2.5, 2500 1963-1977
Triumph GT6 Gold Portfolio 1966-1974
Triumph Stag Gold Portfolio 1970-1977
TVR Gold Portfolio 1959-1986
TVR Performance Portfolio 1986-1994
VW Beetle Gold Portfolio 1935-1967
VW Beetle Gold Portfolio 1968-1991
VW Beetle Collection No.1 1970-1982
VW Karmann Ghia 1955-1982
VW Bus, Camper, Van 1954-1967
VW Bus, Camper, Van 1968-1979
VW Bus, Camper, Van 1979-1989
VW Scirocco 1974-1981
VW Golf GTI 1976-1986
Volvo PV444 & PV544 1945-1965
Volvo Amazon-120 Gold Portfolio 1956-1970
Volvo 1800 Gold Portfolio 1960-1973
Volvo 140 & 160 Series Gold Portfolio 1966-1975
Westfield ☆ Limited Edition

Forty Years of Selling Volvo

BROOKLANDS ROAD & TRACK SERIES

Road & Track on Alfa Romeo 1964-1970
Road & Track on Alfa Romeo 1971-1976
Road & Track on Aston Martin 1962-1990
R & T on Auburn Cord and Duesenburg 1952-84
Road & Track on Audi & Auto Union 1952-1980
Road & Track on Audi & Auto Union 1980-1986
Road & Track on Austin Healey 1953-1970
Road & Track on BMW Cars 1966-1974
Road & Track on BMW Cars 1975-1978
Road & Track on BMW Cars 1979-1983
R & T on Cobra, Shelby & Ford GT40 1962-1992
Road & Track on Corvette 1953-1967
Road & Track on Corvette 1968-1982
Road & Track on Corvette 1982-1986
Road & Track on Corvette 1986-1990
Road & Track on Ferrari 1975-1981
Road & Track on Ferrari 1981-1984
Road & Track on Ferrari 1984-1988
Road & Track on Fiat Sports Cars 1968-1987
Road & Track on Jaguar 1950-1960
Road & Track on Jaguar 1961-1968
Road & Track on Jaguar 1968-1974
Road & Track on Jaguar 1974-1982
Road & Track on Jaguar 1983-1989
Road & Track on Lamborghini 1964-1985
Road & Track on Lotus 1972-1981
Road & Track on Maserati 1975-1983
R & T on Mazda RX-7 & MX-5 Miata 1986-1991
Road & Track on Mercedes 1952-1962
Road & Track on Mercedes 1963-1970
Road & Track on Mercedes 1971-1979
Road & Track on Mercedes 1980-1987
Road & Track on MG Sports Cars 1949-1961
Road & Track on MG Sports Cars 1962-1980
Road & Track on Mustang 1964-1977
R & T on Nissan 300-ZX & Turbo 1984-1989
Road & Track on Pontiac 1960-1983
Road & Track on Porsche 1951-1967
Road & Track on Porsche 1968-1971
Road & Track on Porsche 1972-1975
Road & Track on Porsche 1975-1978
Road & Track on Porsche 1985-1988
R & T on Rolls Royce & Bentley 1950-1965
R & T on Rolls Royce & Bentley 1966-1984
Road & Track on Saab 1972-1992
R & T on Toyota Sports & GT Cars 1966-1984
R & T on Triumph Sports Cars 1953-1967
R & T on Triumph Sports Cars 1967-1974
R & T on Triumph Sports Cars 1974-1982
Road & Track on Volkswagen 1951-1968
Road & Track on Volkswagen 1968-1978
Road & Track on Volkswagen 1978-1985
Road & Track on Volvo 1957-1974
Road & Track on Volvo 1977-1994
R & T - Henry Manney at Large & Abroad
R & T - Peter Egan's "Side Glances"
R & T - Peter Egan "At Large"

BROOKLANDS CAR AND DRIVER SERIES

Car and Driver on BMW 1955-1977
Car and Driver on BMW 1977-1985
C and D on Cobra, Shelby & Ford GT40 1963-84
Car and Driver on Corvette 1978-1982
Car and Driver on Corvette 1983-1988
C and D on Datsun Z 1600 & 2000 1966-1984
Car and Driver on Ferrari 1955-1962
Car and Driver on Ferrari 1963-1975
Car and Driver on Ferrari 1976-1983
Car and Driver on Mopar 1956-1967
Car and Driver on Mopar 1968-1975
Car and Driver on Mustang 1964-1972
Car and Driver on Pontiac 1961-1975
Car and Driver on Porsche 1955-1962
Car and Driver on Porsche 1963-1970
Car and Driver on Porsche 1970-1976
Car and Driver on Porsche 1977-1981
Car and Driver on Porsche 1982-1986
Car and Driver on Saab 1956-1985
Car and Driver on Volvo 1955-1986

BROOKLANDS PRACTICAL CLASSICS SERIES

PC on Austin A40 Restoration
PC on Land Rover Restoration
PC on Metalworking in Restoration
PC on Midget/Sprite Restoration
PC on MGB Restoration
PC on Sunbeam Rapier Restoration
PC on Triumph Herald/Vitesse
PC on Spitfire Restoration
PC on 1930s Car Restoration

BROOKLANDS HOT ROD 'MUSCLECAR & HI-PO ENGINES' SERIES

Chevy 265 & 283
Chevy 302 & 327
Chevy 348 & 409
Chevy 350 & 400
Chevy 396 & 427
Chevy 454 thru 512
Chrysler Hemi
Chrysler 273, 318, 340 & 360
Chrysler 361, 383, 400, 413, 426, 440
Ford 289, 302, Boss 302 & 351W
Ford 351C & Boss 351
Ford Big Block

BROOKLANDS RESTORATION SERIES

Auto Restoration Tips & Techniques
Basic Bodywork Tips & Techniques
Camaro Restoration Tips & Techniques
Chevrolet High Performance Tips & Techniques
Chevy Engine Swapping Tips & Techniques
Chevy-GMC Pickup Repair
Chrysler Engine Swapping Tips & Techniques
Engine Swapping Tips & Techniques
Ford Pickup Repair
Land Rover Restoration Tips & Techniques
MG 'T' Series Restoration Guide
MGA Restoration Guide
Mustang Restoration Tips & Techniques

MOTORCYCLING

BROOKLANDS ROAD TEST SERIES

AJS & Matchless Gold Portfolio 1945-1966
BSA Twins A7 & A10 Gold Portfolio 1946-1962
BSA Twins A50 & A65 Gold Portfolio 1962-1973
BMW Motorcycles Gold Portfolio 1950-1971
BMW Motorcycles Gold Portfolio 1971-1976
Ducati Gold Portfolio 1960-1974
Ducati Gold Portfolio 1974-1978
Ducati Gold Portfolio 1978-1982
Laverda Gold Portfolio 1967-1977
Moto Guzzi Gold Portfolio 1949-1973
Norton Commando Gold Portfolio 1968-1977
Triumph Bonneville Gold Portfolio 1959-1983
Vincent Gold Portfolio 1945-1980

BROOKLANDS CYCLE WORLD SERIES

Cycle World on BMW 1974-1980
Cycle World on BMW 1981-1986
Cycle World on Ducati 1982-1991
Cycle World on Harley-Davidson 1962-1968
Cycle World on Harley-Davidson 1978-1983
Cycle World on Harley-Davidson 1983-1987
Cycle World on Harley-Davidson 1987-1990
Cycle World on Harley-Davidson 1990-1992
Cycle World on Honda 1962-1967
Cycle World on Honda 1968-1971
Cycle World on Honda 1971-1974
Cycle World on Husqvarna 1966-1976
Cycle World on Husqvarna 1977-1984
Cycle World on Kawasaki 1966-1971
Cycle World on Kawasaki Off-Road Bikes 1972-1979
Cycle World on Kawasaki Street Bikes 1972-1976
Cycle World on Norton 1962-1971
Cycle World on Suzuki 1962-1970
Cycle World on Suzuki Off-Road Bikes 1971-1976
Cycle World on Suzuki Street Bikes 1971-1976
Cycle World on Triumph 1967-1972
Cycle World on Yamaha 1962-1969
Cycle World on Yamaha Off-Road Bikes 1970-1974
Cycle World on Yamaha Street Bikes 1970-1974

MILITARY

BROOKLANDS MILITARY VEHICLES SERIES

Allied Military Vehicles No.2 1941-1946
Complete WW2 Military Jeep Manual
Dodge Military Vehicles No.1 1940-1945
Hail To The Jeep
Military & Civilian Amphibians 1940-1990
Off Road Jeeps: Civ. & Mil. 1944-1971
US Military Vehicles 1941-1945
US Army Military Vehicles WW2-TM9-2800
VW Kubelwagen Military Portfolio 1940-1990
WW 2 Jeep Military Portfolio 1941-1945

RACING

Le Mans - The Jaguar Years - 1949-1957
Le Mans - The Ferrari Years - 1958-1965
Le Mans - The Ford & Matra Years - 1966-1974
Le Mans - The Porsche Years - 1975-1982

2157

CONTENTS

Brooklands Books

ACKNOWLEDGEMENTS

This is the fourth in our road racing series covering the great post-war Le Mans races. The first covered the Jaguar years up to 1957. Due to its success it was quickly followed by volumes covering the Ferrari and the Ford and Matra years. This book takes the story forward from 1975 to 1982. During these eight years Porsche took first place five times and came second on a further two occasions.

Descriptions of great motor races often have a national bias - or at the very least, a national flavour - and for this reason we have tried in these books to provide accounts from more than one country. The copyright holders of this material have once again been kind enough to grant us permission to reprint their interesting and factual stories, and our thanks in this instance, go to the publishers of - *Autocar, Autosport, Car and Driver, Motor, Motor Sport* and *Road & Track*. We are also indebted to Anders Ditlev Clausager for the yearly summaries and for the table of results at the back of the book which first appeared in his book, 'Le Mans', published in 1982 but now sadly out of print.

Last but certainly not least, our thanks go to Porsche Great Britain Ltd. who so valiantly came to our aid with the splendid photograph which graces our front cover.

R.M. Clarke

By common consent, a perhaps less interesting Le Mans; the favourite description was 'The Economy Le Mans'. Perhaps the after-effects of the fuel crisis, and the talk about waste of fuel in motor sport, had got through to the Automobile Club de L'Ouest; they decided to run Le Mans according to a fuel-consumption formula - a minimum number of 20 laps between re-fuelling, and limited size of fuel tanks; in consequence the minimum fuel consumption necessary to qualify was above 7 mpg. They were rewarded for their initiative by the C.S.I. withdrawing the world championship status of Le Mans - which in turn meant that the works teams of Matra, Alpine, Ferrari and Alfa Romeo three-litre prototypes all stayed away. Yet one wonders what the fuss was about as after all, every Le Mans race prior to 1960 had been run according to similar regulations restricting fuel consumption, and nobody complained then. Another historical parallel was the 1956 Le Mans race, run under safety-inspired restrictions after the 1955 disaster, as these restrictions also cost the race its championship status then.

Among the makes entered, Porsche was numerically in by far the strongest position; of 55 starting cars, no less than 24 were 911s or Carreras running in the GT categories. In addition there were other Porsches running in the Sports car prototype category; these were three elderly 908 three-litre cars entered by the German Joest-team which were the Porsches with the best chance of a high place among the finishing cars. Otherwise the three-litre class was dominated by the Ford-Cosworth DFV engine which was fitted to six important contenders: John Wyer's two Gulf-Fords (ex-Mirage); two Lolas, of which one was entered and driven by Alain de Cadenet; and two of the Gitane-sponsored Ligiers, while this French team's third car retained the Maserati engine used by Ligiers in previous years.

Among the two-litre prototypes, a V6-engined Alpine-Renault driven by Lombardi/Beaumont attracted attention as the fastest car in practice in this class and was the first Alpine-Renault at Le Mans since 1969; other entries included a Moynet-Simca, four Lolas with Simca-based engines, a BDA-engined Lola, a Tecma and a March-Cosworth. The Japanese Sigma had for the 1975 race forsaken the Mazda rotary engine in favour of a turbo-charged Toyota engine.

As mentioned the GT classes were completely dominated by Porsche Carreras, but there were two Ferrari Daytonas, a Chevrolet Corvette, a Datsun 240 Z and two De Tomaso Panteras. A Porsche Carrera Turbo was the only starter in a new category, the GTX class created for limited-production, non-homologated GT cars; it should have been kept company by three Ferraris entered by Luigi Chinetti and the American N.A.R.T. team but these were withdrawn at the last moment after an argument over qualifying times. The

Touring car category was badly supported; an eye-catching BMW CSL decorated by artist Alexander Calder put in the fastest practice times, and a model not previously seen at Le Mans was a two-litre BMW 2002 saloon. Finally, a Ford Capri and a Mazda.

The Gulf driven by Schuppan/Jassaud went into the lead from the start but after the first pit-stops was overtaken by its team-mate driven by Jacky Ickx and Derek Bell. But the Gulfs retained a 1-2 lead, followed by the Joest Porsche 908; Chris Craft in the Lola he shared with de Cadenet; and the first Ligier-DFV, driven by the triple winner Henri Pescarolo together with Migault. Among the first cars to retire was the two-litre Alpine which ran out of fuel, and the artistic BMW coupe which had been favourite to win the Touring category. Then the Ligier-Maserati was destroyed in a collision with a Ferrari Daytona; fortunately without injury to either driver.

As the evening wore on, the Schuppan/Jaussaud Gulf was delayed with electrical trouble, and a peculiar accident delayed two of the most important entries: the rear bodywork of de Cadenet's Lola fell off without the driver realising what had happened, and Migault in the Ligier struck the debris at 150 mph. Both cars were delayed while repairs were made, and the damage eventually caused the retirement of the Ligier, while the Lola was able to finish the race, albeit in a lowly position. The Bell/Ickx Gulf was still leading, and by early Sunday morning the Schuppan/Jaussaud car was back in second place; only to slip down the field when its ignition was affected by a rainstorm. Nor was the leading Gulf free of problems; with less than two hours to go, it was in the pits with a cracked exhaust system. While a replacement was being fitted the surviving Ligier of Lafosse/Chasseuil steadily reduced the gap between the two cars - but the Gulf was back on the track with one lap in hand, and came home the winner. The average of Ickx and Bell was 118.98 mph and their distance 2,855.55 miles - virtually the same as the 1974 result. The Ligier was second, and the Schuppan/Jaussaud Gulf third, a 1-2-3 victory for the DFV engine. Fourth was the Joest Porsche 908, and this was followed by the GT winner, the first of many Porsche Carreras. The Craft/de Cadenet Lola was fifteenth; a remarkable 31 cars finished the race, with the Moynet-Simca first in the two-litre class, and the BMW 2002 took the Touring car honours.

For the first time since 1959, an all-British car had won at Le Mans - even if sponsored by an American multinational company - and it was an outstanding triumph for John Wyer as it was his fourth win as entrant - Aston Martin in 1959, Ford GT 40 in 1968 and 1969, and now Gulf-DFV. The fastest lap was put in by another British entry: Chris Craft in the Lola, at 130.5 mph.

Le Mans: into the dark?

A FUEL CONSUMPTION figure of at least 7·1 mpg will be a pre-requisite for a good finish at Le Mans this weekend. And as that is beyond the reach of the 12 cylinder Alfa Romeo engine or the turbocharged Porsche and Renault power-units (none of which will be seen at Le Mans). This year's race seems unlikely to be a memorable one.

Who, then, are the main protagonists? Gulf Research Racing will be having their first race this year in an effort to finally put their own car across the line first – in 1968 and 1969 they won with Ford GT40s – and to this end they have worked hard to produce a "slippery" body shape for the GR chassis, one that will hopefully enable them to match last year's speeds by using less fuel. In 1974, the Gulfs' best fuel consumption figure was 6·1 mpg, so this year their Ford DFV engines have been de-tuned still further and will only be producing 375 bhp at 8,000 rpm. Recent tests have shown the '75-spec engines returning a consumption of 7·25 mpg, which should enable the cars to complete the mandatory 20 non-stop laps with a couple of gallons to spare. "Recent tests" is the operative phrase here however, for the cancellation of the Le Mans test weekend has given the Gulf team no chance of confirming its estimates. All their fuel consumption testing will have been done by Wednesday and Thursday this week. The Gulf driver pairing is a strong one, with Derek Bell and Jacky Ickx sharing one car and Vern Schuppan and Jean-Pierre Jaussaud the other.

Three other cars in the Group 5 class will be powered by the Ford DFV engine. The Ligier team will be re-appearing after missing three rounds of the World Championship for Makes, with Henri Pescarolo and Jean-Pierre Beltoise in one car, and Jean-Pierre Jarier and Jean-Louis Lafosse in the second. Guy Ligier is right behind the A. C. de l'Ouest (and against the CSI in its decision to "exclude" him from the Group 4 category) so for him victory at Le Mans would indeed be sweet. Alain de Cadenet will also be using a DFV in the new Lola T380, which was pictured in *Autocar*, 19 April.

Other contenders for outright victory include the two old Porsche 908/3s of the Rheinhold Jöst team. A fast and reliable 2-litre car may be up there as well, and the works Alpine-Renault of Marie-Claude Beaumont and Lella Lombardi looks good. There also hordes of Group 4 Porsche Carreras, several Ferrari Daytonas and a couple of De Tomaso Panteras, which together should provide a far closer race than the leading Group 5 entries.

All in all it's an uninspiring line-up, although there's no doubt that the race will receive as much publicity and will be watched by as many people as ever it was.

LE MANS

Despite the fact that it has lost its championship status from the World Championship of Makes, there is still bound to be a huge crowd gathering in the Sarthe region of France this weekend. Yes, it's time for the running of the Le Mans 24 hour sports car classic once more. Sadly, the race is a pale reflection of its former self but, whatever the quality of the entry, it's quantity rather than quality that the organisers seem to prefer.

Potentially the fastest cars and therefore in with a good chance of victory will be the two brand new Gulf Racing Research GR8 prototypes driven by Derek Bell/Jacky Ickx and Vern Schuppan/Jean-Pierre Jaussaud. The cars, as we've already said, will be powered by specially detuned versions of the Ford Cosworth DFV engine for reliability purposes.

Challenging them in the large G5 class will be a trio of Porsche 908/3 turbos for the regular pairings of Herbert Muller/Leo Kinnunnen (Martini Racing), Reinhold Jost/Mario Casoni plus Jost's spare.

French hopes of an outright win rest with the Gitanes-sponsored Ligiers. Although these cars have proved unable to match the speed of the much lighter sports prototypes so far this season, they will be more suited to the endurance of Le Mans powered by their Cosworth DFV engines. Two, and possibly three, cars will be driven by Jean-Pierre Beltoise, Henri Pescarolo, Jean-Pierre Jarier, Jean-Louise Lafosse and probably Francois Migault.

Apart from the smaller 2-litre G5 class where national interest will be how Marie-Claude Beaumont and Lella Lombardi progress with their Elf Switzerland Alpine Renault A440, there's bound to be a huge dust up in the GT category between the Kremer, Tebernum and Georg Loos Porsche Carreras.

In the Gelo cars will be John Fitzpatrick, Toine Hezemans, Manfred Schurti, Gijs van Lennep and Loos himself. The Tebernum cars will probably be handled by Clemens Schickentanz, Reine Wisell and Hartwig Bertrams while Erwin Kremer usually employs Helmut Kelleners and Jurgen Barth.

Ranged against the Carreras will be the usual hoard of thunderous Ferrari Daytonas, two of them entered by the North American Racing Team.

Britain's back at Le Mans

It was the poorest entry in years – but the 24 Hours was still no pushover

GULF RESEARCH RACING took advantage of one of the least competitive Le Mans 24 Hour races in years to score a resounding first and third finish – but it was no hollow, easy victory. Le Mans wins, by definition, are never that: the team's pre-race preparation was faultless, their race management was good and their drivers did an excellent job. Both Gulf GR8-Ford DFVs had to be nursed as the race drew to a close, and there was always a constant threat from at least one of the works Ligier-Fords. And, most demanding of all, there was always the thought that this was a race Gulf *had* to win. They had tried for the past two years and failed, this year there could be no excuses. The whole production would have to be right from start to finish.

The Gulf team's planning was, of course, greatly affected by this year's "transitional" regulations, in which each competitor had to complete at least 20 laps between fuel stops – and in which cars could be rebuilt during the race. Gulf's DFV engines were tuned to produce around 7·5 mpg, and streamlined bodywork was designed to not only alleviate the 20 less bhp of this year's engines, but also to counter-balance the weight increase of the 1975 cars. An absence of (costly) titanium meant that the Gulf GR8s weighed-in at 750kg, achieved the same maximum speed as last year (194 mph), but were not quite as accelerative.

The Gitanes-Ligier team were three cars strong, two being powered by Cosworth DFV engines (which were 1975 examples, without Ford lettering on the cam covers)

and the other by the old V6 Maserati power unit. Like Gulf, Ligier claimed around 370 bhp from their Ford engines, which nonetheless were being run at slightly higher revs, while the much heavier Maserati-powered JS2 produced only 320 bhp. But unlike the Gulfs, which again used ZF transaxles, the Ligier DFVs were mated to Hewland FG400 gearboxes. Although no match for the Gulfs under braking or acceleration, the Ligiers proved the worth of a closed car design by recording straight line speeds only 4 mph slower than the Gulfs. The Ligier driver line-up had Henri Pescarolo-Francois Migault and Jean-Louis Lafosse-Guy Chausseuill in the Ford-powered cars and Jean-Pierres Jarier and Beltoise in the Maserati, which was generally thought to be a more reliable package.

What of the others? The Ovoro Porsche 908/3 of Reinhold Jöst and Mario Casoni looked threatening thanks to its normally-aspirated flat-8 engine and the addition of a 917/30-like tail section, while Alain de Cadenet's Lola T380-DFV was considered a good outside bet. Its front suspension had been converted to linear rate several weeks before and both Chris Craft and de Cadenet said it improved the handling. The Lola was surprisingly slow on the straight, however, and at 179 mph the team were giving away a lot to the Ligiers and Gulfs. Moreover, the car was still very, very new.

It was Derek Bell who took the lead at the start, his blue and orange Gulf disappearing under the Dunlop bridge with a few lengths' lead over Schuppan. But accelerating out of

Tertre Rouge the second car weaved to the right and nosed ahead: Bell and Ickx had decided that leading from the start gave them no cards to play. In second place, at least, there was something to aim for.

So Schuppan was the early leader of the Le Mans 24 Hours. Bell soon dropped back to a distant second position, and before long was under pressure from Jöst, who was driving his Porsche with much alacrity. Craft settled into an early fourth place, and fifth was Pescarolo, in the first of the Ligiers. But the early race order was academic; many predicted the outright winner would come from the bunch of 14 Group 4 Porsche Carreras at this point down below 11th place.

His lead now around 20 seconds, Schuppan was the first of the Gulf drivers to stop for fuel; he had done 21 laps, it was 5.30 p.m. Jaussaud thus rejoined before Bell assumed the lead. But once Ickx had taken over the second car, the number 11 Gulf soon took the front-running position that it was never to lose: Schuppan reported that his gear lever was jumping out of second gear on over-run, and he and Jaussaud thereafter drove three sections of every lap holding the lever in place.

By the second hour, two prominent runners had struck trouble. The fast 2-litre Alpine-Renault driven by Marie-Claude Beaumont and Lella Lombardi, which had been leading all but one of the Ligiers, ran out of fuel on its 21st lap and remained stranded. The Elf team had consistently completed 26 non-stop laps in practice, so its demise was put down to some form of

Le Mans

Left: Hiroshi Fushida waits patiently while mechanics change the bearings of his Sigma-Toyota turbo. The car was subsequently retired. Top: the second placed Ligier-Ford. Right: Vern Schuppan's Gulf led early laps, lost time in the wet. Below left: Mario Casoni's battle-scarred Porsche. Below right: Chris Craft in the de Cadenet Lola T380

fuel blockage. The other car to lose time was the IMSA-spec BMW CSL of Sam Posey. It fell from eighth place when a brake line came loose, and then retired for good when a prop-shaft coupling broke four hours later.

In the race's early phase, however, Gulf remained bereft of troubles. The drivers were working with so much in hand that not only was the second car well able to keep pace with Ickx–Bell – but the management was also able to provide a bit of frivolity. At one stage, when the two Gulfs were nose to tail, a sign went out for Schuppan-Jaussaud car to drop back. This it did, and the following lap Schuppan was greeted with the signal, ''Good Boy!''

The Ligier Gitanes team, by contrast, were soon in difficulty. At 6.30 pm Beltoise brought in the sixth-place Maserati car to have a brake line repaired, and then shortly afterwards the car was severely damaged when the Frenchman collided with American Harry Jones' Ferrari Daytona. The big car survived with barely a scratch, but the Ligier destroyed itself between the guard-rails at Indianapolis.

But is was around 9.30 pm on Saturday when the race's pattern was substantially altered for the first time. Schuppan broke the order by coming into the Gulf pit with a misfire, and both the spark box and regulator were changed before the trouble was eventually traced to the alternator. That dropped him to fifth place, six laps behind the leading Gulf. Then the de Cadenet team, which had already lost time with a broken exhaust pipe, struck big trouble.

Or rather Francois Migault did. He was streaking down the Mulsanne straight when his headlights suddenly picked out an object in the middle of the road. At around 150 mph there was little he could do but gently swerve, and the Ligier hit what later transpired to be part of the de Cadenet Lola's rear

body section. Migault had an enormous ''moment'' gathering it all together – his headlights had gone out instantly – and he limped the Ligier back to the pits for major surgery. De Cadenet, meanwhile, continued to circulate, unaware that the Lola's rear body hinges had broken and the car was shedding pieces of glass-fibre.

Neither car was to recover from its set-back, for the Ligier later retired when a tyre went flat and he found insufficient clearance between rim and suspension to drive it back to the pits, while the Lola lost more time when a cracked rear upright was found during a brake pad change; the pad change in itself was an annoyance, for the car was fitted with big Lockheed calipers, giving a projected life of 2,000 miles. In the event, the crew changed the rear pads once and the fronts twice.

Schuppan and Jaussaud had little trouble regaining their lost ground – especially as Mario Casoni's Porsche spent 20 minutes being taped up after hitting a slower car, and the Chausseuill Ligier had an excessively long brake pad change – but once back on the same lap as the Ligier the Gulf drivers were told to hold station. As it turned out, this may have been a mistake, for the second Gulf was going to need as big a cushion as possible.

Reinhold Jöst lost more time early on Sunday morning when a front tyre blew and damaged the bodywork, and the Porsche 908 dropped to minus-15 laps when it suffered two more punctures. By this stage, both Gulfs had an ominous back end vibration. The drivers couldn't pinpoint it, and nor could the mechanics – but it was suspected that the differentials were failing.

As the race entered its closing stages, both Gulfs lost laps – and the Chausseuill-Lafosse Ligier moved ever-closer to the lead. Derek Bell brought an anxious expression to the

face of Jacky Ickx by bringing in the leading Gulf with a broken primary exhaust pipe – which left him just two laps ahead – while Schuppan lost a lot of time when his engine went on to seven cylinders during a mid-morning rainstorm. With the remaining Ligier encountering no trouble whatever, that left the second Gulf in an irretrievable third place.

There wasn't a big crowd at Le Mans this year – 80,000 was a mentioned figure – but those who were present felt nothing but admiration for John Wyer and his Gulf team as Derek Bell maintained his lap advantage and came home a fine winner from the Ligier. The third-place Gulf made it a one-two-three for the Ford Cosworth engine, a long-distance result many predicted the power unit would never achieve. Jöst's fourth place was well earned, while fifth outright and first in class was the Gelo Carrera, driven by no less than four ''Porsche Cup'' contenders. And sixth, after a completely trouble-free run, was the well-prepared Harley-Davidson-sponsored Carrera of Nick Faure-Jean Blaton-John Cooper. The Group 4 cars, after all, had played no more than a minor rôle. **PDW**

Le Mans 24 Hours, 15–16 June
1 Gulf GR8-Ford DFV 3·0 (D. Bell-J. Ickx) 336 laps, 2,856·17 miles, 119·01 mph
2 Ligier JS2-Ford DFV 3·0 (G. Chasseuil-J-L. Lafosse) 335 laps, 2,842·39 miles
3 Gulf GR8-Ford DFV 3·0 (V. Schuppan-J-P. Jaussaud) 330 laps
4 Porsche 908/3 3·0 (R. Jöst-M. Casoni-J. Barth) 325 laps
5 *Porsche Carrera RSR 3·0 (J. Fitzpatrick-G. van Lennep-M. Schurti-T. Hezemans) 315 laps
6 Porsche Carrera RSR 3·0 (N. Faure-J. Cooper-J. Blaton) 311 laps
7 Porsche Carrera RSR 3·0 (J. Borras-P. Moisson-H. Cachia) 309 laps
8 Porsche Carrera RSR 3·0 (C. Ballot-Lena-Bienvenue) 304 laps
9 Porsche Carrera RSR 3·0 (C. Bolanos-B. Sprowis-A. Contreras) 304 laps
10 †Porsche Carrera RS 3·0 (G. Maurer-C. Beez-E. Straehl) 295 laps

*Winner, Group 4 class
†Winner, Group 3 class

Towards a new Le Mans

The AC de l'Ouest see bright hopes for the future

ALAIN BERTAUT, his striped business shirt still fresh despite the dust and heat of a scorching Le Mans day, sighed heavily as he stared out from the race control office at the empty pit lane. "I fear," he said, his tone unemotional and methodical, "that to-morrow the crowd will be not so big. I am prepared for that. The *Automobile Club de l'Ouest* is prepared for that. But they also know that the lack of people won't be because of the regulations we've changed this year, or because Le Mans is out of the Championship for Makes. It will be because the spectators are sick of seeing the same cars for the third year running, sick of seeing a . . . a procession."

Alain Bertaut is the man who intends to put Le Mans back where it belongs – in its unique spot on the motor racing calendar. As a serious racing event Le Mans today is a joke – but as a prestigious, ultra-popular shop-window for the sport Le Mans is one of our greatest assets. Bertaut is sure of that. So sure, in fact, that he is staking his reputation, first as a successful long-distance sports car driver and then as a respected motoring journalist – and Le Mans' future – on the hope that the race can exist with its own regulations, outside the World Championship for Makes. This year (and in 1976, as a result of talks which took place a few days before the race), Le Mans is going through a transition period. In 1977 Bertaut's fuel consumption-orientated GT Prototype and GT Production regulations will be fully enforced for the first time – and one year after that, predicts Bertaut, the crowds will begin to return to the *Circuit de la Sarthe*.

Attendances have been down. The epic 1967 Le Mans race saw a recent high of 200,000 paying spectators, but since then, and culminating in the 100,000 people who paid to watch the race in 1974, Le Mans' popularity has been on the wane. Bertaut feels this has reflected the interest shown in sports car racing in general. "No longer", he says, "is there a place alongside formula 1 for sports cars as we have to know them. Three-litre prototypes may be very interesting to watch, but these days they are too close to formula 1. Grand Prix racing has now got itself organized into a really well-run, well-sponsored show; if a sponsor wants to go raving on an international level, there's now no way that he would go into sports car rather than formula 1 racing."

It was the dwindling crowds which first prompted the AC de l'Ouest to ask Bertaut to draw up new regulations. Already very experienced in the running of the 24-hour race and the problems that entail, Bertaut responded by issuing two sets of rules: one for this year's race, another, more radical proposal for the 1977 event. In both, the underlying theme was fuel consumption, and for this Bertaud has been heavily criticized. He is devoted to his cause, however. "Of course, it is not important that the race actually *saves* fuel: that saving is negligible in comparative terms. What *is* important is that

the race is seen to be working towards conserving energy. This is something I've long believed in, not a gimmick we introduced just because of the fuel crisis. The world, and racing, are changing; companies such as Porsche have told me that they would never again spend money on a car like the 917."

But that isn't to say that Bertaut believes racing should improve the breed primarily and provide close racing secondarily. "We have long passed the stage of providing direct feed-back to the production car world. We must forget about that – *direct* feed-back, that is. What we must do instead – particularly as all commercial sponsorship is now centred on formula 1 – is encourage the car manufacturers. They are not encouraged by this year's FIA regulations, or the little-changed rules for next year (except Porsche, who more or less demanded the new Group 5 "silhouette" category) but I believe that if we held the 24-hour race for GT-type cars falling into two main categories only – and with an accent towards fuel economy – we would be heading in the right direction. After all, what have we got to lose? If Le Mans sticks with the FIA Championship our attendances will continue to fall. It's time someone made a stand."

The French Press, in particular, have criticized these GT regulations, which, they say, are too restrictive. What right, they ask, has Bertaut to so closely govern the shape of the next car produced by Alpine or Ford? Freedom of design – and speed – are what Le Mans is all about. This Bertaud counters with the statement that he has already spoken to several big manufacturers – including Ferrari – who have welcomed his plans. "But I would still like to have a round-table discussion later in the year, so that I can hear everyone's views", says Bertaud. "And if there is some thing they do not like, we can change the rules. We mustn't be afraid to do that."

Perhaps that is Bertaud's most striking feature. In a world all wrought up in politics and petty bickering, he is not afraid to admit he may be wrong. Consultation with Goodyear, for instance, has already brought about a change in rim width sizes. And next year's fuel consumption regulations will be worked on a gallons-available basis rather than the minimum number of laps rule.

Yes, we have here a man with a sound idea. For him, the biggest worry is the gamble on Le Mans' reputation to stand as a race in its own right. It needs to do that for at least the next four years, and if last weekend's race is anything to go by, the road will be tough. "But we've done it before," remembers Bertaud, staring across the track at a plaque inscribed *11 Juin, 1955.* A year after the dreadful accident we amalgamated Appendix C and Appendix J for safety reasons. We were excluded from the FIA Championship, but the following year we were given our status again. We were amused to see that the FIA had copied our lead. . . ."

PDW

Le Mans to Ickx and Bell

THERE WILL always be a Le Mans 24-Hour race, I suppose, despite bad economic times, major teams choosing not to compete, rules squabbles and all the other mish-mash that seems to be as much a part of the event as the Ferris wheel and the bread and wine. This year the race was won by Jacky Ickx and Derek Bell who teamed in one of the two John Wyer-prepared Gulf Mirages that totally dominated the event from practice on.

The most recent version of the yearly classic was not a part of the World Championship of Makes. Last year the organizing group in France broke with the FIA and decided to run the race its own way. The result was a decision to require the cars to complete at least 20 laps before refueling. That resulted in a general de-tuning of engines, but Wyer went that obvious trick one better by redesigning the body on the Mirages to give the cars a top speed equal to last year's version while still maintaining the required fuel economy. The second Mirage, driven by Jean-Pierre Jaussaud and Vern Schuppan, was slightly slower than its sister car, but it was still fast enough to keep the field in its wake until late in the race. An ignition problem let the Cosworth-Ford-powered Ligier JS2 of Guy Chasseuil and Jean-Louis Lafosse into 2nd place where it finished, two laps behind the winner.

Both Alfa Romeo and the works Alpine team elected to pass Le Mans which did take some of the glitter off the production this year. However, the three-car Ligier team kept things interesting, as did a smattering of strong Porsche 980/3s and a pair of very fast Cosworth DFV-powered Lolas.

The GT class went to a Porsche Carrera driven by Fitzpatrick/Van Lennep/Hezemans/Schurti. Sam Posey was on hand with a very special BMW 3.0CSL. The car sported a "one-off" paint job designed by Alexander Calder and was insured for a cool half-million. Despite an early stop for a faulty fuel valve, Posey had the car as high as 5th in the early going. However, a rubber coupling in the driveshaft let go after 5½ hours, and that was it.

This race may well have been the last for Wyer—it was his 4th Le Mans victory, one for Aston Martin, two for Porsche and one for Gulf-Mirage. Next year Le Mans will be restricted to GT and touring cars, and it's unlikely Wyer will be dabbling in such machinery.

In a squabble over the classification of his Dino 308, Luigi Chinetti withdrew his entire NART entry—a Boxer Berlinetta, a special one-off Spyder, a Daytona and the Dino. Had Chinetti stayed in, the race would have marked the return to racing of Ronnie Bucknum who was in the NART Daytona and had qualified 18th.

Gulf Wins "Economy" Le Mans

THE COMBINATION of a fuel-consumption formula (all the cars had to run for 20 laps or more without refuelling), the absence of many graded drivers, and—worst—the lack of Matra, Alpine, Ferrari or Alfa Romeo prototypes, all combined to make this year's *Vingt-Quatre Heures du Mans* decidedly a non-event, and the spectators reacted by staying away in their thousands. Victory always seemed within reach of the two well-prepared Gulf Research Racing GR8s, which took turns at leading the race, and on Sunday afternoon the achievement was recorded by Derek Bell and Jacky Ickx. The second car had been delayed with alternator problems, and then by a fault in the differential, and finished in third place behind the Ligier-Ford DFV driven by Jean-Louis Lafosse and Guy Chasseuil.

The Automobile Club de l'Ouest seemed to be in trouble from the very beginning. First they introduced the fuel-consumption formula, virtually dictating a 25% improvement in consumption to the 3-litre teams. Then, having been banished by the CSI from the World Championship for Makes, the ACO had to cancel the vital test weekend because the CSI introduced a clashing sports-car race to the calendar. And when the final entry list was published, it showed a heavy preponderance of Porsche 911 Carreras, which filled no fewer than 28 of the 55 starting places—just over 50% of the total. Just where endurance racing would be now if Dr. Porsche had not founded his own car company is hard to imagine, for with four more Stuttgart cars in the 3-litre prototype class the company was better represented than ever before!

Gulf calculated that they would have to detune their engines to 370 horsepower (at 8,000 r.p.m.) to achieve 7.5 m.p.g., though during practice they found that their calculations were over-cautious and that the GR8s driven by Bell/Ickx and Vern Schuppan/Jean-Pierre Jaussaud were returning about 8.5 m.p.g., and could run 25 laps if necessary

DEREK BELL'S *winning Gulf leads its sister car, driven by Vern Schuppan, Joest's Porsche and a Ligier through the Esses.*

without topping up. Just as well for Guy Ligier, who detuned his DFV engines to 410 horsepower to counteract the heavy weight of the GT bodies on his JS2 models driven by Lafosse/Chasseuil, and Henri Pescarolo and Francois Migault. Another fancied runner was the 3-litre V6 Maserati-powered JS2 (a development of the road car) driven by Jean-Pierre Beltoise/Jean-Pierre Jarier. Private entry hopes were kept high by Alain de Cadenet's Lola-DFV shared with Chris Craft, and the dark horses of the event were the old Porsche 908/3s (which never did develop more than 360 b.h.p. anyway), of which the Reinhold Joest/Mario Casoni/Jurgen Barth entry was easily the most effective.

Speeds were on average 15 sec. per lap slower than last year's, and though visually that mattered little it did detract somewhat from the glamour of the event. The two Gulfs, fastest in practice, soon settled into a

four-minute-per-lap rhythm at the head of the field, with the Ligiers, Craft's Lola and Joest's Porsche 908 in pursuit, none of them hurrying particularly and the drivers audibly taking care of the clutches and gearboxes as they accelerated past the pits. After an hour Schuppan led Bell by 14 sec., followed by Joest, Craft and Pescarolo, with Marie-Claude Beaumont's 2-litre Alpine V6 in sixth place. Half an hour later Mlle. Beaumont became the first, and only, casualty of the fuel-consumption limit when the French car coasted to a standstill half way round its 21st lap.

After the first refuelling stops Ickx and Bell firmly established themselves in the lead, which they never relinquished although their command became tenuous on Sunday morning when the car was delayed 12 min. by a broken exhaust pipe, letting Lafosse's Ligier move briefly on to the same lap. The Schuppan/Jaussaud Gulf was comfortably second until, late on Saturday evening, the alternator failed and half-an-hour was lost in the pits.

In the hours of darkness Alain de Cadenet's Lola lost its rear body section along the Mulsanne Straight, and Migault's Ligier ran over the bits at high speed, damaging its nose section. Both cars were considerably delayed while they were patched up, de Cadenet eventually finishing down in 15th place and Migault/Pescarolo retiring when a puncture put them even lower down the order. Beltoise crashed the Ligier-Maserati heavily after colliding with a Ferrari Daytona, but Lafosse and Chasseuil had no trouble with their car and kept the pressure on the Gulf team all the way to the end.—M.L.C.

PIT STOP *for the second-placed Ligier JS2 of Lafosse and Chasseuil.*

24 HOURS OF LE MANS

1st : D. Bell/J. Ickx (3.0 Gulf DFV GR8) 336 laps, 4,595.6 kms., 191.48 k.p.h.
2nd: J-L. Lafosse/G. Chasseuil (3.0 Ligier DFV JS2)...................335 laps
3rd: V. Schuppan/J-P. Jaussaud (3.0 Gulf DFV GR8).....................330 ,,
4th: R. Joest/M. Casoni/J. Barth (3.0 Porsche 908/3)...................325 ,,
5th: J. Fitzpatrick/G. Van Lennep/T. Hezemans/M. Schurti (3.0 Porsche Carrera) ....315 ,,
6th: N. Faure/J. Cooper/"Beurlys" (3.0 Porsche Carrera)...............311 ,,
7th: J. Borras/P. Moisson/H. Cachia (3.0 Porsche Carrera)..............309 ,,

ULTIMATE MOBILE

Calder's BMW brought new color to racing

PHOTOS BY ELLEN GRIESEDIECK

IT HAS TO be one of the craziest (and most refreshing) ideas of this troubled decade. The famous painter-sculptor Alexander Calder, a French art auctioneer-racing driver, racing driver-artist-writer Sam Posey and one of BMW's superfast racing 3.0CSL coupes are the ingredients of a unique recipe.

It began to happen several months ago at the home of Hervé Poulain, a Paris art auctioneer who also happens to deal in classic cars and race as an amateur. Calder, born in Philadelphia and now 77 years old, is a friend of Poulain's and was having lunch with Poulain and his wife when Poulain casually asked Calder, "Why don't you paint a car?" Calder, not noted for inhibitions, fairly leaped at the idea and demanded to see the car right away. Poulain hadn't even thought of a particular car when he threw out the idea, but the BMW racing coupe

seemed appropriate and he asked BMW for one. The Munich carmaker supplied one happily and shipped the car to Paris, where Calder designed the paint job and workmen applied it to the car.

In the meantime Poulain and the BMW racing department, under Jochen Neerpasch, developed their plans for the coupe. Poulain wanted to race it in the Le Mans 24-Hour race and BMW decided to have Sam Posey co-drive with him. The logistics weren't simple: Le Mans is on the same weekend as the Mosport IMSA event, in which both Posey and Hans Stuck would normally be running two BMW coupes. Neerpasch supplied a fully up-to-date car (though without the anti-lock braking system) and reduced the Mosport entry to one car.

Calder, almost incredibly, charged nothing for the work; it was for a friend. It was his first automotive creation, though not his first motorized one: he had done numerous motor-powered works and he did a Braniff airliner not many years ago. But bringing Sam Posey into the picture was a second stroke of genius, as Sam is an artist himself. Poulain, the catalyst, is as involved with cars as he is with art.

The car was formally introduced at the Louvre (Musée des Arts Décoratifs) at the end of May and then sent to Munich to be displayed with other Calder mobiles in the Haus der Kunst, that city's famous setting for short-term exhibits. It stayed in Munich for just a day before heading for its serious work at Le Mans, but the opportunity to view it there was much appreciated. Aside from the good cheer, the car is fantastic to look at, especially when complemented by other Calder works of like color combination.

In case the Calder BMW met with bad luck at Le Mans, BMW insured it for DM 1,000,000—about $430,000! From there it was to spend the week after the race in the Museum of Modern Art in New York. Whatever befell it, it was bound to be the car to watch at Le Mans.—*Ron Wakefield*

11

LE MANS 24 HOURS

BRITAIN WINS EURO ENDURO

British-built Gulf-Fords finish 1st and 3rd in 24 Hour ' economy run ' Report by Mike Doodson ; pictures by Maurice Rowe

high speed collision and a puncture didn't prevent this 908/3 Porsche (top) from coming 4th but Bell and Ickx (for Britain!) prevented the Lafosse/Chasseuil Ligier JS2 (below) from coming 1st. Half the field comprised Porsches (top right) which de Cadenet in the Lola (right) couldn't completely defy. He came 15th

The best car with the best drivers undoubtedly won the Le Mans 24 hour race which finished at 4 pm on Sunday. But it was a Le Mans which lacked much of the attraction of previous years and reflected the chronic lack of interest which currently plagues this branch of the sport.

Winners of the race—and of the famous *Motor Trophy*—were Britain's own Derek Bell, 33, and Belgium's Jacky Ickx, 30, driving the previously unraced Gulf-Ford Cosworth GR8 belonging to the Slough-based Gulf Research Racing Company. Gulf's 1975 budget made provision for this race only, but the preparation of the car and the ability of its two drivers (both "borrowed" for the occasion from other teams) were more than enough to vanquish the French Ligier-Gitanes teams from Vichy, which after a series of misfortunes had only two of three cars remaining at the finish.

The first three cars home (a second Gulf finished 3rd in the hands of Aussie Vern Schuppan and France's Jean-Pierre Jaussaud) were all powered by Formula 1 Ford-Cosworth engines. These were specially detuned to comply with the "economy" regulations introduced for the first time in what transpired as a vain attempt to attract a different class of entrant.

It is a remarkable tribute to the talents of Cosworth's Keith Duckworth that his famous engine should be so adaptable, for in order to extend the interval between refuelling stops to 20 laps (instead of 16), Gulf Research boss John Wyer was obliged to improve fuel consumption to seven mpg, almost twice that which is achieved in Formula 1.

The latest aerodynamic Gulf body—with a much lower drag co-efficient—enabled the two cars to run at last year's maximum speed in spite of a 40 bhp reduction. And they completed the race with no engine problems whatsoever.

It is nevertheless significant that the Gulfs did not manage to match the previous best distance covered by a 3-litre car (a Matra-Simca, in 1973) in spite of generally good weather.

Derek Bell, who had never previously won at Le Mans, was determined this year to do it as slowly as possible, and right from the start he held back behind even his team-mate Vern Schuppan. Bell was not very happy with co-driver Jacky Ickx, who found it much easier to lap at proper "sprint" speed and managed to ignore most of the pit signals imploring him to go slower.

Electrical troubles on Saturday night delayed the Gulf "hare," however, and from that point onwards Schuppan and his French co-driver Jaussaud (a Le Mans veteran) were faced with a climb back on to the leader board, leaving Bell and Ickx in 1st place.

The all-French Ligier team, which had entered three of its attractive tall-finned coupes, did not have as much faith in the Ford engine as the Gulf people. They put their two sprint drivers, Beltoise and Jarier, into the car which was fitted with a Citroen-Maserati V6 engine. Jarier never got his chance in the race, for Beltoise was pushed off the road during the first stretch when the driver of one of the Ferrari GT cars—an American amateur from Florida—moved over on him under braking at Mulsanne corner and pushed the French car into the guardrail. Beltoise arrived back in the pits livid to report that the car was almost completely destroyed.

An incident involving the amateur British team of Londoners Alain de Cadenet/Chris Craft then cost the faster Ford-engined Ligier of Pescarolo/Migault its chance of challenging the Gulfs.

De Cadenet was getting up to maximum speed along the Mulsanne straight shortly before midnight when the rear bodywork of his new Lola T390 flew off. Completely unknown to de Cadenet, the rear body section flew into the road ("it must have sucked itself over the rear wing like a paper bag") and Migault hit it. Both cars lost over 40 minutes effecting repairs, and the damage ultimately put the French car into retirement.

The British Lola, which at one time had lain 3rd overall, had already lost time having a broken exhaust pipe repaired, and although it was lapping very fast towards the end of the race, in spite of many minor problems, it was never able to make up enough time. It finished 15th.

Thus French aspirations were left in the hands of the sole remaining Ligier, driven by sports car specialist Jean-Louis Lafosse and rallyman Guy Chasseuil. They managed to stay out of the way of stray cars and other obstructions in 2nd place, and the race almost came alive for the sparse French crowd in its last 90 minutes when Ickx brought the leading Gulf into the pits for an unscheduled stop.

For 12 hours the leading Gulf had suffered a serious drive-line vibration which worried both drivers, particularly around right hand corners. The vibration had broken an exhaust pipe, and while the mechanics sweated to fix it the Ligier crept up on their five lap lead.

Urged on by the chauvinistic crowd, the Ligier managed to get on to the same lap, but as it went past the pits to do so Ickx was restarting the engine and preparing to rejoin. There was a desultory "battle" between the two

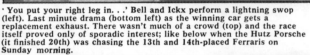

'You put your right leg in. . .' Bell and Ickx perform a lightning swop (left). Last minute drama (bottom left) as the winning car gets a replacement exhaust. There wasn't much of a crowd (top) and the race itself proved only of sporadic interest; like below when the Hutz Porsche (it finished 20th) was chasing the 13th and 14th-placed Ferraris on Sunday morning.

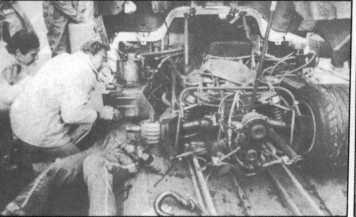

cars, but the Ligier was due for another fuel stop and the gap between it and the Gulf (which also came in, so that Bell could take the "winning" stint) was safe.

Perhaps the finest performance of the weekend came from the German team of Rheinhold Jöst. Since last year, Jost has fielded a five year old short-chassis Porsche 908/3 and often managed to get it into the first three by virtue of steady driving and superior reliability. For Le Mans, he had fitted an attractive long tail body to one of his two Porsches, and it ran almost faultlessly—slowed only by a collision and by several punctures—to finish 4th.

Jöst's partners were the Italian amateur Mario Casoni and Jurgen Barth, son of one-time European hill climb champion and Porsche tester, the late Eddie Barth.

More than half the 55 car Le Mans field consisted this year of Porsche Carreras entered in the Group 4 category. Most of them were driven by rank amateurs, but exceptions were the entries put in by the German entrants George Loos and Erwin Kremer.

Loos' Gelo Racing Team soon had the upper hand with its lead car, driven fast and safely by European GT champion John Fitzpatrick with able assistance

from Dutchmen Gijs van Lennep and Toine Hezemans. A second Gelo entry for Tim Schenken and Howden Ganley ran into trouble on Saturday night before retiring, and second place in the class went to *Motor* contributor Nick Faure, putting his advanced driving technique into a polished race (his first Le Mans) with a Belgian-owned and prepared Carrera. The car was sponsored by Swinford Motors and co-driven by John "BMW" Cooper (spectacular on last year's Avon/*Motor* Tour) and Belgian veteran "Beurlys."

The Le Mans organisers, having freed themselves of the CSI's World Championship of Makes Status by opting for their own "economy" rules, attempted to attract some exciting cars to a special class for GT cars which, because they are made in too small quantities, are not recognised by the CSI.

Three of the four entries in this class were Ferraris entered by Luigi Chinetti of the North American Racing Team. After a disagreement over whether or not one of his cars had qualified for another class, Chinetti—a three-time Le Mans winner himself—withdrew all four cars in a last-minute drama.

This deprived the spectators of the chance of seeing a Ferrari Berlinetta Boxer and two front-engined cars (all prepared in

Chinetti's New York workshop) in action. The sole remaining "GTX" class car was a turbo-Carrera, which duly won the class, albeit many miles behind the much faster driven GT Carreras.

Other interest in the race also disappeared inside the first 90 minutes when the quickest of three all-girl crews, France's Marie-Claude Beaumont and Italy's Lella Lombardi, dropped out.

Mlle Beaumont, an attractive blonde well-known in rallying circles, started the race at the wheel of the sole Alpine-Renault, one of the expensive V6 2-litre sports cars which cleaned up their championship last year.

She was pressing the 3-litre Ligiers for her first dozen laps, and was almost ready to make her first refuelling stop when the little blue Alpine, heavily sponsored by Elf, ran out of fuel. In spite of advice from her mechanics, she was unable to restart the engine, and the car had to be abandoned, refuelling away from the pits being strictly forbidden.

Theories about the cause of the fuel shortage ranged from dirt in the pick-up pipe to fuel being "sucked up" by the special safety sponge inside the tanks themselves. It is quite possible, however, that in being drawn into an

early dice with supposedly faster cars driven by men the lady had used up more petrol than expected.

New regulations for 1976 are still being discussed at Le Mans, but nothing will be settled before September. The organisers are under attack in the French Press for attempting to press their own rules on sports car racing, but the fear remains that sports car racing itself is dying on its feet, incapable of being revived in an era when sports car manufacturers are most notable for the speed at which they go out of business.

RESULTS

**43rd Grand Prix d'Endurance
24 Heures du Mans, 14-15 June 1975**
1 Gulf-Ford GR8 (Derek Bell/Jacky Ickx), 336 laps, 4595.58 kms, 119.0 mph; 2 Ligier-Ford JS2 (Jean-Louis Lafosse/Guy Chasseuil), 335 laps; 3 Gulf-Ford GR8 (Vern Schuppan/Jean-Pierre Jaussaud), 330 laps; 4 Porsche 908/3 (Rheinhold Jöst/Mario Casoni/Jurgen Barth), 325 laps; 5 Porsche Carrera (John Fitzpatrick/Gijs van Lennep/Toine Hezemans), 315 laps; 6 Porsche Carrera (Nick Faure/John Cooper/"Beurlys"), 311 laps; 7 Porsche Carrera (Borras/Moisson/Cachia), 309 laps; 8 Porsche Carrera (Ballot-Lena/Bienvenue/Wollek), 304 laps; 9 Porsche Carrera (" Billy "/Contrera/Bollanos), 304 laps; 10 Porsche Carrera (Maurer/Beez/Straehl), 295 laps, 4037.12 kms, 104.5 mph.

Class winners : Group 5, Gulf-Ford (Bell/Ickx); **Group 4,** Porsche Carrera (Fitzpatrick/van Lennep/Hezemans); **Group 3,** Porsche Carrera (Maurer/Beez/Straehl).

Racing's Darkest Day

• *Twenty years ago, something happened at Le Mans that changed the face of racing forever after. Phil Hill, then a young driver with little more than a string of SCCA successes under his belt, was there to see it.*

Early in May of 1955, the two of them took the boat from Houston, a three-liter Ferrari Monza crated in the hold—Phil Hill the driver and Richie Ginther the mechanic, light-hearted as leprechauns with pocketsful of silver, off to barnstorm Europe. They disembarked at Barcelona and took the train to Modena. There *Il Commendatore* himself got in touch with Hill and invited him to drive a works car in the 24 Hours with Umberto Maglioli. "In a moment," Hill remembers, "it seemed I was a real racing driver, driving a factory Ferrari at Le Mans. It was the best news of my life."

The cars were Aurelio Lampredi's six-cylinder 121 LMs—4.4s, good and quick but unreliable, no match for the Mercedes 300SLRs or the Mike Hawthorn/Ivor Bueb D-Type Jaguar. Fangio and Moss were the mainstays for Mercedes, with John Fitch, Karl Kling and the two Frenchmen, Pierre Levegh and Jean-Claude Simon.

Everyone was worried about the narrow pit straight. Everyone except Charles Faroux, the organizer. Alfred Neubauer, the Mercedes manager, complained to him before the race.

"I think," answered Faroux with a smile, "you're being pessimistic. We've been organizing this race since 1923, and nothing has ever happened." Hill agreed with Neubauer: "It was unbelievably narrow, a two-lane country road with no wall between the track and the pits and cars passing each other 20 feet away from the pit area at full throttle."

At six o'clock, the blue day began to fade, while an implacable Fangio chased Hawthorn and the crowd stayed on tiptoe to watch. Hill put in his ear plugs and strapped on his helmet standing on the plankwood pit counter next to *Il Maestro* Ugolini, the legendary scorer who could keep track of 50 cars for 24 hours without relief. Maglioli was running seventh. Hill was reading over Ugolini's shoulder when a mechanic tugged his trouser leg and said in Italian that someone was shouting to him from the spectator terraces across the track. Hill looked at the sea of heads. An arm waved. It was Tom McGeachin, who lived on the same block in Santa Monica.

And then, as McGeachin looked, Hill suddenly was gone. "I had this extra sense," recalls Hill, "that always warned me something was going wrong just before it happened. It stayed with me all the years I was racing. I'd already worked out what I was going to do if a car got loose in the pits; I was very conscious of self-preservation in those days. So I didn't think, I just jumped backward off the counter and crouched down.

"Then I heard it: bang, thump, crash, again and again, shrieking tires and screams. It went on forever, before the people started coming into the pits, scrambling, tearing at each other. The back door was locked; people were pounding on it hysterically to get out. Thick white smoke billowed across the track from a brilliant fire on the bank opposite. People ran aimlessly across the track through the smoke, dodging cars, waving, shouting. I remember a man tearing a banner off the fence in front of the terraces, a *gendarme* lying on the far side of the track without his legs.

"As I stood there gaping, Luigi Chinetti grabbed me. 'You shouldn't look,' he said. Ginther came up. They herded me out back. I felt annoyed at being treated like a child. Chinetti kept saying, 'You shouldn't see all this.

You have to drive.' Ginther left and came back. 'Maglioli's coming in,' he said.

"It was still chaos. Cars driving by at walking speed through the smoke. Someone said something about a car going into the crowd, but no one was sure what had happened." Then Hill was in his car and pulling onto the track, making his debut with Ferrari amid disaster that dwarfed completely what he was doing. Yet they were watching him through it all, and he had to go quickly to prove himself.

As soon as the road was clear, he started moving. He felt relieved that what had happened seemed not to be affecting him. But as he came over the hill at White House, there was an MG upside down, burning in the middle of the track, and more flags waving through the smoke. It was surreal, an incredible, repetitive nightmare. As he burst through, there was the second pall of smoke over the pits and more flags waving angrily. He slowed to a crawl and turned on the headlights until he had snaked past the fire and the stretchermen. Breaking into waning sunlight, this time shaken and uncertain, he was struck again by the absurdity of what he was doing.

How absurd wasn't apparent until he came to White House for the second time. As he slowed in anticipation, a white Mercedes went past him like a rocket. It was Moss, the golden opportunist, the 23-year-old professional, taking every advantage. It was a lesson that stayed with Hill always, the sight of Moss doing business as usual in the face of total disaster, cold, hard, clear-headed. Hill realized how muddled he was, how ineffectual he had become. This was no seat from which to make value judgments, no place for emotion or equivocation; they only made him a liability. It was too late to worry about being an accessory. Of course he was, and so was everyone in the place; there were no innocents. But he had an obligation to himself and everyone around him as long as he drove. That was all that counted. "I shook myself awake," he said, "and went after Moss, got on with my job while the others got on with theirs."

On the terraces, at least 85 people lay dead or dying with perhaps 150 injured. The race had to go on; evacuation would be impossible otherwise.

Exactly what happened is still hazy. Hawthorn was leading Fangio by 100 yards as they started past the pits on the thirty-sixth lap, at 150 mph. Between the leaders was Levegh's Mercedes, at least a lap down. Twice the Jaguar pits had signaled Hawthorn to come in for fuel, and now his board came out again. Apparently he saw it late but decided to stop anyway. He slipped past Englishman Lance Macklin's Austin-Healey on the left, braked hard and dived for the pits. Macklin, startled by the D-Type slashing across in front of him, swerved left and there was Levegh faced with a closing gap and no chance of slowing in time.

Levegh's real name was Pierre Bouillon. Two years before, the little Frenchman had made himself a legend by driving his Talbot 23 hours unrelieved before he blew the engine, in the lead. Now he raised an arm in warning and went for the hole. There wasn't room. His broad 300SLR mounted the Healey, bounced off onto the low bank in front of the terrace and came apart. The engine and front wheels went into the crowd like chain shot at 100 mph.

Fangio saw the arm shoot up and went to the right. He passed the Healey, but there was the D-type, dead ahead and still slowing (Hawthorn finally stopped 80 yards beyond his pit). He went to the left, grazing the Jaguar; afterward they found green paint on the right front fender of his silver Mercedes.

Hill's Ferrari went out at 11 o'clock, and at midnight word came from Stuttgart and Mercedes withdrew. Hill went back to town and slept. He came down early in the morning. He looked, wondering if he'd see McGeachin, but he didn't. Hawthorn and Bueb still led. They would until the end. Amazingly, now there was no sign of the disaster. "It was as if nothing had happened," Hill says. "The crowd stood packed on the terraces where slaughter had been, watching the cars go by. And when it was over, Hawthorn and Bueb seemed delighted with their victory. Maybe they weren't fully aware of the tragedy—that's possible—or maybe they had been able to force it out of their minds. Anyway, I remember feeling very uncomfortable watching them celebrate." A massive inquiry ended without apportioning blame. The remains of Levegh's Mercedes were impounded for over a year. Many road races were canceled. The Pope called for an end to such a barbarous business. Switzerland, which hadn't been organizing much more than hillclimbs anyway, banned racing entirely. Mercedes completed the season and then quit. The sport was threatened more seriously than it had been since the Paris-Madrid disaster of 1894, particularly such venerable road races as the Mille Miglia and the Targa Florio. And two years later, when the Marquis de Portago killed himself, his co-driver and 11 spectators in the Mille Miglia, the Italian government banned the race. Le Mans 1955 created a new consciousness toward safety in motor racing. Cavalier attitudes went by the board.

Certainly Hill and Ginther's barnstorming summer came to an inglorious end. There were simply not enough races left to run. They came home to California, Hill to a curious footnote to the disaster.

A few days after he returned to Santa Monica, he opened the door to none other than Tom McGeachin.

"My God," said Hill, "I'm glad to see you."

"I wanted to thank you," said McGeachin. "When I saw you disappear, I thought for an instant you'd fallen off the pit counter. Then I realized what you'd done, and for some reason I dropped flat too. I think the car must have gone right over me.

"Everyone around me was killed."

—Charles Fox

11 JUIN 1955

PETE BIRO

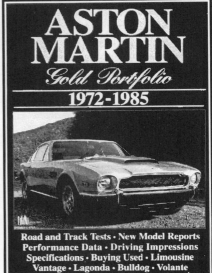
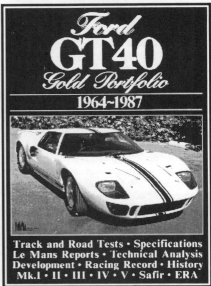

Jacky Ickx clips the guardrail on the way to his excellent victory with Derek Bell in Gulf's GR8.

E MANS 24 HOURS

Bell heads the Gulf stream

By BOB CONSTANDUROS   **Pictures by MOTOFOTO**

has always been called the Vingt Quatre Heures d'Endurance, but this year Le Mans was more of an endurance race than ever, and produced some interesting results. From the middle of the third hour to the end of the race, Derek Bell and Jacky Ickx stroked their car home to win by over a lap at the end of what must have been more of a drive to finish than a race. Their nearest challenger, from the sixth hour, was always a lap behind if not more, and for much of this time, it was their own teamates Vern Schuppan/Jean Pierre Jaussaud in second. Then less than two hours before the finish, the exhaust cracked on the leader's Gulf, but the cushion to the then second placed Ligier of Jean Louis Lafosse/Guy Chasseuil was sufficient, and after his 24 hours a delighted Bell took the flag to head a Cosworth 1-2-3. The surviving Ligier-both he other two had hard luck stories-was delayed by a duff alternator, but was then joined by Schuppan's Gulf delayed with the car pulling to the right, so these two found themselves on the same lap, swapping places for the last four hours of Sunday morning. But a shower of rain on the overcast Sunday soaked the electrics of the Gulf and it was resigned to third. The Porsche 908 of Rheinhold Jost and Mario Casoni had been as high as second, but punctures and a slight collision dropped it to fourth by the end. Behind them came the first of the GT cars, the faultlessly running Carrera of John Fitzpatrick/Gijs van Lennep plus thers.

It was, of course, a race of milestones. The first time that the race was not a round of the World Championship of Makes since inception, because of the first economy regulations introduced. The effect of these was of detuned cars and a sub-standard entry list. The result was a smaller crowd, possibly less actual racing, but an interesting thought that the winner's average speed was less than ½ a kph than that of last year, in near identical conditions. A major milestone was that it was John Wyer's fourth win as an entrant in a career that spans Aston Martins, GT40s and the Gulf, and it was a triumph for this British based team headed by John Horsman who came to conquer, and resoundingly succeeded.

ENTRY AND PRACTICE

Le Mans, the long distance race of many years' standing, was a somewhat different kettle of fish in 1975. The French organisers, the Automobile Club d'Ouest had decided to make their own regulations for 1975 regarding fuel consumption and their ideas caused the CSI to exclude them from the World Championship of Makes. This naturally, had a rather detrimental affect on the entry, even though some of the major participants in sports car racing decided that Le Mans is still Le Mans, that to win this 24 hour "Race" of endurance was to send the world a strong message, and for this season, Le Mans still held some interest.

But back to those regulations again. They referred to a fuel economy measure which required the cars to do 20 laps without refuelling whereas last year, the Matras did around 15 laps per stop, and the Gulfs one more. Thus, a considerable improvement had to be found among the G5 prototypes, and there were some problems down among the Ferraris in the G4 classes.

To qualify, cars had to be seen to do those 20 laps to prove that they were going to do the laps in the race, and thus each car had to well over an hour's racing to qualify, and then do a quick time to get on the grid. With the lack of entry, and this quite hard qualifying effort, many of the top entries really cut down their practice sessions and as the qualifying had to be done in the dark, one often found very few cars on the track early in the day.

Heading the grid, but not necessarily the entry, as far as the French were concerned, were the two specially built Gulf GR8s, powered by their own, and considerably detuned, 3.0 DFVs. For the purposes of fuel economy, and reliability the drivers were only using 8200 to 8400 revs, which compared with last year's 10,400. The new cars, with lengthened wheelbase from last year, but using the same Len Baily designed suspension, had a complete new wind tunnel tested bodyshape along the lines of the Alpine, formulated by team manager John Horsman, and the cars were to run at Le Mans only. The new bodywork, in fact, was so successful, that it lessened the drag co-efficiency from 0.53 to 0.35 and together with narrower tyres, the cars lost very little time in top speed on the Mulsanne straight. To confirm the improvements, Jean Pierre Jaussaud, who was to drive one car with Vern Schuppan, said they felt as nice, and handled as well as the Matras that he drove the previous year. But it was the sister car of Jacky Ickx/Derek Bell which took pole position with a time of 3m 49.4s, Ickx having set the time. This was set on Wednesday evening, and the team didn't bother to bring the car at all on

Thursday. But the other car had a valve spring cap disintegrate in the engine, an apparently rare occurrence, so after the engine was changed, they ran the car on Thursday to try it out, and then encountered a slight brake problem. The disc was picking up residue from the pads, but a change of pad remedied things and all was well. Jaussaud set a time of 3m 51.8s.

The next row held the first of the three car Ligier team, sponsored of course, by Gitanes, who were much in evidence as usual. With no Matras around this year, the team was the focus of much French attention. The cars have been running in their DFV trim throughout the year, so they were well tested, and with former Matra team manager, Gerard Ducarouge in charge, things were well organised, and only the two DFV cars appeared on Thursday. The Ford cars were revving up to 9000 rpm, with the engines producing a measly 380 bhp due to their economy tuning. It was the Jean Louis Lafosse/Guy Chasseuil car which sat on the second row, Lafosse setting the 3m 53.4s.

Beside the Ligier, was Rheinhold Jost's well known Porsche 908/3, Mario Casoni and Jurgen Barth were to help him out in the driving seat. The Porsche, despite being privately entered, had a large staff of Porsche personnel, most of them on holiday, but taking great interest in the proceedings. A new engine came from Germany for them on the Friday evening, after their previous race engine had been overrevved and it was thought better to have it changed. Casoni set their 3m 55.1s, benefiting from a long CanAm tail section.

The third row held the second Ligier with DFV power, that of Henri Pescarolo/Francois Migault, in which Migault set a 3m 57.4s. Beside him was the DFV powered Lola T284 of Heinz Schultess/Herve Bayard on 3m 59.9s. The car had no problems during practice, and it was Bayard who set their time.

Row four was headed by Alain de Cadenet's Lola T380, again with a 3.0 DFV detuned by John Nicholson. De Cadenet had forsaken his own named car for this event, but found, much to his disgust, that the new car was lacking nearly 15 mph in top line speed. There were no Lola personnel in attendance, and though the team tried a number of adjustments, they went back to the original spec, but had to do one or two mods on the all enveloping engine cover to release hot air. Goodyear's Keith Greene in charge of the team at Ruaduin and it was Chris Craft who set their 4m 2.7s. Alain de Cadenet was named second driver with sports car expert Guy Edwards named as the reserve. With a large Union Jack on the rear wing, it looked as though among the team were sponsored by Britain but among the various names helping out were Duckhams and Tic Tac mints, the latter thanks to Guy Edwards.

With them was the first of the 2 litre sports cars, the 2.0 Alpine Renault of Lella Lombardi and Marie-Claude Beaumont. However, Gerard Larrousse had a hand in the proceedings before adjourning to Austria's F2 event, for it was generally said to be he who set the 4m 2.9s although it was attributed to "Beaumont." With many events run by the car already, it wasn't surprising to hear that they ran without problems, using a long tail for the circuit.

Row five held the third Ligier, that of the two Jean-Pierres Beltoise and Jarier. This was fitted as last year's cars were, with the three litre Maserati engine, and both Jean-Pierre's elected to drive this car, as they felt that with the slower speed and previous form, they had a good chance of finishing well up. The Ligier was a late entry on the lists as it had been thought that they wouldn't be able to enter three cars. As such, it was fairly standard.

Alongside the Ligier was the first of the Group 2 cars, the paint adorned BMW CSL to be driven by Herve Poulain/Sam Posey. Poulain is an art fan, and when this IMSA contesting spare car was painted in yellow, orange and red by artist Alexander Calder, he fixed up the drive and BMW arranged Sam Posey to co-drive. Although it was entered by Poulain, Jochen Neerpasch was much in evidence, and to complete the team, the well known veteran Jean Guichet was named as reserve. Posey set the 4m 6s, but Guichet wasn't far behind.

Two two litre cars came next, the ROC Lola T294s of Laurent Ferrier/Xavier Lapeyre and Pierre-Marie Painvin, and France Hummel. Ferrier set their first time of 4m 8s, with Lapeyre setting the 4m 12.9s for the other car. Practice wasn't a particularly happy affair, as the heat affected the often hot Simca engines, and the two cars plus the third team member, had a troublesome time.

Alongside Christian's Poirot's Porsche 908 on row seven was the first of the GT cars, that of

Claude Ballot-Lena/Jacques Bienvenue, in, not surprisingly a Porsche Carrera. The 4m16s set by Ballot-Lena was just 0.7s quicker than the Tebernum Carrera of Clemens Schickentanz/Hartwig Bertrams. This, in turn, had the Claude Haldi/Juan Fernandez Carrera a row down, which Fernandez put into the Armco on the Thursday, but which reappeared for the race. Alongside them was the first of the Ferraris, entered by NART for Carlo Facetti and Ronnie Bucknum to drive.

Another row back was the Lola-Richardson T294 of Nigel Clarkson/Derek Worthington which had a BDA fitted. A veritable cast of stars were in attendance including Geoff Richardson, with former Lola man Patrick Head helping out, and those sons of famous fathers, Adrian Hamilton and Stuart Rolt. Prince Michael of Kent even manned the pumps during the night. Apart from a misfiring practice engine, the car ran well.

Sharing this row was the first of the strong Porsche Carrera team entered by Georg Loos, this one being the Carrera of John Fitzpatrick/Gijs van Lennep. The other cars were driven by Toine Hezemans/Manfred Schurti and Tim Schenken/Howden Ganley, with George Loos joining in when he was needed. Causing much amusement were the pit signals, including a hammer and much hand waving. This was to tell Hezemans that he was going too fast for qualifying, and he was promptly reprimanded . . . until it was found that the time given was someone else's.

Another British based entry was among these, the 2.0 March-Cosworth 75S for Richard and Mike Knight of Winfield racing school fame, sharing with Christian Mons. However, their supposedly demon Cosworth has misfitting heads, and the car has to have a bitza engine built up. After more Porsches and some more G2 cars, came the Porsche Carrera of Nick Faure/John Cooper/Jean "Beurlys" sponsored by Harley Davidson and Swinford Motors. As with many of the Porsches, this one had few problems and sat on the fifteenth row.

The rest of the grid was largely made up of more G2 cars, some slow 2 litres cars and yet more Porsches. Among these was a sprinkling of Ferraris, including the Daytona which Englishman Richard Bond was expecting to drive, but found the drive sold from under him. NART had some more cars too, the Boxer run last year, a Dino (which was to cause problems) and a special Michelotti bodied Daytona. Drivers included Ronnie Bucknum, Lucien Guitteny and Jacky Haran.

Sigma appeared again, this time the low sports car being powered by a turbo charged Toyota engine, but the car, with Japanese drivers, didn't qualify initially, but things were to happen which got it in. What happened was that the organisers told NART that on Thursday night, their Dino had qualified. Come Friday, it didn't appear on the lists. Why? It hadn't qualified. Yes it had, said patron Luigi Chinetti. No, yes, no, it went on all day. Saturday came and Chinetti had another go and this time the organisers got rude, and Chinetti, simply withdrew the lot, letting in three reserve cars at the last minute and making Le Mans very expensive and rather unenjoyable for NART, long time entrants at Le Mans.

RACE

Saturday was another really glorious day, even clearer than the previous scorchers, but something or other was keeping the crowds away, for there wasn't the traffic nor the dust that the vast number of people normally cause. But it would seem that something would overheat — even the driver — in such hot conditions but there were no such complaints when the race got under way. As four o'clock approached, so the cars lined up for their slow rolling lap and immediately there was a problem, for the Schultess/Bayard Lola wouldn't start, and only after the starter had been attended to did the Lola set off, already five minutes behind

The second placed Ligier is a blue against the tall shadows of the early evening on Saturday. Jean Louis Lafosse and Guy Chasseuil drove.

Battle scarred but fourth, Jost/Casoni/Barth had no engine troubles in the Can Am tailed 908 Porsche.

the rest. One of the late entry Porsche Carreras was in the pits for nearly half an hour before it set off.

But up at the front, the two Gulfs got away cleanly as the minute hand clicked on to four o'clock, and at the end of the first lap, Bell led from Schuppan, followed by Pescarolo, then team-mate Lafosse, Jost, Posey, Beaumont, Craft, Beltoise and then a gap to the G4 Porsches. But what did one lap matter in the couple of hundred that would be covered? As the Gulfs slowly pulled away from the Porsche now, early pit visitors in those first couple of laps were the Clarkson Lola with gear selection problems — there are eight rose joints involved — and also the Posey BMW, this latter because the tank was full and a valve had jammed which should let in air, and promptly caused fuel starvation. It took a lap to fix.

By lap three, with the order now Schuppan, Bell, Jost, the Ballot Lena Porsche had a quick visit to the pits, losing the G4 dice which was now headed by Schickentanz from Fitzpatrick, and a whole host of Carreras snapping away just behind. The lappery, amazingly, had begun already and by lap five, there were only seven cars anywhere near in touch, with Beltoise already taking things easy and losing touch with Beaumont's Alpine. Two ROC Lolas had pitted with electrical problems, as they were to for many laps to come.

By lap nine, just forty minutes after the start of the race, there were a mere eight cars on the same lap; how the mighty event has fallen. One of these, Lafosse's Ligier made it seven by pitting, for the red electrical warning light had come on, and while the mechanics checked the complete system, he fell a lap in the six minutes, and it was discovered to be just a faulty light anyway.

After one hour then, the two Gulfs were out in front, followed by Jost's Porsche, Craft in the de Cadenet Lola, the Pescarolo Ligier, Beaumont's Alpine and Beltoise's Ligier, the rest were already a lap down. Fitzpatrick had control of the G4 class but only by 1.2s from Schickentanz, and Schurti had already dropped back with a puncture. The leading cars at that hourly stage had covered one less lap than last year's.

The G3 Carrera of last year's GT winner, Cyril Grandet and Bob Wollek had to come in early after an 'off' and a puncture, but after fifteen minutes, it was time for the first pit stops, and very soon the pit area was alive with cars. Bell, Jost and Craft, covered by a couple of seconds, all came in together, but a late one to come in was Beaumont's Alpine. In fact she never made it, for as she rounded Mulsanne, the engine coughed and died. At first it was thought that she'd tried to do too many laps, but when it was analysed later, in fact part of a rubber seal in the tank had disintegrated causing the fuel pump to block and her race was over. Bayard, who had never got anywhere near his rightful position was another to stop after the rear radius arm pulled out, and his effort was over.

So at the end of the second hour, the two Gulfs still led, now with Bell in front, by a mere 2.1s. Schuppan reported the car jumping out of second from an early stage, but the gear could be held, or just abandoned in favour of third in places. De Cadenet now followed the Gulfs, just in front of Jost and Casoni, and these were the only ones on the same lap. The Pescarolo/Migault Ligier was one lap down, the other two Ligiers two down along with Posey's BMW, now charging along. The Christian Poirot Porsche was next, with Schickentanz leading the GTs by 11s now from Fitzpatrick/van Lennep.

Just after the two hour mark, Beltoise's Ligier

Nick Faure/John Cooper and Jean "Beurlys" had a trouble free run in Beurly's Carrera, but (below), a number of Carreras needed new engines during the race.

hit brake trouble with a pipe coming loose and rubbing the wheel. In fact the problem was so severe that he had to be caught by his mechanics when he came into the pits. The stop cost him 12m. The Japanese Sigma team were in trouble, after running a creditable fifteenth, for they were due for another rebuilding stint as last year when the oil pump fell off and the engine needed new bearings. But after a two hour job, the car still wasn't healthy enough to continue, and they retired. Before the end of this third hour, Beltoise was 'in the news again, for having just got by Harry Jones of Florida in his Daytona, he found Jones nudging him just before the Ford chicane, and in this lefthander, the car was turned off the track into the barrier, and that was that.

So in the third hour, it was still the Gulfs out in front with now just the Porsche 908 for company on the same lap, followed by the two remaining Ligiers, Posey's CSL and then the first of the GTs, the Fitzpatrick car leading Schickentanz. De Cadenet was sitting in the pits having his exhaust rewelded at this stage, an operation which dropped him to twelfth as it took 46 minutes. Vibration had caused it to crack right up by the manifold.

Then it was the turn of the GTs to have their problems. As the sun began at last to cool, Toine Hezemans pitted his Gelo Porsche with a dropped valve, and a few minutes later, it was Schickentanz who had his motor blow up. Schickentanz had a rod through the bottom of the engine, but Hezemans had a new motor fitted. In the two litre class, by the end of the fourth hour, a good class dice had developed between two of the ROC Lolas, still popping and banging, and Nigel Clarkson's Lola, now back on song. But the Knights in the Alroy Racing March weren't having such fun, pitting with alternator problems.

At the eight hour then, Gulfs still led, faultlessly, then the 908 again, the Ligiers, Posey's BMW and now Fitzpatrick in the Carrera with van Lennep. Next up was the Faure/Cooper Porsche, a good effort, partially caused by more problems with Hezemans, having his engine changed and then having a wheel collapse on him at Indianapolis, heralding retirement. Schenken had been having trouble with third gear in his Gelo Porsche, and before this fourth hour had ended, he was in the pits having a new gearbox fitted. It was all go for the Gelo team, although Ganley didn't look too excited by it all. The operation took 45 minutes. Ballot Lena, meanwhile, had a brace of punctures, but the order at the head of the chart looked the same at nine o'clock, except that Posey's BMW had had the transmission broken out on the circuit, and he was out, making the G2 entry very sparse.

Apart from Schenken having more trouble in his Porsche, still with the gears, there was little to report in the fifth hour, but moving on to the sixth, the picture was different. Jaussaud had come in with the second placed Gulf misfiring, and to cure this, the team changed the black box and alternator in a 25 minute stop, during which they changed the pads as well. This dropped the Gulf down to fifth behind the Porsche and two Ligiers, but still the sister car kept charging on and it seemed that nothing would stop it. Fitz and van Lennep still headed the GTs from Faure and Cooper, who were running well, albeit, two laps behind and being caught by the Kremer Carlos Bollanos/"Billy" car.

Clarkson had an engine problem which dropped him right out of the running, and it seemed cruel justice that two fearfully misfiring cars should be leading the class up to 2.0 litres. But one large drama appeared when the De Cadenet team noticed that the bonnet had come off the rear. De Cadenet hadn't in fact noticed what had hap-

Above, an anxious Vern Schuppan talks to team manager John Horsman (with glasses). Schuppan and Jean-Pierre Jaussaud finished third. Below, a day in the life of the Alain De Cadenet Lola, as he spins into the guardrail. After many problems, De Cadenet and Chris Craft finished fifteenth, setting fastest lap.

pened, except that the car wouldn't pull on the straight, and after receiving a signal to pit, duly came in to have another one fitted, a lengthy job. But more dramatic than that was poor Francois Migault who found the residue in the road on Mulsanne, and duly thumped it, ruining the front of the car, and requiring considerable patching, this taking 42m, which dropped him down to eleventh by the seventh hour. De Cadenet and Craft were even further back now, in thirtieth position.

In the GT class, by midnight with eight hours gone, Faure and Cooper had lost their second in class to the Kremer Carrera, but the Gelo car was still charging on, now lying fifth overall in front of the Poirot 908 which was running like all the 908s used to. De Cadenet was still having its rear engine cover properly fixed to prevent the previous accident happening again, losing another eight minutes.

With Frenchmen beginning to take to their sleeping bags under the trees and in the car parks, little took place in the next couple of hours, but the Migault/Pescarolo Ligier was in trouble with the alternator and the bonnet, having two long stops of 19m and 36m, which dropped the Ligier down the leader board, while at the same time, the Jost/Casoni/Barth Porsche had a coming together with a slower car at Mulsanne which took away the lights at around two in the morning. Rebuilding the bodywork took 22 minutes, all of which allowed the second Gulf to catch up. Bell and Ickx were on 159 laps, six more than the sister car, which was now on the same lap as the Ligier with the Porsche, three more laps behind.

Thus, at half distance, it was a Gulf one-two in the lead, then the Lafosse/Chasseuil Ligier, which had run well despite its early problems, and the Porsche 908 still, despite its stop. Then came the Carrera GTs, still with the Gelo car leading the Kremer car by some two laps.

Just into the second half of the race, with dawn just breaking at four, came news of another puncture, this time to Pescarolo, who was admittedly well down but the puncture must have been nasty on the Mulsanne straight, and the car never reappeared. At this stage, there were 37 cars still running, eighteen having retired. The dawn saw a welcome respite from the heat of the previous day, for there were clouds in the sky, and in fact the morning became overcast and cool.

The half way mark also had a further effect on proceedings in the Gelo camp, in that the Schenken/Ganley car was withdrawn as it wouldn't be classified because it hadn't completed 70 per cent of the class leader's distance at this stage. This heralded a change of policy for the winning car, and now as well as the regular drivers, Schurti and Hezemans would drive it for Porsche cup points.

By the end of the thirteenth hour, the positions were much the same as before, although De Cadenet was still fixing his bodywork, this delaying him another 25 minutes, although this British effort was now in nineteenth place.

In the two litre class, there was an interesting change, not in position but the fact that at least

John Fitzpatrick was number one driver with Gijs van Lennep in the Loos Porsche which finished a creditable and reliable fifth. Here he leads more Carreras.

one of the ROC cars was now running really well, although there were other problems. The Knights in the March were having a really bad time, with non-starting, misfiring, and next door, Clarkson was getting a niggle of a misfire, and lost time having brake pads changed, which dropped them out of the running. And before six o'clock, the Jost Porsche suffered a puncture on the straight, normally a car destroying act, but Jost struggled back, fitted a new wheel, and set off immediately, without losing any places, for he was two laps ahead of the next car, the Carrera of Fitzpatrick in fifth.

On the dot of six, Jaussaud arrived in the second placed Gulf complaining of a vibration in the car at the back, but was quickly sent on his way again, coming in again a quarter of an hour later. This time the rear suspension was checked in four minutes and out he went again.

But all this left the second placed Gulf and the surviving Ligier on the same lap after 15 hours of racing at seven o'clock, with the Ligier two minutes ahead. Meanwhile, Billy Whizz (alias Derek Worthington) was having his complete engine changed, which was to lose him 1hr 40m, for the engine had lost all compression in one cylinder, and Worthington and Patrick Head and Geoff Richardson worked hard to change the mill.

Just before 8, the Gulf took its second place back again. In fourth place, the 908 Porsche had yet another puncture, this time a rear, but the tyre was changed with the same speed as before and it kept its place. Fitz was four laps behind in the Carrera, followed by Bollanos "Billy" (2 further laps behind) and Cooper/Faure/Beurlys (one lap behind). But still up front, the Bell/Ickx rode faultlessly on.

Undoubtedly though now, the interest was in

this second place battle, for there was little other racing to watch. At eight o'clock, it was a Gulf one-two, but the Ligier was a mere 1m 15.1s behind Jaussaud and Schuppan. But then Schuppan brought the car into the pits for different wheels to be fitted to try and rid the vibration, and so the Ligier was in second at nine. At ten it was the Gulf, by less than 8s. At eleven, it was the Ligier in second again, for while the Gulf's handling would improve, it would then deteriorate again, and need more time in the pits. It was all brewing up to a good finish.

De Cadenet, with all his problems was in eighteenth place. While the car was singing along, lapping around the 3m 56s mark, it had to have the brakes repadded, and when this happened, half the rear suspension all but dropped out, it was so cracked and the stop dropped them even further back. Then at 11.25, De Cadenet came into the chicane before the pits, tried to get third gear, it slipped out, and in the ensuing moments, round went the Lola, gently kissing the barrier. More delay.

But again, all eyes were on the second placed battle. Schuppan pitted at 11.50, the Ligier at 12 and the Gulf, which had just led the Ligier fractionally before the stop, came out in the lead. But 20 minutes later, rain. In they came, one by one, for intermediates, the odd spin lower down, but nothing to worry either the leaders, nor the second placed battle. But the rain did have disastrous effects on the Gulf of Schuppan, for it got sicker and sicker. Water in the electrics was diagnosed, and the resulting pit stop anulled the battle, leaving the Ligier of Chasseuil and Lafosse to an easy second place, which couldn't be overcome without some sort of problems arising.

But the problems were not with the second Gulf, once it had been dried out, but the smooth running Gulf of Bell and Ickx. Having run perfectly and at an average speed above that of last year's unrestricted winner, the exhaust cracked in the penultimate hour. They had four laps advantage, but this was whittled down to two by the time the new system was fitted. While this was going on, the Bollanos/"Billy" Porsche finally came in for an astonishingly quick engine change by the Kremer team at 2.30, for the car had been going slower, and the Faure/Cooper/Beurlys car had in fact overhauled it for sixth spot. After twenty minutes in the pits, the Porsche went out to a deserved ovation from the crowd.

So now it was just a run to the finish. There were still 31 cars on the track, a fantastic number, at the head of which, the Gulf and Ligier swopped places for the Gulf to finish the 24 hours one lap ahead of the Ligier, for during the pit stop, the Ligier had caught right up, and once back on track, Lafosse unlapped himself once before the finish. The second Gulf was five laps down, before the smooth running Porsche of Jost/Casoni/Barth. The first of the GTs was fifth, the Fitzpatrick/van Lennep Carrera in which Hezemans, Schurti and of course, Loos himself had driven. It had run without problem apart from a cracked tailpipe which had been quickly repaired. The Belgian owned, British/Belgian driven Porsche finished a creditable sixth.

On the two litre side, the rather dated looking Moynet survived through reliability to finish first, albeit in twenty-second position driven by Christine Dacremont, Michelle Mouton and Marianne Hoepfner. Both the English 2 litres finished, the Lola in thirtieth and the March thirty-first, both having had new engines, and the Alroy March having to sort out tyres and a fuel leak at the end. Perhaps a notable finisher was a de Tomaso Pantera, which makes English F5000 preparation look a bit sick.

43rd Vingt Quatre Heures du Mans
Le Mans, June 14/15

1. Derek Bell/Jacky Ickx* (3.0 Gulf-Ford DFV GR8), 336 laps, 191.482 kph;
2. Jean-Louis Lafosse/Guy Chasseuil (3.0 Ligier-Ford DFV JS2), 335 laps, 190.558 kph;
3. Vern Schuppan/Jean-Pierre Jaussaud (3.0 Gulf-Ford DFV GR8), 330 laps, 187.703 kph;
4. Rheinhold Jost/Mario Casoni/Jurgen Barth (3.0 Porsche 908/3), 325 laps;
5. John Fitzpatrick/Gijs van Lennep/Manfred Schurti/Toine Hezemans/Georg Loos* (3.0 Porsche Carrera RSR), 315 laps, 179.499 kph;
6. Nick Faure/John Cooper/"Beurlys" (3.0 Porsche Carrera RSR), 311 laps;
7. Henri Cachia/Jacques Borras/Denis Rua (3.0 Porsche Carrera RSR), 309 laps; 8. Claude Ballot-Lena/Jacques Bienvenue (3.0 Porsche Carrera RSR), 304 laps; 9. Carlos Bollanos/"Billy" (3.0 Porsche Carrera RSR), 304 laps; 10. Edgar Straehl/Christian Beez*(2.7 Porsche Carrera), 295 laps; 11. Charlotte Verney/Yvette Fontaine/Christne Tarnaud (3.0 Porsche 911), 294 laps; 12. Cyrile Grandet/Bob Wollek (3.0 Porsche Carrera), 293 laps; 13. Jean Claude Andruet/Teddy Pilette/Hughes de Fierlandt (4.4 Ferrari Daytona), 293 laps; 14. Marcel Mignot/Harry Jones/Phillipe Gurdjian (4.4 Ferrari Daytona), 293 laps; 15. Alain de Cadenet/Chris Craft (3.0 De Cadenet Lola-Ford DFV T380), 291 laps.

* Class winners.

Dusk falls at Le Mans and the headlamps blaze through the fading light.

Was Le Mans re-born in 1976? With a new set of categories the race was thrown open to a much wider variety of cars than before; the A.C.O. welcomed Group 6, Group 5 and Group 4 cars together with some specially-invented categories like GT prototypes, and even Le Mans prototypes and a special invitation was made to American entrants, so categories were reserved for I.M.S.A. (International Motor Sport Association) specification sports cars, and N.A.S.C.A.R. (National Association for Stock Car Auto Racing) stock cars, as part of a tie-in with the world's other 24-hour race, at Daytona.

It was also the year of the turbo-charger; while turbo-charged cars had been seen at Le Mans before, it was the first time that several of the leading Group 6 entrants had turbo-chargers. Such cars were subject to an equalisation formula; the capacity of a turbo-charged engine was multiplied by 1.4 for classification purposes. The engine of for instance the Alpine-Renault, of two-litres capacity, was thus deemed to be 2.8 litres. The equalisation factor was no new invention and in fact, the formula existed ready-made in the Le Mans rule-book as a hang-over from the heyday of the supercharger.

Porsche-Martini works entries were back; with two Group 6 2.1 litre turbos, the 936 Spyders driven by Jacky Ickx/Gijs van Lennep (both past winners) and Joest/Barth; in addition to a Group 5 2.9 litre 935 turbo, a Carrera-lookalike 'silhouette' car. A similar 935 turbo was privately entered, and there were two 908s: a 2.1 litre turbo, and a normally-aspirated three-litre. In the Group 4 GT category, there were no less than 20 Porsches, split between the 934 turbos and the 911 Carrera RSRs.

Apart from the Porsches, Group 6 included the two-litre V6 Alpine-Renault A442 which was seen at Le Mans for the second time, but now fitted with a turbo; it was driven by Jabouille/Tambay/ Dolhem, and started in pole position, having put in the fastest practice lap. Among the DFV-supporters were the Gulfs which had come first and third in 1975, now under new American sponsorship and running as plain Mirage-Ford-DFVs; and a pair of Lolas, including the car of Chris Craft/Alain de Cadenet. Remaining Group 6 cars were all in the two-litre class, including three Chevrons, three Lolas, a Lenham and a Cheetah-BMW; apart from the last mentioned, using either Simca or Ford-Cosworth engines.

The final categories were the special prototype classes which contained some particularly interesting cars. Running under the main sponsor's name Inaltera, two elegant coupes with three-litre Cosworth-DFV engines were the brainchildren of Le Mans-based constructor Jean Rondeau who himself drove one of the cars together with Jaussaud and

Beckers, while the other was manned by past winner Pescarolo and Beltoise. Another new French contender was the WMP, with a 2.7 litre Peugeot V6 engine; the first Peugeot engined car to appear since the Constantin of 1955. The lion of Sochaux is a reluctant racer; Peugeot's previous Le Mans entries were in 1926, 1937, 1938 apart from the Constantin's lacklustre career of 1952-55. Finally, there was a turbo-charged 2.4 litre Lancia Stratos, the first Lancia at Le Mans since 1951-53; and a Japanese newcomer, a French-entered Datsun 260 Z. But notably not a single Ferrari.

The Alpine-Renault went into the lead from the start, but was soon overtaken by the Ickx/van Lennep Porsche 936. They then stayed firmly in the lead; at one stage they were as much as 16 laps ahead of the number 2 car, although a half-hour pitstop on Sunday at midday to change a broken exhaust system cut this in half. But they were still unassailable, and cruised home to an easy victory; van Lennep's second, Ickx's third and Porsche's third. So most of the interest in the race was in the battle for second place; for two-thirds of the race, the other Martini-Porsche 936 of Joest/Barth had been lying second, but then went out with transmission failure. The Alpine-Renault had held on to third place for a while but had retired much earlier, soon after midnight, when a piston broke.

The two Mirage-Fords had been fairly regularly running in fourth and fifth places, and with the retirement of the two higher-placed cars, moved up; the Lafosse/Migault car held on to its advantage and eventually finished second, but the Bell/Schuppan Mirage had fuel pump troubles and dropped back to finish fifth, while Craft and de Cadenet in the Lola went past them into third place, followed by Stommelen and Schurti in the Group 5 Porsche in fourth place. A Porsche Carrera - the first Group 4 car to finish - was sixth. Both the Inalteras finished, the Pescarolo car eighth after a Porsche 908, the other in twenty-first place. The big disappointment of the race had been the American cars - the stock cars proved to be far too slow, and while the Greenwood Corvette showed a spirited performance, a puncture resulted in a holed fuel tank, and that was that. None of the American cars finished. The Datsun crashed through the barriers at the Mulsanne straight, and its driver, Andre Haller, was killed in the ensuing fire.

The average speed of Ickx and van Lennep had been 123.49 mph, for a total distance of 2,968.88 miles; while the fastest lap was recorded by Reinhold Joest, in the Porsche 936, at 134.076 mph. The first win of a turbo-charged car began the present era at Le Mans; though for van Lennep, this win also marked his retirement from racing. Jacky Ickx by contrast, had not quite finished with Le Mans.

Jacky Ickx takes the Martini-Porsche 936 to his third victory at the Sarthe circuit, and the second for his co-driver Gijs van Lennep.

The voices of experience

Resounding third-time win for Jacky Ickx in Martini's Group 6 Porsche — Great swansong for team-mate Gijs van Lennep — Mirages second and fifth after fuel troubles — Alpine-Renault fast but fragile
Report: BOB CONSTANDUROS — Race data: CHRIS WITTY — Photography: DAVID WINTER

Experience told at Le Mans over a couple of hot days last weekend. Sharing the Martini-Porsche turbo Group 6 car, Jacky Ickx joined the elite ranks of those who have won the 24 Hours three times, and Gijs van Lennep scored his second victory in the race, thus marking his swansong in motor racing in fairytale style. To see two seasoned campaigners spraying Moet & Chandon over the crowd at the end reminded everybody that there really was nothing like experience. Experience at running a team, experience at pacing, even the early race tactics. There were four potential winning teams: JCB Mirage, Alpine, Martini-Porsche and Inaltera. The last-named showed why experience is necessary, the first underpaced themselves, and the Alpine was (and deserved to be) the Porsches' main challenger, but unfortunately, despite tremendous speed, it failed early in the morning with a burnt piston. Under its new guise, Le Mans was definitely a success: interesting cars, even if they did not last, and not a little rivalry between G6 and G5. One has to say that G6 was the winner, but it was a great place to have a contest.

For Britain, there was a share of second place by the Jean-Louis Laffosse/Francois Migault pairing in one of Harley Cluxton's Mirages, but also a splendid amateur effort from Alain de Cadenet/Chris Craft, who brought their newly bodied Tate & Lyle Lola into third overall. The Martini G5 Porsche was fourth in front of the second Mirage, driven by 1975 co-victor (with Jacky Ickx) Derek Bell and Aussie Vern Schuppan. Sadly, Les Vingt Quartre Heures claimed the life of a French Datsun 260Z driver when his car exploded in flames.

LE MANS 24 HOURS

ENTRY & PRACTICE

There's something which attracts drivers from all over the world to Le Mans. And this year, the Automobile Club de l'Ouest came up with the idea that, to get a little bit of everything from all over the world, they would throw their 24-hour race open to the world. It didn't matter what car you had, provided it complied with a recognised FIA formula. The main idea was that, with the Silhouette formula in operation, there were offshoots such as IMSA which could provide an interest in racing against the best of Europe. And where better than at Le Mans?

It was also originally going to be a round of the World Championship of Makes and, with everyone's consent, the offshoot cars would race against the Silhouette cars, normally something that is abhorred; but then, Le Mans is Le Mans. As it happened, for some reason the CSI promptly decided to hold a rival race on the same day at Paul Ricard. As time wore on, it was obvious that *tout le monde* would be off to Le Mans, thank you very much, and that Ricard could keep its race. Ricard cancelled it.

Group 6 cars, keen to show that they were not going to be outdone by G5 cars, were to race against them in their first direct contest. Inaltera decided that Le Mans would be a good race to win in France, and built their machine specially in a GTP class of its own. IMSA, the American sports car series, plus NASCAR, the saloon oval bowl series, decided to show their flag at the French classic, so that, as usual, there was going to be something unique at the Sarthe circuit.

When the entry was announced, then, there were the usual G5 cars, the usual G6 entries, two NASCAR entries, four IMSA cars, some G2 machines, the Inalteras built specially for the race and the victorious Gulf Mirages of 1975, back under the guise of Harley Cluxton's GT Cars business in Phoenix, Arizona, with backing from both JCB Excavators and Total. Suddenly it looked, on paper, an interesting race. It was going to be good just to hear those Southern boys with asphalt-bowl drawls, to see John Greenwood's legendary Batmobile Chevrolet Corvette, a NASCAR pitstop, a G5/G6 battle, and the French trying to beat the French.

So, for their usual weekend, ACO sealed off eight and a bit miles of public road centred on a straight bit of road leading to Tours (called the Mulsanne Straight).

Practice was not quite as long in years past. The reason was said to be that it had been a public holiday on the previous Monday, so that it was a bit difficult to get things done in time. Hence practice began late in the afternoon on Wednesday to midnight, and then for an hour less on the Thursday evening. Friday, as usual, was a rest day, although most teams spent the whole day checking over the cars. Some rest day.

As usual, it was hot. For some teams who had been there for previous days, it was good to get acclimatized, for it was to get hotter and hotter throughout the weekend. The general idea of long-distance practice is not to go out and bust a gut trying to set the fastest time, it's to make sure everything works as it should, to peak efficiency, and get everything ready for the race. Thus it should not be too hectic an affair, and furthermore the times set should not be considered to be of too great importance.

However, it was one hell of a time set by Jean-Pierre Jabouille during the first session. He was partnered by Patrick Tambay in the works Alpine-Renault turbo A442, and during both seassions the car really did look quick, so clean out of the corners and very quick down the straight. The French press got very excited about there being two cars at the race, but the only reason for this was that Alpine were trying a long-tailed car and a short-tailed one. However, the time of 3m 33.1s was so quick that they scarcely bothered to try the shorter one at all. They ran with the same turbo boost as in their unlucky World Sports Car Championship races, while the lengthened tail involved about 40cms more and a much smaller aeleron. For Tambay, sports car racing was a new experience; he had never raced anything with more than one seat. One disadvantage was the small, 120-litre fuel tank.

Porsche and Martini turned up with three cars, this a bit of a surprise. But what in fact they had done was to enlist the help of Reinhold Jost, who also had an entry for a Porsche 908/3 but not a turbo. Porsche came along with their normal car with the new bodywork in G6 version for Jacky Ickx (he had signed his Martini contract before his F1 contract, and thus had to give the Swedish

GP a miss), partnered by Gijs van Lennep, who swore this was going to be his last race. It must have felt good to be on the front row, especially with Porsche and long-distance expert Ickx as teammate. All the Porsches were supported by Martini and the works were running with 1.2 boost on the turbo as opposed to 1.4 (they had used 1.2 when the turbo ran in 1974). The time of 3m 39.8s was six seconds off the Alpine's, but Porsche were not worried.

For one thing, they had another car on the second row. This was the G5 car seen at Silverstone, running the turbo engine too of course, also with reduced boost. They also changed back to air cooling for this race as it was not a G5 championship event, the turbo air cooling taking up more space than the water cooling which is now mandatory on Porsches due to Silhouette ruling. The G5 935 also suffered a blown head gasket, so it was a good effort of Manfred Schurti/Rolf Stommelen to set their 3m 41.7s, this without Dunlop qualifying tyres which Porsche reckoned could pull off about 6s from the time.

Fourth fastest on the grid was a real surprise: two back-of-the-field French Formula 2 drivers in a 3-litre Lola with an ex-Graham Hill Racing DFV. The drivers were Bernard Chevanne and Doctor Xavier Lapeyre, neither fantastic drivers, but they put up a good effort to set 3m 44s in their Lola T286 run by Heini Mader.

The original 936 Porsche of Reinhold Jost/Jurgen Barth headed the third row fitted with the Martini bodywork seen all season on the regular G6 car, once again run by the works and again with reduced turbo boost. They set a 3m 45.4s which was a whole 3s quicker than their neighbours. They were Derek Bell/Vern Schuppan who really had to work for this time. Driving the Mirage again, the identical car which won last year again fitted with a DFV and using 400 more revs than last year (taking it up to 8800), Bell had to nip out in the dark to set his 3m 48.1s, for in the first session they had had a misfire. After the engines were changed, they had another go on the Thursday, but for much of the evening, it was thwarted by gear selection problems, eventually traced to a faulty clutch master cylinder which solved all the problems. Then Bell went out and did his bit.

After all, he couldn't have his place on the grid usurped by the number two car, that of Francois Migault/Jean-Louis Laffosse, even if he was staying at the Migault parental chateau. Both Mirages of course are owned by the amusing young Harley Cluxton, who had raked in JCB support and petrol from Total for the race. The second Mirage did not have its team-mate's problems and set a 3m 51.1s.

They headed the fourth row of the grid with a BMW for company, this the works turbo seen at Silverstone, now "painted" by Frank Stella with a sort of noughts and crosses criss-cross pattern (or a graph sheet with acceleration or power curves on it). Drivers were Brian Redman/Peter Gregg (the American IMSA driver) and Herve Poulain, who also drove the works "art"-decorated BMW last year. Of course, the BMW turbo has not had a very long career, and development problems were rife at Le Mans. They were going to run the car with 1.3 boost, but a valve jammed and gave it 2.0 during the first session, which meant that it wouldn't rev. Then a misfire upset the music in the second, before the motor blew altogether. A second motor was fitted for the race, but practising on the aerodrome early on Saturday morning, the car broke a piston which in turn damaged a valve, and as there were no replacement units, they had to be machined up. Thus the 3m 53.4s time was encouraging, although no-one was confident of a long run.

Heading the fifth row was the car which one felt a lot of people would come to see: the Chevrolet Corvette of John Greenwood, the Spirit of '76. This was not actually the car he runs in IMSA races, but a customer car due for delivery. When the ACO heard that Greenwood was not going to come, they helped out financially: the French helping the Americans to beat the British in Independence year. As with all the Stateside entries, they had one week to get ready before the ship left, which rather thwarted plans to run a narrower car. As it was, this one was quick enough. They had to gear it down from doing 118mph in first after the first practice and reckoned that they might get 215mph on the Mulsanne straight from the 7-litre, 660bhp engine. Helping out Greenwood, who set 3m 54.5s, was his brother Burt and French rally star Bernard Darniche. The latter had driven Greenwood's Corvettes before when the American had come to Le Mans, but Burt was a Le Mans Rookie. After the gearing had been sorted, the car then had the clutch centre fail, a freak fault, and after they had repaired that it ran out of petrol.

A pitstop for the second-placed JCB Mirage driven by Lafosse/Migault.

They shared row five with Alain de Cadenet's now rebodied Lola with DFV power. Le Mans followers may remember that de Cadenet reckoned he was losing as much as 20mph on the Mulsanne straight thanks to the new Lola bodywork, so with the help of development and some testing at a not-so-secret test ground somewhere between London and Bristol, they got things better. A hack DFV was replaced with a new mill for Thursday, as was the suspension, gearbox and so on, all of which rather delayed their practising.

There was what seemed a divorce in the Kremer Porsche camp. Last year, Erwin Kremer got the Mexicans Carlos Bolanos, Billy Sprowls and Alfredo Negrete to drive one of his cars, and once again, bearing loads of loot, they came back, this time driving his smart-looking G5 Porsche turbo with Hans Heyer. As with the works G5 car, they were back on air cooling for the turbo, whose boost they had reduced by 0.2 to 1.2. The car set a 3m 55.7s to head the sixth row.

Beside them was the first of the Inalteras, not built to win the race, said team manager and publicity co-ordinator Vic Elford, just made to give the best presentation for the sponsor. Jean Rondeau, driving the number two car, had really been the man behind the design and mechanic staffing, and in fact in development, the whole caboosh had only been fractionally altered at the rear end. The cars were powered by all-new DFVs from Cosworth giving about 410 to 415bhp and revving to 9500. There were a total of three cars to choose from, and highest on the grid were Henri Pescarolo/Jean-Pierre Beltoise on 3m 56.9s. This wasn't without its problems, for parking his road car in the paddock on the first morning, Beltoise caught a ring on his finger in the steering wheel and the little finger came off worst. It broke, so the French idol was in a little pain.

Back on the seventh row was the first crew over four minutes, Egon Evertz and Leo Kinnunen in the former's Porsche turbo 908/3, on 4m 0.5s. Their main problem was aerodynamics, so once that was sorted out there were hoping for more speed. Beside them was the second IMSA car, the Chevrolet Monza to be driven by Mike Keyser/Ed Wachs. This was an all new car, and although they would not admit it outright, it was really brought out to test it against the turbocharged cars. The car was basically the same as the Monzas run in the States apart from a rear wing. The 351 cu. ins engine would give 550bhp but was reduced to 525 for this race, and 340kmh was hoped for. It certainly seemed to handle well.

Next up on the grid, this the eighth row, was the Georg Loos turbo Carrera for Toine Hezemans/Tim Schenken. A late arrival caused worries, this due to a customs hold-up, and the diff completely seized in the pit road, so their 4m 1.1s was a good effort. It was also the first G4 car. Beside them were Dieter Quester/Albrecht Krebs in the Schnitzer BMW 3.0 CSL raced in G5 this year. They were running to finish, and joining the

strength for the race was Belgian BMW specialist Alain Peltier. They set a 4m 3.8s.

The ninth row held the second Inaltera and the Alpina Faltz BMW 3.0CSL. The Inaltera had immediate problems before even reaching the circuit when a fuel tank was found to be faulty. It was a long job to remove it and then it had to be revulcanized, so Jean Rondeau/Jean-Pierre Jaussaud/"Christine" scarcely had much time to practise on the Wednesday evening, but they made up for it on Thursday and set a 4m 4.2s. Beside them was the Sam Posey/Hughes de Fierlandt/Harald Grohs BMW 3.0 CSL which had big problems with fumes: "It makes you feel sick, I want to burp the whole time. If you'd like me to go into the technical difficulties . . ." Posey went on to say that shortening the tail pipes and having super-lightweight doors which flexed on the fast parts of the circuit meant that the fumes came right in, nice and easily. But they kept trying to rectify it, and ultimately solved it.

Through Mulsanne goes the fourth placed Martini-Porsche 935 of Stommelen/Schurti.

Fast but both fragile: the Alpine A442 turbo of Jabouille/Tambay was a front runner until it burnt a piston, while the following Jost/Barth Porsche 908/936 turbo retired with transmission failure, also while well up.

LE MANS 24 HOURS

The first 2-litre car, that of Francois Servanin/Laurent Ferrier/Fred Stalder, headed the tenth row, and it was good to see this Chevron B36 there, for with its ROC Simca engine now running smoothly, it represented an upturn in the fortunes of the ROC team. Bob Wollek, out of a drive with Heyer in the G5 Kremer Porsche, had a ride in the G4 car with Formula Super Renault ace Didier Pironi and "Beaumont", having to change the gearbox being the main trouble. They set 4m 5.5s.

Row 11 held the Hermetite BMW 3.0 CSL of John Fitzpatrick/Tom Walkinshaw with Holman Blackburn brought into the strength. A misfire meant a new engine, but that was not all — it was a big change-everything day for the team and their 4m 5.6s was not that far off the other Bee-Ems anyway. Their neighbour, the second Chevron-ROC Simca B36 for Fred Stalder/Alain Dufrene/Alain Flotard, was down on 4m 7s but another to be healthy.

After that came a bevy of Porsches, turboed and otherwise, but on the 14th row some British participation in the name of Nick Faure. The British Porsche ace, who finished sixth at Le Mans last year with John Cooper, did not have Cooper on the strength, for after a sponsorship agreement fell through, each driver was asked for more money, and Cooper decided against it. Instead, Faure came up with Hymac, Jean Beurlys, the Belgian, provided the car, and of all people, John Goss, the Australian F5000 driver, brought along Citizen Watches and himself for his first European race ever.

Two rows back was the Lloyds insurance Lola with American National General Agencies sponsorship for Tony Birchenough/Ian Bracey/Simon Phillips in their Lola with Richardson FVC power. After initial practice with a hack engine, they fitted their race mill and found the oil pump cracked, so they were late out on Thursday; and then a specially strong clutch gave out, so there was more hard work for the enthusiastic team.

Another two rows further back were Diego Febles/Alec Poole/Hiram Cruz in an IMSA Porsche. The way this happened was that Puerto Rican Febles drove with Poole for the Spa 500Kms and Poole would drive the Porsche at Le Mans. The ebullient Mr McMahon also put himself on the driving strength although whether he actually held the steering wheel is doubtful. A row back was the rather less dated-looking than last year WPM 76 with V6 Peugeot power, not a great success, despite the presence of Guy Chasseuil and Claude Ballot-Lena. Clemens Schickentanz/Howden Ganley were uncommonly far back in a 1975 Porsche Carrera driving in G5 for Georg Loos, once again troubled by late arrival following customs bothers.

Just one row behind, on the 21st, were Lella Lombardi and the delectable Christine Dacremont in a turbo Stratos sponsored by Asceptogyl, which Lella found a little short on top speed but pedalled quite competently, although one of the two couldn't judge the width of the car.

Yes, there were two NASCAR cars, the Dodge Charger of Hershel McGriff and his son Doug being back on the 24th row, and the Ford Torino of Dick Brooks and Dick Hutcherson (sharing with Bugatti school instructor Marcel Mignot) back on the 28th row. Now there was an education, talking to those boys. You see, there were a few things which had, and were going to, cause problems. For a start, in preparation, they had all had to fit electrics for lights and wipers: "We don't race in the rain in the States". Then there were things like right-hand turns, kerbs, and the like. "I tell you, hauling them hogs around these little tight turns is hard work", said Dick Hutcherson. And what about those legendary pitstops, they were going to be fantastic. "We can do it in 15s if we don't kill the lump". "Oh, but you'll have to". Silence.

There were two full container loads of gear for the two cars, their own tyres, they'd even brought their own food. The McGriffs were taking things more seriously in the Dodge which they race on the West Coast, away from the Grand National series. McGriff is a big timber man from Oregon and this seemed to be his regular car. But they burnt one piston on the Thursday because they had octane problems, so they changed a few things to overcome it.

Sympathetic organization saw the two Dicks make it. Brooks is a regular runner in the Grand National series, from Virginia, and this was just one of three cars he has, probably not his best because some of it had been flipped about ten times at Talladega but he's a top ten runner or so in the series. Hutcherson had scarcely raced for nine years, but at least he had driven and finished Le Mans nine years ago in a GT40. He did know what racing in the dark was like. But seeing the legendary NASCAR heroes trying to get round Arnage made one think about a Jim Russell course on correct racing lines, but the cars are big mothers, the steering is not as precise as it might be, and the driving position is very upright. Anyway, it was certainly good to see them, and a few words was worth a great deal.

So, as usual, 55 cars would line up on the long pit straight for the Vingt Quatre Heures du Mans, and what a varied 55.

RACE

If the previous days had been hot, Saturday was boiling, all the more so for the light dust which thousands of people kick up when they're just wandering around looking at the people and the cars and the people. For those on the boiling hot pit road, there was no dust, but thirst was considerable, ice in demand. One wasn't sure who to feel sorry for most, the drivers who would be encased in boiling cars, or the poor people who had to stand in the sun and look at them. There seemed always to be a fair number of people sitting underneath grandstands in the shade, looking in the opposite direction to the action.

And as four o' clock approached and the drivers sat in their scorching cars alone on the grid, it seemed hotter than ever. Suddenly everyone was closer and crowding in as the cars rolled round on their pace lap and, as four o' clock ticked around on the legendary clock, the pace car pulled in and

Below: the G4 winning Porsche 934 Turbo of Raymond Touroul/Alain Cudini.

Success for Alain de Cadenet/Chris Craft in the former's rebodied Lola-DFV, in which they finished an excellent third.

Jean-Pierre Jabouille/Patrick Tambay/Jose Dolhem (2.8 Alpine-Renault A442 turbo)	3m 33.1s
Jacky Ickx/Gijs van Lennep (3.0 Porsche 936 turbo)	3m 39.8s
Manfred Schurti/Rolf Stommelen (2.9 Porsche 935 turbo)	3m 41.7s
Xavier Lapeyre/Bernard Chevanne (3.0 Lola-Cosworth Ford DFV T286)	3m 44.0s
Reinhold Joest/Jurgen Barth (2.1 Porsche 908/3-936 turbo)	3m 45.4s
Derek Bell/Vern Schuppan (3.0 Mirage-Ford Cosworth DFV GR8)	3m 48.1s
Jean-Louis Lafosse/Francois Migault (3.0 Mirage-Ford Cosworth DFV GR8)	3m 51.1s
Brian Redman/Peter Gregg/Herve Poulain (4.5 BMW 3.0 CSL turbo)	3m 53.4s
John Greenwood/Burt Greenwood/Bernard Darniche (7.0 Chevrolet Corvette Stingray)	3m 54.6s
Chris Craft/Alain de Cadenet (3.0 Lola-Ford Cosworth DFV T380)	3m 55.3s
Carlos Bolanos/Hans Heyer/Billy Sprowls/Alfredo Negrete (2.8 Porsche 935 turbo)	3m 55.7s
Henri Pescarolo/Jean-Pierre Beltoise (3.0 Inaltera-Ford Cosworth DFV GTP)	3m 56.9s
Leo Kinnunen/Egon Evertz (2.1 Porsche 908/3 turbo)	4m 00.5s
Mike Keyser/Ed Wachs (4.4 Chevrolet Monza GT)	4m 00.8s
Toine Hezemans/Tim Schenken (4.2 Porsche 934 turbo)	4m 01.1s
Dieter Quester/Alain Peltier/Albrecht Krebs (3.5 BMW 3.0 CSL)	4m 02.3s
Jean Rondeau/Jean-Pierre Jaussaud/Christine Beckers (Inaltera-Ford Cosworth DFV GTP)	4m 04.2s
Sam Posey/Hughes de Fierlant/Harald Grohs (3.5 BMW 3.0 CSL)	4m 04.4s
Francois Servanin/Laurent Ferrier/Fred Stalder (2.0 Chevron-ROC Simca B36)	4m 05.4s
Bob Wollek/Didier Pironi/Marie-Claude Beaumont (4.2 Porsche 934 turbo)	4m 05.5s
Tom Walkinshaw/John Fitzpatrick/Holman Blackburn (3.5 BMW 3.0 CSL)	4m 05.6s
Fred Stalder/Alain Dufrene/Alain Flotard (2.0 Chevron-ROC Simca B36)	4m 07.0s
Ernst Kraus/Gunter Steckkonig (3.0 Porsche 908/3)	4m 07.0s
Claude Haldi/Florian Vetsch (4.2 Porsche 934 turbo)	4m 07.7s
Francois Trisconi/Georges Morand/Andre Chevalley (2.0 Lola-Ford T292)	4m 08.7s
Hubert Striebig/Anny Charlotte Verney/Heinz Kirschoffer (4.2 Porsche 934 turbo)	4m 12.7s
Nick Faure/"Beurlys"/John Goss (4.2 Porsche 934 turbo)	4m 13.2s
Peter Zbinden/Bernard Cheneviere/Nick Buhrer (4.2 Porsche 934 turbo)	4m 14.9s
Jean-Claude Andruet/Jean Borras/Henri Cachia (4.2 Porsche 934 turbo)	4m 15.3s
Raymond Touroul/Alain Cudini/Rene Boubet (3.0 Porsche Carrera RSR)	4m 17.0s
Daniel Brilat/Michel Degoumois/"Depnic" (2.0 Cheetah-BMW G601)	4m 17.7s
Tony Birchenhough/Simon Phillips/Ian Bracey (2.0 Lola-Richardson Ford FVC T294S)	4m 19.5s
Thierry Sabine/Jean-Claude Andruet/Philippe Dagoreau/Henri Cachia (3.0 Porsche Carrera RSR)	4m 22.0s
Jean-Claude Justice/Jacques Belin (3.5 BMW 3.0 CSL)	4m 22.0s
Jean-Marie Lemerle/Patrick Daire/Alain Levie (2.0 Lola ROC Simca T294)	4m 22.1s
Diego Febles/Alec Poole/Hiram Cruz (3.0 Porsche Carrera RSR)	4m 22.1s
William Vollery/Jean-Pierre Aeschlimann/Roger Dorchy (3.0 Porsche Carrera RS)	4m 22.8s
Guy Chasseuil/Claude Ballot-Lena/Xavier Mathot (2.7 WMP-Peugeot 76)	4m 23.4s
Hartwig Bertrams/Heinz Martin/Egon Evertz (3.0 Porsche Carrera RSR)	4m 24.1s
Clemens Schickentanz/Howden Ganley (3.0 Porsche Carrera RSR)	4m 25.2s
Lella Lombardi/Christine Dacremont (2.4 Lancia Stratos turbo)	4m 25.3s
Thierry Perrier/Guy de Saint-Pierre (3.0 Porsche Carrera RSR)	4m 26.4s
Christian Bussi/Phillipe Gurdjian (3.0 Porsche Carrera RSR)	4m 26.7s
"Segolen"/Marcel Duviere/"Lagagi" (3.0 Porsche Carrera RSR)	4m 27.0s
Georges Schafer/Riccardo Albanesi/Jean-Pierre Adatte/Pierre Laffeach (1.8 Chevron-Cosworth Ford FVC B26)	4m 28.0s
Pierre Laffeach/John Rulon-Miller/Tom Waugh (3.0 Porsche Carrera RS)	4m 28.6s
Hershel Busby/Doug McGriff (7.0 Dodge Charger)	4m 29.3s
Pete Brock/Brian Muir/Jean-Claude Aubriet/"Depnic" (3.5 BMW 3.0 CSL)	4m 29.7s
Claude Buchet/Jean-Luc Favresse/Andre Haller (2.6 Datsun HLS 30/260Z)	4m 30.1s
Joel Laplacette/Alain Leroux/Georges Bourdillat (3.0 Porsche Carrera RSR)	4m 30.2s
Christian Poirot/Rene Boubet/Jean-Claude Lagniez (3.0 Porsche Carrera RSR)	4m 30.9s
Michel Lateste/Jose Thibault/Alain Hubert (1.8 Lenham-Cosworth Ford FVC)	4m 31.9s
Jean-Louis Chateau/Jean-Claude Geurie (3.0 Porsche 934 turbo)	4m 34.2s
Jean-Louis Ravenel/Jean-Marie Detrin/Jean Ravenel (3.5 BMW 3.0 CSL)	4m 36.1s
Richard Brooks/Dick Hutcherson/Marcel Mignot (5.6 Ford Torino)	4m 36.5s
	4m 38.0s
N.B. First driver named started race.	

off they went on lap one. Actually, it almost looked dodgy there and then. Jabouille and Ickx rolled around the first corner side by side, but Jabouille took the initiative and was ahead on the first lap. Ickx and Jost in the two G6 Martini Porsches were next, then Redman's BMW ("It never went better all weekend than on those first two laps") then a gap to Schurti's G5 Porsche, Lapeyre's Lola, de Cadenet, the number two Mirage followed by Greenwood, Bell, Beltoise, the Chevvy Monza and the rest. The Dodge Charger slowed at Mulsanne and ultimately pulled in for ever with a blown engine again. The McGriffs had tried what they could to relieve the octane situation, but it obviously hadn't been enough.

Redman was a pit visitor as the engine was smoking, but after a quick look, out went the car again, although already well down. Fitzpatrick led the BMWs but as they went into lap 4, coming up on backmarkers, Ickx took over the lead, closely followed by Jabouille and Jost, then a gap to Schurti, then Lapeyre, de Cadenet, Greenwood, the Monza and Lafosse with Bell next.

Lapeyre was an early pit visitor, asking for new plugs and a drop down the field which had never been premised by his practice time. It was a sad moment, but finally he had two changes of plugs. Then it dropped a valve and ultimately the head gasket went, and this was the last we saw of it on the leader board. Faure was another pit visitor for a new tyre, and then needed another after a puncture. More important was a puncture to Derek Bell, but that was quickly solved and he was back out again.

After a mere half hour, it looked almost as though the Porsche strategy was to break the Alpine with either of the G6 Martini cars, and thus at least leave the G5 in the lead if the G6s did not survive. For all three of them were way ahead of Schurti's Porsche before a bunch with de Cadenet, the Monza, Greenwood and Lafosse before the Evertz 908, Beltoise's Inaltera, Heyer's Porsche, Jaussaud's Inaltera, Bell catching up again and another nine unlapped cars. The Australian Peter Brock, sharing his BMW with Brian Muir, started his troubles with a broken hub in this first hour.

Redman soon came into the pits again, but the

biggest surprise was that the Alpine had to pit so early due its small fuel load, this after just less than 40 minutes. Schurti wasn't long after him while the sole remaining NASCAR stocker, that of Brooks, pitted rapidly as one would expect. It looked good until the starter jammed. It took 10 minutes to fix that. Further American involvement in the pits included a visit by Greenwood for water . . . on him. He was hot in the big Chevvy.

Thus at hour one the order read Ickx in the Martini Porsche, on 15 laps with Jost's Porsche and the Alpine. Schurti, de Cadenet, Lafosse and now Bell, Greenwood, Kinnunen, Beltoise and Jaussaud were all a lap behind. Walkinshaw led a trio of BMWs while the ROC Chevron of Ferrier led the 2-litre class. An early retirement in that first hour, sadly, was the Monza, whose driveshaft simply twisted around in the middle — a shame, as they were not driving it hard.

The sun still blazed hot throughout the second hour and one to be delayed under it was Posey's BMW, which had to change a windscreen. More BMW trouble came for Redman, who quietly staggered around with the engine being checked for oil all the time and Mr Stella's painting getting blacker and blacker around the rear end. They had to wait until three-quarters of the way through the hour before being topped up, and all that lot escaped so quickly that they retired just into the third hour. The reason was either a machining fault or a cracked block; to some that means the same thing. Early in the second hour, yet more BMW trouble, for suddenly there was no Tom Walkinshaw; the Hermetite car had stopped just after Arnage, and while the engine started, flames belched from the injection trumpets. The BMW mechanics believed it was a broken camshaft, but it was a sad hour for Britain.

In the lead battle, the Alpine's early stop had

The G5 Martini Porsche of Manfred Schurti/Rolf Stommelen had a number of problems, including the suspension collapsing which necessitated body work reworking (above right). However, he finished fourth.

meant that the Porsches moved into a commanding 1-2-3, with the two G6 cars on 30 laps from Schurti's 935 before the de Cadenet of Craft, then the two JCB Mirages and then the Alpine which was being severely handicapped by lengthy stops, in particular a four-minute one for plugs and a new rear wheel. The Lloyds Lola had a lengthy stop here because of fuel vaporization, which dropped it back some 13 places. And Ickx had his first stop (after one and a half hours, so no wonder he was ahead by so much). Tambay had another electrics change briefly during the hour.

Just before the two-hour mark, the Corvette was in trouble, for first there was a puncture, quickly rectified, and then another; but at the same time, Darniche became ill, the heat affecting him too. The Corvette sage continues, so read on. The number two Inaltera had the first of two shock absorbers break, which immediately dropped it back.

Thus, at the third hour, it was Porsche, Porsche and Porsche, the first two on 45 laps and the third on 44. They seemed to have found the Alpine's weak spot, and were quietly showing their own strength. Two Mirages sandwiched the Alpine, also on 44 laps, before the de Cadenet on 43, this having been slowly overhauled although de Cadenet was suffering badly from the heat, which would cause a new nose to be made up overnight. The Everz 908 and Hezemans's Carrera were also

24 hours at Le Mans

Hour 1 (15 laps): 1, Ickx/van Lennep, 131.630mph; 2, Joest/Barth; 3, Jabouille/Tambay; 4, Schurti/Stommelen, 14; 5, Craft/de Cadenet; 6, Lafosse/Migault; 7, Bell/Schuppan; 8, J. Greenwood/B. Greenwood; 9, Kinnunen/Evertz; 10, Jaussaud/Beckers/Rondeau.
Hour 2 (30 laps). Ickx/van Lennep, 129.81mph; 2, Joest/Barth; 3 Schurti/Stommelen, 29; 4, Craft/de Cadenet; 5, Lafosse/Migault; 6, Bell/Schuppan; 7, Jabouille/Tambay, 28; 8, Pescarolo/Beltoise; 9, Jaussaud/Beckers/Rondeau, 27; 10, J. Greenwood/B. Greenwood.
Hour 3 (45 laps): 1, Ickx/van Lennep, 130.347mph; 2, Joest/Barth; 3, Schurti/Stommelen, 44; 4, Lafosse/Migualt; 5, Jabouille/Tambay; 6, Bell/Schuppan; 7, Craft/ de Cadenet, 43; 8, Kinnunen/Evertz, 42; 9, Heyer/Bolanos/Sprowls/Negrete, 41; 10, Hezemans/Schenken
Hour 4 (60 laps): 1, van Lennep/Ickx, 129.945mph; 2, Barth/Joest; 3, Tambay/Jabouille, 59; 4, Bell/Schuppan, 58; 5, Migault/Lafosse; 6, Stommelen /Schurti; 7, de Cadenet/Craft, 56; 8, Bolanos /Heyer/-Negrete/Sprowls; 9, Evertz/Kinnunen, 55; 10, Schenken/Hezemans.

Hour 5 (76 laps): 1, van Lennep/Ickx, 129.751mph; 2, Barth/Joest, 75; 3, Tambay/Jabouille, 74; 4, Bell/Schuppan; 5, Migault/Lafosse, 73; 6, de Cadenet/Craft, 71; 7, Heyer/Bolanos/Sprowls/Negrete, 70; 8, Evertz/Kinnunen, 69; 9, Stommelen/Schurti; 10, Hezemans/-Schenken, 68.
Hour 6 (90 laps): 1, vàn Lennep/Ickx, 128.949mph; 2, Barth/Joest, 89; 3, Tambay/Jabouille; 4, Migault/Lafosse, 87; 5, Schuppan/Bell; 6, de Cadenet/Craft, 85; 7, Bolanos/Heyer/Sprowls/Negrete, 83; 8, Evertz/Kinnunen, 81; 9, Quester/Krebs/Peltier; 10, Stommelen/-Schurti.
Hour 7 (105 laps): 1, Ickx/van Lennep, 128.600 mph; 2, Joest/Barth, 104; 3, Jabouille/Tambay, 102; 4, Bell/Schuppan; 5, Lafosse/-Migualt, 101; 6, Craft/de Cadenet, 98; 7, Schurti/Stommelen, 96; 8, Quester/Krebs/Peltier, 95; 9, Schenken/Hezemans, 94; 10, Bolanos /Heyer/Sprowls/Negrete, 93.
Hour 8 (120 laps): 1, Ickx/van Lennep, 128.363mph; 2, Joest/Barth, 119; 3, Jabouille/Tambay, 117; 4, Bell/Schuppan, 116; 5, Lafosse/-Migault; 6, Craft/de Cadenet, 112; 7, Schurti/Stommelen, 110; 8, Krebs/Quester/Peltier, 109; 9, Schenken/Hezemans, 108; 10, Posey/de Fierlant/Grohs, 107.

Hour 9 (135 laps): 1, Ickx/van Lennep, 128.538mph; 2, Joest/Barth, 134; 3, Jabouille/Tambay, 132; 4, Bell/Schuppan; 5, Lafosse/Migault, 130; 6, Craft/de Cadenet, 126; 7, Schurti/-Stommelen, 125; 8, Hezemans/Schenken, 122; 9, Posey/de Fierlant/Grohs, 121; 10, Zbinden/Cheneviere/Buhrer, 120.
Hour 10 (150 laps): 1, van Lennep/Ickx, 128.096mph; 2, Barth/Joest, 148; 3, Schuppan/Bell, 146; 4, Migault/Lafosse, 145; 5, de Cadenet/Craft, 140; 6, Stommelen/Schurti, 139; 7, Tambay/Jabouille, 135; 8, Hezemans/Schenken; 9, de Fierlant/-Posey/Grohs, 134; 10, Touroul/Cudini/Boubet, 133.
Hour 11 (165 laps): 1, van Lennep/Ickx, 127.910mph; 2, Barth/-Joest, 163; 3, Migault/Lafosse, 160; 4, Schuppan/Bell, 156; 5, de Cadenet/Craft, 154; 6, Stommelen/Schurti, 153; 7, Schenken/-Hezemans, 149; 8, Grohs/de Fierlant/Posey, 147; 9, Touroul/-Cudini/Boubet; 10, Zbinden//Cheneviere/Buhrer, 146.
Hour 12 (180 laps): 1, van Lennep/Ickx, 128.151mph; 2, Barth/-Joest, 178; 3, Migault/Lafosse, 174; 4, de Cadenet/Craft, 169; 5, Schuppan/Bell, 168; 6, Stommelen/Schurti, 167; 7, Schenken/-Hezemans, 162; 8, Posey/de Fierlant/Grohs, 161; 9, Touroul/-Cudini/Boubet, 160; 10, Kraus/Steckkonig, 159.

Hour 13 (195 laps): 1, Ickx/van Lennep, 127.972mph; 2, Joest/-Barth, 192; 3, Lafosse/Migault, 188; 4, Craft/de Cadenet, 183; 5., Bell/Schuppan, 182; 6, Schurti/Stommelen, 181; 7, Hezemans/-Schenken, 175; 8, Touroul/Cudini/Boubet, 173; 9, Zbinden/Cheneviere/Buhrer, 172; 10, Posey/ de Fierlant/Grohs.
Hour 14 (210 laps): 1, Ickx/van Lennep, 128.178mph; 2, Joest/-Barth, 207; 3, Lafosse/Migault, 203; 4, Craft/ de Cadenet, 197; 5, Schurti/Stommelen, 196; 6, Bell/Schuppan, 195; 7, Hezemans/-Schenken, 188; 8, Touroul/Cudini/Boubet, 187; 9, Kraus/-Steckkonig, 186; 10, Haldi/Vetsch, 184.
Hour 15 (225 laps): 1, Ickx/van Lennep, 128.215mph; 2, Joest/-Barth, 218; 3, Lafosse/Migault; 4, Craft/de Cadenet, 212; 5, Schurti/Stommelen, 211; 6, Bell/Shuppan, 210; 7, Hezemans/-Schenken, 202; 8, Cudini/Touroul/Boubet, 200; 9, Kraus/-Steckkonig, 199; 10, Haldi/Vetsch, 198.
Hour 16 (240 laps): 1, van Lennep/Ickx, 128.113mph; 2, Migault/-Lafosse, 233; 3, Schuppan/Bell, 226; 4, de Cadenet/Craft, 225; 5, Stommelen/Schurti; 6, Barth/Joest, 218; 7, Schenken/Hezemans, 216; 8, Cudini/Touroul/Boubet, 213; 9, Pescarolo/Beltoise, 211; 10, Haldi/Vetsch.

Hour 17 (255 laps): 1, van Lennep/Ickx, 128.217mph; 2, Migault/-Laffosse, 247; 3, de Cadenet/Craft, 240; 4, Stommelen/Schurti; 5, Schuppan/Bell; 6, Hezemans/Schenken, 229; 7, Cudini/Touroul/-Boubet, 226; 8, Pescarolo/Beltoise, 223; 9, Posey/Grohs/ de Fierlant, 221; 10, Kraus/Steckkonig, 220.
Hour 18 (270 laps): 1, van Lennep/Ickx, 128.113mph; 2, Migault/-Lafosse, 260; 3, de Cadenet/Craft, 253; 4, Stommelen/Schurti, 252; 5, Schuppan/Bell, 249; 6, Hezemans/Schenken, 242; 7, Cudini/-Touroul/Boubet, 240; 8, Pescarolo/Beltoise, 236; 9, Kraus/-Steckkonig, 234; 10, Zbinden/Cheneviere/Buhrer, 233.
Hour 19 (285 laps): 1, Ickx/ ennep, 128.003mph; 2, Lafosse/-Migault, 269; 3, Craft/De Cadenet, 267; 4, Schurti/Stommelen, 265; 5, Bell/Schuppan, 260/ 6, Hezemans/Schenken, 256; 7, Cudini/-Touroul/Boubet, 253; 8, Beltoise/Pescarolo, 250; 9, Steckkonig/-Kraus, 247; 10, Cheneviere/Zbinden/Buhrer, 245.
Hour 20 (292 laps): 1, Ickx/van Lennep, 127.930mph; 2, Lafosse/-Migault, 283; 3, Craft/de Cadenet, 281; 4, Schurti/Stommelen, 278; 5, Bell/Schuppan, 272; 6, Cudini/Touroul/Boubet, 266; 7, Steckkonig/Kraus, 260; 8, Hezemans/Schenken, 259; 9, Zbinden/-Cheneviere/Buhrer; 10, Beltoise/Pescarolo, 257.

Hour 21 (306 laps): 1, Ickx/van Lennep, 124.389mph; 2, Lafosse/-Migault, 296; 3, Craft/de Cadenet; 4, Schurti/Stommelen, 290; 5, Bell/Schuppan, 286; 6, Cudini/Touroul/Boubet, 279; 7, Steckkonig/-Kraus, 274; 8, Beltoise/Pescarolo, 271; 9, Zbinden/Cheneviere/-Buhrer, 270; 10, Bertrams/Martin/Evertz, 266.
Hour 22 (320 laps): 1, van Lennep/Ickx, 124.281mph; 2, Migault/-Lafosse, 311; 3, Craft/de Cadenet, 309; 4, Stommelen/Schurti, 302; 5, Schuppan/Bell, 299; 6, Touroul/Cudini/Boubet, 292; 7, Kraus/-Steckkonig, 287; 8, Pescarolo/Beltoise, 279; 9, Bertrams/Martin/-Evertz, 278; 10, Grohs/Posey/de Fierlant, 274.
Hour 23 335 laps): 1, van Lennep/Ickx, 124.351mph; 2, Migault/-Lafosse, 325; 3, Craft/de Cadenet, 323; 4, Stommelen/Schurti, 317; 5, Schuppan/Bell, 314; 6, Touroul/Cudini/Boubet, 303; 7, Kraus/-Steckkonig, 300; 8, Pescarolo/Beltoise, 292; 9, Bertrams/Martin/-Evertz, 290; 10, Grohs/Posey/de Fierlant, 286.

Night-time at Le Mans: the lights of the fairground, and of the passing cars heading out into the country again for another lap of over eight miles.

LE MANS 24 HOURS

continued

on terms. The number one Inaltera had a further problem in that it was leaking oil onto the alternator and it needed new belts to stop them slipping, and these then broke. They weren't having much luck. . . .

In this fourth hour, the Inaltera team continued to have the oil problem with the number one car, but the second car broke another shock absorber which had to be cut out. The sun continued to blaze away, despite it being nearly eight o'clock. It transpired that it was Martini's turn to have a touch of the gremlins, and they set about the Schurti/Stommelen car in no uncertain way with firstly an alternator belt failure, which dropped the 935 to sixth overall, just ahead of the de Cadenet and the Kremer G5 Porsche driven by the Mexicans.

Early into the fifth hour, the 935 had more problems, this time when part of the rear suspension fell apart when a mounting broke, and the mechanics had to put the whole lot back together again. And then there was the accelerator cable, but at least the leading two cars were going like trains, and at least it was cooling just a little, even if things were going at full swing in the village. The turbo Porsche being delayed meant that it dropped further down the order, so that at nine o'clock after five hours, the order read Ickx/van Lennep, 76 laps, one less for Jost/Barth, and another down with the Bell/Schuppan Mirage was the Alpine. Seventh was Kremer's turbo Porsche on the same lap as Evertz's 908. The 935 was next in ninth place before Schenken's Gelo Carrera. The first BMW, that of Quester, Krebs and Peltier, was eleventh, before a batch of Carreras. The Lloyds Lola was in more trouble with an oil ring gone, which meant the total loss of 56 minutes.

Then, returning to the press box at nine, a little column of smoke could be seen some four or five miles away. A privately entered Datsun 260Z which, by all accounts, had been handling badly anyway, had left the road on the Mulsanne straight crashing through the guardrails and catching fire. The young driver, Andre Haller, a Strasbourg restaurateur, was dead.

But at the head of the field, there was no change. The Martini Porsches just didn't seem catchable, streaking away from the opposition, if only at a slow, steady pace. The Corvette had been raised on a jack in the pits to try and rectify the damage. The puncture had damaged the rear suspension and the fuel tank, and while the Greenwood crew mended the suspension, the fuel tank was a different matter and after even trying a borrowed one, they regretfully retired. However, the NASCAR Torino was happily touring around, Brooks experiencing his first night racing and the two drivers getting quite enthusiastic about it all.

The dusty lanes of the Le Mans village teemed with people in various states right up to midnight and beyond, and no wonder, because there was little of interest on the course. The leader had a lap over his team-mate and two laps over the following Alpine, which was on the same lap as the first of the Mirages with the second next up followed by the de Cadenet and the G5 Porsche. The Heyer G5 Porsche Turbo was experiencing problems with clutch bother, and after trying to mend it rather than change, they delayed and delayed until finally it had to be changed in a lengthy manoeuvre. Sadly, the Torino was a retirement with transmission delays after a steady if uncompetitive run.

In the next few hours, that is until the light just began to show above the dark countryside and through the trees, little was to happen. The night brought no danger nor excitement for the leaders just continued, round and round, no challenge. However, the BMW of Quester/Krebs/Peltier suddenly quit its eighth place with exactly the same symptoms as the Hermetite car, and in the next couple of hours, just before dawn, the Alpine was suddenly immobilized at its stand. It was a burnt piston, thought at first to be a valve, and a rueful Larrousse explained in front of an equally rueful Francois Guiter of Elf, that the petrol just wasn't of high enough octane, hence the sooting up. They had thought it was a valve, thus the long stop; but no, a piston was too much and the Alpine men retired for coffee in the paddock, their challenge over. Victory, in essence, to Martini and Porsche?

In the next hour, the then third placed Mirage lost three and a half laps too. The alternator had been playing up it was thought, so it was changed. Further investigation revealed a broken internal wire and soon it was singing along again, but having lost a place.

Meanwhile, Britons in Porsches were in trouble too. Poor Nick Faure was in and out of the pits with a loose turbo cooler, then the front bearing seized. Finally, with different diameter tyres, Nick found not surprisingly, that the handling was upset. It took them a while to find the latter. Alec Poole's Puerto Rican Porsche had also had front wheel trouble and needed a new unit, and then had gearbox problems and the crown wheel and pinion gave up. However, Tim Schenken wasn't nearly so troubled and led the G4 category in eighth position with Toine Hezemans, although business partner Howden Ganley had had to quit with a seized diff much earlier on.

The Inaltera number two was not happy at all, because its latest trick was to throw off doors; although there were spares, they did not necessarily fit all that well, and Jaussaud and Christine were particular sufferers.

So when the light began to differentiate between daylight and trees, and paper sellers invaded the pit road with sensationalism, and early stirrers nonchalantly kicked the piles of paper on the stands, the Martini Porsche of Ickx and van Lennep lead by three laps from its teammate, driven by Jost/Barth, who were four laps

Fast in a straight line, the Inalteras proved slightly fragile but it was some achievement to get both the new cars to the finish; this is the eighth-placed Pescarolo/Beltoise model.

ahead of the French driven Mirage. The de Cadenet, still wearing its original rear tyres, was next up, with the Bell/Schuppan Mirage next after its dramas. Then came the 935 Porsche, picking up punctures and hopefully keeping the leading two cars jinx-free by over-compensating. Then came the Gelo Porsche followed by two private French Porsches, the surviving Alpina Faltz BMW completing the top ten. The Inalteras were in 15th and 32nd positions.

As the sun began to give some welcome heat, for the dawn had come with a cold breeze, new life came into the race. The Martini Porsche of Jost and Barth stopped in the pits for nearly 20 minutes with possible valve trouble. The order changed dramatically, and there seemed to be a new purpose to the race. Furthermore, when the Porsche rejoined, it stopped almost immediately with transmission failure out on the circuit. It was the end of a brave run, and slightly messed up the fine one-two which Martini-Porsche were running.

But at eight o'clock, it meant a sudden battle for third place. The JCB Mirage driven by the French team had seven laps over the second team car which was just a lap ahead on paper of the de Cadenet Lola, and in turn, on the same lap as the G5 Martini Porsche.

While all this was going on, there was a lot of action too in the pits. Poor Faure was having everything go wrong, from the wrong-sized tyres through to a holed water pipe caused by a frisky squirrel at Arnage. They lost half the windscreen at one time, and were having tremendous problems with turbo pressure. It was at 2.0 boost instead of 1.1, and Faure was lapping incredibly quickly, except the engine would not last at that rate.

Then there were the two Porsches of the Kremer team, both in a large amount of trouble with clutches, and both being jacked up for attention to them. "I don't like Le Mans," muttered Erwin Kremer who was looking after the G4 car. Then there was Peter Brock and Brian Muir in the former's BMW, which had all sorts of problems with a cracked bellhousing, punctures and vibrations, among others.

As we got to nine o'clock in the morning, the race was really on, but not for long. While de Cadenet suddenly dropped from third to fifth, Bell was quickly back in the pits with the petrol warning light flashing. This was found to be inaccurate, but the petrol pump was changed, while de Cadenet was delayed with a jamming wheel nut in this 18th hour which lost him eight minutes. And suddenly, at the end of the hour, both Mirages were in the pits as was the G5 Porsche turbo of Schurti/Stommelen. The Mirage stops were as a result of this petrol pump trouble, while the Porsche had ignition trouble.

As the dust filled the air as the crowds flocked back for another hot day, the order suddenly changed back to Ickx/van Lennep, looking as though nothing would stop them, ten laps ahead of the French driven JCB Mirage, seven laps ahead of the de Cadenet, one lap ahead of the G5 Carrera which was three laps ahead of the

Bell/Schuppan Mirage. This one suffered worst from the fuel pump problem and had a long stop checking electrics in general, and at one time, the engine completely died on Schuppan. Sixth was the perfectly running Loos Carrera for Schenken and Hezemans, with the Raymond Touroul/Alain Cudini Carrera next up.

The drama continued as the second placed French Mirage had its problems and the Martini G5 Porsche extended its lead to a super-safe 16 laps, but the de Cadenet wasn't losing time and was now just two laps behind the Mirage in third place. The only real problem was that Chris had burnt his foot in the car, and on the ball; he could scarcely feel anything so various medications were being prepared for him. The turbo Martini Carrera had dropped with its ignition problem which was being attended to every now and then; it lost two laps on the stopping Mirage. Bodywork was being patched up all the time after the suspension had collapsed, while before midday, the 20th hour, there was considerable drama yet again.

This time, the leading car tripped up for the first time. The exhaust broke between the manifold and turbocharger but it took just over 20 minutes to fix. In fact, the lead was reduced from 16 laps to 11, but the second-placed Mirage was holding ground over the de Cadenet and this was nine laps ahead of the second Mirage. Drama had struck the following Porsche: Hezemans had only found first and second in the 'box, but the George Loos team set to rebuild the 'box and expected to take about two hours doing it. In fifth spot was the Porsche 908/3 of Ernst Kraus/Gunther Steckkonig which was all of 32 laps behind the leader and 12 behind the men in front. In 20th place should have been the Lloyds 2-litre Lola, which was steady enough after a couple of stops, but just about on the mid-day mark the car suffered badly from fuel stavation. It was thought to be fixed and Bracey made to go back out when it stopped again, and the demon mechanic set to work to get it to go around a lap to its pit.

On the Inaltera front, the number one car of Beltoise and Pescarolo was slowly picking up places with excellent top speed, while the BMW which remained, that of Alpina Faltz, had transmission vibrations. In the next hour, the Kremer Porsche, which should have just been enjoying a downhill run to the finish, suddenly was shown to be on fire and while the pit readied themselves with fire extinguishers, a little plume of smoke from Mulsanne showed that they would not be needed. Hans Heyer said the car was not too badly damaged, but it was probably enough for Erwin Kremer as the G4 was up on stands in the pits, being worked on.

At about midday, the Martini G5 Porsche started sounding horrible, and very shortly afterwards it pitted for a new turbocharger which was very quickly provided by the Porsche mechanics. But it was a stop that helped out the de Cadenet team, because it gave them a safe margin to the G5 car.

As the afternoon approached, the heat really was bad, dust clouds rising as the crowd re-assembled to welcome the victors of this tough race. The usual Le Mans puddles were forming around taps which were left on to provide cooling water. Pescarolo had his second puncture, which was to cause problems for the Inaltera, while the class leading G4 Carrera of Touroul/Cudini was sending up a thin wisp of smoke from the exhaust, although the team were quite confident of their impending class win. Their predecessors, the Hezemans/Schenken car, left the pits after its 2½-hour stop in fine health now, with the gearbox rebuilt. Another, rather quicker mechanical problem was fixed on the remaining G5 BMW, that of Posey/de Fierlandt/Grohs, which caught the crankshaft damper bug previously afflicting the Hermetite car. It was changed in 12 minutes, announced a proud Jochen Neerpasch.

However, for some, it was not all good. The Beurlys team resigned themselves to going out in the final minutes as they had virtually used up Porsche's stock of turbochargers in trying to get the right boost pressure, while the Lloyds Lola had made the pits again only to find that it had lost compression in one cylinder, so they elected to do a final lap too. The Brock BMW, after every complaint, retired with a blown cylinder head gasket early in the afternoon.

So the final hours rolled by with the French-driven Mirage really charging away from the de Cadenet Lola (the Londoner in particular was experiencing heat exhaustion), but they were still ahead of the G5 Martini Porsche, and seemed well assured of third position at least.

And that's the way it all looked as though it was going to end. But with a mere 15 minutes to go, the second placed Mirage appeared with no rear bodywork. This upsets the handling quite a lot, and it was going pretty slowly. The de Cadenet was only a couple of laps behind and obviously gaining now, for the Mirage could not go that fast. A quick decision saw the Mirage in the pits after two further laps, and while there, de Cadenet's Lola came flying by, putting it just a lap behind. The new bodywork was fitted, but then the car wouldn't fire. When it did fire, it sounded ghastly but soon cleared, but the de Cadenet just couldn't quite make it, there wasn't the time. So Harley Cluxton was rewarded with second and fifth, Martini got first and fourth, and de Cadenet and Craft took third for Britain.

44th Grand Prix d'Endurance
24 Hours of Le Mans
Le Mans, France — June 12/13

1. Jacky Ickx/Gijs van Lennep (3.0 Porsche 946 turbo), 349 laps, 2981.20 miles, 124.216mph;
2. Jean-Louis Lafosse/Francois Migault (3.0 Mirage-Cosworth Ford DFV GR8), 338;
3. Chris Craft/Alain de Cadenet (3.0 Lola-Cosworth Ford DFV T380), 337;
4. Rolf Stommelen/Manfred Schurti (2.9 Porsche 935 turbo), 331*;
5. Derek Bell/Vern Schuppan (3.0 Mirage-Cosworth Ford DFV GR8), 326;
6. Alain Cudini/Raymond Touroul/Rene Boubet (3.0 Porsche Carrera RSR), 314;
7. Ernst Kraus/Gunther Steckkonig (3.0 Porsche 908/3-936), 313;
8. Henri Pescarolo/Jean-Pierre Beltoise (3.0 Inaltera-Cosworth Ford DFV GTP), 304*; 9, Hartwig Bertrams/Heinz Martin/Egon Evertz (3.0 Porsche Carrera RSR), 302; 10, Sam Posey/Hughes de Fierlant/Harald Grohs (3.5 BMW 3.0 CSL), 299; 11, Hubert Striebig/Annie-Charlotte Verney/Heinz Kirschoffer (4.2 Porsche 934 turbo), 298; 12, "Segolen"/Marcel Ouviere/"Ladagi" (3.0 Porsche Carrera RSR), 292*; 13, Thierry Sabine/Jean-Claude Andruet/Phillipe Dagoreau/Henri Cachia (3.0 Porsche Carrera RSR), 288; 14, Pierre Laffeach/John Rulon-Miller/Ton Waugh (3.0 Porsche Carrera RSR), 283*; 15, Francois Trisconi/Georges Morand/Andre Chevalley (2.0 Lola-Cosworth Ford T292), 279; 16, Toine Hezemans/Tim Schenken (4.2 Porsche 934 turbo), 277; 17, Joel Laplacette/Alain Leroux/Georges Bourdillat (3.0 Porsche Carrera RSR), 273; 18, Thierry Perrier/Guy de Saint-Pierre (3.0 Porsche Carrera RSR), 273; 19, Bob Wollek/Didier Pironi/Marie-Claude Beaumont (4.2 Porsche 934 turbo), 270; 20, Lella Lombardi/Christine Dacremont (2.4 Lancia Stratos turbo); 265; 21, Jean-Pierre Jaussaud/Christine Beckers/Jean Rondeau (3.0 Inaltera-Cosworth Ford DFV GTP), 264; 22, Tony Birchenhough/Simon Phillips/Ian Bracey/Brian Joscelyne (2.0 Lola-Cosworth Ford FVC T294S), 252; 23, Christian Poirot/Rene Boubet/Jean-Claude Lagniez (3.0 Porsche Carrera RSR), 245; 24, Jean-Louis Ravenel/Jean-Marie Detrin/Jean Ravenel (3.5 BMW 3.0 CSL), 237*; 25, Jean-Marie Lemerle/Patrick Daire/Alain Levie (2.0 Lola-ROC Chrysler Simca T294), 218; 26, Jean-Claude Andruet/Jean Borras/Henri Cachia (3.0 Porsche 934 turbo), 203; 27, Nich Faure/"Beurlys"/John Goss (4.2 Porsche 934 turbo), 168 laps. No other finishers.

Fastest lap: Reinhold Joest (2.1 Porsche 908-3/936 turbo), on lap 19, 3m 48.9s, 134.076mph.

* Class winners

The final drama: a new rear tail section for the second-placed Mirage after 23½ hours.

LE MANS 24 HOURS

Ickx and Van Lennep win for Porsche; De Cadenet and Craft finish third for Britain

Alain de Cadenet and Chris Craft put on a terrific display for a private team, bringing the former's Lola-DFV T380 home third. Here it leads George Schafer's 2-litre Chevron B26. (Le Mans colour photographs appear on page 811.)

Le Mans, June 12th/13th

IF YOU had believed all the advance publicity put out by the AC de l'Ouest, the 1976 edition of the 24-Hours of Le Mans was going to be the most dazzling, original, different looking Le Mans in history. Somehow the race on June 12th/13th didn't work out quite like that, for it was still in essence an event dominated by a handful of very fast sports-racing cars backed up by a large supporting cast of GT and touring cars from the workshops of Porsche and BMW. Yet the organisers had given some welcome thought to brightening-up the image of their race, which had dimmed and tarnished somewhat in recent years as fewer factories, and fewer still Grand Prix drivers, included the race in their competition programmes. Frightened by the relatively poor attendance for last year's race, the ACO had therefore brought in a number of innovations to add a little more sparkle to the gruelling test of endurance round the 13.64 km. Circuit of the Sarthe. The regulations were liberalised to bring in a wider variety of cars than ever before, the organisers audaciously ignoring the FIA's directive that Gp. 6 cars could not be mixed with production based machinery if the race was to stay in either of the two long-distance World Championships. An invitation was sent to America to bring over a handful of the cumbersome NASCAR stock cars that are more used to pounding round all-banked ovals and for the "All American" GT cars that are governed by the rules of the International Motorsport Association.

Yes, despite all these innovations, the entry had the traditional composition of Group 6 sports-racing cars (the FIA has stopped calling them prototypes at last, preferring the more accurate description of "two-seater racing cars"), Group 5 "Silhouette" cars, and Group 4 GT machines. But by insisting on running the one major long-distance event of the year that would pitch all these different classes together, the ACO has succeeded in gathering the most interesting field seen at Le Mans for some seasons, and certainly the most representative entry that would be seen for an endurance race this year.

Fastest in practice, by more than six seconds in fact, was the Alpine Renault A442 shared by Jean-Pierre Jabouille and Patrick Tambay. Rene Arnoux had been nominated as reserve pilot for this car, but when the young Frenchman proved too small to fit snugly into its cockpit, team manager Gerard Larrousse had to call instead on one of his second-string Formula Two drivers, Jose Dolhem. The 2-litre, turbocharged, 500 b.h.p. V6 A442 was almost unchanged from the form in which it has appeared in the World Championship for Sportscars except for a longer, more streamlined tail. Jabouille lapped the circuit

during practice in 3 min. 33.1 sec., making the French, Elf-sponsored car comfortably quickest of the Gp. 6 entries.

The strongest rival to the Alpine was the fastest of three works Martini Porsches, the Germany factory deciding almost at the last possible moment to run not one but two Gp. 6 936 sports-racers as well as their Turbo Carrera based Gp. 5 car. With its 2.1-litre, flat-six turbo engine turned down from 1.4 to 1.25 atmospheres of boost in a bid to lengthen its life, the newer and faster of the 936s had grown a high, neatly flared tail section since its victorious appearances at Monza and Imola, a tall air box on top helping the engine breathe better. This car was to be driven by Jacky Ickx and Gijs van Lennep, and it was Ickx who was second fastest in practice with a lap in 3 min. 39.8 sec. The second Porsche 936 was the original test-bed model raced at the beginning of the season at Nurburgring. Reinhold Joest and Jurgen Barth were its drivers, the former making it fifth quickest during practice at 3 min. 45.4 sec.

Apart from these Gp. 6 cars, the Porsche factory also entered a Gp. 5 935 for Rolf Stommelen and the Lichtenstein driver Manfred Schurti. The 935 also has a turbocharged engine, in its case a flat-six of 2,857-c.c., with such handy extras inside the cockpit as a knob for the driver to control the degree of turbo boost and a lever to adjust

Althought it looked dramatic enough, the turbocharged Lancia Stratos of Lella Lombardi and Christine Dacremont proved disappointingly slow, but at least it finished.

the hardness of the shock-absorbers during the race. Stommelen put the car onto the third place of the 55 car grid, lapping at 3 min. 41.7 sec.

Fourth fastest was the best of several Cosworth DFV-engined cars, an elderly Lola T286 driven by Frenchmen Xavier Lapeyre and Bernard Chevanne. Then, after the second Gp. 6 Porsche, came the two Mirage-DFV GR8s that finished first and third last year but have now been bought by America's Harley Cluxton and sponsored by JCB and Total. Derek Bell and Vern Schuppan held the reins in one of the Mirages, with Francois Migault and Jean-Louis Lafosse sharing the other.

Apart from the Porsche 935, all these were Gp. 6 cars, but next in line for the rolling start was a Gp. 5 BMW CSL with a 600 b.h.p., 3.2-litre turbocharged engine and a graph-like colour scheme that could only be described as imaginative. Serious engine malfunctions cut short the works BMW's efforts on both days of practice, but Brian Redman and Peter Gregg threatened to be very quick once it started to work properly.

Of the few cars that made the trip across the Atlantic in response to the OCO's invitation, two stood out—John Greenwood's brutishly beautiful 7-litre Chevrolet Corvette, with 650 b.h.p. and a maximum speed of over 215 m.p.h., and Mike Keyser's Chevrolet Monza saloon, which is rapidly becoming the car to beat in American GT racing. Much further back down the field lurked two of the huge NASCAR stock cars, but they were neither the latest nor the fastest examples of their breed and as expected proved too heavy, bulky and unwieldy to be at home on a road circuit. In the race, the Dodge Charger lasted no more than a lap and a half before its engine seized spectacularly, but the Ford Torino ran till after midnight before transmission failure put it out.

Apart from the two Mirages, British hopes rested firmly on the Lola T380 with which Alain de Cadenet and Chris Craft had struggled to the finish last year. A purely private entry, sponsored by Tate and Lyle,

Elt and Hammond's Chop Sauce, this machine was to run almost faultlessly throughout the 24 hours. Finished in traditional British Racing Green and proudly bearing a Union Jack on its wing, de Cadenet's Lola had received numerous aerodynamic improvements since last year that were to make the cockpit almost unbearably hot in the intense heat of both Saturday and Sunday, but at least stopped the tail from flying off as happened last year.

The other cars particularly worthy of note were the two Inalteras, pretty French coupés powered by DFV engines which had been built specifically for this one race. To be driven by Henri Pescarolo, Jean-Pierre Beltoise, Jean-Pierre Jaussaud, "Christine" and the project's originator Jean Rondeau, the Inalteras were much heavier than the Gp. 6 cars, for although there are no intentions whatsoever to put them into production as road cars they were made for the "Touring Car Prototypes" class invented by the organisers for precisely this sort of machine. Add in two dozen Gp. 4 and Gp. 5 Porsches, both turbocharged and otherwise, half a dozen BMW CSLs and a smattering of other makes, and you will gather that it was a very mixed bag that took the flag at four o'clock on Saturday afternoon.

Jabouille's Alpine took the lead immediately at the start, coming round with a comfortable lead over the Porsches of Ickx and Joest and the Turbo BMW of Redman after the first lap. The BMW lasted no more than three circuits before a serious oil leak from the engine box forced it into the pits, heralding its imminent departure, but the opening laps still saw a fine tussle as Ickx closed up on the Alpine, got by, led it for half a lap, and then dropped back as Jabouille repassed.

After only ten laps, Jabouille made his first refuelling stop, worried that the high track temperatures might be affecting his car, but all was well and he set off again in third place. The Alpine was not to lead again, however, for although it was the fastest car on the circuit between pit stops a spot of electrical trouble was to lose it several minutes before two hours were up. Having regained third place quite swiftly and then held it comfortably for several hours, the Alpine eventually retired at 1.15 on Sunday morning when a piston broke up.

After a dynamic start that took it into third place for a few miles, Lapeyre's Lola was soon back in the pit road with a damaged engine, and so the Porsche 936s of Ickx/van Lennep and Joest/Barth were left a long way clear of the rest of the field throughout the first quarter of the race. By the end of six hours, Greenwood's Corvette had gone out after a fine run in sixth place when a burst tyre ruptured its fuel tank, the Monza had retired with a broken driveshaft, and both the Inalteras had had trouble. Then the Stommelen/Schurti Porsche 935 also ran into a spate of dramas, as an alternator belt broke, a rear suspension pick-up point gave out, and a battered rear wing had to be patched up. French amateur André Haller sadly died after his Datsun 260Z crashed on Mulsanne Straight and caught fire, but a string of lesser incidents proved harmless, although several drivers were suffering from burns caused by the stifling temperatures—it was

reckoned to be the hottest Le Mans for years.

Throughout the second quarter of the race, the Porsches of Ickx/Van Lennep and Joest/Barth ran beautifully, and by half distance the former led the latter by two laps, with Lafosse/Migault a further four laps adrift in the better of the Mirages. The other Mirage, the one handled by Bell and Schuppan, suffered a series of electrical failures but nevertheless lay fifth behind de Cadenet's Lola, which was going superbly after an alternator belt had been changed. Apart from a wheel that stripped its thread on Sunday morning, this was to be the only mechanical problem afflicting the Lola throughout the race, a record that says much for the standard of preparation achieved by de Cadenet's private team. By half distance, however, the Porsche 935 had also solved its problems for the time being. Schurti and

Despite being a brand new team in its first race, Inaltera enjoyed the luxury of a ready-to-race spare car in the paddock as well as two cars in the race. Despite a variety of troubles, the most spectacular of which was a driver's door that blew open at speed, the French debutants got both their coupes to the finish.

Stommelen were therefore again sixth, making ground fast on the three British cars in front of them.

Nothing, it seemed, could stop the two works Porsches at the head of the field; but at ten past seven on Sunday morning the second placed car of Joest/Barth stopped on the circuit with a broken driveshaft, only a few minutes after it had left the pits with an obvious engine defect. So now British cars lay second, third and fourth, and with the Porsche 935 still making ground on the Mirages and de Cadenet's Lola, a tremendous battle for second place developed.

As Sunday morning wore on the Bell/Schuppan Mirage lost more time when its mechanical fuel pump gave up the ghost. The Lafosse/Migault Mirage had one costly pit stop when its throttle linkage, the high pressure electrical fuel pump and a fuel pressure relief valve all had to be restored to working order, while the Porsche team achieved the staggering task of changing the complete turbo unit in their 935 in only ten minutes.

But still the leading Porsche of Ickx and Van Lennep continued its inexorable progress, the better part of a hundred miles ahead of its nearest pursuers. Then, just before noon, that car made for its pit with a crack in the

exhaust pipe that ran from the engine to the turbocharger. It lost twenty minutes before it rejoined the race, but it was twenty minutes the team could afford to lose, and with no further dramas Ickx and Van Lennep finally won by 11 laps from Lafosse and Migault. The latter's Mirage nearly lost second place, when its rear bodywork blew off three laps from the finish after a mounting bracket snapped. It was replaced just in time to keep its position, even after the engine had refused to fire for many seconds after that last dramatic stop, and finally staggered away misfiring.

After a tremendous closing burst which won them the prize for covering the greatest distance during the last quarter of the race (another innovation this year), Craft and de Cadenet came a fighting, heroic third, drawing cheers not only from the large British contingent at the finish but from many of the French as well. It really was a splendid performance from such a small team whose drivers' feet had been burned and blistered by the heat of the pedals. Fourth were Stommelen and Schurti in the Porsche 935, leaving Bell/Schuppan to bring their failing Mirage into fifth place and French amateurs Touroul/Cudini/Boubet to come sixth and winners of the Group 4 GT class with their Porsche Carrera RSR.—J.C.T.

Results :
LE MANS 24 HOURS
349 laps—4,769.92 kilometres

1st : J. Ickx/G. Van Lennep (2.1 t/c Porsche 936)— 349 laps (198.75 k.p.h.)
2nd : J-L. Lafosse/F. Migault (3.0 Mirage-DFV GR8) .... 338 laps
3rd : C. Craft/A. de Cadenet (3.0 Lola-DFV T380) .... 337 ,,
4th : M. Schurti/R. Stommelen (2.9 t/c Porsche 935) .... 331 ,,
5th : D. Bell/V. Schuppan (3.0 Mirage-DFV GR8) .... 326 ,,
6th : R. Touroul/A. Cudini/R. Boubet (3.0 Porsche Carrera RSR) .... 314 ,,
7th : E. Kraus/G. Steckkonig (3.0 Porsche 908/3) .... 313 ,,
8th : H. Pescarolo/J-P. Beltoise (3.0 Inaltera-DFV) .... 305 ,,
9th : H. Bertrams/H. Martin/E. Evertz (3.0 Porsche Carrera RSR) .... 302 ,,
10th : S. Posey/H. Grohs/H. de Fierlant (3.5 BMW CSL) .... 299 ,,
Fastest Lap : J-P. Jabouille (2.9 t/c Alpine-Renault A442), 3 min. 49.3 sec. (214.15 k.p.h.), recorded on lap 7.

44ᵉ Grand Prix d'Endurance 24 Heures du Mans

Jacky Ickx and Gijs van Lennep win the new, improved Le Mans

BY JOHN G. RETTIE

THE 24 HOURS of Le Mans race has traditionally been Europe's premier racing event, drawing huge crowds of racing fans, curiosity seekers and revelers. Over the past 10 years much of the glamour and glory of Le Mans has been dissipated as the race cars have become less identifiable, the classes more confusing and various manufacturers have

up with the more nimble racers, but what the hell, it was a good opportunity to go to France.

The leading contenders for victory included the three Porsche factory entries: two turbo 936s (one for Jacky Ickx and Gijs van Lennep, the other for Reinhold Jöst) and a turbo 935 to be driven by Rolf Stommelen and Manfred Schurti.

dropped out. The Le Mans organizers have attempted to overcome the waning interest with some changes in the classes this year with categories for Group 6, 5 and 4 cars, unhomologated production cars (GTX) and Le Mans prototypes (GTP) built to special dimension and weight rules. Finally, through an agreement with Bill France and the Daytona 24-hour race, as well as in recognition of the American bicentennial, two NASCAR stockers and two IMSA GTs were invited to compete.

John Greenwood showed up with his Spirit of Le Mans Corvette (R&T March 1976), number 76, appropriately enough, and many said it was the best-looking car in the race. The other IMSA competitor was Mike Keyser in his Monza (see R&T August 1976) with an extra large wing on the trunk. Greenwood and Keyser have driven at Le Mans previously, so it was not an entirely new experience for them.

It was a whole new racing encounter for the good ol' NASCAR boys, however. Dick Brooks and Dick Hutcherson brought their Ford Torino and Hershel McGriff and his son Doug entered their Dodge Charger. It was a foregone conclusion that these unwieldy cars had little chance of keeping

Porsche's primary adversaries would be a turbocharged Alpine Renault A442, driven by Jean-Pierre Jabouille and Patrick Tambay, and two Mirage Fords.

The Fords were last year's winning cars and they had been bought as a complete team by Harley Cluxton of Grand Touring Cars, Phoenix, Arizona. Derek Bell, who won last year, would team with Vern Schuppan in one car while the second would be piloted by Francois Migault and Jean-Louis Lafosse.

BMW was represented by six 3.0CSLs, three from the factory and three from privateers, with the most graphically exciting one being the Brian Redman/Peter Gregg car. It had been turned over to American artist Frank Stella and he came up with a striking black-and-white paint job that looked like a 3-dimensional graph complete with power curves!

One very sad fact about this year's Le Mans was the absence of Ferraris for the first time since World War II. Some of that disappointment was countered by the new GTP cars, the Inalteras. This project began two years ago under the impetus of French driver Jean Rondeau. Now the team is managed by former driver Vic Elford, and sponsored by Inaltera, the largest wallpaper manufacturer in France. The GTP cars are heavier than the Group 6 cars and are not allowed to have wings, so they had little chance of an overall win, even in the hands of a driver like 3-time Le Mans winner Henri Pescarolo.

Four o'clock Saturday afternoon came with the temperature in the 90s, the organizers counting the crowd to see if the new Le Mans had drawn the people in, the drivers complaining about the heat and Bill France with the starter's flag in his hand. The Alpine Renault was on the pole after having toured the course in 3 min 33.1 sec (143.2 mph) during practice and holding off the works Porsches. John Greenwood was starting in 9th position after demonstrating in practice that his Corvette might not be the quickest through the corners but he could outrun everyone down the 3-mile Mulsanne straight where he

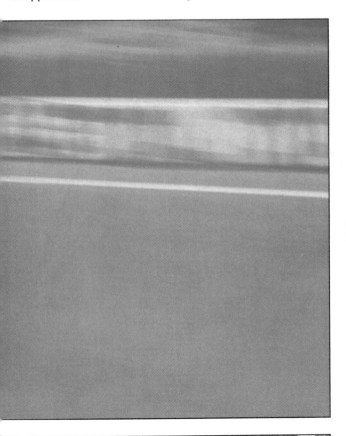

Jacky Ickx takes his turn in the winning Porsche 936 (left). Unretired NASCAR ace, Dick Hutcherson, follows a Porsche through Tertre Rouge (left, below) in his Torino GTX entry. Mike Keyser (above) driving his modified IMSA Monza leads John Greenwood's Corvette down the hill from the Dunlop Bridge and into the esses.

was clocked at 215.6 mph!

In the early going, Jabouille in the Alpine Renault and Ickx in the Porsche 936 swapped the lead several times, followed by the Porsche 935, the other 936 and Brian Redman in the BMW. Unfortunately, Redman's car lasted only three laps before he stopped to find out why it was smoking so badly and discovered the cylinder head was leaking oil, putting the car out of commission. The two IMSA entries, Greenwood's Corvette and Keyser's Monza, were having a race of their own back about the 10th position and putting on a good show for the spectators. It was brief, however, as the Monza broke a halfshaft on the 12th lap and Keyser spent the rest of the 24 hours selling Camel GT T-shirts.

The NASCAR folks saw their hopes dashed early on when McGriff's Charger quit on the first lap with an engine oil leak. The Ford Torino stuck it out until about the halfway point when its gearbox packed up. R&T Contributing Editor Sam Posey had better luck driving one of the BMW Group 5 cars, but not much. The car's engine and transmission gave Sam fits throughout the 24 hours but he was able to nurse it home to finish 10th overall and 4th in his class.

Getting back to the leaders, Ickx took the lead on lap 10 when Jabouille pitted the Alpine, and stayed there the rest of the way. Ickx's co-driver, Van Lennep, had announced his retirement before the start and it was a good way to finish, winning his second Le Mans. Second place went to Cluxton's Ford Mirage with drivers Migault and Lafosse, and 3rd was captured by British privateer Alain De Cadenet in a Lola DFV. It was a dream come true for De Cadenet who had been racing at Le Mans for years in private entries. Incidentally, Le Mans is the only race he enters!

Privateer at Le Mans

British interest at Le Mans this year centred around four teams: the two JCB Mirages, Alain de Cadenet's private Lola with Tate & Lyle sponsorship, the Dorset Racing 2-litre Lola, and Hermetite's Group 5 BMW. There were other drivers, but these were the teams.

Of all these, it was perhaps most gratifying for the British to see Alain de Cadenet's 3-litre Lola team taking its best result yet: third overall. After a year in a Ferrari 512, and three years with the Gordon Murray-designed Duckhams special, the second year with the Lola has at last reaped some real success for this very determined amateur, who co-drives with Chris Craft.

Each year, de Cadenet gathers around him a team of equally enthusiastic skilled part-timers. If that seems derogatory, it's not meant to be. They are all highly skilled at their own jobs, but they just gather together to help Londoner de Cadenet at this one race. Heading the team for the past two years has been Keith Greene, at one time no mean racer himself, but more recently team manager of the Hexagon F1 team, team manager of the Crowne Racing 2-litre sports car championship winning team, Brabham team manager, Goodyear tyre supervisor and part-time team manager for Damien Magee's Hexagon F5000 team. This year, for the second time, Greene took a week's holiday from Paul Michaels's Superbike centre (attached to Hexagon in Highgate), and disappeared off to France to spearhead the de Cadenet effort. Greene spoke with BOB CONSTANDUROS about life with the de Cadenet team before, during and after the Le Mans 24 Hours.

Driver cooling was a major problem in the de Cadenet Lola during Les Vingt Quatre Heures. Here, de Cadenet is about to get a jugfull.

You came third at Le Mans. Was that a disappointment, or was it where you expected to finish?
For me, we did it almost to perfection! That is, we came third, but we might have come second. When we were running true to form, we were out there in front of the Mirages. I did have hopes of coming second. But then you can't combat that sort of thing, when they march off down the pit lane with 25 mechanics.

The biggest compliment we had came from a German, the Porsche team manager and engineer, who came up and congratulated us, which for a German is unbelievable. But then he knows that his lot spent DM3,000,000 doing Le Mans, and we were only ten laps further back, having spent three million farthings....

Starting from the beginning, you weren't really happy with the Lola after last year's race, were you?
Last year, Alain more or less had the Lola as Eric Broadley designed it, which was all a bit of a guesstimation job: it was long-tailed, and they hoped it would do all sorts of miles an hour with only 400bhp. The trick suspension was no problem as such, except that the uprights were fabricated and we broke one during the race.

But our main problem in 1975 was bodywork: vibration, and hinges breaking up. For 17 hours of the race, we had the whole thing rivetted up solid. Pop rivets had pulled out and the split pin brackets just lifted the monocoque. There was so much air inside the body that it was really tearing every single mounting off. As you know, Alain lost the complete rear tail early in the night.

After that, I did screeds of all the things we learned and job lists for what we had to do last year, and that's what choked me. Although I thought everything was done, in fact it wasn't. The car was going to be MIRA-tested and wind tunnel-tested, to find out this and that; none of this happened. We just wasted a whole year. Then eventually it did a show or two, and then finally

Keith Greene — Le Mans team manager.

Alain got it together and remade up his mind to do Le Mans again this year. And then, of course, they started pulling the car to bits.

So this year, we wanted to make the front shape better, reduce the weight of the tail and its length, and make a much better wing, because last year the wing was actually mounted on the body. This year it was mounted on the back of the gearbox so it was completely separate; the body came off without us touching the wing at all.

Anyway, Alain got all busy making up suspension and rear uprights in demon metals and tried to do the underneath parts properly. I did a couple of test days with him at Silverstone in the final six weeks or so, and we just messed about with aluminium really, until we changed the bodywork from the back of the radiator duct to the windscreen.

We were also looking for straight line speed when we tested the car. In fact, Alain totally misled me anyway, because he failed to take into account the diameter of the tyre — he didn't fail to take it into account, but he got it wrong by an inch, which is 400 revs, which is quite a lot of miles an hour. He was determined to pull this 28/28 ratio and he got the tyre diameter wrong. We were only pulling 8200/8300 revs in practice on a 28/28, and we were only getting tyre growth to around 27ins as well, so we poked in a 27/28 and it pulled 9000 revs, which is about 200 miles an hour.

The trouble is, there is nowhere to test before Le Mans?
You can't test anywhere! MIRA can't cope, there's nowhere. You could possibly do a deal with motorways which aren't yet open, although that would still create hassles because it's a public road built with public money.

Nobody used to say that they learned at the Le Mans test weekend. They all jerk at it and say, "We're not going to be bothered to go to that." But in actual fact, you need the weekend to do Le Mans.

I only know how to do my job list, because I've done it a few times. Otherwise, where would you be? And even now I'm making amendments. I mean, I dropped a clanger: I didn't have enough driver cooling in case it was super-hot. I put some in, but it wasn't enough. I put in a deflector plate inside to make an air space between the radiator and the bulkhead, but their feet were the big problem. Fried, right? Well, God knows, they wouldn't have been able to drive at all if I hadn't happened to put that one plate in.

There wasn't really enough practice for us, because there was so much we wanted to do. In the past, Alain has always wanted to run everything fresh for the race. I won't have it. Every-

Opposite: The British-built JCB Mirages of Jean-Louis Lafosse/Francois Migault and Vern Schuppan/Derek Bell in the pits at Le Mans. Like last year, both cars finished, this year with the French-driven car in second position, and the second car fifth after petrol pump problems. Overleaf: The 3-litre de Cadenet Lola of Alain de Cadenet/Chris Craft, sponsored by Tate & Lyle and Hammonds Sauce, which finished a fine third under the team management of Keith Greene.

Sugar for endurance

A scenic view of the de Cadenet Tate & Lyle Lola as it nears the end of a hot lap at Le Mans.

Privateer at Le Mans

continued

thing going in the race has to be run, as far as I'm concerned. I made that clear last year. This year was even worse, because we had all these uprights and suspension and things in these demon spec materials.

In testing, the car was handling beautifully. The way to have it at Le Mans is fast, smooth and easy to drive, without doing anything silly. OK, we got all that and then Alain wanted to change everything. So I thought to myself, OK, he's gone to all this trouble, so even though I had said that I was not starting the race on anything that I hadn't tried, that's what we did. We had to fit *all* new front suspension, *all* new rear suspension, *all* new driveshafts, *all* new bellhousing, *all* new gearbox, *all* new engine and *all* new clutch. All that was left of the car when we set about it at Le Mans at 6 o'clock on the Thursday morning was the tub!

We also had to do all the other bits I'd made. I was steaming around trying to get a bit of air over the top with all these fabrications I'd been making while the others were doing the normal changeover. It was just hard work, flat out. I did a little calculation: we did 857 man hours from Monday morning until Sunday night after the race, that's 122 hours for each of the seven of us.

Who makes up the team, in fact?
John Anderson is the mechanic who's been with Alain all year, he does a bit on his vintage car, or works on the Lola, or whatever; he's from New Zealand. This year he had a mate who won some sort of scholarship for driving, again from New Zealand, a fellow called Howard who's built his own F2 car but can't find an engine. He worked for Alain for the last three or four weeks up to and including Le Mans. Then we had John Gardener and John Hewitt, who are more or less Doctors of Engineering (unbelievable, you should see their place in Sussex — they rebuild Bugattis and Frazer Nashes). They're both machinists and engineers *par excellence* and they had another of their machinists along, a fellow called Anthony who was pretty green, at his first race meeting. Then I had Dave who works for Dan Margulies as a vintage mechanic *cum* run around; he was my gofer, looked after the spare parts and so forth, and he'a a bit of an electrician as well. And I worked as well while I was there, little bits of fabrication and so on.

What I tried to do was to pick the job which was best suited to the individual, I gave them all job lists individually until I came to the last day, when I gave them all total job lists.

Drivers Alain de Cadenet (left) and Chris Craft.

What is this about the Cosworth DFV being of tremendous vintage, the engine Bruce McLaren used to win the 1968 Belgian GP at Spa?
It's engine number 913, the same block and crank that we ran last year, and seven of the rods are the same. It's the most perfect line-bored block they've ever seen down at Nicholson-McLaren Engines, and the rods, despite an ovality test at the big end, are the truest set of rods, apart from the one which was tossed and replaced. The engine has done all sorts of mileage. Alain's had it for years, I don't know whether he's used that one for every race; he's got two, 934 and 913, and 913 is the race engine.

We did what Thursday practice we had time for with it, and then all the race. He just did seven laps between ten and eleven on the Thursday night to check it out. It was beautiful, sweet as a nut. Three hours after the race, when they found the car in the *parc fermé*, John Anderson just got in, switched on, turned the key, and drove it.

Mind you, the foreman at Nicholsons builds it and he's fantastic. It's become his annual thing, to do that engine himself, and he really takes some care. It's his own personal pride.

Only one DFV failed in the race (in a French-driven Lola) but that was a full-house mill; they were third on the grid, easy to do that. You see, we only use 8500 revs in the gears and nine in top.

How did you plan to tackle the race?
We just planned to run between 3m 55s and 4m as near as possible and just stay up there, routine stop and stay up there, routine and stay up there. We had a fixed team to refuel, check the oil, retape the ducts which moved around, and give it a water feed down to the high pressure mechanical pump to stop vaporization.

In fact, this year we didn't lift the tail or the nosecone once throughout the entire race. Not once. We put in about a gallon and a half of oil, which can go in from the cockpit behind the passenger seat, and we changed front brake pads through the wheel arches; we never had to change rear pads. We changed front wheels for a fatigue

reason, along with pads and rear wheels. This we really need not have done, which was a great shame as it cost us second place as it happened, because the wheel nut seized on. It took eight and a half minutes to get it off.

We made up a new nosecone during the night for extra driver cooling, but when the play-acting was over (like the walking on one toe, the *crapolada*, the tension and excitement, the banter), I established that the problem was their feet, and a new nose wouldn't have helped. Also, I knew that if we changed the nose it was going to take about four minutes to screw it on. I tried to talk Alain out of putting on the new nose and we had a bit of a row about it. But you get all that because there's tension. I had two alternatives: to walk out and jack it in, or to stick. I thought, no, it's just because they're tense and their arses are all sore, so I then got all the birds out there to give them a big team wave and they forgot all about it then.

At about the same time, things were quite tense in the pit. The Goodyear people came over to me with the regulations and pointed out that the Porsche was illegal, paragraph numbers in the regs and everything. On the Silhouette car, all or any of the coolants have to be within the original dimensions of the chassis. And also, it had to have the original bonnet: any Porsche Carrera bonnet out of the car park must fit that car.

I hate those sort of things, those specific things which are cheats, but cheats which aren't going to improve the performance necessarily. OK, fractionally, maybe; but when you're talking about 400 against 600bhp you're not really in the same ball park anyway. If they run strong and clean, you aren't going to win, because a good biggy is always going to beat a good littly.

Do you prefer doing something like Le Mans to doing a Grand Prix?
Different. It's very hard to say. You get right into something like Le Mans. When you realize, at about eleven, that you can do something, like there's no reason why not, and you think that everything's been done, and you've looked at all the job lists and you know what's needed because you've done it all before, then it's quite satisfying. I never blinked my eyes for 24 hours, I timed every single lap. If somebody asked me to do that two weeks before, I knew I would have said I would do it, but I wouldn't have been able to say for sure. I'm older, it's quite a strain. They all go out to the team dinner on the Sunday night, but it's always the same for me: shower, shampoo, lie down, POW, gone. Just used up.

A GP produces a different sort of tension. Le Mans is very tense because all the time you've got to be conscious of all these little regulations, you've got to know, not "hang on, I've got to look it up in a book". That puts on a tension. When I go to Alain's team, there are always ups and downs, but I run it totally unless he doesn't actually want me to do it. Otherwise, what I say goes. Which is different from what GP's used to be like for me . . . .

How do you feel about the team's achievement now, in retrospect?
I always think things are quickly forgotten in motor racing, no matter who you are or what your achievement. It's rather sad in a way. Monday morning, it's all great, everyone's happy, Tuesday it's pretty good, Wednesday, there's still a number of people to see, Thursday, there's a team dinner somewhere or other so that revives it. But by the following Monday, it's history.

It was rather like when we won the European 2-litre championship. One week later it was still great, two weeks later we might never have won. It never did Chris Craft any good, it never did me any good, it never did anyone any good, really.

It's sort of like Le Mans itself. If you see the 450,000 people there at 4 o'clock on the Sunday afternoon, and then you go there at 4 o'clock on the Monday afternoon, 24 hours later, not a soul, just a lot of waste paper. It's weird. And the achievement is like that in a way.

Now Alain has come this close . . .
I should think he'll want to go back.

And what could you see winning?
A turbo. I just see it in my mind that a Ford DFX might be an amusing tool with some nice little sports car job underneath. Cosworth might be interested, they couldn't believe the first year when we even finished with a DFV. They said absolutely, totally, 100 per cent no way will that engine, whatever you do, do that number of hours. But Keith Duckworth was absolutely shattered when we did it. I'd like to shatter him again. □

Le Mans gets a boost

Photographs Ron Easton

As turbocharged cars make the running

and a Group 6 Porsche outlasts its production-based counterparts

PORSCHE were hedging their bets. At the end of last year they were looking to their ultra-powerful turbocharged 3-litre Group 5 "silhouette" Carrera to win Le Mans. Then, when it became clear that the CSI intended to proceed with the madness of running two sports car racing championships in 1976 they built a Group 6 spyder, the 936, to have a contender in both categories. They intended that both should run at Le Mans.

But just a week before this, the 44th *Vingt Quartre Heures du Mans*, the Group 5 Carrera 935 suffered serious engine troubles at the Nurburgring. Porsche hurriedly prepared a second 936. Then their engineers gave the 935 the all-clear for a Le Mans attempt. They had three race-ready cars; why not race them all? Reinhold Jöst, a faithful and successful Porsche privateer, had an entry in the Group 6 category at Le Mans. The second works Martini Porsche 936 was entrusted to him. So Porsche had a foot in both camps, with a bit more weight among the faster Group 6 cars. It

was, in retrospect, more than they needed.

Their number one 936, driven by two previous Le Mans winners, Jacky Ickx and Gijs Van Lennep, ran through the 24 hours comfortably ahead of the field. Ickx said that they had never had to push it hard, that their aim had been to go steadily and consistently throughout. Only mechanical problems would stop that. They had just one — a broken exhaust pipe before midday on Sunday. It took 33 minutes to replace the complete exhaust system on one side of the flat-six engine. Their lead was cut from 16 to eight laps. That was still more than enough.

Le Mans were also hedging their bets. The CSI's parallel-but-never-to-meet World Championship for Makes and World Sports Car Championship were no good to them. Neither could bring the sort of field they needed to restore some confidence in this most famous of motor races. Nor, the A.C. de L'Ouest recognised, would the 1975 fuel consumption regulations used last

year. Freed from Championships and at such difference with the CSI that a World Championship Grand Prix was allowed to be staged the same weekend, they decided to throw Le Mans open to almost anything with four wheels and all-enveloping bodywork. Thus there were categories for Group 5, Group 6, Group 4 GTs, unhomologated production cars (GTX) Le Mans prototypes (GTP) built to special dimensional and weight rules, and thanks to a tie-up with the World's only other 24-hour sports car race at Daytona, two categories for American IMSA and NASCAR modified production cars. They trebled the prize fund, introduced six-hour classifications with £1,000 prizes which produced four races-within-the-race. They tried every trick in the book to get the best of what was available. In that context, the organisers did well.

Only Porsche's works Group 5 car, driven by Rolf Stommelen and Manfred Schurti, seemed likely to be able to mix with the Group 6 cars on speed alone. As it turned out, this car had the troubles that the winning

Porsche lacked. Four punctures in quick succession, a sticking throttle, broken rear suspension mounting causing it to bounce into the guard rail, ignition troubles, and finally a failed turbocharger, dropped this impressive machine well down from a best placing of third early in the race and it finished fourth, 18 laps behind its winning Group 5 teammate.

The Le Mans prototypes were, by definition, bigger, heavier and slower than the Group 6 cars, and the locally built Inalteras, managed by Vic Elford and including three-times winner Henri Pescarolo among their drivers, were never in contention for the lead, though both finished. The IMSA and NASCAR challenge made no mark on the race, retiring early.

Whilst the number of Group 5 and Group 4 Porsches in the entry list and the retirement record in the first few hours had suggested that the event might become a Porsche club race towards its end, these normally reliable 911 variants had all sorts of problems. Clutches, gearboxes and turbochargers were

37

the most popular failures and interestingly the unturbocharged and two years old Carrera RS of Raymond Touroul and Alain Cudini was the best placed at the finish, sixth.

So it was that the leading positions were disputed throughout by the Group 6 cars. Fastest of all on the basis of practice times was the single turbocharged Alpine Renault A442 driven by Jean-Pierre Jabouille, Patrick Tambay and Jose Dolhem. Renault were anxious that this single-car effort should not be billed as a Porsche versus Alpine confrontation. Le Mans had not originally been on their race schedule and they had carried out no special preparation for the 24-hours; unlike the works Porsches, the car was in its normal 500 bhp, 1000 Km race tune with a rev limit of 9,800 (700 lower than usual) as its only concession to the length of the race.

In practice the Alpine did 3 min 33.1 sec, 143.1 mph, which was over six seconds quicker than the Ickx-Van Lennep Porsche that joined it on the front row for the rolling start. The Alpine led the field in the opening laps but it was soon in trouble and lasted only until 1 a.m. before retiring with a broken piston.

With so much more powerful supercharged opposition, the Cosworth DFV-engined Group 6 cars could do no more than sit it out and count on fast reliability for a good result. Last year's winning Gulf GR8s were entered by their new owner Harley Cluxton of Phoenix Arizona, re-named Mirages, sponsored by JCB and Total, run by John Horsman, formerly team manager of Gulf Research Racing, and driven by Derek Bell and Vern Schuppan and Jean-Louis Lafosse and Francois Migault. But neither these or the De Cadanet Lola-DFV driven by Chris Craft and Alain de Cadanet could hope to beat the Porsche 936 if it kept going. By 12 hours, half distance, the De Cadanet was sandwiched between the two Mirages, and the trio held third, fourth and fifth places, behind the two 936s. That remained the pattern. Lafosse and Migault finished second, the De Cadanet team a delighted third, while troubles for the Bell-Schuppan Mirage dropped it back to fifth.

Taking a special interest in this team at Le Mans this year was the man who had initiated these and earlier Mirages, nurtured drivers like Jacky Ickx and Derek Bell, and been behind no less than four Le Mans wins. Now retired from racing, but probably more knowlegeable about this event than anyone else, **John Wyer** spent this year's race as a very special contributor to *Autocar*. He takes up the story of that long, hot weekend at La Sarthe. Now read on . . .

Results

A WINNER RETURNS

JOHN WYER'S

chronicle of Le Mans 1976

Friday, La Chartre sur le Loir. *Practice is over, the cars scrutineered, the entry confirmed. It is a day of preparation, of fine tuning and checking for a racing team. Of reflection on the significance of what is about to happen for journalists, as Wyer discovers:*

"This is a decisive year for the ACO. Sports car racing and Le Mans have reached the bottom of the trough and I think they are on the way up now. This year's entry is a good deal more interesting than last year. They had to fragment it into all those different classes to get a representative entry and to be sure they have enough cars to have some running on Sunday . . . What's wrong is the international regulations, not Le Mans. There are just too many classes, Le Mans this year could not do anything else but open up.

We have got to find some formula for getting the two classes of so-called sports cars (Group 5 and 6) together. Everyone is looking for a lead here and the ACO have done a courageous thing in trying to give that lead. They have devised the GTP Le Mans prototype class. This is desirable, allowing manufacturers to come in with cars that have not yet been homologated. Le Mans is trying to define what a sports car is today and have imposed minimum height regulations and various other things to produce a sensible regulation of what a sports car should be. They have framed the rules quite well — the minimum height is about right, it lets in cars like the Lotus Europa and the Ferrari 308GTB which are the modern idiom of a sports car. There are not many of these cars this year (only the two Inalteras, an interesting but slow WMP specialising the Peugeot-Renault-Volvo V6 engine, and a turbocharged Lancia Stratos for two girl drivers), but I think that it will grow and that there will be some interesting cars. GTP can't compete with Group 6 for the cars are bigger and heavier. But longer term, when people get used to the idea of running something closer to the usual run of production cars, Group 6 has got to go. There doesn't seem to me to be much logic in Group 5 either; I would have thought it better to relax the regulations for Groups 2 and 4. We need to reduce the spread of categories.

The link with Daytona is sensible, for a car that is good for Le Mans is good for Daytona and Sebring. I am considerably less sure about the links with NASCAR. But linking with other truly long distance races makes sense. If they give a lead, other race organisers might follow because they are all unhappy about putting on races for either of the CSI championships. Le Mans has given a lead before. It could do it again, though it is not as strong as it was.

So this year's is a rag-bag. Which category would I choose to go for a win? The small independent really has no choice — he must go for Group 6. If he wants to enter Group 5 he has to ally himself to a major manufacturer.

Porsche are in both categories. That is the way they operate; their racing programme is technically-orientated and they love technical exercises: the more they have, the happier they are. To have cars in Groups 4, 5 and 6 makes their engineers very happy. But I am not sure that it is good strategy if you are going out to win the race. It is better to decide what gives you the best chance and concentrate all efforts on that.

I would have gone for their Group 5 car — the 935. With 2.8 litres (effectively 4.1) and 545 bhp it is not as highly stressed as the 2.1-litre 520 bhp engine of the 936 — and for that reason has the best chance. But they would have a better chance if they had three of those cars

Wyer's pre-race favourite — the Group 5 Martini-Porsche 935. It ran for the last half of the race with a crudely patched rear wing after a suspension breakage had spun it into the guard rail. This and other problems relegated this powerful turbocharged Carrera to fourth place at the finish

instead of one. One car at Le Mans is a tremendous hostage to fortune.

There is only one entry from Renault — the turbocharged Alpine. I can understand why Renault want to play it down but it is a very serious effort and I am sure they are hoping for a good result. They have no experience of it over 2,000 km so obviously they will be biting their nails after that point. The car is quick, but I would look upon it as a trial horse.

I cannot see the sense of BMW's late entry of the very powerful (700 bhp) turbocharged CSL. It isn't fast enough to be competitive with the Group 5 Porsche or to lead the race, the transmission is known to be suspect for this sort of power and Brian Redman reports that it is by no means an easy car to drive — the power comes in very suddenly. BMW's experiments with turbocharging are interesting but could be done without exposing it to the publicity of Le Mans. I never thought that going out to make a grandstand display in the first four hours did you much good at Le Mans.

The JCB Mirages were bought by Harley Cluxton specifically for Le Mans and then some races in North America. They are last year's cars with no important changes, and still running the BD3 camshafts used in the DFVs last year for the fuel consumption limit. They are geared to 9,000 rpm instead of 8,000 but with these cams the curve is so flat between eight and nine that the maximum power is still only 402 bhp. There is no reason why they should not do well, but they will be playing a waiting game.

The number of cars using turbochargers is interesting but I don't think there is any reason to suppose that this should make them unreliable; from the point of view of engine bearing load they are better than a normally-aspirated car. The trouble is the equivalence of 1.4. There is absolutely no logic in having an equivalence of 2 to 1 for formula 1, and 1.4 in this kind of racing. I don't want to see them banned — turbocharging is a useful and legitimate way to go — but I think a 2 to 1 equivalence would even things out.

It is notable and regretable that there are, for the first time since the War, no Ferraris in this race. I talked

to Mr. Ferrari about this last autumn and he was waiting to see which way the regulations went. He is happy about running in Groups 4 and 5 but not at present with factory entries, because of the effort going into the formula 1 programme. The Groups 4 and 5 categories would certainly be more interesting with the inclusion of the Boxer and 308 Ferraris.

Saturday, 3.30 p.m.: The Welcome — Le Mans' exclusive enclosure for invited guests. Wyer wears an Invitée d'Honneur badge as well as his Press armband but is so well known here that he needs neither. The mid-afternoon sun is scorching. How will that affect the pace, the cars and drivers? In 20 minutes the cars come out on to the circuit for the pace lap and as they return, strung out over perhaps a mile and 55 engines sing their loudest, Wyer methodically starts his Heuer chronograph. It is 3.58 p.m.: for Le Mans 1976, Zero Hour. Jabaulle in the Alpine leads. Lap times are in the high 3 min 50 secs.

Nobody is racing at all yet. I expected the race to start slowly in this sort of heat but to look exciting between the Group 6 Alpine and Porsches — at least until you put a watch on it and find that they are only in the mid-50s. Alpine are under some pressure to make a show with a French car in front of a French crowd.

Everybody is cautious in this temperature. It is important not to get the whole thing soaked in heat for there is a risk of fuel vapourization at the first pit stop. It is always

important to stay out of trouble in the heavy traffic of the opening laps and for that reason one tends to put the more experienced of the driver-pairing in the car for the first stint. It's no good having someone starting who wants to tear out in front . . .

Saturday, 6.30 p.m.: The pits. Still very hot. The Alpine's early lead is lost for good in a pit stop to introduce some more air to the radiators on lap 10. Ickx leads in the Porsche from team-mate Jöst, their cars identical apart from the funnel air box rear section of the leader. Two of the American cars — the massive but slow NASCAR Dodge Charger and the fast TMSA Chevrolet Monza are already out, and Greenwood's fast Corvette follows them into retirement soon after.

> The only surprising thing so far is how early the Alpine ran into trouble — I expected it to put on a show for four hours at least. But

Above: "They can congratulate themselves in every way." A splendid performance by uncomfortably overheated Chris Craft and Alain De Cadenet brought their modified Lola-DFV home in third place. Sponsored by Tate & Lyle, it carried the motto "sugar for endurance". Success was sweet

Left: Le Mans' modern idiom of a sports car — the Inalteras were built to the new GTP regulations and used Cosworth DFV engines. Unraced before Le Mans, they did well to finish despite such setbacks as a door blowing off, lights failure and broken shock abosrbers

Below: John Greenwood's spectacular IMSA Corvette held eighth place in the first hour but was forced to retire with holed fuel cell after a tyre puncture on the Mulsanne Straight, where in practice it was unofficially fastest of all at 215 mph

now it has problems — they have been changing plugs in the pits. Alain de Cadenet's car is fourth, though I suspect both the Mirages behind him could overtake if they wanted to but they are obviously running to orders. There have been several punctures, including one on Bell's Mirage on the sixth lap.

The turbo BMW has a serious oil leak. It will be hard put to make the distance (in fact, it soon retired with a cracked block). I was surprised to see the Group 5 935 Martini-Porsche come in on the 11th lap. We are assured that this was routine. Being a Group 5 car it has only 120 litres tankage compared to the Group 6s' 160 litres. Combined with heavy fuel consumption and covering 15 laps an hour, stopping every 11 laps will mean an awful lot of stops.

The first three Porsche pit stops were efficient — around 50 sec is par. The fuel delivery rate should be the limiting factor in a routine pit stop and the organiser's pumps run

at 3 litres a second. A driver and wheel change can be completed in the refuelling time but a pad change — needed three times in the 24 hours for a car like the Mirage, takes 2 mins — or more.

It is always astonishing how much time at Le Mans is spent standing still. Ideally, 20 routine stops should not amount to more than half an hour. But if at the end of the 24 hours your car has been stationary for less than an hour you have done very well — in 1969 when our GT40 narrowly beat the Porsche and the pressure was on throughout, we managed this. Last year we were running for 22 hrs 40 minutes — 1 hr 20 mins stopped is a hell of a long time. . . .

Saturday, 9.30 p.m. Mulsanne Corner. A visit to the signalling pits at Mulsanne provides an opportunity to watch the cars at close quarters. The order has not changed much except that the Alpine, repaired, is back in third place behind the two Group 6 Porsches and the two Mirages are running fourth and fifth having overtaken the De Cadenet Lola. Earlier, at 9 p.m., an ominous cloud of black smoke scarred the still-shimmering blue sky in the direction of the kink in the Mulsanne Straight. Unaccountably, a Datsun 260Z had run wide on the dirt and hit the Armco barriers at very high speed. The car burst into flames. The

driver, Andre Hallaire, lost his life. We were unaware of the outcome of this accident as we discussed the rôle of the signalling pits:

" I can't see any reason why signalling cannot be done from the pits themselves these days. There is the Ford chicane slowing the cars down coming on to the start straight and an Armco barrier in front of the pits. The signalling pits, miles away at Mulsanne, are a throwback to the past. It is all part of Le Mans' way of making life as difficult as they can — you need more people to run the signalling pit for the week and the communication with pits proper is through some pre-World War I telephones that the French PTT rent out at vast cost. Tonight, things have been simply terrible with everyone

"Ideally pit stops should be limited by the speed of fuel supply." The single Alpine-Renault Turbo, the fastest car on the circuit, was soon a regular pits visitor with overheating and engine troubles, culminating in its retirement after 10½ hours

getting crossed lines. Porsche and BMW, I think, now use a direct radio link.

In our teams, signals from the Mulsanne station were kept purposely simple. If a driver is going in for an unscheduled stop and he knows he just points up the road when he passes here.

Midnight: The Press Tribune, *high above the circuit opposite the pits. A clear night, though with a strong breeze. Lights sweep round the circuit while the departure of the turbocharged Porsches is signalled by the cherry red ovens glowing beneath their tails. The De Cadanet Lola has dropped to four laps behind the Mirages, after a long stop to fit some cold air ducting to the tightly enclosed cockpit — Chris Craft has been driving hard, but in considerable discomfort from personal overheating and burnt feet. With eight hours gone, Wyer assesses the situation:*

" That three turbocharged Group 6 cars are in front is much as one might have expected. It is surprising that the Group 5 Porsche is so far back in seventh place, ten laps behind the leaders. That is unexpected — and leaves it a lot of ground to make up. From a tactical point of view, the Mirages are extremely well placed, both on the same lap and within three minutes of one another. Fourth and fifth places at midnight is a good position to be in. It just depends on those three turbocharged cars up in front, whether they keep going. The Alpine is in trouble but the Porsches look strong.

Night time doesn't slow the cars down, really. On a clear night like

"Unexciting as a spectacle but intensely interesting technically." Sensible strategies brought both Group 6 JCB Mirages (née Gulfs) to the finish and kept this second placed car at the same pace as the leader in the closing hours of the race

this cars run at the same speed as in the daylight. The reference points are very clear and lights are very good now; the Mirage has four headlamps, two very long range driving lights and two lights giving a spread to pick up the apex of corners — all quartz halogen of course.

The cars are easier for the timekeepers to pick up at night as well, with reflective number panels and the identification lights — which we put on the tail. It is no good having them on the front for they get confused with the headlamps.

During the night, drivers take two refuelling spells at a time as a matter of course. Some drivers take two stints in a row during daylight but we have always made this entirely a driver's option — he decides when he comes into the pits. At night, the second driver does not need to be ready to go into the car at every pit stop and can get at least an hour's sleep. We have never found driver fatigue a factor in this race. In fact, by the end of the race, the drivers are always much fresher than the crew. We have tried shifts for the mechanics, but if the cars are running they like to stay up the whole time.

Sunday 11 a.m.: Goodyear Rest Centre, *in the paddock. Discussions were delayed while JW awaited the outcome of problems in the Mirage pit. The Alpine had finally retired with a burnt piston at 2.30 a.m. while the Group 5 Porsche 935 ran through*

its series of troubles during the night. At half distance (4 a.m.) the order had been:
1. Porsche 936 (Ickx-Van Lennep), 180 laps; 2. Porsche 936 (Jost-Barth), 178; 3. JCB Mirage (Lafosse-Migualt), 174; 4. De Cadanet Lola (Craft-De Cadanet), 169; 5. JCB Mirage (Bell-Schuppen), 168 laps; 6. Porsche 935 (Stommelen-Schurti), 167 laps.
36 cars were left in the race, 21 of them Porsches though many of the Group 4 and private Group 5 911s were in serious trouble. The Jost-Barth 936 retired at Mulsanne after 16 hours racing, during 15 of which it had held second place. Wyer reflected:

" So far the race has worked out pretty well the way I saw it except that the Ickx-Van Lennep Group 6 car is still going strongly and running very easily, while the works Group 5 Porsche has run into trouble and is falling back.

The Lafosse-Migault Mirage had a long stop earlier due to failure of its high pressure fuel pump. It wouldn't start after a routine stop because there was no fuel pressure. The No. 11 Bell-Schuppan Mirage in fifth place had all sorts of electrical problems during the night, starting when the alternator fell apart. More recently Bell came in and said that the engine had cut out completely. The Mirage has two sorts of low pressure fuel pumps — a Porsche one and a Bendix as a back-up. They switched to the Bendix and the engine cut out again. It took three more stops to discover that both pumps had failed, one of which hadn't been used. This car has also lost its clutch, so it is difficult to see how it can improve on its position.

The French-driven Mirage is going well again but at 10 laps down they are in no position to apply any pressure on the leader. This is the usual pattern with four or five hours to go, where the leader has a comfortable cushion and can afford to adjust his speed to that of the nearest competitor. The leader has the faster car, so both play it out to the finish. It isn't very exciting as a spectacle but it is immensely interesting technically.

Sunday 3.30 p.m. — The pits. *Wyer*

watches anxiously the activity in the JCB Mirage pit, as the Bell-Schuppan car has new rear bodywork fitted. The rear glass fibre moulding was breaking up. Replacement was a wise precaution for, with 10 mins of the race to go, Francois Migault lost the engine cover completely on the other car and had to make a last-minute pit stop for a replacement. The leading Porsche has had its only trouble of the race but remains 10 laps in the lead, while the De Cadanet Lola, still sounding as sweet as when it started despite the great age (8 years) of at least some of its DFV engine, lies a splendid third and has been almost within striking distance of the second place Mirage.

" Porsche had to change an exhaust pipe on the leading car, and they lost seven laps or so. Ickx thought that the turbocharger had gone and radioed the pits tell them so, but it was found to be the exhaust pipe downstream of the turbocharger.

Alain De Cadanet is going magnificently. The car is running fairly slowly now — over 4 mins — so I think they would be very happy to finish third. That will be a great achievement. Alain is an old style Le Mans privateer who has this one race a year. He is a highly professional amateur if you will forgive the apparent contradiction. They have learnt a lot over the years, the car has gone very well and been well controlled and their stops have been good. I think that they can congratulate themselves in every way. It is pleasing to see that because of the long Porsche stop he wins the fourth of the six hour intermediate prizes.

In conclusion:

Before the race started I had the feeling that Group 6 had to go, but now one is bound to say that it would have been a very much less interesting race without the Group 6 cars.

In general, it was a more interesting race than last year and I detect that people have started coming back to Le Mans this year — it was well supported by entrants, the public, and a large section of the Press, despite there being a Grand Prix in Sweden. It's still not what Le Mans was in the mid-1960s. But I think it is beginning to climb back. □

Alpine-Renault staged their first major attack on Le Mans, with three works-entered, and a fourth privately-entered but works-supported, cars; all were the two-litre V6 turbo model A44Zs, running in Group 6. Martini-Porsche countered with two 936 turbos in Group 6, supported by a 935 Group 5 car in addition to the four privately-entered 935s, of the Loos and Kremer teams. Other Group 6 entries included the two Mirages from the 1975 and 1976 races, but now re-vamped with Renault turbo engines. The DFV brigade included two Inalteras, now running in Group 6 a Lola; and a Lola-based but much modified car entered by Alain de Cadenet under his own name.

Among the two-litre cars were three Chevrons, two with the ROC-Chrysler-Simca engines; two Lolas; and three cars with BMW-based engines, from Osella, Cheetah and Sauber. A BMW 320 saloon ran in Group 5. The various GT sports car categories, Group 4 and I.M.S.A., included two BMW 3.0 CSLs, a Ferrari Boxer entered by the N.A.R.T. team - after a year's absence by the Ferrari marque - and sundry Porsches, of the 934 turbo and Carrera models. The total number of Porsches in the race was 27. In the GT prototype class, there was a third Inaltera, two WM-Peugeots, a Lancia Stratos, an Alpine-Renault A.310, and Robin Hamilton's 5.3 litre Aston Martin V8 - the first Aston Martin at Le Mans since 1964.

The main battle was naturally expected to be between Renault and Porsche, with the possibility of a DFV-engined car joining the fray. Renault's number one car, driven by Jean-Pierre Jabouille and Derek Bell which had started from pole position, took the lead initially, with the Martini-Porsche 935 of Schurti/Stommelen acting as pursuit car in accordance with the works team's strategy. But the 935 soon fell back with various mechanical problems and eventually retired after three hours with a blown gasket. However, the 936 allocated to the old masters - the combination of two triple winners, Ickx and Pescarolo - moved into second place following the leading Alpine; the other 936, driven by Barth/Haywood was third, and then came the remaining two works Alpine-Renaults.

The Barth/Haywood Porsche pitted to have its fuel pump changed, and when it rejoined the race had dropped well down the field; that left effectively only one of the Martini team cars in the running, the Ickx/Pescarolo 936. Pescarolo briefly challenged Jabouille for the lead; but apparently, he over-revved the Porsche's engine, and the car was withdrawn after less than three hours. The Alpine-Renault works cars were now in a 1-2-3 lead, followed by a Porsche 935, the two Mirage-Renaults and the first Inaltera. Was it going to be an Alpine walkover? It certainly seemed that the odds against a Porsche victory were staggering.

But then a quick decision was taken in the Martini-Porsche camp. The Barth/Haywood 936 was called in, and Jacky Ickx put behind the wheel. This was in accordance with the regulations that three drivers per car were permitted, and the same driver might drive two cars in the same team. At the time, the 936 was lying fifteenth, but in Ickx's hands it moved inexorably up the scoreboard - according to one report, Ickx flew, and in the course of a magnificent drive not unnaturally put in the fastest lap of the race, at 141 mph. Shortly after midnight, the Porsche 936 went into fourth place, just behind the leading trio of Alpine-Renaults.

During the hours between midnight and dawn, the Porsche team played a waiting game; soon rewarded as within the space of three hours, first the Jaussaud/Tambay Alpine retired with a blown up engine, and then the Depailler/Lafitte car went into the pits for a gearbox repair; when it got back on the track, the Ickx/Barth/Haywood Porsche was in front. Then at 9 am, the leading Jabouille/Bell Alpine expired with piston failure, and the Porsche went into the lead; the Depailler/ Lafitte Alpine might still have challenged, but with four hours to go, the last Alpine-Renault engine went the way of its team-mates engines. From then on there was nothing to touch the Porsche; after what seemed a miracle, the tables were completely turned on the Alpines, and Ickx's fourth Le Mans win seemed a reality.

But the drama of the race was not over; with less than an hour to go, the Porsche came into its pit in a cloud of smoke. A piston had broken; however, as there was no time to undertake an engine rebuild, it was decided to stay in the pit until 3.50 pm, and then Jurgen Barth eased the car round two final laps of the circuit, to take the flag as winner at 4 pm. Ickx, Barth and Haywood were winners, at an average speed of 120.95 mph, and a total distance of 2,902.81 miles.

While the Alpine-Renault team had suffered a total defeat, at least the Mirage-Renault of Schuppan/Jarier finished second; third, and winner of the Group 5 class, was the Ballot-Lena and Gregg Porsche 935. The local hero Jean Rondeau, together with Ragnotti, brought his Inaltera-DFV home in fourth place as first French car; followed by Chris Craft and Alain de Cadenet in the De Cadenet-Lola in fifth place. Sixth was a Chevron-ROC which won the two-litre Group 6 class, and seventh the highest-placed Group 4 car, a Porsche 934. Then came a BMW 3.0 CSL, as winner of the I.M.S.A. category. Among the remaining finishers were the other two Inalteras, the Ferrari Boxer in fifteenth place, and Robin Hamilton's Aston Martin in sixteenth place after a completely reliable run. A total of 21 cars finished, although the two-litre Lola last home did not classify.

1977 was one of the most exciting and dramatic Le Mans races in modern times; the victory of Jacky Ickx was hugely popular, despite the French disappointment with their national cars. At 32, Ickx with four Le Mans wins had reached a level previously only attained by his fellow Belgian Oliver Gendebien who had won Le Mans in 1958, 1960, 1961 and 1962. The major point of interest over the next few years before every Le Mans race would be, will Ickx make it his fifth victory?

LE MANS 24 HOURS
Porsche — by 90 miles

Not even a three-car £400,000 assault by Renault on the coveted endurance crown could prevent Porsche (and Jacky Ickx) from pulling off their 4th victory at Le Mans this year, even though the winning car did the last two laps at walking pace

Report by Mike Doodson

DRIVING an inspired race which recalled some of the excitement of when he won his first Le Mans 24 Hours for Ford in 1969, Belgian long-distance ace Jacky Ickx carried the works Martini-Porsche team to a resounding 4th victory at the Sarthe in this year's race.

It was also Ickx's own personal 4th Le Mans victory, equalling the record of his illustrious fellow countryman Olivier Gendebien, now a silver-haired sexagenarian who applauded Ickx all the way from the pit lane.

However, despite having completed only 13 of the permitted hours behind the wheel, Ickx was happy to watch, tired and apprehensive, as his German team-mate Jurgen Barth completed the final two laps to glory in a car which was very sick. A disintegrating piston kept it in the pits — albeit with a secure lead — for half of the last hour of the race.

"Waiting to see if the car would last for the remaining two laps was no fun at all," said Ickx. Asked if he would be returning to try for a 5th, he would not answer, except to say "I haven't made up my mind" — perhaps forgetting that a shower and a good night's sleep quickly alters

the less pleasant memories of Le Mans.

The winning Porsche was not the one in which Ickx had started the race. That blew up after less than two hours with Henri Pescarolo at the wheel. The Belgian lost no time switching to the sister long-tailed 936 which Barth was sharing on a one-off basis with American Hurley Haywood, taking the place of regular Martini-Porsche teamster Jochen Mass.

Indeed, the race was barely under way when Porsche's chances of another win started to look thin; their 935 coupe, in the hands of Stommelen/Schurti, lost 12 minutes with rocker shaft trouble in the first hour, and soon retired with a blown head gasket.

When Ickx moved into the sole remaining Martini car, this, too, had lost half an hour while a fuel pump was replaced. Faced with a scramble back from 41st place, Ickx responded with all the panache for which he made his name as a teenager.

Throughout Saturday evening Ickx constantly broke the lap record, and didn't let up the pressure even when heavy rain fell at dawn on Sunday, sending many

Left: three hours to go and already the winning Porsche is showing smoky signs of the piston failure which demanded that the last two laps be taken at walking speed. But still the car won from Jarier and Schuppan's Renault turbo-powered Mirage, above. Right: the Porsche trio of Ickx, Barth and Haywood celebrating victory. Below: Saturday night at the drive-in

experienced Le Mans hands — but not Ickx — off the road in the treacherous conditions.

"In the rain, it is quite difficult," he grinned, adding: "It was half dry and half wet, so choosing tyres was the problem."

The Martini car moved into the lead at 9.27 on Sunday morning, and as rivals retired, began to establish a commanding lead. This proved to be of vital importance as the hours ticked by, for with less than 50 minutes to go before the flag came out to end the Grand Prix d'Endurance, Haywood brought the hard-worked Porsche into the Martini pit with a sick-sounding flat-six turbo motor.

Almost 40 minutes had gone before Barth chugged away on five cylinders, with French spectators applauding madly, to complete the last two laps at walking pace. The second-placed car, the Schuppan/Jarier Mirage Renault, had sliced six laps from the Porsche's lead, but the Stuttgart car's winning margin was nevertheless a commanding 11 laps, almost 90 miles.

This last minute drama went some way to reward the weary French spectators whose patience had been worn thin by what can only be described as a disastrous performance from the turbo-Renault cars of which they had expected so much.

Local newspapers went so far as to headline their Saturday night editions with predictions of a "Renault walkover" and reports of "Porsche knocked out". But these began to look a bit sick when the turbo-Renaults hit trouble with piston failure — something which the Regie's technicians blamed on low quality fuel when it eliminated their single car last year — and one by one pulled up with massive engine blow-ups.

First of them to stop was the Tambay/Jaussaud car at 3 am on Sunday, when in 3rd place. Six hours later it was the turn of the Jabouille/Bell car, which had held the lead unchallenged for no fewer than 17 hours. "The car was going perfectly," said Derek: "Jean-Pierre had just taken over from me half and hour before and I had taken a shower and washed my hair.

"Suddenly, going down the Mulsanne Straight at full chat the piston blew. I know how Jean-Pierre must have felt. I was bitterly disappointed, particularly for everyone who had worked so hard; our team manager Delfosse was in tears."

With the leading Alpine out, Ickx's long pursuit suddenly paid off when the Porsche moved into the lead. The sole remaining Alpine, remnant of an assault which has cost Renault an alleged £400,000 in 1977 alone, had been delayed by a half hour stop to replace a gearbox on Sunday morning, and it lasted until mid-day when Jacques Laffite was sidelined by a third engine failure in the car he was sharing with fellow F1 "regular" Patrick Depailler.

By a lucky chance (see separate story) the two Mirages being run with Renault factory support happened to be running rich, which undoubtedly saved them from the Alpine troubles, even if it had handicapped them on fuel consumption and top speed.

Unhappily, one of them (Posey/Leclere) ran out of fuel — or at least showed symptoms of it — on Saturday evening, and after some minor delays in the pits, was unable to match the winning Porsche for speed. Nevertheless 2nd place (Schuppan/Jarier) went a small way to compensating Renault for its monumental commitment.

RESULTS

45th Grand Prix d'Endurance
Le Mans 11/12 June 1977
1 Martini Porsche 936 turbo (J Ickx/Hurley Haywood/Jurgen Barth), 342 laps, 2903 miles (121 mph); 2 J Mirage-Renault turbo (V Schuppan/J-P Jarier), 331 laps; 3 Porsche 935 turbo (Claude Ballot-Lena/P Greig), 315 laps; 4 Inaltera Cosworth (J Rondeau/J Ragnotti), 315 laps; 5 de Cadenet Special Cosworth (Alain de Cadenet/Chris Craft), 315 laps; 6 Roc-Chrysler B 36 (Pignard/Dufrenne/Henry), 303 laps. **Fastest lap:** Jacky Ickx, 3 m 36.8 sec, 140.76 mph (new record). 55 starters, 19 qualifiers.

Class winners

Group 6: Martini Porsche 936 turbo (Ickx/Haywood/Barthu). **Group 5:** Porsche 935 turbo (Ballot-Lena/Greig). **Group 4:** Porsche 934 turbo (Wollek/"Steve"/Gurdjian), 298 laps. **IMSA:** BMW CSL (Xhenceval/Dieudonne/Dini), 291 laps. **GTP:** Inaltera Cosworth (Rondeau/Ragnotti). Index of efficiency: Chevron-Chrysler (Pignard/Dufrenne/Henry) 0·960 on co-efficient.

Renault: not quite a £½m disaster

A SLIP up in the otherwise seemingly perfect three million Franc operation of the Regie Renault's six car assault on the 1977 Le Mans Grand Prix of Endurance may, amazingly, have turned out to be the sole reason for the survival, in 2nd place, of the one Renault car which managed to last out the race.

British engineer John Horsman, in charge of the two Renault-engined Mirages of Harley Cluxton's Arizona-based Grand Touring Cars team, revealed as the race drew to its close — with one of his Mirages surviving what had become a nightmarish disaster for the state-owned Renault company — that his two cars had been "gulping fuel" at a totally unexpected rate.

One of them, co-driven by US veteran Sam Posey, actually ran out of fuel within one lap of a scheduled stop on Saturday evening. Posey worked in vain at the track side to coax the last few pints of petrol into the fuel injection system, but was forced to abandon the struggle. Happily, the other car lasted to the finish despite a fuel consumption at least 20 per cent more than that of the works Alpine entry.

"We think that the only difference between us and the works team was our inability to make the air work properly for us," said Horsman mysteriously. "We had no opportunity in the States for the high speed testing over 160 mph which is so important at Le Mans, and it looks as though the design of our car's bodywork meant that not enough air could get into the turbocharger intercooler, with the result that the engine was running too rich."

In racing, running rich means running cool, and it was burnt pistons which put all three of the works Alpine-Renaults out of the race. It was a problem which had also eliminated the sole Alpine Renault which was run as an experiment in last year's race, but on that occasion Renault technicians blamed slightly poor quality fuel for the piston failure which eliminated them on Sunday morning.

A further indication of "woe", which for Horsman's Anglo-American team turned out to be a happy accident, was an inexplicable loss of top speed for his cars which

in Ford-engined guise not only won the "economy" Le Mans race of 1975, but had also achieved a reputation as particularly "slippery" and efficient in comparison even with the extensively tested works Alpines with their long-tailed bodies.

"We were using bigger Goodyear tyres than the Michelins on the Alpines," said Horman "but that doesn't account for a speed differential of 22mph compared with the 205mph which they were pulling down the Mulsanne Straight." The difference of only six mph can handicap a car down the long Mulsanne Straight by up to 2 sec.

Though obviously happy to have proved the well-placed faith of Renault technicians to get a car to the finish, which was well proven yet again this year, Horsman mourned with the French engineers in their anguish. Glancing towards the fabulously equipped Renault pits, where dedicated mechanics gathered up their tools, Horsman said: "I feel so sorry for them after they worked so hard right from the end of last year. It would be a terrible shame if a big company like Renault were to get disappointed by a setback like this and disappear from racing."

This of course, is unlikely since Renault announced just over one month ago that within the next few weeks it would be entering the world of Formula One Grand Prix racing with a turbocharged car running on Michelin tyres developed in the prototype programme. What it could mean, though, is that Renault are going to find it difficult to run a complicated turbocharged engine in its more highly stressed 1.5-litre GP version.

No jubilation for Jabouille who, with Derek Bell, led the race for 17 hours before his works Renault Alpine blew up

ASIDES . . .

● The 1977 Le Mans 24 Hours was less than one lap old when the first retirement was posted. A works backed but separately run **Alpine turbo Renault** — actually the chassis which had done an estimated 18,645 miles of endurance testing — **caught fire** on the Mulsanne Straight when a fuel pipe burst. Didier Pironi, 25 year old Alpine protege, who

Above: Porsche had their problems — Ickx in the sole remaining Martini car had to scramble up from 41st place after losing 30 minutes — but they weren't as bad as Renault's, whose three works cars had their 500 bhp 2-litre turbo engines expire. This is the Bell/Jabouille car which led for over half the race. Below: Stommelen in the Porsche 935 about to take the Group 5 BMW 320i shortly before retiring with a blown head gasket

was to have shared the car with his F2 Martini Renault team-mate Rene Arnoux, hopped out in time to watch the pompier extinguish the blaze, but that spelled fini for his weekend.

● Dorset Racing Associates, a group of experienced British amateurs who had hoped to qualify last year's 3rd placed **de Cadenet Lola,** had an **unexpected tragedy** on their hands on the evening of the first practice when a French friend of the equipe, who had been acting as their translator, took a shower in the paddock medical centre and passed out from what turned out to be gas fumes. Rushed to hospital, he never recovered consciousness and died the following day. Several other team members had showered just before him and felt unwell.

● Attempts by the **Automobile Club of the West** to fuse the two remaining 24 hour races on the international calendar (Daytona and Le Mans) **seem doomed.** There were no NASCAR stockers at Le Mans this time, no real IMSA GT cars like the fabulous Greenwood Corvette which wowed the crowds last year, and the only US-style feature of the two Group 2 Luigi BMWs in the IMSA class were the screen retaining pins and safety nets in the drivers windows which the club insisted upon in accordance with the American regs.

● Chauvinism strikes: **Derek Bell,** the only non-Frenchman in the works Alpine Renault squad, was posted after practice as having set **fastest time** in the official qualification sessions. When the grid was drawn up, however, Bell's fellow driver Jean Pierre Jabouille appeared as the fastest after all.

● New York Ferrari distributor Luigi Chinetti Jnr has settled the **spectacular quarrel** which he had two years ago with the ACO, and returned to the Sarthe with a race prepared **Ferrari Boxer BB** which raced surprisingly well in the hands of two Frenchmen into 16th place, though no match for the fast BMWs and Porsches in the IMSA class.

● Chill weather with a constant threat of rain which held off until dawn on Sunday, **discouraged the crowds** from Le Mans this year. Officials of the organising club must be worried about what sort of race they will be able to promote in 1978, with **Renault switching to F1,** and Porsche reportedly going to Indianapolis instead. Harley Cluxton will be back though, after two 2nd place finishes in two years. "It's not the race I'm hooked on," he said, "It's the food, which is always great."

● Although **Jacky Ickx was so exhausted** after his fabulous drive that the Porsche doctor forbade him to take the winning car across the line, Jacky seemed more thrilled with his 1977 victory than the ones he scored in '69, '75 and '76. "I like the idea of being 41st and trying to catch up," he said: "not for winning but just so that you can go as hard as possible."

● The excitement got through even to self confessed endurance race-hater **Jochen Mass,** who was in the Le Mans pits as a cameraman with a German film crew. Toting an expensive and heavy piece of equipment, Jochen said: "When the car dropped back to 41st place, I felt like jumping in and driving it myself, because normally here no one ever tells you to **go flat out.**" Jochen may reconsider his personal ban on 24 hour races, which followed the pair of exciting tyre blow outs during the Daytona 24 hours.

de Cadenet foiled

BRITISH hopes of outright victory at Le Mans rested on Alain de Cadenet and Chris Craft in the new sports car developed with *Motor*'s help.

Once again de Cadenet — and particularly Craft, who did most of the driving — put on a performance which anyone who is not used to their uncanny Le Mans durability, would not have expected. Even so, the team had run out of development time. Explained Alain: "Like everyone else we really can't find anywhere to test for this place with its huge great long straight".

Having qualified lower than Alain would have liked, Chris Craft started the race with a slightly increased rev limit (just over 9000rpm, compared with the 10,000 used by the F1 "sprinters"), but early set-backs, like nine minutes lost adjusting the clutch, and 20 minutes tightening exhaust manifold bolts, put them out of touch of the leading Renault cars.

On Sunday morning, when the track was still half wet and half dry, Chris went off the road and damaged the nose frame, brake ducts and bodywork sufficiently to keep the valiant little car out of the race for an hour.

Additional problems with the exhaust ("The vibes are so bad that the whole lots just crystallised", said team manager Keith Greene) dropped the London-based team behind the much more heavily sponsored French Inaltera coupe (like the de Cadenet, powered by a Cosworth DFV) in 4th place.

An equally brave show was put on by the Aston Martin DBS built in Burton-on-Trent by Aston dealer Robin Hamilton. The £35,000 effort, helped out at the last minute by the London-based SAS chemical group, looked ludicrous at the Silverstone 6 Hours, but despite a weight twice that of a Renault Alpine, the smart car ran almost faultlessly. The longest stop was to replace two cracked rear brake discs, which took 15 minutes each.

"I'm absolutely thrilled with it", said Hamilton, who shared the driving with Dave Preece and Aston veteran Mike Salmon, whose last Le Mans appearance, in 1964, ended in a nasty fire.

Less lucky, ironically, were the three Britons who bought ready-made cars. Having found some expensive sponsorship for their rides in a German-prepared Porsche 935, Londoners Guy Edwards and Nick Faure were left without so much as a lap in the race, since their car inexplicably blew up under Porsche expert John Fitzpatrick after less than an hour.

Jacky Ickx became the second man (the other is another Belgian, Olivier Gendebien) to win LeMans four times when his turbocharged Porsche limped across the finish line. After his own car had broken, Ickx took the Hurley Haywood/Barth 936 from 41st to first as the leading squadron of Alpine-Renaults dropped out. Only 45 minutes before the finish, the car holed a piston and sat in the pits while its immense lead dwindled. Mechanics plugged the fuel line to the offending cylinder and the car stuttered two final laps to be classified a finisher. It was also Ickx's third consecutive win.

24 HOURS OF LEMANS FOR THE 45th TIME

Few converts are made in an atmosphere of hasty improvisation.

At the end of the first lap, Jabouille's Alpine-Renault hurtles past the pits, followed by Stommelen's Porsche 935 and Ickx in the 936.

Ickx is not denied

Le Mans hat-trick for Jacky Ickx—Barth/Haywood share winning Martini-Porsche 936—All four Alpine-Renaults retired after Jabouille/Bell led race for 17 hours —Schuppan/Jarier second for Mirage-Renault—All Inalteras finish—Craft/de Cadenet fifth—Report: BOB CONSTANDUROS—Photography: DAVID WINTER.

To win the Le Mans 24 Hours is an achievement in itself, and precious few are the racing drivers who manage to pull it off more than once. Last weekend, Jacky Ickx reaffirmed his status as one of the truly great sports car drivers when he won his fourth Le Mans, and his third in succession. At the end of a gruelling race, Le Mans belonged to him alone last Sunday afternoon as the clock reached four o'clock. Not for the first time in a career of frequent virtuosity, Jacky Ickx was The Man.

After co-driver Henri Pescarolo had blown up Ickx's Martini Porsche 936, the Belgian ace was put into the works team's second-string car driven by Jurgen Barth and Hurley Haywood. During the night, thanks mainly to a magnificent stint by Ickx, the car climbed inexorably up the leader board until, with eleven hours remaining, it had taken over second place behind the Alpine-Renault of Jean-Pierre Jabouille/Derek Bell, which had led the race from the start. At this stage the prospect of Ickx's hat-trick, in fact, seemed remote, for the French car was many miles in the lead. But, at 9.27am on Sunday, France's hope was pushed away, its engine broken. Having been written off as a likely winner, the Porsche survived a dramatic final hour piston failure, and Barth nursed it to the finish to claim a remarkable victory.

Le Mans was an unmitigated disaster for the Alpine-Renault team. They lost one car on the very first lap, and although the surviving three led the race at the ten-hour mark, each dropped out in its turn with engine failure. The second place won by the sole surviving Mirage-Renault, driven by Vern Schuppan/Jean-Pierre Jarier, did nothing to alleviate French sorrow.

More engine failures eliminated all the fancied Porsche 935 Group 5 cars, and third place was taken by the unrated 935 of Claude Ballot-Lena/Peter Gregg. This car withstood a late challenge from the Inaltera of Jean Ragnotti/Jean Rondeau and from the De Cadenet Lola of Chris Craft/Alain de Cadenet, which had been seriously delayed at various times during the race, yet failed by but 90 seconds to repeat the Englishmen's 1976 third place. A 2-litre Chevron was sixth overall ahead of a Group 4 Porsche and one of the "IMSA" BMW CSLs of the Luigi team.

Of the other British entrants, the Robin Hamilton team was the only one to come away from the Sarthe with a real sense of achievement, for the Aston Martin droned on and on and never once looked like failing to finish.

LE MANS 24 HOURS

The unique Le Mans 24 Hours is no longer part of any championship, yet it receives immense publicity throughout the world, and attracts strange entries with sometimes unfamiliar drivers. This year's race was no exception but anyone running through the entries could see that the promise of a real race was greater than in the last few years.

Walking through the paddock during the three days before the race is a strange experience. No matter how many races have taken place in the Group 5 and Group 6 calendar, Le Mans is a whole new event. Cars that used to be blue are now green, they are not necessarily driven by the regular drivers, and they are almost certainly sporting new sponsorship. In quite a few cases, they have not been seen since last year's Le Mans race, and might not be seen again until next year's.

In the paddock, there were fleets of tyre company vans. Dunlop and Goodyear had at least five vehicles each, and Michelin, with their heavy Renault duties, had their own camp. And talking of camps, the Renault effort has to be seen to be believed. Renault made a huge effort this year. They entered three cars with star drivers, all turbocharged two litres with long, long tails for straight-line speed. Massive publicity back-up kept everyone well-informed of every move, and Renault made no secret that they intended to win Le Mans. Down at the bottom end of the paddock, a large area was fenced off and tents erected under which uniformed mechanics tended the cars, while there were rest areas for the drivers, a seperate press office, and even a hole cut in the fence to sell goodies to the public outside the paddock. Matra-Simca came to Le Mans in quite a big way during their years, but not quite like Renault. . . .

Surprisingly, the French cars did not run at one, two and three, but further back in the line-up, at seven, eight and nine. The driver pairings were Jean-Pierre Jabouille/Derek Bell (the only non-Frenchman), Patrick Tambay/Jean-Pierre Jaussaud and GP drivers Patrick Depailler/Jacques Laffite. Their pits,

48

emblazoned with the legend Renault Sport, were a real sight, the tools beautifully mounted under each pit counter so that a mechanic could find what he wanted very quickly. The cars were nearly identical, only the colour coding of the wing mountings and the interior of the overhead airboxes distinguishing the different cars, apart from the race numbers.

Renault had also paid Harley Cluxton from Arizona a bag of gold to use Renault V6 engines in the two Mirages which he ran in 1976 but, unlike last year when he had fine back-up from JCB and Total, he was definitely the poor relation in comparison with the Renault works team. The cars were essentially the same as last year, but in order to accommodate the Renault engine they had been extensively re-worked around the rear end. John Horsman was again running the JCB-sponsored team, with John Wyer in attendance and a reasonable amount of Renault help. The names of nearly ten different sponsors were on the cars, Gitanes, Motorola, Total, GTC.(Cluxton's own company), Elf and Renault being just some of them. With Renault's help more star names were included in the team, the pairings being Vern Schuppan/Jean-Pierre Jarier and Sam Posey/Michel Leclere. Jean-Louis Lafosse was allegedly meant to bring more sponsorship, but did not do so, and Cluxton, Wyer and Elf and Renault lawyers were involved in court cases for two days of the week when he did not get a drive.

Apart from an A310 further down the field, there was just one other Alpine. Just after the Pau F2 race, Martini F2 team mangager Hughes de Chaunac was asked if he would run the *muletta* Alpine-Renault which had done all the testing, for his two F2 men Didier Pironi and René Arnoux. Didier had done Le Mans before in a Porsche, but René could not drive the lone Alpine last year as he was too short. De Chaunac had four days to prepare the car, and was frankly unused to long distance team mangagement, but with Bendix sponsorship he got the car together and was making his customary efficient job of it. Some believed that this car was to be used as the "hare" in the race, to break Renault's adversaries, but de Chaunac naturally wasn't telling.

The adversaries, without doubt, were Porsche. From the Martini works team came two 936s (the model that won last year) and the Silverstone-winning 935-77. One could not forget the Renault presence at the Sarthe, but one could almost miss Porsche in the paddock. Their rapid de-camp after practice was over would have done a retreating army proud, but whatever, they were the very strong opponents. The two 936s were essentially based on last year's winning car but with a twin turbocharged 2.1-litre engine, and a great long tail. Martini-Porsche's line-up was a *coup* in itself, certainly when it came to the number one car: Jacky Ickx and Henri Pescarolo, both three times winners of Le Mans. What more could any team manager wish for. The other car was driven by Jurgen Barth, a factory man, Hurley Haywood, the American Porsche driver, and Eberhard Braun, who is also a factory driver. The 935-77, in its usual pristine condition, was to be driven by Rolf Stommelen and Manfred Schurti.

Porsche's assistance privately was naturally immense, and there were 29 Porsches entered in total. The main support (or opposition, depending on which way you look at it) involved the Georg Loos and Kremer teams. Loos found two drivers for his second Porsche 935 in Hans Heyer and Klaus Ludwig, both well-known for their exploits in long distance saloon races, while his number one pairing was Tim Schenken and Toine Hezemans, both of whom drive for Loos regularly.

Erwin Kremer's team, however, was somewhat different. That king of sponsorship, Guy Edwards, brought along *Penthouse*, Rizla and Denim aftershave money to sponsor the Kremer 935 that was crashed at Mugello, the body of which had been rebuilt to the same specification as their German Group 5 contending car. As well as Edwards, John Fitzpatrick, Kremer's regular long distance man, and Nick Faure, the Porsche specialist who finished sixth at Le Mans two year ago, were due to drive, while Bob Wollek was waiting in the sidelines, although due to drive a Group 4 Porsche with a couple of unknowns.The G4 car also had British sponsorship from Burton's of London.

Not to be discounted was the Inaltera team. Since last year's debut race, they had been to Daytona for the Group 5 event there but this year entered cars in both Group 6 and in the Grand Touring/Prototype class. Team manager Vic Elford had found that cars could be extensively lightened when preparing them for Daytona, and Cosworth had managed to find them some more power from the DFVs, so things looked very hopeful for the wallpaper and paints manufacturing firm. Running at number one was Jean-Pierre Beltoise with American Al Holbert, and at number two were the ladies, Lella Lombardi and Christine Beckers. The heavier (by 110 kilos) GTP

One of the highlights of the race: Ickx's stirring drive in the Barth/Haywood 936 after his own had been retired.

car was driven by Jean Ragnotti and designer Jean Rondeau.

Then, of course, there was the de Cadenet team. Alain's new car is not really a Lola; it does have some of Eric Broadley's ideas, but also some of Len Bailey's and some more of Gordon Murray's, the Brabham designer having of course designed the first car de Cadenet ran. The chassis was built up by John Thompson and then finished off by de Cadenet's chief mechanic, John Anderson. But, "It's been the biggest nightmare to make the car, this year I really wonder why one does it," said de Cadenet. His reasons for saying that were the biggest catalogue of bungling by British racing car component manufacturers of which this reporter has ever heard. Wrong sizes, wrong parts, shoddy material, leaking containers, the team had had them all, and despite a year's preparation half of the mechanics were still making up parts during the first practice. Sponsorship came from Hammonds Sauce and from Tate & Lyle again, hoping for even better things this year after de Cadenet's third place in 1976. Sharing the driving with the patron (who was driving a Le Mans winning Bentley on the road) was Chris Craft, and Gordon Spice, who could be seen on the first day of practice shaking his head and wondering how he would ever get into the car, was named as the reserve. An example of how flat wings were being worn this year was the de Cadenet car, whose wing was virtually flat, an extension of the body, as it were.

The final quick Group 6 car was the T286 Lola of Xavier Lapeyre/Patrick Perrier, who were also quick last year at Le Mans with their DFV engine. This year they had only one motor, so that would have to do practice and race, but they certainly set a reasonable time.

A host of 2-litre sports cars were headed by the well-prepared ROC/Chrysler-engined Chevrons from Annecy, driven by a number of Frenchmen and the lightest cars in the race. The Osella-BMW PA5 was obviously quick in the hands of Alain Cudini, who has great experience, and shared with rally lady Anna Cambiaghi. Meanwhile a short, plumpish man could be seen at sunrise and sunset turning all shades of colours as he blew a bugle and one of the Chandler Ibec International/Team Lloyds mechanics raised or lowered the Union Jack—Ian Bracey being as English as only he can. His Chevron co-drivers, standing in line beside him during this ritual, were Tony Charnell, John Hine and Robin Smith. Dorset Racing brought two cars, one a 2-litre Lola for Ian Harrower, Martin Birrane, Ernst Berg and Richard Down, the other last year's de Cadenet Lola with DFV power,

which Simon Phillips would share with Richard Bond, Tony Birchenough and Brian Joscelyn.

Among the other cars were a Group 5 Porsche for Anny Charlotte Verney, which she shared with G1 Leyland driver René Metge and Danny Snobeck. There was a works tended and rather ugly BMW 320i for Herve Poulain and Marcel Mignot plus the two Luigi BMW 3.0 CSLs, far too "fresh" from the European Touring Car Championship race at Brno, with Tom Walkinshaw and Spartico Dini boosting normal drivers Eddy Joosen/Claude de Wael and Jean Xhenceval/Pierre Dieudonné. Charles Ivey brought along his Modsports Porsche for the IMSA class, sharing with John Cooper, John Rulon-Miller and Peter Lovett, while NART's Luigi Chinetti brought Ferrari back to Le Mans with a Boxer for François Migault and Lucien Guitteny.

Along with the Inaltera and a Lancia Stratos turbo for Marianne Hoepfner and Christine Dacremont in the GTP class was the Robin Hamilton-built, SAS-sponsored Aston Martin V8, which had the dubious honour of being the heaviest car at scrutineering. With Hamilton was former rallycross driver David Preece, and they asked Mike Salmon to return to Le Mans to co-drive too. There were, of course, many others, some 60 cars in all at scrutineering, of whom 55 would start.

PRACTICE

Practice, as usual, was on Wednesday and Thursday evenings, six hours each time, but the weather played its hand and cut the time down to Thursday evening, and that was all. Very uncharacterstic Le Mans weather greeted those turning out to watch on Wednesday, and the drizzle later turned to heavy rain, which dampened everyone's enthusiasm for testing. In fact precious little took place, and most people just looked forward to a better morrow.

Fortunately it was a lot better, sun greeting the spectators who massed around the circuit. Even though there was quite a rush to get out on to track at the start of practice, because it was thought that it might rain shortly after, there was quite a lot of competition at the end. Eventually, 18 cars got under the 4 mins mark, as opposed to 12 last year.

Despite sounding as though they would never make the end of the pit road every time they went out, it was the Renault team who had the academic advantage of being on pole position, Jabouille setting the 3m 31.7s, for Bell only did a few laps. The Depailler/Laffite car was alongside, 1.2secs behind, while the

Henri Pescarolo coasts to a halt in the smoking number one Porsche 936, having over-revved the engine after taking over from Ickx. Below: One of the drives of the race came from Patrick Depailler in the Alpine-Renault. Here he follows the IMSA class-winning BMW of Dieudonné/Xhenceval.

second row was shared by the Ickx/Pescarolo Porsche 936 and the third Alpine of Tambay/Jaussaud, the former giving Renault their only problems by slightly over-blipping the throttle. Renault's fourth car, the Arnoux/Pironi "hack", was on row three, sharing it with the Martini Porsche 935 which was due to run at a lightly reduced turbo boost, 0.2 down on normal at 1.3. All the Martini Porsches were running their race engines in this second practice.

The second 936 provided Porsche with their only problem when Braun put it off the track during the wet session, but it was not badly damaged and it reappeared in pristine condition. Sharing its fourth row was the first of the Loos 935s with the second just behind the Heyer/Ludwig car needing a new engine during the second session after having a practice battle with the works Martini 935. The battle was then taken up by the second car, but the Schenken/Hezeman model was a little slower. The Lapeyre/Perrier Lola had trouble with the alternator which delayed them during the night sessions, but they were on the fifth row of the grid.

On the sixth were the two Mirages with their Renault engines. They really had a problem, firstly with fuel pumps which delayed both cars out on the circuit, and then with a lack of revs. The drivers, however, were finding that their helmets were being sucked upwards, so with a longer airscoop the Mirage team were hoping to pick up the airflow which was apparently creating turbulence around the bulkhead behind the driver. That, they hoped, would find them the 1000 revs they were missing. The quickest Inaltera was in the seventh row, the team's main problem being that the new setting up geometry was maladjusted and actually set the cars up wrongly, so they had to start all over again. Beltoise's car was suffering from overheating, and the other two cars were back on the tenth row. Fourteenth fastest was the *Penthouse* Rizla Porsche 935, but that too was not running smoothly, so the Kremer team fitted another engine and the car was qualified rather slowly at reduced turbo pressure.

One row behind was the De Cadenet Lola, which was still virtually being built as mentioned earlier. However, it ran perfectly cleanly and the team was relatively happy. Two more Porsches filled the next positions before the first 2-litre and the final car under 4mins, this the Osella which Cudini put on the night row. Claude Haldi and Florian Vetsch did well to get their Porsche 934 to 21st position in one practice session, while John Hine qualified the Lloyds Chevron 27th, although not as quick as a Cheetah and two of the ROC Chevrons. However, they had an engine tighten up towards the end of the session.

The poor Dorset Racing Association team really did have a miserable time. Their 2-litre Lola holed an engine, although it finished up 34th fastest, but the new acquistion had an engine change after the wet session which took twice as long as expected as the two DFVs were different, and they only made it out for the final 30mins of practice, when they set the 36th fastest time. But it was the slowest Group 6 time, and the car became a reserve in favour of slower cars further back but in different classes, which seemed strange.

The Luigi team had trouble converting their Group 2 cars to IMSA spec, using funny little bits of metal on the windows, the only modification it seems which might have been overlooked. Sixtieth fastest was the Aston Martin, whose straightline speed seemed lacking; it was easy down on 4m 31.8s, but not outside the 133 per cent qualifying rule. Finally the SAS Aston was allowed to start, because Jean-Louis Chateau had only qualified himself and not his two co-drivers, and was consequently chucked out.

Race day was blustery, not at all like last year when everyone boiled, but there was fair cloud covering through which the sun shone occasionally. The reduced crowd attendance was very disappointing, and it looked as though Le Mans would be quiet in comparison to years past.

RACE

The cars lined up in the usual colourful array under cooler skies than normal—at least the dreadful heat of the previous year would not be a problem. At the end of the rolling start, the French cars chanelled nicely into line through the final curve but the German team was having none of that, and as the course car drew off, Ickx drew up alongside the third Alpine as they went off on the first lap, and Stommelen pulled the 935-77 up past Arnoux.

At Mulsanne, little René pulled his Alpine off the road on fire, not a pleasant situation with a full fuel load. An oil line to the turbo had split, and the whole car was quickly ablaze, but the flames were soon extinguished, although not before enough damage was done to put the young Frenchman out of the race. Meanwhile Jabouille was in the lead followed by the Martini Porsche 935, then Ickx, the two other Alpines, the other 936 and then the two Georg Loos cars. A lot was to happen during this first hour. Rondeau brought the GTP Inaltera into the pits for about 5mins to have the clutch adjusted, the Lloyds Lola had a problem with the oil pressure in its new engine, and the number one Loos Porsche driven by Schenken blew its brand new engine after only four laps.

At the head of the field, Jabouille was pulling away from Stommelen, and Ickx was next before the two further Alpines, then Schuppan in the Mirage tied up with the French 3-litre Lola of Lapeyre and the surviving Loos 935 before the Inaltera of Beltoise.

But at eight laps, Stommelen was in the pits: the problem, which delayed the car for some time, was a loose rocker shaft. The 935-77 once it went out again, was not very quick because it had lost some oil, and the regulations stated that this could not be replaced until 16 laps had been completed, so Rolf just had to run slowly.

On the ninth lap, both the French Lola-DFV and the second G6 Inaltera pitted. The former needed a new front wheel after losing a weight, and the latter had an early stop for fuel. By lap ten, there were only 12 cars on the same lap, and less than an hour gone. By the 11th lap, the Martini 935 was back in the race having lost three laps, but at least the works 936s were splitting the Alpines.

With just 12 laps completed, the Tate & Lyle Lola came in with a dragging clutch, and during the ensuing stops to re-adjust it the team lost a crucial 15mins. By lap 13 both the GTP Inaltera and the Schuppan/Jarier Mirage were in the pits for refuelling, leaving but eight cars on the same lap. The first of these to be lapped was the Kremer Porsche driven by Fitzpatrick, which shortly after came into the pits sounding dreadful. A burnt cylinder liner was diagnosed, and before the end of the first hour the car was pushed away, Edwards and Faure having not raced it.

In the second hour it was the turn of the second Martini Porsche to hit trouble. At 5.15 it pitted with a broken injection pump, and it took 24mins to change it. Thus at two hours the order was Jabouille, Ickx and the Depailler/Laffite Alpine all on the same lap, before the third Alpine a lap down, then the second Loos Porsche another lap down in company with both Mirages and Beltoise's Inaltera. The 2-litre class had lots of troubles, and for their part the Lloyd's team now had an overheating problem. Dorset Racing had had a couple of punctures, and then the gear linkage broke, but the Osella was running well in 12th position.

The field had been decimated by early retirements, and the competition seemed to have left the race even at this early stage. However, there was a Porsche among the Renaults, and that at least was good.

By the third hour, the leading Porsche had slightly slowed. Apart from dropping behind the Jabouille Alpine, the Depailler/Laffite car was catching it easily, and passed it going into that hour. So at 7 o'clock it was the three Renaults in front, then the Porsche, two Mirages, the Loos Porsche 935 and Beltoise's Inaltera in eighth place. Even so JPB was three laps behind already.

The Britons had had their fair share of dramas. After the oil pressure worry, the Lloyds Chevron was overheating, and ultimately they replaced the head gasket in the pits, while Dorset Racing too had an overheating problem. One noticeable engine note

circulating was that of the Aston Martin, some way back but healthy after having a spoiler modification removed in the early laps. The De Cadenet was back in 22nd position, and had an overheating problem due to being run too lean; they lost nine more minutes getting the mixture right.

Before the hour was out, Pescarolo pulled off the faster Martini Porsche 936 with a blown engine, and the rev counter revealed why.

At eight, then, with darkness and the cold drawing in, it was the three Elf Alpine-Renaults out in the lead followed by the remaining Porsche 935 of Georg Loos, which had been handed over to Hezemans and Schenken, and then the two Mirages which had benefited from their modifications after practice, although not by much. The second of them was four laps down on the leader, which seemed a long way.

With the number one Porsche out, there was nothing that could actually challenge the Renaults for the lead. What a situation after four hours! However, the Martini 936 had climbed back up to tenth place before a cylinder head gasket blew—picking up 14 places in an hour. What could it do in Jacky Ickx's hands?

It soon became clear. Ickx drove the car for the next three hours, and flew. How long could the 936 take that sort of treatment? It was a source of real excitement, for now there really was a hare which was racing through the field. At one time, despite being 15 laps down, Ickx was pulling back 10secs on the leaders per lap. They seemed so safe, with a huge lead, but then strange things happen at Le Mans. . . .

By 9 o'clock in the evening, with night setting in and the funfairs and bars in full swing, the Martini Porsche was up to ninth, just ahead of the De Cadenet. Things had been made easier for the German team, for Sam Posey had inexplicably run out of fuel out on the circuit, when there should have been ample in the tanks, and he just could not get the car going again, so had retired from sixth position. The sister car was third, for the Jaussaud/Tambay Alpine had had its inlet manifold work loose, and it had to be screwed up, they had dropped to sixth place.

Shortly before nine came the news that all the Lloyds efforts had come to naught, for with Ian Bracey driving the car blew up out on the circuit, and their race was over. The Dorset Racing Lola, however, was going well after its early bothers. The British-entered Porsche had had its bothers too, with a shortening fuel pump which just allowed John Cooper to stagger around to the pits, but that was fixed and the car went on its way.

The Mirage had had a couple of boring complaints. An alternator bracket broke, and they thought it was the alternator itself, which was changed. Then the brake pads were renewed and the piston slipped out of the caliper, so that lost a little more time.

But the talking point of the moment in the late evening hours was Ickx. At 10 o'clock he had taken the 936 up to sixth place, broken the lap record by six whole seconds, and was really showing his class. The task was made easier when the Inaltera of Beltoise, the only one that had run trouble-free, pitted, and on restarting caught fire. The car needed a considerable rebuild before it could go out again. A short circuit was to blame for the fire.

Despite their earlier bothers, by total darkness, 11 o'clock, the Alpine-Renaults were running one-two-three, albeit several laps apart, with the Tambay/Jaussaud car five laps down on the leader. Such had been the casualties of the race that there was absolutely no danger to the leaders. Jabouille and Bell were thoroughly enjoying the race and were completely trouble-free. The same could be said for the fourth-placed Loos Porsche, while the Mirage was healthy again. De Cadenet's Lola was in seventh place before more Porsches and the Lombardi/Beckers Inaltera, and the gap from first to tenth was 13 laps.

Both the 320i of Poulain/Mignot and the Xhenceval/Dieudonné/Dini CSL were still in the running for BMW, although the latter had gearbox trouble. However, its sister car had stopped out on the circuit with a holed piston. The Aston Martin was still running but there was a worry about cracking discs; if these had to be changed, it would mean a fairly lengthy stop.

All eyes (or those that were still open) were on the progress of the flying Martini Porsche. It was a bit of a face-saver for Martini—even though Count Rossi had gone home—and in the night hours it was interesting to see the car creeping up the leaderboard. At 1am it went into the same lap as the fourth-placed Alpine of Tambay/Jaussaud. Then the latter car disappeared altogether before 2am with a blown motor, loss of oil pressure. "What I'm frightened about is that all the cars are the same", said Gerard Larrousse, team manager of the Alpine-Renaults.

At 3am, the Martini Porsche was in third place. It had been as low as 41st!

At 4 o'clock there were four hard laps to catch up on the second-placed Alpine of Laffite and Depailler. It would be a while before we saw any more place-changing.

At the 12-hour mark, the second-place Alpine had four laps over the Porsche still. In turn, the 936 had four laps over the G5 Loos Porsche, which had four laps over the Mirage. De Cadenet was just behind, but didn't look like moving up a place. Behind the Porsche 935 of Ballot-Lena/Gregg, running smoothly throughout, was the Inaltera of Rondeau/Ragnotti, which had quietly chiselled its way up after earlier problems. In eighth position, they were 16 laps behind the leader.

At 5 o'clock, the Martini-Porsche moved up another place, this time at the expense of the Laffite/Depailler Alpine, which had to change fifth gear in the pits. It took over half an hour. Still, the Porsche was six laps behind the leader. The Loos Porsche was still going well in the hands of number one strings Schenken and Hezemans, with Hans Heyer co-driving, and behind them were the Mirage (another four laps adrift) and the De Cadenet Lola, another two laps away. Among the night retirements were de Wael/Joosen/T. Walkinshaw, who had a holed piston in their Luigi BMW, but the other car was up to 13th and leading the IMSA class.

Into the early morning, there came rain, at times quite heavy. Jabouille worried the Alpine team by spinning three times out of the final bend in sight of his pit, but he didn't make any contact. The day had dawned overcast and really rather unpleasant, but

Alain de Cadenet and Chris Craft once again finished in the money. This year the de Cadenet Lola came home fifth, only 90 seconds away from third place, where they finished last year. Alain is driving here.

still the cars went charging around. At 6am there were 33 cars still in the race. With few cars on the circuit, it was sometimes possible to hear the Aston going down the Mulsanne Straight from the pits, such was its unique V8 noise. However, the quality was lacking a little throughout now: the 10th placed car at 6am was 41 laps behind the leader!

The rain meant stops throughout for wet tyres, but even so, poor Craft found some water with which his Goodyears couldn't cope, and went off quite quickly on the new part of the circuit. The whole of the nose section was damaged and it took just over an hour to get it all repaired, which dropped them back to ninth from their sixth place. Throughout the night, Dorset Racing had all sorts of bothers with the gearbox, but the car was plodding on gamely back in 29th position, which at 7am was last. All three Inalteras were running, the most promising being that of Jean Ragnotti and Rondeau, who after a clutch adjustment early on were running like a train in eighth position.

Little took place between eight and nine in the morning. The leading Alpine of Jabouille/Bell was keeping station with the remaining Martini Porsche, although the Depailler/Laffite machine was just a couple of laps further back. In fact, that was the way they looked as though they would finish, but it was not to be.

Going down Mulsanne the leading Alpine (driven by Jabouille at the time) suddenly erupted in smoke, and staggered back to the pits. After a quick look, the team sent it out with five cylinders operating, for the sixth was holed. But it was obvious that, with falling oil pressure, there was little to be done. The car was sadly pushed away having completed almost 7½ hours in the lead, a real credit to drivers Jabouille and Bell. It was a very sad moment for Renault, who had tried so hard to win and then seen their hopes gradually disappear. At 9.27, the Porsche went into the lead, and the faces in and around the Renault pits were very, very long. . . .

In an effort to try to brighten the scene, the sky cleared and out came the sun. The spectators stirred in their damp sleeping bags and began to drift back to the circuit, to be greeted with the sight of the white Martini Porsche leading with Haywood and Barth doing most of the driving, while Ickx rested. This car had a two-lap lead over the Alpine-Renault of Laffite/Depailler. Would Renault push the second car in order to challenge the Martini Porsche? The answer would be yes, but we would probably have to wait a while.

Still running in what was to become third position was the Georg Loos Porsche 935, which had been going really well and without problems. In fact a visit to the pit revealed just lots of lovely ladies, no drivers, mechanics or team managers. They had every reason to be pleased, but not complacent, and they were soon put on their mettle. Just before 11am, with five hours to go, the car smoked dreadfully and came into the pits. The turbocharger was changed in just 12m, but when the car went out it smoked badly once again, and was soon back. Another lap failed to change matters, and it came back into the pits; oil was getting into a cylinder, so that was immobilised.

Meanwhile, there had been an interesting scene in the Maritni Porsche pits when Haywood tried to take over from Barth and got the rough treatment to hang on for a while. Shades of Pierre Levegh. The gaps were so large between one car and another that even a 30m pitstop made little difference. When the Loos Porsche finally got going again after half an hour's delay, it had dropped just one place to the sedate but reliable Mirage-Renault. The two Jeans in their Inaltera had really gone well and were in fifth, while sixth, after a half-hour stop to change the turbo-charger earlier in the morning were Ballot-Lena/Gregg in their Porsche 935, 31 laps behind the leader. The De Cadenet car came next three laps down, while the first 2-litre car, a Chevron B36, was eighth. Luigi's remaining BMW, which had its gearbox changed in 21mins during the night was tenth, just in front of the 320i which was still reliable. Following the two further Inalteras (which had been delayed) and countless Porsches were the Aston Martin, still booming around, and the Ferrari Boxer, which had not had a happy run at all and would not start after its pitstops. Finally, 24th was the Dorset Racing Lola, pitting less frequently and eight laps down on the car in front.

Before midday came the news that the Loos Porsche had finally succumbed out on the circuit with a broken injection pump, and as the final four hours started the news came of the retirement of the final Alpine-Renault of Laffite and Depailler, a final blow of immense proportions for Renault. Its reason for retiring so close to the end was another holed piston, which befell Depailler. The V6 engine failures must have led the team to think seriously about their petrol, which differed on the Mirages.

The Martini Porsche now led the Mirage-Renault

Above: Co-driving with Jabouille, Derek Bell kept the Alpine-Renault in the lead for many hours, but unfortunately their luck was out. Below: Jean-Pierre Beltoise in the Inaltera which he shared with Al Holbert; the team achieved a 100 per cent finish. Bottom: Vern Schuppan has come close to victory at Le Mans more than once. This year, co-driving with Jarier, he finished second with the Mirage-Renault.

by a whole 17 laps at 1pm, with the Alpine still classified third, the Inaltera fourth (16 laps behind the second-placed car) and the Porsche of Ballot-Lena/Gregg fifth, in effect in fourth position. Just behind came the De Cadenet car, sounding fairly horrible as the exhaust had broken in a number of places and was wired together, but once again, Alain and Chris looked to be heading for another finish. Next was the Chevron of Pignard/Dufrene/Henry, which was a good effort for a 2-litre, even though they were 40 laps down. Right at the back still was the Dorset Racing Lola, which had had untold troubles with everything from gearbox to engine to suspension.

The final two hours were run in the hottest weather of the weekend. There were 23 runners still, until Anny Charlotte Verney parked her troublesome Porsche out on the circuit. It certainly wasn't going to be a close finish, but the race had been fascinating; retirements and heartbreaks had been considerable.

The final hour, in fact, unfolded in a most curious way. There seemed nothing to stop the Martini Porsche, and everyone (with the notable exception of

Chris Craft) was really driving for that chequered flag which would fall at 4 o'clock. But just as the thin blue line of gendarmes was taking up position opposite the pits to "control" the crowd after the race, a puff of smoke came from the leading car, and then huge clouds of white smoke. The 936 headed dramatically for the pits, where the mechanics raised the rear and started work. It looked like a turbo problem, but it was a holed piston. The Porsche had a lead over the Mirage of 19 laps, and the team could afford to wait until right at the end before going out to do two slow laps, and still finish first. Hurley Haywood got out of the car, the turbo boost was turned down and Jurgen Barth prepared himself for that all-important final stint.

As the 21 remaining cars went round, most of them conserving themselves and assuring a finish, the Porsche was prepared. It sat in the pits with all eyes directed on it, for the suspense was terrific: was it capable of getting round?

The drama in the Porsche pit directed attention away from the progress of the Tate & Lyle Lola, for Chris Craft now had the Inaltera firmly in his sights and was chasing that car for fourth place as hard as he could go. In fact, in the dying minutes of the race the Inaltera got onto the same lap as the third-placed Porsche 935, and Craft did the same.

Among those still on the circuit was the Aston

Martin, which had surprised many of the pundits, not because of its speed but because of its stamina. The loving care the mechanics had spent on it brought it home in the hands of Robin Hamilton, Dave Preece and Mike Salmon. The Berlinetta Boxer of NART had been having quite a dice with the Aston throughout the 24 hours, but now had drawn away. Last, but not least, was the Dorset Racing Lola, still somehow getting round despite its many problems.

So it was all down to the finish, after all. At 3.50 Jurgen Barth was strapped in, and the crowd was cleared from around the Porsche. It started cleanly, with no smoke to speak of, and gently motored down the pit lane, the smoke increasing as Barth accelerated around the first curve. It was going to be a slow couple of laps, applauded all the way by the colourful crowd. In fact, the car came round with two minutes to go to four o'clock, bang on schedule, and completed another lap to become the winner of the 45th Vingt Quatres Heures du Mans.

Schuppan in the Mirage finished the event just astern of the winning car, still 11 laps down, but third place was unexpectedly close. Craft's mighty effort to catch the GTP Inaltera failed by a mere 41s, and in fact the Englishmen finished less than 90s behind the third-placed car. It had been a problematical Le Mans for the De Cadenet team, but once again they had put in an impressive performance.

45eme Grand Prix d'Endurance
24 Heures du Mans

June 11-12, 1977: 24 hours over 8.475-mile circuit. **No of starters:** 55. **No of finishers:** 21. **Winners:** Jacky Ickx/Jurgen Barth/Hurley Haywood (2.1 Porsche 936 turbo), 342 laps, 2898. **Average speed:** 121.04mph. **Fastest lap:** Ickx, 3m 36.8s, 140.72mph. **Previous year's winners:** Jacky Ickx/Gijs van Lennep (2.1 Porsche 936 turbo), 349 laps, 2963.89 miles. **Existing lap record:** Francois Cevert (3.0 Matra-Simca MS670B), 3m 39.6s, 138.94mph (1973). **Qualifying record:** Arturo Merzario (3.0 Alfa Romeo 33TT12), 3m 31.0s, 144.61mph (1973).

	1	2	3	4	5	6	7	8	9	10	11	12	13	14	15	16	17	18	19	20	21	22	23	24
1	9 15 134.9	9 31 133.03	9 46 132.67	9 62 132.00	9 78 132.26	9 93 131.73	9 108 131.34	9 123 131.20	9 139 131.50	9 154 131.27	9 170 131.17	9 185 130.89	9 199 130.18	9 213 129.53	9 227 128.27	9 240 127.67	9 255 127.29	9 262 123.71	4 278 124.19	4 294 124.66	4 308 124.55	4 323 124.48	4 337 124.40	4 342 121.04
2	3 15	3 31	8 46	8 61	8 77	8 92	8 107	8 122	8 137	8 153	8 168	4 183	4 193	4 207	4 220	4 233	4 247	4 261	8 276	8 289	8 291	10 305	10 318	10 331
3	4 15	8 31	7 45	7 61	10 74	39 88	7 103	7 118	7 133	4 143	4 163	8 179	4 191	4 204	8 216	8 230	9 245	39 257	10 267	8 278	40 289	40 288	40 302	40 315
4	8 15	7 30	3 44	39 59	39 73	7 88	39 102	39 117	4 132	4 148	39 160	39 175	39 188	39 202	39 214	39 227	39 240	39 255	10 264	39 269	88 275	88 287	88 301	88 315
5	7 15	11 29	10 44	10 59	1 73	10 85	4 101	4 116	39 131	39 145	7 158	10 171	10 184	10 198	10 211	10 222	10 235	10 249	88 248	88 274	40 285	5 300	5 315	5 315
6	1 14	39 29	11 44	11 58	7 73	4 84	10 100	10 114	10 129	10 142	10 156	5 170	40 182	88 195	88 200	88 209	88 221	40 235	40 247	40 260	5 271	26 280	26 293	26 303
7	11 14	10 29	39 44	1 58	40 70	40 84	5 99	40 112	40 126	5 140	5 153	40 167	40 178	40 188	5 199	40 206	40 218	40 232	5 244	5 257	39 269	58 273	58 286	58 298
8	39 14	1 29	1 43	40 56	60 69	5 83	40 98	60 110	5 125	40 140	40 153	88 159	88 172	88 185	88 197	26 205	26 217	26 231	26 242	26 255	26 268	71 267	71 279	71 291
9	10 14	2 28	40 42	88 55	5 69	60 82	60 97	5 110	60 122	88 135	88 146	7 158	26 171	26 183	26 194	5 203	5 215	58 230	58 234	58 247	50 260	50 264	50 275	50 287
10	14 14	40 28	41 42	60 55	5 69	2 82	2 95	2 109	88 122	59 133	59 146	26 158	21 161	25 172	58 183	58 196	58 208	58 221	71 229	71 242	71 255	61 258	61 270	61 281

FASTEST 30 QUALIFIERS

9	Jean-Pierre Jabouille/Derek Bell	2.0 Alpine-Renault A442 turbo	3m 31.7s
8	Patrick Depailler/Jacques Laffite	2.0 Alpine-Renault A442 turbo	3m 32.9s
3	Jacky Ickx/Henri Pescarolo	2.1 Porsche 936 turbo	3m 33.0s
7	Patrick Tambay/Jean-Pierre Jaussaud	2.0 Alpine-Renault A442 turbo	3m 34.8s
6	Rene Arnoux/Didier Pironi	2.0 Alpine-Renault A446 turbo	3m 38.6s
41	Manfred Schurti/Rolf Stommelen	2.8 Porsche 935-77 turbo	3m 39.3s
4	Hurley Haywood/Jurgen Barth	2.1 Porsche 936 turbo	3m 40.0s
39	Hans Heyer/Klaus Ludwig/Toine Hezemans	2.8 Porsche 935 turbo	3m 40.3s
38	Tim Schenken/Toine Hezemans	2.8 Porsche 935 turbo	3m 43.8s
14	Xavier Lapeyre/Patrick Perrier	3.0 Lola-DFV T285	3m 45.2s
10	Vern Schuppan/Jean-Pierre Jarier	2.0 Mirage-Renault turbo	3m 47.0s
1	Jean-Pierre Beltoise/Sam Posey	2.0 Mirage-Renault turbo	3m 47.4s
42	John Fitzpatrick/Guy Edwards/Nick Faure	2.8 Porsche 935/2 turbo	3m 47.5s
5	Alain de Cadenet/Chris Craft	3.0 De Cadenet Lola-DFV	3m 48.3s
40	Claude Ballot-Lena/Peter Gregg	2.8 Porsche 935 turbo	3m 49.2s
58	Bob Wollek/"Steve"/Philippe Gurdjian	3.0 Porsche 934 turbo	3m 56.4s
29	Alain Cudini/Anna Cambiaghi	2.0 Osella-BMW PA5	3m 59.6s
2	Christine Beckers/Lella Lombardi	3.0 Inaltera-DFV	4m 0.5s
88	Jean Ragnotti/Jean Rondeau	3.0 Inaltera-DFV	4m 0.7s
60	Claude Haldi/Florian Vetsch	3.0 Porsche 934 turbo	4m 1.0s
26	Michel Pignard/Jacques Henry	2.0 Chevron-ROC/Chrysler B36	4m 3.4s
59	François Servanin/Laurent Ferrier	3.0 Porsche 934 turbo	4m 5.4s
85	Marc Sourd/Xavier Mathiot	2.7 WMP 77 turbo	4m 6.1s
25	Andre Chavalley/Wink Bancroft/François Trisconi	2.0 Cheetah-BMW G501	4m 8.3s
25	Michel Dubois/Alain Flotard	2.0 Chevron-ROC/Chrysler B36	4m 9.7s
22	John Hine/Tony Charnell/Ian Bracey/Robin Smith	3.0 Chevron-Richardson FVD B31	4m 9.8s
30	Christian Blanc/Georges Morand/Frederic Alliott	3.0 Lola-T296	4m 10.4s
56	Cyril Grandet/Jean-Louis Bousquet/P. Dagoreau	3.0 Porsche 934 turbo	4m 12.3s
21	Eugen Strähl/Peter Bernhard	3.0 Sauber-BMW C5	4m 13.2s
71	Jean Xhenceval/Pierre Dieudonné	3.2 BMW 3.0 CSL	Qual 41st
61	Christian Gouttepifre/Philippe Malbran	3.0 Porsche Carrera	Qual 45th
50	Hervé Poulain/Michel Mignot	2.0 BMW 320i	Qual 51st

FINISHERS

1	Jacky Ickx/Jurgen Barth/Hurley Haywood	2.1 Porsche 936 turbo	2898.62 miles
2	Vern Schuppan/Jean-Pierre Jarier	2.0 Mirage-Renault turbo	2805.39 miles
3	Claude Ballot-Lena/Peter Gregg	2.8 Porsche 935 turbo	2669.78 miles
4	Jean Ragnotti/Jean Rondeau	3.0 Inaltera-DFV	2669.78 miles
5	Chris Craft/Alain de Cadenet	3.0 De Cadenet Lola-DFV	2669.78 miles
6	Michel Pignard/Jacques Henry	2.0 Chevron-ROC/Chrysler B36	2568.07 miles
7	Bob Wollek/"Steve"/Philippe Gurdjian	3.0 Porsche 934 turbo	2525.70 miles
8	Jean Xhenceval/Pierre Dieudonné	3.2 BMW 3.0 CSL	2468.37 miles
9	Herve Poulain/Michel Mignot	2.0 BMW 320i	2432.46 miles
10	François Gouttepifre/Philippe Malbran	3.0 Porsche Carrera	2381.61 miles
11	Christine Beckers/Lella Lombardi	3.0 Inaltera-DFV	2364.66 miles
12	Jean-Pierre Delaunay/Jean Guerin	3.0 Porsche Carrera	2330.76 miles
13	Jean-Pierre Beltoise/Al Holbert	3.0 Inaltera-DFV	2330.76 miles
14	Jean-Louis Ravenel/Jacky Ravenel	3.0 Porsche Carrera	2330.76 miles
15	Xavier Mathiot/Marcel Mamers	2.7 WMP76	2322.28 miles
16	François Migault/Lucien Guitteny	4.4 Ferrari 365 GT4 BB	2271.43 miles
17	Robin Hamilton/Dave Preece/Mike Salmon	5.3 Aston Martin V8	2203.63 miles
18	Anny-Charlotte Verney/Dany Snobeck	3.0 Porsche Carrera	2153.77 miles
19	Jean-Louis Bousquet/Philippe Dagoreau	3.0 Porsche 934 turbo	2144.30 miles
20	John Hotchkiss/Robert Kirby	3.0 Porsche Carrera	2084.97 miles
NC	Ian Harrower/Martin Birrane/Ernst Berg	2.0 Lola-Cosworth T294S	1796.80 miles

CLASS WINNERS

Group 6 over 2000cc	Ickx/Barth/Haywood	Porsche 936
Group 6 up to 2000cc	Pignard/Henry	Chevron B36
Group 5	Ballot-Lena/Gregg	Porsche 935
Group 4	Wollek/"Steve"/Gurdjian	Porsche 934
GT Prototypes	Ragnotti/Rondeau	Inaltera
IMSA	Dieudonné/Xhenceval	BMW 3.0 CSL

Les Vingt-Quatre Heures Du Mans

Le Mans, June 11th/12th

DRAMATIC ENDINGS are nothing new in motor racing, even if they are less frequently encountered in long, drawn out endurance races than in the more hectic excitement of Formula One and Formula Two events. But the finish to the 45th edition of the 24 Hours of Le Mans that took place on June 12th was exceptional by any standards, with the winning Porsche 936 suffering a virtual engine failure 45 minutes from the end. After half an hour's stay in the pits, during which time its turbocharger was switched off to minimise the risk of further damage, the Group 6 Porsche staggered round two final laps on five cylinders to take the chequered flag – not merely as a finisher but as the comfortable though crippled victor of a race marked by wholesale mechanical carnage amongst the faster cars.

For the three drivers of the victorious, Martini sponsored Porsche it was an historic and memorable occasion. Having taken over the car late on Saturday night and then smashed the lap record in his bid to regain lost time, the Belgian Jacky Ickx took his third consecutive win in the 24 Hours, and his fourth ever, a feat only previously achieved by fellow Belgian Olivier Gendebien. As for Ickx's two co-drivers, the result gave Jurgen Barth the first major victory of his racing career, while for the American Hurley Haywood, Le Mans was his first ever race in Europe.

As last year the organisers of this classic test of speed and endurance, the Automobile Club de L'Ouest, cocked a proverbial raised finger or two at the CSI by ignoring their loss of championship status and running their famous race for a mixture of production-based machinery and out-and-out two-seater racing cars, colloquially known as sports cars, though more from custom then logic. The result was that the ACO was rewarded with the most open field of cars seen at the Sarthe for several years, indeed the most competitive entry seen for any long distance race this season or last.

The essence of the race was a massive confrontation between Renault and Porsche. Ever since their calamitous failure to win a single round of last year's World Sports Car Championship, Renault had concentrated their entire Group 6 programme on this one race. Throughout the winter and spring their cars underwent long endurance tests at Paul Ricard, and when the team turned up at Le Mans it presented not just three, as expected, but four of the long-tailed Alpine A442 sports cars. Resplendent in Regie Renault's vivid sunshine yellow livery, and adorned with advertising for Elf, three of these cars were brand new, full works entries. For drivers, they had Derek Bell and Jean-Pierre Jabouille in one car, French Formula One stars Patrick Depailler and Jacques Laffite in another, and Patrick Tambay and Jean-Pierre Jaussaud in the third. The fourth car, although technically a private entry and painted in the blue of Gitanes, was in fact

the "mule" used for the bulk of the pre-race proving programme. Its drivers were two men with growing reputations in Formula Two, Didier Pironi and Rene Arnoux. However, beneath the skin all four Renault Alpine A442s were virtually identical, being powered by the turbocharged, two-litre, 520 b.h.p. V6 Renault Gordini engine that is now in its third year of competition.

Against this French onslaught, Porsche ranged a team of three factory entered cars, all turbocharged and all supported by Martini. The two Group Six sports-cars, the 540 b.h.p. 936 models destined for Jacky Ickx/Henri Pescarolo and Jurgen Barth/Hurley Haywood, were in fact the same chassis as ran at Le Mans last year, albeit with extensive modifications to their bodywork and their 2142 c.c. flat-six engines. The third works Porsche was a 935/77, the Group Five "Silhouette" car that usually contests the World Championship for Makes. Rolf Stommelen and Manfred Schurti were to be the drivers of this car, which although heavy could reach speeds as high as 220 m.p.h. thanks to its twin turbocharged 2.85 litre motor, which produces up to 650 b.h.p. on full boost

Yet the race did not only lie between Renault and Porsche. After finishing second in each of the two previous years, the two Mirages entered by American enthusiast Harley Cluxton could not be ignored, despite their relative lack of straight line speed, especially as their previous Cosworth DFV engines had been replaced this year by more powerful turbocharged Renault units. Vern Schuppan was to share one car with Jean-Pierre Jarier, while Sam Posey and Michel Leclere had the other. Nor could one altogether ignore the DFV-powered Inaltera coupes built in the town of Le Mans itself, for which Jean-Pierre Beltoise and Al Holbert, Lella Lombardi and Christine Beckers, and Jean Rondeau/Jean Ragnotti were the three sets of drivers.

From a British point of view, our hopes rested on the very special 3-litre Lola-DFV that Alain de Cadenet had had built for himself and Chris Craft. In addition though, the very fast Kremer prepared Porsche 935 had an all British crew, with John Fitzpatrick, Guy Edwards and Nick Faure to share the cockpit duties, while Tim Schenken was destined to drive both of Georg Loos' rapid Gelo Porsche 935s at different stages of the race in conjunction with Toine Hezemans and Hans Heyer.

The first session of practice, on Wednesday evening, was blighted by incessant rain, with the consequence that times set then were of little true significance, though Manfred Schurti raised a few eyebrows by taking the works Porsche 935 round faster than any of the supposedly quicker Group Six "sports cars". In the second six hour session of practice, on Thursday evening, the Renault Alpine team moved swiftly into its stride, with Jabouille gaining pole in 3 min. 31.7 sec.

Ickx takes over the winning Porsche from Barth, above. Below, winners Ickx, Barth, Haywood.

and Depailler claiming the other front row grid position with a lap 0.8 sec. slower. Ickx was a tenth of a second slower again to keep the best of the 936s on the inside of the second row, but then came the two other Alpine A442s and Stommelen's Porsche 935/77 before one got to the second Porsche 936 on the grid.

When the race began at its traditional hour of four o'clock on Saturday, the two Alpines of Jabouille and Laffite took immediate command at the head of the swarming pack of cars, but before half a lap had been completed the hard trying Stommelen had got the works 935/77 up to third place. By the end of the first lap he was second, chasing Jabouille for all he was worth. For half an hour the pursuit continued, though Jabouille slowly prised open a few seconds' advantage, but after eight laps the second placed Porsche was in the pits, for a rocker shaft was loose and was causing a persistent loss of oil. The Porsche lost over three laps before it could rejoin, and although it then began to make up many of the lost places it eventually retired three hours later when a head gasket blew. Already Tim Schenken's Gelo Porsche had retired in a spectacular engine failure, leaving the Australian to share the team's other Porsche with Hezemans and Heyer for the rest of the race. The fourth Alpine-Renault, the one that started with Pironi at the wheel, was also *hors de combat*, having caught fire half way round the opening lap when an oil pipe feeding the turbocharger fractured.

With Stommelen's Porsche effectively out of contention after little more than half an hour, Jabouille's Alpine enjoyed a 25 sec. advantage over the Porsche 936s of Ickx and Barth. The remaining Alpines were fourth and fifth, easing their pace while the drivers carefully watched how the pacemakers fared ahead of them. John Fitzpatrick's Kremer Porsche Turbo became another victim of engine failure, the car retiring

The Ickx/Pescarolo Porsche 936 looks for a way past the Luigi BMW and the lone Aston Martin.

with burnt cylinder liners after less than an hour, but the Mirages were beginning to look handily placed although well behind the works Renault and Porsche entries.

The Porsches had a much greater range than the Alpine-Renaults, so that when Jabouille had to refuel and hand over to Bell after 18 hours, Ickx took the lead for the German team, relinquishing it to Bell again only when Pescarolo took over from him five laps later. By this time all the leading cars had completed their first round of scheduled refuelling stops, and Bell's Alpine had a 35 sec. lead over Pescarolo's Porsche, with Depailler and Jaussaud further back. The second Martini Porsche 936 was now several laps behind, however, for after 18 circuits of the 8½ mile track it had had to have its fuel pump changed, which took over ten minutes.

The way Depailler was trying, he seemed certain to pass Pescarolo, but no sooner had he caught the Porsche than his Alpine needed to stop for a second time to take on more petrol. So Pescarolo clung on to second place. and though Bell was practically a minute ahead Henri knew that the French car would have to stop again long before his own. On the 39th lap Bell came into the pits, making way for Jabouille, who accelerated back into the race at exactly the moment that Pescarolo's Porsche blasted into the lead. When they reappeared sweeping through the long curves that now by-pass the old White House section and lead into tight Ford Esses before the pits, a mere four seconds separated the two leaders. Next time round, Porsche's lead had hardly shrunk at all, but a lap later it was Jabouille in the lead with Pescarolo fighting to stay in his slipstream.

Two-thirds of the way round that 44th lap, as the yellow car and the white one sped towards Arnage, Pescarolo revved the Porsche too hard. In a billow of oil smoke its engine expired, and with a shade under three hours gone, the Renault team held the top three places. With the Mirages already a couple of laps behind, it looked uncomfortably like a stranglehold on the race that Renault were not likely to lose.

It was approximately an hour later when the Alpines had their first hint of trouble: the third placed car of Tambay and Jaussaud lost over ten minutes in the pits while a loose inlet manifold was tightened up.

Sam Posey's Mirage mysteriously ran out of petrol on Mulsanne Straight five laps before it was due to take on more, and then the Inaltera shared by Beltoise and Holbert burst into flames for a few seconds during a pit stop, though it suffered remarkably little damage and was soon on its way again. The Inaltera with the all girl crew was in trouble too, electrical failures delaying it on more than one occasion during Saturday evening.

Porsche, meanwhile, had decided that with only one works car left running, but running faultlessly, they should use Ickx to inject more pace into the Barth-Haywood partnership. The outcome was dramatic to say the least. Ickx immediately began to fly round the circuit, making up ground fast on all but the Alpines, and shattering the lap record to leave it. 2.8 sec. below the previous best-ever race lap recorded by Cevert's Matra in 1973. By the end of the seventh hour of the race, the Porsche was fourth again, headed only by those three Alpines.

Just before three o'clock on Sunday morning came the first of the engine failures that were to eliminate the entire works Renault team. The third placed Jaussaud/Tambay car was the first to go, and an hour and a half later Depailler brought the second placed Alpine into the pits for its gearbox to be rebuilt. A pinion had to be replaced, and by the time the car was running

The Jabouille/Laffite Renault Alpine 442. Le Mans was a disaster for the Renault team. All four 442s, developed specially for a Porsche confrontation, succumbed.

again the Porsche had swept past. Only the Jabouille/Bell Alpine lay ahead of the Porsche now, though that car had six laps in hand and was going quickly enough to keep that distance constant.

With the dawn came rain, but the only victim was Chris Craft, whose Lola aquaplaned off the road and lost several positions while body and chassis damage was repaired. A few minutes past 9 a.m. Jabouille brought the leading Alpine into the pit lane trailing ominous clouds of smoke. After a brief inspection and one final slow lap, the car was wheeled away, another victim of piston failure. So the Porsche of Ickx, Barth and Haywood inherited the lead – but Depailler and Laffite were still chasing hard in the sole surviving Alpine and were still only two laps behind. Then, alas for French hopes, that car's engine also expired approaching Arnage with a fraction over four hours to go.

The entire Renault team was out, and the works Porsche 936 was left with a huge lead over the Schuppan/Jarier Mirage, apparently set for a comfortable victory. But 45 minutes from the end it too slowed dramatically amidst a sudden cloud of smoke as a piston broke. It limped to its pit, remained there for half an hour, and only ten minutes before the flag came out staggered away for two final laps that would ensure the victory that Ickx, Barth and Haywood so richly deserved.

With Barth driving as gently as he could, the Porsche finally cruised over the line on five cylinders to win by 11 laps. There were those amazed that it had done two laps instead of only one, and others surprised that Barth, not Ickx, was given the crucial task of bringing the crippled car home. But Porsche do nothing without a good reason: the car had to do two laps, for the rules stated that in order to count, any competitor's final lap had to be completed within a

certain percentage of the time taken for its penultimate one; and as for Ickx, he had already used up his maximum permitted time at the wheel.

Second after an almost entirely trouble-free run was the Mirage of Schuppan and Jarier, the Mirage benefiting from the retirement five hours from the finish of the Gelo Porsche driven by Hezemans, Heyer and Schenken. That car, too, had sustained a valve failure, the broken valve also destroying the turbocharger; ironically, the thing that eliminated it was a fuel pump that suddenly stopped working. The last two hours of the race were much enlivened by an exciting dash for third place, with the Porsche 935 of Claude Ballot-Lena and Peter Gregg and the Inaltera of Rondeau and Ragnotti both being hauled in hand over fist by Chris Craft in the de Cadenet Lola. Despite problems with the nuts that held on the exhaust system, and despite the earlier loss of time following Craft's spin in the rain, the Lola failed to catch the third-placed Group-Five Porsche by only 92 sec., while the fourth positioned Inaltera was a meagre 41 sec. ahead at the finish.

Sixth overall, and easy winners of the 2-litre Group 6 class, were Michel Pignard, Jacques Henry and Alain Defrenne with a Societe ROC prepared, Simca engined Chevron B36. Seventh and winner of the Group 4 category was the Kremer Porsche 934 Turbo driven by Bob Wollek, Philippe Gurdjian and "Steve". Eighth and victor of the IMSA class was the Luigi Racing BMW CSL shared by Jean Xhenceval, Pierre Dieudonne and Spartaco Dini; while in 17th place out of the 21 finishers, the Aston Martin V8 entered by Robin Hamilton for Dave Preece, Mike Salmon and himself upset almost every prediction by keeping going to the finish. And that, after all, is what Le Mans is really all about.

J.C.T.

Results:

24 HOURS OF LE MANS   342 laps   13.64 kilometres per lap   4664.9 kilometres   Weather varying between warm and dry, and cold and wet

1st :	J. Barth/H. Haywood/J. Ickx (2.1 t/c Porsche 936)*	194.802 k.p.h.
2nd :	V. Schuppan/J. P. Jarier (2.0 t/c Mirage-Renault)	
3rd :	C. Ballot-Lena/P. Gregg (2.9 t/c Porsche 935)*	331 laps
4th :	J. Rondeau/J. Ragnotti (3.0 Inaltera-DFV)*	315 laps
5th :	C. Craft/A. de Cadenet (3.0 De-Cadenet Lola-DFV)	315 laps
6th :	M. Pignard/J. Henry/A. Defrenne (2.0 Chevron-Simca B36)*	315 laps
7th :	B. Wollek/"Steve"/P. Gurdjian (3.0 t/c Porsche 934)*	303 laps
8th :	J. Xhenceval/P. Dieudonne/S. Dini (3.2 BMW CSL)*	298 laps
9th :	H. Poulain/M. Mignot (2.0 BMW 320i)	291 laps
10th :	C. Gouttepifre/P. Malbran/R. Touroul (3.0 Porsche Carrera)	287 laps
		281 laps

Class winners

Fastest lap: J. Ickx (2.1 t/c Porsche 936), 3 min. 36.8 sec.   226.94 k.p.h.

The pretty Inaltera of Beltoise/Holbert, one of three of the Le Mans-built cars.

LE MANS 24 HOURS

No time to lose

STORY & CAPTIONS BY SAM POSEY

PHOTOS BY ELLEN GRIESEDIECK

THE FIRST REQUIREMENT for a driver at Le Mans is to appear at Scrutineering at the time his car is there. For each team there is a different appointment time. The cars pass slowly through a dozen checkpoints, being measured, weighed, filled with fuel, emptied of fuel, prodded and poked. Meanwhile, the team's drivers present their medical cards, licenses and insurance papers. Le Mans scrutineering can take more than four hours but the inspectors themselves, glacially formal Frenchmen wearing dark ties and blue suits, seem to relish the tedium.

When everything has been approved, the team is photographed for posterity by a battery of photographers representing publications from all over the world. Our Renault Mirages were posed with French and American flags that symbolized the cooperation between Renault, which made our engines, and our Phoenix-based team. In other contemporary forms of racing commercialism is everything, but at Le Mans no one begrudges you a touch of patriotism.

First Practice

THERE ARE only two practice sessions for Le Mans but each is six hours long. The first runs from 6:00 p.m. to midnight Wednesday; the second from 5:00 to 11:00 p.m. Thursday. Thanks to long summer evenings, it's light until 10 o'clock and there's a nice balance be-

tween daylight and night running.

This year rain was threatening as practice began. It was still dry at the pits but after a while cars started coming by streaked with water. The word was that it was raining toward the end of the long Mulsanne straight.

Ordinarily I am not afraid to race in the rain, but I am afraid at Le Mans. I don't mind going through the slow parts of the track in the rain; but when I'm going 180 mph or more and the car is aquaplaning and I can't see properly, *that* makes me worry. Also, I drove in the 1970 race when rain came down relentlessly for 20 of the 24 hours, numerous cars were wrecked, a corner worker was killed and conditions were so bad that the winner, Hans Hermann, announced immediately afterward that he

Second Practice

THE SECOND day of practice was clear. Fuel pump problems stranded both the Mirages far from the pits but because the cars were radio-equipped, it was possible to find out where they were and send mechanics to make repairs.

Once the cars were running right it became obvious that their top speed was as much as 15 mph slower than the Porsche prototypes and the Renault Alpines. Since we had the same engines as the Alpines we began to worry that the Mirage's problem was aerodynamic drag. (Ironically, in our testing at Phoenix, we had been able to evaluate almost every part of the car, but the shortness of the Phoenix track kept us from checking the car at top speed.) Trying to reduce drag,

ager, and drew up a plan for what could realistically be done in the time left before the race. The air scoop would be extended to pick up less turbulent air. Cockpit pressure would be relieved by venting the area behind the driver's head. The front part of the cockpit cowling would be reshaped. None of this work, however, would be allowed to interfere with the regular preparation of the cars. We knew the strong cards held by the other teams were already on display while ours—fast pit work and a proven chassis—wouldn't be played until the race itself.

Interlude

A FEATURE of the Le Mans schedule is that on Friday, the day before the race, the track is closed in order to give

was retiring from racing. So when I see rain at Le Mans I tense up reflexively, but this year the rain played only a minor role. The shower at the beginning of practice dried off well before anyone was under pressure to go really fast, and the track stayed dry until another shower which came at dawn in the race. At that point only Jacky Ickx took any real risks. It could be argued that he was the only driver on the track at the time in a strategic position which justified chance-taking (he was engaged in a flat-out pursuit of the leading Alpines). But it's probably closer to the truth to say that Ickx drove as he did in the rain because he is one of the few drivers in racing today who seems to thrive on danger.

we flattened our rear wings but this made the cars unstable without giving us any more speed. Another problem was extreme wind turbulence in the cockpit.

When practice was over we assessed the situation. After so many months of work and hope it was hard to admit we weren't as fast as we had anticipated. The only solution to our problems seemed to lie in a total redesign of the body, and there obviously wasn't time for that. At this point, team owner Harley Cluxton displayed his instinct for leadership. During a long dinner at our hotel he extracted from the drivers and the crew every useful bit of information relating to our problems. Then the next morning he met with John Horsman, the team man-

A traditional team portrait showing owner Harley Cluxton (center) with drivers Vern Schuppan (far left), Jean-Pierre Jarier (center left), Michel Leclere (center right) and me (far right). Harley was telling jokes out of the side of his mouth, Bogart style, but I was feeling subdued. This was due in part to jet lag and in part to the genuine emotion I felt at being part of a major American Le Mans team.

the teams time for the final preparation.

Our team stayed in La Chatres, a small town a half hour south of the track. On this day it seemed as if the whole life of the town was given over to watching us prepare for the race. Old men and women, many of them carrying long rolls of French bread which made them look as if they had stepped straight out of a travel poster, stood immobile for hours at the entrance to our garage. And a steady stream of kids ran back and forth between the garage and the hotel, checking the progress on the cars and hoping to get a driver's autograph.

For the drivers, Friday was a day off, although at one time or another each of us visited the garage to see how things were going. I wandered around town looking in store windows at French pastries and mopeds, everything priced bewilderingly in francs. I also went jogging. The streets were narrow, with old stone sidewalks, and I saw disbelief registering on the faces of the townspeople who saw me galloping by in my shorts and T-shirt.

Every now and then through the day I could feel my mind sliding. Instead of being aware of whatever was going on, I'd be thinking about the race.

We're Off

THE RACE didn't start until 4 p.m. but because of the vast crowds it was necessary to leave for the track around noon. Leaving the hotel I felt as though I was embarking on an expedition because in addition to all my usual driving equipment, I also took blankets, pillows and some special food.

The paddock area behind the pits was crowded, and the pits were even more so. The crowds, the noise, the excitement, made the whole thing feel very much like Indianapolis just before the start, but with one important difference. At Indy the start is the beginning of a 500-mile sprint, and in its explosive power it is the logical continuation of the immediate pre-race tension. But at Le Mans the start, really, is nothing. It is merely the moment you put your 24-hour "system" into action. For a handful of drivers—the inexperienced, or a few who, for tactical reasons, are assigned sprinting roles by their teams—the start means going fast, but for everyone else it is as if you are a clock which, having just been wound, now begins to run smoothly, regularly.

Vern Schuppan and I were side-by-side at the start but in a lap it was apparent that his car, which was fitted with stiffer springs, was faster and gradually he drew away. I was furious that my co-driver Michel Leclere and I had made this technical blunder, but it was too late to do anything. On the plus side, however, the revised cockpit cowling sharply reduced the wind buffeting. I was delighted that after several years of driving GT cars at Le Mans I was now back in a full-fledged prototype, with a solid chance to beat my previous best finish

Our hotel, the Hotel de France. No team had finer accommodations. The restaurant was of top quality even by French standards. Arriving back from practice after 2 a.m. we still found the restaurant ready to serve us fabulous multicourse meals and an endless supply of French wine.

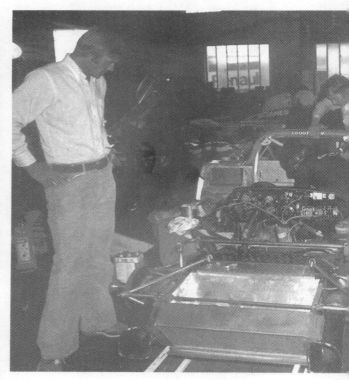

The view out of my room, with my fireproof underwear drying on the windowsill. Matisse would have loved it.

(3rd in 1971 with a Ferrari 512M), and even had a chance to win.

Every long-distance team has its complements of timers and other supporting personnel, but in the case of our team, Harley had encouraged some of our financial backers to handle these jobs, with the result that we had some extremely intelligent people, including a doctor, a lawyer and a banker, in the pits. John Horsman had organized this eclectic group and as team manager he received a constant flow of reports about fuel consumption, tire and brake pad wear, lap times and overall standings. In addition, because Renault had asked for regularly updated information about their sensitive turbocharged engines, the drivers radioed reports on boost pressure and exhaust gas temperature as well as all the regular engine functions.

By 8 p.m. the light of the long evening slanted across the track. One Renault Alpine was out, a victim of an early fire, and Ickx's Porsche had also succumbed. The remaining Alpines controlled the race. Our Mirages had moved up to 5th and 6th. I was headed down the Mulsanne with more than 50 miles to go before a scheduled fuel stop when I

The day before the race the team worked in a controlled frenzy. The idea was to modify the cars' bodywork while leaving enough time to get through the extensive checklist of routine maintenance. The garage, which is virtually next door to the hotel, was for years John Wyer's headquarters, and it was magical to think that 20 years ago Aston Martins littered the floor and 10 years ago it was Fords.

You leave in the morning and you return in the evening— but it's the *next* evening.

noticed the fuel warning light begin to flicker. Odd. Two hundred miles an hour on the ultra-smooth Mulsanne is a little like being in the cockpit of a low-flying plane and with a pilot's deliberateness, I checked the instruments. The fuel pressure was correct and I recalled that our drivers' instruction manual, which I had memorized before the race, said that with the warning light flashing I should be able to make it to the pits without slackening my pace. Okay. But in a moment the light was on steadily.

I slowed and glanced at the fuel pressure. It was falling. I activated the reserve pump but the pressure continued to drop. The engine was dying. I coasted around the corner at the end of the straight and pulled off to the side.

In the next two hours with the aid of a full complement of tools that we carried onboard, I checked everything I could, but the fact remained that there were streaks of gas along the underside of the outboard tank and I was all but certain we had had a leak and I was out for good: Le Mans regulations don't allow refueling on the course.

One possible explanation for the inadequacy of our top speed was that compared to an Alpine (left), the Mirage was bigger and boxier. When an Alpine passed us on the straight it went by so fast it looked like a dart you had thrown out ahead of you.

Eventually someone was sent for me and I took the long, slow ride to the pits via the narrow back road. There John Horsman sensed my crushing disappointment at being out and asked me to stick around in case a reserve driver was needed for the remaining car. It was at best a tenuous relationship with the team but I was thankful for it. I couldn't bear to leave.

By then it was 11 p.m., dark, and the Alpines were facing a challenge by Ickx who, having taken over the second Porsche, was storming through the field. Our remaining Mirage was still 5th.

During the night the order remained the same, but the Porsches drew closer to the Alpines. Then in the early morning rain Ickx sliced into 3rd. Just before dawn the 1st-place Alpine whispered into the pits and died. By noon all three were out. They had dominated the first three-quarters of the race, but at Le Mans minutes can be like hours and hours like months and by early afternoon, with the crowd having flowed back into the grandstands like a returning tide, it was almost as if the Alpines had been in some other Le Mans, not this one.

The demise of the Alpines put the Porsche of Ickx, Hurley Haywood and Jürgen Barth firmly in the lead. Our Vern Schuppan/Jean-Pierre Jarier Mirage was 2nd, miles behind, but running so well that I knew I would never be needed as a relief driver so, early in the afternoon I walked up the pits toward the 1st turn.

Looking back along the track toward

the Ford chicane, I could see the cars popping into sight at random intervals. They seemed to hang there suspended in the distance before crystalizing into a discernible form, a particular car, which then rushed toward me. Only then could I hear the sound of the engine winding through the wide-spaced gears and the long hesitation on the upshift. The cars seemed freed by then of that earlier urgency when tenths of seconds still mattered. Still, as the cars fled up through that first turn, they transmitted to anyone watching them an unmistakable sense of power generated seemingly without effort. As I watched them pass, climbing through the long right turn, I could almost imagine I was still driving in the race. Vividly I could feel how it had been to crest that first hill under the Dunlop bridge and rush steeply down toward the Esses. I could remember how the heavy braking between the earth embankments caused a compression of energy which was released split seconds later as the car catapulted itself along the tiny straight into Tertre Rouge.

The last hours went by with no change as the race drew to a close. Then with less than 40 minutes to go, Haywood brought

All through the night our surviving Mirage came and went from the pits, always right on schedule.

Adjacent to the Esses is a carnival, with kids waiting in line to be frightened by Dracula or perhaps to ride the bump cars. Ferris wheels turn in the night sky and every four minutes or so the fat lady heaves herself to her feet. It is as if she is synchronized mysteriously with the passing of a particular car on the track.

the leading Porsche into the pits trailing smoke. Holed piston. Le Mans regulations require that in order to be classified as a finisher, a car must be running at the finish and must cross the line under its own power.

The mechanics disconnected the turbo and removed the sparkplug from the broken cylinder. Just before 4 o'clock they sent the crippled car out onto the track. It was a strange time, waiting to see if the Porsche could make it. It seemed that the race had passed beyond the point where the outcome would be determined by the relative qualities of the men competing in it; instead it was as though the whole thing was in the hands of fate.

With Jarier in the Mirage for the finish, Harley and I stood with Vern and watched for the Porsche. It reappeared but—too soon! The checkered flag hadn't yet been waved and now the car was committed to another lap. Vern, who had the most to gain if trouble struck the Porsche, was also the most composed; I was in anguish. As much as I wanted our Mirage to win, and would have done anything I could have to help, I knew that to have been part of the winning team, but not to have driven the car, would undoubtedly be the most frustrating experience of my career.

Then the Porsche came around again, this time to win.

With less than an hour to go in the race, Hurley Haywood brought the leading Porsche into the pits, trailing a cloud of smoke. Dazed and exhausted he waited while the mechanics worked on the stricken car.

LE MANS 1978

Sometimes Le Mans history seems to repeat itself, and there were many similarities between the 1977 and 1978 races. Once again, the major battle would be between the two big works teams Porsche and Renault. Even if Le Mans was still without championship status, the A.C.O.'s 24-hour race once again asserted its pre-eminence in the world of endurance racing, in terms of its entry record, and the publicity it attracted.

Alpine-Renault first tried for an overall victory at Le Mans in 1968-69, with a three-litre V8-engined car, which was just not fast enough. They came back in 1975 with a two-litre V6, which then was fitted with a turbo-charger, blossoming out as the A442 and now the A443. Four of these cars in various models were entered; of these, the Jaussaud/Pironi car ran with a high almost all-enveloping windscreen known as the bubble top which proved in practice to be worth another 10 mph down the Mulsanne straight. The Alpine-Renaults all ran on Michelin radial tyres.

Against the Alpine-Renault team, the other main contender was the Martini-Porsche team which had three 936 Spyders - one of which was driven by Jacky Ickx and Pescarolo - with a supporting 935 in Group 5. Apart from the Renaults and Porsches, the other Group 6 cars consisted of a new Lola for Alain de Cadenet and Christ Craft, and de Cadenet's old car in the hands of Faure, Philips and Beasley; a third British contender, also using the Cosworth-DFV engine, was the Ibec-Hesketh-Ford with a Postlethwaite-designed chassis and driven by Grob, Edwards and Bracey. Finally, the two Mirage-Renaults which had been seen in 1977.

The majority of the two-litre Group 6 cars were British-made if not necessarily British-entered; there were no less than seven Lolas, of the 294, 296 and 297 types; four Chevrons, with Chrysler-Simca or Ford engines; and finally, one each of Cheetah, Osella-BMW and Sauler-BMW. By contrast both Group 5 and Group 4 were entirely Porsche-dominated; Group 5 was made up of eight Porsche 935s, including the Martini-Porsche entry, while Group 4 consisted of four Porsche 934s and three Carrera RSRs.

The GT prototype class held one Inaltera, together with Jean Rondeau's newest design which also used a Cosworth-DFV engine but which ran under the constructor's own name; in addition there were three WM-Peugeots, with their 2.7 litre turbo-charged V6 engines - one was a new car and the other two had been seen at Le Mans in previous years. Finally the I.M.S.A. category held five Ferrari 512 BB Boxers, two Porsche 935s, a single Porsche Carrera and the only American car in the race, a Chevrolet Monza. If Porsche still dominated the field with 21 cars, there was at least a lot of variety among the other 34 cars.

Apart from the 24-hour race itself there was a half-hour race on Saturday morning for historic Le Mans cars; won by Stirling Moss in a not-quite-appropriate Maserati 250 F single-seater Grand Prix racing car entered by JCB, with Willie Green and Martin Morris coming second and third, both in D-type Jaguars. After ten entries at Le Mans in the period 1951-61, with the best results two second placings, Moss had the satisfac-

tion of winning a race at Le Mans, after 16 years in retirement.

Although Ickx had set the fastest lap time in practice and started from pole position the race began badly for Porsche; within a few laps two of the 936s were in the pits, Ickx's own car and the Haywood/Gregg car. So the Alpine-Renault of Pironi/Jaussaud went into the lead, followed by the Jarier/Bell sister car, while the Barth/Wollek Porsche 936 held on to third place followed by the remaining two Renaults. For most of the early part of the race, Alpine-Renault had a 1-2-3 lead with the Barth/Wollek Porsche in fourth place. Then the Ickx/Pescarolo Porsche went into its pit again with a serious gearbox problem; and in a repeat of the 1977 race, the Martini-Porsche team leader decided to put his best driver into the highest-placed Porsche. Ickx joined Barth and Wollek, and with his assistance, that car had gone into second place by midnight, after the Jabouille/Depailler Alpine-Renault which was now race leader. Soon after, the Jarier/Bell Renault had to be withdrawn with a broken differential.

On Sunday morning, the Ickx/Wollek/Barth Porsche lost its fifth gear as had the original Ickx/Pescarolo car the previous evening but it took little more than half an hour to rebuild the gearbox. Similarly, the Pescarolo car had had its gearbox rebuilt and had rejoined the race with Jochen Mass co-driving; but he crashed the car on Sunday morning. Then disaster overtook the Renault team when the Jabouille/Depailler car blew its engine after twelve hours as raceleader; however, the Pironi/Jassaud car which had gained second place while the Porsche gearbox was being rebuilt, now moved back into the lead. And although the Ickx Porsche was able to reduce the leader's margin in the final hours of the race, Jaussaud and Pironi drove home to Renault's first victory in the 24-hour race. Their distance was 3,134.51 miles at an average of 130.6 mph. The fastest lap in the race was driven by Jean-Pierre Jabouille in the other Alpine-Renault, at 142.44 mph.

Second and third places were taken by the Porsche 936s. of Ickx/Barth/Wollek and Haywood/Gregg/Joest, while the only other surviving Alpine came fourth. The next four places were filled by Porsche 935s, of which the Redman/Barbour car in fifth place won the I.M.S.A. category and the Busby/Cord/Knoop car in sixth place was the first Group 5 car home. Ninth place, and victory in the GTP category, went to the Rondeau. The first two-litre car was a Chevron-Chrysler-Simca in eleventh place, followed by a Porsche Carrera in twelfth place which won the Group 4 category. Of the British contingent, the de Cadenet/Craft Lola succeeded in finishing in fifteenth place after a host of problems, while the Ibec-Hesketh blew its engine on Sunday morning. A total of 25 cars finished but only 17 classified under the minimum distance rules.

So Renault had achieved their ambition; winning the most prestigious French race. Immediately after the race, Renault's managing director Bernard Hanon made known that the team was retiring from sports car endurance racing, in order to concentrate on Grand Prix racing. Porsche, having suffered defeat at the hands of an arch-rival, went home and began thinking about next year's Le Mans.

Moment of truth

The Renault-Porsche, Franco-German rivalry at Le Mans will reach new heights next weekend, and there will be four British prototypes, too. QUENTIN SPURRING discusses the cars involved in a classic confrontation.

Le Mans is about a lot of things, every one exceptional. To many people, most of all it is about national pride. Now the only remaining proper endurance sports car race in the world, it is also the premier motoring event in France. And the French—represented these days by Renault—have had to endure the strains of *Deutschland Uber Alles* at the Sarthe, both last year and the year before.

Next weekend's 24 Hours will be the 46th since a French car won the first event, in 1923. Cars from only five nations have won Le Mans in this 55-year period. Counting all the Ford entries as American ones, Britain and Italy have won 13 apiece, France 10, Germany five and USA four. For Renault, the historical superiority of France over Germany loses significance when *marque* achievements are counted. Ferrari have scored the most wins at the Sarthe, nine; next come Bentley and Jaguar with five, followed by Alfa Romeo, Ford and Porsche with four; Matra have won three, Lorraine and Bugatti two each, and Chenard & Walcker, Lagonda, Delahaye, Talbot, Mercedes, Aston Martin and Gulf-Ford one each. Renault? Nil.

In the third year of the full-scale Renault Le Mans programme, national pressure therefore weighs heavily on the shoulders of the state-owned company's competitions director, Gérard Larrousse. In the face of opposition from Porsche even stronger than last year's, he has to win this time. In his own words, "The sales battle in Europe has never been so tough. The commercial fall-out of a race like this is far more obvious than the technical spin-offs, for a victory at Le Mans is one that cannot be doubted. It is a unique 24-hour endurance test. Le Mans, more than any other race, adds up to the moment of truth for a car builder and his machinery."

The main Renault effort will be directed by the official factory team of four Alpine-built chassis, developments of the A440 project initiated in 1972. Three of the cars will be versions of the A442 which first appeared in 1975. The cars have been modified since last year's race in over 40 areas, including a series of aerodynamic changes to the bodywork. The A442 power unit is the familiar 1997cc, cast-iron block, 90deg V6, with four valves per cylinder; its single turbocharger gives the water-cooled, Gordini-developed unit a power output of about 500bhp at 9900rpm in Le Mans tune. Last year, the fast works Alpine-Renaults suffered a depressing series of piston failures at Le Mans, and over 30 modifications have been made to the engine over the winter, including a lot of new work on the heat endurance of the pistons themselves and redesigned valvegear. The Hewland TL200 five-speed gearbox is retained.

Renault have tested the latest A442A cars extensively at Paul Ricard, and they expect a top speed of just over 220mph down the Mulsanne Straight this weekend. These will not be the fastest Renaults, however.

Timing its announcement for maximum publicity, Renault have taken the A440 concept a stage further with an all-new car, designatd the A443, the existence of which was officially revealed only last Wednesday. The A443 has a 15cms longer wheelbase than the A442-series cars, different bodywork and wider front wheels, but most significantly it will be fitted with a new version of the Gordini V6, with a capacity of 2140cc. A top speed of 233mph is projected for this car, which was tested for the first time at Paul Ricard last week. The drivers were to have been F1 men Jean-Pierre Jabouille/Patrick Tambay, but Patrick's foot has not healed sufficiently to be risked for 24 hours, and he will not now drive. The A443 will be just about the quickest thing there if the estimated top speed is correct.

Renault have not released power output figures for their 2.1-litre engine, but it is thought that the A443 will derive its maximum speed mainly from its aerodynamics. The French design team have evolved a new semi-enclosed cockpit, the 'dome' of which is made from Plexiglass so that the drivers are still visible. In addition, the A443 has brush skirts fitted. Both these features have been incorporated in one of the 2-litre cars, which will be driven by Jean-Pierre Jaussaud/Didier Pironi, and has been designated A442B. The other modified A442-series cars (A442A) will be crewed by Derek Bell/Jean-Pierre Jarier and by Guy Frequelin/ Jean Ragnotti, the latter car sponsored by Calberson.

Apart from the massive investment by the state-owned car manufacturer itself, further backing for Renault's Le Mans project (which is now confirmed for 1979, incidentally), comes from Elf, Cibié and their tyre supplier, Michelin. It's certainly an all French affair: Renault must think very highly of our own Derek Bell.

A second string to Renault's bow, once again, will be the Phoenix, Arizona, based Grand Touring Cars Inc team of Harley Cluxton. Cluxton's two Mirage M9 chassis (one of which finished second last year) will again be directed at Le Mans by John Wyer and John Horsman, and they have also been much modified over the winter and extensively tested (at Mid-Ohio). The cars are now lower, shorter and narrower, with new cockpits and fuel supply systems and resited radiators, plus a large number of other detail changes. Power, once again, comes from the 1997cc Renault-Gordini V6, and the latest engines have been supplied to the GTC team. It now seems that Vern Schuppan will forsake his clashing USAC date in favour of partnering Jacques Laffite in one of the cars while, as in 1977, the other one will be shared by Michel Leclere/Sam Posey.

The Mirage team is again backed by the British JCB excavator company, and will run on Goodyear tyres.

Three Martini-Porsche factory prototypes will oppose the six Renault-powered cars in the Group 6 class. The 936 cars have also been considerably modified since one of them won Le Mans last year, the major changes being longer tails and the installation in two of the 700kgs chassis of the latest version of the famous flat-six. The unit is of 2142cc capacity, and is similar to the larger Group 5 engine which made such a superb debut at Silverstone last month in that it has four valves per cylinder and water-cooled heads (although the aluminium 911-block remains air-cooled, as on the G5 machine). As usual, it drives through Porsche's own five-speed gearbox. In this form, Porsche tell us that the engine develops around 580bhp at 8500rpm with its twin KKK turbochargers set at 1.4 boost.

Even though they have done a 40-hours test with it at Paul Ricard, Porsche are not over-confident about this engine which, of course, has never been raced. The four-valve 936s will be slower in a straight line than all the Alpine-Renaults at about 212mph. They will be driven by 1977 winner Jurgen Barth with G5 driver Bob Wollek, and by Jacky Ickx—chasing an unprecedented fifth (and fourth straight) victory at the Sarthe—with Henri Pescarolo, himself a three-times Le Mans winner.

The third works 936 will retain last year's two-valve engine, which produces around 560bhp, and the car should be very little slower in a straight line. The winning chassis (001) which won in 1976 and 1977, this one will be entrusted to American pairing Hurley Haywood (one of the 1977 winning drivers) and Peter Gregg, in recognition of Porsche's huge American market. All three 936 entries will run on the latest Dunlop tyres which have been developed during development testing at Paul Ricard. An unwilling Jochen Mass and Reinhold Jöst are the reserve drivers.

So, Porsche *versus* Renault. The prototypes do not end there, however, and (apart from Jorg Obermoser's latest Ford-Cosworth engined Toj SC303) the rest of the 3-litre class comprises British entries. Alain de Cadenet has flown the Union Jack at Le Mans for six years now, for which every British enthusiast should be grateful. Next weekend, there will be no fewer than three De Cadenet modified Lolas, all of course with Cosworth DFV power. Alain himself will co-drive his latest car with Chris Craft.

Like his previous cars, Alain's latest Le Mans challenger is based on the Lola T380 chassis, developed extensively by Len Bailey and built by John Thompson. The all-new car—the specification of which includes such things as on-board air-jacks—has been assembled at Buxted, Sussex, by Dick Crosthwaite and John Gardner, whose company is responsible for those Kougar Jaguar-based sports cars. The latest car, which has been tested at Silverstone in recent weeks, will again use Nicholson built Cosworth engines, tuned this year to give 460bhp (previous De Cadenet Lolas had their DFVs tuned down to about 400bhp). The team will again be managed by Keith Greene. Unfortunately, no sponsorship—not even from the motor racing trade—could be found to back Alain's 1978 Le Mans project, save for nominal (although welcome) support from British Rail Sealink. It really makes you wonder what our industry is thinking about.

The 1977 De Cadenet Lola is now owned by Peter Lovett and prepared to the latest specs. Lovett will drive along with John Cooper (with sponsorship from Cooper Industries). The third entry is the Simon Phillips owned 1976 car, for which Phillips has attracted sponsorship from BATCO France, and which he will drive along with John Beasley and Nick Faure.

Finally, the Ibec Racing Developments entry, the new Hesketh built Ibec IBH1 which is to be driven by Ian Bracey, Ian Grob and Guy Edwards. DFV-powered and sponsored by the Alexander Howden insurance firm and by Chrysler UK, the car has been designed by Harvey Postlethwaite and is based on his 308B Formula 1 chassis. It was run for the first time at Donington last Friday, and more details can be found in *Pit & Paddock*.

All the likely winners are in the 3-litre G6 category, but there is also the intriguing prospect of the performance of the new *langheck* Martini-Porsche 935-78. This car, of course, has had a perfect qualifying and race at Silverstone last month, the 6 Hours being used as a competitive shakedown for Le Mans. In 3213cc form, the four-valve flat-six (with the turbos turned down for Le Mans) pushes out at least 750bhp at 8200rpm, making this one of the most powerful cars in the race. Last year, Manfred Jantke used his G5 entry as a 'hare'. If he has similar plans for 1978, his equipment is ideal, for the 935-78 could reach 230mph down Mulsanne, pretty much as fast as the newly announced Alpine-Renault. Its drivers will

Facing page: the rivals. The Martini-Porsche team tests the 936 prototype at Paul Ricard (top), in readiness for the defence of Germany's Le Mans 'title' from French attack by Alpine-Renault and Mirage-Renault.

LE MANS PAST WINNERS

Year	Drivers	Car	Speed	Distance
1958	Oliver Gendebien/Phil Hill	3.0 Ferrari 250TRV12	106.12mph	2547.76 miles
1959	Roy Salvadori/Carrol Shelby	3.0 Aston Martin DBR1 S6	112.57mph	2701.65 miles
1960	Oliver Gendebien/Paul Frere	3.0 Ferrari 250TR/60 V12	109.19mph	2620.64 miles
1961	Oliver Gendebien/Phil Hill	3.0 Ferrari TR/161 V12	115.90mph	2781.70 miles
1962	Oliver Gendebien/Phil Hill	4.0 Ferrari 330TR/LM V12	115.25mph	2765.73 miles
1963	Lodovico Scarfiotti/Lorenzo Bandini	3.0 Ferrari 250P V12	118.50mph	2834.60 miles
1964	Jean Guichet/Nino Vaccarella	3.3 Ferrari 275P V12	121.60mph	2906.20 miles
1965	Masten Gregory/Jochen Rindt	3.3 Ferrari 250/275LM V12	121.80mph	2917.70 miles
1966	Bruce McLaren/Chris Amon	7.0 Ford Mk2 V8	125.40mph	3009.50 miles
1967	Dan Gurney/A. J. Foyt	7.0 Ford Mk4 V8	135.48mph	3251.58 miles
1968	Pedro Rodriguez/Lucien Bianchi	5.0 Ford GT40 V8	114.93mph	2764.23 miles
1969	Jacky Ickx/Jack Oliver	5.0 Ford GT40 V8	129.40mph	3105.60 miles
1970	Dick Attwood/Hans Herrmann	4.5 Porsche 917K F12	119.29mph	2863.15 miles
1971	Helmut Marko/Gijs van Lennep	5.0 Porsche 917K F12	138.11mph	3315.20 miles
1972	Henri Pescarolo/Graham Hill	3.0 Matra-Simca MS670 V12	121.45mph	2915.06 miles
1973	Henri Pescarolo/Gerard Larrousse	3.0 Matra-Simca MS670 V12	125.67mph	3016.13 miles
1974	Henri Pescarolo/Gerard Larrousse	3.0 Matra-Simca MS670B V12	119.96mph	2856.07 miles
1975	Jacky Ickx/Derek Bell	3.0 Mirage-Ford GR8 V8	119.67mph	2847.60 miles
1976	Jacky Ickx/Gijs van Lennep	2.1 Porsche 936 F6	124.22mph	2981.20 miles
1977	Jacky Ickx/Jurgen Barth/Hurley Haywood	2.1 Porsche 936 F6	121.04mph	2898.62 miles

preview

The Porsche 936—Le Mans hat-trick?

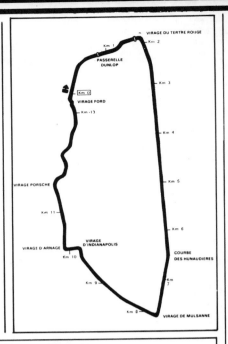

Moment of truth

be Rolf Stommelen/Manfred Schurti.

Sharing the G5 class with the fourth works Porsche are 935-77A models entered by the regular 'customer' teams. Three come from Erwin Kremer (who loses his two lead drivers to the G6 Porsche effort), and it is good to see Britain's Martin Raymond and Mike Franey among the drivers, together with American Jim Busby. Only one is entered by Georg Loos, crewed by our own John Fitzpatrick with Toine Hezemans. Other 935 entries—the teams' regular World Championship of Makes cars—come from Konrad Racing, ASA Cachia and Mecarillos.

Apart from Hervé Poulain's BMW 320i, the final G5 entry is the AMG Mercedes 450 SLC, to be driven by Clemens Schickentanz/Hans Heyer—the latter a regretted absentee from the Loos Porsche team.

Fifteen more G5-type cars are entered in the IMSA class, among them two Porsche 935s from Dick Barbour's team, with none other than Brian Redman and Bob Bondurant among the drivers. Luigi Chinetti has entered a Ferrari 308 GTB and one of *five* Boxers, while Charles Ivey Engineering are running their Porsche Carrera for Larry Perkins/Gordon Spice/Jay Rulon-Miller in this class.

In the unique 'Grand Tourisme Prototype' (GTP) category the revised Aston Martin will be crewed by owner Robin Hamilton and Dave Preece, now with a turbocharger on its 7476cc V8 engine; the car finished on its debut last year, and for 1978 the team is hoping for 200mph plus between Tertre Rouge and Mulsanne Corner.

As usual, there is plenty of British interest in the 2-litre G6 class, all but three of the entries being British-made Lola and Chevron chassis. Dorset Racing once more have two Lolas in the field, one driven by Bob Evans/Martin Birrane/Richard Down and one (co-sponsored by Kelly Girl) by Tony Birchenough-/Ian Harrower/Juliette Slaughter, the last-named the first British lady at the Sarthe for many years. The Mogil Motors Chevron will be there for Tony Charnell/Robin Smith, but these three all-British cars face stiff class opposition. Apart from the ROC Chevrons, the Swiss-built works Sauber-BMW will be quick, with F2 ace Marc Surer among its drivers. So will the British entered, works prepared Italian Osella-BMW, in which BMW (GB) are running Tom Walkinshaw/Dieter Quester, and Tolemans Rad Dougall/Ted Toleman.

There are 67 confirmed entries, of which 55 will start on their 8.475-mile pace lap at 3.50pm on Saturday. Last year, Jean-Pierre Jabouille put his works Alpine-Renault on the pole; he is likely to set the pace again during qualifying today and tomorrow. And if the Renaults last, we expect them to win the race for France. The French know very well, though, that Porsche will be right up there to take advantage of the merest mechanical slip-up.

Radio coverage

BBC radio are giving Le Mans almost the sort of coverage it used to get in the old days of the Jaguars and Raymond Baxter, when every schoolboy used to smuggle his transistor into the dormitory to listen to the bulletins through the night. Simon Taylor will be on the air with reports before, during and after the race, including two on the BBC's World Service. Provisional times are:

Saturday 8.10am, Radio 4—preview in *Sport on 4*
2.55pm, Radio 2 (LW only)—The start
5.25pm approx, Radio 2 (LW only)
12 midnight, Radio 2 (LW only)

Sunday 3.30am, World Service (232m, 276m, 371m or 464m MW)
7am, Radio 1 & 2 (247m, LW and VHF)
8.30am, Radio 1 & 2 (247m, LW and VHF)
10.45am, World Service (232m, 276m, 371m or 464m MW)
12 noon, Radio 2 (LW and VHF)
3pm, Radio 2 (LW and VHF)—The finish
7pm, Radio 2 (LW only)—review in *Sunday Sport*

1978 LE MANS 24 HOURS

Entrant	Car	Drivers		
Group 6 2001-3000cc				
Renault-Sport	Alpine-Renault A443	Jean-Pierre Jabouille	Patrick Depailler	
Renault-Sport	Alpine-Renault A442B	Jean-Pierre Jaussaud	Didier Pironi	
Renault-Sport	Alpine-Renault A442A	Jean-Pierre Jarier	**Derek Bell**	
Renault-Sport	Alpine-Renault A442A	Guy Frequelin	Jean Ragnotti	
Martini Racing Porsche System	Porsche 936-78	Jürgen Barth	Bob Wollek	
Martini Racing Porsche System	Porsche 936-78	Jacky Ickx	Henri Pescarolo	
Martini Racing Porsche System	Porsche 936-77	Hurley Haywood	Peter Gregg	
Alain de Cadenet	**De Cadenet Lola-Ford**	**Alain de Cadenet**	**Chris Craft**	
Alain de Cadenet	De Cadenet Lola-Ford	**Peter Lovett**	**John Cooper**	
Grand Touring Cars Inc	Mirage-Renault M9	Vern Schuppan	Jacques Laffite	
Grand Touring Cars Inc	Mirage-Renault M9	Sam Posey	Michel Leclere	
Simon Phillips/BATCO France	**De Cadenet Lola-Ford**	**Simon Phillips**	**John Beasley**	**Nick Faure**
BP Racing	Toj-Ford SC303	Jörg Obermoser	Pierre-François Rousselot	
Ibec Racing Developments	**Ibec-Ford IBH1**	**Ian Grob**	**Guy Edwards**	**Ian Bracey**
Group 6 up to 2000cc				
Chuck Graemiger	Cheetah G601	Plastina	Grandjean	Luini
Jean-Marie Lemerle	**Lola T294**	Jean-Marie Lamerle	TBN	
Agence Locomotiv	**Lola T296/7**	Anna Cambiaghi	Jean-Claude Geurie	M. Renier
PP Sauber AG	Sauber-BMW C5	Marc Surer	Eugen Strähl	Peter Bernhard
Pronuptia	**Lola T296**	TBN	TBN	
Pronuptia	**Lola T294/6**	TBN	TBN	
GVEA	**Lola T296**	Georges Morand	Eric Vuagnat	Christian Blanc
Mogil Motors/Kores Racing	**Chevron-Ford B31**	**Tony Charnell**	**Robin Smith**	Frederic Alliot
Dominique Lacaud	**Lola T297**	Dominique Lacaud	Jean-François Auboiron	Michel Lateste
ROC Modylook	**Chevron-Chrysler B36**	TBN	TBN	
ROC La Pierre du Nord	**Chevron-Chrysler B36**	Michel Pignard	Alain Dufrene	
ROC La Pierre du Nord	**Chevron-Chrysler B36**	Fred Stalder	TBN	
Dorset Racing with Kelly Girl	**Lola-Ford T294S**	**Tony Birchenough**	**Ian Harrower**	**Juliette Slaughter**
Dorset Racing/Cloud Engineering	**Lola-Ford T294S**	**Richard Down**	**Martin Birrane**	**Bob Evans**
BMW (GB) Racing/Tolemans	Osella-BMW PA6	**Tom Walkinshaw**	Dieter Quester	**Rad Dougall**
Group 5				
AMG Motorenbau GmbH	Mercedes 450 SLC	Clemens Schickentanz	Hans Heyer	
ASA Cachia	Porsche 935-77A	Claude Ballot-Lena	Jean-Louis Lafosse	
Konrad Racing	Porsche 935-77A	Franz Konrad	Volkert Merl	
Martini Racing Porsche System	Porsche 935-78	Rolf Stommelen	Manfred Schurti	
Porsche Kremer Racing	Porsche 935-77A	Jim Busby	Knoop	Chris Cord
Porsche Kremer Racing	Porsche 935-77A	Philippe Gurdjian	Dieter Schornstein	'John Winter'
Porsche Kremer Racing/Fisons	Porsche 935-77A	**Martin Raymond**	**Mike Franey**	'Steve'
Weisberg Gelo Team	Porsche 935-76A	**John Fitzpatrick**	Toine Hezemans	
Mecarillos Racing Team	Porsche 935-76A	Claude Haldi	Herbert Müller	
Group 4				
Mecarillos Racing Team	Porsche 934	Blessy	Delautour	Hennken
Auto Daniel Urcun	Porsche 934	José Dolhem	Jean-Claude Lafevre	Cyril Grandet
'Segolen'	Porsche 934	'Segolen'	Christian Bussi	
Christian Gouttepifre	Porsche Carrera RSR	Christian Gouttepifre	Raymond Touroul	René Boubet
Georges Bourdillat	Porsche Carrera RSR	Georges Bourdillat	Alain-Michel Bernard	
Joël Laplacette	Porsche Carrera RSR	Joël Laplacette	Courage	Salamin
Anny-Charlotte Verney	Porsche Carrera RSR	Anny-Charlotte Verney	Hubert Striebig	
Florian Vetsch	Ferrari 308 GTB	Florian Vetsch	TBN	
Harvé Poulain	Porsche 934	Edgar Dören	Hervé Poulain	Marcel Mignot
Jean-Louis Ravenel	Porsche 934	Jean-Louis Ravenel	Jacky Ravenel	
Grand Touring Prototype				
André Chevalley Racing	Inaltera-Ford M378	André Chevalley	François Trisconi	
Jean Rondeau	Rondeau M378	Jean Rondeau	Bernard Darniche	
Bernard Decure	Alpine-Renault A310	Bernard Decure	TBN	
WM AEREM	WM-Peugeot P76	Christine Dacremont	Marianne Hoepfner	
WM AEREM	WM-Peugeot P77	Marcel Mamers	Raulet	
WM AEREM	WM-Peugeot P78	Christian Debias	Xavier Mathiot	Marc Sourd
IMSA				
Wynn's Belgium	Chevrolet Monza	Brad Frisele	Robert Kirby	John Hotchkiss
'Beurlys'	Ferrari 512 BB	'Beurlys'	Teddy Pilette	
Ecurie Grand Competition Car	Ferrari 512 BB	François Migault	Lucien Guitteny	
Luigi Chinetti Snr	Ferrari 512 BB	TBN	TBN	
Pozzi Thomson JMS	Ferrari 512 BB	Jean-Claude Andruet	Spartaco Dini	
Pozzi Thomson JMS	Ferrari 512 BB	Claude Ballot-Lena	Jean-Louis Lafosse	
Dick Barbour Racing	Porsche 935	**Brian Redman**	Bob Bondurant	
Dick Barbour Racing	Porsche 935	Dick Barbour	TBN	
Holly Cars LSA	Porsche 935	TBN	TBN	
Whittington Bros Racing	Porsche 935	Bill Whittington	Don Whittington	Reinhold Jöst
Garage du Bac	BMW 3.5 CSL	Alain Cudini	Pierre Dieudonné	
Charles Ivey Engineering	Porsche Carrera RS	Larry Perkins	**Gordon Spice**	Jay Rulon-Miller
Thierry Perrier	Porsche Carrera	Thierry Perrier	Belliard	Mouetron

Note: British cars and drivers in bold type.

Let battle commence

*— on the most
intriguing
Le Mans in years*

by Peter Windsor

LE MANS 1978 will be a battle of the giants — a straight fight between Porsche and Renault. As a non-championship all-comers race, the outright winner seems likely to come from the Group 6 category (in which Renault have four entries and Porsche three) although the Group 5 Porsche 935/78, so impressive at Silverstone, must be considered to have an outside chance, particularly if the race resembles last year's. The Group 6 class is 13-cars strong, which leaves two Mirage-Renaults, three de Cadenet-Cosworths and the Ibec-Cosworth to fight out the minor placings. All these cars are covered in our review, particularly as four of them happen to be British. In addition, Robin Hamilton will be running a turbocharged version of his spectacular Aston Martin V8 in the GT Prototype category, and hoping for a class win, while famous Porsche entrants like George Loos and Erwin Kremer will be running 935s in Group 5. It is going to be a remarkable Le Mans, the 1978 edition, and *Autocar* will be reporting it in full next week. Meanwhile, peruse the contenders. They are both intriguing and powerful.

Martini Porsche

Porsche have entered three of their 936 models and one 935/78. Two of the 2.1 litre 936s will be fitted with four valves per cylinder and water-cooled heads — the system already race-proven on the 935 — while the third, the Gragg-Haywood car, will be virtually as driven to victory last year. As ever, Porsche have already completed more than enough testing — up to 30 hours without problem with the new 936. This car might be slightly slower in top speed than the bigger-engined, 850 bhp 935, but, even so should be doing over 230 mph on Mulsanne straight. The 936 will also score heavily over the 935 in that it runs for 80 minutes between fuel stops (rather than for the 45 minutes of the smaller tanked-935) which means that it will start with something like a nine-lap advantage.

Dunlop will be providing the tyres for both cars, and report that tyre sizes for the 936s are still something of a question mark. Porsche are keen to use the large 16 in. rear tyres — so that they can run larger brakes — but, if so, this would be a new development for the 936. As we went to press, it looked as though the two new 936s would start with 16 in. rims and the older car on 15s. The 935/78, which could be making its last racing appearance if the Group 5 Championship continues to decline, will be on its familiar, huge, 19 in. rear tyres.

A Porsche win would set two significant records. Dunlop would score their 25th Le Mans victory and Jacky Ickx would have a hat-trick in Porsches, as well as an unprecedented fifth Le Mans win. Ickx and Prescarolo, of course, start with a total of seven wins behind

Two-time winning Group 6 Porsche 936 has been developed over the winter

them; Bob Wollek will be having his first works drive after some excellent performances for the Kromer team, and Gregg and Haywood have between them won four Daytona 24 Hours races.

Car No. 5
Martini Porsche 936 turbo (*Bob Wollek-Jurgen Barth*)
Car No. 6
Martini Porsche 936 turbo (*Jacky Ickx-Henri Pescarolo*)
Car No. 7
Martini Porsche 936 turbo (*Peter Gregg-Hurley Haywood*)
Car No. 43
Martini Porsche 935 turbo (*Rolf Stommelen-Manfred Schurti*)

De Cadenet-Cosworth DFV

Alain de Cadenet's plans were in a state of flux even as we closed for press — which suggests that the team might be less effective this year than in the past. Under the organization of Keith Greene, De Cadenet is running one car for himself and maybe Chris Craft, and this will be the latest Len-Bailey version of the 1977 de Cadenet, featuring weight-saving and a longer chassis. Last year's car will be driven by Peter Lovett and John Cooper, and managed by Adrian Hamilton, while the de Cadenet Lola, which finished third in 1976, will be in the hands of Simon Phillips and John Beasley. Because of engine problems, Phillips and Beasley failed to qualify with this car last year.

Alain de Cadenet's Lola-Cosworth is largely unchanged from that which ran last year

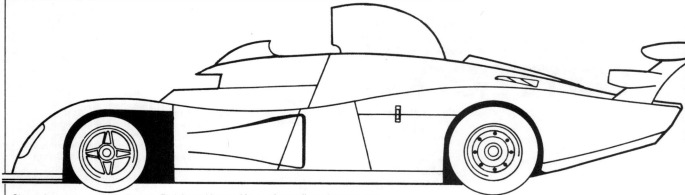

Shape of things to come from Renault. Their latest idea provides an almost all-enveloping cockpit

Renault Sport

To win the race they lost last year, Renault Sport have entered four cars for the 1978 race. Three have the type number A442, as in 1977, but one, recently announced as Renault's "secret weapon", has been named the A443. Complete with its semi-enclosed cockpit, it is depicted in the drawing above.

The A443 has been billed for a top speed of 233 mph — a mere 2 mph slower than that anticipated by Porsche. . . . Like the Porsche, it is of larger engine capacity (2,140 cc compared with the 1,997 cc of the A442 and, again like the latest Porsche 936s, it is fitted with a longer tail. Its wheelbase is thus 6 in. longer than the A442s'. It also runs wider front rims and has a new cockpit surround.

Of the three A442s, one is a B-type, featuring last year's shorter chassis but the revised cockpit bodywork. The other two are as the cars appeared last year. Since last June, the V6 turbocharged engine has been given 30 modifications, from revised valve spring design to the position of the spark plug lead supports. Bench tests have been supplemented by three test sessions at Paul Ricard (2,174 miles and 4,350 miles) and Mid-Ohio (1,864 miles), and a total of nine turbo' engines have been built.

Last year's engine failures centred around piston breakages, so this year's units will be running with more heat-resilient materials and valve springs designed to improve the mechanical and thermal resistance of the exhaust valves. Additionally, the engine's torque has been systematically increased (in concert with lessons learned from formula 1 development and the latest Garrett turbocharger).

Reflecting the renewed importance of Le Mans, the Renault team features no less than five active formula 1 drivers, although Patrick Tambay's participation is dependent on the condition of his injured leg. Because of the Brands Hatch formula 1 outing on 7-8 June, the Renault drivers will be making two trips to England in two days, in that way taking in both Brands and Le Mans practice.

Car No. 1 (Red)
Renault Alpine V6 turbo A443 *(Jean-Pierre Jabouille-Patrick Tambay)*
Car No. 2 (White)
Renault Alpine V6 turbo A442B *(Patrick Depailler-Didier Pironi)*
Car No. 3 (Blue)
Renault Alpine V6 turbo A442 *(Jean-Pierre Jarier-Derek Bell)*
Car No. 4 (yellow)
Renault Alpine V6 turbo A442 *(Jean-Pierre Jausaaud-Guy Frequelin-Jean Ragnotti)*
All fitted with Michelin radial racing tyres.

Grand Touring Cars Inc.

Long-tailed hybrid: British chassis, French engine and American entrant — the GTC Mirage

American exoticar agent, Harley Cluxton, is a again backing a two-car Le Mans team, and is again utilising the combined resources of Mirage and Renault. His engines will be the standard 1.9 litre turbocharged units, but his chassis are very different from last year in that they have been shortened, lowered and narrowed. Such a reduction in frontal area has also necessitated a revised fuel system and oil and water radiator layout. The Mirage-Renault effort will be managed by John Wyer and John Horsman, will be sponsored by Elf, Gitanes and JCB and will use Goodyear tyres.

24-hour testing on the banking at Mid-Ohio has produced excellent results, including a 206 mph top speed, and STC's driver line-up is a strong one.

Car No. 10
Renault-Mirage M9 turbo *(Vern Schuppan-Jacques Laffite)*
Car No. 11
Renault-Mirage M9 turbo *(Sam Posey-Michel Leclere)*

Ibec Hesketh 308LM — Cosworth DFV

Car No. 19 (dark blue)
That's the name that will be on the car, at any rate. When we visited the Ibec team at the Lyncar workshops last week, little remained on the chassis that could accurately be described as Hesketh-derived. Lyncar took over the project only five weeks ago, and in that time have re-designed the front of the monocoque, grafted on a new front suspension layout and revamped the rear of the car. And not because of inter-company rivalry. Upon arrival at Lyncar, the Le Mans Hesketh reeked of a chassis built up around spare, defunct formula 1 parts. Drive-shafts and Hewland gearbox were to formula 1 spec, and thus undersized. The oil tank was too small, and so, too, were the brakes. The turning circle was larger than that allowed in the Le Mans regs.; the front track was too wide for the bodywork.

Credit, then, goes to Lyncar for not only meeting the schedule imposed on them, but for having such an excellent first shake-down run with the car. At Goodwood last week, the revised chassis had a trouble-free run, registering completely normal cooling

Let battle commence

temperatures from radiators mounted in the side of the (original spec. — and very attractive) bodywork.

The Ibec is straightforward in concept, as well it needed to be. But the team is well-composed and experienced, from Lyncar's Martin Selator and Ray Stokoe to chief mechanic, John Anderson. Anderson worked for Alain de Cadenet's Le Mans team and is thus seasoned with the sort of detail information — like pit equipment — that only several Le Mans outfits can provide. Guy Edwards is the right sort of driver for the car in that he is superenthusiastic about the three-year project and also able to think of finishing foremost, while Ian Crob hasn't driven with DFV power before, but is intelligent enough to learn. Reserve driver is the outfit's mentor, Ian Bracey, who unfortunately broke his foot while training for Le Mans last month. Goodyear tyres will be used.

Finishing touches to the Ibec chassis at the Lyncar works

Aston Martin V8 turbo

Car No. 70

This isn't a works entry — although a 1979 Le Mans effort by the Newport Pagnell firm is more than just a dream. Meanwhile, Aston *afficionado*, Robin Hamilton, is making a second attempt to run well at Le Mans — and to do that he at least needs to improve on last year's creditable effort. His 1977 car was built and developed by his own team of mechanics and, despite being new to the event and running an overweight car on a minimal budget, he finished third in class and 17th

GTP outsider. Robin Hamilton's 750 bhp turbocharged Aston Martin V8 on test at Donington last week.

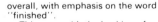

overall, with emphasis on the word ''finished''.

This year, with the backing of Link Systems, the team have high hopes of a GT-P class win. The car is better, the budget is larger. The Aston's engine is now turbocharged and produces around 750 bhp and an estimated top speed of 220 mph, while the braking system, such a problem in 1977, is larger and water-cooled. The car is also lighter and has been fitted with a bigger fuel tank.

An Aston — and British — it is. ''A fearsome beast.'' as Hamilton describes his car, it also is.

Historics

On the Saturday morning before Le Mans' 4.00 pm start, two historic car races will be held, featuring machinery and drivers from Le Mans past — and Stirling Moss, 250F-up. Moss will be driving the JCB car driven with success by William Greene. Jaguar will also be playing a part in the festivities, for not only will there be D-types present but also a 1953 C-type, to be driven on the pace lap by Duncan Hamilton and Tony Rolt. This will mark 25 years since the most significant of the Jaguar Le Mans wins — the one in which disc brakes arrived and the race average speed leapt up by 10 mph.

Les Vingt-Quatre Heures du Mans

Renault victorious at last

The Ragnotti/Frequelin/Dolhem Renault-Alpine A442 finished fourth.

Le Mans (Sarthe) June 10th/11th

THE LE MANS 24 Hours has always been considered as the most important long distance race in the world, right from its inception in 1923. Never has its pre-eminence been more pronounced than this year, however. Held on the weekend of June 10th and 11th, the Automobile Club de L'Ouest's annual test of speed and endurance round the Circuit of the Sarthe was the only long distance race of this season to attract a major, full works effort from such factory teams as still support sports car racing.

Those few works teams – two, to be precise – did the 24 Hours of Le Mans proud. Both Porsche, hoping to complete a hat-trick at Le Mans, and Renault, striving desperately to avenge last year's humiliating defeat, entered four cars each, and there was a strong supporting cast of private and semi-private teams to back them up. Porsche's four cars consisted of three open Gp. 6 machines, labelled 936s, plus the very latest, 3.2-litre 935, the Gp. 5 car that won at Silverstone in May on its maiden outing and the engine of which develops anything between 750 and 850 b.h.p., depending on the setting of its twin turbochargers. Huge yet dramatic looking in its Martini liveried coupe-style bodywork, the 935 was to be driven by Rolf Stommelen and Manfred Schurti.

The 936s were powered by relatively puny 2.1-litre flat-six engines; but, like the 935, two of them had the very latest 12-valve, twin overhead camshaft, water cooled cylinder heads, as well as a separate turbocharger for each bank of cylinders. In this form the 936 motors produced around 580 b.h.p., and they propelled the cars entered for Jacky Ickx/Henri Pescarolo and Bob Wollek/Jurgen Barth. The remaining works Porsche was the 936 that won at Le Mans last year; it still had the older, rather less powerful single turbo engine, and was driven by Hurley Haywood, Peter Gregg and Reinhold Joest.

Against this powerful German onslaught, Renault fielded a quartet of their Alpine V6 sports-racers, although their plans took a knock when Patrick Tambay had to withdraw from the 24 Hours because of fire extinguisher burns suffered in the F2 race at Pau. Tambay's injury caused some hasty rearrangement of cockpit crews in the Renault camp, and in the end Patrick Depailler shared a car with Jean-Pierre Jabouille, Didier Pironi with Jean-Pierre Jaussaud, Jean-Pierre Jarier with Derek Bell,

and French rally star Jean Ragnotti with Guy Frequelin and Jose Dolhem.

The extreme speeds reached on the long straights of Le Mans have always nurtured technical novelties designed to snatch another 10 k.p.h. on Mulsanne or a shade more stability through the notorious kink. This year it was Renault's turn to come up with the most interesting aerodynamic experiment: a perspex windshield that almost completely enclosed the cockpit. In practice the best of the Renaults, a new car called the A443 that was powered by a 540 b.h.p., 2.1-litre engine, attained a staggering 228 m.p.h. on Mulsanne with the new "bubble top" in position. Without the semi-enclosed cockpit, the same car could manage no more than 216 m.p.h. (By way of comparison, the works Porsche 935/78 achieved 227 m.p.h., Ickx was radar trapped at 214 m.p.h. in the quickest of the Porsche 936s, and during the race though not in practice Alain de Cadenet's very special Lola-DFV was unofficially timed at over 220 m.p.h.).

Yet the Renault-Alpine A443 lapped the 13.64 kilometre circuit virtually as quickly without the rooflike "bubble top" as with it, and the drivers were far from happy with it. It made the cockpit hot and claustrophobic, and afforded them reduced visibility at night. Thus, for the race, Jabouille and Depailler used conventional open bodywork for their 2.1-litre engined A443, while Pironi and Jaussaud had the controversial high windshield fitted to their otherwise conventional 2-litre engined A442.

Outside the big budget works teams from Renault and Porsche, variety was the keynote of the entry, although Porsche Turbos and Carreras inevitably accounted for almost a third of the field. But there were plenty of Group 6 sports-racers as well – a pair of turbocharged, Renault V6 propelled Mirage M9s for Vern Schuppan/Jacques Laffite and Michele Leclere/Sam Posey; a trio of Cosworth DFV

powered de Cadenet Lola T380s for Chris Craft and Alain de Cadenet himself, Simon Phillips/Nick Faure/John Beasley, and Bob Evans/John Cooper/Pete Lovett; Ian Bracey's brand new IBEC-Hesketh 308LM, driven in the race by Guy Edwards and Ian Grob; and no fewer than 15 2-litre cars, including the very swift Sauber-BMW of Marc Surer, Eugen Straehl and Harry Blumer, and its main class rival, the BMW (GB) Racing entered works Osella-BMW shared by Tom Walkinshaw, Dieter Quester and Rad Dougall. Among other smaller 2-litre sports-racers were a pair of British entered, Ford FVC powered Lolas and the Chevron-BDG B31 run jointly by Tony Charnell and Robin Smith.

Other entries of special interest included a trio of Peugeot V6 powered WMs in Le Mans' unique "Grand Touring Prototype" class, little French coupes built specifically for the 24 Hours and two of which were turbocharged. For the same category local resident Jean Rondeau had built another DFV engined coupe that he named after himself this year, having lost the Inaltera sponsorship that supported his team in 1976 and '77. One of the old Inalteras was there too, although now a private entry, as were five Ferrari Berlinetta Boxers, the sleek 4.9-litre flat-12 machines looking very purposeful though not, alas, entered by the Maranello factory.

Early in the first practice session, on the Wednesday evening before the race, Jacky Ickx shattered the lap record when he took his Porsche 936 round in 3 min. 27.6 sec., at an average speed of almost 147 m.p.h. That was 3.4 sec. better than the previous best ever lap of the current circuit, set by Arturo Merzario in a 3-litre Alfa Romeo during training for the 1974 race. The following day, on Thursday evening, the Renaults responded, as Depailler set a 3 min. 29.4 sec. lap in the slightly larger engined Alpine A443, still equipped with the semi-enclosed cockpit cover at that stage.

On the Wednesday, Stommelen had achieved 3 min. 30.9 sec. in the Group 5 Porsche 935 which remained third quickest overall, but on the second day of practice the car cooked its engine and holed a piston after being driven to the paddock through slow traffic on public roads. It was a fine, flag waving gesture, but that journey meant the team would have to run in a freshly rebuilt engine during the early stages of the race, preventing Schurti and Stommelen from realising the 935's full potential when it was most needed.

Alongside the Porsche 935 on the second row of the 55 car grid was the 936 of Wollek and Barth, after which came the Pironi/Jaussaud Renault-Alpine, the Gregg/Haywood Porsche 936, the other two Renault A442s, and then the best of the Mirages driven by Vern Schuppan.

How hopes of victory faded for the major British entry: gearbox problems on the De Cadenet-Lola.

When the race began in a rolling start at the traditional hour of four o'clock, Jabouille shot away from the outside of the front row to head a trio of Porsches into the Dunlop Curve. The new Renault was clearly appointed as "hare", for Jabouille completed the first lap a gargantuan 11.6 sec. ahead of the others, led by Ickx and Pironi and then Schurti, Leclere and Ragnotti.

With every lap Jabouille extended his advantage, but the Porsches were immediately in trouble. Both Ickx's 936 and Haywood's similar but older car came into the pits at the end of lap two and again after the fourth tour. The former needed attention to a sticking accelerator linkage and excessive fuel pressure (cured by switching off one of the car's two fuel pumps). The latter also had faulty accelerator linkage, and then returned for its turbocharger boost to be lowered from a wildly high 3 atmospheres to a more normal level of around 20 lb./p.s.i.

Jabouille led the race for almost an hour, but had to stop after 14 laps to refuel and to change the rear tyres. Pironi inherited the lead, returning it to the Jabouille/Depailler car when he himself refuelled and made way for Jaussaud on the 19th lap. Depailler, however, was in the pits again five laps later to report a serious vibration thought to be coming from the front bodywork. Another circuit proved that was not the cause, so he stopped again on lap 25 for a complete change of wheels. This time the problem was solved, but the two stops in consecutive laps dropped the number one Renault to eighth place, and left Jaussaud in a lead that he and his partner Pironi would hold almost without interruption until the seventh hour.

It was shortly after quarter distance that the Jabouille/Depailler Renault-Alpine regained the lead, by which time the Renault works team had annexed a position of crushing dominance, holding the top three places ahead of the works Porsches. Yet in reality their position was not as strong as it looked. Five hours after the start, the fastest Porsche, driven by Ickx and Pescarolo, had broken fifth gear, ensuring a 46 minute delay while the damage was repaired. Before that car had rejoined the race, the slowest of the 936s, the Haywood/Gregg car, required a new turbocharger, costing some 13 minutes while the unit was replaced. So far, so good for Renault. But during the seventh hour Porsche had decided to move Ickx into what was then their best placed car, the 936 of Wollek/Barth lying fourth behind the Renaults. With Ickx at the wheel, the leading Porsche was up to second place by midnight, and Renault's stranglehold no longer looked secure.

The threat to Renault's supremacy intensified when, at three in the morning, the A442 of Jarier and Bell had to be withdrawn with a broken crown wheel and pinion. But six hours later Porsche's challenge fell apart, when the Ickx/Wollek/Barth 936 broke its fifth gear, just as its sister machine had the previous evening. This time only 37 minutes were needed to rebuild the gearbox, but it left Renault firmly first and second again, although their fourth car, the Ragnotti/Frequelin/Dolhem machine, had also lost time because of a stripped gear.

Then at 10 o'clock on Sunday morning came the disaster that Renault team manager Gerard Larrousse must have feared. In an almost exact replica of last year's race, the Jabouille/Depailler Alpine A443 that had led continuously for 11 hours stopped at Mulsanne with a broken engine, a piston having failed.

Now the Renault "with the bubble on top", the semi-enclosed Pironi/Jaussaud car, again inherited the lead. Fortunately for the French team it was still running like a train, with an eight lap advantage over the repaired Porsche of Ickx, Wollek and Barth. It was still going strong six hours later when the chequered flag came down on the yellow and black car to mark Renault's first ever win at Le Mans. Its winning margin had shrunk to five laps, but that was more than enough to be safe, although Pironi was in a state of near collapse from heat exhaustion and actually fainted after crossing the line. Jaussaud was overcome with emotion on the victory rostrum at the realisation struck him that, at the age of 41, he had at long last achieved his life's ambition of winning an important motor race. The Michelin radial shod car had covered a record distance for the current circuit, completing 5,044 kms. in the 24 hours.

The Porsche 936 of Ickx, Wollek and Barth came a solid second, and after its change of turbocharger the Haywood/Gregg/Joest Porsche followed it home third. Hindered towards the end by their car's desire to leap out of fourth gear, Ragnotti, Frequelin, Dolhem and (for a brief late spell) Jabouille steered their A442 to a distant fourth place.

The fortunes of the others had been chequered in the extreme. Many cars had crashed, particularly on Mulsanne. In the worst of many enormous accidents on that five kilometre straight, the quickest of the French WM-Peugeots flattened a great length of guard-rail and broke into three pieces, seriously injuring its driver, Christian Debias. Having taken over the 2-litre class lead during the early hours of Sunday morning, Tony Charnell was incredibly lucky to escape totally unhurt from the wreck of his Chevron, which had hurtled right over the barriers and into the trees beyond after a suspension failure. Initially delayed by electrical problems, the Osella PA6 had fought back into a strong lead of the same class only for Quester to crash at high speed shortly after midnight and cut his face nastily.

In an American entered Porsche 935, Oliver Garretson lost control at the kink on Mulsanne and rolled over and over in an accident that lasted for almost half a mile. And at almost the exact moment that the leading Renault-Alpine retired on Sunday morning, the worst placed works Porsche 936 smashed into the guard rails at Porsche Curve while Jochen Mass was at the wheel. Mass had taken it over on Saturday night when Ickx switched to the car that came second; his progress back up the field had already been reversed as the car refused to give full power or revs. as the night wore on.

Mechanical misfortunes, too, were legion. The Leclere/Posey Mirage was abandoned out on the circuit before darkness fell when its electrical system packed up. The other Mirage, of Schuppan and Laffite, lost hour after hour with alternator failure, throttle linkage failure, gear linkage failure and finally turbocharger failure. Yet it kept going and finished tenth! After reaching seventh place at one point in the early laps, the Craft/de Cadenet Lola successively suffered lost wheel balance weights, major electrical troubles, and then serious problems with both clutch and gearbox, all of which conspired to leave it hobbling into 15th place at the finish; nevertheless it was the first all British team to finish.

The two-year-old de Cadenet Lola of Phillips, Faure and Beasley was excluded after dropping way behind with major gearbox and gear selection difficulties, while last year's de Cadenet car was not even allowed to start. It was excluded by the ACO's somewhat quaint qualifying rules in preference for a slow but French driven Porsche Carrera – even though John Cooper had been equal 18th fastest in practice with the Lola. The new Ibec 308LM ran well between bouts of misfiring, tyre blistering, balance weight losing and miscellaneous electrical faults, until its Hesketh DFV cried enough on Sunday morning, only a few minutes after the team had had to mend a split brake pipe. The Sauber that headed the 2-litre division for the first three hours at least finished, but only after a gearbox strip-down and a long spell of misfiring and overheating.

Most of the Porsche Turbos fell prey to mechanical mishaps, too, with holed pistons very much in fashion among the customer 935s. The works car of Schurti and Stommelen, placed fifth on Sunday morning, limped to the finish with a broken piston seal that consumed oil in vast quantities, though it held together to finish eighth. The Georg Loos entered 935 driven by John Fitzpatrick lost time during the first hour when a hub bearing needed replacement and retired during the second when its engine broke. A little later the Kremer Porsche 935 shared by Englishmen Martin Raymond and Mike Franey and Frenchman "Steve" dropped out for similar reasons.

Avoiding all misadventures, however, Brian Redman brought the Porsche 935 he shared with Americans Dick Barbour and Jon Paul into a fine, class winning fifth place, narrowly beating the similar Kremer car of Californians Jim Busby, Chris Cord and Rick Knoop. In spite of his almost unparalleled endurance racing record elsewhere, this was Redman's first ever finish at Le Mans. For all the many British enthusiasts at the circuit, that was probably the most cheering result of all. –J.C.T.

24 HOURS OF LE MANS

Winners' distance—369 laps, 5,044.53 km.

1st :	D. Pironi/J-P. Jaussaud (2.0 t/c. Renault-Alpine A442) .... (210.19 k.p.h.)	369 laps
2nd :	B. Wollek/J. Barth/J. Ickx (2.1 t/c. Porsche 936/78)*	364 laps
3rd :	H. Haywood/P. Gregg/R. Joest (2.1 t/c. Porsche 936/77)	362 laps
4th :	J. Ragnotti/G. Frequelin/J. Dolhem (2.0 t/c. Renault-Alpine A442)	358 laps
5th :	B. Redman/D. Barbour/J. Paul (3.0 t/c. Porsche 935/77A)*	337 laps
6th :	J. Busby/C. Cord/R. Knoop (3.0 t/c. Porsche 935/77A)*	336 laps
7th :	A. Guarana/P. Gomes/M. Amaral (2.9 t/c. Porsche 935/76A)	329 laps
8th :	M. Schurti/R. Stommelen (3.2 t/c. Porsche 935/78)	326 laps
9th :	B. Darniche/J. Rondeau/J. Haran (3.0 Rondeau DFV M378)*	294 laps
10th :	V. Schuppan/J. Laffite/S. Posey (2.0 t/c. Mirage-Renault M9)	293 laps
11th :	M. Pignard/L. Rossiaud/L. Ferrier (2.0 Chevron-Chrysler B36)*	284 laps
12th :	A-C. Verney/X. Lapeyre/F. Servanin (3.0 Porsche Carrera)*	279 laps
13th :	A. Chevalley/F. Trisconi (3.0 Inaltera DFV)	279 laps
14th :	G. Spice/L. Perkins/J. Rulon-Miller (3.0 Porsche Carrera RS)	278 laps
15th :	C. Craft/A. de Cadenet (3.0 De Cadenet-Lola DFV T380)	273 laps
16th :	F. Migault/L. Guitteny/F. Vetsch (4.9 Ferrari 512 Berlinetta Boxer)	262 laps
17th :	C. Bussi/"Segolen"/J-C. Briavoine (3.0 t/c. Porsche 934)	259 laps
18th :	E. Straehl/M. Surer/H. Blumer (2.0 Sauber-BMW C5)	257 laps
19th :	S. Plastina/M. Luini/J-D. Grandjean (2.0 Cheetah-BDG G601)	250 laps
20th :	G. Bourdillat/A. Bernard/L. Favresse (3.0 Porsche Carrera)	241 laps
21st :	B. Sotty/G. Cuynet/J-C. Dutrey (2.0 Lola-BDG T294/6)	238 laps
22nd :	M. Elkoubi/P. Yver/P. Streiff (2.0 Lola-BDG T296)	232 laps
23rd :	M. Lateste/J-F. Auboiron/D. Lacaud (2.0 Lola-BMW T297)	217 laps
24th :	J. Winter/D. Schornstein/P. Gurdjian (3.0 t/c. Porsche 935/76A)	182 laps

*Class winners

Fastest Lap: J-P. Jabouille (2.1 t/c. Renault-Alpine A443) on lap 226 in 3 min. 34.2 sec. (229.24 k.p.h.)

55 starters—24 finishers.

Renault makes the grade

The pressure from Porsche didn't rattle Pironi and Jaussaud, who stayed cool and made sure that Renault's seven-figure gamble paid off — by five laps and at record speed. Mike Doodson reports from Le Mans, photography by Maurice Rowe

USING Porsche's own weapons — immaculate preparation and a refusal to leave anything to chance, at whatever the cost — the Régie Renault clobbered its German rival at Le Mans on Sunday with a flag-to-flag victory which blotted out the humiliation suffered by the French team in last year's race. It is no good asking what might have happened if Renault's million-pound investment had not paid off, for as the race wore on it was plain that failure formed no part of their plan.

The task of holding off Porsche fell in the end on Renault's most interesting pair of drivers, a combination of age and experience which owed more to similiar physical shape than any amalgamation of temperament. But Didier Pironi (26) and Jean-Pierre Jaussaud (41) — thrown together when Patrick Tambay's burned leg forced him to withdraw — complemented each other perfectly.

Driving Renault number 2, a developed "B" version with slightly altered bodywork from last year's A442, they were content to follow the senior Renault pairing of GP "regulars" Jean-Pierre Jabouille and

Patrick Depailler in the brand new A443 Alpine-Renault. Although it raced without its bubble canopy (too hot and difficult to see out of), the A443's slightly larger, more powerful V6 engine and different bodywork enabled Depailler/Jabouille to command the race from the moment when Jabouille hustled past Jacky Ickx Martini Porsche and in front of 54 others even before the rolling start had been flagged away.

On practice form, Ickx should have been able to retaliate instantly. The 1978 version of the Martini Porsche 936 which he was driving is a good 80 horsepower stronger than the 510 bhp Renault, and only 15 kilos heavier: on Wednesday he had hurled it round the 13.64 km track in a record 3m 27.6s, and not even a determined Depailler with *carte blanche* from Renault comps boss Gérard Larrousse to beat it was able to get closer than 3m 28.4s.

Nevertheless, at the end of one lap, Jabouille was already getting away from Ickx, and when the Porsche made for its pit next time round there were three Renaults, numbered 1-2-3, holding their number order (Jabouille, Pironi,

Jarier) so cheekily that it would have annoyed the Porsche men if they hadn't got their heads inside Ickx's engine compartment trying to sort out a fuel pressure problem.

Victims of their own success, Porsche were looking sick. "After the Porsche victories of 1976 and 1977, it would be wrong to expect a hat-trick this year," had said team manager Jantke. "For reasons of capacity and racing budget, our extent of testing has had to be kept smaller than that of race favourites Renault and Mirage. We are expecting an exciting race, but we know

it's not going to be an easy one."

After two stops with the same problem (the fuel pressure was too high, and a pump had to be disconnected), Ickx was back in 14th place, and his French team mate Bob Wollek — a capable rather than a great driver — was holding to his fixed lap time in 3rd place behind the leading pair. But Porsche had suffered a blow to their image, for another early stop had been made by their number 3 pair, Americans Gregg and Haywood, with throttles jammed by the dust on the warm-up.

Looking for an unprecedented fifth Le Mans win, Ickx was not about to give up, but even though delays with his own car later caused him to be switched into the Wollek/Barth 936, the highest he could get with it was 2nd place before that, too, succumbed to the problems which had dropped Ickx back before. Fifth gear broke up (it was a new part, adapted for the more powerful twin turbo '78 version of the 936) and there was a 36 minute delay to replace it while the turbos themselves were removed to provide access to the transmission.

Renault's darkest moment came on Sunday morning, when even Larrousse must have started to get an uncomfortable feeling as hitherto reliable cars started to give trouble.

First of the Renault problems came when one of the two back-up Mirages (Schuppan/Leclère) stopped before dark on Saturday with electrical failure. Laffite brought in the Mirage that he was sharing with Schuppan for a new alternator; it set fire to the wiring as soon as the engine was started, and effectively Renault was not now without its back-up team.

Then one of the works cars was suddenly in trouble: at 3 am Derek Bell's A442 stopped on the Mulsanne straight with a broken final drive, dropping out of a 3rd place which he and Jarier had found uncomfortable to maintain because the handling had been so awful ("we didn't spend enough time sorting it out in practice," he confessed).

If Jabouille was worried about this failure, he didn't show it. At 7 am he set a new circuit record, and by 9 am the A443 was 25 miles ahead of Pironi/Jaussaud, lapping superbly when the amateur idiots could be persuaded to look in their mirrors.

Then, without any warning, Depailler dribbled to a halt at Mulsanne in a cloud of smoke and pulled in under the noses of the signallers there as the scent of breakfast wafted from their tents and motorhomes. Depailler didn't notice the aroma: he was sniffing out cooked engine or gearbox, and calling up his pit on the car's on-board radio. But the problem (officially described as "gearbox jammed") was more than the little tool kit could fix, and soon the marshals were pushing the yellow Alpine away.

Now it was Jaussaud and Pironi against the Porsches, for Ickx had helped to bring the Wollek/Barth

twin-turbo 936 into 2nd place behind the number 2 Alpine, and the '77-spec single-turbo version of Americans Gregg and Haywood, which hadn't had the 5th gear problem, lay 4th ahead of Renault's "reserve" Alpine, in the hands of rallymen Guy Frequelin and Jean Ragnotti with Jose Dolhem, had already been delayed when 3rd gear had broken while Depailler slipped off to bed.

For six hours more, the leading order was not to change. Larrousse did not permit his two leading driv-

Above: Mulsanne, Sunday morning and the French-entered, Brazilian driven Porsche 935 of Gomes/Guarana/ Amaral chases Rondeau's class-winining GTP to Indianapolis corner. Right: Brian Redman on his way to the Group 5 class win with Dick Barbour

ers to react against some hard work by Ickx and his mates, who whittled away until the Alpine's nine-lap lead was down to five. In a boring finish to what had promised to be a splendid scrap, Renault stayed ahead without having to do anymore than keep its corporate cool and make sure that the drivers were well informed.

In the classes, however, there was action like the battle between the Porsche factory and its customers

Left: Gregg in the 3rd-place Porsche 936. Below: watched carefully by a marshal, Depailler unsuccessfully tries to revive the Alpine A443 at Mulsanne with advice from a Renault mechanic

for the Group 5 "Silhouette" honours. To the great satisfaction of the customers, the Martini 935 "Moby Dick" which had won at Silverstone was soon in trouble. It had fallen foul of scrutineers earlier in the week ("Group 5½," said one of them) and with Stommelen/Schürti driving had kept going fast enough, despite stops every 40 minutes for fuel, to lead the class. Later it was dropped way back by a mysterious misfire and an oil leak which could only just be satisfied by a sumpful of fresh oil every 16 laps, the minimum permitted by the rules.

The Group 5 battle lost John Fitzpatrick — all the way back from a race in Australia— when his Kremer entry burned a piston, leaving Brian Redman (sharing with corpulent Californian entrant Dick Barbour) to get the decision only after a long struggle with the third and last Kremer entry of four Americans.

As usual, the under 2-litre cars proved to be too fragile for such a long race. Fastest in practice had been the Italian works-prepared Osella-BMW entered by BMW (GB)and Tolemans Delivery Service for Walkinshaw/Dougall/Quester, but some unscheduled early pit stops allowed the unusual Swiss-built Sauber-BMW of top F2 driver Marc Surer to get well away.

Quester was lucky to walk away from the wreck of the Osella when it spun four times at the 150 mph Mulsanne "kink", allegedly when

one of its Pirelli tyres failed, and hit the rails. Although the Sauber staggered to the finish on three cylinders, the class was eventually won by a French-driven Chevron with one of the unusual (and hitherto unreliable) ROC Chrysler-based racing engines.

In the "GT Prototype" class developed by the AC de l'Ouest especially for Le Mans, a major disappointment was the withdrawal of the Hamilton Preece Aston Martin turbo, which had not been tested sufficiently. French designer Jean Rondeau has built a new Cosworth-engined 3-litre coupe bearing his own name but looking very similiar to the Inaltéras which he designed for the new GTP class in 1976, and he proceeded to have a good battle with one of his old cars, which have now passed into other hands.

For a while, they were joined by another French-built coupé, the attractive Peugeot V6-engined WMs, two of which were turbocharged. But after a serious accident involving one of the WM drivers on Sunday morning, the surviving example was however withdrawn.

Thus Rondeau, who was sharing the driving of his car with three-time European rally champion Bernard Darniche, again won the GTP category. Last year his two Inaltéras finished, and now a finish for his new car indicates that his GTP cars are reliable even if the GTP weight and wing rules prevent them from matching the faster Porsche turbos in Groups 4 and 5.

A major disappointment in GTP — which attracted a healthy 15 entries this year — was the poor showing of the five Ferrari Boxer BBs. Two of these, entered by French Ferrari importer Charles Pozzi, had been breathed on at Maranello, while two more were

Above: Ferrari's Strongest entry at Le Mans since 1972 included two works-prepared Boxers from Pozzi. Transmission proved to be a problem (this is Andruet/Ballot-Lena/Dini). Below: once again the best-placed Britons, de Cadenet and Craft scraped home 15th after cooking a gearbox

The tension . . . and the tears: 24 hours of emotion

For one little man, the sound of a **brisk "Marseillaise"** booming across the Le Mans track to mark the end of 24 hypertense hours was to prove too much. **Jean-Pierre Jaussaud** simply sank his head in his hands and wept tears which touched even the hearts of the screaming fans who had invaded the track below the victory balcony. Jaussaud with his big-hearted grin and gendarme's moustache has long been a popular driver, but one who despite some splendid races (including a memorable but all-too-brief rush into the lead with one of **Ken Tyrrell's** Matra F2 cars at Crystal Palace in '68) has never been able to follow so many of his countrymen into F1. Now, at 41, there cannot be much left for him in the sport except the happy memory of a race in which — when he was hurriedly promoted to take over **Tambay's** place — he can hardly have expected to have brought victory alongside Renault's youngest driver, 26 year old **Didier Pironi.** Such is the luck at Le Mans . . . Despite a completely dry 24 hours, this year's Le Mans brought a **record crop of accidents,** many of them when cars left the track at horrendous speeds along the Mulsanne straight. In two of the incidents, cars actually vaulted the guardrails, and one driver, French hillclimb champion **Christian Debias,** was badly injured. His turbocharged WMP-Peugeot coupe, running in the GT Prototype "Le Mans" class, ran along the

top of the guardrail and broke up in the trees beyond on Sunday morning. Debias was taken by helicopter to hospital in Tours with **severe head injuries:** his team immediately withdrew its second car . . . Luckier after a no less spectacular shunt, in the same straight, was Scotsman **Tony Charnell,** whose 2-litre Lola also went flying into the trees, scattering everything attached to the chassis, including the engine, as it went. Charnell found himself sitting unhurt in the wreck . . . reluctant Le Mans racer **Jochen Mass,** who had been hoping not to be called into the Martini-Porsche team, lost his "reserve" status on Friday evening when he was nominated to join **Henri Pescarolo** in the second twin-turbo 936 prototype which had been delayed in Ickx' hands after **fuel injection** and **gearbox troubles.** By Sunday morning, Mass and "Pesca" had recovered most of the 15 laps the car had spent in the pits and were up to 6th, but then Mass went missing and **Chris Craft** brought back stories of a big crash on the new section of the circuit before the pits. The 600 horsepower Porsche had all but ploughed its way between the guardrails, destroying its rear chassis section and leaving two straight black lines on the tarmac. Mass could not suggest a cause for the incident . . . Lancastrian hero **Brian Redman** returned to Le Mans for what was to be only his second race of 1978 (he

won at Sebring in March) and added a Group 5 class win to an impressive record which is increasing in spite of a resolve to retire following the serious head and other injuries when his Can-Am Lola flipped in Canada a year ago. "I always said I'd never become one of those drivers who went slowly down the other side of the hill," said Brian half-seriously before the 24 hours, in spite of which he has agreed to share a Group 1 VW Scirocco saloon with Jacky Ickx in the Spa 24 hours at Francorchamps, next month . . . Britons did not fare well at Le Mans this year. Our best hope, Sussex farmer **Derek Ball,** held 2nd place in the works Alpine he was sharing with **Jean-Pierre Jarler** for nine hours until transmission problems culminating in final drive failure forced them out at 3 o'clock in the morning . . . Somehow **Alain de Cadenet** and **Chris Craft** managed to finish in the brand new de Cadenet-Lola which had been built at the very last minute. The car started the race with known clutch linkage problems, had to stop with electrical trouble during the night, and only managed to crawl across the line in 15th place after some heroic asbestos-hands work in the pits to replace red-hot gearbox internals . . . Last year's de Cadenet/Lola, very smartly turned out in red for a team which included **Simon Phillips** and **Nick Faure,** had already retired with similar troubles after an excellent run at the

beginning of the race. The car was briefly driven by one time top club racee **Martin Raymond,** who had diplomatically explained to a large party of supporters from Fison's, his sponsors, why the failure of a piston in his German Kremer-prepared Porsche 935 after only a couple of hours could hardly be blamed on Herr Kremer . . . The much-trumpeted **Ibec-Hesketh** retired on Sunday morning when its Cosworth engine failed. Disappearing wheel weights and blistered Goodyears hampered its early progress, but a pleasant surprise for the team was the driving of 25 year old London Ian Grob, who proved faster than team mates Guy Edwards and Ian Bracey and did not slow up noticeably even after his brakes had twice failed at Mulsanne . . . Brands Hatch PR lady **Juliette Slaughter** shared a 2-litre Lola with Dorset entrant **Tony Birchenough** and two of his friends until its engine failed on Sunday morning. "A very silly race" was her verdict on Le Mans, though she did not need the gearshift diagram which an Italian team manager had to produce for a couple of his (happily non-qualified) lady drivers in practice . . . MOTOR contributor **Bob Constanduros** was persuaded to help out with the English-language commentary at intervals in **Jean-Charles Laurens'** incredible 24 hour French information service. Bob's knowledge was appreciated by the British contingent.

sent by New York Ferrari distributor Luigi Chinetti. Transmission problems kept most of them in the pits for too long, but even when they were running they didn't look as impressive as one has come to expect of Ferraris at Le Mans.

It is on the GTP cars that the AC de l'Ouest is relying to keep its race alive and well in future years, perhaps when major manufacturers like Renault and Porsche have moved on to different fields (F1 and Indy respectively, it's rumoured), but it is difficult to see it proving a major public attraction.

Already the club is pleading poverty. This year they were required by the local authority to employ policemen and firemen to a total value of over 1 million francs (£125,000). Whatever Renault and Porsche decide about a possible renewal of this year's battle (and the chances are that they won't be at the Sarthe in '79), that's too much money to spend on controlling a crowd which may never again go to see a race which is as important as this year's Le Mans was to Renault.

Result

46th Grand Prix d'Endurance
Le Mans — 10/11 June
1 Renault-Alpine A442B turbo (Pironi-Jaussaud), 369 laps in 23 hrs 55 m 17.9 s (131 mph);
2 Martini-Porsche 936 Turbo (Ickx-Wollek-Barth), 364 laps;
3 Martini-Porsche 936 turbo (Gregg-Heywood), 362 laps;
4 Renault-Alpine A442A turbo (Fréquelin-Ragnotti-Dolhem), 358 laps;
5 Porsche 935 turbo (Redman-Barbour), 337 laps;
6 Porsche 935 turbo (Busby-Gord-Knoop), 336 laps;
7 Porsche 935 turbo (Guaranã-Gomes-Amaral), 329 laps;
8 Martini-Porsche 935 turbo (Stommelen-Schurti), 326 laps;
9 Rondeau M378-DFV (Rondeau/Darniche/Haran), 294 laps;
10 GTC Mirage-Renault M9 turbo (Schuppan-Laffite), 293 laps.

Fastest lap: Jean-Pierre Jabouille (Renault-Alpine A443 turbo), on lap 226, in 3 m 34.02 s (142.45 mph), new circuit record

Class winners: Group 6 —Renault-Alpine A442B turbo (Pironi-Jaussaud); Group 6 under 2 litres — Chevron-ROC Chrysler (Pignard/Rossiaud-Ferrier), 284 laps; Group 5 — Porsche 935 (Redman-Barbour); Group 4 GT — Porsche Carrera (Lapèyre-Servanin-Mlle Verney), 279 laps; GT Prototype "Le Mans" — Rondeau M378-DFV (Rondeau-Darniche-Haran)

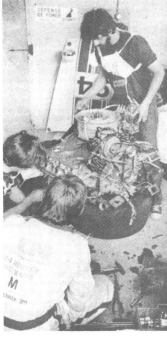

Above: time eventually ran out for this Porsche crew trying to fix an engine, but the de Cadenet team (under Keith Greene, top right) broke records to get this jigsaw puzzle of gears back together in time to take the flag. Below: Mass' bent Porsche 936 after its crash (note the guardrails). Below right: race-winning Renault V6 turbo ready for fitting

12th time lucky Moss

He shouldn't really have been allowed to race a single-seater Maserati, but who cared? Fifteen years after his last major accident, and after 11 unsuccessful attempts to win Le Mans, Stirling Moss came back to win a thrilling half-hour Historic race on Saturday with his JCB entered 250F. He is seen (left, centre) with 2nd man Willie Green and 3rd man Martin Morris, who both drove Jaguar D-types

Le Mans 1978

The winning Pironi/Jassaud Renault about to enter Tertre Rouge.

of doing the same before breaking and giving in to the Porsches. Some critics even argued that Renault shouldn't try Le Mans this year, concentrating on Formula 1 instead, but the Alpines went back and they won. The car which finished 1st was one of the familiar 500-bhp, 2.0-liter turbocharged A442s in long-tail Le Mans trim, taking the lead during the 19th hour when the new A443 blew its 540-bhp, 2.1-liter turbo engine on the Mulsanne Straight. The winning car did borrow a bit from the A443, more specifically the front end, which included a plexiglass windscreen that was almost a complete roof, leaving openings only at the very top and in front for ventilation and vision. Patrick Depailler and Jean-Pierre Jabouille found that cover made them overly warm and caused weird reflections at night, problems that hadn't been solved because Renault was trying to keep the new car secret and hadn't extensively tested it. The pair of Grand Prix drivers appealed to Renault Team Manager Gerard Larrousse, and he allowed them to run with a normal open cockpit and gave the more aerodynamic design to Jassaud and Pironi.

Renault's greatest challenge came, of course, from Porsche, which entered three 936s and their incredible 3.3-liter, 750-bhp 935/78 coupe. While all three 936s looked identical, two were full 1978 models with twin turbos, two camshafts per water-cooled head and 580 bhp, while the third, for American drivers Hurley Haywood and Peter Gregg, was more a 1977 model with a single turbo, one cam for each air-cooled cylinder head and less horsepower. The 935 is an astounding rule-bender which, in the hands of Rolf Stommelen, was 3rd fastest qualifier overall and second fastest on Mulsanne, hitting 221 mph, the Alpine A443 managing 228 mph.

Considering the potential of the Porsches, you can imagine everyone's shock when both Jacky Ickx and Hurley Haywood stopped on the 2nd lap of the race because of sticking throttles in their 936s. They went out and a few laps later both were back in again with problems. So it went for the Porsches, the two newer 936s needing new 5th gears and one eventually being stuffed by Jochen Mass. The "Big Bertha" 935/78 started slowly on a brand new engine and suffered various problems during the 24 hours, finally finishing 8th.

Renault's backup team of Harley

I T WAS HALF-WAY through the playing of *Le Marseillaise* to celebrate the French victory at Le Mans this year that 43-year-old co-winner Jean-Pierre Jassaud broke into tears. On the elevated winner's platform at the start-finish line, Jassaud, who shared the driving with Didier Pironi, just couldn't hold the emotion back any longer and he cried, bringing cheers from his countrymen. Now if that all sounds a bit corny to you, first, you aren't much of a romantic and, second, you don't appreciate just what winning the 24-hour event means to the French.

Matra had its wins on the Sarthe circuit in 1972, 1973 and 1974 and last year a Renault-Alpine got within a few hours

Before the start, the Busby/Cord/Knoop Group 5-winning Porsche showed its true colors.

frustrated and the car finished 10th.

Though the most talked about honors went to the French, a number of Americans deserve a great deal of credit for their efforts. Gregg and Haywood finished 3rd in their 936, teamed with Reinhold Joest. Auto dealer Dick Barbour and John Paul were matched with Britain's Brian Redman in a twin-turbo Porsche 935/77A and had the distinction of being not only 5th, but also the first privately owned finisher and winner of the special IMSA class. Just behind them in 6th and winning in Group 5 were Americans Jim Busby, Chris Cord and Fred Knoop driving a similar 935, their position behind the Barbour car being set only in the final few hours. The Whittington brothers, Dick and Bill, had their 935 well positioned early on, but had to stop for four hours in the pits to virtually rebuild half the car's engine after it suffered from a common disease

racing, the former being the creator of the Monterey historic races and the latter one of the quicker competitors in his Cooper Monaco. Last year, Akin was competing in a vintage car event at Sebring and got to wondering if he and Earle couldn't hold their own in the more contemporary cars. So they discussed it and struck a deal to buy George Dyer's old RSR and run it in the long-distance races in 1978. They finished 6th at Daytona, 5th at Sebring and 5th again at Talladega and before they knew it they were top competitors for the FIA's World Challenge for Endurance Drivers. After Talladega, Barbour suggested they might like to share his second car with Garrettson and, so, almost by accident, they were at Le Mans.

"I had to learn to stop looking at the road signs and thinking that I'd only read about this place before," Earle said. "Also, this is less gentlemanly and more

After 2nd-place finishes in 1976 and 1977, Harley Cluxton's Mirages had problems this year.

Cluxton's Phoenix-based Renault-Mirage M9s got to Le Mans and immediately had severe handling problems they hadn't encountered in earlier high-speed testing. They eventually got most of the bugs sorted out, but used valuable practice time doing so. The new M9s were down in 9th and 12th during qualifying, but promised a top five finish to complement the 2nds they managed the last two years. Then one car suffered an alternator problem early on, stranding driver Michel Leclere on the course, and keeping R&T contributing editor Sam Posey from his stint in the car. The same problem cropped up in the Jacques Laffite/Vern Schuppan Mirage and while they managed to get that fixed and make an excellent drive back through the pack during the night, a variety of problems early Sunday morning kept the team very

among 935s at Le Mans, a holed piston; they got the car underway again, but later crashed.

Brad Frissell's IMSA Monza, decked out in the bright colors of Wynn's International, was noisy and spectacular and qualified in 26th spot, which may not sound too impressive unless you know 56 cars started in the race. A favorite of the fans, the Chevy, was in 18th spot by lap 8, but suffered from a leaking transmission seal and was withdrawn later when the block cracked. Luigi Chinetti entered one of the five Ferrari 512 Boxers in the race (Gregg Young was one of his drivers), all of which sounded and looked better than they ran, with only one Boxer finishing and that in 16th position.

Then there is the story of Steve Earle, Bob Akin and Bob Garrettson. Earle and Akin are really graduates of vintage car

race oriented than in the U.S., so we had to learn to drive smoothly and give the other drivers plenty of room." As Akin explained it, their racing has been a policy of no dicing, keeping a steady pace and minimizing unnecessary pit stops. If they could just continue that, they felt they could manage a good final position. It sounded to be quite an awakening for the pair of gentlemen drivers, a matter of, "Well, here we are . . ." All that ended, unfortunately, around 4:00 a.m. when Garrettson made a mistake at the kink on Mulsanne at close to 200 mph and wrapped the 935-bodied RSR into a little ball, happily without injury.

Overall it was an interesting Le Mans, with just enough tension near the end, everyone wondering if the Renault would last to the checker. It did and the home crowd loved it.—*John Lamm*

Jean-Pierre Jaussaud and Didier Pironi brought victory home to France for the first time since 1974 with a record-breaking win in the Alpine-Renault A442B.

Renaults reign

Jaussaud/Pironi win at record speed for France—Porsches never lead after early delays but finish second and third—Another Alpine-Renault fourth—Redman/Barbour fifth in best-placed Porsche 935—British prototypes and Mirage-Renaults fail—Report: BOB CONSTANDUROS—Photography: JEFF BLOXHAM.

Soon after four o'clock last Sunday the *Marseillaise* was played at Le Mans for the first time since 1974, and Jean-Pierre Jaussaud broke down on the victory balcony, to the applause of a wildly ecstatic crowd. It was a perfect afternoon for the French. The veteran 41-year-old Jaussaud, who must have all but given up hope ever of winning a race of this importance during a career which must surely be approaching its end, had partnered the 26-year-old *comingman* Didier Pironi to a famous victory for Renault, Elf and Michelin.

The long-awaited Renault/Porsche duel lasted throughout the 24 Hours, but the rivalry was never as intense as had been expected. The Martini-Porsche team was in trouble from the start, with two of their cars in the pits as early as the second lap. Thereafter the Renault-powered Alpine cars always had the upper hand. After leading for most of the first six hours, the winning Elf-backed car of Jaussaud/Pironi was always in the first four and moved into the lead when its sister car, crewed by Jean-Pierre Jabouille/Patrick Depailler, went out with an engine failure during the 19th hour. Their lead of seven laps over the second-placed Porsche 936, driven by Jacky Ickx/Bob Wollek/Jurgen Barth, was reduced only to five laps by the end of another gruelling Le Mans.

Ickx joined his team-mates when his own 936, co-driven by Henri Pescarolo, was seriously delayed in the pits, and this car was later crashed out of the event by Jochen Mass. The other works Porsche Group 6 car finished third in the hands of

Hurley Haywood/Peter Gregg/Reinhold Jöst, having also been delayed.

The Alpine-Renault of Derek Bell/Jean-Pierre Jarier having dropped out with broken transmission, the fourth works car driven by Jean Ragnotti/Guy Frequelin/Jean-Pierre Jabouille finished fourth behind the two Porsches. Brian Redman, driving a new Porsche 935/77A in the IMSA class with Dick Barbour, drove an exceptionally fine race to finish fifth overall ahead of three more G5-type Porsches. An engine problem afflicted the works Porsche G5 car and dropped it to an eighth place finish after, as had been predicted, it had proved to be one of the fastest cars on the track.

Harley Cluxton's Mirage-Renault team suffered a series of setbacks which resulted in a tenth place finish for Vern Schuppan/Jacques Laffite after the second Gitanes-backed machine, that of Michel Leclere/Sam Posey, had retired with an electrical failure.

The British 3-litre prototypes failed this year, neither of the De Cadenet Lolas which made the start featuring, and the new Ibec-Hesketh finally dropping out with a broken engine after all kinds of problems. The 2-litre G6 category was being led by the British-entered Mogil Motors Chevron when Tony Charnell had a terrifying accident on the Mulsanne Straight, from which he emerged completely unscathed; the class was won by a French driven Chevron-Simca, while the DFV-powered French Rondeau car won the GTP class and finished ninth overall.

ENTRY

Le Mans 1978: the great race, the long-awaited battle between Renault and Porsche. The preparations were long and exhaustive, tracing every little problem, test circuits, days in the wind tunnels, on the motorways of Europe, trying to extract that extra top speed for the Mulsanne Straight.

Mulsanne is what Le Mans is all about. The cars have to be fast and stable on the straight. Henri Pescarolo, driving a works Martini-Porsche 936 with Jacky Ickx, summed up the essential problem of all the teams: "We have handling problems, but when you're trying to make a car fast for a long straight like Mulsanne, then it doesn't go around corners very well. The straight takes priority here over everything else. An extra ten miles an hour over 5.6 kilometres makes a lot of difference to your lap time!"

Le Mans starts early, weeks—even months—before the cars finally arrive at the circuit. And these days the efforts of the factory teams seem to be bigger than ever. Even the privateers are spending more money now on their outings to the Sarthe area of France. From the preceding Friday to the first day of practice on the Wednesday, the paddock begins to fill up; this year, the Le Mans paddock seemed finally to have outgrown itself for, prior to Wednesday's six-hour session, the teams had a lot of trouble fitting themselves into the tarmac area behind the pits. Huge transporters were squeezed between caravans and private cars. Jurgen Barth tried to arrange the entire Porsche team, having to kick out one team from their space; these in turn, had to move on to another's. Motor homes blocked the road, awnings resting on one another, vehicles lapped the paddock trying to find some space, and then competing cars arrived from their garages nearby only to find no space to park. The ultimate threat to move on was a fork-lift truck; if you weren't in the right place, in moved this machine, and bodily moved the offending car, motor home or van. Its threat became greater when it dropped a Renault 5 from about eight feet; and damaged a Ferrari!

Finally the teams found their slots, out came the cars, and the final preparations began. Regie Renault again had their enclosure at the bottom of the paddock. Under Gérard Larrousse, the Renault-Elf attack was naturally well patronised by the French. With their World Cup football team out of the contest, the national pride was directed towards the yellow cars. Larrousse's team of drivers was strong. Running at number one were Jean-Pierre Jabouille/ Patrick Depailler in a new Alpine-Renault A443. Long-tailed for the Mulsanne Straight, with a perspex cockpit cover that all but made the car enclosed, it was the flagship of the French effort. It had a new 2.1-litre single-turbo engine which was fractionally bigger than their other 2-litre engines, and the bodywork stretched far behind the wheels, super-slippery for that straight. Jean-Pierre Jaussaud/Didier Pironi had the same bodywork, but a 2-litre engine, and this car named an A442B; the other two works cars, those of Jean-Pierre Jarier/Derek Bell and Guy Frequelin/ Jean Ragnotti/José Dolhem, were A442A cars, fairly similar to last year's 442s. These were the cars on which the hopes of Renault, Michelin and France rested.

Grand Touring Cars of Phoenix, Arizona, were also upholding French honour, as they did last year. The two revised M9 Mirages now had long tailwork, and were also using the 1997cc turbo engine. The driver line-up made use of Frenchmen, too: Australian Vern Schuppan was joined by Jacques Laffite, and Michel Leclere shared with the USA's Sam Posey.

The French, naturally, had their 'reserves.' Jean Rondeau, the man who built the Inalteras, had designed a new car, again round the Ford-Cosworth DFV engine, and had sponsorship from SKF Bearings; his co-driver was rally man Bernard Darniche. Of course, the WM team again brought a new car, complete with a turbocharged Peugeot engine, as well as the cars built for the last two 24-hour races. Then there were the French-entered Ferrari Boxers, built up with a lot of help from the factory. The French concessionaire Charles Pozzi was running two cars, with Jean-Claude Andruet/Spartaco Dini driving one, and Claude Ballot-Lena/Jean-Louis Lafosse the other. Ecurie Grand Competition Car built up another for François Migault/Lucien Guitteny. After last year's showing, one had little hope for the Boxers, but these cars proved to be rather more competitive than before.

Naturally, there were a fair number of 2-litre cars from the French. As well as various privateers, there were the three Racing Organisation Course Chevrons, complete with Simca-Chrysler engines, and a two-car Lola team from Pronuptia, who make wedding and maternity outfits. The French, then, had a fair sprinkling of drivers throughout the classes.

At the head of the field, though, the rivalry was intense. Larrousse's opposing Brigadeer was Manfred Jantke of Martini-Porsche. His reply to the four Alpine-Renaults was a three-car works team of Porsche 936s, plus the Porsche 935/78 seen at Silverstone. The new 2.1 flat-six engine from Porsche, with four valves per cylinder and water-cooled head, has been much publicised, and this design was in use on three of the cars: those of Pescarolo/Ickx, Barth/Bob Wollek, and the 3.2-litre 935 for Rolf Stommelen/ Manfred Schurti. Hurley Haywood, co-winner with Barth and Ickx last year, was sharing a two-valve 936, last year's car, with fellow-American Peter Gregg. While these superb cars, in the red, white and blue of Martini, were naturally the spearhead of the effort, Porsche had many, many more models to rely on. Another seven 935 models completely dominated the Group 5 class, five 934s and a brace of Carreras filled the Group 4 class, and another couple of 935s and a Carrera contested the IMSA class.

The main Porsche Group 5 effort was in the hands of the works team, naturally, but there were twin-turbocharged 935s from several prominent German teams. Georg Loos finally only brought one car, to be driven by John Fitzpatrick/Toine Hezemans/Klaus Ludwig. The Kremer team still had their two renting drivers, Dieter Schornstein and John Winter, in one of their cars, but Fisons Agricole were sponsoring one of the 935s for Martin Raymond. With him were 'Steve' and Mike Franey, the latter sponsored by Road & Racing Accessories. Jim Busby/Chris Cord/Fred Knoop were in the third Kremer 935, and the American Whittington brothers, Bill and Don, hired Reinhold Jöst's 935.

The English always seem to be the underdogs at Le Mans these days. But they had four cars in the over 2000cc class, challenging the might of Porsche and Renault. 'Made in Britain' was the only livery in practice on Alain de Cadenet's new John Thompson built Lola, which he shared as usual with Chris Craft. Once again, it was turned out in British Racing Green, and was powered by a Nicholson DFV, this year a unit developing 460bhp in an all-out effort to keep with the turbo cars. De Cadenet's 1977 Lola was in the hands of John Cooper/Peter Lovett, with Bob Evans also down to drive, and this dark green car only had support from Lovett's sports car business. The 1976 De Cadenet Lola was decorated in the colours of BATCO; owner Simon Phillips, in between racing his historic cars, was with Nick Faure and John Beasley. Finally, there was the new Ibec-Hesketh, designed by Harvey Postlethwaite and built and run by Martin Slater of Lyncar. Again DFV powered, it was driven by Ian Grob/Guy Edwards, with the injured Ian Bracey doing a few laps. Sponsorship came from Alexander Howden/Lloyds of London and Chrysler UK.

Although most of the 2-litre sports car chassis were built by British constructors, only four teams were actually British entered. Tony Charnell's Mogil Motors team had their regular Chevron B31 for the boss himself, Robin Smith who built the engines, Richard Jones and Frenchman Fred Alliot, who brought the Kores sponsorship. Dorset Racing had ADA to look after their car, Ian Harrower/Tony Birchenough/ Brian Joscelyne being joined by Juliette Slaughter in the Lola, suitably decorated in Kelly Girl colours.

Cloud Engineering brought Richard Down's Lola for Down himself, Martin Birrane (suffering from an injured wrist), Bob Evans and Richard Bond. Finally, Toleman's fixed up to hire a very nice little Osella-BMW from the works for Tom Walkinshaw, Ted Toleman, Rad Dougall and Dieter Quester to drive. There were other British drivers about of course, including Raymond and Franey in their 935, Brian Redman in one of Dick Barbour's two IMSA 935s, and Gordon Spice, sharing Charles Ivey's Rivet Supply sponsored Carrera with Larry Perkins and John Rulon-Miller.

For the Americans, there was not only Harley Cluxton's Gitanes Mirage team, but also Dick Barbour's well-prepared Porsche 935s. The number one car, brand new, was for Redman/Barbour, while the second (single-turbo) machine was to be driven by Oliver Garretson/Steven Earle/Robert Akin. Luigi Chinetti also entered a Boxer for a team of Frenchmen plus former CanAm and Formula 2 driver Gregg Young. Finally, Brad Frisselle brought the only real American car in the race, his Falconer & Dunn powered IMSA Chevrolet Monza entered by Wynn's, for himself and Robert Kirby.

The Swiss had their involvement too, of course. Chuck Graemiger brought one of his little Cheetah 2-litre cars, and Eugen Strähl his effective Sauber-BMW. This car was driven by Marc Surer, the F2 driver, teamed with Strähl himself and Harry Blumer. Claude Haldi/Herbie Müller had their Mecarillos Porsche 935 as usual.

Brazil and Belgium provided an interesting car each. Alfred Guarana, Paulo Gomes and Mario Amaral came over from South America to hire the ASA Cachia Porsche 935 (with single turbo), and put in some promising times. Jean Beurlys had a Boxer built up in Belgium which ran in yellow colours for Beurlys/Teddy Pilette to drive; Nick Faure also drove it in practice.

PRACTICE

Practice at Le Mans is a long affair. There are usually six hours on the Wednesday, starting at six o'clock, and another five hours on the Thursday, also starting at six. Many people regard these 11 hours as time

The Martini-Porsche team did not challenge the French as intensely as expected. Here, braking for Mulsanne Corner, the Barth/Wollek/Ickx 936 has just taken second place from the Haywood/Gregg/Jöst machine late on Sunday morning.

simply to wear out a car, but Le Mans plays its own tricks: you can test for days anywhere but, when you get to the Sarthe, it all starts again. So the practice time is often jealously used. Tyres are scrubbed, drivers have to qualify during the day and at night, full tank settings have to be made, there are new adjustments to the cars, the long business of aerodynamics.

All these factors must have been right for four times winner Jacky Ickx. Less than three hours into practice, Ickx chopped 1.2secs off Arturo Merzario's outright record of 3m 31.0s, and half an hour later he took another 2.2secs off that too. His 3m 27.6s was a sensational effort by the Belgian long distance specialist, and everyone waited for Renault to reply. Jean-Pierre Jabouille got down to 3:28.4 the next day, but it wasn't enough to take pole position, so Martini-Porsche started from a position of strength in the war of nerves between the two camps. They had their problems, however: a wheel fell off Ickx's car at the end of the first session, and the car was involved in a small accident at the end of the second session with the Sauber, out at Mulsanne.

But Porsche's main problem was centred around the rapid Group 5 car. Stommelen set a fabulous time, but halfway through the second session the 935/78 blew a piston. This upset Porsche somewhat, worrying about their other engines, but in fact the problem was caused by the fact that the car had been driven to the circuit in traffic: this low-rev running had overheated the flat-six, and practice had finished off the piston.

For Renault, practice was disappointing. Their drivers were having a hard time, for Pironi, Jabouille and Depailler were flying to and from Brands Hatch taking in the Formula 1 test sessions, and then practising in the evening in France. But their main problems were aerodynamic ones. They had the inevitable handling troubles, but on the fastest car the plastic bubble was causing the drivers to get claustrophobia, and had to be abandoned. It had been giving a 15kph speed advantage on the straight. Without it, the car had to be retuned.

Interestingly, the Mirage-Renault team had a similar problem. A flap used to deflect air from the driver

Most successful Brit was Brian Redman who shared the IMSA class winning Porsche 935 with Dick Barbour.

had to be removed as it was upsetting the windflow on to the rear body work, and only then did the team start to get into reasonable times.

The English had a mixture of success and failure. De Cadenet's own car had not been properly tested, and there was still a lot of sorting to be done. However, like all the Lolas, it really looked quick in a straight line. Phillips's red car had fuel pump trouble in the first session, as did Cooper's green machine. But in the second session, Cooper, Evans and Lovett really tried, and picked up 19th quickest time. For some reason, the organisers decided to exclude two cars from the over 2000cc division of the Group 6 class and, after the slow Toj-DFV (which blew its one engine anyway), Cooper's De Cadenet was next. The organisers had given assurances to various teams that all Group 6 cars would get in unless very slow, but

this was a reversal of the decision. To take a G6 car to Le Mans and try to qualify against the works teams seems to be inadvisable now, and if they are not careful the Automobile Club de L'Ouest may be left with just the works cars, and will miss out on the privateer who cannot take the chance of not qualifying. Meanwhile, of course, just as last year, various slow and rather common Porsche Carreras, and all but one of the 2-litre G6 cars, got a race.

The Ibec-Hesketh also gave problems, with a half-opening throttle in the first session, and the inevitable handling difficulties. But all three drivers qualified, despite the roll oversteer, and a cracked plug electrode which also delayed the team's practice.

The 2-litre class was really between the Sauber and the Osella. Surer set a fine time in the Sauber in the first session, but Ted Toleman had an unfortunate accident: his driving shoe was cracked, and it caught in one of the Osella's pedals coming into the Ford chicane, causing the car to go off the road and hit the barrier. It was repaired by the end of the session and (using qualifying Pirellis) the next day Quester set the fastest time in the class. Toleman decided not to drive (it was his first visit to Le Mans and he had twisted his ankle in the accident), so Dougall and Walkinshaw flew in from F2 testing at Donington to qualify themselves in the car. The Sauber got stuck in the paddock for most of the second session, and scarcely practised before having a slight coming-together with the Porsche 936 at Mulsanne.

Dorset Racing's Lola qualified well, Harrower setting the time, while Juliette Slaughter did well to qualify and also drove well during the night. Cloud Engineering, though, had a bad time . A rear suspension breakage when Down was driving down the Mulsanne Straight put the car into the barrier, and the impact all but wrote off the Lola. For the next two days, the mechanics struggled manfully—and successfully—to build it up again. The Mogil Motors team was also impressive, with Smith, Jones, Charnell and Alliot really having a go.

The Group 5 class was naturally dominated by the Martini 935/78, but George Loos's Weisberg team also put in a respectable time, while the Kremer brothers were just pacing their cars ready for the real event. In the IMSA class, Redman set another good time, his American team seemingly thoroughly enjoying the Le Mans experience. The Monza was impressive, but then blew a new engine in the second session. The Ferraris in the IMSA class were quick in a straight line and all qualified well.

As well as Cooper's De Cadenet, there were other unfortunate non-qualifiers. Alain Cudini/Pierre Dieudonné were meant to drive an ex-Luigi BMW CSL, but were just not fast enough. The Mercedes from AMG, this time using a five-speed gearbox (soon replaced by three-speed again), was scarcely changed from Group 2 form, and failed to make the grade.

RACE

Le Mans is comparatively quiet during the practice days. The crowds are local people, the hard race fans have not yet arrived. By Friday night, though, the pace is beginning to pick up. The British arrive in their droves: Minis piled high with camping gear, smart Range Rovers cruising around the roads, the enthusiasts in their Lotus Sevens, the unprepared sleeping in their cars. There are the back-packers, idly sitting around, wondering what to do next. The Americans arrive with enough booze to sink a battleship, often with neither sleeping bags nor tents. The

A night refuelling stop for the fast works G5 Porsche, which was later delayed.

place becomes a big arena of friends; if you don't have any, you soon make them.

The sun was shining on race day, with white clouds occasionally drifting across to cool the spectators. The dust rose from their feet as they casually picked their way around the fairground and the goody stands, or bought small bottles of beer for large amounts of francs. A quarter of a million spectators gradually gave Le Mans its life.

As the crews moved away from the shining cars on the grid, protected by a thin blue line of policemen, the signal was given, the engines roared into life, and the cars, shimmering under the sun and looking the millions of dollars they were worth, moved off on the warming up lap. As they came out of the Ford Chicane, it was clear that Jabouille was going to take the initiative.

Across the start line it was Jabouille, Ickx, Wollek, Schurti, and Pironi. Normally, the opening laps of a 24-hour race mean nothing. But who should be heading for the pits at the end of the second lap, but Jacky Ickx! And then, Hurley Haywood too.

Ickx had too much fuel pressure, so they shut off one of the pumps; Haywood had a sticking throttle. A couple of laps later, both were back in, this time for further adjustment to Ickx's car, and to cure too much turbo boost (three atmospheres!) on Haywood's. Porsche were in trouble.

Jabouille led, Pironi second, Jarier third, a Renault 1-2-3; then came Wollek, Ragnotti and Leclere. Walkinshaw made a couple of stops for adjustment to the electrics on a new engine, but in fact needed a new black box to cure the misfire. The new De Cadenet and the Kelly Girl Lola needed new tyres early on, and the Chevrolet Monza needed a new tyre after hitting a barrier. Behind the two Mirages came the Group 5 leaders, Schurti in the Martini-Porsche (running in the rebuilt engine) and Fitzpatrick in George Loos's 935. The rest were strung out in their own mess behind, and by lap 12 they were all lapped.

There was plenty of action in the pits. It was quite remarkable: the De Cadenet heading for the pits, the Hesketh too, and then Fitzpatrick. The Loos Porsche needed a new wheel bearing, while both the British sports cars were having wheel or tyre trouble: Grob had lost a tyre, and Craft had a wheel weight shoot straight through the bodywork.

Meanwhile, there was the progress of Ickx. As he came up through the field, after an hour, he was in 23rd position, a lap later 20th, then 16th, 12th and 11th in successive laps. But the Renaults continued to be the front runners, Jabouille, Pironi and Jarier.

Jabouille seemed to pit very early: Renault were expecting the 2.1 car to consume more petrol than the well-tried 2-litre, so he brought it in early just in case. Pironi took over the running ahead of Jarier, and Wollek was the only nigger in the Renault woodpile. The Calberson Alpine followed in fourth place and then came the two Mirages, not that fast, but steady, sandwiching the Martini 935 as they came up to the second hour. Jabouille, from the pits, brought up the tail of those still unlapped. The Renaults certainly had the upper hand.

The activity in the pits was exceptionally high. Fitz had a wheel hub go, and later the car staggered in, smoking, just before six: so the Gelo mechanics pushed the car away with a burnt piston, and Loos and Fitz were soon flying home. Into the third hour, Pironi led Jarier, Wollek, Frequelin and Jabouille. The rest were lapped.

They included the first of the Mirages, that of Schuppan/Laffite, but its sister car (Leclere/Posey) was missing. Posey stopped at Mulsanne in last year's race with no petrol; this time, it was Leclere's turn to stop, with a broken alternator. Although the car somehow returned to the pits, it was retired, the first blow for Renault.

But the French were in charge. Even the Porsche reserves were having no luck. The Fisons-sponsored Kremer 935 staggered into the pits in a similar state to the Loos car, and was driven into the paddock with another broken engine. And then the second Mirage pitted, the first of many stops, this one with the same problem as the sister car: electrics. During the next hour, all the electrics were changed. They were busy in the Chevrolet Monza pit again, too: this time the problem was brakes. However, it was not long before the car was back in the pits, the big V8 making a dreadful row, and ultimately being pushed away with a cracked block, a legacy of their practice problems.

At seven, there were five cars on the same lap: Pironi/Jaussaud, the sister car of Bell/Jarier, the Wollek/Barth 936, the Calberson Renault and finally Jabouille/Depailler. The works 935 was sixth, ahead of the Ickx/Pescarolo 936, the De Cadenet, the Haywood/Gregg 936 and the Americans in their Kremer Porsche.

Jabouille had been delayed by a couple of stops. He felt a vibration at the front, and changed the bonnet section, which had caused a mild problem in practice. But that did not cure the vibration, so they changed wheels, and that solved the problem.

As well as the Monza and the two 935s, a further retirement was the Richard Down 2-litre Lola. A shunt after a blow-out damaged the already second-hand chassis, and the mechanics wheeled the car into retirement.

After Walkinshaw had pitted a couple of times at the start, the team then had to change the lights after another car kicked up some stones and broke them. After tyre problems, the Hesketh-Ibec team had a fuel pressure problem, with too much air in the system. The BAT De Cadenet Lola lost an hour with the gear linkage broken in two places. Alain de Cadenet's new car had to stop for attention to the clutch pedal, and the Kelly Girl Lola team, as well as coping with a tyre blow-out, had to take out the crown wheel and pinion and rebuild the gearbox internals. Later they lost a lot more time tracing a vibration. Tony Charnell's 2-litre Chevron had overheated from the start, and they modified a nose section to try to get some more air to the engine. The two Barbour Porsche 935s had varying stories: Redman and Barbour himself were fine, racing only for the IMSA class, but the sister car had hit a couple of kerbs, which had punctured two tyres, and caused a longish delay.

Ickx's fine run through the field came up to a snag at exactly nine o'clock: he came into the pits with fifth gear inoperative. It took nearly 45 mins to replace. The BAT De Cadenet Lola was in trouble, with no fourth gear, and they vowed to change the whole gearbox if another ratio should go; they were already a long way behind. Early in the sixth hour, the team decided to rebuild the gearbox, which was unfortunately a bad move. The Hesketh team were desperately searching for someone from Lucas, for three spark boxes had been tried to cure their misfire, and the car would only rev to 8800rpm.

Porsche fortunes took another turn for the worse 20mins before the seventh hour. With Ickx's car still immobile, waiting for its new fifth gear, Haywood's 936 came into the pits belching smoke and fire, like an angry dragon. One of the turbo axles had broken, but in comparison with its sister car's delay it was brief: 10mins to replace it.

With this new swing in their favour, the Renault team looked strong. Of the first six, Porsche's only

Martin Raymord's Kremer-Porsche leads the 2-litre G6 class winning Chevron out of the Ford chicane.

Before he destroyed the rapid Toleman/BMW works Osella, Dieter Quester is hounded by Jacky Ickx's Porsche.

LE MANS 24 HOURS

healthy 936 was in fourth place, and the 935 of Schurti/Stommelen was sixth. Ickx was down in 17th place. What to do for Porsche's golden boy? Manfred Jantke put him in with Wollek/Barth, and finally persuaded first reserve Jochen Mass to take over from Ickx with Henri Pescarolo. So Ickx joined the main challenge to the Renaults running out front. Behind his fourth-placed car came the Calberson Frequelin/Ragnotti Alpine, a lap down on the first three as darkness fell on the Sarthe. Schurti/Stommelen and Haywood/Gregg were ready to back up Ickx from their sixth and seventh places, while Craft/de Cadenet were the only drivers with a normally aspirated car in the first 15. A brace of 'American' driven Porsches filled ninth and tenth places, Busby/Cord/Knoop second in the Group 5 class, and Redman/Barbour leading the IMSA class. Haldi/Müller

were 11th, the second Kremer car was 12th, and then came the 936 formerly driven by Ickx. The Brazilians were 14th in their 935, and Schuppan/Laffite were 15th after their electrical troubles.

The 2-litre prototype class had been the property of the neat Swiss Sauber, but early in the evening Surer found he couldn't change gear. They took out the gearbox and found a bent pin inside, but the whole business of renewing it lost the team an hour's running. The ROC Chevron B36 of Pignard/Rossiaud/ Ferrier took over the class lead, but that in turn had to have its injection pump fixed. So the Toleman/BMW GB Osella found itself not only in 16th position overall, but also leading the class.

In the minutes up to midnight, the De Cadenet Lola pulled into the pits for a 25mins stop, the gear linkage fouling the 'box; it dropped the team three places, to 11th. They might have dropped farther down the field, but two 935s were also in trouble, each with a broken driveshaft: Haldi/Müller were on one side of the control tower having a new one fitted, and Schornstein/Winter/Gurdjian were on the other.

Quester's 2-litre sports car lead did not last long.

Just before one in the morning, a tyre apparently exploded on the Osella at Tertre Rouge, and Dieter had one of the biggest accidents of his career. He cut his face, but otherwise was unhurt.

The British teams were in more trouble. Craft had a chassis vibration but, more seriously, no clutch, while the Ibec team, over 2½ hours, changed all the electrics and finally cured their dreadful misfire.

Among the front runners, Ickx's transfer began to pay dividends. By 12.30, he had moved ahead of Pironi/Jaussaud for third place, and an hour later he slotted into second position. The pace was rapid. Derek Bell pointed out that the race was being run at a very quick pace, and a swift calculation brought attention to the fact that the final mileage at the current rate would be over 3,230; the previous year's was less than 2,900.

Maybe Ickx was forcing the pace, the sole Porsche in among a quartet of Alpines. But the French were soon down to three. The crown wheel and pinion went in Bell's car, which alarmed the Renault camp: could the same thing happen to the other cars? Marie-Claude Beaumont pointed out that the cars were all built differently so that the eventuality of one failure spreading through the team would be avoided. But it was still worrying, and the mechanics went out to Tertre Rouge to check out the car.

The new De Cadenet Lola dropped out of the leader board towards 2pm. This time, the whole clutch had to be changed; the thrust bearing had failed. The hardworking mechanics took 105mins to do the job. The older De Cadenet was in trouble too, this time needing a new alternator, and then suffering a recurrence of the gearbox problem. Another 30mins was spent in the pits.

The 2-litre class fortunes continued to change through the cold early hours. A French Lola inherited the lead, but not long after its accelerator cable broke out on the circuit, allowing Charnell's Chevron to take the class lead, in 18th position overall. Fellow 2-litre man Brian Joscelyne had had the motor explode to end a busy weekend for the Kelly Girl team, and the Rivet Supply Porsche Carrera was in need of a new gearbox. The Hesketh team was in fine fettle without the misfire.

With one Renault down, the pendulum seemed to swing fractionally away from the French in these hours. True, Jabouille/Depailler had a good lead, but Ickx/Wollek/Barth were in second place for Porsche ahead of Pironi/Jaussaud and Frequelin/Ragnotti. Then came three more works Porsches, and more privateers to back them up. Tenth was the Laffite/Schuppan Mirage-Renault.

But Porsche's challenge was weakened at four by the Pescarolo/Ickx/Mass 936 visiting the pits for an electrical check-up. The activity in the pits was phenomenal: there was always a massive job going on, and yet the retirement rate was not very high. But the 936 slipped down the order, ending up ninth. Then it made another stop with problems with the lights, dropping it farther down the order.

Early into the second half of the race, with 38 cars left, the sole remaining Mirage came into the pits for the first of many stops. The throttle linkage had fallen to pieces, and it took over an hour and a quarter to fix it. Meanwhile, another car that had had long stops was being pushed away, the BAT De Cadenet of Simon Phillips's team, which had run out of time and was way behind the 70 per cent rule.

Even the dawn brought its problems. As the sun came up to reveal the inert bodies lying on a reasonably comfortable bit of French waste ground, both the De Cadenet and the Charnell Chevron spent

Second Alpine-Renault to finish was the fourth-placed Calberson car of Ragnotti, Frequelin and Jabouille.

Above: Alain de Cadenet, who finished 15th despite major transmission bothers, leads the Jacques Laffite/Vern Schuppan 2-litre Mirage. Below: A fine performance by Brazilians Alfredo Guarana/Paulo Gomes/Mario Amaral was rewarded with seventh overall.

LE MANS 24 HOURS

time in the pits. The main feed to the alternator shorted against the former chassis, and stranded Alain out at Arnage. While the team was planning to pack up and go home, Alain sorted it out; but when he got back to the pits and it was sorted properly, it had eaten 41mins out of their racing. The starter motor had to be replaced on the Charnell car, and that took them 20mins; even so, they remained in the lead of the 2-litre class, with four laps advantage over the next man.

Although there was a lot going on in the pits, the order had remained fairly steady through the night, and Jabouille/Depailler had consolidated an advantage of two laps over Ickx/Wollek/Barth. Pironi/Jaussaud were in third place and, although José Dolhem had helped out the Calberson team, they were well down in fourth place. Haywood/Gregg and Schurti/Stommelen completed the top six. Busby/Cord and Knoop had moved up to seventh, in front of the final Porsche 936, while Barbour/Redman had lost their second 935 team-mate when Garretson had an enormous 200mph accident just after the Mulsanne kink, which went on for 700yds during which he rolled several times. Fortunately the driver was unhurt.

Then the second-placed Porsche 936 began to have problems. It came in twice, the mechanics looking for play in the front wheels, but sorting it out for Wollek to remain in second place. The Haywood car had not been revving properly, and that had a four-lap stop, but it did not lose its place either. However, one of the Kremer Porsches was out, the Schornstein/Winter/Gurdjian car losing a piston after getting into the top 12.

Before seven o'clock in the morning, the 2-litre class leader, Charnell, had a very nasty accident towards the end of the Mulsanne Straight when, it seems, a bottom link pulled out of the rear of the chassis at 165mph. The car spun backwards against the kerbing and flew over the barrier and into the trees. Charnell was very lucky indeed to be unhurt,

although the Chevron was naturally very badly damaged.

The British privateers with their DFV-powered cars again had troubles. De Cadenet and Craft had another wheel-weight fly through the bodywork like a bullet, as had also occurred some hours earlier. Ian Grob went straight on up the escape road at Mulsanne with a real lack of brakes on the Ibec-Hesketh; the genial Grob came grinning back to the pits, quietly explained the problem, and the Lyncar mechanics set to bleeding the brakes.

The Mirage-Renault had a number of problems, delaying it considerably. Trouble with the gears and the turbo, plus its electrical problems, dropped it back to 19th place. The Ibec-Hesketh was 23rd, the De Cadenet one place farther back, and the Rivet Supply Carrera, with a new gearbox fitted, in 28th position.

Next, the front runners began to run into difficulties. The Group 5 Schurti/Stommelen Porsche came in with bodywork fouling one of the rear tyres. At about the same time, the Calberson Alpine lost third gear, which took 20mins to replace. And then the 935/78 Porsche had a misfire; in 12mins the mechanics changed the injection pump. But even while they were working, Wollek brought the second-placed 936 into the pits with no fifth gear; it took nearly 40mins to replace. The balance had swung firmly over to Renault.

Hesketh traced their brake problem to a leaking brake pipe, and they changed it, plus a top link that was pulling out.

At the same time, there was a really bad accident on the Mulsanne Straight when Christian Debias crashed his WM 78 in the biggest possible way. The barrier was uprooted, the car was split into three pieces, and Debias was lucky to get away with his life. He was taken to hospital unconscious, but the latest reports on his condition are favourable.

In the morning hours, the shivers ran through the Renault team again: the leading Alpine went out with a holed piston.

It gave no comfort to Porsche, though. Mass's 936 suddenly spun out on him, into the guardrail near the Porsche Curve; it severely damaged the car, but Mass

was unhurt. Another 3-litre G6 car retired at the same time, when the Hesketh finally called enough and broke its crank on the Mulsanne Straight.

Going into the final five hours, Renault did not seem to have cause for worry. The Pironi/Jaussaud machine now inherited a seven-lap lead on the low-revving Haywood/Gregg 936. Before noon, the healthy 936, that of Wollek/Ickx/Barth, passed its sister car, but by then the Renault's advantage was eight laps. Renault's next car was three laps behind the two Porsches, though, and it would be of little good if the leading car was delayed.

The works Martini 935 broke a seal in a cylinder head and had lost out badly to two more 935s. The IMSA car of Barbour/Redman was fifth, and Barbour's compatriots, Knoop/Busby/Cord were on the same lap, now leading the G5 class in their Kremer car. The Martini works 935 was six laps behind these two, and the Brazilians in their 935 were just two laps behind the works car. The 935/78's cylinder head failure was irreparable, and all the team could do was to keep filling it up with oil and run it at low revs. Steadily the order dropped down.

Jabouille now had a run in the car which Frequelin and Ragnotti had driven, but it had to make up three laps against the Martini Porsches. Brian Redman was earning a lot of praise from the Dick Barbour team for his consistent lapping as he held off his entrant's compatriots in the Kremer Porsche. The Brazilians, Alfredo Guaranara/Paulo Gomes/Mario Amaral, were just as pleased with their own efforts.

The final few hours were very uneventful, save for the last efforts of the more mechanically stricken. Immediately de Cadenet/Craft had started off with their new clutch, it failed too. On their next pitstop, they couldn't get started again, so John Hewitt, one of Alain's faithful mechanics, built up a gearbox to get the car home. In the final hour, Alain went out to finish the course, which he did despite finding a box of neutrals out on the circuit. The Sauber that had run so well early on was stricken with a three-cylinder engine, but Marc Surer was sent out to do the final stint and get the car home. There was no chance of catching the 2-litre car in front of them, so one of the French-entered ROC Chevrons was set to pick up the class win and 13th position overall.

One of the interesting things about this year's race was the last performance of Jean Rondeau. This year, he brought his own car home to ninth overall position. Last year, all three Inalteras finished, cars that he designed. Furthermore, André Chevalley, who bought the Inalteras, entered one for himself this year, and that finished too. Quite a record.

But the day belonged to Renault. They had tried for so long, and succeeded just when many people thought they had run out of time (and money). Furthermore, they won what was a very evenly matched competition with the crack Porsche team.

From an insider's point of view, the race was fascinating. The activity in the pits was tremendous, and the changing face of the race held the interest throughout. But this is not something that is easy to share with spectators, and one can only hope that the English and other foreign visitors enjoyed the 24 Hours as much as the patriotic French. This format is, after all, what the CSI have now itemised as next year's sports car formula.

With luck, experience at other events will make some of the British competitors a little more prepared for Le Mans next year. If they are to spend money on this type of racing, then it should be spent wisely, with the maximum benefit. Foreigners might like our British spirit, but the professionalism needs sharpening up.

46eme Grand Prix d'Endurance 24 Heures du Mans

June 10/11, 1978. 24 hours over 8.475-mile circuit. **Organisers:** Automobile Club de l'Ouest. **No of starters:** 55. **No of finishers:** 25. **Winners:** Jean-Pierre Jaussaud/Didier Pironi (2.0 Alpine-Renault A442B), 369 laps at 130.60mph, 3134.52 miles. **Previous year's winners:** Jacky Ickx/Hurley Haywood/Jürgen Barth (2.1 Porsche 936/77 turbo), 342 laps at 121.04mph, 2898.62 miles. **Previous distance record (8.475-mile circuit):** 3016.13 miles (1973).

QUALIFYING

No	Drivers	Car	Time
5	Jacky Ickx/Henri Pescarolo	2.1 Porsche 936/78 turbo	3:27.6
1	Jean-Pierre Jabouille/Patrick Depailler	2.1 Alpine-Renault A443 turbo	3:28.4
43	Rolf Stommelen/Manfred Schurti	3.2 Porsche 935/78 turbo	3:30.9
6	Jürgen Barth/Bob Wollek	2.1 Porsche 936/78 turbo	3:35.2
2	Didier Pironi/Jean-Pierre Jaussaud	2.0 Alpine-Renault A442B turbo	3:35.7
7	Hurley Haywood/Peter Gregg	2.1 Porsche 936/77 turbo	3:37.3
3	Jean-Pierre Jarier/Derek Bell	2.0 Alpine-Renault A442A turbo	3:37.9
4	Guy Frequelin/Jean Ragnotti/José Dolhem	2.0 Alpine-Renault A442A turbo	3:42.7
10	Jacques Laffite/Vern Schuppan	2.0 Mirage-Renault M9 turbo	3:45.8
8	Alain de Cadenet/Chris Craft	3.0 De Cadenet Lola-DFV	3:46.5
47	John Fitzpatrick/Toine Hezemans/Klaus Ludwig	3.0 Porsche 935/77A turbo	3:46.9
11	Michel Leclere/Sam Posey	2.0 Mirage-Renault M9 turbo	3:48.3
19	Ian Bracey/Ian Grob/Guy Edwards	3.0 Ibec Hesketh-DFV 308LM	3:50.2
44	Jim Busby/Chris Cord/Fred Knoop	3.0 Porsche 935/77A turbo	3:50.7
12	Nick Faure/John Beasley/Simon Phillips	3.0 De Cadenet Lola-DFV	3:51.4
90	Brian Redman/Dick Barbour/John Paul	3.0 Porsche 935/77A turbo	3:52.6
94	Don Whittington/Bill Whittington	3.0 Porsche 935/77A turbo	3:52.8
78	Xavier Mathiot/Marc Sourd/Christian Debias	2.7 WM-Peugeot P78 turbo	3:52.9
71	François Trisconi/André Chevalley	3.0 Inaltera-DFV	3:53.9
46	Martin Raymond/Mike Franey/'Steve'	3.0 Porsche 935/77A turbo	3:54.9
48	Claude Haldi/Herbert Müller/'Nico'	3.0 Porsche 935/77A turbo	3:55.8
34	Dieter Quester/Tom Walkinshaw/Rad Dougall	2.0 Osella-BMW/Osella PA5	3:56.2
41	Alfredo Guarana/Paulo Gomes/Mario Amaral	2.0 Porsche 935/77A turbo	3:59.5
23	Marc Surer/Eugen Strähl/Harry Blumer	2.0 Sauber-BMW/Mader C5	4:00.1
33	Bob Evans/Martin Birrane/Richard Down	2.0 Lola-Richardson FVC T294	4:02.0
84	Brad Friselle/Bob Kirby	5.7 Chevrolet Monza	4:02.3
27	Tony Charnell/Fred Alliot/Robin Smith/Richard Jones	2.0 Chevron-Smith BDG B31	4:03.3
77	Jean-Daniel Raulet/Marcel Mamers	2.7 WM-Peugeot P77 turbo	4:03.5
45	John Winter/Dieter Schnornstein/Phillipe Gurdjian	3.0 Porsche 935/77A turbo	4:04.2
31	Michel Pignard/Lucien Rossiaud/Laurent Ferrier	2.0 Chevron-Chrysler B36	4:04.2
28	Michel Lateste/Jean-François Auboiron/Dominique Lacaud	2.0 Lola-BMW/Mader T297	4:04.5
91	Oliver Garretson/Steven Earle/Robert Akin	3.0 Porsche 935/77A turbo	4:05.2
68	Gerhard Holpp/Edgar Dören/Hervé Poulain	3.0 Porsche 934 turbo	4:07.1
89	Claude Ballot-Lena/Jean-Louis Lafosse	4.9 Ferrari 512 BB	4:07.3
88	Jean-Claude Andruet/Spartaco Dini	4.9 Ferrari 512 BB	4:07.3
29	Michel Dubois/Daniel Gache/Julien Sanchez	2.0 Chevron-Chrysler B36	4:07.8
69	Gregg Young/Jean-Pierre Delaunay/Jacques Guerin	4.9 Ferrari 512 BB	4:07.9
69	Willy Braillard/Philippe Dagoreau/Jacky Ravenel	3.0 Porsche 934 turbo	4:08.0
30	Jacques Henry/Albert Dufresne/Max Olivar	2.0 Chevron-Chrysler B36	4:08.3
61	Guy Chasseuil/Jean-Claude Lefebvre/Marcel Mignot	3.0 Porsche 934 turbo	4:09.1
72	Guy Darniche/Jean Rondeau	3.0 Rondeau-DFV M378	4:09.4
32	Ian Harrower/Juliette Slaughter/Tony Birchenough	2.0 Lola-Richardson FVC T294S	4:10.4
85	Teddy Pilette/'Beurlys'/Nick Faure	4.9 Ferrari 512 BB	4:11.7
26	Michel Elkoubi/Pierre Yver/Philippe Streiff	2.0 Lola-Smith FVC T296	4:11.7
26	Georges Morand/Christian Blanc/Eric Vaugnat	2.0 Lola-Smith FVC T296	4:12.2
21	Jean-Marie Lemerle/Alain Levie/Pierre-François Rousselot	2.0 Lola-Chrysler T294	4:13.7
97	Larry Perkins/Gordon Spice/John Rulon-Miller	3.0 Porsche Carrera	4:14.7
25	Bruno Sotty/Gerard Cuynet/Jean-Claude Dutray	2.0 Lola-Smith FVC T294/5	4:15.8
86	François Migault/Lucien Guitteny	4.9 Ferrari BB512	4:15.9
20	Sandro Plastina/Mario Luini/Jean-Daniel Grandjean	2.0 Cheetah-Cosworth BDG G501	4:19.3
66	Anny-Charlotte Verney/Xavier Lapeyre/François Servanin	3.0 Porsche Carrera	4:19.6
60	'Segolen'/Christian Bussi/Jean-Claude Briavoine	3.0 Porsche 934 turbo	4:21.6
76	Marianne Hoepfner/Christine Dacremont	2.8 WM-Peugeot P76 turbo	4:22.8
65	Antoine Salamin/Gerard Vial/Joel Laplacette	3.0 Porsche Carrera	4:25.0
64	Georges Bourdillat/Alain Bernard	3.0 Porsche Carrera	4:28.2

FINISHERS

1	Alpine-Renault A442B	G6	Jean-Pierre Jaussaud/Didier Pironi	3134.52 miles
2	Porsche 936	G6	Jürgen Barth/Bob Wollek/Jacky Ickx	3087.04 miles
3	Porsche 936	G6	Hurley Haywood/Peter Gregg/Reinhold Jöst	3070.02 miles
4	Alpine-Renault A442A	G6	Jean Ragnotti/Guy Frequelin/Jean-Pierre Jabouille	3041.23 miles
5	Porsche 935/77A	IMSA	Brian Redman/Dick Barbour	2862.91 miles
6	Porsche 935/77A	G5	Jim Busby/Chris Cord/Fred Knoop	2853.93 miles
7	Porsche 935/77A	G5	Alfredo Guarana/Paulo Gomes/Mario Amaral	2789.34 miles
8	Porsche 935/78	G5	Rolf Stommelen/Manfred Schurti	2763.69 miles
9	Rondeau-Ford M378	GTP	Jean Rondeau/Bernard Darniche/Jacky Haran	2497.30 miles
10	Mirage-Renault M9	G6	Vern Schuppan/Jacques Laffite/Michel Leclere	2490.28 miles
11	Chevron-Simca B36	G6*	Michel Pignard/Lucien Rossiaud/Laurent Ferrier	2409.80 miles
12	Porsche Carrera RSR	G4	Anny-Charlotte Verney/Xavier Lapeyre/Frank Servanin	2372.34 miles
13	Inaltera-Ford	GTP	André Chevalley/François Trisconi	2367.53 miles
14	Porsche Carrera RS	IMSA	John Rulon-Miller/Larry Perkins/Gordon Spice	2361.92 miles
15	De Cadenet Lola 78	G6	Alain de Cadenet/Chris Craft	2317.44 miles
16	Ferrari 512 BB	IMSA	François Migault/Lucien Guitteny/Florian Vetsch	2224.09 miles
17	Porsche 934	G4	'Segolen'/Christian Bussi/Jean-Claude Briavoine	2200.20 miles
NC	Sauber-BMW C5	G6*	Marc Surer/Eugen Strähl/Harry Blumer	2178.72 miles
NC	Cheetah-BMW G601	G6*	Sandro Plastina/Mario Luini/Jean-Daniel Grandjean	2125.50 miles
NC	Porsche Carrera	G4	Guy Chasseuil/Jean-Claude Lefebvre/Marcel Mignot	2047.65 miles
NC	Lola-Ford T294/6	G6*	Bruno Sotty/Gérard Cuynet/Jean-Claude Dutrey	2020.01 miles
NC	Lola-Ford T296	G6*	Michel Elkoubi/Pierre Yver/Philippe Streiff	1969.21 miles
NC	Lola-Ford T297	G6*	Michel Leteste/J-F Auboiron/Dominique Lacaud	1842.41 miles
NC	Porsche 935/77A	G5	Dieter Schornstein/John Winter/Philippe Gurdjian	1550.23 miles
NC	Chevron-Ford B31	G6*	Tony Charnell/Robin Smith/Richard Jones/Fred Alliott	1533.27 miles

* 2-litre G6 class.

Jean Rondeau's latest car won the GT Prototype class.

Anny-Charlotte Verney's G4 class-winning Porsche.

	1	2	3	4	5	6	7	8	9	10	11	12	13	14	15	16	17	18	19	20	21	22	23	24
1	2 15 laps 135.50 mph	2 31 133.16	2 47 133.12	2 62 130.07	2 79 134.58	2 94 132.95	1 109 132.62	1 125 132.58	1 140 132.72	1 156 132.88	1 172 132.79	1 187 133.08	1 203 132.62	1 219 132.62	1 235 132.86	1 251 133.24	1 266 132.95	1 279 132.92	2 293 130.95	2 309 131.16	2 324 131.05	2 339 130.89	2 354 130.75	2 369 130.60
2	3 15	3 31	3 46	1 62	3 78	2 93	6 109	3 124	6 139	6 155	6 170	6 186	6 201	6 217	6 231	6 247	2 263	2 278	7 286	6 301	6 317	6 333	6 349	6 364
3	6 15	6 31	6 46	3 62	6 77	1 93	3 109	6 124	3 139	3 155	2 170	2 184	2 199	2 215	2 231	6 246	6 262	7 270	6 286	7 301	7 317	7 332	7 347	7 362
4	1 15	4 30	4 46	6 62	1 77	6 93	6 108	2 123	2 139	2 154	4 167	4 183	4 198	4 213	4 228	4 241	4 254	4 270	4 283	4 298	4 314	4 329	4 344	4 358
5	4 15	43 30	4 46	43 61	4 76	43 92	43 107	4 122	4 137	4 152	43 166	7 178	7 193	7 208	7 223	7 239	4 252	4 267	1 279	90 281	90 295	90 309	90 323	90 337
6	11 15	11 30	43 45	5 61	5 76	4 92	4 106	43 121	43 136	43 151	3 162	43 175	43 190	43 205	43 220	43 235	43 245	5 255	44 267	44 281	44 295	44 309	44 323	44 336
7	10 15	1 30	5 45	4 61	43 76	7 89	7 102	7 116	7 132	7 147	7 162	5 170	44 182	44 197	5 211	5 227	5 242	44 253	90 267	43 275	41 286	41 300	41 315	41 329
8	43 15	10 30	8 45	8 59	8 74	8 88	8 100	90 113	44 127	44 141	5 155	44 169	90 182	90 196	44 211	44 225	5 240	5 251	90 262	43 273	43 288	43 298	43 311	43 326
9	8 14	8 30	7 44	7 58	7 74	8 74	44 85	44 99	48 111	90 126	90 140	90 155	5 169	5 180	90 196	90 210	90 224	90 238	90 248	43 259	41 254	71 263	66 275	72 282	72 294
10	78 14	5 30	44 43	44 57	44 71	90 85	90 99	44 111	5 125	5 140	90 154	10 167	41 176	41 189	41 202	41 217	41 231	41 244	41 255	5 250	66 263	66 272	72 279	10 293

LE MANS
1979

In the absence of the Alpine-Renaults or indeed any other works supported Group 6 team, Porsche was the undoubted favourite; their two 936 cars were entered in co-operation with Essex Motorsport. Additionally, the two 935s entered by the German Kremer organisation were supported by the Porsche company; one of these was a very special K3 type with 'ground-effect' aerodynamic bodywork, driven by the German Klaus Ludwig and the American Whittington brothers. The 936s were in the hands of experienced Le Mans veterans, no one more so than Jacky Ickx who shared one car with Brian Redman, while an international complement of drivers crewed the other car - Wollek, Haywood and Barth.

This year, all of the other Group 6 entrants favoured the Cosworth-DFV engine; there were three Lolas entered by various equipes; Alain de Cadenet's own car which he shared with a new co-driver, Francois Migault; three examples of the Le Mans-built Rondeau M379s; the two Mirages which had shed their Renault engines and returned to Cosworth-DFV power getting sponsorship from the French Ford company and therefore racing as Ford M-10s. Finally, two Japanese cars, Dome-Zeros, with four British drivers - Craft/Spice and Evans/Trimmer. An Anglo-German entry which despite the use of a 3.5-litre turbo-charged engine had been given special dispensation by F.I.S.A. to run as a Group 6 car was an exciting lightweight BMW M.l, prepared by March engineering for Guy Edwards; but it failed to qualify, proving disappointingly slow in practice.

The two-litre cars were as usual a mixed bunch of five Chevrons, six Lolas, two Cheetahs and a Toj, using either Chrysler-Simca, Ford or BMW engines. Group 5 numbered nine cars - all Porsche 935s and Group 4 consisted of five Porsche 934s. The I.M.S.A. category held another five Porsche 935s, four Ferrari Boxers and a BMW M.l which did make it into the race; driven by Winkelhock/Poulainj Mignot and painted by Andy Warhol. It was however *not* sponsored by Campbell's Soups. Apart from this the I.M.S.A. car getting most media attention was a Porsche 935 entered by Dick Barbour, and driven by himself together with Stommelen and 53-year old Hollywood star Paul Newman. Finally, the GT prototype category held four cars - three WM-Peugeots, and the turbo-charged Aston Martin V8 of Robin Hamilton which had first come to Le Mans in 1977. Among the non-qualifying entrants had been a Mazda RX-7 rotary engined coupe which the Mazda company had entered in the I.M.S.A. category, and a SAAB turbo entry in the GT prototype category failed to materialise.

As there was going to be the election for the European Parliament on Sunday 10 June, the time of the race was brought forward two hours to allow the French time to vote after the finish of the race at 2 pm Sunday afternoon. The circuit had been slightly shortened and was now 8.47 miles long; the alteration was a newly-laid out Tertre Rouge corner, leading into the Mulsanne straight.

Porsches filled the first four positions on the grid: the two 936s, followed by the 935s of Ludwig/Whittington and Schurti/Heyer. Then came the Schuppan/Jaussaud Mirage-Ford, a Rondeau, another Porsche 935, the Bell/Hobbs Mirage-Ford, a second Rondeau and the De Cadenet. The race sorted itself out soon after the start, the two Porsche 936s took the lead with the Mirage-Fords in third and fourth places. But none of the favourites were to last out the race. The first car to hit trouble was the Ickx/Redman Porsche 936; a tyre blew out, and there was considerable damage to bodywork and one of the radiators. The car got going again after a pit stop of 80 minutes but was later stranded on the circuit, and was disqualified when Ickx accepted outside assistance. The Wollek/Haywood/Barth 936 similarly had to spend a long time in the pit in the early stages of the race; although it got going again and at one stage had re-captured second place, it had to retire with further engine problems.

After the initial Porsche troubles set in the Bell/Hobbs Mirage-Ford took the lead while the Schuppan/Jaussaud car had the gearbox break. But the Bell/Hobbs car also ran into trouble and had to have its exhaust system replaced; and after a quarter of the race had been run, the Group 5 Porsche 935 of Ludwig/Whittington went into the lead, followed by the similar car of Schurti/Heyer. At one stage, there were five Porsche 935s leading the first Group 6 car. This set the pattern for the rest of the race; with the fastest Group 6 cars either out of the race, or seriously delayed, the Porsche 935s retained their grip on the race. Then Sunday morning brought a spell of wet weather with it; as so often before, rain was the great equaliser at Le Mans, effectively reducing the advantages of the fastest cars.

The Ludwig/Whittington Porsche 935 led for most of the rest of the race and came home a comfortable winner, albeit at the slowest speed for a Le Mans winner since 1958, 108.10 mph for a distance of 2,590.928 miles. They were followed by an I.M.S.A. Porsche 935, the Barbour/Newman/Stommelen car - and naturally, the fact that Paul Newman came second in his first Le Mans was the biggest Le Mans story for years; Motor's headline 'The Day the Winner Came Second' spoke for itself. But with a third 935 in third place, and a Group 4 934 in fourth place, the 1979 Le Mans was a notable triumph for Porsche; their fifth win elevating the Stuttgart sports car manufacturer to the same level as Bentley and Jaguar in the Le Mans history.

In this year of debacle for the Group 6 cars, the best-placed Group 6 car was the Rondeau which came fifth, followed by the BMW M.l, another three Porsches and a second Rondeau. A total of 22 cars finished. Of the British entries, the De Cadenet had been forced to abandon within the first hour of the race with gearbox failure, and the Aston Martin broke its engine in a big way, after suffering loss of oil pressure. Two British cars were first and second among the two litres, and one of the DFV-engined Lolas also survived, to finish in twentieth place. The lesson learned from the 1979 Le Mans race was that once again, endurance had proved more important than speed.

THE SPORT
PETER WINDSOR

Le Mans countdown

Porsche versus an interesting private entry in this year's 24 Hours

NEXT WEEKEND'S Le Mans 24 hour race will unquestionably be the year's premier long-distance race, and even for the highly-favoured will be a difficult race to win. That much will be the same. Different, however, will be the start time — 2.00 pm in deference to the French elections — and the shape of the circuit, for a new corner at *Tertre Rouge* has taken exactly 100.32 feet from the overall lap distance. This marks the seventh circuit change since the first event in 1923, and was brought about by the close proximity of the new South-East Le Mans by-pass. *Tertre Rouge* is now less sharp than it used to be, and should contribute to higher speeds on the first part of the Mulsanne straight.

Feeling this change perhaps more than any others will be the drivers of the works Porsche 936s — the fastest cars entered for this year's race. Despite their braking problems at .the Silverstone Six Hours (or perhaps because of the problems they have already encountered) Porsche are by far and away the favourites for Le Mans. Two 936s have been entered, to be driven by the potent driver combinations of Jacky Ickx-Didier Pironi and Brian Redman-Hurley Haywood. Their sponsors, of course, will be Essex petroleum, the Monaco-based firm that also support Team Lotus. Jacky Ickx is currently the unofficial lap record holder at Le Mans, thanks to his 3 min 27.6 sec lap in Wednesday's practice last year, although the fastest race lap stands to Jean-Pierre Jabouille's Renault at 3 min 34.2 sec. The Porsche should break 210 mph on the straight.

Renault won't be at Le Mans this year, so Porsche's major opposition will come from semi-works and private teams. American dealer Harley Cluxton will be the foremost "private" entrant, for he returns to Le Mans with the Mirage chassis that won in 1975, but modified with Cosworth DFV engines and sweeping long-tail bodywork. Cluxton's Mirage GTC Cosworths will be backed by local Ford dealers and driven by Derek Bell-Vern Schuppan and David Hobbs-Jean-Pierre Jaussaud, both of which are strong pairings.

Also in the over 2-litre Group 6 class are a number of strong British-based entries, including two Japanese Dome-DFVs (Gordon Spice-Chris Craft and Tony Trimmer-Bob Evans), a Fisons-sponsored Lola-DFV for Martin Raymond, Ray Mallock and Simon Phillips, plus the De Cadenet-DFV which went so well at Silverstone. This will be driven by De Cadenet himself and Francois Migault. Ian Bracey, who in 1978 announced a two-year deal with a Hesketh chassis, has unfortunately been forced to scratch following the loss of his sponsorship. His drivers were to have been Rupert Keegan, Divina Galica and Richard Bond. Bracey's 1978 sponsor, Alexander Howden, will instead be appearing on the sides of a March-prepared BMW H1. This car is entered for the Group 5 category, although whether it will run here or in the TMSA class will be decided at Le Mans scrutineering. In any event, the March-BMW (a connection which sounds familiar!) is perhaps the most interesting car in the field. Designed and built by March Engines in Oxford, the M1 was conceived last August and first tested in February. It has been built from scratch as a Group 5 car, complete with maximum-regulation bodywork, and is sponsored by a Guy Edwards package comprising ICI, Alexander Howden insurance (Edwards drove

for Bracey in 1978!), Arena sportswear and *Newsweek*. Like the works Porsches it will be running on Dunlops, and already it has been tested in darkness as well as daylight. Drivers are Guy Edwards, Dieter Quester and Ian Grob.

Jean-Pierre Beltoise will be teaming with Henri Pescarolo to drive the DFV-powered Group 6 coupé that used to be called an Inaltera. This year the car has been re-named in favour of its sponsors — ITT Oceanic — and will be supported by a similar car driven by rally stars, Bernard Darniche-Jean Ragnotti. The Inaltera factory has now been taken over by Jean Rondeau, who will be driving a third car in the GTP class in conjunction with Giacomo Agostini.

Porsche 935s dominate Group 5, and, as ever, look like providing the closest racing. George Loos has entered two cars — for Manfred Schurti, Bob Wollek and John Fitzpatrick — and so has his arch-rival, Erwin Kremer. The latter's driver line-up is weaker though, for Klaus Ludwig will be paired with rent-a-drivers. Also in the Group 5 class is a Porsche 935 driven by Jean-Pierre Jarier.

The IMSA class contains the race's other interesting entries. Six Ferrari 512BBs face a host of American Porsche 935s and the BMW M1s — and this year stand a good chance of victory. The Ferraris ran into chronic tyre trouble with their Michelins at Daytona, but, since then, have been extensively tested at Paul Ricard. They are now longer and lighter, have better front aerodynamics and larger radiators, and should be capable of at least 190 mph on Mulsanne. Clay Regazzoni is among those listed to drive the BBs, so watch for spectacular results. In addition to the March-BMW, the works will also be taking an interest in the M1 entered by Herve Poulain — but mainly for aesthetic reasons: Poulain's car has been painted by Andy Warhol! Amongst

Night practice for the March-prepared BMW M1, which has been entered in Group 5 but, due to its non-homologation, seems likely to run in the IMSA class. A Guy Edwards package deal brings together a number of sponsors, the bodywork is the most extravagant seen on an M1

the Porsches, actor Paul Newman is slated to drive with Dick Barbour.

And then there is the GT Prototype class — the category designed by Le Mans for cars without a home. Three of the interesting W.M.s have been entered here, each fitted with a twin turbo V6 Peugeot-Renault engine. W.M. stands for the two men who built the cars — Gerard Welter and Michel Meunier — and this year they are looking for around 500-510bhp from their new turbo layout.

The GTP class is six cars strong and the strongest, in terms of power is unquestionably the Aston Martin V8 turbo entered by Alan Hamilton. Hamilton, Dave Preece and Mike Salmon will drive the 225 mph, twin turbo car, and this year feel confident of winning their class. "We are aware that we are racing what is essentially a heavy road-going car," says Aston dealer Hamilton, "but the car is not as heavy as some people think. Weight could be reduced to the minimum, but this would certainly affect our reliability."

A full report of the Le Mans 24 Hour race will be published in *Auto car* next week. Readers can meanwhile keep track of the race by tuning in to BBC radio. Transmissions can be heard at the following times:

Saturday, 9 June — race preview and start at 1.30 pm on *Sport or Two*. Further reports at 5.30 pm with interviews and live coverage in *Sports Desk* at 7.30 pm. Final news at 11.02 pm.
Sunday, 10 June — reports at 8.03 am, 10.02 am, 12.02 am and in 1.00 pm news. Race round-up in *Sunday Sports Special* at 5.30 pm.

Above: The IMSA Ferrari 512BB has undergone extensive testing since Daytona, where it was beset with tyre problems
Right: Alan Hamilton is looking for a GTP class win with his twin turbo Aston Martin V8
Far right: Porsche will be running two 936s in Essex colours, with Jacky Ickx hunting for an unprecedented fifth Le Mans win

LES VINGT-QUATRE HEURES DU MANS

A Question of Endurance, Not Speed

SOME aspects of the international racing scene may change with almost frenetic haste from month to month, but other facets of the sport seem to remain reassuringly constant from one year to another. One of those unchanging constants is the magic of the 24 Hours of Le Mans. The ACO's annual epic of speed and endurance on the famous and historic Circuit of Le Sarthe took place this year on June 9th/10th, and had all its usual character and charismatic allure, even though the entry hadn't quite the quality of the past two years.

Owing to the recent construction of a new road junction on the Route Nationale that forms the three-and-a-half mile long Mulsanne Straight, the old Tertre Rouge Corner had been replaced by an ever so slightly less acute twin apex bend, shortening the circuit from 13.64 to 13.61 kilometres (8.47 miles). Another divergence from tradition was a change of starting time, moved forward from four o'clock to two o'clock in order to give the French plenty of time to cast votes for the EEC's new European Assembly.

As far as the entry was concerned, it was very much a case of Porsches against the rest. Of the 55 starters, no fewer than 19 emanated from the Stuttgart manufacturer, their ranks headed by the two Essex Petroleum sponsored factory 936s. These are the long-tailed open Group 6 sports-racers with twin-turbocharged flat-six engines of 2.1-litre capacity that won at Le Mans in 1976 and 1977, although soundly beaten last year by a Renault. The two works cars were little changed since that defeat, apart from a change to the Essex livery of white, red and blue, although sturdier fifth gears had been fitted to avoid the failures that probably cost them the race a year ago. Drivers for the two Porsche 936s were Jacky Ickx (trying for a record fifth victory in the 24 Hours), his partner Brian Redman, France's Bob Wollek and America's Hurley Haywood.

All the other quick Porsches entered were 3-litre 935 Turbos. Some were in the Group 5 division, others in the IMSA category, although the differences between "European" and "American" models are in fact few and subtle. Among the swiftest of more than a dozen 935s in the list of starters were a pair of Gelo cars from Cologne, driven by Manfred Schurti/Hans Heyer and John Fitzpatrick/Harald Grohs/Jean-Louis Lafosse, and an American twin-turbo 935 entered by Dick Barbour for Rolf Stommelen, Barbour

Brian Redman waits while the Porsche mechanics attend to the consequences of tyre failure on the Dunlop Curve!

himself and enigmatic filmstar Paul Newman.

The quickest 935 of all, however, was a very special car. Built by the Kremer family at their workshops in Cologne, the 935K3 had substantially different bodywork, giving improved aerodynamics and even a small measure of "ground effect", and an air-cooled as opposed to water-cooled intercooler unit. Driving the white, Philippe Selvet sponsored machine, was Kremer's regular German Championship driver, Klaus Ludwig, plus two Americans from Fort Lauderdale, Florida, whose names were practically unknown in Europe before the race: the Whittington brothers, Don and Bill.

Against the Porsches were ranged a string of Group 6 sports-racing cars all powered by the ubiquitous Cosworth DFV engine. From Harley Cluxton's Grand Touring Cars Incorporated stable in Arizona came a pair of Ford-France-entered Mirage M10s, developed from last year's M9s but substantially improved (or at any rate altered!) in numerous respects. Down to drive the Mirages were Derek Bell/David Hobbs and Vern Schuppan/Jean-Pierre Jaussaud. From Britain came Alain de Cadenet's latest Le Mans contender, the De Cadenet that had finished second at Silverstone in May. As then Francois Migault was de Cadenet's co-driver.

From France came a trio of Rondeaus, built in Le Mans itself by Jean Rondeau and his partner Charles James. One of the attractive DFV-

powered coupes was actually entered as a "GT Prototype", but apart from different sized wheels it looked practically identical to the pure Group 6 cars. Henri Pescarolo/Jean-Pierre Beltoise handled one Rondeau M379, rally stars Bernard Darniche/Jean Ragnotti another, and Jean Rondeau/Jacky Jaran the "GTP" entry. Finally, from Japan, came a pair of ultra-long, low and narrow Dome Zero R1s, DFV-powered sports-racing machines with canopy-topped cockpits that were built specifically for the long fast straights of Le Mans. As at Silverstone where the Dome made its racing debut, Chris Craft and Gordon Spice were the team's main drivers, with Bob Evans and Tony Trimmer in the second car.

Very comfortably fastest in the 12 hours of official practice, as expected, were the two works Porsche 936s. Bob Wollek won pole with a 3 min. 30.61 sec. on Wednesday night, and Jacky Ickx returned a 3 min. 31.37 sec. on Thursday — neither time approaching the 3 min. 27.6 sec. set by Ickx last year in a virtually identical car on a fractionally longer (yet arguably slower) circuit. Nor was the Porsche team without its dramas in practice. Minutes after setting his pole position time, Wollek had a frightening moment at around 200 m.p.h. when a rear tyre deflated suddenly on Mulsanne Straight. More by luck than judgement perhaps, he hit nothing, but it was worryingly reminiscent of Jochen Mass's high speed accident at Silverstone, when a rear tyre had come off the rim after going down without warning. The result was a night of hard work for Porsche's mechanics repairing a battered car, and some modified rear rims that were made up for the race. Ickx's car had its dramas too, an engine having to be changed after Redman had over-revved it.

An eyebrow raising third quickest in practice was the Kremer Porsche 935K of Ludwig and the Whittingtons, the German driver recording 3 min. 36.64 sec. The Group 5 "Special Production Car" proved quicker on Mulsanne than any of the Group 6 cars except Ickx's 936, and that had been only a whisker better on top speed, at around 220 m.p.h. Another Porsche 935, the Gelo entry of Schurti and Heyer, was fourth in line at 3 min. 36.65 sec., following a couple of engine failures for Georg Loos's team during the first, seven hour long practice session. Only after the two 935s did one come to the

Bell up on the kerb in the Mirage-DFV: he and Hobbs led the race in the early stages.

best of the DFV propelled machines, the Mirage M10 of Schuppan/Jaussaud setting a 41.63 on Wednesday with so little fuss that it was left back at base in Le Chartre for the second session on Thursday.

The opening laps went very much as planned, the two Essex Porsches taking a commanding lead before they reached the Esses on lap one. At the end of the first lap, Ickx headed team-mate Wollek by inches, but more than ten seconds passed before Ludwig, Bell, Schuppan and Migault howled past the long line of pits. By the end of lap three the expected order had established itself, with the two Porsche 936s striding away at the head of the field and the Mirages of Bell and Schuppan in third and fourth.

Not until the first round of refuelling stops, early in the second hour, was there any upset in that order. Ickx lost a couple of minutes at his first scheduled pit stop while his rear wheels were changed — the modified rims fitted to his car since practice seemed to be fouling brake calipers, themselves altered since Silverstone where excessive rear brake wear had almost sent Brian Redman into the wall. But it was on laps 43 and 44 that the order changed dramatically. Having taken over from Wollek, Haywood stopped to have his seat more securely fixed, and Schuppan's Mirage stopped out on the circuit with a broken gear selector shaft. (Although repaired, the car was later excluded for falling too far behind.)

Then Redman, having relieved Ickx a few laps earlier, suffered a tyre blow-out in the Dunlop Curve. He spun the car deliberately, and came to rest without smashing into the barriers; but the car was badly damaged on one side nevertheless, the radiator serving one bank of cylinders being slashed off by the torn and tattered rubber. Redman nursed the battered machine back to the pits for repairs, but 80 minutes were lost.

So in spite of its unscheduled stop for seat adjustment, the Wollek/Haywood 936 enjoyed a good lead until the fourth hour, when it began to misfire. By the time the fuel injection pump, the fuel filter and other parts of the injection system had been replaced, it was restored to full health. But over an hour had slipped away in the

meantime, and it left the Bell/Hobbs Mirage with a big advantage over the best Group 5 machines. For close on two hours the Mirage held the lead, Bell and Hobbs being joined by Schuppan out of the other car as afternoon turned to evening. At a little past quarter distance, however, the blue Mirage lost that lead when its exhaust system had to be replaced — and the net result of that was little short of sensational.

As dusk turned to darkness, the Kremer 935K of Ludwig and the Whittingtons thus held the slenderest of advantages over the Gelo 935 of Schurti/Heyer. Throughout the night the two rival teams from Cologne fought spiritedly for the lead, first one car heading the order, then the other — and all the time, the second Gelo Porsche was close at hand.

Hardly had darkness fallen over the restaurants and fairground of the Circuit of the Sarthe than the Mirage team ran into trouble again. The car that was still well placed was bedevilled by an over-charging alternator, causing one headlamp failure after another. The first time it happened, Schuppan left the road at Porsche Curve; fortunately damage was slight, so the car continued, but it lost more time when the problem repeated itself.

Soon after midnight light rain began to sprinkle down, and not long after half distance it turned into a ferocious thunderstorm that threatened to leave the track awash. Now it really was a matter of endurance, not speed. Regaining places steadily after its earlier delays, Ickx's Porsche was stranded on the circuit when its electrics failed. Ickx persuaded the car back to life but was disqualified soon afterwards for receiving external asssistance away from the pits.

The Gelo team lost both its cars in quick succession early in the 15th hour of the event, when the red 935s were second and fourth. First Fitzpatrick's suffered a spectacular turbocharger failure that lit up the whole tail end in flames: damage was minimal, but the marshals smothered it with so much extinguishant that the car had to be withdrawn. Less than 15 minutes later Schurti was in the pit road reporting an engine failure in the other car, leaving the Ludwig/Whittington

Kremer Porsche in front by literally miles from the Stommelen/Barbour/Newman team.

As night turned reluctantly into a grey, wet dawn, the surviving Mirage was one of numerous cars suffering acute misfires, suffering internal engine damage as a consequence. With seven hours to go, the Wollek/Haywood 936 had recaught so much lost ground that it had moved into second place again, albeit 13 laps behind the leaders. Yet it, too, went sick, and finally retired with something seriously amiss inside the engine during the 19th hour.

Nothing, it seemed, would stop the Kremer Porsche out front — until it ground to a halt on Mulsanne Straight while Don Whittington was at the wheel. The belt that drove its fuel injection pump had broken, and whilst a spare was on board, all Don's attempts to fit it so that it stayed on proved futile. Eventually he coaxed the stricken car back to the pits by removing and shortening the alternator belt. Shortly after noon, the leading Kremer car was back in the race, its lead reduced from 15 laps at one stage to only three.

It might well have lost the lead during the hour or so it spent out of action, had not the second placed Barbour Porsche encountered problems of its own. Chiselling away the leaders' advantage by the minute, it had come in for a routine wheel and pad change, only to have a wheel nut jam solid and refuse to budge. The nut had to be sawn off, keeping the car in the pit road for 23 minutes.

As the race ran to its conclusion, the Stommelen/Barbour/Newman car encountered more serious problems in the closing stages. With 20 minutes to go, Stommelen slowed abruptly to a crawl; after a couple of creeping, misfiring laps, he stopped a few yards short of the finish line and waited patiently for the chequered flag to appear, taking care to keep his engine running. Only four or five laps from home, the second placed 935 had holed a piston — but Stommelen's action ensured that it would still finish second, over six laps behind the vicorious Kremer 935K3 of Klaus Ludwig, Don and Bill Whittington. Third was another Kremer prepared Porsche 935, driven by Frenchmen Francois Servanin, Laurent Ferrier and Francois Trisconi, while fourth was the GT class winning Porsche 934 of Swiss drivers Herbert Mueller, Angelo Pallavicini and Marco Vanoli.

So what of the others? The De Cadenet had gone out, in effect, after only six laps, after a bearing in the gearbox had failed. Why had it failed? — because someone had forgotten to drill a hole in a pinion to let oil reach the bearing; bad preparation in other words. The two Domes fared little better. Craft's, running seventh on the opening lap, had caught fire on the second because a lead to the distributor had been improperly secured; eventually the mess was cleared up and the car set off again only to run out of petrol later at Mulsanne! In the other car, Trimmer climbed through the order to be fifth after a few laps, but in so doing he ignored the rising temperature gauge needle.

The Rondeaus were in trouble right from the start, Ragnotti's car throwing off wheel balance weights with gay abandon and Pescarolo's stopping on the warm-up because of fuel vaporisation. The third car, the GTP Rondeau, finally retired with a damaged chassis after swiping the guard-rails at Tertre Rouge, but the two Group 6 cars plugged on gamely despite numerous set-backs. The team's persistence was well rewarded, for Ragnotti/Darniche ended up fifth and winners of the Group 6 class, while

Continued on page 89

Class win for Messrs. Charnell/Jones/Smith in their Chevron B36-Cosworth.

Results:

LE MANS 24 HOURS — 306.7 laps — 4,169.71 Km.

1st: K. Ludwig/D. Whittington/B. Whittington (3.0 t/c Porsche 935K3)	306 laps
2nd: R. Stommelen/D. Barbour/P. Newman (3.0 t/c Porsche 935 77A)	300 laps
3rd: F. Servanin/L. Ferrier/F. Trisconi (3.0 t/c Porsche 935/77A)	292 laps
4th: H. Mueller/A. Pallavincini/M. Vanoli (3.0 t/c Porsche 934)	291 laps
5th: J. Ragnotti/B. Darniche (3.0 Rondeau M379 DFV)	287 laps
6th: M. Mignot/M. Winkelhock/H. Poulain (3.5 BMW M1)	284 laps
7th: D. Schornstein/E. Doeren/G. von Tschirnhaus (3.0 t/c Porsche 935/77A)	283 laps
8th: B. Garretson/E. Abate/S. McKitterick (3.0 t/c Porsche 935/78)	278 laps
9th: J. Hotchkiss/B. Kirby (3.0 t/c Porsche 935/78)	275 laps
10th: H. Pescarolo/J-P. Beltoise (3.0 Rondeau M379 DFV)	274 laps

Winners average speed: 173.913 k.p.h. (108.2 m.p.h.)
Class winners: Ludwig/Whittington/Whittington; Stommelen/Barbour/Newman; Ragnotti/Darniche; T. Charnell/R. Smith/R. Jones (2.0 Chevron B36 Ford BDG); J-D. Raulet/M. Mamers (2.6 t/c WM P79 Peugeot); Mueller/Paliabicini/Vanoli.

88

SPORTWEEK
Circuit scene Mike Doodson

Porsche 936-01, right, will be chasing a third Le Mans win. Brand new German challenger (from Oxford!) is the March Engines-built lightweight M1 BMW coupé, seen below

Le Mans:
Porsche and Paul Newman to the rescue

THE WITHDRAWAL of the works Porsche and Renault teams, last year's million-dollar Le Mans rivals, caused more than a little mid-winter anguish in the HQ of the Automobile Club de l'Ouest. With no big names to promote, and world sports car racing in the doldrums as a result of frequent incomprehensible rule changes, the chances of this year's Grand Prix d'Endurance being a classic looked slim.

At the last minute, however, the race has taken on an unexpected tenseness. Not only have the seemingly limitless petro-dollars of US tycoon David Thieme persuaded Porsche to return (in the colours of Thieme's Essex Overseas Corporation), but the race has gained its single most promotable personality with the announcement that Hollywood actor Paul Newman would be taking part.

At 53, Newman is almost certainly the oldest man in the race. This is no stunt, though: he's been an amateur racer of some repute, winning a SCCA title only two years ago, and always entering

under the self-effacing name of "P J Newman". Le Mans is the climax of his motor racing career, and the adulation of the masses is something which neither he nor the ACO will want.

Inevitably, the Essex-Porsches (driver pairings confirmed this week as Ickx/Pironi and Redman/Haywood, with Mario Andretti under a Goodyear ban) must be favoured to win. The 936/1 which proved unexpectedly fragile at Silverstone has been rebuilt: victory for this car would be its third at the Sarthe circuit.

The most serious opposition to the Porsches comes from Arizona attorney Harley Cluxton's team under veteran Le Mans engineer/manager John Horsman. Essentially

they're the same Mirage M10s which won in '75 and were metamorphosed in '77 with Renault engines. Now redesigned again to accept their original Cosworth-Ford V8s, they're entered by a consortium of French Ford dealers simply as Ford M10s. The experienced driver pairings are Schuppan/Jaussaud and Bell/Hobbs.

Other, less proven, entries in the Group 6 (Sports 2-seater) class include two of the Japanese Dome coupes, now with all-British driver pairings of Craft/Spice and Bob Evans/Tony Trimmer under the cool management of the able Keith Greene. Similar French coupes, developments of the ambitious but hitherto unsuccessful Inaltera project, are the Rondeaus for old-timers

Beltoise/Pescarolo and rallymen Darniche/Ragnotti.

Ian Bracey has had to withdraw his Ibec-Hesketh, but last-minute sponsorship has enabled Alain de Cadenet to share his quick Lola-based "Special" with local driver Francois Migault, albeit without Craft and Green's support. A similar well-prepared de Cadenet-Lola is in the hands of British trio Raymond/Mallock/Phillips.

But perhaps the most exciting "British" entry of all is the BMW M1 coupe entered by ICI Vymura/Alexander Howden Insurance and Arena Sportswear for Guy Edwards/Ian Grob/Dieter Quester. Not to be confused with the Procars, this is the forerunner of BMW's 1980 Group 5 "Silhouette" entries, and is built by March Engines of Oxford on a lightweight spaceframe. Testing has not gone as well as it might, though surprisingly it's been the turbo-engine which has given trouble.

Inevitably, turbo-Porsches in various stages of tune dominate the entry, with eight of them in the Group 5 class (drivers include Jean-Pierre Jarier and our own John Fitzpatrick); another eight in the "IMSA" class (which Paul Newman is contesting along with co-drivers Rolf Stommelen and his chubby but quick team boss Dick Barbour); and six in the GT category.

Le Mans news flashes

● No fewer than six **Ferrari 512 BB "Boxers"** have been entered. One of them is due to be shared by Clay Regazzoni with a yet-to-be-announced co-driver.

● Returning to Le Mans in the special GTP (Grand Touring Prototype) class after a year's absence is the **Aston Martin DBS turbo** prepared in Burton-on-Trent by Robin Hamilton. Denying criticisms that the car is overweight, Hamilton says: "this year we've got speed as well as reliability ... I am confident that after 24

hours this time we'll win our class." We certainly share Hamilton's contention that the public appreciates what at least resembles a true road-going car, and wish him and co-drivers Dave Preece and Mike Salmon the best of British.

● All the fastest Porsches, the Group 6 BMW M1, Hamilton's Aston Martin and the two Domes are running this year on **Dunlop rubber.** Due to a conflict with his Goodyear contract, Mario Andretti will not now be starting the race as he would have liked at the wheel of a works Essex-Porsche 936.

All-British, and proud of it: the much revised turbo version of the Aston Martin which finished 17th two years ago. Drivers are Robin Hamilton, Dave Preece and Mike Salmon

LE MANS:—
Continued from page 88
Pescarolo/Beltoise were tenth. Another car to profit from simply keeping going in the face of adversity was the works run "Procar" style BMW M1 handled by Winkelhock, Poulain and Mignot. It lost hours while clutch, gearbox and all four brake discs were changed, and misfired horribly throughout Sunday, yet it still finished sixth.

The four Ferrari 512 Berlinetta Boxers had mixed fortunes. Private entries, the rebodied "Boxers" had nevertheless been developed by the factory at Maranello and Fiorano specifically as

endurance racers. Crashes left the 512BB entered by Le Mans veteran Jean Beurlys for Nick Faure, Steve O'Rouke, Bernard De Dryver and himself to finish 12th.

It was to the 2-litre Group 6 class that one had to look to find British success. First in class were Tony Charnell, Robin Smith and Richard Jones, whose Mogil Motors entered, Ford BDG-engined Chevron B36 survived wet electrics and repeatedly flattened batteries to finish 17th. Right behind them, im both the class and the overall

order, was the Dorset Racing Association team of Tony Birchenhough, Richard Jenvey, Brian Joscelyne and Nick Mason, whose Lola-BDG T297 had gone very crisply indeed after losing almost an hour in the opening stages with a cracked rotor arm.

So that was the 24 Hours of Le Mans for another year. Thanks to the failure of all the favourites, it had proved a better race than anyone expected. — J.C.T.

The day the winner came second

Yes, that's Paul Newman (spot him, left) with the champagne at Le Mans. As an actor, he's a pretty fine driver . . .

Report by Mike Doodson
Photography by
Maurice Rowe

End of the road at last (above) for Le Mans winner Klaus Ludwig as the flag marshals salute him at the *Virage Porsche*

left: only half an hour earlier, his Kremer mechanics worked frantically to replace thrown injection belts

THE NAMES were hardly familiar. Klaus Ludwig, a 28 year old German with a hatful of German championship successes to his name; two wealthy American brothers, Don (33) and Bill (29) Whittington from Fort Lauderdale in Florida; and a big bottle of champagne on the podium. Don was interviewed politely, and he thanked his entrant, Erwin Kremer, for a fine job of preparation. They had won Le Mans — the Whittingtons in only their second year of car racing — and for a moment the glory was theirs.

But while Bill deliriously unpicked his victory garland and scattered carnations to the crowd below, back came the cries. "New-man, New-man," they echoed, and after a decent interval for the winners to be fêted, the second garlanding ceremony was initiated, with the 2nd place trio of drivers.

Leading them out on to the balcony he came. The silver hair, the blue eyes, the slight figure could be no greater contrast than the one with that of his burly entrant, Dick Barbour. Paul Newman, 53 year old Hollywood star, had done what he came to do: race at Le Mans and finish honourably. He acknowledged the help of Barbour and of Rolf Stommelen, the "rock" of their driving strength, and modestly embraced them. He permitted himself a quiet smile, possibly the first of the weekend.

This will always be remembered as the year of Paul Newman. Why, at one stage before lunchtime on Sunday, when Don Whittington was struggling to jury-rig an injection pump drive belt on the stranded leading car out in the country, Newman, Barbour and Stommelen were gobbling up its 14 lap advantage and heading for a possible win.

Don fixed it, and anyway the Newman car lost several laps more as the result of a jammed wheelnut. The euphoria died away somewhat, dampened by another shower of rain, though not enough of it to explain entirely why this year's winners covered fewer miles than anyone at Le Mans since 1958. No matter. A hero had been born — hardly of his own making — and no doubt a script writer is at this moment attempting to improve on reality.

The diversion could hardly have come at a better time for Porsche. Coaxed back into the race by the financial blandishments of Essex petroleum (whose money also seemed to have bought up Le Mans itself this year), the works team and its museum-piece 1976-vintage type 936 prototypes was on to a hiding to nothing. By general consensus, including that of their drivers, the two 936s were unbeatable.

The Porsche's first worries came in practice, however. Insufficiently tested, they'd been fitted with stronger 5th gears (to overcome *last* year's Le Mans problem), repainted in Essex red, white and blue . . . and run into a tyre problem. Bob Wollek, a last-minute replacement for Tyrrell contractee Didier Pironi, lost a rear Dunlop when it leaped off its rim and took much of the long-tail Porsche bodywork with it: shades of the frightening accident which Jochen Mass suffered (at appreciably lower speed) at Silverstone. Much to-ing and fro-ing between Le Mans and Porsche's Weissach workshops ensued.

Come Sunday afternoon, they sped away, leaving the rival 3-litre prototype Group 6 cars panting at a pace which they couldn't match and which ultimately blew up all but two of them. Within three hours, though, the Porsche winning machine was looking decidedly frail: the number 2 car (Wollek/Haywood) was suffering from fuel starvation and Brian Redman, who had just taken over the number 1 car from his old partner Jacky Ickx, got a big fright when another tyre parted company with a wheel just after Dunlop's own bridge, and he was faced with a four-mile drive back "home" on nothing more than three good tyres and a bare metal rim.

Porsche's concern over tyres (which was shared by the drivers) had put into action a last-minute attempt at changing the specification of the wheels. Just how desperate the modifications were was proved when Ickx stopped for fresh tyres and was unable to leave the pit . . . because the rims had jammed hard up against the brake calipers. Already, the 936s were losing their grip on the race. And though Wollek fought back to 2nd place after four hours, the lead passed to the slower but less troublesome Ford (née Mirage) 10 of Derek Bell and David Hobbs.

It was other teams' setbacks rather than Porsche speed which enabled the Wollek/Haywood car to race back after a complete rebuild of its fuel injection system into 2nd place, after 17 hours of the 1979 Le Mans. By then, the Ickx/Redman car had been excluded for receiving outside assistance (while Ickx was trying to fix a broken injection belt), and Wollek-Haywood's good work was undone at breakfast time on Sunday by a sudden, massive engine failure. Porsche, one imagines, will not be anxious to return to Le Mans.

By rights, the Fords should have been able to take over the race and stroll home. After two years with Renault power, Harley Cluxton's Mirages in blue paint — handsomely sponsored by a consortium of French Ford dealers — were back with Cosworth engines, 20 per cent less frontal area and some useful drivers.

Yet here, too, lack of race testing showed up early. Jean-Pierre Jaussaud in the car he was sharing with Vern Schuppan went for 3rd gear, and the ZF gearbox refused to engage. Jaussaud lost half a dozen laps (and a lead which he'd held for three hours, since the Wollek Porsche's trouble until now, tea-time on Saturday) while he struggled to find a gear to get him back to the pits. There, a transmission rebuild took three hours, and eventually put the car out of the regulation time limit.

Schuppan was put into the other Ford in place of David Hobbs, who was less comfortable (and slower) in the revamped car than his team mates. Towards midnight, its headlights failed without warning as the Australian rushed through the tricky "new" return section after White House, bounced off the barriers on both sides of the road, and made a long stop for fresh body panels, attention to the electrics and other remedial work.

But this was not the end of the Ford's trouble. An intermittent engine problem suggested that team manager John Horsman had

perhaps taken too much of a gamble by specifying F1-tune DFV engines, and when a broken first gear was added to their problems, the Arizona-based team could hope only for a finish.

In this, watched by team associate John Wyer, they were to be disappointed. When Bell made his final pit stop, the combination of ropey engine and non-existent gears made it impossible to start the final lap. Poor Bell, who had been unwell (and certainly looked it), had to retire at the end of the pit lane, and the team was deprived even of the honourable 16th place it held at that stage.

With so many early retirements and woes, the eventual winner had taken over the lead as early as the seventh hour. This much-modified Porsche 935 has already shown its terrific speed in German national championship races, and here at Le Mans it wa renewing its season-long rivalry with the similar 935s prepared at Weissach by mechanics of the George Loos team, Ludwig's employer last year.

For two hours on Saturday, the Kremer car had kept station with the two leading Loos entries, one of which (Schurti/Hayer) held the lead for two hours before half-distance.

Then, before dawn on Sunday, both Loos cars retired almost simultaneously with spectacular engine failures, one of which (Fitzpatrick/ Grohs/Lafosse) lit up the sky in front of the pits. The unfortunate John Fitzpatrick, realising that it was probably a turbocharger failure which could be repaired, was mortified when French marshals smothered it with gritty powder, putting him out of the race whether he liked it or not.

The Kremer car was now securely in a lead which it was to hold for the final 14 hours of the race. Amazingly, the two Whittingtons were able to maintain much of Ludwig's pace, a remarkable achievement considering that until 15 months ago both had raced only motorcycles and aeroplanes. And Don's unexpected mechanical aptitude was called into play by the involuntary Sunday lunchtime stop when the fuel injection belt broke.

"It was the longest half hour of my entire life," he said: "it felt like three whole days." Another toothed belt (robbed from the alternator) failed "ten feet" from the first spot, and only a cobbled-up arrangement got him back to the pit, where the professional mechanics soon had the 750 horsepower Porsche back in the race.

But although the 2nd place Newman car had whittled 10 laps off the leader's 14 lap advantage, their own problems prevented Hollywood scoring the fairytale victory. Within sight of the finish, with only one lap needed to mop up the final quarter-hour, Stommelen passed the pits with a dreadful misfire. At walking speed, he completed two laps, then waited before the line for the flag to appear.

When it did flutter, he crossed over to take a 2nd place which will surely be remembered longer than any victory. The 1979 Le Mans 24 Hours made history from otherwise unmemorable ingredients.

Above: after most of the Group 6 cars had raced themselves to a standstill, the French Rondeaus were still running. This is Ragnotti/Darniche braving the wet

Above: Tertre Rouge has been clipped, and so have the Mulsanne's trees. Newly reprofiled corner is 30 metres shorter than before

Above: the bagpipes will skirl (with an English accent) for Tony Charnell and his class-winning Chevron crew from Dumfries

Above: last of the Porsches? After their all too brief showing, the two veteran 936s are now surely destined for a museum

'Motor' trophy for Scotland's valiant

Klaus Ludwig: German winner

BRITISH hopes faded early at Le Mans with retirements which several teams will want to forget in a hurry. First to go was the **de Cadenet-Ford,** newly sponsored in a barrage of double-page publicity by the **Daily Express,** which lasted for six laps in 6th place, until French co-driver **François Migault** brought it in with a seized (and brand new) gearbox, a problem quickly traced to an oil union which had not been drilled. Owner **Alain de Cadenet,** a Le Mans finisher in the last three years, looked through bloodshot eyes (he'd already been up all of one night), at the broken 'box and blamed himself. "That's six months of the hardest work I've ever done in my life down the drain," he

announced ... At least de Cadenet made no rash promises, unlike Aston Martin dealer **Robin Hamilton,** who had forecast a finish and a class win for his ponderous DBS turbo. Alas, the Aston disappointed, for not only did the promised 225 mph fail to materialise, but Hamilton's mechanics couldn't trace an oil leak, and the big car expired out on the circuit under veteran **Mike Salmon,** who had enthused after night practice about its "intriguing ability to light up the sky every time you lift off the throttle" ... Though Japanese in design, the two **coupe Domes** had British drivers who didn't last very long: two cars proved to be more than the largely British team under Keith Greene could manage, and both of them (**Craft/Spice** in one, **Trimmer/Evans** in the other) were retirements long before nightfall ... The two French-designed **Rondeau-Cosworth** coupes were the only healthy survivors in the Group 6 over 2-litre class, maintaining an enviable record established when they were known as **Inaltéras.** Both entries had a stack of problems, and rallymen **Ragnotti/Darniche** surprised by both qualifying and finishing ahead of single-seater experts **Pescarolo/Beltoise** ... Valiantly struggling through to the finish despite such setbacks as the loss of its alternator, a broken front hub and a rear brake caliper which fell off and vanished, the Fison's sponsored ex-de Cadenet Lola of **Martin Raymond** and **Ray Mallock** was credited with 20th place ... With England's hopes suffering so many

setbacks, it was left to the 2-litre Chevron entered by **Mogil Motors of Dumfries** to bring home the bacon for Britain. Prepared and driven by Scotsmen **Robin Smith** and **Richard Jones** at the Mogil HQ (prop: Wolverhampton-born **Tony Charnell**), the little Chevron survived various stops to be classified in 18th place, winner of the 2-litre class and the **"Motor" trophy** ... One British-built car which didn't even make it into the race was the long-awaited **March-built BMW M1.** After a minimum number of practice laps by **Ian Grob** and **Guy Edwards** — under the scrutiny of March director **Robin Herd** it failed to qualify for the Group 6 class, for which — because it's over 3-litre capacity — it had to be specially approved by the FISA in Paris ... One M1, however, did make it into the race. This was the works-owned "Procar" specification example entered for rapid German driver **Manfred Winkelhock** and a pair of Frenchmen. Despite running for half the race on five of its six cylinders (and having to undergo a complete gearbox-rebuild), the somewhat unlovely M1 with its **Andy Warhol**-created paint scheme came home in a completely unexpected 6th place overall ... The winning Porsche 935 incorporates some works-inspired tweaks, which according to Ex-Kremer driver **Bob Wollek** were acquired by team boss **Erwin Kremer** as a result of a close examination of last year's "Moby Dick" which he's been asked to take to an exhibition. The car incorporates some F1-type "ground effect"

aerodynamics which require fixed side skirts ... French journalists complained of being brushed off by **Paul Newman,** but he explained to me that it would be unfair to allow one journal to interview him at the expense of others. "I came here to race, not to talk," he said, "and anyway I didn't have too much to do with the success of this car." This didn't prevent the actor from taking the "dead man's watch" just before dawn, though he was relieved after half an hour when torrential rain flooded the track ... After lots of pre-race publicity, F1 men **Didier Pironi** and **Clay Regazzoni** both failed to show up. Pironi's Tyrrell team mate **Jean-Pierre Jarier** briefly drove a short-lived Porsche 935: "Ken says it's alright if I drive a saloon car, but only as third driver," said Jarier ... A nasty accident on Saturday night resulted in a marshal being taken to hospital in "grave" condition after he'd been struck by the crashing Lola-ROC of 2-litre class leader **Marc Sourd,** a top French hill-climber. The accident occurred at the revised (30 metres shorter) Tertre Rouge corner before the Mulsanne straight ... The European elections and the loss of the Renaults which won last year were variously blamed for the poor crowd at Le Mans this year. The heavy Sunday morning rain didn't help either, and it seems that it will take more than Paul Newman to bring the crowds back to Le Mans. The 2 o'clock start was not a great success, unless you include journalists with deadlines to meet ...

Vern Schuppan gets instructions from John Horsman in the (Mirage) Ford M10 which suffered disqualification in the closing seconds of the race

One of the two French-entered Ferraris: this one (Andruet/Dini) led the IMSA class in the 6th place overall before its retirement

RESULTS
24 Heures du Mans
Le Mans, 9/10 June 1979

1 2.4 Kremer Porsche 935 turbo (Klaus Ludwig/Don Whittington/Bill Whittington), 306 laps (2590.932 miles) in 23 hours 57m 58.6s at 108.10 mph; **2** 2.4 Barbour Porsche 935 turbo (Rolf Stommelen/Dick Barbour/P L Newman, 299 laps); **3** 2.4 Kremer Porsche 935 turbo (François Servanin/Laurent Ferrier/François Trisconi), 292 laps; **4** 2.4 Kores Porsche 934 turbo (Georges Bourdillat/Roland Ennequin/Alain Bernard), 291 laps; **5** 3.0 VSD/Canon Rondeau-Cosworth M379 (Jean Ragnotti/Bernard Darniche), 287 laps; **6** 3.5 Poulain BMW M1 (Manfred Winkelhock/Marcel Mignot/Hervé Poulain), 284 laps; **7** 2.4 Sekurit Porsche 935 turbo (Dieter Schornstein/Edgar Dören/Gotz Tschirnhaus/Gerhard Holup), 283 laps; **8** 4.2 Barbour Porsche 935 turbo (Oliver Garretson/Edwin Abate), 278 laps; **9** 2.4 Barbour Porsche 935 turbo (Robert Kirby/John Hotchkiss;, 275 laps; **10** 3.0 ITT Oceanic Rondeau-Cosworth M379 (Henri Pescarolo/Jean-Pierre Beltoise, 274 laps; **11** 2.4 Haldi Porsche 935 turbo (Claude Haldi/Rodfrigo Teran/Herbert Loewe), 270 laps; **12** 4.9 Ferrari 512BB (Nick Faure/Bernard de Dryver/Steve O'Rourke/"Beurlys"), 269 laps.

Sport sidelines

● As we closed for press Olympus Cameras and Wolf Racing announced that the Finnish driver **Keke Rosberg** would be taking over the GP seat vacated by James Hunt for the rest of the 1979 season.

● Guy Ligier has dismissed as "not serious" suggestions that Jacques Laffite would shortly be flying to Brazil to persuade Copersucar, sponsors of **Emerson Fittipaldi's** Grand Prix team, to release Emerson so that he can take the place of injured Ligier driver Patrick Depailler.

● Testing at Silverstone last week, the Renault team and **Jean-Pierre Jabouille** had a most unusual failure: instead of the engine blowing up, the chassis did! Team manager Jean Sage believes that a build-up of vapour between the car's bag tank and its outer skin may have accidentally ignited: "the trouble is that it is not the first time this has happened, though it is the most serious incident of its type that we experienced at Silverstone," he said.

● Reigning Aurora AFX champion **Tony Trimmer,** now living in the USA, had his first race outing of the year (albeit not for very long) at Le Mans with Dome. He hopes to find work in the States now that his position at Melchester Racing has been taken over by Desire Wilson.

D OWN ON MY knees in the rain, an
umbrella is clamped between
my neck and shoulder, the borrowed Canon camera balanced on my
knee and I'm making notes up under
the umbrella so they won't smear in the
drizzle. My feet are soaked and I think
I'm coming down with a head cold, but
I'm hanging on to every word from the
public address announcer, trying to
understand the French and impa-
tiently waiting for the English transla-
tion. Here we are in the 20th hour of
the 24 Hours of Le Mans and it's more
exciting than a great number of half-
hour sprint races I've attended—but
more on that in a moment.

A great deal of that excitement was
because the 1979 *Vingt-Quatre Heures
du Mans* was truly an American Le
Mans. We were there in large numbers,
thanks in no small part to the *Voitures*

IMSA class which attracted cars meant
to represent our International Motor
Sports Association. In combination
with that was the World Challenge for
Endurance Drivers, which makes
points earned at Le Mans in June as
important as those picked up at, for
instance, the 6-hour RS race held three
weeks later at Daytona.

Leading the list was the 4-car
Porsche 935 team of California automobile dealer Dick Barbour, who was
teamed with Rolf Stommelen and Paul
Newman in a twin-turbo version. The
other three were single turbos headed
by the Sebring-winning trio of Bob
Akin/Rob McFarlin/Roy Woods plus
Bob Garretson/Ed Abate/Skeeter
McKitterick and Bob Kirby/John
Hotchkiss. Pitted next to the Barbour
team was Ted Field's single-turbo Interscope Porsche 935, which was

looked after by the Interscope team
and Vasek Polak and had Field teamed
with John Morton and Milt Minter.
Also listed in the IMSA group were six
Ferrari 512BB Boxers. Only four
showed up, with one from Luigi Chinetti's North American Racing Team
and having Floridian Preston Henn as
one driver, while Peter Gregg took a
holiday from his 935 ". . . to keep in
touch with the competition" by driving
one of the Charles Pozzi Ferraris.

In the Group 5 class, where the cars
are only slightly different than IMSA,
Don and Bill Whittington were teamed
with German Klaus Ludwig in one of
the Porsche-Kremer Racing twin-turbo
935s (properly a 935K3), the car sporting Kremer's special "wing" bodywork
and an air-cooled intercooler. In this
group Randy Townsend shared a 2-
turbo 935 with his former Can-Am

AN AMERICAN LE MANS

And the race came complete with a Hollywood script

BY JOHN LAMM
PHOTOS BY THE AUTHOR

The flag-draped Barbour team (below), Harley Cluxton's Mirage-Ford (right) and the winner's stand (lower right) as the Moët flies.

teammate, Jean-Pierre Jarier, and Raymond Touroul.

The big guns in Group 6 were, of course, the Mirage M10s and Porsche 936s. The former are based in Phoenix, Arizona and sponsored by a consortium of French Ford dealers. Team owner Harley Cluxton had brought former Le Mans winner Derek Bell to race with David Hobbs, while Vern Schuppan was matched with last year's winner, Jean-Pierre Jassaud. The Stuttgart-based 936s were sponsored by American David Thieme's Essex Motorsports, which also bought an amazing amount of wall space for advertising at the track. The Porsche pairings had Jacky Ickx and Bob Wollek in one and Brian Redman and 4-time Daytona 24-hour winner Hurley Haywood in the other, with Jürgen Barth the third driver for both entries.

It was obvious right from the outset that the American influence would be considerable if from nothing more than our numbers. This was the sort of year at Le Mans when you might just as easily be greeted with "Hi, how are you?" as *"Ah, comment ça va?"* Then there was Dick Barbour's "Pete-air-bilt" rig, appropriately chromed and polished and drawing a seemingly endless line of onlookers who climbed up to stare at the cockpit. Underlining it all was the presence of Paul Newman, who found that, just as in the U.S., he couldn't escape the photographers and autograph seekers for a short time to just be P.L. Newman, race driver. It reached the point where the gendarmes had to be called to clear the *paparazzi* from the Barbour pits so the cars could be properly serviced during the stops.

One of the Barbour Porsches in the miserable drizzle of Sunday morning (below). The Sebring-winning team (bottom) of, left to right, Rob McFarlin, Roy Woods and Bob Akin suffered engine failure. Hurley Haywood (bottom, left) in a Saturday stint in a Porsche 936. At left Harley Cluxton and a bespectacled John Horsman smile through their troubles.

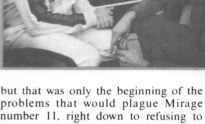

There were two changes of some note at Le Mans this year, one being the redesign of the Tertre Rouge corner and the other a 2:00 p.m. starting time. The former turned this famous right-hand turn onto the Mulsanne Straight into a 2-part, modern-looking corner with little of the charm of the old one. The early starting time was to accommodate the European parliamentary elections.

The colorful line of race cars that twisted through the Virage Ford for the early start was headed by the Porsche 936s, the 935s already making their presence known by filling the second row. In 3rd spot was the Ludwig/Whittington/Whittington car in which they'd cranked up the boost from the race setting of 1.20 bar to 1.45 bar and sent the German out to run a lap just 3.27 seconds slower than the 936s. In a race of 24 hours, however, starting spot isn't particularly critical as each team rushes off to the fate the 24 hours have planned for them.

In the case of the 936s, it started with supreme control over the event that turned too quickly to embarrassment because of a grand variety of ills that included a loose driver's seat, the sort of tire deflation that almost destroyed one of the cars weeks earlier at Silverstone and a mysterious misfire. The 936s kept struggling back from each *malade* until Ickx was disqualified in the early morn-

ing hours for receiving outside help and the Wollek/Haywood car's engine went sour, then dead just before 9:00 a.m. Finally the two gallant machines became museum pieces.

There's only one way to describe the fate of the Mirage team and that's pure rotten racing luck. Mind you, they had their moments of glory, leading for some three hours in the sunshine of late Saturday and spending more time out front than the 936s, but then it all came apart. The point of a race like Le Mans is to filter out all the variables and leave only the knowns for the 24 hours. No one knows that better than team manager John Horsman and his former boss John Wyer, who is the master of the subject. Yet the team was plagued by failures that had never threatened before. For the first time in what Wyer estimates to be 20,000 miles of racing, a ZF gearbox broke, virtually eliminating one car. An exhaust pipe broke on the other car and then lights went out on Vern Schuppan's around midnight when he was on the quick section after Arnage. "It was one of those situations where there is very little you can do," Schuppan explained. "It got very quiet so I knew I was on the grass. I had the steering over at full lock and was waiting to see what I would hit." Despite bouncing off Armco on both sides of the track Schuppan made it back to the pits,

but that was only the beginning of the problems that would plague Mirage number 11, right down to refusing to start to make the required 1 lap within the last 15 minutes of the race to be qualified as a finisher.

Other American runners suffered failures, the 5th hour being particularly rough, with the Akin/McFarland/Woods and Townsend/Jarier/Touroul Porsches losing to engine failure and the NART Ferrari finishing in the pits after Henn put it off the road. During the 13th hour, the Interscope Porsche also had its engine fail, after having climbed into the 6th place an hour before, and early Sunday morning the Ferrari Gregg was sharing crashed while Michel Leclere was driving after a steady run up to 10th spot.

During all this, the Porsches of Garretson/Abate/McKitterick and Kirby/Hotchkiss whistled along to what would be 8th- and 9th-place finishes respectively, giving the Barbour team (with the Stommelen/Barbour/Newman Porsche) three finishers in the top 10, a feat no private team has managed in Le Mans history. Yet, all that took on a secondary air to what was happening between the mostly American driven cars at the head of the list.

After the Mirage dropped from the leader board during the 9th hour, the Porsche-Kremer Racing 935 of Whittington/Ludwig/Whittington took over 1st spot. It gave up that position for a while around midnight to one of the 935/77As of arch-contender, George Loos, but then took command again and began to reel off quick laps. By 10:30 in the morning the Kremer car had a 15-lap lead on the 2nd-place 935 of Stommelen/Barbour/Newman. Then at 10:40 came the announcement that Don Whittington had stopped on the Mulsanne Straight near Les Hunaudières Restaurant and when Barbour went by the next time his crew gave him the thumbs ups.

The announcer commented that Whittington was trying to fix his 935, but that was met with some doubt in the pits, considering the complexity of a modern Porsche Group 5 car. At least there was an American-run car in the lead, but then just after 11:00 a.m. that car pitted and had trouble. The right front wheel was jammed on the hub and the only way to get the car back in the race was to replace the entire hub. Twenty-two minutes later the red number 70 Porsche went back out, Stommelen trying to put on laps in a hurry. By 11:30 they had cut the Whittingtons/Ludwig lead to 9 laps, but by around 11:45, the announcer said Whittington was on his way to the pits.

The crowd loved it, cheering Don to the Kremer pits where the mechanics pulled off the engine cover and went to work. As Don, soaking wet and his face smudged with grime, explained it, his injection pump belt broke shortly after he started on the Mulsanne. He fitted the spare belt, but it broke after the car had gone only 10 ft. Now the 935 was on the track, the other cars going by at 200 mph, but Whittington went back to work. He noticed the alternator belt was about the same size as the pump belt and took it off with a screwdriver, almost cutting the belt. When he found the belt too large for its new job, he took a roll of tape and built up the size of the pump pulley until the belt fit. Then he had to set the timing about right, get the car started, load up all the tools and limp back to the pits. He added, "I was out there a lifetime."

Dick Barbour walked up the Kremer pits to watch over the shoulder of the crowd as the Kremer mechanics rushed to get number 41 working again. They belted Bill Whittington in and to still more cheers he headed back to the track. Barbour turned and, with more than a little hope in his voice, said, "It doesn't sound too healthy." At that point the Kremer car had a 4-lap lead on the Barbour car, a margin the second car could have wiped away if it hadn't needed that hub change.

The drama wasn't quite over, for at 1:40 p.m. the Barbour car stopped on Mulsanne and then started up again very slowly. It had a 10-lap lead so there was little chance of losing 2nd place before the 2:00 p.m. finish, but the rules say you have to make 1 lap in the last 15 minutes. Stommelen, driving the 935 with a blown headgasket, sputtered around for 2 laps, then stopped short of the finish line and waited a few minutes for 2:00 p.m. and finally slowly crossed the line for 2nd place.

Don Whittington and Klaus Ludwig had been waiting at the track Armco in front of their pits as Bill circulated and the crowd grew restless for the finish. Lines of gendarmes set up along pit row and between the stands and the track, but when the flag dropped they didn't raise a finger to stop the fans who poured out of the main grandstands as the last car passed at racing speed.

On the cool-down lap at Le Mans, the corner workers come out on the track and hold out their flags to the cars that have endured the 24 hours. Bill Whittington said he had tears in his eyes as he drove under the flags on that last lap and when he and the other drivers returned to the front straight they were enveloped by the massive crowd that traditionally storms the straight. It was drizzling again as the drivers tried to work through the press of people, and many cars needed to be rescued by crew members. Whittington said he reached the point where he was sure he could have let out the clutch on the 935 and not moved. He also saw the crowd climbing on the Porsche, starting to ruin the bodywork and he got upset, but then decided it wasn't important, not now. He abandoned the car and made his way to his driving partners and then the winner's stand.

Rob Walker would have been appalled, because the Whittingtons and Ludwig mercilessly sprayed the Moët & Chandon. There were hugs and cheers all around and the drivers pulled the flowers from their wreaths and threw them down to the crowd. After a false start with "Le Marseillaise," they played "Deutschland Uber Alles" and Ludwig was obviously moved and for a moment could only stop and look quietly at the crowd.

After the overall winners left, Stommelen, Barbour and Newman appeared and the scene started again, Barbour delighting in a champagne shower and Newman opening his eyes wide for a big slug of Moët. The crowd continued to call for more as the trio stripped their wreaths and tossed the flowers. The crowd didn't even begin to thin until the Barbour team retreated to the team's compound, where the celebrating began.

And the only complaint I heard from any American was that despite it all, the French never played "The Star-Spangled Banner."

Winners Don Whittington and Klaus Ludwig (above) figuratively and literally bite their nails during the last hour. Don (left) splashes back to the pits after his Mulsanne repairs. Dick Barbour (below) waits as the car he shared with Rolf Stommelen and Paul Newman whistles to 2nd.

LE MANS 24 HOURS

OVERWHELMING winners at Le Mans after leading continuously throughout the last 13 hours of the race were Klaus Ludwig, Don Whittington and his brother Bill in the Kremer Porsche Racing team's 935K3 (above). They won by seven laps, despite losing over an hour when the drive to their car's fuel injection pump broke. Best placed Group 6 car at the finish was the Rondeau M379 of Jean Ragnotti and Bernard Darniche (left), one of three such coupés in the race. The only one of four Ferraris to make the chequered flag was the 512 Berlinetta Boxer (below) shared by Nick Faure, Bernard de Dryver, Steve O'Rourke and Jean "Beurlys", Faure and O'Rourke being the highest placed British drivers in the final results.

Le Mans 24 Hours:

A night to remember

Drama, dreams, a downpour;
Le Mans very much up to, even above standard

By Maurice Hamilton and Michael Scarlett
Photographs: Ron Easton

BILL WHITTINGTON propped himself against the grey breeze-block wall in the dank alley-way behind the Le Mans pits, peered into an empty paper cup and then raked the gravel with his right foot as he gave the question some thought.

"How do I feel about leading at Le Mans?" he echoed. "It's, aw . . . how can I describe it . . . it's, aw, jus' somethin' I never dreamed would happen. Never."

The 29-year-old American from Fort Lauderdale had just finished an early morning stint in the Kremer Porsche 935, bringing the car back safely for his brother, Don, after having driven through some of the most appalling weather conditions ever seen at Le Mans. His hollow-eyed expression mirrored he effort expended in driving through walls of spray while peering through a foggy windscreen.

His energy may have been sapped but his aches and pains were washed away by the elation of leading. "My brother and I have always been inter-ested in auto racing thanks to our Dad. He raced sprinters and although he won at Phoenix and places like that, he was really just a kind of country boy. Don and I figured that if we could get enough coins together then we could go auto racing. We've managed that OK — I was second in the IMSA series last year and Don was fourth — but to be asked by a professional team like Kremer to run Le Mans — and then to lead it . . . boy, that's somethin' I'll always remember."

Above: On its winning way — the Porsche Kremer Racing 935 Turbo group 5 car of Klaus Ludwig-Don and Bill Whittington

Below left: They're off; leading the rolling start, the Wollek / Haywood Porsche 936, followed by the winning 935, then the Darniche / Ragnotti Rondeau

Below: Crucial stop for the Barbour / Newman / Stommelen IMSA 935. A front wheel bearing is in trouble as a glum Dick Barbour (helmet unstrapped having left car) next to actor-racing driver Paul Newman watches; Stommelen is in driving seat

Le Mans 24 Hours

Memories. That's what Le Mans is all about. It's the event which counts; the cars take second place and the drivers an almost incidental third. The Le Mans 24 Hours is a time for recollection; a time when the past is allowed to catch up with the present. And if your powers of recollection are rather weak, there are *aides-memoires* at the turn of every corner, on the walls of every hotel.

The Hotel Moderne in central Le Mans has always been a motor racing haunt and journalists, drivers and motor racing personalities find it difficult to beat the irresistible urge to return to the hotel that fed and watered the Bentley team in the twenties. On the Thursday night before this year's race there was a gathering in a long narrow room and the false ceiling slung under ornate plasterwork summed up the situation — the

Above: Ickx leads Essex Porsche team mate Wollek in the superbly turned out 936 Turbos early in the race when they looked to have such easy domination

Right: The Ickx/Redman 935 when things had started to go wrong for them — a tyre has destroyed itself and a large section of Porsche bodywork flaps up and down, flailed by tread rubber

past was there if you cared to look for it. The Moderne has been retextured, repainted — and remembered. A plaque presented by the Bentley Boys and partially covered in ivy, is tacked to the courtyard wall, signifying fifty years of racing at Le Mans.

Paul Frére, winner in 1960, was present to examine a dog-eared photograph; Gordon Wilkins, a former Technical Editor with *Autocar*, talked with sharp recall about his first racing experience at Le Mans when his

weekend's racing cost him the princely sum of £100.

By contrast, the French-domiciled American President of Ford France arrived, tousle-haired, wearing jeans and sweater, and enthusing about the atmosphere within Cluxton's two-car team. Ford France had gathered support from 250 of their dealers and Cluxton's Ford M10s were garaged at La Chatre-sur-Le Loir. The cars were fettled in the *Garage Central* located in a narrow side street and the whole scene of race preparation seemed out of keeping with the serene town. Besides, why should a team make their base 15 miles from the circuit?

The answer lay around the corner within the portals of the smart provincial *Hotel de France* where a photographic tapestry told the story of Aston Martin days in La Chatre; recorded an impressive gallery of visiting drivers ranging from Moss

and Collins enjoying dinner to Pedro Rodriguez dressed in a dapper suit and reading a newspaper outside the front door.

Cluxton was optimistic despite practice problems with overheating rear tyres thanks to overactive downforce plus engine problems which restricted Derek Bell to a mere 15 minutes competitive running on Thursday evening. Sadly, his optimism was ill-founded.

Bell felt unwell during the first few

hours of the race (which started at 2pm this year in deference to the forthcoming European elections the following day) although the smart blue and white M10s ran comfortably in third and fourth places for the first few hours. The first hint of trouble struck the Jaussaud/Hobbs car at just before 5pm when last year's winner was stranded out on the circuit with no forward gears.

Twenty minutes of beating the stout gearbox with an equally stout hammer carried in the cockpit produced a workable cog for the persistent Frenchman and he trundled back to the pits for a complete gearbox rebuild. The lengthy stop dropped the car to last place 60 laps behind the leader and number 10 was eventually withdrawn during the evening when it was realised they would not complete the minimum distance necessary for classificiation.

The Bell/Schuppan car had been leading the Essex Porsches until a broken exhaust pipe dropped it to sixth place. The two drivers were fighting back when a disaster struck Schuppan in the early hours of darkness. The electrics failed just as the Australian was hustling through Porsche Curve and in the ensuing darkness the M10 cannoned off the barrier. A major rebuild at the front and rear was called for. Cluxton began to look extremely frustrated. Once again, a Ford M10 began a climb back up the lap chart but then the weather stepped in during the early hours of Sunday morning and let loose the first of several torrential downpours. Several cars did not take kindly to the wet conditions and the M10 was one of them.

The track conditions were simply horrifying, cars passing the pits leaving huge plumes of spray; drivers treating throttles with respect; en-

gines popping and banging Clucton's problems were compounded by a loss of engine compression and the car was in fourteenth place when Schuppan made the final pit stop to hand over to Bell. Vern eased himself out of the cockpit his soaking overalls steaming and peppered in gravel as Bell took over. The car made another stop just before 2pm and the team suffered the final ignomony when Bell was unable to coax the car out of the pit lane. It was not classified as a finisher after 23 hours and 56 minutes of racing.

Further down the lane, the Essex Porsche boxes were empty. Both 936s were already loaded on the Mercedes transporter following an uncharacteristic race for Porsche. Initially both Ickx and Bob Wollek (drafted onto the team following the enforced absence of Didier Pironi) had strolled into an easy lead as they circulated line astern in impressive fashion. The first chink in the smart

long-tailed bodywork occurred when Brian Redman had an almighty moment when a rear tyre deflated as he swept up to the Dunlop Bridge (appropriately enough although Brian probably didn't see it that way).

"I just don't know how I spun there and got away without hitting anything," he said, looking more

Showing how wet Le Mans can be for both cars and spectators — the second place 935 streams past stands-full of umbrellas

Unhappy Aston

ANOTHER CAR which ended up as a GT prototype, the Robin Hamilton turbo Aston Martin was not a happy one. Never fast, it rumbled round until a mysterious oil leak which its pit crew could not find or cure started it on a series of stops from around 4pm on Saturday. A porous sump casting was suspected, they said, in spite of apparently successful running for eight hours before Le Mans. Finally Mike Salmon took it out at 5pm, to end up with a broken engine at what they nowadays officially call Porsche corner — as on the other recent part of the circuit near White House. We met him walking back, genial in spite of an early end to his nth Le Mans, and less than complimentary about the car. He said it was over-geared, and too wide ratio'd for the turbo installation that brought the power in at just below 5,000 rpm — with only 1,500 rpm to go before the rev limit of 6,500. On its last lap ''it wouldn't pull more than 4,000 rpm along Mulsanne — oil pressure went, I tried to nurse it back but there were tinkling noises . . .''

relaxed than he had done following his lurid moment at Silverstone a month previously. He had made his way slowly back to the pits but the trailing rubber smashed the bodywork to bits and wrecked a water radiator. Another lengthy rebuild job in the pit lane. Another prelude to a storming comeback from Ickx.

Ickx's class was clearly demonstrated during the first thunderstorm at around 2am. While other drivers conserved themselves and their cars, the Porsche number 12 would fishtail up the straight, wheels spinning as Ickx demonstrated his incredible car control. The Belgian's enjoyment was brought to a halt at 3am when the Porsche broke a timing belt out on the circuit. Ickx carried out a repair job but a sheepish grin and hurried consultations with Norbert Singer in the back of the pit indicated that there was perhaps more to the matter than the official Porsche line. The organisers had their own version of the

incident and the Porsche was disqualified for receiving outside assistance.

Hopes of Essex glory were washed away by the rain when the remaining 936, recovering from a lengthy delay to rectify fuel injection bothers, gradually lapsed on to five cylinders and the team abandoned the struggle at dawn. It hadn't been a particularly happy weekend for Essex who endeavoured to inject a touch of the unusual, not to say the bizarre, into the weekend. A laser show coupled with a massive slide presentation was scheduled to be run against a backcloth of helium balloons flying at the back of the enclosure opposite the pits. The balloons didn't quite form the most stable background and the whole mystifying sequence of events was rounded off by music blasting from a mountain of amplifiers.

The unreal quality was totally in keeping with Le Mans as was the appearance of Paul Newman — or P. L. Newman as the stitching on his Simpsons informed us. The actor wasn't there for the posing, however, as his taut expression and overactive heavy men demonstrated. The man simply wanted to race and the flying fists in the pit lane were prompted by some of the pushiest and most unsavory photographers seen for some time. Newman did his share of driving at the team's set speed although it was noticeable that one particular stint lasted no more than 35 minutes — and that just happened to coincide with a thunderstorm at 4.30 am. Newman handed the IMSA 935 over to team patron Dick Barbour — a colossus of a man — who urged the red car through the spray.

Meanwhile the Whittington brothers were leading the field just two laps ahead of John Fitzpatrick. The Englishman was forced to retire the Loos 935 when the car caught fire in the pit lane and the Stommelen/Barber/Newman car moved into second place. The white Kremer car seemed secure with a thirteen lap lead as the brothers changed over and it was then that Bill took a few moments to consider his unbelievable position. He said they owed a lot to Klaus Ludwig who was ''a great guy with a super sense of humour'' and to the enthusiasm of the Kremer team which was fantastic. He was almost reluctant to say that the car had run perfectly. Just three minutes later, the loudspeakers announced that the Porsche had stop-

Fertile, like dragon's teeth

ONE BRITISH SURVIVOR, the Fisons Lola of Simon Phillips, finished 20th, 65 laps behind the winner after a race-long chapter of *ennui*. It had misfired throughout, had no back brakes after half distance when a caliper support broke, destroyed a front wheel bearing (blamed on heat from over-used front brakes), lost any alternator output, so had to change batteries at every fuel stop. At the last hours, they'd run out of racing batteries, so someone acquired a Cortina one from the paddock; they ended in third gear, having lost fourth and fifth.

The sadly short-lived de Cadanet of Alain de Cadanet / Francois Migault at the Ford chicane, in front of the Herve Poulain BMW M1. Also out of luck were the British -based Japanese Domes; they were both early retirements on Saturday

One of the Pozzi-JMS Racing Ferrari 512 BBs overtaken approaching the Dunlop bridge by two open seaters; although an IMSA car, its special bodywork makes it unrecognisable as a Boxer

Turn again Whittington

DON WHITTINGTON is a tall, craggy American of obvious abilities, as his similarly capable brother Bill explained. This was his second Le Mans, and a rather luckier one than last year which ended in a crash. When the 935 stopped near Les Hunaudières, he diagnosed the injection pump failure, and had a go at fitting the spare without being able to move the pump. The spare broke, so that left only the belt on the alternator. Trouble was that the injection belt is a cogged one, necessarily because upon it depends injection timing, while the alternator belt is both longer and a plain type.

He took up extra belt length by wrapping tape round the pulley. He primed the cylinders for starting by turning the pump over by hand. It would not start, the belt slipped, so he used more tape. The tape chewed up the second time, but it worked. What about pump timing? ''Well, I timed it.'' He could clearly cope with things mechanical? ''Yeah — I took my bike to bits as a kid — I fix my car, the engine of my plane'' (he runs a close-circuit-record-holding World War Two Mustang fighter). He was stuck out on Mulsanne for nearly an hour, a 15 lap lead disappearing steadily as the Barbour car drove on. ''I was out there a lifetime.'' But that was the car's only glitch; before and after the belt bother, it had been ''perfect all the time — it's so fast — we've been running it easy.''

My kingdom for a hole

APART FROM the group 6 2-litre class-winning Chevron of Mogil Motors, it wasn't the best of races for the few British cars there. The most obviously British apart from the Aston was of course Alain de Cadanet's faithful DFV-engined group 6 open seater sponsored by the *Daily Express* and Sealink and dark green in colour. While team mate Migault was driving in the first half hour, it started jumping out of gear. Struggles at the pits with the gear linkage were not the answer, so they eventually opened the gearbox — nowadays never the easy job Mike Hewland meant it to be with wings, alternators and everything else fixed on the box. The pinion bearing had failed, allowing the pinion shaft to move endways, disturbing gear location, apart from what it must have been doing to the final drive teeth.

The reason for the failure was sad. The previous engine and gearbox had done a successful 15 hours' running including the Silverstone Six Hours. Working through Friday night, they changed what turned out afterwards to be a perfectly fit drive assembly — just to make sure — running it for the first time on Saturday morning, driving from their garage in Le Mans proper to the circuit. A banjo connection for the external oil feed pipe to the pinion bearing had been welded up out of a collar and pinion some time before — but someone had forgotten to drill through the collar, starving the bearing. The cold dreariness of retirement is brought home hard to the unfortunate entrant by a little form which is brought to him to sign. It's headed ''abandon''; de Cadanet signed it slowly and carefully, and like 33 other entrants was politely presented with a carbon copy.

Jochen Neerpasch was on hand to see the Hervé Poulain-entered BMW M1 come sixth in its first Le Mans, in spite of a misfire caused by suspected valve trouble in one cylinder

101

Le Mans 24 Hours

ped out on the circuit. Over in the paddock, Mrs Dick Barbour accepted the news with mixed feelings; a win looked possible but anything could happen at Le Mans. Newman walked round the corner of the giant Peterbilt truck:

"Hey Paul, did ya hear that?" she yelled.

"You bet your ass I heard," he said, smiling for the first time.

There were three hours remaining and if the Kremer car remained out of action for one hour, Newman could

Last minute leak

DICK BARBOUR is a bulky man. At 25 to 2 on Sunday afternoon, he looked less than happy. How was the car going (it was lying second)? "I'm sorry you asked me that. We started a head gasket going ten minutes ago." They made it of course — but it was tense in the Barbour pit.

win Le Mans. Barbour muscled the Porsche through the crowds in the pit lane as he came in to hand over to Stommelen. Then the unbelievable happened — again. The left front wheel bearing broke and the frantic mechanics could not remove the nut. Newman stopped smiling. Twenty minutes later and Stommelen was on his way. Ten minutes after that and applause from the crowd announced the arrival of the leading Porsche. Don Whittington climbed from the cockpit looking as though he had been rolling in the mud; his overalls soaked; his face smeared and frowning. More lightening spanner work; more applause as the car left the pit lane. Two laps in the lead. Surely that would be that. Not quite. The Stommelen car blew a head gasket with half an hour to go and crept across the line while Klaus Kremer and the brothers Whittington finally won Le Mans 1979 with the sort of performance that memories are made of.

Above: Most of Le Mans is still ordinary public road, closed for the occasion; the car nearest camera is the Rondeau M 379 of Jean Rondeau himself and J. Haran (which did not finish)

Right: A dramatic, cruel moment for the last surviving Mirage Ford; with very little compression and only a few minutes left to get back on to the track in order to qualify as a finisher (it would have been 11th), the car is desperately unwilling to start. It does so, then stalls; here the mechanics are pushing it back to its pit after it had stalled on driver Derek Bell. A second attempt to get away failed after some furious revving with four minutes to go

Nearer the right sort

IN SOME old fashioned opinions, it was poetically just that a Porsche 935 should have won. Although a "special production" (group 5) car — a heavy distortion of a true production car — it did look distantly like the sort of ordinarily available production car that Le Mans ought to be for. It would have been poetically just-er if the Barbour 935, an IMSA car, had done it; IMSA machines are a very little bit less remote from the real thing, paying lip service to reasonable costs even if the IMSA deal is obviously in Porsche's pocket. But even these seem too great an exaggeration of the road car you can buy from your Porsche (or Jaguar or BMW or Lotus) dealer.

We still believe that *Les Vingt-Quatre Heures* could be fascinating, and more crowd-grabbing, with a field of exclusively genuine production sporting cars. Engine mods perhaps — but not special engines. Racing wheels and tyres — but only ones that fitted the standard wheelarch. No bodywork changes. Le Mans is so different from anything else; could stand the change. Turning a blind eye to the absence of any real French challenge, might not Le Mans' presently continuing divorce from reality perhaps be part of the explanation for that small crowd this year?

Klaus Ludwig (garland, light overalls) holds hat on in victorious delight; the Whittington brothers (Bill next to Ludwig, then Don with bottle) prepare a further shower for crowd below

Le Mans 24 Hours 10/11 June 1979

1 **Porsche 935 4.5 t/c** (K. Ludwig — B. Whittington — D. Whittington) 306 laps, 4169.71 km, 108.11 mph.
2 **Porsche 935 4.2 t/c** (D. Barbour — R. Stommelen — P. Newman) 299 laps, 4074.32 km *(winner IMSA class)*.
3 **Porsche 935 4.2 t/c** (F. Servanin — L. Ferrier — F. Trisconi) 292 laps, 3978.99 km.
4 **Porsche 934 4.2 t/c** (A. Pallivicini — H. Muller — M. Vanoli) 291 laps, 3965.32 km *(winner Group 4 class)*.
5 **Rondeau M. 379-Ford 3.0** (J. Ragnotti — Darniche — J-P Beltoise) 287 laps, 3910.81 km. *(winner Group 6 class)*.
6 **BMW M1 3.5** (M. Mignot — H. Poulain — M. Winkelhock) 284 laps, 3869.93 km.
7 **Porsche 935 4.2 t/c** (D. Schornstein — E. Doeren — G. Tschirnhaus) 283 laps, 3856.30 km.
8 **Porsche 935 4.2 t/c** (O. Garretson — S. McKitterick — E. Abate) 278 laps, 3788.17 km.
9 **Porsche 935 4.2 t/c** (R. Kirby — J. Hotchkis) 275 laps, 3747.29 km.
10 **Rondeau M. 379-Ford 3.0** (J-P Beltoise — H. Pescarolo) 274 laps, 3733.66 km. 11 **Porsche 935 4.2 t/c** (C. Haldi — H. Loewe — R. Teran), 270 laps, 3679.15 km. 12 **Ferrari 512 BB 4.9** (N. Faure — B. De Dryver — S. O'Rourke), 269 laps, 3665.53 km. 13 **Porsche 935 4.2 t/c** (A. Plankenhorn — J. Winter — P. Gurdjian), 268 laps, 3651.90 km. 14 **WMP 79 3.7 t/c** (M. Mamers — J. Raulet — S. Saulnier), 267 laps, 3638.27 km *(winner GTP class)*. 15 **Porsche 935 4.2 t/c** (J. Guerin — F. Alliot — J-P Schlessor), 264 laps, 3579.40 km. 16 **Porsche 934 4.2 t/c** (G. Bourdillat — G. Ennequin — A. Bernard), 258 laps, 2515.64 km. 17 **Chevron B36-Ford** (A. Charnell — R. Jones — R. Smith), 258 laps, 3515.64 km *(winner Group 6 2-litre class)*. 18 **Lola T297-Ford 2.0** (R. Jenvey — N. Mason — B. Joscelyne — A. Birchenhough) 253 laps, 3447.50 km. 19 **Porsche 934 4.2 t/c** (A. C. Verney — P. Bardinon — R. Metge) 242 laps, 3297.61 km. 20 **Lola-Ford 3.0** (M. Raymond — R. Mallock — S. Phillips) 241 laps, 3283.99 km.

The chief innovation for the 48th 24-hour race was a much revised set of regulations, drafted by the A.C.O. to encourage efficiency and reliability rather than speed. While there was not a return to the old fuel consumption restrictions as such, the maximum tank capacity was fixed at 120 litres (approx. 26 gallons) for all cars and the rate of delivery from the pumps installed at the pits was reduced to 50 litres per minute, so the length of the average pit stop was increased from 40 seconds to two and a half minutes. It is interesting to note that the least time spent in the pit by a car in the 1980 race was 45 minutes in contrast to the record ten minutes that the Macklin/Thompson Aston Martin DB 2 spent at its pit during the 1952 race. Then there was a ban on the replacement of major components (engine, gearbox etc) from the start of official practice to the end of the race which put a stop to the practice of using one engine for qualifying and another for the race itself, and also to those lightning engine changes that team mechanics had entertained pit-watchers with in the 1970s.

Another new regulation shortened the official practice period to two hours, and cars had to qualify on the basis of the average lap times recorded by all named drivers; if more than two drivers, the third could be dropped to improve the average speed to enable a car to qualify. One driver eliminated because of this rule was Desire Wilson who had an accident while practising in Alain de Cadenet's car; she was unhurt and the car was rebuilt for the race but the A.C.O. officially recorded a lap time which was more than twice what the team thought it should be. After this and similar episodes the atmosphere was somewhat strained in the British camp, and some teams were talking in terms of suing the A.C.O. because of the discrepancies in officially and unofficially recorded lap times, which led to a number of British teams not qualifying.

Again, there was noticeably little direct works involvement at Le Mans in 1980; only two factory teams appeared, Porsche and Lancia, and neither company fielded Group 6 cars. Porsche ran a team of three 924 Carrera turbos (in itself a major milestone: for the first time a front-engined water-cooled Porsche at Le Mans!) in the GT prototype category while Lancia concentrated efforts on Group 5 which held the world championship status - three mid-engined Beta Monte Carlo coupes, with turbo-charged 1.4 litre Fiat-based engines. Apart from the unsuccessful Stratos entry in 1976-77, this was the first Lancia entry at Le Mans since 1953.

The number of cars entered in Group 6 was reduced, with six cars over two litres and eight in the two-litre class. Heading the list was a single Porsche, a specially-built 908/936 cross-breed sponsored by Martini Racing, and entered for Reinhold Joest to drive together with Jacky Ickx who had let himself be tempted out of 'retirement' by the prospect of winning a fifth Le Mans. All the other big Group 6 cars used the Cosworth-DFV engine - two Rondeaus, the De Cadenet, a Swiss ACR based on the Lola T380 and a much-improved Japanese Dome with British drivers Craft and Evans.

In the two-litre class there were four Lolas and two Chevrons with various engines, an Osella-BMW entered by March engineering and co-driven by Mark Thatcher, and a Toj-BMW. Group 5 held seven Porsche 935s apart from the Lancias; Group 4 four Porsche 934s and a Porsche 911 SC which ran on ethanol. The GTP category had the Porsche 924s, three WM-Peugeots and an extra Rondeau. A Grand Touring Production (GTX) category was revived for the benefit of a single BMW M.1 entry although another three examples of this model ran in the I.M.S.A. category together with the modified March-BMW M.1, eight Porsche 935s,

a rotary-engined Mazda RX-7 and five Ferrari 512 BB Boxers. Among those who did not get a race was a sixth Ferrari Boxer which had a holed cylinder block and had to withdraw under the rule forbidding engine replacements after the practice session. Also a second De Cadenet entered by Nick Faure, Ian Bracey's Ibec-Cosworth and a Janspeed Triumph TR7V8 turbo which had been entered in Group 5 with the enthusiastic co-sponsorship of the TR Register. This would have been the first Triumph at Le Mans since 1965, so the failure of this car to qualify was a particularly intensely felt disappointment.

The Pescarolo/Ragnotti Group 6 Rondeau started from pole position just as a thunderstorm passed over the circuit - this was to be another wet Le Mans and many competitors suffered from misfires, damp ignition systems and similar maladies. A Porsche 935 soon went into the lead, with a challenge coming from an unexpected quarter - a BMW M.1 driven in spirited fashion by Hans Stick until he was involved in a slight collision and had to stop for repairs to bodywork. The Ickx/Joest Porsche was gaining and got briefly ahead in the early evening before stopping on the circuit with a broken fuel injection pump belt; a contingency for which the team had been prepared so Ickx was able to continue after fitting the spare carried in the car. With the delay the car had gone right down the scoreboard, but once under-way again Ickx did not tarry, putting in some very quick laps including the fastest lap of the race at 138.30 mph, and before the first half of the race was over the Porsche was leading again, now followed by the Rondeau of Jaussaud/Rondeau, a Porsche 935 and the Martin/Martin/Spice Rondeau GTP car the Pescarolo/Ragnotti Group 6 Rondeau had retired with engine failure.

Sunday morning dawned with more rain, and a further mishap for the Porsche 936 which lost its fifth gear - a recurring Porsche problem in past races - losing half an hour in the pit which permitted the Rondeau to go into the lead. The French car was to retain this position. There was some further drama when quick showers washed over the circuit in the afternoon; both the leading Rondeau and the Ickx/Joest Porsche spun and fetched up against the Armco barriers though neither car suffered much damage and both were able to continue. While many teams made hurried tyre changes, the Rondeau stayed on slicks and was rewarded when the sun came out drying the circuit in the last half hour of the race. The Rondeau won and Jean Rondeau became the first constructor to win Le Mans in a car bearing his own name, while his co-driver Jaussaud could celebrate his second victory in a French car. Their average speed was 119.30 mph and the total distance 2,863 miles.

The Ickx/Joest Porsche followed, while the Martin/Martin/Spice Rondeau was third and winner of the GTP category. Fourth was a WM-Peugeot and next came the first I.M.S.A. car, a Porsche 935, with one of the works Porsche 924s in sixth place and the De Cadenet seventh. This was the first British car to finish. A total of 25 cars finished, including two BMW M.1s but only one of the Lancias. Also among the finishers were the Ethanol Porsche, the Mazda RX-7 and the Dome which was last car home after having spent four hours in the pit.

An outstanding memory from this Le Mans was the live television coverage, broadcast via a helicopter link from a camera mounted in the WM-Peugeot which finished in fourth place. The colour pictures were shown in the pressbox and also projected on a huge screen in the 'Village'. Suddenly everybody could experience the thrill of driving down the Mulsanne straight at 190 mph in the rain.

Fifth Le Mans for Ickx?

The older de Cadenet chassis will be driven by its entrant Nick Faure with Richard Jones and Bernard de Dryver co-driving.

Given the fact that there will be no big-buck rivalry between major manufacturers for overall victory and the sports-prototype class, perhaps the most significant aspect of the 1980 Le Mans 24 Hours will indeed be the emphasis on efficiency, reliability and equal performance which, claims the ACO's press release mysteriously, are "the most striking innovations" in the new regulations.

The Automobile Club de l'Ouest conceived its surprisingly prestigious Index of Thermal Efficency back in 1959, and has now applied the thinking to the race as a whole. Every car competing on the Sarthe road circuit next weekend will be restricted to 120 litres of fuel. In addition, they will have to refuel using equipment supplied by the ACO which will flow at a constant 50 litres per minute, so that every routine pitstop will consume a minimum of 2 minutes.

The ACO's release also informs us of the good news that "The wall has been opened for all types of fuel," but only one car — the French entered Group 4 Porsche 911SC (see entry list) — will actually run on an alcohol fuel.

Changes have also been made to the rules covering replacement parts. The days of qualifying engines are at an end, for the teams may not now change engines after the start of qualifying on Thursday morning until after the race has finished. This rule also applies to gearboxes, and to turbochargers in that turbos may be replaced only once (a move which caused the works Porsche team, at least, to have a lot of harmless fun with the organisers by deliberately complicating the question of twin-turbo cars).

The rule which has formerly disqualified delayed cars for not having covered a minimum distance after 12 hours has also been discarded.

The fastest car in the race will be the Porsche 936 with which Jacky Ickx has been tempted out of retirement. Lured by Martini money and the prospect of becoming the first man ever to win Le Mans five times, the great Belgian driver, partnered by the efficient Reinhold Jöst,

must be rated among the favourites. The car has been supplied by the Porsche factory in Zuffenhausen, and it has been updated (reportedly losing 30 kilos) and race-prepared by Jöst's very efficient Liqui-Moly backed team.

I would be as pleased to see Jacky better the record of four wins he shares with his compatriot Olivier Gendebien as I would be to see a victory at last for Alain de Cadenet. Under these new regulations, Alain, with his normally aspirated DFV-powered Group 6 car, must stand the best chance yet, and he will be sharing the driving with the experienced but under-employed Frenchman François Migault and with Desiré Wilson. The famous wins at Monza and Silverstone will have done much be boost the impecunious De Cadenet team's confidence, especially that of Desiré, who is making a name for herself as a top-level professional this year, and who could become the first woman to win Le Mans as well as the first to win a Formula 1 race.

Also in the G6 class, Ian Bracey has entered his considerably updated Ibec, but the main opposition to the De Cadenet and the turbo Porsche will probably come from the French Rondeau entries, with their hugely experienced drivers, including two previous winners. Chris Craft reports after testing

at Suzuka that the latest version of the ungainly Japanese Dome is a far more competitive proposition, while the last of the DFV-engined G6 cars will be the Swiss ACR, the Lola-based car which made such a fast if brief debut at Silverstone. Mark Thatcher, thankfully, is no longer down to drive the older De

Past Winners

1979	Klaus Ludwig, Don Wittington, Bill Wittington	Porsche 935
1978	Jean-Pierre Jaussaud, Didier Pironi	Renault A442
1977	Jacky Ickx, Hurley Haywood, Jurgen Barth	Porsche 936
1976	Jacky Ickx, Gijs Van Lennep	Porsche 936
1975	Jacky Ickx, Derek Bell	Gulf Mirage Ford GR8
1974	Henri Pescarolo, Gerard Larrousse	Matra MS670
1973	Henri Pescarolo, Gerard Larrousse	Matra MS670
1972	Henri Pescarolo, Graham Hill	Matra MS670
1971	Helmut Marko, Gijs Van Lennep	Porsche 917
1970	Hans Herrman, Richard Attwood	Porsche 917

This is the 'British' Porsche of Derek Bell, Tony Dron and Andy Rouse.

Le Mans Preview

Cadenet now owned by Nick Faure.

The Sports 2000 driver might, apparently, appear in the 2-litre G6 section, however, as a third driver in the Osella, which would have started very much the favourite to win the class. In this French-dominated category (which as usual still include three Talbot-powered cars), the Dorset Racing Lola is also in with a good chance.

Under the ACO's class-by-class qualification system, the works Porsche team may have some fears that one of its off-the-pace (184mph is slow these days) Carreras may not qualify, thanks to the withdrawal from the GTP class of the Aston Martin powered entry for which the brave but ill-advised Dave Preece must take the blame. The latest Porsches are described elsewhere in this issue. Gordon Spice and the Martin brothers, who so successfully race his Belga-backed G1 Capris in Belgium, are sharing a Rondeau in this important category, and the intriguing WM cars, powered by turbo Peugeot engines, have been updated. The Rondeau is the likely class winner.

The very powerful Porsche 935 cars in the G5 and IMSA classes could produce the overall victor. This year there will be 15 of these cars, and the fastest will be the Kremer K3 versions, particularly those driven by Stommelen/Plankenhorn/Ikuzawa (many well-wishers will watch Tetsu's one-off comback). Garretson/Rahal/Moffat and Fitzpatrick/Redman/Barbour. It would be nice to see the BMW France M1 Coupé, which made its debut recently at the Nürburgring, on the pace for Didier Pironi (if he has a licence!), although that is too much to ask of the March Engines entry, newly modified though it is. While it may be pressed to qualify, the British Triumph TR8 turbo's debut will be full of interest, and so will be the performance of the works Lancias, even though Riccardo Patrese and Eddie Cheever will not be driving them. One of the Lancias is powered by a supercharged engine originally intended for rally use in a Fiat 131.

QDS

LE MANS 24 HOURS 1980 Entry list

Group 6 over 2000cc

Entrant	Car	Driver	Driver	Driver
Equipe Liqui-Moly	Porsche 908/3 Turbo	Reinhold Jost (D)	Jacky Ickx (B)	—
Ian Bracey	Ibec-Cosworth P6	Tiff Needell (GB)	Ian Bracey (GB)	—
Alain de Cadenet	De Cadenet-Cosworth LM	Alain de Cadenet (GB)	Desiré Wilson (ZA)	Francois Migault (F)
André Chevally Racing	ACR-Cosworth	André Chevalley (F)	Francois Trisconi (F)	Patrick Gaillard (F)
Nick Faure	De Cadenet	Nick Faure (GB)	Richard Jones (GB)	Bernard de Dryver (B)
Jean Rondeau	Rondeau-Cosworth	Henri Pescarolo (F)	Jean Ragontti (F)	—
Jean Rondeau	Rondeau-Cosworth	Jean-Pierre Jaussaud (F)	Jean Rondeau (F)	—
Dome Co Ltd	Dome-Cosworth RL80	Chris Craft (GB)	Bob Evans (GB)	—

Group 6 up to 2000cc

Entrant	Car	Driver	Driver	Driver
Jean-Phillippe Grand	Chevron B36	Jean-Philippe Grand (F)	J. Heuclin (F)	—
Racing Fans	Cheetah G601	Sandro Plastina (I)	Mario Luini (I)	M. Frischknecht (I)
Hubert Striebig	Toj SM01	Hubert Striebig (CH)	Michel Pignard (F)	—
R.O.C. Ste Yacco	Lola-Talbot T298	Florian Vetsch (F)	Michel Dubois (F)	Christian Debias (F)
R.O.C. Ste Yacco	Lola-Talbot T298	Marc Sound (F)	B. Verdier (F)	—
R.O.C. Ste Yacco	Chevron B36	Bruno Sotty (F)	Philippe Hesnault (F)	N. Del Bello (F)
Patrice Gaulupeau	Lola T298	Michel Lateste (F)	P. Lenormand (F)	J. Terrien (F)
Michel Elkoubi	Lola T298	Michel Elkoubi (F)	Pierre Yver (F)	Paul Perrier (F)
Scuderia Torino Corse	Osella-BMW PA8	Lella Lombardi (I)	Vittorio Brambilla (I)	—
Dorset Racing Associates	Lola T297/8	Peter Clark (GB)	Nick Mason (GB)	Tony Birchenough (GB)
Jean-Marie Lemerle	Lola T298	Jean-Marie Lemerle (F)	Jean-Pierre Malcher (F)	—

Grand Touring Prototype (GTP)

Entrant	Car	Driver	Driver	Driver
Simon Phillips Racing	DP Aston Martin LM	Dave Preece (GB)	Simon Phillips (GB)	Richard Jenvey (GB)
WM Esso	WM-Peugeot 79/80 Turbo	Guy Frequelin (F)	R. Dorchy (F)	J.L. Bousquet (F)
WM Esso	WM-Peugeot 79/80 Turbo	Marcel Mamers (F)	Jean-Daniel Raulet (F)	J.L. Bousquet (F)
WM Esso	WM-Peugeot 79/80 Turbo	Daniel Morin (F)	Serge Saulnier (F)	J.L. Bousquet (F)
Jean Rondeau	Belga-Rondeau-Cosworth	Jean Michel Martin (B)	P.H. Martin (B)	Gordon Spice (GB)
Porsche System	Porsche 924 Carrera GT	Derek Bell (GB)	Tony Dron (GB)	Andy Rouse (GB)
Porsche System	Porsche 924 Carrera GT	Peter Gregg (USA)	Al Holbert (USA)	—
Porsche System	Porsche 924 Carrera GT	Manfred Schurti (D)	Jurgen Barth (D)	G. Steckkonig (D)

Grand Touring Production (GTX)

Entrant	Car	Driver	Driver	Driver
BMW Zol	BMW M1	Francois Servanin (F)	Laurent Ferrier (F)	Pierre-Francois Rousselot (F)
Garage du Bac	BMW M1	Fred Alliot (F)	Jacques Guerin (F)	—

Group 5

Entrant	Car	Driver	Driver	Driver
Janspeed/ADA/TR Register	BL Triumph TR8 Turbo	Ian Harrower (GB)	John Sheldon (GB)	John Brindley (GB)
Malardeau Krèmer Racing	Porsche 935 K3	Xavier Lapeyre (F)	Anny Charlotte Verney (F)	Jean Louis Trintignant (F)
Gozzy Kremer Racing	Porsche 935 K3	Rolf Stommelen (D)	Tetsu Ikuzawa (J)	Axel Plankenhorn (D)
Porsche Kremer Racing	Porsche 935 K3	Danny Ongais (USA)	Ted Field (USA)	Jean-Louis Lafosse (F)
Charles Ivey Racing	Porsche 935 K3	John Cooper (GB)	Peter Lovett (GB)	Dudley Wood (GB)
Gelo Racing Team	Porsche 935	Bob Wollek (F)	TBN	
Meccarillos Racing	Porsche 935	Claude Haldi (CH)	Bernard Beguin (F)	Volkert Merl
Vegla Racing Team	Porsche 935	Dieter Schornstein (D)	Harald Grohs (D)	Gotz von Tschirnhau (D)
Lanica Corsa	Lancia Beta Monte Carlo	Hans Heyer (D)	Bernard Darniche (F)	Piercarlo Ghinzani (I)
Lancia Corsa	Lancia Beta Monte Carlo	Giorgio Pianta (I)	Walter Rohrl (D)	—
Jolly Club — Lancia Corsa	Lancia Beta Monte Carlo	Carlo Facetti (I)	Martino Finotto (I)	—

IMSA

Entrant	Car	Driver	Driver	Driver
All Canadian Racing	Chevrolet Camaro	Mo Carter (CDN)	D. Valentine	M.E. Edwards (CDN)
Douglas Rowe	Chevrolet Corvette	TBN	J. Bienvenue	Doug Rowe (USA)
Luigi Chinetti Snr	Ferrari BB512	TBN	TBN	
Ch. Pozzi — JMS Racing	Ferrari BB512	Lucien Guitteny	Gerard Bleynie	J.P. Llbert
Ch. Pozzi — JMS Racing	Ferrari BB512	Jean-Claude Andruet (F)	Claude Ballot-Lena (F)	—
Ch. Pozzi — JMS Racing	Ferrari BB512	Pierre Dieudonne (B)	Jean Xhenceval (B)	—
Steve O'Rourke	Ferrari BB512	Steve O'Rourke (GB)	Mike Salmon (GB)	Vic Norman (GB)
Scuderia Supercar Bellancauto	Ferrari BV512	Spartaco Dini (I)	F. Violati (I)	Renzo Zorzi (I)
Dick Barbour	Porsche 935 K3	Dick Barbour (USA)	John Fitzpatrick (GB)	Brian Redman (GB)
Dick Barbour	Porsche 935 K3	Bob Garretson (USA)	Bobby Rahal (USA)	Allan Moffat (AUS)
Dick Barbour — Wynn's Int.	Porsche 935 K3	B. Kirby	B. Harmon	Scherwin
JLP Racing	Porsche 935 K3	John Paul (USA)	John Paul Jr (USA)	Guy Edwards (GB)
Diego Febles Racing	Porsche 934	A. Gonzalez	Diego Febles (PR)	F. Romero
Alpha Cubic Racing	Dome Toyota Celica Turbo	N. Tachi (J)	F. Sato (J)	C. Totani (J)
March Engines Ltd	BMW M1	Patrick Neve (B)	Michele Korten (D)	—
BMW France	BMW M1	Didier Pironi (F)	Dieter Quester (A)	—
Dominique Lacaud	BMW M1	G. Pollini	Dominique Lacaud (F)	—
Herve Poulain	Porsche 935	Danny Snobeck (F)	Hervé Poulain (F)	P. Destic
Lubrifilm — Whittington Bros.	Porsche 935 K3	Angelo Pallavicini (CH)	Don Whittington (USA)	Bill Whittington (USA)
Racing Associates Inc	Porsche 935 K3	Charles Mendez	Leon Walger	Skeeter McKitterick
Racing Associates Inc	Porsche 935 K3	Bob Akin	Bob Woods	R. Cooke

Group 4

Entrant	Car	Driver	Driver	Driver
Georges Bourdillat	Porsche 934	Georges Bourdillat (F)	Roger Ennequin (F)	Alain Bernard (F)
ASA Cachia	Porsche 934	Christian Bussi	Bernard Salam	—
Thierry Perrier	Porsche 911 SC (Methanol)	Thierry Perrier (F)	Roger Carmillet (F)	—
Equipe Almeras Freres	Porsche 934	Jean-Marie Almeras (F)	Jacques Almeras (F)	M. Hoepfner

Reserves

Entrant	Car	Driver	Driver	Driver
Z & W Enterprises	Mazda RX7 (IMSA)	Pierre Honegger (USA)	Ernesto Soto (USA)	Mark Hutchins (USA)
Carlo Pietromarchi	De Tomaso Pantera (G5)	Maurizio Micangeli (I)	Carlo Pietromarchi (I)	Gianfranco Brancatelli (I)
Racing Team Schulthess	Saab Turbo (GTP)	Stig Blomqvist (S)	O. Stromberg (S)	Heinz Schulthess (S)

Ian Bracy, Tiff Needell and Tony Trimmer at Silverstone.

Ian Harrower, John Sheldon and John Brindley will be debuting the TR8 Turbo.

Rondeau's reward . . .

Made in Le Mans, raced at Le Mans and now . . . after gaining an uncanny reputation for reliability . . . victor at Le Mans. Jean Rondeau scores an historic triumph at the wheel of his own car, shared with veteran Jaussaud. Ickx has to settle for 2nd place in his last race as the new Porsche 924s do well in their first

Report by Mike Doodson. Photography by Maurice Rowe

HEAVY RAIN and numerous changes of lead were the most notable early features of this year's Le Mans 24 hour race. By lunchtime on Sunday, however, a fierce David and Goliath battle had developed between the turbocharged Martini Porsche of four-time winner Jacky Ickx and the Rondeau-Cosworth of local heroes Jean Rondeau and Jean-Pierre Jaussaud.

The partisan crowd seemed almost equally divided between its loyalty for Ickx, in what he said was his last ever major race, and for the little Rondeau — a smart coupe built in Le Mans itself. The biblical allegory was to be appropriate again on this occasion, for the Rondeau drivers aim proved true, and after yet another rain storm had obliged Ickx to withhold a desperate last-minute challenge it was to be the French team that felled the German giant.

The race was undoubtedly decided in the pits. The Porsche, a detuned version of the works-entered 936 prototypes, ran into two of the problems already encountered by its factory predecessors in recent years: a broken fuel injection pump belt and a shattered top gear. Together, these failures cost Ickx and German owner Reinhold Joest almost an hour in time lost both in the pits and out on the circuit.

Meanwhile, the immaculate Rondeau droned on, its Cosworth-Ford V8 engine sounding as crisp as ever. After it had taken the lead at exactly 10 am on Sunday (when the Porsche was stuck in the pits with its transmission still in pieces) it was not to be headed. Indeed, it was the Rondeau that spent the least time in the pits — a paltry 45 minutes — of the entire 55 car field. It would surely have been even less if the organisers had not introduced a new rule requiring "filling station" rates of refuelling instead of the now forbidden high pressure system.

Bidding for a repeat of last year's Porsche 935 victory, early race leaders included the German-entered old-shape design of Bob Wollek-Helmut Kelleners and the American entry of hefty Californian Dick Barbour, who was sharing with British long-distance experts John Fitzpatrick and Brian Redman.

Having lost the race last year when team boss George Loos increased the turbocharger pressure to engine-

blowing heights, Wollek backed off in the face of the challenge, only to be let down yet again by engine failure. He had not expected it to last, for the Loos car was a hastily-prepared 935 more normally used in German championship sprint events.

The Barbour entry, prepared to "K3" specification in Cologne by Loos's arch-rivals, the Kremer brothers, got into a scrap with a similar entry driven mainly by Rolf Stommelen and returning Japanese driver Tetsu Ikuzawa. But the Stommelen car was also destined to retire with engine failure, and although the Barbour entry eventually finished fifth it had sounded far from healthy for many hours. Having scored a memorable second place with actor Paul Newman as his co-driver last year, Barbour has vowed to return to Le Mans until at last he wins this most fascinating race.

Despite two "offs" when Rondeau was at the wheel, the neat French prototype scored a convincing victory, celebrated in the traditional way, below

Left: Joest helps Jackie Ickx into their 2nd place Porsche. Above: John Fitzpatrick led away from pole in Dick Barbour's 935 K3

On paper, a strong challenge was expected from a Group 6 sports/racing class which should have included several British crews. At least three of these were eliminated or weakened by some suspicious pre-race manoeuvring on the part of the organising club (*see separate story*). In the event, perhaps the most entertaining performances were those put up by a pair of Procar-type BMW M1 six-cylinder coupes — appreciably less powerful

"We'll sue if we must" say angry Brits

THE ARRIVAL of bailiffs to remove the timekeepers' records of qualifying times was another "first" at this year's Le Mans. Angered by what he regarded as dishonest attempts by the Automobile Club de L'Ouest to eliminate the De Cadenet car which had been entered for him to share with Richard Jones and Belgian Renta-racer Bernard de Dryver, London illustrator Nick Faure called for French legal advice, and the bailiffs' visit was the result.

Rumours of wangled times started after the Thursday evening practice session, the only period of official qualifying. Roly-poly London insurance broker Ian Bracey was close to tears after race officials "corrected" the times for his 3-litre IBEC-Cosworth car driven by experienced F1 men Tiff Needell and Tony Trimmer. The same officials also managed to "lose" the single lap in dry conditions recorded by the quick South African girl Desire Wil-

son, who was down to share the leading De Cadenet with its constructor and Frenchman Francois Migault.

In both cases the teams involved had independent evidence that their originally published times would have qualified their cars. Adding to the less than savoury atmosphere was the revelation that the car which benefited from their non-qualification was a Swiss-built special sponsored by none other than Longines, whose electronic equipment (when it worked) was being used by the ACO for official lap timing.

Leading driver in the Swiss car was sometime Ensign F1 man Patrick Gaillard, who was asked to practise while wearing a crash helmet belonging to one of his less-than-capable Swiss co-drivers. An unhappy Gaillard — who learned about fair play during the two years he spent racing in Britain — told your correspondent: "Sometimes, I am not proud to be French".

continued over

continued over

After a major rebuild the De Cadenet Ford finished a remarkable 7th

than turbo-Porsches — in the rain that fell during the early hours after the start.

Inevitably, the fastest BMW driver in the wet was none other than Hans Stuck in a Marlboro-sponsored M1 shared with new German star Hans Georg Burger. A second M1, sponsored in beautiful "map" livery by the French BMW importers, was almost equally well driven by a team which included GP star Didier Pironi. Both were to be delayed for repairs following accidents, and among the other problems to strike them was the familiar BMW affliction of flying crankshaft

dampers. The two "Procars" finished on five or fewer operative cylinders in 14th and 15th places.

Underlining the importance of reliability and safe driving was the arrival in 3rd place of a second Rondeau (a third, driven by former winner Henri Pescarolo, retired with valve failure) in the hands of two Belgian saloon car drivers, Jean-Michel Martin and his brother Phillipe, who shared the wheel with British all-rounder Gordon Spice. And fourth place, ahead of the Barbour Porsche, was taken by the French home-built WM prototype driven principally by rallyman Guy Frequelin.

LE MANS 24 HOUR RACE

Above: the winner hounds 21st place Mazda RX7 and 25th place Dome through the Sunday morning spray

Rondeau who?

NEVER BEFORE in the 57 year history of the Le Mans 24 hours has a constructor achieved victory at the wheel of one of his own cars. In the early years of the race, W O Bentley left the job to his "Boys" and after the war both John Cooper and Colin Chapman tried — but failed — to do it.

Yet for Jean Rondeau, the quiet 34 year old engineer and interior decorator, this year's race win is the culmination of a five-year programme which he plans to continue. "I'm interested in the new endurance championship which is being talked about," he says, "but the whole thing seems to be angled at major manufacturers."

Rondeau, born in Le Mans and still resident there, saw his first 24 Hours as a three year old toddler in arms. Having won the race at his fifth attempt, he has now set himself a new target: "I want to build a new car — and I would like it to have a French Matra V12 engine." In fact his current project began in 1976, when he was commissioned to build a team of Le Mans cars in the GTP class for the French wallpaper makers Inaltera. Developed over the years into full group 6 prototypes, not even the withdrawal of Inaltera's

sponsorship in 1978 deterred Rondeau, whose cars have always had an uncanny reputation for reliability.

His driving is perhaps less predictable. Twice in this year's 24 Hours his enthusiasm got the better of him, and in the very wet last half hour of the race he managed to spin between the barriers under the Dunlop bridge without causing any serious damage. Yet Jean-Pierre Jaussaud chose to share the wheel with Rondeau, despite a difference of as much as 35 seconds per lap in their times. "I didn't want to share with Pescarolo because I had two unlucky races with him in the Matra days."

One Matra association did, however, pay off for the local team. Matra's top racing engine man, the imperturbable Jean-Francois Robin, managed the popular French victory.

The '80s first supercar?

A PORSCHE might have finished second at Le Mans, but far more significant was the performance of the works entered 924 Carrera Turbo on its competition debut. It was significant not only because of the actual results achieved (the three 924s finished 6th, 12th and 13th) but also because it signalled the end of the air-cooled rear drive 911 series as the basis of Porsche's motorsport activities.

The race cars were based around the newly announced — and thus unhomologated — 924 Carrera GT road car, and the 320 bhp machines had been the subject of a typically thorough development campaign at Paul Ricard. A number of high mileage tests had been undertaken, one of which ended after 29 hours. The bulk of the testing responsibilities fell on the more-than-capable shoulders of Derek Bell, and he was due to drive the "British" entry with saloonists Andy Rouse and Tony Dron. The other two cars were to be in the hands of American and German drivers, but plans went awry when Porsche tester Gunther Steckkonig was struck down with a liver infection and US racer Peter Gregg had a road accident on the way to the circuit, leaving him with a worrying double-vision problem. Eventually, Rouse and Dron shared the English car, Bell teamed up with Al Holbert for the USA, whilst the Teuton twosome were Manfred Schurti and Jurgen Barth.

Without the necessary homologation the cars were forced to contest the GTP class whilst being prepared to what were essentially the stricter Group 4 regulations in a warm up to a major sportscar assault next year. All went well until a mysterious valve burning problem slowed both the American and UK cars to the tune of some 30 seconds per lap.

The sweet running German entry made up considerable time during the frequent heavy rain showers and was only delayed when Barth collided with a hare down the Mulsanne Straight, necessitating a lengthy stop to repair the front of the car. Sixth place made a sufficiently impressive debut, however — and it was precisely the position in which the calculating Porsche technicians thought it would finish.

Below: "old" super Porsche — Ickx's 936 look-alike — heads "new" super Porsche, the 924 Carrera Turbo which Andy Rouse and Tony Dron took to an encouraging 12th

Fast lady scares Thatcher

Porsche's sixth overall with the best-placed of their three all-new **Carrera 924 Turbos** was encouraging, but it was worrying that the burned valve troubles had not shown up in the course of the 29 hour test during the winter at Ricard ... **Derek Bell** took over the co-driver's seat alongside **Al Holbert** in the "USA" 924 after **Peter Gregg** was hurt en route to Le Mans in a road accident, leaving Le Mans newcomers **Andy Rouse** and **Tony Dron** alone in the "GB" entry. Both acquitted themselves well, especially in the frequent heavy rain showers, but the damaged valve was losing them more than half a minute per lap ... **Colin Chapman** was a surprise visitor to Le Mans in the Essex pit. The last time he was at the Sarthe was as a **competitor**, in 1962, when the ACO found an excuse to turn down his entry on spurious technical grounds *after* it had shown alarming speed in practice. Having sworn then never to return, it seems that important business — possibly FISA president **Jean-Marie Balestre** ... **Ford** had a surprise at Le Mans, for on paper it looked like another turbo-Porsche victory. But most of the heavy-metal German Turbo-Motors wilted (again), and Ford Europe PR man Box Sicot was looking much happier at the finish than earlier ... **Lancia's** two works entries were **early retirements** with broken oil pump belts, leaving the semi-works entry of **Finotto/**

Ickx: "My last Le Mans"

SECOND PLACE in his last Le Mans wasn't quite good enough for Belgian veteran Jacky Ickx. With four victories behind him already, Ickx, 35, was planning on a fifth victory, which would have been a unique achievement in the race and a fine opportunity for him to finally step down.

Ickx's Porsche prototype, shared with its German owner Rheinhold Joest, was entered by Martini Racing. Looking very like the 936 prototypes which he had raced in the previous three Le Mans events, it was built by Joest on a spare works 936 chassis left over from last year, though the official designation is "908/80" in deference to Porche modesty.

The engine was *not* one of the semi-watercooled units developed by Porsche in an unsuccessful bid to beat Renault in 1978. Instead, Joest was restricted to one of his own aircooled two-valve units.

A broken fifth gear caused a 28 minute pit stop when the car had been leading for eight hours, and at 10 am on Sunday the Rondeau passed into the lead. Though Ickx did his best to catch up — putting in a hurry-up drive of a quality rarely seen at Le Mans — the

combination of too little power, sudden rain showers and too much time lost meant that he would have to be satisfied with second place.

"This is definitely my last race," said Ickx: "next year I think that I will not have the same motivation. But I have not finished with the sport altogether (a reference to the Spa-Francorchamps Circuit, where he is manager) and I may even be seen on a big rally too."

So near and yet so far (again) . . .

LAST YEAR Dick Barbour looked set to win Le Mans. On Sunday morning, the leading Porsche of Klaus Ludwig and the Whittington brothers was delayed with a broken drive belt, and suddenly victory appeared to be within the grasp of the portly Southern Californian Datsun dealer and co-drivers Rolf Stommelen and Paul Newman. Then a front wheel nut jammed on during a crucial pitstop, and any hopes of a win were dashed.

This year Barbour teamed up with expatriate English racing drivers John Fitzpatrick and Brian Redman to drive a new Porsche 935 K3 and lead his three car attack on the Sarthe. Former Solihull VW garage owner Fitzpatrick — who now lives in San Diego — showed the team's intent by hurling the Sachs Sporting Shock Absorbers-backed Porsche around to pole position and initially leading the race. According to the team, the only weak spot in the

Above: the 5th place Fitz/Barbour/Redman 935 doesn't merit a glance at Mulsanne . . .

Kremer built car were the headgaskets, and these proved to be the car's undoing. One let go around midday on Sunday, a cylinder was immobilised, the turbo boost backed off, and the car had to be cruised to a fifth place finish.

For Barbour and his fifteen man crew, it was a poor reward for their hard work. With only four professional mechanics — the rest of the outfit being enthusiastic Porsche Club of America members who donate their spare time to the project — they had not only prepared the lead car, but also transformed last year's second place 935 into the lighter and stiffer chassied

K3 variant, complete with the power releasing air-to-air (rather than water/air) turbo intercoolers. Crewed by Bob Garretson, former F2 driver Bobby Rahal and Australian saloon car champ Allan Moffat, the machine ran well until retiring after 10 hours with similar head gasket troubles.

After the race, the crew were looking forward to a trip to that mecca for Porsche freaks, the factory's Weissach test facility, before going on to contest the Norisring German Group 5 race next Sunday. After that it's an APEX flight back to the USA, before initial plans are laid for next year's Le Mans.

Facetti to carry the company colours in a return (after 25 years) to the big race. Racing for points in the group five "silhouette" championship, the two Italians were delayed by several pre-cautionary stops to have fresh belts fitted, and had to be content with a third place in class . . . One of the three turbo-Peugeot WM prototypes which started the race was fitted with a TV camera which broadcast via a helicopter-link to closed circuits which could be viewed in the press stand. The sight of rallyman Guy Frequelin thundering down Mulsanne with his digital speedometer registering over 190 mph in the rain — in full colour — was enough to change several motor noters' minds about becoming racers . . . British fans seemed to form an even larger proportion than usual of the attenuated spectators this year, and Union Jacks were waved opposite the De Cadenet pit regardless of the fact that a Frenchman, Francois Migault, was co-driving the familiar all-green car. It was most unfortunate that

Desiré Wilson was not allowed to drive the car, for she not only qualified the car handsomely in her one lap on a completely dry track, but also climbed out of it as coolly as any man after she'd clipped a kerb on the next lap and started a series of rolls which scared the wits out of a following Mark Thatcher. The De Cadenet crew under Murray Smith did a splendid job of repairing the car for the race, and had a rear cross member not forced a one-hour pit stop (it was almost certainly cracked in Mrs Wilson's accident) there was every chance of a De Cadenet victory at the Sarthe . . . Chris Craft, De Cadenet's one-time regular co-driver, was similarly unlucky to run into transmission bothers with the Japanese Dome-Cosworth he was sharing with ex-Lotus star Bob Evans. The Dome had been substantially altered since last year but its sister car, a somewhat outrageous prototype masquerading as a Toyota Celica, did not qualify in the hands of some unknown Japanese drivers.

RESULTS
48th Le Mans 24 Hours Race. June 14/15 1980

		laps
1	Rondeau M379 B (Jean Rondeau/Jean-Pierre Jaussaud)	338
2	Porsche 908/80 turbo (Reinhold Joest/Jackie Ickx)	336
3	Rondeau M379 B (Jean-Michel Martin/Phillipe Martin/Gordon Spice)	329
4	WM 79/80 turbo (Guy Frequelin/Roger Dorchy)	318
5	Porsche 935 K3 turbo (Dick Barbour/John Fitzpatrick/Brian Redman)	317
6	Porsche 924 turbo (Jurgen Barth/Manfred Schurti)	316
7	De Cadenet Ford (Alain de Cadenet/Franciois Migault)	313
8	Porsche 935 turbo (Dieter Schornstein/Harald Grohs/Von Tschirnhau)	313
9	Porsche 935 K3 turbo (John Paul/John Paul Junior/Guy Edwards)	312
10	Ferrari 512 BB (Pierre Dieudonne/Jean Xhenceval/Herve Regout)	312
11	WM 79/80 turbo (Max Mamers/Jean-Daniel Raulet)	311
12	Porsche 924 turbo (Andy Rouse/Tony Dron)	310
13	Porsche 924 turbo (Derek Bell/Al Holbert)	305
14	BMW M1 (Didier Pironi/Dieter Quester/)	293
15	BMW M1 (Hans Stuck/Hans Georg Burger)	283
16	Porsche 911 methanol (Thierry Perrier/Roger Carmillet)	280
17	Chevron B36 (Bruno Sotty/Phillipe Hesnault/N Del Bello)	276
18	Lola T298 (Florian Vetsch/Michel Dubois/Christian Debias)	272
19	Lancia Beta turbo (Carlo Facetti/Martino Finotto/Bernard Darniche)	272
20	Porsche 935 turbo (Herve Poulain/Danny Snobeck/Patrick Destic)	271

Winners' average speed: 119.266 mph. Distance covered: 2,862.026 miles.

A French victory

Historic victory for Jaussaud and driver/constructor Rondeau — Ickx's fifth narrowly thwarted — Qualifying controversy foils Britons — Works Porsches all finish — Qualifying: QUENTIN SPURRING — Report: MARCUS PYE & MARK HUGHES — Photography: JEFF BLOXHAM.

There were two attractions above all others at last weekend's Le Mans 24 Hours for most of the spectators at the Sarthe circuit. Two years on from Renault's 1978 win, there were two well-prepared teams capable of bringing another French success, the Rondeau and WM-Peugeot teams both entering three cars. And Jacky Ickx, of course, had returned to try to win Le Mans for the fifth time, sharing Reinhold Jöst's Porsche 936 'look-alike'. Through the night a grand battle had shaped up between the Jean Rondeau/Jean-Pierre Jaussaud Rondeau and the Ickx/Jöst Porsche, Jacky driving with characteristic perfection to maintain a slender one lap lead over the black Rondeau.

That one car would weaken seemed inevitable, and in the 18th hour the Porsche slowed, arriving in the pits for a 25mins stop to replace fifth gear. The Rondeau inherited a five lap lead, which seemed just too much for Ickx to make up, but the weather was looking increasingly uncertain . . .

Two short, heavy showers in the last three hours provided first rate drama. Shortly after 1.00pm, the leading two cars were the first to arrive at a soaking Dunlop Curve, and incredibly both slithered broadside into the armco, thankfully without causing substantial damage. With 40mins remaining, Ickx was just over a lap down on Jaussaud when an equally sudden shower sent almost everyone into the pits for tyre changes. The Rondeau stayed out on slicks . . .

Matters were decided by the wind. The sun quickly returned, the track dried, and Ickx dropped two laps by the 4.00pm finish. Jean-Pierre Jaussaud had won his second Le Mans in a French car, and Jean Rondeau had become the first driver/constructor ever to win the 24 hour race.

The Rondeau team's effort was truly impressive, for the Gordon Spice/Martin brothers car finished third and won the GTP class, while the Henri Pescarolo/Jean Ragnotti car hauled itself into the lead shortly before 1.00am, only to blow its Cosworth engine within an hour. The other three car French team also put on a fine show, the WM-Peugeot which had served as a camera car bringing Guy Frequelin/Roger Dorchy into fourth place.

Of the 15 Porsche 935s entered in various guises, the American John Fitzpatrick/Brian Redman/Dick Barbour car was easily the quickest, but its fuel thirst and a motor struggling on five cylinders in the closing hours prevented it from finishing higher than fifth, although it had led for two hours late on Saturday evening. Impressive reliability nonetheless, for only four 935s finished.

The works Porsche 924 Carrera Turbos fared much better, all three finishing — two of them were sapped by a loss of compression in one cylinder, but the Jurgen Barth/Manfred Schurti/Eberhard Braun car came home in sixth place.

Thousands of British supporters travel to France each year to back the handful of loyal British entrants, led by Alain de Cadenet's gallant outfit. That the team even reached the grid was incredible, for Desiré Wilson rolled the car in a horrific accident which would have written off many lesser chassis. Non-stop work readied the car for the race, and incredibly de Cadenet and

François Migault came through 24 hours to finish seventh.

The Pete Clark/Nick Mason/Martin Birrane Dorset Racing Lola overcame an enormity of problems to finish, having led the class briefly. The massive Steve O'Rourke/Simon Phillips/Richard Down Ferrari 512BB survived the distance, while the John Cooper/Peter Lovett/Dudley Wood Porsche 935 K3 dropped out after 12 hours with head gasket failure. There should have been more British starters, but three cars failed to qualify in circumstances which may well be resolved in court (see *Pit & Paddock*).

Among the unreliable 935s, one displayed an astonishing turn of speed in the wet opening two hours — the Loos car of Bob Wollek/Helmut Kelleners soon gained the lead, although it hit problems and eventually retired with a broken engine. Hans Stuck, too was mighty in the wet, rapidly hauling his BMW M1 into second place, but he was later to be considerably delayed with a serious crankshaft vibration. The works Lancias were appalling, both running their bearings before the two hour mark, while the vastly improved Dome never recovered from a gearbox rebuild during the first four hours.

QUALIFYING

Three things made qualifying something of a lottery, and gave rise to a great deal of unpleasantness and controversy.

First, there was the ACO's very sensible new rule which said that starting positions would be based on the *average* best lap times of all the drivers in each car. As usual, the organisers were operating a class-by-class qualification system. The teams had until 10am on Friday morning to declare if they wished to drop drivers from their cars, in order either to improve their grid positions or to make sure that their cars had qualified.

This resulted in much confusion. For a start, the ACO showed itself to be incapable of satisfactorily policing what was universally accepted as a very wise regulation, designed to eliminate drivers who were dangerously off the pace. The officials were not able to keep track of who was driving each car and when during the qualifying session, and to add to the chaos and bad feeling there were accusations of drivers switching team cars and even helmets. In addition, teams trying to make the decision about whether to drop drivers had no idea what others in the class were intending to do, which caused some to take an unnecessary risk to ensure that all their drivers got a race, and also left some drivers without a race when they might have qualified with ease.

Second, there was the new 'efficiency' rule, which

| WCM | WORLD CHAMPIONSHIP OF MAKES
LE MANS 24 HOURS | 7 |

Jean Rondeau negotiates the Ford chicane in the superbly reliable winning car — Pescarolo's sister machine was leading when it went out.

The first lap — early leader was John Fitzpatrick in Dick Barbour's Porsche, which fought off an attack from Pescarolo's Rondeau.

banned engine and gearbox changes from the start of qualifying on Thursday afternoon until the end of the race. Naturally, this added to the nightmare of the team managers, who were wary of pushing their drivers lest this kind of failure occurred.

Third, because of the efficiency rule, qualifying was confined to the single five-hour session on Thursday — and the weather was inconsistent. The session started out raining, and finished in ideal conditions, warm and humid. This produced a rush by the team managers to get *all* their drivers out during the last hour or so, when conditions were at their best. Some of them failed in this, and drivers with slow times after only practising on a wet or damp track were discarded. Thankfully, there were not many cars with mechanical troubles encountered towards the end of the session.

In the 3-litre G6 class, the best lap was one in 3m 41.4s by Jacky Ickx, but the highest average qualifier — pole position for France — was the Pescarolo/Ragnotti Rondeau. The sister car was fortunate with the weather, losing much time early in the session with suspected black box failure, but getting out in the last half-hour for both Jaussaud and Rondeau himself to set good times when the track was at its best.

The Martini team introduced a new angle to the driver qualification saga, putting Michel Leclere into the 908/J80 and using his time to qualify despite Jöst's slower effort in the damp — then the team used Leclere only as a reserve!

The Japanese team was also fortunate with the weather. During Wednesday's unofficial session, Craft had had the frightening experience of a tyre coming off the unpegged rim on Mulsanne. During the rain early in the Thursday practice, it happened again, but Chris was able to get back the Dome to the pits and both drivers qualified later — although the Japanese slicks were turning on the rims! The tyres were both pegged and glued for the race . . .

The De Cadenet team also had a hectic time. After the Wednesday session, the mechanics had worked an all-nighter replacing the engine and gearbox, and after both de Cadenet and Migault had set comfortable qualifying times they found another night's work on their hands — and this a desperate one. Desiré Wilson went out late in the session to do her time, and on her third lap she lost the car at the Ford corner, flat in fourth. She put a wheel on the dirt, and shot across the track in front of an alarmed Pete Clark in the DRA Lola; as the car hit the barrier on the other side of the track, the rear dug into the sand, and the De Cadenet flipped through the air.

The car must be immensely strong. Not only was

NOTES ON THE CARS

Year after year, the exclusive magic of Le Mans goes to work. Irrespective of the rules formulated with such an independent air by the Automobile Club de l'Ouest, and irrespective of the general state of endurance racing worldwide, Le Mans attracts a massively oversubscribed entry, representing the cream of the world's sports car teams. This year, the ACO permitted a total of 70 cars to attempt to qualify (although three of these entries were scratched), and it was interesting that the best supported category came from the IMSA class initiated by John Bishop and Bill France in the USA.

There were 22 IMSA-type cars (of which half actually came over from North America), twelve Group 5, eleven 2-litre Group 6, nine GTP, eight 3-litre Group 6, four Group 4, and two GTX. Of these, it was originally intended that 50 (rather than the normal 55) would start the 24 Hours, but the ACO ultimately decided, in controversial circumstances, to revert to the old figure.

Group 6/3000cc

The most interesting car in the 3-litre prototype group was the so-called Porsche 908/J80, with which Jacky Ickx was attempting to win Le Mans for an unprecedented fifth time. The impetus for this one-off project came from Reinhold Jöst's Liqui-Moly backed team, and from Martini, the most famous of Porsche's Le Mans sponsors, eased out after many successful seasons by the overkill of Essex the year before.

With Martini money, Jöst persuaded Ickx out of retirement and the Porsche factory team in Stuttgart to assist in the return of what is essentially a Martini-Porsche 936 (of the 1977 front-radiator type) to the Sarthe. Officially, the Dunlop-shod car was built in the Liqui-Moly team's base near Karlsruhe, Germany. It consists of a 908/936 type chassis, its 936/77 bodywork supplied direct from Stuttgart, and it is powered by one of the air-cooled, two-valve, twin-turbo 936 engines of the type used by the factory team in 1977. This unit has been used in Jöst's familiar old 908/3 sports-prototype with which he has been contesting the 1980 WCM events. The gearbox and brakes are both of the type used on the 917. Having tested extensively at Hockenheim, Jöst was very confident about his team's prospects, believing that this power unit, tuned to produce only about 550bhp on low boost, would be the best compromise between the need for sheer speed and the ACO's new regulations concerning fuel.

Sleek G6 bodywork is an obvious benefit at Le mans, but from this class many felt that the French Rondeau entries, with their normaly aspirated and less thirsty Cosworth DFV engines, represented the more sensible comprmise. Jean Rondeau's purposeful cars have become a regular feature at

this race, and this year's refuelling rules gave him his best chance yet of the overall win.

Based at Champagne, only 10 miles east of Le Mans, Rondeau's team had once again attracted heavy sponsorship for its two G6 entries. Both these Goodyear tyred cars raced here in 1979, but since last year they have been updated to M379B specification, with longer rear bodywork, new wings and revised ducting. They remain quite heavy, about 65 kilos over the G6 weight limit, although this was about 13 kilos less than the Porsche.

The engines, prepared by Heini Mader (who described them as similar to 1978 spec for F1), were small-valve DFVs tuned to give a reliable 460bhp. Under team manager Jean-François Robin and crew chief Philippe Beloou, the cars were painstakingly prepared in the exclusive area of the paddock formerly reserved for the *gloire de la France* teams of Renault and Matra, which added to the formidable appearance of the operation. The G6 cars were backed by Le Point ITT, and had done a 26-hour test at Ricard.

Another favoured team — ask the ACO — was André Chevalley Racing, which was running the attractive G6 car which made its debut at Silverstone. Since then, while the team has still not done any testing, the two main problems seem to have been solved, the Swiss-built car (its chassis based on the Lola T380 design) having been fitted with larger brakes and with new rear bodywork, made of the very rigid Kevlar material in order to avoid the flexing troubles experienced in England. Its power unit, again, is a Mader developed DFV.

The Longines backed ACR was one of three Lola-based G6 cars, the others both bearing the increasingly proud name of De Cadenet, and displaying their Lola pedigree to decreasing extents. Nick Faure is now the owner of the former John Cooper/Pete Lovett car which was originally built in 1976. Since Faure bought it three months ago, the car has been completely refurbished by his K&K Automotive organisation, the actual work being carried out in a private garage in Newbury. For Le Mans, the Pepsi/Diagrit Diamond entry was set up in Bridgewater, Somerset, at the M&H factory, which supplied the tyres. The power unit is a very torquey Alan Smith DFV.

The latest De Cadenet, coming to Le Mans with a real chance of a victory to add to those gained at Monza and Silverstone, was in its usual trim, under the team management of Murray Smith. Sponsored by Antar, Sealink, Ford Europe, Sodis and *Le Parisien Liberé* magazine, the team received the additional backing from Pepsi Cola France when, to the disappointment of Pepsi's 500 guests, the Faure car was excluded after qualifying. As usual, the 'De Cad' is powered by a Nicholson engine.

Above: Having borrowed a replacement tail section, the O'Rourke/Phillips/Down Ferrari 512BB ran reliably to the finish. Below: John Paul, chasing Claude Ballot-Lena's rapid Ferrari 512BB, in the Porsche 935 he was sharing with his son and Guy Edwards.

Desiré unharmed (and undeterred!), but the chassis was only slightly dented but as straight as a die after the shunt. Fortunately, the team had plenty of spares, including body sections and wing, and was able to fabricate other new parts and rebuild the car's suspension for the race. In disgraceful circumstances (see *Pit & Paddock*), however, Desiré was excluded from the race.

Patrick Gaillard found the ACR well off the pace in a straight line, pulling only 9400rpm (500 revs down) on Mulsanne. With his slower co-drivers, he seemed to have a problem qualifying, but the Swiss car was the last in the class to get in. From the teams which failed, there were accusations that the ACO had made a mistake with the time credited to owner André Chevalley — and even that the time had been deliberately falsified.

The unlucky cars (again) were the Faure De Cadenet and the Ibec. Bernard de Dryver was fastest in the Pepsi car, but in the final hour the car lost fourth gear, and the average made them the first non-qualifier. The Ibec broke its CWP on Wednesday, and the replacement unit proved unsatisfactory. As official practice got under way, the car would pull only 8400rpm down Mulsanne. But there is no doubt that the ACO properly cocked up the times for this car.

For a while, the club had Tony Trimmer's best lap credited to Ian Bracey, who did not even drive. When the team pointed this out, they lost the time as well, and the new average was not quite good enough, for Tiff Needell never drove in the dry because of an electrical failure. Both Trimmer and Tiff Needell were furious, and Bracey actually accused the French of cheating (see *P&P*).

The anger of these British teams was increased when the ACO announced on Friday that 55 cars would start after all. The club admitted the slow Mazda and ethanol Porsche on the grounds that these cars were of "special technical interest", and discretionary selection was also applied to three more cars, the 'German' works Porsche 924, the second works Lancia and the slowest of the three factory Kremer-Porsche K3/80 cars.

The Norbert Singer managed Porsche team had an unhappy few days leading up to the race. First, Gunther Steckkonig, who was due to drive with Schurti and Barth, was rushed to hospital with a kidney failure.

Notes on the cars continued

The third British G6 entry was Ian Bracey's Ibec, having its first outing here in revitalised form. The chassis — originally based on the Hesketh 308 tub — has been very extensively modified now, and the car features relocated oil coolers, modified rear suspension, new front suspension detail work, and revised body sections, the changes effected by ADA Engineering and by Gordon Horn's team itself; producing a much neater package all round. With a similar power output to the other DFVs, the Ibec's engine is race-prepared by John Dunn's Swindon firm. The team had some chunking problems with the Ibec's M&H tyres.

Finally in this class, the Japanese entered, British driven Dome RL80. This is an entirely new car from Dome's designer Masao Ono and built at this determined team's factory in Kyoto. Powered, as before, by a DFV prepared also in Japan by Shinji Kondo, the windcheating car looks similar to last year's model, but it is about 18ins shorter and 3ins wider. The new chassis and better suspension and aerodynamics produced dramatic improvements both in handling and straightline speed during extensive tests at Suzuka, including one for 18 trouble-free hours conducted by its Le Mans drivers. The new car is again fitted with Japanese Dunlop tyres, which caused their own problems during practice.

Group 5

There were no fewer that 15 Porsche 935 cars, seven of which were in the G5 class, although essentially the same as their IMSA equivalents. As we have come to expect, the Kremer and Loos entries were among the very fastest cars here.

Erwin Kremer entered three of the latest K3/80 models, one of which (that driven by Ongais/Field/Lafosse) had made its debut in such an impressive fashion at Silverstone, the other two being brand new. The new breed of Kremer-Porsche features revised rear suspension pickups, designed to keep the front end down under hard acceleration. It also has the last word in 3.2-litre 935 engines, fitted with Kugelfischer fuel injection (replacing the Bosch system), and a revised induction system with larger inlets. The twin-turbo package results in yet more power and, even here where the boost must be set at around 1.2 or 1.3 bars, there is a comfortable 650bhp or so on tap. With the latest 'wing-car' bodywork, featuring the high fences channelling the airstream onto the rear wing, the combination was impressively effective down Mulsanne.

Georg Loos's rival team, also based in Cologne, had a singleton entry, supported to the hilt by Pirelli, whose tyres the Gelo team is using this year in the German G5 series. The

car was the team's regular 3.2-litre DRM machine with its 'pinched' front wheel arches, and was sponsored at Le Mans by Kraus hi-fi. As before, Loos was running his car more or less as supplied by the factory, and this is not as highly developed as the glorious K3s.

The other two 935s in the class were the familiar machines of the Meccarillos and Vegla teams, both two-year-old single-turbo versions with 3-litre engines, and Dudley Wood's Charles Ivey Racing entered K3. This is the ex-John Winter car which finished third here in 1979, and it retains its 3-litre twin-turbo power unit.

Very conscious of its World Championship of Makes points lead, Cesare Fiorio's factory Lancia team discarded its plan to run a supercharged engine in one of its Beta Monte Carlo G5 cars, and fell back on the known quantity of the 1.4-litre turbo power unit for both its entries. With finishing the prime target, the KKK turbo on each car was set at only 1.2 bars, compared with the 1.4 (sometimes 1.5) used in the six-hour events, so the Fiat 131 based engines just had to last with only about 350bhp being produced. The tattily prepared cars were not fast in a straight line (175mph), but as far as ease and comfort were concerned their superb handling made them the ideal tool for Le Mans. Fiorio's men were also looking after the Jolly Club entry here, and Facetti/Finotto car now also running on Pirelli rubber having moved over from Goodyear.

Finally in G5, the Triumph TR8 turbo came to Le Mans looking the part but lacking development.

IMSA

The stars of the IMSA class were undoubtedly the Dick Barbour team cars, and particularly the brand new Sachs-sponsored Porsche 935 K3/80 to be driven by Barbour/Fitzpatrick/Redman. Like the other new K3 run by the Kremer team itself, this machine was fitted with the

Dome-DFV — Craft/Evans.

latest rear suspension, and also with the latest Kugelfischer injection. After using this motor for Wednesday practice, however, the team — noticeably boosted by the full-time arrival of John Fitzpatrick — decided that the new engine was too much of an unknown quality, and reverted to its 3.2 Bosch engine, built in the USA.

The team had two more K3s, the Apple Computers backed machine for Rahal/Moffat/Garretson being the car with which Barbour finished second in 1979 with Paul Newman and Rolf Stommelen, still fitted (like the third, Wynn's sponsored entry) with the twin-turbo 3-litre. Judge the extent of the San Diego based team's competitiveness by the fact that yet another K3/80 (this the Sebring 12 Hours winner, no less) was brought along to the Sarthe as a sort of mobile spare parts depot . . .

The other K3/type Porsches in the class were also 3-litre twin-turbo cars. Charles Mendez's Racing Associates Inc. team was making its first trip to Le Mans with two Hawaiian Tropic sponsored entries, the Akin/Cooke/Miller car being the one which won the pole at Daytona last year for Carlo Facetti/Martino Finotto. The other was built up in the States mid-season last year by Franz Blam Racing, and both have now been brought up to K3/80 spec except for the engines.

The 1979 winning Whittington brothers took over Angelo Pallavicini's entry to run their aptly named 'Warthog II', the original being the car which won last year. The second generation 'Hog was built to K3/80 spec at the team's Fort Lauderdale base, and was sponsored here by Sun Systems.

Hervé Poulain's car came straight from the factory and was near standard, which cannot be said for the 'Grand National' 935 of the JLP Racing team, the blue and yellow car seen at Silverstone. A rebuilt wreck, the car is immensely strong and heavy (some 60 kilos over the weight limit), reinforced by a massive NASCAR-type roll cage as part of the chassis structure. The car bore the logos of *Newsweek*, for the third driver was Guy Edwards.

The IMSA class was reinforced by the appearance of two works-prepared BMW M1 Coupé entries, run here by the Munich based factory team under competitions boss Dieter Stappert. Both cars, claimed the team, were built very close to the Group 4 regulations, although the suspension front and rear was more highly developed and the wings were mounted further back. The engines, too, were the 470bhp, Paul Rosche built endurance type motors as supplied to the March Engines team, although the straight-six units were fitted with a different exhaust system which made them sound less crisp than that in the March entry. The BMW France entry was the ex-Quester 1979 Procar rebuilt; the Lacaud machine (running here in Marlboro colours) the 1980 car which ran at the Nürburgring.

The return of an official BMW team to Le Mans was

More serious was a road accident which befell Peter Gregg as he drove from the team's hotel to the circuit for Wednesday practice. Gregg, who received a nasty knock on the head when his car rolled in a ditch, tried to drive on Thursday but after only a lap decided to give the race a miss, his vision impaired. Derek Bell was switched to the 'American' car to join Al Holbert.

Porsche then decided to qualify one of their test drivers, Eberhard Braun, as a reserve for all three cars, but after misreading the regs put him only in the German entry, which he was not told to drive fast. The result was that Braun could only drive the German car, and his time left the car a non-qualifier when the team did not drop him on Friday morning. The ACO let it in.

The club told Cesare Fiorio that the 2-litre G5 cars were to be considered as a separate class for qualification purposes, and the Lancia competitions boss understandably kicked up a hell of a fuss when his second car was excluded on these shaky grounds. The ACO let it in.

Jean-Louis Trintignant was way off the pace with the Kremer car he shared with Anny-Charlotte Verney and Xavier Lapeyre, but he is a famous film-actor. The ACO let it in.

Among the IMSA cars, John Fitzpatrick set the best lap time of the whole field with a 3:40.2, and the laps of Dick Barbour and Brian Redman were good enough to put the car on the front row alongside the black Rondeau. The JLP Porsche driven by John Paul, his 20-year-old son and Guy Edwards, had to have extensive rear end damage repaired after Paul Snr had crashed on Wednesday. The March BMW team was fortunate when the gear selector fork broke during the official session just as the track was drying, for it happened when Mike Korten was within reach of the pits, and freewheeled in for it to be repaired.

Neither of the Canadian Chevs qualified, the team manager accusing the drivers of not trying, while the Dome Toyota never looked like getting in, having no fifth gear throughout the official session. The Chinetti Ferrari threw a rod which, although the team tried to get an engine change past the scrutineers, allowed in the British Ferrari. The Mendez Porsche had to have a new fuel pump before it could get out towards the end of the session.

In Group 5, the only casualty was the Triumph, which was only just getting sorted towards the end of the second practice, the car suffering from a severe vibration and other teething troubles. The best time, surprisingly, came from Harald Grohs with a 3:45.0 in

Above: Two fine British performances came from the amazing seventh placed De Cadenet (pictured with Alain at the wheel), and the Clark/Mason/Birrane Dorset Racing Lola, which briefly led the 2 litre G6 class. Below: Hans Stuck presses on in the Marlboro BMW.

ACR-DFV — Gaillard/Chevalley/Trisconi.

significant not only for its own sake, but also because it showed up the March Engines M1 programme in such bad light. The British built car, of course, features a purpose made chassis and bodywork, which is still being hacked about as the March team pursues a hopeless development programme. The latest changes to the Marlboro and Philippe Salvet sponsored machine are designed to give greater speed and stability. The modification which repositioned the fuel tank horizontally behind the driver (instead of along the backbone of the chassis) is retained. The wheelbase is as before, but the track has been lessened by 6ins both front and rear, which has necessitated new suspension, although the actual geometry is as before. The tail is 10ins shorter on the new bodywork. While speed is improved, at 194mph the car was no faster than standard-bodied works cars down Mulsanne, and because of the 'shorter' suspension required by the narrower track there is increased tendency to roll.

Half a dozen beautiful Ferrari Boxers graced the IMSA class, including one from NART's Luigi Chinetti Jnr., and three new cars entered by the French Ferrari importers, Charles Pozzi, and run by JMS Racing. The superbly prepared Steve O'Rourke entry (the ex-Ecurie Francorchamps Le Mans car) was again a credit to Rosso Racing, the second fastest Boxer in a straight line.

Two Canadian entries were the spectacular low-line Camaro which raced in the USA rounds of the WCM, built up by Brad Francis's Descon team in Concord, Ontario, and a brand new Corvette, also fitted with one of the powerful 7-litre Descon prepared Chevrolet V8s.

Alongside the G6 car, the Dome company was running the turbocharged Toyota Celica which was built in Japan based on the ex-Stommelen Schnitzer German G5 car, which was sold to that country when Tom Hanawa took over the project for his Le Mans Co.

Also adding a Japanese flavour was the Z&W Enterprises Mazda RX7, this the car built by Holman & Moody to the order of Pierre Honegger, which we saw at Silverstone. The Carolinan organisation still believes in making 'em strong:

the Mazda, at 1020 kilos, was 80 kilos over the limit, and only the works BMWs in the class were heavier.

GTP

The basis of the FISA's new Group C, the GTP class was surprisingly poorly supported, with only three *marques*. The favourite was the third Mader-powered Rondeau, this a brand new car to the latest G6 spec, but ballasted to comply with the GTP weight limit. Weighing in at 810 kilos to the 765 of the G6 cars, the GTP entry differed only because of the stiffer rear suspension. Sponsored by Belga cigarettes and driven by the Martin brothers and by Gordon Spice (whose Capris the Martins race in the Belgian touring car series), the car was administered by the former De Cadenet team manager, Keith Greene.

As described in Tony Dron's track test in last week's issue, the production based Porsche 924 Carrera GT entries, with their mildly tuned 320bhp engines, formed the basis of a straightforward development exercise by Manfred Jantke's factory team from Stuttgart, with an eye very much on the future. This was the first time that the team (which has not missed Le Mans since 1961) was not going for an outright win since 1975, when the 911 Carrera Turbo was used here. All three cars were brand new, the Ricard test car being used only as a development prototype, and they were finished only just in time for their press launch a week before arriving.

The intriguing Esso-sponsored WM cars get faster each year. The cars have been extensively modified since 1979 in the Thorigny (near Paris) factory run by Gerard Welter and Michel Meunier. Apart from a host of detail chassis and suspension modifications, they are fitted with new rear bodywork, developed in the interests of sheer speed at the St Cyr l'Ecole, the wind tunnel facility used by the Renault and Ligier F1 teams. The basis of their engines is still the unlikely PRV six-cylinder, and the units are now fitted with twin KKK turbos. This is not a full-race engine, but the big capacity of the V6 motor enabled the little French team to achieve an easy 500bhp from only 1.2 boost, and the cars are light (the lightest only 3 kilos over the 875kgs limit) and very fast on the straight.

Others

In the 2-litre G6 category, the Dorset Racing team with its immaculate Lola T297/8 had its work cut out this year, with very strong opposition in the class than it won last year. After Wednesday practice, the team switched from its Swindon BDX to the probably more reliable (but 20bhp less powerful) Richardson BDG engine used at Brands and Silverstone. Martin Birrane bought sponsorship from Frox clothing to add to DRA's Stelrad backing.

Apart from the Walter Wolf Racing run Cheetah, which was

fitted with a BD-series engine prepared in Geneva by Marc Frischknecht, the DRA team's opposition relied on either ROC/Simca or BMW power. Far and away the fastest car in the class, predictably, was the factory Osella PA8, in which Lella Lombardi was joined by the inexperienced Mark Thatcher, making his debut at Le Mans exactly 52 weeks since his first race, a Lords versus Commons event at Brands Hatch. Thatcher added the sponsorship of British Car Auctions and Kelly Girl to the regular Alpilatte and Lana Gatto backing for the Osella, and had personal deals with Diagrit Diamond and Hertz.

Managed by Luis Peano (and in the race also by Giorgio Stirano) of the F1 team, the Osella drivers found that, with the 290bhp short-stroke Osella/BMW engine running at an unstressed 8600rpm, they could easily pull 198mph down Mulsanne with the purposeful, Pirelli-shod car. The Osella prepared motor had been back to the Munich factory for some long-distance conversion by Paul Rosche.

Also with their engines set at rather more than 280bhp, the ROC team fielded two Lolas and a Chevron with some experienced Le Mans drivers and a lot of sponsorship this year from Yacco. Years of perserverance with the Simca based engines now seems to be paying off and, with the exception of the Italian works car, the ROC team enjoyed the most professional preparation in the class, all three cars being completely stripped and rebuilt at the end of qualifying.

There were two BMW M1s in the GTX category, which they filled, so we will have to wait until next year before this particular IMSA inspired class attains the kind of popularity here that it enjoys in the USA. The Porsche 911SC accepted as a Group 4 entry, along with the four 934 cars, had its engine converted to run on a 50-50 mixture of petrol and ethanol, a distillation of sugar beet. The car was very slow, but the decision to take this advantage of the ACO's new rules (the only team to do so) guaranteed the Perrier team qualification.

Porsche 935 K3 — Cooper/Lovett/Wood.

For Jacky Ickx, bitter disappointment. Gearbox problems cost the popular Belgian his fifth win at the Sarthe, the Porsche leading comfortably at the time.

the old Vegla car, the next average from the Kremer K3 of Danny Ongais/Ted Field/Jean-Louis Lafosse. In the Gozzy Kremer car, Tetsu Ikusawa did a good job after his long lay-off, while 20-year-old Dale Whittington drove 'Warthog II' in place of his injured brother, Bill. The Charles Ivey car suffered a cwp failure on Wednesday, but qualified well the next day. Teo Fabi damaged the Chardonnet entry in unofficial practice on the Porsche curve, but the rear end was rebuilt overnight.

The ACO's attitude towards Porsche's problem put in all the GTP cars, the fastest driver being Guy Frequelin (3:48.7) in reportedly the best car in a straight line, the lead WM turbo, which was clocked at a remarkable 217mph.

The transfer of the ZOL M1 to the G5 class left only the similar Garage du Bac BMW the only runner in GTX, while all four G4 entries were allowed to race, the Diego Febles entry rebuilt after a major front-end shunt at Arnage on Wednesday.

Finally, in 2-litre G6, Jean-Marie Lemerle's Lola T298 broke its ROC engine, and the other non-qualifiers were Patrice Gaulupeau's Lola-BMW T298 and the Racing Fans Cheetah-Ford. The best time in the class came from Michel Pignard in Hubert Striebig's Toj-BMW at 4:2.9, while Mark Thatcher went a long way towards silencing his critics when he was just 6secs slower than Lella Lombardi's 4:5.6 with the factory Osella.

The ACO's decision to limit every car to a tank capacity of 120 litres, and to compel the teams to refuel using equipment flowing at 50 litres a minute, made this a very open race indeed, and gave new meaning to tactics. While the normally aspirated cars had a theoretical advantage here, the turbo cars would be faster between more frequent stops, and if it ever came to the crunch the turbo teams would be able to screw up the boost for any final dash . . . Despite the fact that the Martini-Porsche team was obviously not showing its hand during qualifying, however, most of the wise money was on the DFV powered G6 cars.

LES VINGT-QUATRE HEURES

By mid-morning on Saturday the bustling activity of the paddock began to filter into the pit lane and by noon all 55 starters for the 48th Vingt-Quatre Heures du Mans had assembled in echelon formation in front of the vast crowd. The NART Ferrari BB was withdrawn with an incurable engine problem allowing the British-entered Ferrari a run as reserve in the IMSA category. Owing to the changeable weather conditions of the previous three days, few people were fooled by the glorious sun two hours before the 4.00pm start, and when the skies darkened they suspected the worst. Torrential rain flooded the circuit as the cars were pushed to their grid spaces, the Sarthe becoming the hub of an enormous thunder storm on the 'pace lap'.

Pescarolo's Rondeau took the initiative as the swarm lunged for the start line, the ACO timing the 'off' to perfection. Fitzpatrick swept through to lead at the Dunlop curve by making the most of the rolling start. Looking more like offshore power boats with huge rooster tails in their wake they streamed back into the Ford chicane to complete the first lap over 6mins later, the track treacherously awash in all parts. Fitz, Pescarolo, Ikusawa and Wollek in their Porsche 935 derivatives filed through before Rondeau, Ickx in the 936-bodied 908 (happy to make such a leisurely start), Frequelin's WM, and de Cadenet. Then came Stuck, from Rahal, Ongais, Mamers and Gaillard's ACR. The rest of the field continued to appear for another couple of minutes! Already in trouble was Striebig, whose Toj had staunchly refused to fire on the grid and was pushed to the pits for attention, wet electrics being to blame.

Naturally, sodden ignition systems proved to be the most common malady in the opening hour, poor de Cadenet's machine rapidly descending the lap charts as an awful misfire set in. Although the Toj got away eventually, Ballot-Lena was in after his first lap (as was Gonzalez's 934) to have his Ferrari's ignition dried; indeed all three Pozzi-entered 512BBs lost around 20mins in the first hour for the same reason. O'Rourke's Ferrari entered for a plug change and a plastic bag, which served admirably in keeping the distributor dry.

The camera in the Frequelin/Dorchy WM showed what conditions were like on the *ligne droit:* downright evil. There was no question of taking the infamous Mulsanne kink flat out, for even Ickx was lifting there. John Paul admitted that the only way he knew where he was heading in the spray was by following the road markings, and at one point he put his 935's wheels onto the grass at 180mph — what he thought was the central line was in fact showing the edge of road . . .

Patrick Perrier's little Lola established an early lead in the 2-litre G6 division over Lombardi's Osella

misfiring which, despite duplicated electrical components, had to stop for the engine bay to be mopped out. Ghinzani's Lancia followed the lead of team-mate Heyer's troublesome car by stopping to report similar oil pressure problems; while it was oil pump belt failure which put the Austrian out after only an hour, fan belt breakage and consequent overheating dealt the ultimate blow for the second works car at the two hour mark. Not an impressive record for Cesare Fiorio's team — neither Markku Alen nor Bernard Darniche, the team's imports from the rally world, got to drive.

Lapping the midfield runners as early as lap 7, Fitzpatrick, now with Wollek in tow ahead of Pescarolo, had taken this group clear of Ikusawa's lurid pink device and Ickx, who was soon to be challenged by a determined Stuck in the Marlboro-backed BMW. No-one was driving more exuberantly than the lanky German who quickly disposed of Frequelin's resistance in the WM 'camera car'.

The Dick Barbour team received Fitz for his first fuel stop after 11 laps (only 50 mins), the Englishman opening the routine pit calls and falling to fifth place behind Wollek's Gelo 935, the rapid Rondeau of Pescarolo and the incredible Stuck. Fighting the Marlboro-liveried car every inch of the way with delicate fingertip control, this was exemplary stuff, Hans slithering round to great effect in a constant powerslide. Ikusawa was showing great verve too, while Ickx was prepared to conserve his mount in preference to displaying his unrivalled wet weather talents. *Quel dommage!*

Wollek, Pescarolo and Stuck refuelled within the space of four laps, allowing Fitzpatrick to set the pace once more. Least well off after the stops was Pescarolo, who lost time having a rear wheel changed and rejoined in sixth. Way down the order, in 37th position after the first hour, de Cadenet had suffered greater misfortune as his DFV spluttered and banged continuously until the BRG car ground to a halt at Mulsanne. An electrical problem with the damaged master switch (a legacy of the car's flip on Thursday) was diagnosed, and Alain informed his anxious pit crew by telephone from the signalling boxes at Mulsanne itself!

The Bellancauto Ferrari of Spartaco Dini had retired at the 90min stage, the result of an 'off' at White House. Charles Mendez's American 935 went off the road soon after Arnage and clobbered the armco hard enough to damage the rear suspension. He was limping back to the pits, he explained, when marshals at the Ford chicane waved him off the track — the engine stalled and wouldn't restart because the starter motor had also been damaged, so his race was over. Mike Sherwin retired the third Barbour car when he hit the spinning Chevron of Yves Courage coming on to the Mulsanne, reportedly flying over the car.

Another temporary casualty during the first hour was the angular Dome, which Craft gamely struggled with despite having lacked second and third gears from the start. When Japanese mechanics pounced on the car, the problem was quickly traced to a broken pinion bearing, whch necessitated a new cwp assembly and a stop of several hours. Feeling that it was an excellent dry

weather car, Craft was anxious to resume as the weather was improving.

Mercifully the rain had stopped mid-way between fuel stops for the leaders, Fitzpatrick ahead of the brilliant Wollek again before handing over to Brian Redman who took the wheel with the car now in third place. Redman effortlessly made up the distance to Stuck, hurtling by just as Wollek refuelled to put the Sachs Sporting machine back on top. Pescarolo, Ickx and Stommelen were running close, while in the 2litre G6 division Sourd's ROC-engined Lola maintained a tenuous advantage over Perrier's BMW-powered Lola, with the Dorset Racing car one lap back at this stage. As for the Osella, it had repeated electrical problems before a new battery was fitted, and Thatcher assumed control.

Among the Porsche 935s, John Paul Jnr was experiencing problems with the electronic and mechanical 'brain' of a new fuel injection system (which the team had hoped would give better fuel consumption) until the electronic circuit was by-passed. The 'British' 924, now with Dron at the helm, received new front bodywork in an extended fuel and tyre halt.

Positions after 3 hours: 1, Wollek/Kelleners, 39 laps; 2, Stuck/Bürger/Lacaud, 39 laps; 3, Barbour/Fitzpatrick/Redman, 39 laps; 4, Ickx/Jöst, 39 laps; 5, Ikusawa/Stommelen/Plankenhorn, 38 laps; 6, Pescarolo/Ragnotti, 38 laps; 7, Frequelin/Dorchy, 38 laps; 8, Field/Ongais/Lafosse, 38 laps; 9, Pironi/Quester/Mignot, 37 laps; 10, Rondeau/Jaussaud, 37 laps.

De Cadenet's marvellous stint was starting to look more rewarding when he brought his Cosworth special, now running beautifully, in for new tyres all round, as did Trisconi who relieved Gaillard in the ACR. Neve took over from Korten in the March Engines M1 which was as unreliable as ever, having stopped several times to replace a punctured rear tyre, to diagnose a steering problem and to attempt to cure vibrations at both front and rear — a bent front wing had to be straightened before the Belgian could continue. His countryman Martin, J. M. was moving up in the Belga Rondeau after replacing a couple of out-of-balance wheels. A leaking head gasket troubled Sourd's Lola which spent half an hour in the pits with cylinder head off although Marc handed over to Bernard Verdier shortly before they realised that the problem would be terminal. Redman's routine stop to install Barbour behind the wheel put Wollek's partner Kelleners at the head of the pack six laps after the German took over.

All the while Jöst was nonchalantly creeping up on the leading 935s, Reinhold taking over from Ickx in a typically tidy fashion. After shadowing Barbour for a couple of laps he set after Kelleners, finding no resistance as the open car moved into the lead at 7.50pm. Behind Barbour, and on the same lap as those ahead of him, Ragnotti maintained the pressure which Pescarolo had built up while Plankenhorn (with Stommelen), Jaussaud (with Rondeau) and Dorchy (with Frequelin) were engaged in another scrap with the other WM-Peugeots running close behind.

Alas for Stuck, who had been denied the race

Porsche drivers do it in the wet. Two 935's raise a cascade of spray in the rain-sodden 1980 race. Inset: Rondeau, Jaussaud and Moet on the balcony after the Rondeu's historic win. 1980.

Bob Wollek disputed the lead early on, the brilliant Frenchman running his regular German G5 series Gelo Porsche.

WCM WORLD CHAMPIONSHIP OF MAKES
LE MANS 24 HOURS **7**

leadership by mere feet several times during the pit stop sequences, he did not bargain for the attentions of Grohs, who had taken over the Vegla 935 from von Tschirnhaus a while earlier. Despite being a couple of laps adrift, Göt decided to thwart Hans's advances and blocked the BMW driver for a couple of laps. Stuck did get by briefly, but the Porsche repassed the M1 on the following lap before a clash in which the nose of Stuck's car was badly bent. He limped in slowly for the mechanics to replace the front spoiler, radiator and windscreen. Hans-Georg Bürger then took up pursuit.

Shortly after this incident, Claude Haldi's smart Meccarillos 935 retired with a broken camshaft just as it seemed that a lot of places could be made up. Then de Cadenet came in, strapping Francois Migault into the car after a heroic 3¾hr stint in which Alain had hauled the team up to 24th place.

The BMW France M1, now in the hands of Mignot, Chief Instructor of the Le Mans Ecole de Pilotage, spun at Tertre Rouge, damage to the front end necessitating a change of steering rack in the pits at the moment when Jöst handed the leading Martini Porsche back to his Belgian partner. At the four-hour mark, therefore, Ickx held a slender lead over the Barbour Porsche, Kelleners and Pescarolo, a lap clear of Ikusawa's Kremer Porsche and the second ITT Le Point Rondeau of Jaussaud. Making strong impressions just outside the top 10 were the 'American' and 'German' 924 Carreras while Dudley Wood's K3 — after a fine start by John Cooper — was in front of many teams with more experience of 935s.

Serge Saulnier, in the third of the beautiful WM-Peugeots, lying 10th overall, stopped for a new throttle cable while the smooth Thatcher handed back to Lella again, the pretty Osella slowly hauling back lost time after its earlier dramas. A longer stop for Redman had Barbour away, refuelled, and Craft, at last with an operational gearbox in the speedy Dome, also came into repair a throttle linkage fault. Another windscreen for Burger's BMW and Don Whittington's call to fix a fuel leak preceded the retirement of the March M1 after Neve shunted it at Mulsanne.

Around 9.30pm, the leading Porsche of Ickx slowed dramatically at the back of the circuit, the great Belgian leaping out to find a broken fuel injection belt. Spares are carried as a precaution for gremlins such as this and 14mins let jacky was on his way once more, stopping at his pit for a proper adjustment to be made. So began a fight back up the leader board which would be remembered for a long time, and Jacky set off again with a string of quick laps around the 3m 41.0s mark.

Shortly before six hours were up the BMW France M1 hit trouble, Mignot bringing it in first for body repairs and Quester three laps later to check the suspension, knocked askew in Mignot's earlier excursion. Further evidence of fuel pressure problems on the 935s came when Stommelen complained of fluctuation and fuel starvation on the circuit, the pink Gozzy Kremer car sitting idle while the injection system was looked over.

Positions after 6 hours: Pescarolo/Ragnotti, 84 laps; 2, Barbour/Fitzpatrick/Redman, 84 laps; 3, Rondeau/Jaussaud, 83 laps; 4, Wollek/Kelleners, 83 laps; 5, Field/Ongais/Lafosse, 81 laps; 6, Ickx/Jöst, 81 laps; 7, Rahal/Moffat/Garretson, 80 laps; 8, Frequelin/Dorchy, 80 laps; 9, Martin/Martin/Spice, 80 laps; 10, Mamers/Raulet, 80 laps.

Dorchy's petrol stop was used to replace the WM's front brake pads and also to alter the TV cameras which had served their purpose for an Esso film, the 8min stop dropping the quickest of the Peugeot-powered machines down the field. Chevalley handed back the understeering ACR to Gaillard, but the car had dropped well down the field after two long stops, the first to replace the starter motor, and the second to repair collapsed suspension after a wishbone broke — in all, over an hour and a quarter was lost.

Moving up very impressively now, the second Rondeau was right on the pace and just a lap behind Pescarolo's leading chassis, ahead by nearly a minute after recent fuel stops. The Barbour car split Jean Rondeau's pair and the Wollek/Kelleners 935 was pressing the second one hard — he was in a hurry to get back on terms with his rival K3, now with Fitzpatrick up once more. Into fifth place after a solid reliable run was Danny Ongais in the orange Interscope-Kremer K3, half a minute ahead of Ickx, while the older 3-litre 935 of Apple Computers trio Bob Garretson/Bobby Rahal/Allan Moffat was showing reliability and speed at this stage. Two-thirds of the WM equipe sandwiched the well-driven Rondeau of Spice and the Martin brothers while Migault, forging on in the De Cadenet, was now 11th and gaining.

Frantic activity in the WM pit saw the cars of Mamers and Morin re-equipped with fresh brake pads, Bousquet taking over the latter's car, running 13th. At the same time Jaussaud arrived for similar attention to his Rondeau while Rahal, running a splendid seventh, stayed in during a fuel stop. With Jöst now out again and closing the gap to Jaussaud, the scene up front was shaping up for a grand battle into the night.

Second to the Perrier/Yver Lola still, the Dorset Racing Lola had five laps to make up when the car came in for lighting repairs. De Cadenet relieved Migault for his second stint as Pescarolo took over from Ragnotti, while the sole-surviving Lancia, the Jolly Club car of Facetti, spent nearly an hour in the pits having a pinion in the gearbox replaced and new brakes before Finotto continued. Lapeyre's Porsche, like several others, had a new nose cone fitted while Poulain's came in for a new turbo rotor to be fitted, which lost the 935 more than 40mins.

The well drilled team work in the Porsche pits had all three cars running through routine stops quickly although Ongais's Kremer car was abandoned with piston failure from fifth place. The Charles Ivey K3 fell from ninth overall when first Cooper then Lovett came in to have the alternator changed and the battery had to be changed twice in an effort to trace a persistent misfire. Until this point the British team's tactics had paid off — Cooper reckoned that they were running a lower boost than any other 935 in the interests of reliability, and the car had run like clockwork.

Lella Lombardi's crew had to repair the rear lights before Thatcher could rejoin the race, the Osella clearly the quickest 2-litre car on the circuit. The fuel pressure problems on Stommelen's car continued until the Kremer team changed the injection pumps before entrusting the car to Plankenhorn. Wollek also hit problems soon after nightfall, the injection belt jumping off the Gelo car just as it passed the pits — Bob matched Ickx's time of 14mins to replace it after carrying out repairs by the side of the road at the Dunlop curve dropping his outfit to 17th overall. By midnight Dudley Wood's Porsche had had still more electrical components replaced, spoiling a commendable run, and the class-leading 2-litre Lola also lost 5mins in the pits, bringing the Dorset Racing car ever closer — now but three laps behind.

Both Haywood (in the Whittington Brothers' 935) and Rondeau received new oil while Barbour, his car having displaced the Rondeau pair at the top of the field before the eight hour mark, was still there an hour later. The big disappointment, as far as the partisan spectators were concerned, was that Pescarolo had abandoned his Rondeau out on the Mulsanne when the head gasket suddenly blew. Now the all-French effort rested firmly on the shoulders of Jaussaud and Rondeau himself. Much talk, however, surrounded the de Cadenet, which was running perfectly through the night and had moved up to fifth. And fourth place was not far away. For the de Cadenet was gaining on the heavier GTP spec Rondeau of the Martin brothers and Gordon Spice.

Positions after 9 hours: 1, Barbour/Fitzpatrick/Redman, 126 laps; 2, Rondeau/Jaussaud, 126 laps; 3, Ickx/Jöst, 126 laps; 4, Pescarolo/Ragnotti, 124 laps; 5, De Cadenet/Migault, 123 laps; 6, Rahal/Moffat/Garretson, 122 laps; 7, Martin/Martin/Spice, 122 laps; 8, Stuck/Bürger/Lacaud, 121 laps; 9, Whittington/Haywood/Whittington, 120 laps; 10, Barth/Schurti/Braun, 120 laps.

Garretson's Porsche expired with piston failure just before 10 hours were up, by which time the battle for the lead had hotted up once more, Jaussaud, Ickx and Barbour (after a puncture) now on the same lap and four ahead of Migault. The other Rondeau, the Whittington Porsche and Bürger's recovering BMW (which had had the crankshaft damper replaced) were also in touch. Bell and Holbert moved up to lead the three Porsche 924s in their American-entered car when the 'German'-liveried car struck a hare which necessitated a new radiator and nose section, dropping it to the back of the trio.

Peter Clark fought his way on to terms with Perrier's Lola, the Stelrad-backed Dorset Racing machine having the honour of class leadership by 2.00am after Perrier stopped to cure a misfire by changing the alternator. Nick Mason had major problems an hour later though, for he spun the Lola at the Ford chicane, barely 100 yards from the pit entrance. He was unable to restart as the clutch fluid had drained away and he could not select a gear. Rather than give up altogether, Nick laboriously drove the machine back on the starter motor and the team resumed at unabated pace after making up a new clutch pipe.

Not to be forgotten, however, among the British entrants, was the O'Rourke/Phillips/Down Ferrari 512BB, which was going smoothly until a rear tyre blew out on the Mulsanne while O'Rourke was driving. He got the car back to the pits with its damaged bodywork, and the team negotiated to use the rear section of Spartaco Dini's car. A problem in matching up incompatible connections between the light wiring delayed them for longer than necessary, but a now red and green car was out again within the hour.

Positions after 12 hours: 1, Ickx/Jöst, 170 laps; 2, Rondeau/Jaussaud, 169 laps; 3, Barbour/Fitzpatrick/Redman, 167 laps; 4, Martin/Martin/Spice, 165 laps; 5, De Cadenet/Migault, 164 laps; 6, Wollek/Kelleners, 163 laps; 7, Stuck/Bürger/Lacaud, 160 laps; 8, Lapeyre/Verney/Trintigant, 160 laps; 9, Bell/Holbert, 160 laps; 10, Saulnier/Morin/Bousquet, 160 laps.

The order was now well established up front, Jst and Ickx extending their lead to two laps over the Rondeau/Jaussaud pairing, with the Fitzpatrick/Redman/Barbour 935 maintaining its position yet unable to

The quicker ITT Le Point Rondeau of Pescarlo was leading well when a leaking head gasket put it out.

match the pace of the G6 cars. The Whittington Porsche finally succumbed to a broken differential, the Sun System team having got the engine out before deciding that the damage was irreparable, while yet more electrical problems befell Wollek and Kelleners. Dudley Wood's 935 was another to fall foul of head gasket failure at half-distance, the engine losing one bank of cylinders without warning. The car could have limped on for a couple of hours, but 12 more hours would be asking too much, so the team withdrew.

Mamers suffered throttle difficulties which dropped his car to the back of the WM group, while Plankenhorn, in the pink and white Kremer K3, eventually had to abandon it with a blown engine after persistent fuel system problems. Frequelin's WM was the next team car to call in for throttle rectification while Redman dropped in for attention to the fuel injection and was replaced by Barbour. At 5.45am Thatcher brought the Osella in for a new fuel injection pump, the Prime Minister's son having replaced Lombardi 30mins previously. At this point the troublesome ACR was finally wheeled away, with the suspension broken again. Wollek's swift Gelo Porsche went also, this yet another 935 to suffer piston failure.

Positions after 15 hours: 1, Ickx/Jöst, 215 laps; 2, Rondeau/Jaussaud, 214 laps; 3, Barbour/Fitzpatrick/Redman, 210 laps; 4, Martin/Martin/Spice, 207 laps; 5, De Cadenet/Migault, 206 laps; 6, Saulnier/Morin/Bousquet, 202 laps; 7, Bell/Holbert, 201 laps; 8, Rouse/Dron, 200 laps; 9, Lapeyre/Verney/Trintignant, 200 laps; 10, Barth/Schurti/Braun, 199 laps.

Soon after dawn, a gripping situation occurred whereby both the leading cars found themselves on the same lap. In a real battle of team tactics the lead changed hands several times. Ickx clambered aboard the Porsche at 7.06am and 20mins later Jaussaud was in the Rondeau. A stone wedged itself in the clutch cable of the third-placed Barbour Porsche, which spoiled its chances at this stage so that it fell into the clutches of the Spice/Martin *frères* Rondeau. This Belga/backed car had deposed the de Cadenet from fourth place, running smoothly after an earlier stop to change an alternator belt. Alain's car was still motoring reliably, having held fourth place for three hours, and even running second briefly when the leaders pitted. So far there were thankfully no more signs of weakness from the flip.

The little Osella's race came to an abrupt end in the 16th hour when Thatcher, sent out on some sticky qualifying tyres, lost the car at Tertre Rouge, locked up, and half spun, graunching the nose against the barriers. Although he was prepared to continue — in a race which will have helped his race discipline no end — the battery was dead and it refused to budge. Considering Mark had controlled the moment when a front stub-axle decided to break on Saturday, his was a good performance.

All three works Porsche 924 Carrera Turbos were established within the top 10 by now, Bell and Holbert running seventh with Rouse and Dron (in whose company they had run during the night) a place behind — only Ms Verney's Porsche split them from their sister car. This was a superb performance so far from the works team, and a tribute to their impeccable preparation.

The lead was finely balanced, for even a swift fuel stop meant half a lap lost, and the squabble over third place continued with the 935 keeping the upper hand over the Belga Rondeau. The list of casualties continued to grow as light rain set in on Sunday. The Lapeyre/Verney/Trintignant K3 was still running cleanly (Anny-Charlotte well on her way to a seventh Le Mans finish from as many starts?) while the Belgian-crewed blue Ferrari was disputing 14th place closely with Raulet's WM. The three surviving M1s — Guerin had the accident he had been threatening for some time early on Sunday — were together, the BMW ZOL entry (with a gearbox/clutch malady) narrowly leading Quester/Pironi/Mignot and the much-delayed Stuck/Bürger/Lacaud trio.

With just seven hours remaining, a major reversal of fortunes began to unfold. At two laps to the good the leading Porsche looked far from comfortable, even though Jaussaud had made a routine halt for brakes and new tyres all round on the second-placed Rondeau.

Meanwhile, after superb calculated driving through the night by de Cadenet and Migault, Francois came in at 8.35am to report that something had broken at the rear, since the car was weaving badly. A crossmember had broken and the engine was being supported by an exhaust pipe only on one side — it looked as if the race might have been over for the battle-scarred team, but the enthusiastic crew set to the task of effecting makeshift repairs. The stop cost 55mins, and all hope of a top three finish was gone, but still they soldiered on...

Verney took over from Trintignant in the yellow Malardeau Porsche, already with a savaged rear wing, and then retired it when the gearbox broke shortly

Above: The reliable Vegla 935 of Schornstein is harried by the 2-litre Lolas of Sourd and Perrier in the first hour. Below: Korten's disappointingly slow March-BMW M1 chases Dorchy (and SFP camera) in the quickest WM-Peugeot. Bottom: The Dron/Rouse 924 Carrera lifts a wheel at Mulsanne corner

before 9.00am. As healthy cars became even thinner on the ground, the works Porsche team was hitting problems — both the British and American 924s had lost compression in one cylinder, probably because the rings had worn, and were stuttering around 40secs off their previous pace. Team manager Norbert Singer was hopeful they would finish, albeit slowly.

The BMW France M1 still sounded crisp, as did the Dorset Lola — now easily the quickest survivor in its class. It had, however, suffered a rear blow out with Birrane at the wheel, and ran for a while with the rear body patched up minus wing. Birrane found the handling evil, but the hard-worked team soon had a new wing ready. A second puncture an hour later was thankfully not so violent. The rotary Mazda continued on its raucous way, although the rotor seals were failing, while the WM reliability was still a talking point.

Few were expecting the drama which occurred at 9.55am for Jöst made an unscheduled stop shortly after he took the Martini-Porsche out — and just when he looked to be helping Jacky Ickx to an historic fifth victory in the French classic. It was a gearbox malfunction... could the Liqui-Moly men fix it in the 6mins before the Rondeau was due to take the lead? The answer was no, for the white car remained stationary for 25mins — the black car rushed over the line at 10am precisely to the delight of all Frenchmen present. The fifth gear pinion had broken on the Porsche and had to be changed. Jöst explained that he could not have carried on without top gear, for one slow lap had been 4mins off the pace — he feared that the linkage was also faulty, but there was nothing the team could do about that.

Positions after 18 hours: 1, Ickx/Jst, 258 laps; 2, Rondeau/Jaussaud, 257 laps; 3, Barbour/Fitzpatrick/Redman, 250 laps; 4, Martin/Martin/Spice, 248 laps; 5, Saulnier/Morin/Bousquet, 244 laps; 6, Rouse/Dron, 240 laps; 7, Barth/Schurti/Braun, 239 laps; 8, Frequelin/Dorchy, 239 laps; 9, Bell/Holbert, 237 laps; 10, Paul/Paul/Edwards, 237 laps.

Jaussaud, looking for his second victory at the Sarthe, backed off cautiously, not wishing to stress the car any more than absolutely necessary. Rondeau first and third — for the attractive Belga-sponsored machine of Spice and the Martins was running faultlessly — would be a victory well worth celebrating. With his new fifth gear fitted, Jöst gave chase as hard as he dared, simply flying away from an unmoved Jaussaud on the road. Fitz took the wheel of the remaining Barbour K3 — the troubled JLP Racing 935 was still running but the other American-entered machine, the Akin/Miller/Cooke 935 had been raised on jacks, soon to be retired with a broken gearbox — in an attempt to wrest back third place, after a stop to rectify a distributor fault.

Serge Saulnier's WM lost a well-deserved fifth place when he pirouetted off the circuit at the Ford Chicane with a little over four hours remaining, while the surviving Pozzi Ferrari, still resplendent in European University colours, climbed to eighth place in the hands of Pierre Dieudonné/Hervé Regout/Jean Xhenceval. On the subject of Ferraris, the Rosso Racing *équipe* were certainly making the most of their late admission to the race, persevering despite a multiple of sins in what was, by the end, a real 'tank-tape special'.

But for the American Mazda reducing its speed to

LES 24 HEURES DU MANS
QUALIFYING

No.	Entrant	Drivers	Capacity	Chassis	Class	Tyres	Time
15	Jean Rondeau/ITT Le Point	Henri Pescarolo (F)/Jean Ragnotti (USA)/*Gordon Spice (GB)*	3.0	Rondeau-DFV M379B	G6	Goodyear	3:47.9
70	Dick Barbour Racing	John Fitzpatrick (GB)/Brian Redman (GB)/Dick Barbour (USA)	3.2	Porsche 935K3t/c	IMSA	Goodyear	3:48.4
42	Gozzy Kremer Racing	Tetsu Ikusawa (J)/Rolf Stommelen (D)/Axel Plankenhorn (D)	3.2	Porsche 935K3t/c	G5	Dunlop	3:49.8
9	Martini Racing Liqui Moly	Jacky Ickx (B)/Reinhold Jöst (D)/*Michel Leclere (F)*	2.1	Porsche G6/80t/c	G6	Dunlop	3:50.0
16	Jean Rondeau/ITT Le Point	Jean Rondeau (F)/Jean-Pierre Jaussaud (F)/*Gordon Spice (GB)*	3.0	Rondeau-DFV M379B	G6	Goodyear	3:50.2
8	Alain de Cadenet	Alain de Cadenet (GB)/Francois Migault (F)/*Désiré Wilson (ZA)*	3.0	De Cadenet Le Mans	G6	Goodyear	3:50.6
12	Dome Company Ltd	Chris Craft (GB)/Bob Evans (GB)	3.0	Dome-DFV RL80	G6	Dunlop (J)	3:50.7
41	Porsche Kremer Racing Team	Ted Field (USA)/Danny Ongals (USA)/Jean-Louis Lafosse (F)	3.2	Porsche 935t/c	G5	Goodyear	3:51.3
5	Ecurie WM Esso	Guy Frequelin (F)/Roger Dorchy (F)/*Jean-Louis Bosquet (F)*	2.6	WM-Peugeot 79/80t/c	GTP	Michelin	3:51.9
45	Gelo Racing Team	Bob Wollek (F)/Helmut Kelleners (D)	3.2	Porsche 935t/c	G5	Pirelli	3:53.1
49	Vegla Racing Team	Dieter Schornstein (D)/Harald Grohs (D)/Götz von Tschirnhaus (D)	3.0	Porsche 935t/c	G5	Dunlop	3:54.0
7	Ecurie WM Esso	Serge Saulnier (F)/Denis Morin (F)/*Jean-Louis Bousquet (F)*	2.6	WM-Peugeot 79/80t/c	GTP	Michelin	3:54.5
1	André Chevalley Racing/Longines	Patrick Gaillard (F)/André Chevalley (CH)/Francois Trisconi (CH)	3.0	ACR-DFV	G6	Goodyear	3:55.7
71	Dick Barbour Racing	Bobby Rahal (USA)/Allan Moffat (AUS)/Bob Garretson (USA)	3.0	Porsche 935K3t/c	IMSA	Goodyear	3:56.1
6	Ecurie WM Esso	Max Mamers (F)/Jean-Daniel Raulet (F)/*Jean-Louis Bousquet (F)*	*2.6*	WM-Peugeot 79/80t/c	GTP	Michelin	3:56.5
73	JLP Racing	John Paul (USA)/John Paul Jnr (USA)/Guy Edwards (GB)	3.0	Porsche 935K3t/c	IMSA	Goodyear	3:56.8
77	JMS Racing/Charles Pozzi	Claude Ballot-Lena (F)/Jean-Claude Andruet (F)/*Pierre Dieudonne (B)*	5.0	Ferrari 512BB	IMSA	Michelin	3:58.4
46	Meccarillos Racing Team	Claude Haldi (F)/Bernard Beguin (F)/*Volkert Merl (D)*	3.0	Porsche 935t/c	G5	Dunlop	3:58.9
17	Andrew Company/Belga	Jean-Michel Martin (B)/Philippe Martin (B)/Gordon Spice (GB)	3.0	Rondeau M379B-DFV	GTP	Goodyear	3:59.0
44	Charles Ivey Racing	John Cooper (GB)/Peter Lovett (GB)/Dudley Wood (GB)	3.2	Porsche 935t/c	G5	Dunlop	4:00.0
85	Sun System Whittington Brothers	Don Whittington (USA)/Hurley Haywood (USA)/Dale Whittington (USA)	3.2	Porsche 935K3t/c	IMSA	Goodyear	4:00.1
68	Racing Associates Inc	Charles Mendez (USA)/Skeeter McKitterick (USA)/*Leon Walger (RA)*	3.0	Porsche 935K3t/c	IMSA	Goodyear	4:02.5
84	Lacaud BMW Motorsport	Hans-Joachim Stuck (D)/Hans-Georg Bürger (D)/Dominique Lac'aud (F)	3.5	BMW M1	IMSA	Dunlop	4:02.5
76	JMS Racing/Charles Pozzi	Pierre Dieudonné (B)/Jean Xhenceval (B)/Hervé Regout (B)	5.0	Ferrari 512BB	IMSA	Michelin	4:02.6
83	BMW France	Dieter Quester (A)/Didier Pironi (F)/Marcel Mignot (F)	3.5	BMW M1	IMSA	Dunlop	4:02.7
51	Scuderia Lancia Corse	Hans Heyer (A)/Bernard Darniche (F)/*Teo Fabi (I)*	1.4	Lancia Beta t/c	G5	Pirelli	4:03.2
43	Malardeau Kremer Racing	Xavier Lapeyre (F)/Anny-Charlotte Verney (F)/Jean-Louis Trintignant (F)	3.0	Porsche 935K3t/c	G5	Dunlop	4:04.1
53	Jolly Club Lancia Corse	Carlo Facetti (I)/Martino Finotto (I)/*Bernard Darniche (F)*	1.4	Lancia Beta t/c	G5	Pirelli	4:05.2
69	Racing Associates Inc	Bob Akin (USA)/Ralph Kent-Cooke (USA)/Paul Miller (USA)	3.0	Porsche 935K3t/c	IMSA	Goodyear	4:05.3
52	Scuderia Lancia Corse	Piercarlo Ghinzani (I)/Gianfranco Brancatelli (I)/*Markku Alen (SF)*	1.4	Lancia Beta t/c	G5	Pirelli	4:06.6
95	BMW ZOL	Laurent Ferrier (CH)/Francois Servanin CH)/Pierre-Francois Rousselot (F)	3.5	BMW M1	IMSA	Goodyear	4:08.2
28	Torino Corse	Lella Lombardi (I)/Mark Thatcher(GB)	2.0	Osella-BMW PA8	G6	Pirelli	4:08.6
82	March Racing	Mike Korten (D)/Patrick Neve (B)/Manfred Winkelhock (D)	3.5	March-BMW M1	IMSA	Goodyear	4:09.4
3	Porsche System	Derek Bell (GB)/Al Holbert (USA)/*Eberhard Braun (D)*	2.0	Porsche 924 Carrera t/c	GTP	Dunlop	4:10.8
24	ROC Yacco	Marc Sourd (F)/Bernard Verdier (F)/*Florian Vetsch (F)*	2.0	Lola-ROC T298	G6	Goodyear	4:10.9
75	JMS Racing/Charles Pozzi	Lucien Guitteny (F)/Gerard Bleynie (F)/*Jean-Claude Libert (F)*	5.0	Ferrari 512BB	IMSA	Michelin	4:11.1
96	Garage du Bac	Frédéric Alliot (F)/Jacques Guerin (F)	3.5	BMW M1	GTX	Dunlop	4:11.7
89	Hervé Poulain	Danny Snobeck (F)/Hervé Poulain (F)/Philippe Destic (F)	3.0	Porsche 935t/c	IMSA	Dunlop	4:13.5
72	Dick Barbour Racing/Wynns	Bob Kirby (USA)/Siegfried Brunn (D)/Mike Sherwin (USA)	3.0	Chevron-BMW B36	IMSA	Goodyear	4:14.0
20	Jean-Philippe Grand	Yves Courage (F)/Jean-Philippe Grand (F)	2.0	Lola-BMW T298	G6	Goodyear	4:14.3
79	SC Supercar Bellancauto SRL	Spartaco Dini (I)/Fabrizio Violati (I)/Maurizio Micangeli (I)	5.0	Ferrari 512BB	IMSA	Michelin	4:14.4
27	Michel Elkoubi/Primagaz	Patrick Perrier (F)/Pierre Yver (F)/*Michel Elkoubo (F)*	2.0	Lola-BMW T298	G6	Goodyear	4:16.0
23	ROC Yacco	Michel Dubois (F)/Christian Debias (F)/Florian Vetsch (F)	2.0	Lola-ROC T298	G6	Goodyear	4:16.0
2	Porsche System	Andy Rouse (GB)/Tony Dron (GB)/*Eberhard Braun(D)*	2.0	Porsche 924 Carrera t/c	GTP	Dunlop	4:16.5
*74	Luigi Chinetti Snr/NART	Preston Henn (USA)/Jean-Pierre Delaunay (F)	5.0	Ferrari 512BB	IMSA	Michelin	4:16.7
29	Dorset Racing Associates	Pete Clark (GB)/Nick Mason (GB)/*Martin Birrane (GB)*	2.0	Lola-BDX T297/8	G6	Dunlop	4:17.1
4	Porsche System	Jurgen Barth (D)/Manfred Schurti (FL)/Eberhard Braun (D)	2.0	Porsche 924 Carrera t/c	GTP	Dunlop	4:17.1
25	ROC Yacco	Philippe Hesnault (F)/Bruno Sotty (F)/Daniel Laurent (F)	2.0	Chevron-ROC B36	G6	Goodyear	4:17.4
22	Hubert Striebig	Michel Pignard (F)/Hubert Striebig (F)/Mario Ketterer (A)	2.0	Toj-BMW SMO1	G6	Dunlop	4:18.9
94	Equipe Almeras Freres	Jacques Almeras (F)/Jean-Marie Almeras (F)/Marianne Hoepfner (F)	3.0	Porsche 934t/c	G4	Michelin	4:23.3
91	ASA Cachia	Christian Bussi (F)/Bernard Salam (F)/Cyril Grandet (F)	3.0	Porsche 934t/c	G4	Goodyear	4:26.3
80	Diego Febles Racing	Armando Gonzales (PR)/Diego Febles (PR)/Francisco Romero (YV)	3.0	Porsche 934t/c	G4	Michelin	4:26.4
90	Georges Bourdillat	Georges Bourdillat (F)/Alain Bernard (F)	3.0	Porsche 934t/c	G4	Goodyear	4:36.1
86	Z&W Enterprises Inc	Ernesto Soto (YV)/Pierre Honegger (USA)/Mark Hutchins (USA)	2.3	Mazda RX7t/c	IMSA	Goodyear	4:37.6
93	Thierry Perrier	Thierry Perrier (F)/Roger Carmillet (F)	3.2	Porsche 934t/c	G4	Kleber	4:37.6
78	Rosso Racing/Emka Productions	Steve O'Rourke (GB)/Richard Down (GB)/Simon Phillips (GB)	5.0	Ferrari 512BB	IMSA	Dunlop	4:19.7

Drivers in italics practised but did not race

*Did not start because of holed cylinder block — rules do not permit engine changes between qualifying and practice. — car 78 started in its place as first IMSA reserve

Did not qualify: Tony Trimmer (GB)/Tiff Needell (GB) (3.0 Ibec-DFV P6), 3:53.7; Bernard de Dryver (B)/Nick Faure (GB)/Richard Jones (GB) (3.0 De Cadenet LM-DFV), 3:56.7; Mo Carter (CDN)/Murray Edwards (CDN)/Dick Valentine (CDN) (7.0 Chevrolet Camaro), 4:16.8; Sandro Plastina (CH)/Mario Luini (CH)/Marc Frischknecht (CH) (2.0 Cheetah G601), 4:17.2; Jacques Bienvenue (CDN)/Bill Adams (CDN)/Doug Rowe (CDN) (7.0 Chevrolet Corvette), 4:22.6; Nobuhide Tachi (J)/Fumiyasu Sato (J)/Chiyomi Totani (J) (2.8 Dome Toyota Celica Turbo), 4:27.9; John Sheldon (GB)/Ian Harrower (GB)/John Brindley (GB) (3.5 Triumph TR8 Turbo), 4:37.1; Jean-Marie Lemerle (F)/Max Cohen-Olivar (F)/Jean-Pierre Malcher (F) (2.0 Lola T298), 4:52.7.

Above: Jean-Michel Martin's third-placed GTP-winning Rondeau chases Questers' mobile map of France' BMW M1 and Ghinzani's ill-fated Lancia. Below: Dorchy hands over to Frequelin as the WM mechanics fettle the sleek Esso camera car which finished fourth.

continued

walking pace and coughing out steam every time it stopped, the race remained in balance until around 1.00pm, when the Fitzpatrick/Redman/Barbour Porsche came in with a misfire — the mechanics inspected the engine and then left the car unattended in the pit lane, to all intents and purposes discarding its fourth place.

Sheer consistency had brought the Frequelin/Dorchy WM back to fifth overall while the German Porsche 924 (the only survivor with compression in all four cylinders) had overcome its rivals to lie sixth, a lap behind that WM and two clear of the other. Laurent Ferrier retired the BMW ZOL M1 with a melted piston — leaving 27 cars running.

Positions after 21 hours: 1, Rondeau/Jaussaud, 300 laps: 2, Icky/Jöst, 296 laps; 3, Martin/Martin/Spice, 291 laps; 4, Barbour Fitzpatrick/Redman, 287 laps; 5, Frequelin/Dorchy, 281 laps; 6, De Cadenet/Migault, 278 laps; 7, Barth/Schurti/Braun, 278 laps; 8, Paul/Paul/Edwards, 278 laps; 9, Dieudonne/Xhenceval Regout, 278 laps; 10, Rouse/Dron, 276 laps.

Then came the rain for the third time in the race, but on this occasion it was only a freak shower on part of the circuit, heavy enough to waterlog the Dunlop curve in an instant. First on the scene at 1.10pm was the leading car with Rondeau at the wheel. Its pace reduced only fractionally, the light car aquaplaned off course, scraped the line of armco barriers on the outside of the circuit and spun harmlessly . . . only to miss being clipped by Jöst's Porsche by a fraction. Reinhold had come past the pits as quickly as usual and realising that an excursion was inevitable, guided the Porsche squarely sideways into the barriers, catching them a glancing blow and, like his predecessor emerging none the worse for the experience. Yver's 2 litre G6-leading Lola appeared next, oblivious to the hazards of the corner and he too was helpless as he sped like a lemming to the cliff. Somehow the Lola spun twice without hitting anything (a stroke of luck!), while John Snr in the John Paul *père et fils* Porsche rammed the barrier with a front corner and spent half an hour having the damage straightened. Yver took 12mins to reappear after his incident, now with a dreadful misfire and he got only as far as the Mulsanne straight after pitting, throwing the class lead towards the remaining ROC cars.

Redman's car burst into life out of the blue and began circulating again, the driver choosing slicks like the majority of the others. Brian Redman explained the circumstances of the stop: "We thought about retiring before the engine blew itself apart, but when we looked carefully we found it was a valve problem in only one cylinder — we disconnected that cylinder, reduced the boost to nothing and ran 1500revs down on five cylinders."

Confusion reigned in the WM pit as both of their survivors stopped at least three times to change tyres, without noticeable improvement. The never-say-die attitude of the de Cadenet team was rewarded by a promotion to sixth place shortly before the storm in which Regout also rotated the 512BB Ferrari which then required temporary bodywork repairs to each end.

Jaussaud was put back in the leading car with 90mins remaining, and a lead of something like 8mins to protect, and Ickx was back in the Jöst Porsche. This was surely to be the showdown. The speed of the second placed car on the track, not to mention some very slick pit work, brought the deficit down to a lap with an hour remaining. The slower but reliable ROC Chevron and Lola had taken over the 2litre G6 lead when the Perrier/Yver Lola, which had sounded terribly rough for some laps, expired on the circuit with a blown engine. Both Yacco oil-backed cars had overhauled the DRA Lola, still running sweetly. In all, 25 cars were running now, nearly half of which had sounded critically ill; the Mazda in particular had been circulating at about 70mph for the last three hours.

Ickx piled on the pressure, trying his heart out and taking several seconds per lap from Jaussaud and unlapping himself with 40mins remaining. With approximately 15 laps to run, therefore, Jacky needed to close on the leader by about 14secs on each tour, an enormous and seemingly impossible task with Jaussaud fully aware of his progress and responding accordingly. At 3.25pm, however, a whole new complexion was put on the matter then the heavens opened again, turning the road into a skating rink within seconds.

Pussyfooting round at almost walking pace just to stay on the circuit, the Rondeau was still losing time to Ickx. The luckier drivers who were close to the pits when the rain came ducked in for wets again and made up plenty of ground on those right round the back. With Ickx's famed reputation for brilliant wet-weather driving, the shower could have been a godsend had it lasted longer, but blue sky wasn't far away. The rain was still falling heavily when Jacky came through the Ford chicane, and the white car was seen to hesitate momentarily as its driver weighed up the problem before swerving in for wets — a last ditch effort.

One of the last cars through was Jaussaud's, and the Frenchman too had a big decision to make. Casting his glance to the clear blue sky behind the rain cloud, Jean-Pierre elected to stay on slicks, gambling on the track drying quickly once the shower was over. And this it did, on-line at least. Due to his stop Ickx was now a lap behind again, although his pace was undeniably quicker than Jaussaud's, who was conserving his machine now victory was at hand.

He failed to judge the startline clock accurately though, crossing it 30secs before 4.00pm, so an extra tour was necessary before the local team could celebrate a rousing victory, their delight expressed freely as their hero came home. Immediately the track was invaded by spectators, the winning Rondeau lost in a sea of excited faces. Jean Rondeau's beam could not stretch any wider when the Belga car of Martin/Martin/Spice came in third after a very reliable run, and winner of the GTP category.

Fourth was the Frequelin/Dorchy WM which, like its 11th placed sister machine, had made several shambolic tyre stops as the conditions varied, nevertheless gaining a lap on the leading Porsche, which Redman had taken over from Barbour for the final 20mins. A splendid sixth fell to the first of the trio of works Porsche 924 Carrera turbos, crewed by the German drivers, while Francois Migault struggled home in an overjoyed seventh with the Alain de Cadenet's ailing machine — a quite outstanding achievement considering their hour-long stop at breakfast-time on Sunday. Waved on by Union Jacks brandished by team manager Murray Smith from the pit lane, Migault was less than a lap clear of Grohs in the Vegla 935 and being cheered on in the closing minutes by hundreds of jingoistic Britons. The rapid German came in for wets during the last rain storm (during which Schornstein was due to take over), and as he announced that he was enjoying it immensely, the team owner let him continue. John Paul's attractive Newsweek 935 and the solo Pozzi Ferrari completed the top 10.

A disappointed Dorset Racing team had to settle for third in class, a lap clear of O'Rourke's Emka Ferrari for which a finish was reward in itself after its earlier dramas. All three British Racing Green cars finished, even if one did have a splash of Italian scarlet! Bringing up the rear of the field — and only two laps short of jumping a rung despite over four hours spent in the pits — was the amazing Dome of Craft and Evans, who simply refused to give up as 30 of the 55 starters had been forced to do.

48eme Grand Prix d'Endurance 24 Heures du Mans

June 14/15. 24 hours over 8.475-mile circuit. **Organisers:** Automobile Club de l'Ouest. **Number of starters:** 55. **Number of finishers:** 25. **Winners:** Jean-Pierre Jaussaud/Jean Rondeau (3.0 Rondeau-DFV M379B), 338 laps at 119.225mph, 2861.40 miles. **1979 winners:** Don Whittington/Bill Whittington (3.2 Porsche 935 K3 Turbo, 306 laps at 108.10mph, 2590.93 miles. **Distance record:** (8.475-mile circuit): 3134.52 miles (1978).

FINISHERS

Pos	Drivers	Class	Car	Distance
1	Jean-Pierre Jaussaud/Jean Rondeau	G6	Rondeau-DFV M379B	2861.40 miles
2	Jacky Ickx/Reinhold Jöst	G6	Porsche G6/80	2844.63 miles
3	Jean-Michel Martin Philippe Martin Gordon Spice	GTP	Rondeau-DFV M379B	2784.98 miles
4	Guy Frequelin/Roger Dorchy	GTP	WM/Peugeot 79/80 Turbo	2692.39 miles
5	John Fitzpatrick/Brian Redman/Dick Barbour	IMSA	Porsche 935 K3 Turbo	2683.69 miles
6	Jürgen Barth Manfred Schurti Eberhard Braun	GTP	Porsche 924 Carrera Turbo	2674.99 miles
7	Alain de Cadenet/Francois Migault	G6	De Cadenet LM-DFV	2649.52 miles
8	Dieter Schornstein/Harald Grohs/Götz von Tscirnhaus	G5	Porsche 935 Turbo	2649.52 miles
9	John Paul/John Paul Jnr/Guy Edwards	IMSA	Porsche 935 K3 Turbo	2641.44 miles
10	Pierre Dieudonné/Jean Xhenceval/Hervé Regout	IMSA	Ferrari 512BB	2641.44 miles
11	Jean-Daniel Raulet/Max Mamers	GTP	WM-Peugeot 79/80 Turbo	2632.74 miles
12	Andy Rouse/Tony Dron	GTP	Porsche 924 Carrera Turbo	2624.66 miles
13	Derek Bell/Al Holbert	GTP	Porsche 924 Carrera Turbo	2581.79 miles
14	Didier Pironi/Dieter Quester/Marcel Mignot	IMSA	BMW M1	2480.50 miles
15	Hans Stuck/Hans-Georg Burger/Dominique Lacaud	IMSA	BMW M1	2396.00 miles
16	Thierry Perrier/Roger Carmillet	G4	Porsche 911SC (ethanol)	2370.52 miles
17	Bruno Sotty/Philippe Hesnault/Daniel Laurent	G6	Chevron B36	2336.35 miles
18	Michel Dubois Christian Debias Florian Vetsch	G6	Lola T298	2302.79 miles
19	Martino Finotto/Carlo Facetti	G5	Lancia Beta Monte Carlo	2302.79 miles
20	Dany Snobeck/Hervé Poulain/Philippe Destic	IMSA	Porsche 935 Turbo	2294.09 miles
21	Ernesto Soto/Pierre Honegger/Mark Hutchins	IMSA	Mazda RX-7	2251.84 miles
22	Pete Clark/Nick Mason/Martin Birrane	G6	Lola BDG T297/8	2226.36 miles
23	Steve O'Rourke/Simon Philips/Richard Down	IMSA	Ferrari 512BB	2218.29 miles
24	Georges Bourdillat/Alain Bernard	G4	Porsche 934 Turbo	2099.60 miles
25	Chris Craft/Bob Evans	G6	Dome-DFV RL80	2082.21 miles

Pos ▼ / Hours ▶	1	2	3	4	5	6	7	8	9	10	11	12	13	14	15	16	17	18	19	20	21	22	23	24
1 (car)	45	45	45	9	9	15	15	70	70	16	9	9	9	9	9	9	9	9	16	16	16	16	16	16
(laps)	13 laps	26	39	54	69	84	99	113	126	141	155	170	185	200	215	230	245	258	272	284	300	312	325	338
2 (car)	84	70	84	70	15	70	16	15	16	9	16	16	16	16	16	16	16	16	9	9	9	9	9	9
(laps)	12	25	39	54	69	84	98	113	126	141	155	169	184	200	214	229	243	257	267	282	296	309	324	336
3 (car)	15	84	70	45	70	16	70	16	9	70	70	70	70	70	70	70	70	17	17	17	17	17	17	17
(laps)	12	25	39	54	69	83	98	112	126	141	153	167	181	196	210	222	236	250	262	277	291	302	316	329
4 (car)	70	42	9	15	45	45	9	9	15	8	17	17	8	8	17	17	17	17	70	70	70	5	70	5
(laps)	12	25	39	54	68	83	95	110	124	137	150	165	178	192	207	221	234	248	261	273	287	293	306	318
5 (car)	42	9	42	42	16	41	9	71	8	17	8	17	17	8	8	7	7	5	7	5	70	70	15	70
(laps)	12	25	38	53	68	81	95	108	123	136	150	164	178	192	206	221	230	244	258	267	281	293	306	317
6 (car)	5	15	15	16	42	9	71	8	71	85	85	45	3	45	7	7	8	2	5	4	8	4	4	4
(laps)	12	25	38	53	68	81	95	108	122	135	150	163	174	189	202	216	229	240	253	266	278	290	304	316
7 (car)	9	71	5	5	5	71	17	17	17	84	45	84	45	7	3	3	3	4	7	4	7	8	8	8
(laps)	12	24	38	52	67	80	94	108	122	135	149	160	174	188	201	215	228	242	252	264	278	290	302	313
8 (car)	52	5	41	41	41	5	8	85	84	71	7	43	7	2	2	2	5	8	8	73	2	76	49	49
(laps)	12	24	38	52	66	80	93	106	121	134	148	160	174	188	200	214	227	239	251	264	278	287	300	313
9 (car)	16	83	83	6	6	17	44	7	85	7	3	84	2	43	43	4	3	73	73	76	76	49	49	73
(laps)	12	24	37	52	66	80	93	106	120	134	147	160	173	187	200	214	225	237	250	264	278	287	300	312
10 (car)	53	16	16	7	71	6	3	4	4	45	43	7	43	4	4	5	73	2	76	2	49	76		
(laps)	12	24	37	51	66	80	92	106	120	134	148	160	173	186	199	212	224	237	250	264	276	300	312	

1980 24 HEURES DU MANS

Le Mans, as seen from the cockpit of a Porsche 935 K3 BY BOB AKIN

Vintage and endurance racer Bob Akin wrote this first-person account of what it's like to drive a Porsche 935 K3 at the Le Mans 24 Hours.

LE MANS IS SPECIAL. Unique in the world of racing. Rushing from one afternoon to the next through the lush French countryside, past the little restaurants, their checkered tables just a few feet beyond the guardrail, past the offices and factories; diving into the dark forests, braking, shifting, sliding through the difficult sections and out onto the long straights. The blaze of color and the crush of the enormous crowd. The flags of all nations and the all-night carnival. Daytime, sunset, darkness, dawn—and another day. Exactly 8.4 miles connecting the towns of Le Mans, Mulsanne, Arnage and back to Le Mans. Mostly in top gear, often over 200 mph. To drive a good car at Le Mans is an experience beyond adequate description. And those who have been there never forget.

It had rained intermittently all week and as the 4:00 p.m. start approached on Saturday it began again—a cloudburst complete with thunder and lightning. Subsiding to a drizzle before the 55 cars moved off behind the Porsche 928S pace car, the storm had left the track with huge puddles at every depression, curb and apex. All wipers were on and some lucky ones in closed cars had defogging fans. Everyone was on rain tires, some with intermediate treads, others with deeply grooved full rains. Onto the 3.5-mile Mulsanne straight the field began to pick up speed and string out. Spray filled the air and visibility diminished to a few yards. Ahead of me Don Whittington's Porsche 935 K3's hazard lights flashed, giving me something to follow in the mist. Miles before the starting line we were all at racing speed. Only the first few rows held any semblance of order. On the 1st lap the run down Mulsanne posed a frightening dilemma: I couldn't see, but I knew I had to maintain speed or risk being hit from behind. Mirrors were useless and lane changes risky. The only option was to follow the guardrail by looking along the side of the road and drive into the thickest part of the spray, knowing there was a car up there somewhere and hoping he could see where he was headed.

The crashes began at once. Mike Scherwin, driving one of Dick Barbour's Porsche 935s, ran headlong into a 2-liter sports racer that had spun sideways on the Mulsanne. The big turbo climbed up and over the little car, soaring into the air and came down squarely on its nose, eventually crushing itself against the guardrail. The drizzle soon turned to heavy rain and those of us

on intermediate tires were in serious trouble. It was a time for great care and reserve, yet there were some driving with reckless abandon; passing, spinning, recovering to pass and spin again. A Ferrari 512BB managed to run Charles Mendez' 935 K3 into the rail, damaging the rear suspension on the Porsche and putting the 512 out for good. Mendez managed to get going again and slowly moved toward the pits. With only a few hundred yards to go, Le Mans officials directed Mendez to pull off the course and shut off his engine. Reluctantly he obeyed the wildly gesturing marshals. Minutes later, when they gave him permission to move on, the engine would not start. Regulations prohibit any outside help and the driver cannot go beyond 10 meters from the car. With no way of replacing the dead battery and not allowed to push the car, Mendez finally walked to the pits, disqualifying the car. He had run only 50 minutes.

Fuel stops began in less than one hour and the John Fitzpatrick/Brian Redman/Dick Barbour 935 K3 (the second of three Barbour entries) relinquished the lead Fitz had bravely accumulated to Bob Wollek/Helmut Kelleners in one of the latest factory 935s. Hans Stuck in a BMW M1 was soon 2nd as he displayed his rain talents and the M1's better fuel economy. Meanwhile, the pole-sitting Henri Pescarolo/Jean Ragnotti Rondeau-Cosworth DFV had fallen to 3rd.

Fitzpatrick had started on the front row next to the Pescarolo Rondeau. Under a new rule the average of the drivers' best times determine the starting position. Fitzpatrick/Redman/Barbour had the best combined qualifying times, while the French Rondeau team was a bit slower, but this was easily fixed by simply dropping their third and slowest driver and, presto, to the delight of all France, its countrymen were on the pole. Now, theoretically the same option was available to Fitz, Redman and Barbour, but when you own the team and bring three cars across the ocean, you can't blame Dick for wanting to drive. Thus, they placed 2nd on the grid. Of course, all this is nonsense in a 24-hour race because a car driven at qualifying speeds would never finish anyway. But the new rule created much confusion and protests. Rumor had it that one team had hired a Paris law firm which in turn had seized the timing sheets for careful scrutiny.

The rain stopped in the second hour, the sun came out and the track dried quickly. Everyone stopped for dry tires and the speeds began to pick up dramatically. After two hours Fitz, Brian and Dick were back in the lead with Stuck hanging onto 2nd but in deep trouble now that the 935s could get the power down. My car was running in midfield with Ralph Cooke driving when one of the little sports racers made contact, neatly amputating the left rear fender. The replacement, along with the rewiring of the taillight, cost us 30 minutes and put us far back in the field. But the car was running perfectly and the track was dry. It had become a beautiful summer evening and my second driving stint was very nice indeed.

Four-time Le Mans winner Jacky Ickx was paired with Reinhold Joest and Michel Leclere in a Porsche 908/80. Jacky had started 3rd and was running with the leaders when the injection pump drive belt broke. I recall passing him once as he was going very slowly. The next lap he was stopped. Then I passed him twice while he had the back of the car open. Next time he was underway again, the talented Ickx having made temporary repairs to get back to the pits.

But the pride of Stuttgart was not the 908 nor the legion of 935s, most of which sported the Kremer bodywork and other modifications, or the factory's latest super trick answer to the Kremer K3. No, Porsche's major effort this year centered on a team of three beautifully prepared and exhaustively tested 924 Turbos. Although not nearly as fast as the 935s, the 924s were surprising, with top speed of about 180 mph, excellent cornering (particularly in the rain) and good fuel economy.

Fuel consumption was made more significant this year by a subtle change in the metering system which dispenses fuel from a central reservoir to each pit. Fuel flow was restricted so it now took nearly 2 minutes to refuel the 935s, compared to around 20 seconds last year. Consumption for the Kremer cars is frightful; down to 3 mpg from 4 last year because of the more effective intercooler providing a denser charge. We had planned on only 12 laps between stops while the 924s were going 22 laps on a tankful.

In the rainy first hour these little, surprisingly stock-looking cars had it all their way, moving up to 15th, 22nd and 28th. Had the wet conditions continued they might have won, yet even in the dry they continued to run well, finishing 6th, 12th and 13th; the last car being the Derek Bell/Al Holbert car which had been as high as 6th before going off on three cylinders in the last hours.

Peter Gregg was originally scheduled to drive with Holbert in what was to be the All-American 924. Porsche had even loaned Peter a slick, greenish-gold 924 to drive to and from his hotel in La Lude, about 20 miles south of the track. On the first day of practice, Peter was heading for Le Mans with artist Frank Stella and Peter's girlfriend, Ann Derby, clipping along (as everyone does) at about 75 mph on a clear straight road when, abruptly, a Citroën, approaching from the opposite direction, turned across his path to enter a driveway on Peter's side of the road. Seeing the onrushing Porsche, the driver panicked and slammed on his brakes, stopping directly in Peter's path. Peter swerved left, grazing the Citroën, then corrected to the right. He almost made it, but the rear end got loose and one rear wheel caught in the drainage ditch. The car was launched end over end, bouncing once on the rear window and ending up on its side.

Fortunately all three wore seatbelts and Stella was not injured. Ann sustained minor injuries. Peter woke up on the stretcher as they were taking him to the hospital in Le Mans. He was treated for a concussion, severe whiplash and minor cuts. Complaining of double vision, Peter attempted to practice on Thursday nevertheless, but after one lap which he described as a "psychedelic movie," he parked the car and Derek Bell was transferred from one of the other 924s to take his place.

Americans were at Le Mans this year in record numbers but for the most part they didn't fare well. The Barbour/Redman/Fitzpatrick car, having led off and on during much of the race, went on five cylinders by mid-Sunday morning, and its ability to finish was in doubt. Losing ground but still maintaining a respectable pace, Dick's newest turbo managed 5th overall when 4:00 p.m. finally arrived. Barbour's 3rd car, driven by Bobby Rahal/Allan Moffat/Bob Garretson was out before dawn with still another broken engine.

The Kremer team entry for Ted Field and Danny Ongais retired after 6 hours with engine failure. Last year's Cinderella winner, Don Whittington, was teamed with speedy Hurley Haywood and youngest Whittington brother Dale while Bill sat home with a broken ankle from his crash at Indy. Their 935 K3

ran well until the differential gave up at 4:00 a.m. Sunday.

John Paul, co-driving with his son John, Jr. and Guy Edwards, recovered gradually from early mechanical problems to finish 9th in spite of a crash during a rain shower late in the race.

Canadian Mo Carter's fast and reliable IMSA Camaro went well during qualifying but somehow his good times were caught up in the timing fiasco. On Friday after qualifying, Mo took a trip to the Normandy beaches, returning late that night to discover he would not be allowed to start. A terrible disappointment for Mo when you think of the time and expense involved in bringing a team across the Atlantic.

Preston Henn suffered a similar fate when his Ferrari 512BB self-destructed in Thursday's qualifying. Now the rules prohibit an engine change after the start of qualifying, but the crew set about to swap it anyway, hoping the officials would be charitable in this case. No dice. On race day there was a big crowd of important looking people peering into the back of the car and shaking their heads.

Five of the latest 512BBs made it to the grid. Sentimental favorites, the latest version was reported to be a few hundred pounds lighter and a bit more powerful. I recall racing against them last year at Daytona and Le Mans and working fairly hard to get ahead, driving one of Barbour's older single turbos. The new 512s may be faster than their predecessors, but the new Porsches can just blow them away. The 935 K3 stops and corners better and, while the Ferrari has good top speed, it takes the entire 3.5 miles of the straight to gather itself up. The Porsche comes around Tertre Rouge, gets up on the boost and it's gone! Nevertheless, Ferraris always provide variety and entertainment. Someone is always building one in the pits just before the race is to start. This year two mechanics were squatting on the nose of a blue 512, still screwing it together as others pushed it to its place on the grid.

The Mendez/Woods/Akin team had entered two 935s. The car Roy Woods and I have been driving this year is a 1979 edition which was updated to Kremer K3 specifications last winter using the kit available from Kremer. This is no small feat, involving almost all-new body panels, extensive suspension alterations, new chassis pieces, a different oil cooler, replacement of the water-cooled intercooler with the advanced air-to-air edition, and many other detail changes. The sister car, which Mendez has driven with Redman at Daytona, Sebring and Riverside, is a total kit car—built from scratch at Franz Blam's race shop in Atlanta.

The author in the Mendez/Akin/Woods Porsche 935 K3.

We simply bought all the components and bolted it together. All considered, I think we saved about $49.75 by doing this instead of ordering a ready-made one from Kremer, but we have the satisfaction of knowing that both cars are carefully assembled and first-class in every respect.

For Le Mans we fitted 3.0-liter endurance engines and brought two spare 3.1-liter versions which we hoped to save for Watkins Glen. The shipping schedule made preparation for the Glen necessary in France after Le Mans because the boat would not arrive in New York with much time to spare. All engines were twin turbos which are much easier to drive than the singles. Throttle response is so much improved that an experienced turbo driver can eliminate the effect of the lag entirely.

The cars, engines, tires, wheels, spares, etc, were packed into our gigantic van hauled by a new red-white-and-blue long-nose Kenworth tractor. This is a good rig and the French went wild over it. No one could believe a truck could be so big—its size caused some routing problems on the way from Le Havre to Le Mans.

In the Charles Mendez/Leon Walger/Skeeter McKitterick car only McKitterick had been to Le Mans before, driving last year for the Barbour team and finishing 8th. Roy Woods, who had been with me last year, had canceled out suddenly and we were fortunate to sign up Paul Miller who was vacationing in Europe and just happened to have his driving gear with him. So, in my car, Miller and Cooke were new to Le Mans while I had raced there twice before.

Mendez' unfortunate fate in the first hour was a bitter disappointment to everyone, especially Leon and Skeeter who never even got a chance to drive.

My race ended at 11:00 a.m. when the transmission pressurized itself and pumped its oil out into the catchtank. Cooke brought the car in and a quick inspection revealed the situation was hopeless. All through the night and into Sunday morning the car had run perfectly; Miller, Cooke and I taking turns of two tankfuls or about 1 hour 45 minutes each. I had one close call during the night when the fuel reserve warning light went on just as I passed the pits. Normally, this means you have about 4 miles of fuel left—a depressing thought on an 8.4-mile track. I slowed down, kept to the right and coasted down the hills, expecting the engine to stop any time. But, somehow, the reserve was enough to get me around to the pits again.

After a driver change my routine was to debrief the crew, check our position and my lap times during the last run, then leave the pits for some food and rest. An access hall runs the length of the pits with doors at the rear of each enclosure opening into this dimly lighted, dank, tunnel-like area which is crowded with extra body parts, wheels and tires, and, at night, sleeping crew. The hallway exits into the paddock where, at any hour of the day or night, there is an immense crowd. Appearance of anyone in a driving suit causes a stir of the usual autograph requests. It feels good to change out of the Nomex and then rejoin the crowd unnoticed.

The team had arranged for two small campers—one for eating and one for sleeping. After soup and a sandwich I could sleep soundly for about two hours before someone would wake me in time to get ready again. Walking back to the paddock from the quiet campground I stared at the stars, thankful for the good weather and a healthy car. I had a fresh set of Nomex underwear for each drive and a new outer suit for every other session. Visine helped erase the last remnants of sleep and an electric shave before the dawn made me look halfway presentable.

Reentering the crowd, conspicuous in my bright red suit highlighted with sponsors patches, I felt fresh and relaxed. The access hall to the pits got progressively worse as the race went on, mainly because the crew was using it as a urinal as the toilets were far off. Body panels, once neatly arranged against the walls were now replaced by smashed bits and pieces of fiberglass. Inside the pit enclosure I would check the progress of the car and the laps remaining before the next stop. When the car passed the pits to start on its last lap I would take a drink of water and pull on my helmet, the fueling crew would get ready for the hose and vent bottle, and the Goodyear man would stand ready to check the tires. Everyone would watch the crowded pit lane for the approach of the distinctive four headlights.

When the car arrived there was time to discuss the condition of the car and the track with the exiting driver while fastening the harness and plugging in the radio. Oil level, tires and brakes checked, windshield washed. Ready. Hand on ignition switch. A strange feeling of quiet solitude as I waited for the fueling to finish. Finally the hose was pulled free, the engine fired and the battle was joined once again.

We did not expect the car to break. We were moving up well from nearly last in the third hour to 15th. Now the car sat quietly in the pit. My son Bobby, who had worked all week with the crew, decided the car needed a bath and set out with a bucket and sponge to clean the battered racer. Some of us headed out into the midway of shops and amusements that adjoin the paddock to sample the champagne and Grand Marnier crepes. Others stayed to watch the final hours unfold.

In 1978 the French government spent millions to gain a Le Mans victory for the turbo Renaults. Following its win, Renault withdrew from sports car racing to concentrate on Formula 1. That same year Jean Rondeau, an industrialist from Le Mans, entered a home-built prototype with a detuned Cosworth DFV. The car finished an impressive 9th, with Rondeau himself co-driving. In 1979, slightly improved editions finished 5th and 10th.

Now, as the last six hours began, the Rondeau driven by Jean-Pierre Jaussaud and Rondeau led, with the 908 of Ickx/Joest in the pits with gearbox trouble. All through the night these two had swapped the lead, but now, with the 908 losing 30 minutes to repairs, it seemed the impossible dream might come true. But Jacky had another charge left in him, with the taste of a fifth Le Mans victory strong on his lips. In the final hour he was back on the same lap, but a fuel stop, more rain and more gearbox trouble halted the onslaught. Jean Rondeau had accomplished an incredible feat: building and driving his own car to win his hometown race—which just happens to be the biggest sports car race in the world.

Rational people may justifiably ask why Americans have tried so hard, committed such vast sums of money and labored so long in an effort to win Le Mans. Some, like Briggs Cunningham, never did win. Others, like the Whittingtons, won on their second try. There are other 24-hour races, but none come close to this one in personal impact and special meaning. Each one of us thinks of Le Mans in special terms. Carrying away memories that will endure long after we have found different ways to amuse ourselves. For me the magic of Le Mans comes after dark, when the traffic thins and there are long stretches, sometimes several laps, between passing or being passed. Alone. At 200 mph. Somewhere in the night.

48th 24 HOURS OF LE MANS
Le Mans—June 14-15, 1980

Driver	Car	Laps
1 Jean-Pierre Jaussaud/Jean Rondeau	Rondeau	338
2 Jacky Ickx/Reinhold Joest/Michel Leclere	Porsche 908	336
3 Jean-Michel Martin/Philippe Martin/ Gordon Spice	Rondeau	329
4 Guy Frequelin/Roger Dorchy	WMP turbo	318
5 Dick Barbour/John Fitzpatrick/Brian Redman	Porsche 935 K3	317
6 Manfred Schurti/Jürgen Barth	Porsche 924 Carrera GT	316
7 Alain de Cadenet/Francois Migault	De Cadenet	313
8 Dieter Schornstein/Harald Grohs/Götz von Tschirnhaus	Porsche 935 K3	313
9 John Paul/John Paul, Jr/Guy Edwards	Porsche 935 K3	312
10 Pierre Dieudonne/Jean Xhenceval/ Herve Regout	Ferrari 512BB	312

Works Porsches were back in Group 6, with a pair of 936s; there was a notable return of a Porsche 917 built by Kremer Racing as a replica of a ten-year old car in a British museum; the hoped for return of Ford to endurance racing was frustrated as the new C.100 with its claimed 250 mph top speed could not be ready in time; and there was universal relief when the A.C.O. gave way over the complicated qualifying rules and decided to accept the 55 fastest cars, on the basis of the fastest time achieved irrespective of individual drivers' times and without worrying about fixed quotas for individual categories. These, and Ickx's entry together with Derek Bell in one of the works Porsches, were the highlights of Le Mans previews in 1981.

The Group 6 entry was headed by the two Porsche 936s with 2.6 litre turbo-charged engines based on Porsche's abortive Indianapolis project and four-speed gearboxes which it was hoped would be more robust than the previously troublesome five-speed boxes. Then there was the 917 and for good measure a Porsche 908 as well. Against these were ranged assorted cars with Cosworth engines, some of which used the new 3.3 litre DFL engine. There were three Rondeaus, a Lola, a Lola-based ACR, two De Cadenets, a Dome-Zero and an Ibec. The two-litre class attracted precisely four cars, three Lola-BMWs and a Renard-Delmas-Simca.

In Group 5 there were six Porsche 935 turbos, four BMW M.1s and four Lancia Beta Montecarlo turbos. Group 4 held another two BMW M.1s, a Porsche 934 and a Porsche 924 Carrera. A particularly interesting new car in the GT prototype category was a Porsche 944 turbo, with Porsche's own 2.5 litre engine which was then still on the secret list. Other GTP entries included two Rondeaus in addition to their two Group 6 cars, while WM-Peugeot's entries were also divided in two categories: two GTP cars, and two in the new Group C category which was effectively a preview of the 1982 Le Mans regulations. Finally the American-style I.M.S.A. category was as usually well supported with 13 cars. Four Porsche 935s and five Ferrari Boxers were what you would expect but they were kept company by a Porsche 924, a Chevrolet Camaro and two Mazda 253s based on the RX-7 with 320 bhp 2.6 litre rotary engines. These cars were entered by Tom Walkinshaw racing.

Porsche had come back with a vengeance. The grid was headed by the two 936s with the Ickx/Bell car in pole position; the 908 was third, then came the two Group 6 Rondeaus followed by two Porsche 935s. The start was at 3 pm - as had happened before to allow sufficient voting time in the following day's election. Ickx and Joest in the Porsche 936 and the Porsche 908 respectively went into a 1-2 lead while the other 936 in the hands of Jochen Mass went almost straight into the pit with a misfire which was eventually traced to a faulty plug. After the first pit stops the 908 took the lead but in the third hour was overtaken by a Porsche 935. Both of these cars were to retire soon afterwards while the Ickx/Bell Porsche 936 went into the lead in the fourth hour of the race - a lead it was never to relinquish. The sister car of Mass/Schuppan/Haywood kept pace and for a long time was in second place only to drop back in the second half of the race when it was delayed for an hour while a new clutch was fitted. The car eventually finished thirteenth, and Haywood put in the fastest lap of the race at 142.47 mph.

With the second Porsche 936 dropping back the two Rondeau three-litre cars which for a long time had been shadowing the leaders moved into second and third places. The margin of the Ickx/Bell 936 was so great that little short of wholesale mechanical disaster there was no hope for any other car to snatch victory; and this year the Porsche 936 behaved faultlessly, without any of the niggling mechanical problems that had proved Ickx's undoing in the previous three years. When Jacky Ickx and Derek Bell finished the race as winners, the crowd was delighted - the Belgian driver became the first driver to win at Le Mans five times and went straight into the record books. For his British co-driver it was a second win - Bell had shared Ickx's victory in the Gulf-Mirage-Ford in 1975. And for Porsche it was a notable sixth win - the German make now had the second greatest number of Le Mans wins, after Ferrari's nine. The winners' average was 124.9 mph and the total distance 2,998 miles.

The two GTP Rondeaus followed in second and third places with the number two car winning the GTP category. A Porsche 935 was placed fourth and won Group 5. A fifth place, and a win in the I.M.S.A. category, was achieved by a Ferrari Boxer and was this marque's best showing at Le Mans for a number of years. A further Porsche 935 followed and the works Porsche 944 was seventh, with a Lancia Montecarlo in eighth place. Although there was a British driver in the winning car the best British car was Guy Edwards's Lola T600 with a 3.3 litre Cosworth-DFL engine which finished sixteenth. The best Group 4 car was a Porsche 934 in eighteenth place and the two-litre class was won by a Lola which came nineteenth. The total number of finishers was 21, but this did not include either of the De Cadenets, nor the Ibec.

Two tragedies marred the 1981 Le Mans. After an hour's racing the Belgian driver Boutsen lost control of his WM-Peugeot near the end of the Mulsanne straight when he was travelling at around 220 mph. The car hit the barrier and disintegrated partially; while Boutsen was unhurt, three marshals were hit by debris and one died from his injuries. An hour later, just after 5 pm about a mile further back from the Mulsanne straight the other accident happened to the Rondeau of Jean-Louis Lafosse which went out of control while accelerating. The car first hit the barrier on the right and then rebounded across the road into the barrier on the left; the second impact virtually broke the car in two and Lafosse was killed.

Le Mans 1981; the 49th race possessed many of the qualities of a classic Le Mans race but with the prospect of the new Group C regulations and increased works support, many commentators preferred to look forward to the 50th race in 1982.

Derek Bell hustling the travel-stained Porsche 936/81 towards a conclusive victory — he and Ickx were over 10 laps clear of the rest

The Jacky and Derek spectacular

Jacky Ickx scores a record fifth victory with twice-triumphant Derek Bell in the Porsche 936/81 that didn't have problems. The threat from the new big-bangers fails to materialise and the little French Coupes can only hang on valiantly in a tough race marred by accidents

Report by Mike Doodson. Photographs by Maurice Rowe

CELEBRATING THIRTY years at Le Mans, Porsche returned at the weekend to the classic French circuit for the first time since 1979 as a works team. The Germans went home to Stuttgart with a stunning 13-lap victory over opposition teams who knew that only a major mechanical failure on Porsche's part would give their much less powerful cars a chance. No two drivers ever had a more trouble-free run to victory than Porsche drivers Jacky Ickx and Derek Bell enjoyed on Sunday afternoon. For Ickx, there was the added joy of having briefly left retirement in order to become the first man in history to win six times at the Sarthe Circuit.

Hot weather and uncertainty about their latest flat six engines (originally developed for 500 miles of racing at Indianapolis) made no difference to the inexorable progress of the winning Ickx/Bell Porsche 936, although a spate of accidents and two fatalities cast a shadow over their achievement and destroyed any chance they might have had of setting a new distance record. A second works 936, however, was much less fortunate, for it was delayed first by misfiring (traced early in the race to a damaged spark plug), and then by a long stop for a new clutch (the original one had been improperly installed). As if to prove that troubles come most often in threes, the second 936 was making amazing progress back up through the field when it was

again forced to make a long unscheduled pit stop — this time with fuel pump failure.

Chasing the factory Porsches proved to be a wearing and expensive business for the opposition, particularly as this year's race was dry throughout and unremittingly hot through the long daylight hours. With high averages to maintain, and no rain to take the strain off engines and transmission, even the most methodically prepared machinery was bound to wilt. The organisers classified as finishers a mere 20 of the original 55 starters, and several of those would not have survived another half hour.

The only two cars to head the winning Porsche both retired early. American Ted Field, driving his Porsche 935 like a man possessed, lasted less than five hours before it seized under American Don Whittington (a member of the winning 1979 crew). Ironically, perhaps, it was Whittington's younger brother Dale who was at the wheel of Reinhold Jost's privately entered (and less powerful) Porsche 936 when it crashed early on Saturday evening, returning to the pits on three wheels and a brake disc after a solid brush with the guardrail.

The Porsche 935s, super powerful coupes built to the soon to disappear group 5 "silhouette" rules, were outclassed this year largely on lack of top speed (they would only do 190 mph or so!), not to mention their once every 50 minute fuel stops.

It was the French Rondeau-Cosworth and WM-Peugeot cars

which promised to chase the two Porsche 936s most effectively, and indeed for a while they valiantly demonstrated their potential.

The five Rondeau cars, two of them with 3.3-litre DFL versions of the classic Cosworth V8 F1 engine, had a good combination of speed and economy, but the two big-engined versions were destined to retire, and a third car was involved in a fatal accident when it was crashed by French long distance expert Jean-Louis Lafosse.

The WM team, whose homemade coupes rely on a combination of turbocharged Peugeot V6 engines and very low frontal area for their inordinately high top speed, was devastated by a crash in the first hour in which a marshal was killed in an incident involving one of their cars. Neither team was as reliable as in recent years, and although the two surviving Rondeaus took second and third places behind the winning Porsche, they were almost 125 miles behind at the finish.

Perhaps the most praiseworthy effort, however, came from the Martini Lancia Team. Starting their three works cars in the 2-litre class (using highly stressed turbo versions of the 1.4-litre Lancia engine producing well over 200 bhp per litre), they managed to bring one car over the line despite some hard treatment by a cockpit crew of F1 youngsters which included American Eddie Cheever and Italian Michele Alboreto. With maximum points in the class, the Lancias now look unassailable in the World Championship for Makes for the second year in a row.

Above: high flyers and low-level dicers brightly illuminated on a hot summer's evening as some play while others work through the night

Above right: Gordon Spice shared this Rondeau with Migault and finished a creditable 3rd, 19 laps behind the winner

Sarthe sidelines

WILL JACKY Ickx return to Le Mans for an attempt at a sixth victory? "After announcing my retirement here last year, I'm not going to make any more stupid statements," said the Belgian, who broke his fellow countryman **Olivier Gendebien's** record of four Le Mans wins on Sunday. Friends suggest, however, that Ickx — now fully occupied with his construction business in Brussels — is most *unlikely* to be back... Ickx's co-driver **Derek Bell**, however, admitted that he would "probably" be returning. Bell, 39, collapsed in a dead faint on the victory podium ("it must be the champagne," he joked) after what he described as "a marvellous run, with no problems whatsoever"... The two veterans, who teamed up for Bell's first Le Mans victory (1975, with a Gulf-Ford), were so strict about keeping to the pace set for them by Porsche competitions boss **Manfred Jantke** that they failed to beat the distance record set by Renault in 1978, despite the great speed potential of the "Indy" engined Porsche. Nevertheless, Bell couldn't resist the temptation to give the car its head during his final stint "I wanted to feel what it was like the last time I drove it," he confessed, "and it just screamed along"... The **two works Porsches** were sponsored this year by *Jules*, a new man's fragrance, launched

last year by Christian Dior, and already a market leader in France... Not all the Porsches at Le Mans this year worked as perfectly as they might have done and one of them failed even to qualify. This was the **Canon Cameras** sponsored **924 Carrera GTR** entered for Britons **Richard Lloyd** and **Tony Dron** to share, which was called in during qualifying because Porsche engineers believed that a mistake had been made in the setting of the computer that controls the fuel injection... Porsche spokesmen remained curiously silent about the exact specification of a **2.5 litre engined 924** which was entered in the GTP section, finishing 7th overall in the hands of factory drivers **Walter Röhrl** and **Jurgen Barth** (joined by racing dentist Sigi Brunn). It is believed that the 16-valve engine will shortly be announced in an upmarket version of the front engined car, to be called the "**944**"... Was there something wrong with the **120 octane aviation fuel** supplied to the teams this year? That was the question being asked by several competitors after they suffered fuel pump troubles. Both of the Cosworth-engined de Cadenets were afflicted, and so was the Otis Lifts sponsored Rondeau driven by Britain's top saloon car driver **Gordon Spice** and Le Mans regular **Francois Migault**. Spice was making a comeback to racing after a serious road accident while

Above: victory in the prestigious Group 5 class went to Englishmen John Cooper and Dudley Wood with a little help from yet another Belgian, Claude Bourgoignie

returning from Belgium several weeks ago... Two equally disappointed Brits were **Chris Craft** and **Bob Evans** in the Japanese-built Dome-Cosworth. Although the Japanese personnel all wore blue and white happy jackets with letters imploring the gods to look favourably on the project, nothing could be done after an electic misfire dropped the car from 8th to 26th position, and ultimately out of the race altogether with a valve broken in the team's only engine...The Japanese influence was nevertheless unusually strong this year, for although the two **RX7 Mazdas** that qualified were eliminated, there were two interested observers from **Bridgestone Tyres**, whose products had filled the first two places at the Pau F2 race the previous Monday... The **Peugeot Citroen Group** was giving its overt support for the first time this year to the **four WM prototypes** built, in their spare time, by a group of Peugeot employees. The twin turbo Douvrin-type PRV V6 engines fitted with special cylinder heads this year, gave the tiny little coupes even more speed than usual, but two were early casualties of serious accidents... With the **Ford C100** which he will be supervising not ready for this year's 24 Hours, British entrant **Alain de Cadenet** was co-opted into one of his last year's open prototypes entered by **Belga Cigarettes** for the Belgian Martin

Brothers. They ran as high as 4th place before their engine, alas, let them down after 18 hours... Former Grand Prix drivers **Hans Stuck** and **Jean-Pierre Jarier** took an early bath when their works entered BMW M1 resplendent in the superb red livery of **BASF Tapes** (have you seen the TV commercial yet?), was put off the road by German co-driver **Helmut Henzler**... of the six **BMW M1s** entered, only one managed to survive to the finish. Driven by Frenchmen **Phillipe Alliot** and **Bernard Darniche**, along with Venezuelan motorbike ace **Johnny Cecotto**, it lumbered to the line, having outlasted similar cars driven by such diverse names as **Marc Surer** and **Dieter Quester**... spare a thought for Americans **Pierre Honegger** and **Fred Stiff**, who put their truck in a ditch on the way to the circuit, rammed the engine and gearbox back into the bulkhead of their **Mazda RX7** in a paddock accident, were eleven seconds quicker than last year — when they finished the race — in practice, and still failed to qualify... another **notable non-qualifier** was the eccentric **Ardex**, a front engined two seater designed by French aerodynamicist Max Sardou. He was responsible for the bodywork on the Lola T600, and his self-built creation matched oddball aerodynamics with seemingly erratic cornering behaviour...

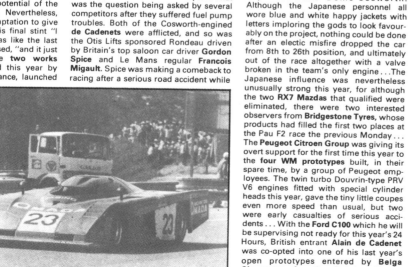

ight: Chris Craft and Bob Evans had a problematic weekend with the Dome Zero, retiring after 12 hours

Above: the 2nd place Rondeau M379 rounds Mulsanne corner ahead of Walter Röhrl in the Porsche 924 which he and Barth took to 7th place

Above: the Ferraris surprised many with their speed and durability. This is the 5th place car passing the Belga-backed De Cadenet which retired

Yarborough's massive Camaro is hounded by Edward's Lola T 600, above, which went on to take 16th place after an eventful race, below

Return of the big bangers

THE AMERICAN IMSA sportscar series is currently being dominated by the British-built Cooke-Woods Lola T600-Chevrolet, driven by skilful expatriate Lancastrian Brian Redman. Despite a claimed 600 bhp from the mildly tuned 5.7 litre Chaparral Chevy V8, the Californian team claim that their primary advantage comes from the car's good handling ground effect chassis. Couple that fact to a host of durability worries concerning the Chevy and an idea of a Lola-Porsche alternative for Le Mans seems clearer.

For the past few years, the American team has run Porsche 935s at Le Mans, and is thus familiar with the quirks and needs of the complex twin-turbo flat-6 engine. It was for that reason that the decision was taken to fit a 935 motor — rather than a Cosworth-Ford already proven in the similar Lola run by Guy Edwards — into a second T600 chassis for Le Mans.

Even though the hard-pressed crew — headed by former English F3 racer John Bright — worked solidly on the car for two months, it was lack of time that destroyed any chances the ambitious project may have had. Such was the schedule that no testing was possible prior to Le Mans; this was an all-new car-engine combination which was completely untried before the first practice session.

There an improperly assembled driveshaft CV joint had failed after half a lap. For the second session, Redman — teamed with American Can-Am racer Bobby Rahal — managed to complete a greater mileage but with no more success. On the advice of Lola designer Eric Broadley the car was tried without the ground effect underside panels to reduce drag — and hence increase top speed on the vital Mulsanne straight — while simultaneously lessening a debilitating engine overheating problem. Finally, the engine lost its turbo boost and Redman and Rahal were thus spectators for the weekend.

However, the potential within the car is enormous. Assuming that its size and frontal area were similar to that of the early seventies Porsche 917 (which was capable of around 240 mph along the straight), then the Lola's extra 200 bhp and ground effect grip meant that the car should have been aiming for a 250 mph top speed. It should not be forgotten that 5 litre sportscars such as the Porsche 917 were eventually banned for being *too* fast . . .

Due to the complexities of sportscar regulations, there was a 917 running at Le Mans this year, ten years after Gijs van Lennep and Helmut Marko took their experimental magnesium chassis 917 to victory at the Sarthe. The new car was built by the German Kremer brothers, who used an old Gulf 917 which had lain in a British motor museum through the seventies as a pattern. The 1981 917 had a space-frame chassis built from thicker gauge tubes than the original, revised aerodynamics and a slit cut in the roof to comply with the new sportscar rules, but was otherwise similar to the original car.

It even ran 1971's gear ratios, which proved to be hopelessly long and left the car driven by Frenchmen Bob Wollek, Xavier Lapeyre and Guy Chasseuil struggling to break the 180 mph barrier on the straight. That handicap was exacerbated by the new rear wing which created too much drag, and the engine inlet trumpets being starved of air. The result? A lowly eighteenth on the grid, which was matched by a lacklustre race ending with a broken crankshaft just before the seven hour mark.

If the two new — or to be precise, newly built — overtly powerful cars failed to impress on the track, then the winning Porsche 936/81 presented quite another story. The cars looked similar to the 936 chassis last raced in 1979 — indeed one had been removed from the Porsche museum for this race — but appearances proved deceptive. The flat-6 turbo engine was from the aborted Porsche Indianapolis project, detuned to 640 bhp, and matched with a Type 920 Can-Am gearbox. That potent combination was sufficient to combine phenomenal cornering performance with acceleration enough to touch 235 mph on the Mulsanne and a staggering 175 mph at the Dunlop bridge after the pits: Jacky Ickx's pole position time represented an average speed of just over 147 mph.

There's no question about it. The big bangers are definitely back at Le Mans.

Right: it looked great but lacked top speed — the 1981 Porsche 917 went out with a broken motor

Derek Bell: 'This car is absolutely incredible'

DEREK BELL enjoys powerful racing cars and driving at Le Mans. Combine these two factors, add in a super-professional team and you have one relaxed, enthusiastic racing driver.

"This car is absolutely incredible. The Renault that I drove in 1978 was tremendous, but it didn't have the power of this Porsche. A Porsche 935 has a fantastically brutal feeling of power, but not much handling. This car just has both. It's got 640 horsepower and good handling too. It's good to drive.

"But it would seem that the more power you have, the more throttle lag you get from the turbocharger. Because we've got so much power, when you actually press the throttle you must wait for the power to come in. And because we're using a four speed gearbox, for a lot of corners you have to come up say in third, rather than change down to second and up to third in the middle of the bend. You can't do that as it throws the balance of the car.

"So you go in off the power — you can hear the tyres squealing! — and suddenly the power comes on and it goes from understeer to beautiful, neutral steer. Then the trouble is you've got to get over to the other side of the road for the next corner — so you lift off and lose power. It's not easy to drive, but it is consistent. You know exactly what it's doing — you just pray

and hope you don't hit oil while you're doing it.

"It makes lapping people very difficult. They see you whistling up at 235 mph, you outbrake them and then have to sit and wait for the power to come in . . .

"I don't think the cars are too quick. The slower cars are going so much quicker nowadays; the speed differential is still only 50 mph. There's nothing going much slower than 180 mph — it's just the fact that there are some lousy drivers out there.

"I had some astonishing trouble with one car. I came up behind him, and he pulled over to the right behind a slower car. I was flashing my lights at him, and as I went to go by, he pulled out! I just backed off — it's not worth taking the chance. But there has been some pretty oafish driving this year.

"It's a magnificent feeling to drive this Porsche here. I'm just so lucky to drive such a beautiful car. The team are super, they are just so professional. "Yes, it's a super car. Everything's been just great."

Great, that is, until after the race. Then, on the victory rostrum, Bell — like Didier Pironi in 1978 — fainted due to both the heat and sheer physical effort required to drive a turbocar at Le Mans.

Horsepower advantage or not, Le Mans still demands the utmost from car, driver and team.

Above: the Porsche 936 may be a great 24 hour race car but Bell fainted from exhaustion on the rostrum

RESULTS

49th Le Mans 24 Hour Race
June 13-14
Sarthe Circuit, 8.466 miles

		laps
1	Ickx/Bell/Barth (*Jules*-Porsche 936/81 3.7 litre)	354
	2998.9 miles at 125.45 mph	
2	Haran/Schlesser/Streiff (*L'Automobile*-Rondeau M379C 3.0 litre)	340
3	Spice/Migault (*Otis*-Rondeau M379C 3.0 litre)	335
4	Bourgoignie/Cooper/Wood *Travel Cruiser*-Porsche 935 K3 4.2 litre)	330
5	Andruet/Ballot-Lena/Regout (*Pozzi*-Ferrari 512 4.9 litre)	328
6	Verney/Garretson/Cooke (*BP*-Porsche 935 K3 4.2 litre)	327
7	Rohrl/Barth/Brunn (*Boss*-Porsche 924 GTP 3.5 litre)	323
8	Cheever/Alboreto/Facetti (*Martini*-Lancia Beta 2.0 litre)	322
9	Diedonne/Xhenceval/Libert (Ferrari 512 4.9 litre)	320
10	Grohs/Schornstein/Tschirnhaus (*Vegla*-Porsche 935/2 4.4 litre)	320

Fastest lap: Hurley Haywood (*Jules*-Porsche 936/81 3.7 litre) in 3m 34.00s/142.47 mph.

Accidents cloud Le Mans' sunshine

IT WAS the first time that the organising Automobile Club de L'Ouest had used pace cars to "neutralise" the field during accident periods as in American racing, and it was significant that the big Mercedes 500 SEL "safety cars" (not a happy epithet) appeared no fewer than four times during the race, for a total of just over 50 minutes.

Significant because there have never been so many powerful cars competing in this classic race, and those who felt that there was a good chance of disaster were proved right. Accidents cost one driver, Rondeau Team member Jean-Louis Lafosse, and one marshal, Thierry Mabilat, their lives and five other marshals were hospitalised, one of them with injuries that obliged surgeons

subsequently to amputate one of his arms.

The long-tailed Porsche 917 of ten years ago may have been faster, albeit marginally, than the modern 936 with its 620 horsepower engine, but cars like the aerodynamic Rondeau-Ford, WM-Peugeot and Porsche 935 coupes, are very little slower — and they formed almost half the field this year. It has always been contended that there aren't enough drivers with ability to race these 450 plus bhp cars and successive attempts have been made to curb the power of the long-distance cars — with a conspicuous lack of success. The ACO wants fast cars on its fast circuit and the drivers respond without complaint to the challenge which they present.

However good a driver he may be, of

course, he becomes a passenger when something goes wrong with his car. The first to discover the truth of that dictum this year was Belgian Thierry Boutsen the works March F2 driver who is regarded as Jacky Ickx's own protege. With fewer than 13 laps of the race run, Boutsen's WM-Peugeot went out of control at top speed, probably in excess of 190 mph, striking the barrier on both sides of the long Mulsanne Straight, and killing the unfortunate marshal as he stood behind it with two colleagues, both of whom were also taken to hospital, one with severe arm injuries.

Boutsen, still unable to believe he had survived the incident without a scratch, told the team's designer that the front end of the car had "dropped on to the road." Later that night, one of the remaining WMs broke its suspension, though not with such appalling results.

Lafosse was much less fortunate. Half a lap before his accident, he had been off the road in an incident which his co-driver, rallyman Jean Ragnotti, believes may have damaged either the steering of his Rondeau, or possibly a tyre. The car evidently turned at right angles into the barrier at a point on the straight where it was doing approximately 140 mph, and Lafosse died instantly as the car disintegrated. Three marshals, all standing behind the barrier, suffered broken legs.

"I have mixed feelings about winning this race," said Derek Bell of the incidents. "The truth is that it's the long, long straight that's responsible. But if Le Mans was just a matter of going round and round, that would make it just another circuit . . ."

Right: the well mangled Lancia Monte Carlo of Gabbiani and Pirro

Lafosse: his Rondeau disintegrated

OBITUARY

Forty year old French driver Jean-Louis Lafosse was killed at Le Mans late on Saturday afternoon when his Rondeau struck the barriers along the Mulsanne straight. Lafosse began racing in 1966 with a Renault Gordini, was part of the winning European F3 team in 1971 and during the past decade had concentrated on sportscar racing. He had finished second at Le Mans in 1975 and 1976, being partnered on the latter occasion by Francois Migault in a Mirage-Ford GR8.

The old firm on form

Ickx achieves his fifth victory at Le Mans, sharing with Bell — Lafosse dies in one of three Mulsanne accidents — GTP Rondeau cars second and third — British-entered Porsche fourth — Lancia's 2-litre honours — Rondeau-DFLs fail — Qualifying: QUENTIN SPURRING — Race: MARK HUGHES & MARCUS PYE — Photography: JEFF BLOXHAM.

Jacky Ickx took his historic fifth win in a Porsche 936 shared with Derek Bell.

Last year, Jacky Ickx came out of retirement with the sole aim of winning Le Mans for the fifth time. He finished second. When he received a 'phone call a few months ago from Porsche's Manfred Jantke, offering him a drive in one of the 2.6-litre works 936s, he was eager to accept another chance, especially as his co-driver was to be Derek Bell, with whom he last won in 1975. At the Sarthe last weekend, everything went perfectly for Ickx and Bell as they won by the huge margin of 14 laps after a totally trouble-free race. The new engine (an endurance version of Porsche's abortive Indy unit) was mated to the strong four-speed CamAm gearbox and never missed a beat, the car needing only routine stops for fuel and tyres.

A second works Porsche 936 had been entered for Jochen Mass/Hurley Haywood/Vern Schuppan, but a weakness in the German team's armour dropped this car to the back on the first lap when a broken spark plug was found. Two long stops later in the race — for a new clutch and adjustment to the fuel injection — dropped the car to 13th place at the finish. Reinhold Jöst's 908/80 had led briefly after Ickx's first pit stop, but retired in the sixth hour when a front wheel fell off.

After their all-French victory last year, the crack Rondeau team entered five cars, two powered by the new Cosworth DFL engine. Although the two slower GTP class entries finished second and third in the hands of Jacky Haran/Philippe Streiff/Jean-Louis Schlesser and Gordon Spice/François Migault, the team's enthusiasm was dampened by a fearful accident which claimed the life of Jean-Louis Lafosse during the third hour. The experienced Frenchman was killed instantly when his Calberson-backed car inexplicably went out of control on the Mulsanne Straight; two marshals were also hurt by flying debris. The pair of larger-engined cars were early front-runners, but both suffered delays of nearly two hours due to failures in the belt drive to the fuel pump, and further problems put them both out by the eight hour mark.

Lafosse's crash was one of the three incidents which called out the pace cars in the first four hours. Earlier, Belgian Thierry Boutsen had escaped unhurt from an incredible accident at top speed through the infamous Mulsanne kink. His pretty Peugeot-engined WM was destroyed as it bounced along the barriers, and sadly three marshals were injured by the wreckage, one of them fatally. The other Mulsanne incident also involved a WM, Jean-Daniel Raulet's car being eliminated when it collided with Beppe Gabbiani's Martini Lancia under braking for the corner.

A superb run from John Cooper/Dudley Wood/Claude Bourgoignie brought the overjoyed Charles Ivey crew's Porsche 935 into fourth place — there were British drivers in three of the top four cars — ahead of the Jean-Claude Andruet/Claude Ballot-Lena Ferrari Boxer. The only other British-entered car to finish was the Guy Edwards/Emilio de Villota/Juan Fernandez Lola T600 after a troublesome drive to 16th position. The fancied Porsche-engined T600, which was to have been driven by Brian Redman, was unable to qualify.

Lancia still lead the World Endurance Championship for Manufacturers thanks to the eighth-placed Eddie Cheever/Michele Alboreto/Carlo Facetti car winning the 2-litre class, but Porsche claimed maximum points in the larger class due to the British 935's fourth place to stay second.

ENTRY & PRACTICE

"This is a very, very interesting Le Mans, because it has assembled together so many different types of cars, and because it shows us some of what is going to happen in endurance racing in the future. I have been able to change my mind because I have been given the opportunity to drive this new Porsche, to undertake Le Mans with a team that I know will never put me to risk. Porsche have produced the best racing car they have ever made, in my opinion — and that means that it is the best car in the field without a doubt." Jacky Ickx was brimming full of enthusiasm for his attempt on a fifth victory in the 24 Hours. "You know, I don't mind if I don't win," he said on race morning. "With this car I know that I am going to enjoy myself, anyway."

Jacky, sharing the lead Porsche 936-81 with his 1975 co-winner Derek Bell, had every reason to be confident. Midway through the first of the two four-hour practice sessions, Manfred Jantke sent him out on Dunlop's Q-tyres, and he took the white 936 round over half a second under the 3m 30.07s qualiying record which Bob Wollek set with one of the 2.1 works cars in 1979. On race rubber, Bell had no difficulty in lapping almost 2secs beneath Ickx's 1979 lap record of 3:36.11, the British ace clearly delighted to be back with a front-running Le Mans entry.

Firmly established on the pole, the Ickx-Bell car was joined in the front rank by a Q-tyre lap by Jochen Mass in the second session, the German joined here by Hurley Haywood (in place of the injured Rick Mears) and a surprised, but very pleased, Vern Schuppan. And the privately entered Reinhold Jöst Porsche 936 replica, running the familiar old 2.1 flat-six turbo, added to the frustration of the *Gloire de la France* Rondeau team by qualifying third, also under the lap record.

Manfred Jantke, beaming broadly, enthused about his new engine, the stillborn 2.65-litre twin-turbo flat-six which was intended to achieve a German win at Indianapolis. "We have not really had to modify the engine very much," bubbled Manfred. "Basically we have just converted it to run on petrol instead of methanol. That meant work on the ignition, injection, things like that, but we have done nothing to the engine itself. It is a much, much better engine for long life than the 2.1, for three reasons. First, the bore/stroke ratio is much improved for balance. Second, we do not have to run it on high boost. Third, there has been a dramatic improvement in operating temperatures.

"On low boost we can achieve 650bhp very easily and the engine produces massive torque. It is the most impressive new engine we have ever had, and now we need to look no further for our power unit in Group C.

"The new unit has not been run for a long test in a car because we were short of time. But it has done over 60 hours continuous running on the bench, and also we did a 31-hour on-car test on a rolling road. We used a team of mechanics to change gear manually, simulating the Le Mans circuit, and we even included pitstops which were as close to the real things as we could manage. The engine never missed a beat."

The Ickx-Bell Porsche was the fastest car at Le Mans last weekend, shooting the Mulsanne Straight speed trap at 236mph, and hitting 172mph at the Dunlop Bridge after the pits straight. During qualifying, Schuppan felt a slow puncture (his first thoughts confirmed by Porsche's natty dashboard warning light system), and slowed towards the end of his lap to bring the sister car into the pits next time around: "I thought maybe the lap would be about four minutes, but it turned out to be a 3:43! You know, it took us two days to get down to that kind of time with the Mirage . . ."

After qualifying, it looked as though Porsche were going to make this a processional Le Mans. With unstressed engines, the factory entries — late recipients of sponsorship from Jules perfume — were also equipped with the very robust 917/30 CanAm gearboxes, heavy four-speed units designed to cope with up to 1000bhp, and a far cry from the five-speed 'box which has shown itself to be Porsche's Achilles' heel so often in the past. Porsche had proven chassis, the only significant revision to which were new rear wings atop their broad fibreglass backs, as well as fast and experienced drivers, power and reliability.

The opposition — particularly that from the Rondeau encampment — was quite properly demoralised. Of course, there were the clichés about Le Mans being a long, long motor race. "I am not impressed by a car that can outqualify the rest," offered an apparently serious Jean-Pierre Jaussaud. "I am impressed by a car that is the winner at the end."

Pole position? Five seconds in hand over the best Rondeau? Pah!

In the unlikely event of the works team needing a buffer, it had the Jöst 908/80, the replica of a 1977 spec 936 twin-turbo with which Ickx had finished second here last year. The very experienced, Karlsruhe-based German, after a great deal of to-ing and fro-ing, ended up with the youngest Whittington brother, Dale,

Qualifying

Pos	No	Car-Engine	Tyres	Class			
1	11	2.6 Porsche 936-81 tc	Dunlop	G6	Jacky Ickx (B) Derek Bell (GB) *Jurgen Barth (D)*	**3:29.44**	3:39.59
2	12	2.6 Porsche 936-81 tc	Dunlop	G6	Jochen Mass (D) Vern Schuppan (AUS) Hurley Haywood (USA)	3:35.22	**3:32.61**
3	14	2.1 Porsche 908-80 tc	Dunlop	G6	Reinhold Jöst (D) Dale Whittington (USA) Klaus Niedzwiedz (D)	**3:34.51**	3:43.47
4	26	3.3 Rondeau-Ford M379C	Goodyear	G6	Henri Pescarolo (F) Patrick Tambay (F)	**3:35.16**	3:37.93
5	24	3.3 Rondeau-Ford M379C	Goodyear	G6	Jean-Pierre Jaussaud (F) Jean Rondeau (F)	3:39.74	**3:36.17**
6	59	3.2 Porsche 935 K3 tc	Goodyear	G5	Don Whittington (USA) Ted Field (USA) Bill Whittington (USA)	**3:36.54**	3:46.29
7	60	3.0 Porsche 935 tc	Dunlop	G5	Harald Grohs (D) Götz von Tschirnhaus (D) Dieter Schornstein (D)	**3:37.15**	3:52.86
8	82	2.7 WM-Peugeot P81 tc	Michelin	Group C	Michel Pignard (F) Serge Saulnier (F) Thierry Boutsen (B)	3:51.64	**3:37.89**
9	5	2.7 WM-Peugeot P79/80 tc	Michelin	GTP	Guy Frequelin (F) Roger Dorchy (F)	3:43.85	**3:39.74**
10	25	3.0 Rondeau-Ford M379C	Goodyear	G6	Jean Ragnotti (F) Jean-Louis Lafosse (F)	**3:40.32**	3:53.94
11	83	2.7 WM-Peugeot P81 tc	Michelin	Group C	Jean-Daniel Raulet (F) Max Mamers (F)	3:49.67	**3:40.80**
12	18	3.3 Lola-Ford T600	Goodyear	G6	Guy Edwards (GB) Emilio de Villota (E) Juan Fernandez (E)	3:47.92	**3:42.40**
13	61	3.0 Porsche 935 K3 tc	Dunlop	G5	Edgar Dören (D) Jurgen Lässig (D) Gerhard Hölup (D)	**3:42.66**	3:54.03
14	22	3.0 ACR-Ford 80B	Goodyear	G6	Patrick Gaillard (F) Bruno Sotty (F) André Chevalley (CH)	**3:43.43**	4:08.35
15	7	3.0 Rondeau-Ford M379C	Goodyear	GTP	François Migault (F) Gordon Spice (GB)	3:45.77	**3:43.99**
16	4	2.7 WM-Peugeot P79/80 tc	Michelin	GTP	Xavier Mathiot (F) Denis Morin (F) Charles Mendez (USA)	4:01.14	**3:44.14**
17	41	3.0 Porsche 935 K3 tc	Dunlop	IMSA GTX	Marcel Mignot (F) Michael Chandler (USA) Preston Henn (USA)	**3:46.22**	3:58.15
18	10	4.9 Porsche 917 K-81	Dunlop	G6	Xavier Lapeyre (F) Bob Wollek (F) Guy Chasseuil (F)	3:53.51	**3:46.54**
19	20	3.3 De Cadenet-Ford LM	Dunlop	G6	Alain de Cadenet (GB) Philippe Martin (B) Jean-Michel Martin (B)	**3:46.69**	4:00.52
20	23	3.0 Dome-Ford Zero RL81	Dunlop	G6	Bob Evans (GB) Chris Craft (GB)	3:48.22	**3:47.43**
21	50	3.5 BMW M1	Dunlop	G5	Hans-Joachim Stuck (D) Jean-Pierre Jarier (F) Helmut Henzler (D)	**3:47.63**	3:53.77
22	52	3.5 BMW M1	Dunlop	G5	Marc Surer (CH) Dieter Quester (A) David Deacon (CDN)	**3:47.90**	3:52.03
23	55	3.0 Porsche 935 K3 tc	Dunlop	G5	John Cooper (GB) Dudley Wood (GB) Claude Bourgoignie (B)	**3:48.02**	3:52.99
24	66	1.4 Lancia Beta Montecarlo tc	Pirelli	G5	Piercarlo Ghinzani (I) Hans Heyer (D)	**3:48.14**	4:28.71
25	40	2.8 Porsche 935 tc	Dunlop	IMSA GTX	Gunther Steckkonig (D) Kenper Miller (USA) Maurizio de Narvaez (COL)	**3:48.20**	3:52.79
26	21	3.0 De Cadenet-Ford LM	Dunlop	G6	Nick Faure (GB) Martin Birrane (GB) Vivian Candy (IRL)	**3:48.90**	4.00.11
27	27	3.0 Ibec-Ford P6	Dunlop	G6	Tiff Needell (GB) Tony Trimmer (GB) *Ian Bracey (GB)*	3:50.25	**3:49.94**
28	8	3.0 Rondeau-Ford M379C	Goodyear	GTP	Jacky Haran (F) Jean-Louis Schlesser (F) Philippe Streiff (F)	**3:50.61**	3:52.54
29	49	4.9 Ferrari 512 BB	Michelin	IMSA GTX	Alain Cudini (F) John Morton (USA) Philippe Gurdjian (F)	3:55.12	**3:52.60**
30	43	3.0 Porsche 935 K3 tc	Goodyear	IMSA GTX	Bob Akin (USA) Paul Miller (USA) Craig Siebert (USA)	**3:52.61**	3:56.88
31	65	1.4 Lancia Beta Montecarlo tc	Pirelli	G5	Michele Alboreto (I) Carlo Facetti (I) Eddie Cheever (USA)	**3:54.09**	3:58.52
32	57	3.0 Porsche 935 tc	Dunlop	G5	Claude Haldi (CH) Mark Thatcher (GB) Hervé Poulain (F)	3:57.51	**3:54.32**
33	42	3.2 Porsche 935 K3 tc	Goodyear	IMSA GTX	Anny-Charlotte Verney (F) Ralph Kent-Cooke (USA) Bob Garretson (USA)	4:00.09	**3:55.15**
34	45	4.9 Ferrari 512 BB	Michelin	IMSA GTX	Maurizio Flammini (I) Duilio Truffo (I) Fabrizio Violati (I)	4:03.52	**3:55.66**
35	51	3.5 BMW M1	Dunlop	G5	Philippe Alliot (F) Bernard Darniche (F) Johnny Cecotto (YVEN)	**3:55.68**	4:04.47
36	46	4.9 Ferrari 512 BB	Goodyear	IMSA GTX	Pierre Dieudonné (B) Jean Xhenceval (B) Jean-Paul Libert (B)	4:00.96	**3:56.72**
37	47	4.9 Ferrari 512 BB	Michelin	IMSA GTX	Claude Ballot-Lena (F) Jean-Claude Andruet (F) Hervé Regout (F)	3:56.98	**3:56.89**
38	53	3.5 BMW M1	Dunlop	G5	David Hobbs (GB) Eddie Jordan (IRL) Steve O'Rourke (GB)	**3:56.99**	3:59.36
39	35	6.4 Chevrolet Camaro	Goodyear	IMSA GTO	Cale Yarborough (USA) Bill Cooper (USA) Bob Mitchell (USA)	4:22.33	**3:59.57**
40	48	4.9 Ferrari 512 BB	Michelin	IMSA GTX	Mike Salmon (GB) Steve Earle (USA) Simon Phillips (GB)	4:03.60	**3:59.68**
41	71	3.5 BMW M1	Dunlop	G4	Christian Danner (D) Leopold von Bayern (D) Peter Oberndorfer (D)	4:07.57	**4:00.14**
42	31	2.0 Lola-BMW T298	Goodyear	G6	Yves Courage (F) Jean-Philippe Grand (F)	4:08.07	**4:00,42**
43	1	2.5 Porsche 944 LM tc	Dunlop	GTP	Walter Rohrl (D) Jurgen Barth (D)	4:02.66	**4:01.03**
44	67	1.4 Lancia Beta Montecarlo tc	Pirelli	G5	Beppe Gabbiani (I) Riccardo Patrese (I) Emanuele Pirro (I)	4:49.53	**4:02.22**
45	33	2.0 Lola-BMW T298	Goodyear	G6	Pierre Yver (F) Michel Dubois (F) Jacques Heuclin (F)	**4:02.81**	No time
46	30	2.0 Lola-BMW T298	Goodyear	G6	Max Cohen-Olivar (MOR) Jean-Marie Lemerle (F) Alain Levié (F)	4:09.37	**4:03.00**
47	72	3.5 BMW M1	Dunlop	G4	Pierre-François Rousselot (F) Laurent Ferrier (F) François Servanin (F)	4:04.09	**4:03.76**
48	36	2.0 Porsche 924 Carrera GTR tc	Dunlop	IMSA GTO	Manfred Schurti (FL) Andy Rouse (GB) *Siegfried Brunn (D)*	**4:04.09**	4:11.89
49	38	2.6 Mazda 253i	Dunlop	IMSA GTO	Win Percy (GB) Yojiro Terada (J) Hiroshi Fushida (J)	4:12.79	**4:04.79**
50	69	1.4 Porsche 935 L1 tc	Dunlop	G5	Axel Plankenhorn (D) Jan Lundgardh (S) Mike Wilds (GB)	4:10.44	**4:06.92**
51	37	2.6 Mazda 253i	Dunlop	IMSA GTO	Tom Walkinshaw (GB) Tetsu Ikusawa (J) Peter Lovett (GB)	4:10.66	**4:07.16**
52	70	3.0 Porsche 934 tc	Michelin	G4	Valentin Bertapelle (F) Thierry Perrier (F) Bernard Salam (F)	4:22.23	**4:08.88**
53	68	1.4 Lancia Beta Montecarlo tc	Pirelli	G5	Martino Finotto (I) Giorgio Pianta (I) Giorgio Francia (I)	4:12.51	**4:09.01**
54	32	2.0 Renard-Delmas-Simca RD31	Goodyear	G6	Hervé Bayard (F) Louis Descartes (F) Bruno Preschey	5:21.33	**4:15.57**
55	73	2.0 Porsche 924 Carrera GTR tc	Dunlop	G4	Jacques Almeras (F) Jean-Marie Almeras (F) Jean-Pierre Sivel (F)	No time	**4:19.91**
Non-qualifiers							
	62	3.0 Porsche 935 tc*	Dunlop	G5	Jacques Guerin (F) 'Segolen' (F) Christian Bussi (F)	**4:03.89**	4:09.03
	16	3.5 Ardex-BMW S80*	Michelin	G6	Jean-Marie Lateste (F) Patrick Perrier (F)	4:22.67	**4:05.02**
	17	3.2 Lola-Porsche T600 tc*	Goodyear	G6	Bobby Rahal (USA) Brian Redman (GB)	No time	**4:18.30**
	75	2.0 Porsche 924 Carrera GTR tc	Dunlop	G4	Tony Dron (GB) Richard Lloyd (GB)	4:21.30	**4:20.01**
	39	2.3 Mazda RX-7	Goodyear	IMSA GTO	Dirk Vermeersch (B) Frederick Stiff (USA) Ray Ratcliff (USA)	5:45.51	**4:21.97**
	74	2.0 Porsche 924 Carrera GTR tc	Dunlop	G4	Colin Bond (AUS) Peter Brock (AUS) Jim Richards (AUS)	4:48.48	**4:24.95**
	90	5.7 McLaren-Chevrolet M12/6B	Goodyear	IMSA GTP	Hervé Regout (F) Michel Elkoubi (F)	**5:13.06**	No time

NB: First named drivers set best qualifying times. Drivers in italics did not race. *Failed to qualify on 110% rule in class.

and Ford DRM driver Klaus Niedzwiedz in his 540bhp car, sponsored here by Technocar forklift trucks, much to the detriment of the car's aesthetics.

Good looks have always been a strong point of Jean Rondeau's Le Mans team and, for the most part, the local constructor has managed to resist the temptation to turn his five entries into the mobile bill boards which abounded here. After his 1980 win, Rondeau's sponsorship is now stronger than ever before. Many detail vehicle alterations over the past year resulted in improvements in lap times of up to 10secs but the cars, designed by Philippe Balooue and Hubert Rohée, were well off the Porsches' pace in both sessions.

Two of the team's G6 entries, the Otis sponsored M379C of Rondeau/Jaussaud and the Oceanic/*Le Figaro* car of Pescarolo/Tambay, were fitted with the new 3.3-litre DFL engines, the former's supplied by Cosworth (and overseen by Dick Scammell) and the latter's assembled by Heini Mader from a Cosworth kit. The G6 cars were right on the weight limit, with shorter windscreens than their GTP sisters and more wing front and rear. The other three were all equipped with Mader prepared DFVs, the shorter tail GTP entries weighing around 60 kilos more than the G6 cars. The Spice/Migault Otis backed car was actually the 1980 winning chassis.

Goodyear were making a substantial effort to assist Rondeau, but not even the American qualifying rubber could put the French cars among the German.

Keith Greene, the team's British team manager, gave Migault a set of Q-tyres late in the second session and moved the car further up the grid. François, however, was still 4secs away from being the fastest GTP driver. For their sheer professionalism — extending this year to on-board TV giving visual display of any serious hazard on the circuit — Rondeau outclassed the relatively small WM team, but the little Gerard Weltier/Michel Meunier prototypes are astonishingly fast.

Thorigny based WM had five cars at the Sarthe, one used as a spare and two of them — not, as it turns out, both entirely new chassis — prepared to the new Group C specifications (well, as far as these are known at this stage . . .). Once more backed by Esso France money and Michelin know-how, the WMs this year had formal backing from Peugeot, recognition of the privateers' notable success in recent years with the unlikely 'PRV'

A fabulous fourth place went to John Cooper/Dudley Wood/Claude Bourgoignie in this British-based Porsche 935.

road car V6. Peugeot, in fact, supplied the team with new engines for the race, still with the 2.7 block but with entirely new, four-valve cylinder heads. Mated to the five-speed ZF gearbox, the twin-turbo unit was producing over 500bhp and the faster Group C car, in which Belgian F2 driver Thierry Boutsen was a late replacement for Richard Dallest (injured in a road accident), was hitting 223mph down Mulsanne.

Leaving aside the several mechanical problems encountered by Ian Dawson's GRID Racing team during qualifying, the top speed of the Ultramar/Banco Occidental Lola-DFL T600 was a major disappointment, and ample illustration that unique design parameters are demanded by the 3½-mile section of the RN158 which has for so long perplexed teams in the 24 Hours. Purpose built for Le Mans, the WMs most certainly are, but Eric Broadley's T600, pending a good deal of further development, is a short-track car. The big T600, in which Spaniard Juan Fernandez Garcia was engaged as a third driver, was quick through the swerves, as can be seen from

its lap times: it may have been 13 secs off the pole position pace but, after all, it was losing 45mph on top speed to the front row Porsches!

Out of Tertre Rouge and onto the daunting Mulsanne Straight, the T600 accelerated well until hitting a brick wall at a mere 175mph, one of the slowest top speeds in the field. In the second session, the team fitted taller Goodyears and a top gear as high as they could find, but the terminal velocity could be improved to only 191mph. Ground effect is not the answer to everything.

A new air scoop to ram air into the engine compartment did not help, and the team's problems were increased by a mysterious recurrence of the Lola's fuel pickup malady, which virtually brought the car to a halt after hard braking for Mulsanne Corner.

Of the other Group 6 entries, the Swiss ACR was surprisingly fast round the lap in Patrick Gaillard's hands, although its top speed was an unspectacular 205mph. André Chevalley's Longines sponsored entry has had both chassis and front body revisions over the winter, and the

suspension has been completely redesigned, the car now 100 kilos heavier than before. Fresh from an eight-hour test at Ricard, the Lola based ACR might have qualified better had Chevalley not blown an engine.

Alongside the downright tragedy of the American Lola-Porsche's failure to qualify (see *Pit & Paddock*), the performance of the Kremer brothers' new Porsche 917 was a relatively minor disappointment. On Wednesday, the car, although handling really well, would pull only 7000rpm (1000 down) on Mulsanne. Failing to find any fault with the 4.5 flat-12, the team, backed by BF and Malardeau, fitted its 4.9 unit for the second session, but encountered the same problem, the beautiful yellow machine reaching only 180mph on the straight on its long fourth gear. Discussions with the Porsche personnel revealed that the factory team had had the same difficulty a decade ago, and after practice the problem was identified: the engine was being starved of air. The team cut out small holes in the engine cover, confident of at least another 30mph on race day.

The British sports-prototype team fared a good deal better than in recent years, qualifying with ease despite the usual myriad of little mechanical problems which are brought about from lack of funds rather than lack of expertise. The well financed Belga De Cadenet, the newest and most powerful of the 'Brits', with a DFL for this race, was also the fastest, the Martin brothers joined by alain de Cadenet in the absence of the new Ford C100. The team, now managed by Murray Smith, enjoyed its customary circumspect practice, like the others saving its best cards for race day.

Tony Birchenough's four-year-old De Cadenet, looking the part in BRG with backing from Air Florida and Frost Clothing, suffered from a fuel feed problem on its Smith DFV, but is still very fast and the DRA team was in less difficulty than Ian Bracey's Gordon Horn managed Ibec, a car still itching to show its potential. Substantial detail revisions to both chassis and body have slimmed the Eden-engined, Hesketh 308 based P6 by 23 kilos, and the car remains one of the most stable windcheaters in the game here. The team, however, encountered both gearbox and engine misfire problems during qualifying and, unable to trace a chronic misfire in the Thursday session, its drivers were both frustrated not to be able to prove that the Ibec could have gone 10secs faster.

From the pits: the Ted Field/Don and Bill Whittington car was the swiftest by far of the Porsche 935s.

Masao Ono's "new" Dome Zero turns out to be last year's chassis fitted with a new, carbonfibre body of identical, angular shape. The new body is 15 kilos lighter than before but the longtail Dome, tested at Fuji before the race by its two British drivers, has new front wheels to allow for bigger and heavier brake assembly, which cancels out the saving. Backing again came from Amada Tools.

The intiguring Ardex, to the disappointment of many, failed to make the grade. The extraordinary front-engined chassis, with its huge undertray and air tunnels, did enough to command respect for Max Sardou's adventurous aerodynamic theories, but the car hit the same ground-effect snag as the Lola on Mulsanne, and needed more than the 470bhp available from its BMW straightsix to overcome the problem. Although it was qualified within the fastest 55 overall (51st), it was excluded on the 110% rule, such was the pace of the three G6 Porsches.

The fastest Group 5 and IMSA GTX cars once again proved to be a force. Indeed, the remarkable speed of the two best Porsche 935s caused real qualifying headaches under the same 110% ruling for some of the Ferrari Boxer teams, and actually caught out Christian Bussi's old 935-77.

Alongside the charismatic 917, the Kremer team aligned a K3 which suggested that the Cologne team's 935 development is far from closure. Incorporating Kremer's latest bodywork and suspension ideas, and almost uniquely fitted with a 3.2 power unit for a race in which most of the 935 teams were running 3-litre engines, the Gozzibacked Interscope-Kremer entry was remarkably fast in the hands of Ted Field and the Whittington brothers, and even Harald Grohs in the rapid ex-Jöst Vegla Porsche could approach its speed.

Like Kremer, the Cooke-Woods Racing team was also running a prototype and a 3.2-litre 935, this the Daytona winning K3 sponsored here by BP. Bob Akin had managed to replace his Coca-Cola car, destroyed at the Nürburgring, by building up a new K3 at the Kremer factory, using a new chassis and spares from his own huge Kenwood transporter. It was 7secs faster than Akin's 1980 entry here straight out of the box.

Preston Henn's Thunderbird Swap Shop K3, the ex-Fitzpatrick 1980 IMSA championship winning car, was, however, clearly the fastest of the 'American' Porsches.

Of the British Porsche 935 drivers, John Cooper and Dudley Wood, joined by Claude Bourgoignie whose entry they had taken over, had their regular unspectacular practice with the Charles Ivey Racing K3 (sponsored by Travel Cruiser and Olney Galleries and sporting a new 3-litre power unit with many of the latest factory modifications), while Mark Thatcher performed well with Claude Haldi's chisel-nose 935.

BMW's newly revitalised opposition to Porsche in Group 5, which had reaped such benefit at the 'Ring, was once more spearheaded by the two Peter Sauber built spaceframe M1s which had made their débuts in Germany. Throughout qualifying, there was nothing to choose between the BASF GS Tuning and Sauber/Würth entries, although Hans Stuck — his prayers for rain unanswered on this occasion — emerged with the fastesr lap. With a strong works presence and excellent preparation, the lightweight M1s could do with a modicum of ground-effect (there being plenty of space for air tunnels) and, more important, with a whole lot more power, which the chassis could undoubtedly handle.

Team owner Reinhold Jöst at the wheel of his Porsche 908/80, which led briefly but retired when one of the front wheels fell off at high speed.

Dieter Stappert's BMW team is experimenting with engines, and the feeling is that another 40bhp or so would put the M1s well onto the pace of the best 935s.

Steve O'Rourke's Michael Cane Racing M1, a Procar conversion, is about 90 kilos heavier than the Sauber spaceframe machines in spite of its extensive use of carbonfibre, and was a whole 10secs slower. Now in the blue livery of SDC Builders and co-driven by Eddie Jordan, the EMKA M1 benefited a good deal from the presence in the team of David Hobbs, the most experienced Le Mans driver at this year's event, with 13 races behind him. The EMKA car was just slower than Zol'Auto's M1, another converted Procar driven by an F3 driver, a rally driver and a motorcycle champion.

Cesare Fiorio's factory Lancia team, freshly in the lead of the World Championship again after the 'Ring, decided after all to run all its cars in the 2-litre G5 class to be as sure as possible — in the memory of the almost disastrous Le Mans 1980 — of maximum points in what might yet be the last Makes round of the present series. There were three Martini entries plus the ostensibly privateer Jolly Club/Lubrifilm car, the regular top-line driver strength boosted by Carlo Facetti and Martino Finotti, whose amazing Ferrari was scratched because it had been heavily damaged at the Nürburgring. There was a degree of children-unwillingly-to-school among the works team drivers, but Fiorio was uncompromisingly going for a finish, the only opposition in the class once again coming from the nice but underpowered Tuff-Kote Dinol 'baby' Porsche 935. All the

Martini cars featured the lightly modified aerodynamics and were fitted with detuned versions of the 1.4 engines, producing only about 400bhp on low boost pressure. After engine problems, the Lubrifilm car caused some concern but qualified nevertheless in the second session, but all the Martini cars were well in, and Fiorio even ventured some of his cars out with Pirelli Q-tyres. So equipped, Piercarlo Ghinzani set an outstandingly good time, once he had recovered from an astonishing, if brief, period of hooliganism.

Mike Wilds, on his first visit to Le Mans, again thoroughly enjoyed himself with Jan Lundgardh's 'baby', despite its lack of power.

The big Ferrari Boxers in the IMSA GTX class were in their element, the fastest of them exceeding 210mph down the straight. All but two followed the familiar, well-proven 512 BB theme. The Belgian-driven Rennod Racing car, a new machine built to the order of its American owners Bon Donner and Paul Pappalardo, has been modified by Jim Robinson and François Sicand to run to the same spec as the Rennod team's Daytona entry, with the wider rear and the new suspension to take the bigger Goodyear tyres. This modification is good for the Daytona banking, but slowed the BB on Mulsanne. The fastest Ferrari was the Luigi Chinetti/NART entry — among whose drivers was former TransAm champion John Morton — rather than the special bodied Bellancauto car, in which former F2 ace Maurizio Flammini got a drive after all.

A sensation of practice was NASCAR star Cale Yarborough, imported by Terry Labonte's Grand National en-

trant, Billy Hagan, to drive a new Camaro similar to the one run by Hagan's Stratagraph team at Dayona. Built by Dennis Frings, the Chevrolet had the only stock-block V8 in the field, a 620bhp unit which really shifted its 1100 kilos down the straight. Braking was not a strong point, and the Camaro drivers spent some time in the Mulsanne Corner escape road, also losing much of first practice with engine and transmission bothers. On Thursday, however, Yarborough drove magnificently, forcing the brute into the race through sheer tenacity and car control.

Fastest in Group 4 — over 3secs better than the Zol'Auto M1 — was the Helmut Marko entered BMW, with its aristocratic German drivers and BMW protégé Christian Danner. There was no real challenge to the BMWs from the Porsche 924 entries.

Porsche's participation with road car based cars was not only at the other end of the field, it was also at the other end of the efficiency scale. Last year, on their debut, the works 924 Carrera turbocars had suffered from burned exhaust valves (although all three finished), and the works engineers had developed a new cylinder head to eliminate the problem. When Richard Lloyd's Canon Cameras 'customer' car was co-opted into the works team, its regular engine (on which GTI Engineering had already resolved the difficulty with apparent success) was replaced by one of the new works engines — which proved to be unreliable, the same over-fuelling problem recurrent. In spite of a positively heroic late effort by Tony Dron, the British 924 failed to qualify.

So also did the new car which had been bought by Alan Hamilton to run here under the Porsche Cars Australia banner, which was equipped with the same revised engine. The combined talent of three of that country's top touring car drivers was not enough to do the job in the circumstances, although the older Eminence Racing Team entry got in by the skin of its teeth.

The other two works 924s both qualified, both with the latest aerodynamic treatment, the faster in GTP and the slower in IMSA GTO. The latter, essentially, has the same running gear as the G4 cars, co-driven by Sigi Brunn, driving at Le Mans after all in spite of the traumas at the 'Ring. The most interesting of all these Porsches, however, was the GTP entry, an entirely new conception.

The basis of next year's Group B car, the '944' was driven through a 935-type gearbox by Porsche's brand new engine, a 2479cc version of the single-turbo four. With a 16-valve, twin-cam head, the narrow-stroke, long-bore unit was producing around 420bhp at 6500rpm. Although the new car is around 20 kilos heavier than the works GTR, the 944LM was capable of almost 190mph.

At Le Mans with Tom Walkinshaw Racing for what will hopefully be a long string of 24 Hour outings, a veritable crowd of Mazda personnel was on hand to oversee two of the new RX-7 based 253i cars, powered by the very effective 320bhp rotary engines. The car Win Percy drove was the newer model which had made such an impressive debut at Silverstone, the other one the original 'muletta' which had done all the testing in Japan.

The Z&W team's journey to the Sarthe was wasted, for the team's overweight RX-7 was off the pace, and the Chevrolet-engined, CanAm chassis M6 GT McLaren should never have been given an entry. Paul Canary's club racing car in the USA, it was both unkempt and ineffectual.

In stark contrast, the Primagaz Lolas were among the best prepared racing cars we have ever seen, and the fastest of four 2-litre G6 entries which made the grade.

Porsche at the other end of the spectrum: a night stop for the reliable, but under-powered, 924 of Manfred Schurti/Andy Rouse/Siegfried Brunn.

THE 24 HOURS

The qualifying days had been blessed with glorious weather, but, as the sun climbed higher into the sky before the start, it was warmer than ever for the race. The build up at Le Mans is unique: the noise, the colour and the people combine to sharpen the atmosphere to a fever pitch when the cars form up for the rolling start.

As the pace car peeled into the pitlane at 3.00pm to the very second, Jacky Ickx eased the pole position works 936 ahead of Pescarolo's Rondeau, Mass's 936, Field's 935, Jöst's 908/80, Boutsen's WM, the two Rondeaux of Jean Rondeau and Ragnotti, Gaillard's ACR, Mamers's WM and Dören's Wera 935.

At the end of that first lap, Ickx had a clear advantage from Pescarolo, but there was one man already into the pits. The Porsches had looked invincible during qualifying, but here was a chink in the armour straight away, for Mass had a chronic misfire. The mechanics checked the fuel injection, but it took a second call on lap 3 before a damaged spark plug (the ceramic was cracked) could be traced, Mass dropping back to second from last but now happy with the car and keeping pace with Ickx. Behind him was the other pit caller on the first lap, Darniche's BMW M1 in for the first of several stops to bleed the clutch and change first one plug and then all six.

Jöst, anxious not to lose touch with the more powerful but bodily similar Ickx car, disposed of Field and Pescarolo for second place on the following lap and looked comfortably able to hold station 5secs behind. Already making good progress was John Cooper, up two places from 15th on lap 1, and Gaillard, who displaced the Otis and Calberson backed Rondeaux on lap 3.

Another favoured car became a pits visitor on the third lap, de Villota bringing the Lola T600 in to rectify a faulty gear linkage and dragging clutch. The problem could not be fully solved, but the Spaniard resumed with pace slightly reduced by the need for careful gearchanges.

Pescarolo dropped another place to Field at Tertre Rouge on lap 6, but all five Rondeaux were running crisply . . . until last year's winner, Rondeau, himself, started to slip back, his blue car spluttering as a result of the fuel pump drive having broken. He pitted on lap 9, and Keith Greene's efficient crew set about a repair job which ended up taking 88mins: the chance of a repeat victory had almost vanished.

Meanwhile, the expected reliability of the WM team was also beginning to look suspect, with both Boutsen and Morin stopping briefly, the former to have a fractured fuel pipe repaired. The other two cars were going strong, Mamers holding a steady sixth and Frequelin, in the live camera car, 10th.

The first routine stops began 45mins into the race, Ickx's thirsty 2.6-litre car being one of the first in for fuel, but no driver change. A flurry of pitstops kept the situation confused for a while, but Ickx soon settled into fifth place behind the longer-legged Jöst Porsche and the three Rondeaux of Pescarolo (1min behind Jöst), Ragnotti and Migault, the Belgian waiting to regain the lead when the French cars stopped for fuel. When the Rondeau stops finally occurred after 75mins, Pescarolo and Ragnotti led for a lap each before Ickx was back in front, 30secs ahead of the Jöst car.

The first confirmed retirement came just before the hour was up, when Cale Yarborough found that even his heroism could not prevent the mighty Camaro ploughing straight on at Arnage with

brake failure, but he had enjoyed his visit to the Sarthe. Also with brake problems, Frequelin's WM became the third of that team's cars to falter, its discs overheating badly and causing fade. Gaillard also had to cure a vapour lock on the ACR, losing his encouraging fifth place, and later dropping still further back when the rear anti-roll bar broke.

It was at 16.17pm that the race lost its momentum for the first of several periods under the pace car. The departure of three Mercedes course cars kept the field in control for half an hour while the wreckage from a fearful accident at the Mulsanne kink was cleared up. The quickest of the WMs in the early stages had been hurled into the barrier when a front suspension component broke, and Boutsen was a helpless passenger as the car scraped along the armco past a marshals' post. The cockpit section was not heavily damaged, but the front and rear disintegrated, debris hitting three marshals. One sadly died and another was badly hurt.

While the leading pace car picked up on Tambay's Rondeau, several cars made for the pits for more fuel, including Ickx for a driver change to Bell, so that the two hour mark saw the leading positions revised again to show Jöst in front from Field, Bell, Tambay, Spice and de Cadenet. The last was entirely happy with the Belga car's progress, having enjoyed a spirited fight with Craft's Dome during the first hour.

A number of British entries had hit problems during the opening two hours, none having been delayed more than the

Ibec, which had gone well in Trimmer's hands for the first hour before it started jumping out of third gear. The gearbox was stripped and a damaged selector was found, the car dropping to the very back of the field and only starting to haul itself back up several hours later after two more gearbox rebuilds.

The Phillips Ferrari in the hands of Steven Earle was delayed for 23mins to replace a holed radiator, while Hobbs's BMW M1, the Michael Cane Racing car, lost time when the clutch had to be bled. Hobbs had selected first instead of third because of the clutch at the Esses on one lap, damaging the nose frame and front bodywork. The Ivey 935 had made superb progress up to eighth in Cooper's hands, but slipped to 16th when it picked up a puncture with Wood driving.

Exactly an hour after Boutsen's accident at the kink, the pace cars appeared again, this time to lead the field slowly through the scene of a horrifying crash near Les Hunaudières involving Lafosse's Rondeau. It seems that the Calberson car inexplicably went out of control at over 200mph, and poor Lafosse died instantly, trapped as the car destroyed itself. Surer was among those following, and he described the accident as the worst he had ever seen.

The positions remained stable for the 20mins that the pace cars were out, but, almost as soon as the yellow flags disappeared, the leading car, now driven by Niedzwiedz, was forced into the pits with a cracked turbo fan, which took 12mins to replace and cost the 908/80 21 places. The ultra-reliable Interscope-

entered 935 was left in front, but Bell was on the same lap and closing swiftly as the Englishman settled into the groove, the 936 running "absolutely perfectly".

The highest placed Rondeau was now Spice's third-placed GTP car, which was running to its driver's liking apart from an alarming tendency to weave under braking. But only one other Rondeau remained in the top 10 by the three-hour point, Haran's steady L'Automobile machine in eighth place. Tambay had been holding fourth place, but the same problem that had afflicted the sister DFL-engined car struck, and the car lost the best part of two hours repairing the fuel pump drive. Unique to the DFL engine, this problem is thought to have been caused by insufficient cooling to the pump, which is mounted low on the block near the exhaust manifold.

Measured driving by de Cadenet had hoisted the Belga car to fourth place by this stage, and there were no complaints about its performance. The Dorset Racing de Cadenet was not so fortunate, slipping to 31st after being slowed in the first hour by persistent overheating, and then being delayed when the fuel metering unit belt broke. As it would have required unbolting the engine to change the belt, it was decided to run with the electric fuel pump in permanent use, even though this meant restricting maximum revs to 7,800.

Over the course of the fourth hour Bell continued to hold station from Migault, while the balance of pitstops on positions at four hours put the Vegla 935 of Schornstein/Grohs/von Tschirnhaus into third place from the NART Ferrari, which had made a faultless but unnoticed advance up the order. The next 10 cars were all on the same lap, but the significant intruder was the second works 936, up into ninth spot after a solid stint from Schuppan.

Another WM bit the dust when the camera car handled by Dorchy suffered a small engine fire at Mulsanne corner, so the four car team was reduced to two survivors. At 7.00pm, however, the third serious incident on the Mulsanne occurred, and a third WM was out of the race. Just before braking for the 90 degree corner, Raulet's WM collided with Gabbiani's Martini Lancia, knocking the Italian into a spin towards the inside barrier. Although the WM was relatively undamaged, it was out of the running, while the Lancia was heavily modified at both ends. Shortly before this incident, which brought out the pace cars yet again, the Henn 935 had retired when the fuel injection failed.

Positions after four hours: 1, Ickx/Bell, 56 laps, 120.97mph; 2, Spice/Migault, 55 laps; 3, Schornstein/Grosh/von Tschirnhaus, 54 laps; 4, Cudini/Gurdijan/Morton, 54 laps; 5, Field/Don and Bill Whittington, 53 laps; 6, Jöst/Dale Whittington/Niedzwiedz, 53 laps; 7, Haran/Schlesser/Streiff, 53 laps; 8, Morin/Mendez/Mathiot, 53 laps; 9, Mass/Schuppan/Haywood, 53 laps; etc.

Over the next hour, Haywood took over the second 936 and continued the rise to the top, gaining six places and reducing the deficit to second-placed Migault to a

Alain de Cadenet shared his car with the French Martin brothers, but retired early on Sunday morning.

It was early in the race, when the crowds were still thick on the terraces, that the pace car came out for the first time. It leads Tambay, Edwards and Verney.

Gordon Spice finished third for the second year in succession, in a GTP class Rondeau shared with François Migault.

ngle lap. Behind him, in fourth place, at the astonishing NART Ferrari, and then two more cars crewed by British drivers, the Ivey 935 and the Belga De Cadenet.

Right at the tail of the field, the two DFL Rondeaux were repaired after their fuel pump failures, but the team patron's own car then started slipping out of fourth and fifth gears, necessitating a 10mins halt to rectify a loose nut on the primary shaft of the 'box.

As soon as the pace cars had disappeared, the fifth-placed pink 935, now in the hands of Don Whittington, began to smoke signal that its days were numbered, and it soon expired with a burned piston. The Ivey and Vegla cars were left to sort our 935 honours between themselves!

Over the next hour and a half, with Ickx and Bell drawing inexorably further away, there were to be three significant retirements, the most cruel being to the lost 908/80, which had been set for a strong comeback after its turbocharger problems. Dale Whittington was driving when a front wheel came off at high speed; he managed to limp back to the pits with the front bodywork in tatters, but the car was beyond immediate repair. Yet another front runner was gone.

Soon after, the Nürburgring-winning BMW M1 was crashed by Henzler. He too was able to soldier back to the pits, only to find that the spaceframe had cracked too badly for a makeshift repair to be possible. It had been a lacklustre performance from the red BASF machine, partly because of a clutch problem which had afflicted most of the M1s, despite the use of a new spec bleed valve designed to improve reliablity!

The most exciting new car in the race, the Porsche 917 replica, also retired soon after the six hour point after a spectacular performance in the brilliant Bob Wollek's control. Unfortunately, the car was as spectacular when Lapeyre was driving, so much so that he put it far enough off the track to twist the engine frame: end of race.

Remaining in the shadows so far had been the quicker Martini Lancias of Cheever/Alboreto/Facetti and Patrese/Heyer/Ghinzani, moving hand in hand gradually up the order. Cesare Fiorio admitted that they were content to run at a very comfortable gait, since maximum 2-litre class World Championship points seemed there for the taking if the cars

held together, especially as the possible challenge from the Lundgardh/Plankenhorn/Wilds 'baby' Porsche had evaporated with piston failure. Patrese's stop to change the intercooler looked like a flaw in the plan, but he was motoring again within 12mins.

The Porsche 924s, as ever, were also maintaining a low profile, with the Schurti/Rouse/Brunn car having crept up to 11th place by six hours. The Rohrl/Barth 944 GTP was equally dependable in 16th place, but the Almeras-prepared machine, which had transmission problems from the very beginning, was retired. The gearbox had been rebuilt, but the car stopped twice on the circuit once out again.

Mass moved into second place during the seventh hour — a fine climb from virtually last place — to hold position four laps behind Ickx/Bell. A lap behind now were the Spice/Migault Rondeau and — a superb effort — the Cooper/Wood/Bourgoignie 935. As twilight approached, signalling lights at the Dunlop Curve warned of oil at the Esses, which, it transpired, had been deposited by de Villota's Lola, until now running swiftly, albeit down in the 30s. There had been an oil leak, caused by an undersized 'O' ring, from the scavenge tube, and the inaccessibilty meant that repairs took

almost an hour.

The two DFL Rondeaux, meanwhile, had hit further problems, which ultimately caused their retirements. Pescarolo was driving when the Oceanic car stopped out on the circuit with a recurrence of the fuel pump dramas, and his efforts to re-start flattened the battery. Team-mate Rondeau, now happy with the gearbox, found the handling of his car deteriorating so badly that he stopped to have everything checked over. Suspension, brakes and steering were examined carefully but no reason could be found for the car's consistent, violent tugging to the left, leading Keith Greene to ponder whether the extra stresses imposed by the DFL engine had cracked the chassis. It was decided that to continue was pointless.

As darkness began to close in, the two works Porsches looked intent on stretching their lead through the night, still running faultlessly and charming their drivers. For Ickx/Bell in particular, it all seemed rather easy: Spice, Cooper and Haran did not appear to have much chance of hanging on. Reliability continued to take the two quickest Ferraris on their way, Andruet/Ballot-Lena now leading from the NART car.

Further down the field, the two De Cadenets were now motoring well

(although the Belga car had been delayed by second, third and fourth gear selection problems), while the Dome lost a lot of ground — it dropped to 24th — when it was unable to start in the pits. Craft, however, was full of praise for the car's cornering.

Positions after eight hours: 1, Ickx/Bell, 116 laps, 123.37mph; 2, Mass/Stuck/Haywood, 113 laps; 3, Spice/Migault, 111 laps; 4, Cooper/Wood/Bourgoignie, 110 laps; 5, Haran/Schlesser/Streiff, 109 laps; 6, Andruet/Ballot-Lena/Regout, 109 laps; 7, Jean-Michel and Philippe Martin/de Cadenet, 108 laps; 8, Cudini/Gurdjian/Morton, 108 laps; 9, Grohs/Schornstein/von Tschirnhaus, 108 laps; 10, de Narvaez/Miller/Steckkonig, 107 laps; etc.

The BMW M1s were afflicted with two problem areas: clutches and crankshaft dampers. Having suffered a sticky clutch in the early stages, Hobbs then felt a vibration in the engine just before eight hours were up, but the EMKA crew were able to install a new damper in half an hour before any damage had been done. The Danner/Oberndorfer/Bayern G4 M1, however, had retired with that very problem an hour earlier.

The Ivey 935 dropped a few places soon after one third distance when the headlights started to flicker: rather than fiddle with bulbs, the crew changed the whole nose section, but the glimmer

The long-awaited Porsche 917 'replica' made an indifferent debut, but certainly looked the part with the brilliant Bob Wollek at the wheel. Lapeyre later put it off the road.

A finisher in 16th place, but not without many mishaps along the way, was the Edwards/de Villota/Fernandez Lola T600.

persisted. Through the night, the nose was changed three times, with new bulbs in each time. In much greater trouble, and not looking forward to the night, the Ibec crew had stripped the gearbox three times, but still it overheated: the car was pushed to run for an hour without a long stop for attention, but Trimmer and Needell were willing to struggle on.

Still Ickx and Bell pressed on into the night, both driving with consummate skill and consistency. The gap to Mass/Schuppan/Haywood remained steady at four laps until early morning, and the two Rondeaux stayed in touch throughout the night. Their only difficulty was with visibility, as the deep screens collected a lot of oil and grime, particularly from that slick at the Esses.

Behind the steady Vegla Porsche, the NART Ferrari led all the Boxers, all of them fairly reliable apart from the Flammini/Violati/Truffo car which endured all manner of fuel and electrical difficulties. Before the half way point, though, the Phillips Ferrari was to retire out on the circuit, with a structural failure.

The ACR, which had looked so promising at the start, developed worsening clutch problems which eventually caused the car's abandonment. An hour later, the second of the TWR-run Mazdas was also out after a mechanically traumatic race: severe problems with the rotary engine on top of earlier differential and gearbox rebuilds spelled the end. The team's other car had retired much earlier, after three hours, when Terada stopped with terminal transmission problems on the Mulsanne.

As the race approached half way, little changed at the top, apart from the fine progress of Anny-Charlotte Verney in the Cooke-Woods 935, up to ninth having been one of the lowly-placed 935s at first. The second Jöst car, the 935, dropped out when an oil leak caused an engine fire which engulfed the back of the car, Steckkonig leaping out unharmed. And the WM team, having a quiet time with their single car, suddenly had work on their hands when Mendez pitted with a broken front wishbone. He had had quite a fright when it snapped in the middle of Indianapolis, and it proved to require nearly an hour's work, Morin resuming in 19th position.

At half distance, the positions were as follows:

Positions after 12 hours: 1, Ickx/Bell, 176 laps, 124.69mph; 2, Mass/Schuppan/Haywood, 172 laps; 3, Spice/Migault, 168 laps; 4, Haran/Schlesser/Strieff, 166 laps; 5, Andruet/Ballot-Lena/Regout, 165 laps; 6, Jean-Michel and Philippe Martin/de Cadenet, 164 laps; 7, Cudini/Gurdjian/Morton, 163 laps; 8, Cooper/Wood/Bourgoignie, 163 laps; 9, Verney/Garretson/Kent-Cooke, 162 laps; 10 Schurti/Rouse/Brunn, 160 laps; etc.

After running as high as fifth, the Belga De Cadenet was delayed by the failure of its mechanical fuel pump, a problem the sister car shared. An extra electrical pump was fitted in compensation, and the injection was adjusted, Alain getting away again after two stops amounting to around 15mins. The Dorset car, meanwhile, had been developing a tendency to slip out of fourth gear at crucial moments, so Candy's routine stop was extended to examine the gearbox's insides. This car's new electric fuel pump was also causing pressure problems.

In last place, with considerably less than half the leader's distance completed, lay the Ibec, its troubles mounting further into the night. Trimmer at last got out around 3.00am after lengthy rebuilds of the gearbox, only for the master switch to fail on the Mulsanne on the first lap, cutting the lights and the engine. Tony pitted once more, and on his first lap out again the rear bodywork

fell off: there was nothing for it but to close the show and retire. . .

Retirement was the last thing in the mind of the works Porsche team: they were invincible, or so it seemed. Both cars pounded round four laps apart, building up a cushion of eight laps by 6.00am over the Spice/Migault and Haran/Schlesser/Strieff Rondeaux. Both French cars ran trouble-free through the night, apart from Spice being slowed slightly as his Cosworth was hitting the rev limiter early, allowing his team-mate into second place.

The unexpected, however, happened soon after 6.00am, when Schuppan pulled the number two 936 into the pits with a clutch problem which took over an hour to cure, the car regaining the track with Haywood at the wheel. The disc mechanism had broken, so the Porsche had to have a new clutch, but the car now lay in 12th place.

The Ivey Porsche reached fourth place again as a result of this delay, a place ahead of the surprisingly swift Verney/Cooke/Garretson 935. But others had suffered further problems during the night. A long stop when the spindle in the turbo rotor broke cost the Vegla 935 its place in the top 10, while the Lola T600's tale of woe continued . . . but at least it was still going. Edwards went off the road at the Esses shortly after 4.00am and had to have the rear bodywork taped together. And then half an hour later it split its first oil cooler. The Dome also had a troubled night, Craft having to pit with a chronic misfire which was traced to a broken valve spring. Japanese mechanics swarmed over the car, but its English

drivers were doubtful that they could rectify it, and were proved right.

Positions after 16 hours: 1, Ickx/Bell, 237 laps, 123.75mph; 2, Haran/Schlesser/Strieff, 224 laps; 3, Spice/Migault, 223 laps; 4, Cooper/Wood/Bourgoignie, 219 laps; 5, Mass/Schuppan/Haywood, 218 laps; 6, Verney/Garretson/Kent-Cooke, 218 laps; 7, Cudini/Gurdjian/Morton, 218 laps; 8, Andruet/Ballot-Lena/Regout, 216 laps; 9, Rohrl/Barth, 215 laps; 10, Schurti/Rouse/Brunn, 213 laps; etc.

The Lancias were well in the 2-litre hunt, the leading pair level on laps once again as a result of Alboreto's stop for a throttle cable and a new fuel pump, but worse was to occur when the other car still running, Patrese's, became a Martini

on the rocks. Its misfire was traced to head gasket failure.

With two thirds distance over, and the sun already warming up, Ickx/Bell had a staggering lead of 13 laps over the Haran/Schlesser/Strieff Rondeau, and Spice/Migault were just a lap further back. Then came the Ivey and Cooke-Woods 935s, and the NART Ferrari, which as dawn arrived had been showing signs of weakness. First it was slowed by a clutch problem, then it had to struggle back to the pits for a new left rear tyre, and, finally a fatigued Gurdjian put it into the barriers soon after the Porsche curve. The end of a superb run.

Above: La Gloire de la France? It didn't look like that when the quickest of the Rondeau cars, pictured with Henri Pescarolo at the wheel, suffered a two hour delay and ultimately retired. Below: So nearly a finisher, the O'Rourke/Hobbs/Jordan BMW M1.

Another valiant effort had been con- ded shortly before, when the Belga : Cadenet, after an hour's delay for ore fuel pump attention, blew up after ulsanne corner with one of the Martin others at the wheel. Almost at the same ne, the sister Dorset Racing car gave up e ghost after a more troubled run when e gearbox casing split and leaked all its . Its broken exhaust delay before that s trivial in comparison.

After losing all that ground, Haywood d Schuppan put in two storming stints, ch lapping around 10secs quicker than e leading 936 to climb back up to fourth ace within two hours. Deposed from at fourth place was the Ivey car, which d run strongly throughout the early orning apart from a 13mins halt to ange the crankshaft pulley drive to the ternator.

As the 20 hours mark approached, the orsche 924s held eighth and 11th places, though the lower-placed Schurti/ ouse car was emitting the three- linder splutter — the result of a burned haust valve — with which we were so miliar last year.

The 'shovel nose' 935 had reached 14th ace in the care of Haldi/Thatcher/ oulain, but a good run finished with tirement on the Mulsanne: Haldi was riving, and claimed that the rear wheels mmed when the differential broke, ausing him to clobber the armco near es Hunaudières.

Another blow to British hopes was the tirement of the EMKA BMW after 20 ours with a broken engine. It was a name in particular for Steve O'Rourke, ho had flown over from London in the arly hours of the morning having asterminded the last night of Pink

How the Frequelin/Dorchy WM retired at Mulsanne Corner . . .

Floyd's 'The Wall' concert. His first stint began at 7.37am, and the car was out of the action by mid-morning. Two other BMWs retired with engine failure, the Surer/Quester/Deacon car (after an extraordinary string of clutch, brake and engine traumas) and the Servanin/Rousselot/Ferrier car.

Positions after 20 hours: 1, Ickx/Bell, 296 laps, 125.45mph; 2, Haran/Schlesser/Streiff, 283 laps; 3, Spice/Migault, 280 laps; 4, Mass/Schuppan/Haywood, 275 laps; 5, Cooper/Wood/Bourgoignie, 273 laps; 6, Andruet/Ballot-Lena/Regout, 272 laps; 7, Verney/Garretson/Kent-Cooke, 271 laps; 8, Rohrl/Barth, 269 laps; 9, Cheever/Alboreto/Facetti, 267 laps; 10, Dieudonné/Xhenceval/Libert, 266 laps; etc.

With the final four hours to go, Ickx and Bell led by 13 laps, and were slowing their pace all the time for a safe finish. Schuppan's second 936, meanwhile, was securely in fourth place, when the motor cut out on the new section near the Porsche Curve. The fuel flow had suddenly gone full rich, and the engine refused to rev above tickover, so Vern had to radio to the pits for instructions to get him back. He lost 45mins out on the circuit tinkering with the injection, and then a further 42mins in the pits having a new fuel pump fitted. Once on the move soon after 1.00pm, the car was fine.

The leading car continued, as it had throughout the race, without drama, although a few hearts must have fluttered when Bell made an unscheduled stop an hour and a half from home for a new rear tyre. The Englishman drove for the last two hours at a very relaxed pace and was able to cruise to a highly emotional win with 14 laps in hand. Derek Bell had won Le Mans for the second time, and the great Jacky Ickx for an unprecedented fifth time: the jubilation after the race was more delirious even than last year's all-French win.

Very little changed during the last four hours: no more cars retired, and there were few place changes as teams concentrated on reaching the finish. One car, the Akin/Miller/Siebert 935, actually stopped after the 24 hours when there was a small electrical explosion behind the dashboard, but it was classified 11th.

Some teams made a point of finishing in style — the Rondeaux and the two Primagaz Lolas travelled to the finish in convoys — while some had to do everything in their power to survive. The Zol G5 BMW spent hours having its gearbox rebuilt, but it was out there at the end, the only BMW to finish. Others put up with their cars falling apart and soldiered on: the Lola T600, for example, did remarkably well to finish, running in the closing hours without second and fourth gears.

A final word should go to the British survivors. There were six at the finish — Bell, Spice, Cooper, Wood, Rouse and Edwards — and four of them were in the first four cars. Spice repeated his third place of last year, while Cooper and Wood put in a sterling effort for fourth place.

49th Grand Prix d'Endurance 24 Heures du Mans

June 13/14. 24 hours over 8.467 mile circuit. **Organisers:** Automobile Club de l'Ouest. **Winning average speed:** 124.93 mph. **Distance covered:** 2996.8 miles. **1980 winners:** Jean-Pierre Jaussaud/Jean Rondeau (3.0 G6 Rondeau-DFV M379'B), 338 laps at 119.2265 mph, 2861.40 miles. **Distance record (8.467 mile circuit):** 3134.52 miles (1978).

Pos	Drivers	Car	1	2	3	4	5	6	7	8	9	10	11	12	13	14	15	16	17	18	19	20	21	22	23	24	Laps	Retirements
1	Ickx/Bell	11	5	3	2	1	1	1	1	1	1	1	1	1	1	1	1	1	1	1	1	1	1	1	1	1	354	
2	Haran/Schlesser/Strieff	8	6	9	8	7	11	12	7	5	5	4	4	4	4	4	4	2	2	2	2	2	2	2	2	2	340	
3	Spice/Migault	7	4	5	3	2	2	2	3	3	3	3	3	3	3	3	3	3	3	3	3	3	3	3	3	3	335	
4	Bourgoignie/Cooper/Wood	55	17	11	16	12	5	5	4	4	8	8	11	8	6	6	6	4	4	4	5	5	4	4	4	4	330	
5	Andruet/Ballot-Lena	47	19	19	13	15	8	9	8	6	7	9	9	5	9	9	8	8	7	8	7	6	5	5	6	5	328	
6	Verney/Garretson/Cooke	42	30	27	19	15	15	13	14	12	12	11	10	9	7	7	7	6	5	5	6	7	6	6	5	6	327	
7	Rohrl/Barth	1	39	21	27	21	18	16	16	14	14	14	13	11	8	8	9	9	8	9	8	8	7	7	7	7	323	
8	Cheever/Alboreto/Facetti	65	31	26	29	23	19	18	17	15	15	15	14	15	14	13	13	13	12	12	10	9	8	8	8	8	322	
9	Dieudonné/Xhenceval/Libert	46	18	14	15	16	13	14	13	13	13	13	15	13	12	10	12	12	13	13	12	10	9	9	9	9	320	
10	Schornstein/Grohs/von Tschirnhaus	60	28	18	5	3	7	7	10	9	6	5	7	16	15	14	11	11	10	10	9	12	13	12	11	10	320	
11	Akin/Miller/Siebert	43	27	30	26	17	16	15	15	17	18	18	18	19	17	17	14	14	14	14	13	13	12	10	10	11	320	
12	Schurti/Rouse	36	25	23	25	14	12	11	11	11	11	12	12	10	11	11	10	10	11	11	11	11	10	11	12	12	315	
13	Mass/Schuppan/Haywood	12	50	40	24	9	3	3	2	2	2	2	2	2	2	2	2	5	9	7	4	4	11	13	13	13	312	
14	Morin/Mendez	4	10	10	11	8	10	10	12	16	16	16	16	12	18	19	18	16	16	16	16	15	14	14	14	14	307	
15	Finotto/Pianta/Schon	68	40	37	38	31	24	22	22	23	21	21	23	26	23	22	21	18	19	18	18	16	16	15	15	15	292	
16	de Villota/Edwards/Fernandez	18	51	46	39	33	23	23	31	32	33	31	30	29	26	26	26	25	24	23	21	20	17	16	16	16	287	
17	Alliot/Darniche/Cecotto	51	53	49	44	39	30	29	30	27	26	26	25	22	20	20	20	23	25	25	23	21	20	19	18	17	277	
18	Perrier/Bertapelle/Salam	70	49	45	40	36	27	27	26	26	27	25	26	23	21	21	23	22	22	20	20	18	18	18	17	18	274	
19	Grand/Courage	31	44	34	33	27	22	20	20	19	20	23	22	21	19	18	19	17	17	17	17	17	19	20	19	19	272	
20	Yver/Dubois/Heuclin	33	45	48	52	50	47	41	41	38	38	37	36	33	33	31	29	28	28	28	26	24	23	23	20	20	203	
21	Descartes/Bayard/Preschey	32	55	52	46	43	37	35	36	35	35	35	33	31	30	29	28	27	27	27	25	23	22	22	21	21	187	
	Haldi/Thatcher/Poulin	57	38	25	30	24	21	19	18	21	19	20	20	17	16	16	15	15	15	15	14	14	15	17			260	Accident
	Cudini/Gurdjian/Morton	49	20	13	7	4	4	4	5	8	4	6	8	7	5	5	5	7	6	6	15						247	Accident
	O'Rourke/Hobbs/Jordan	53	16	31	32	42	32	28	29	33	32	30	29	28	25	24	25	20	20	19	19	19	21	21			236	Engine
	Servanin/Rousselot/Ferrier	72	32	42	45	41	33	32	33	29	28	28	27	27	24	23	22	21	21	21	22	22					212	Engine
	Martin/Martin/de Cadenet	20	14	6	4	11	6	6	6	7	9	7	5	6	10	15	17	19	18	22							210	Engine
	Surer/Quester/Deacon	52	37	20	28	19	17	17	21	20	23	27	28	25	27	25	24	24	23	24	24						207	Engine
	Patrese/Heyer/Ghinzani	66	23	24	18	22	20	21	19	18	17	17	17	14	13	12	16										186	Head gasket
	Birrane/Faure/Candy	21	26	33	31	32	35	31	28	25	25	24	24	24	28	28	27	26	26	26							171	Gearbox casing
	Craft/Evans	23	15	8	14	26	26	26	23	24	24	22	21	20	12	27											154	Engine
	de Narvaez/Miller/Steckkonig	40	21	16	6	10	9	8	9	10	10	10	9	18													152	Fire
	Phillips/Salmon/Earle	48	52	50	42	37	28	24	22	22	19	19															140	Structural failure
	Violati/Flammini/Truffo	45	48	44	37	30	29	33	34	30	30	33	31	30	29	30											118	Breakdown
	Chevalley/Gaillard/Sotty	22	24	32	36	28	34	30	27	28	29	29															114	Clutch
	Ikuzawa/Walkinshaw/Lovett	37	46	36	41	45	42	36	35	34	31	32	32														107	Engine/gearbox
	Lemerle/Cohen-Olivar/Levie	30	43	47	47	44	36	34	32	31	34	34	34	32	31	32	30	29	29								104	Electrics
	Needell/Trimmer	27	34	51	53	49	46	42	40	37	37	36	35	34	33	33	31										95	Head gasket
	Wollek/Lapeyre/Chasseuil	10	13	12	9	20	14	25	25																		82	Engine frame
	Jöst/Whittington/Niedzwiedz	14	1	1	22	6	25																				60	Accident
	Jaussaud/Rondeau	24	54	55	51	47	44	38	37	36	36																58	Handling
	Stuck/Jarier/Henzler	50	8	41	23	18	31																				57	Accident damage
	Field/Whittington/Whittington	59	7	2	1	5																					57	Engine
	Raulet/Mamers	83	9	28	17	25																					50	Accident
	Lundgardh/Wilds/Plankenhorn	69	42	38	35	29	38																				49	Engine
	Danner/Oberndorfer/Bayern	71	22	22	20	40	41	39	38																		49	Crankshaft damper
	Dören/Holup/Lässig	61	11	15	10	34	39	37	39																		48	Breakdown
	Gabbiani/Pirro	67	35	35	34	35																					47	Accident
	Frequelin/Dorchy	5	12	29	21																						46	Engine
	Henn/Chandler/Mignot	41	29	17	12	38	40																				45	Breakdown
	Pescarolo/Tambay	26	2	4	43	46	43	40	42																		41	Flat battery
	Almeras/Almeras/Sivel	73	47	43	49	48	45																				30	Gearbox
	Ragnotti/Lalosse	25	3	7	48																						28	Accident
	Terada/Fushida/Percy	38	41	39	50																						25	Transmission
	Saulnier/Boutsen/Pignard	82	43	53																							15	Accident
	Hagan/Cooper/Yarborough	35	36	54																							13	Accident

On the apex

*A precision drive
to a record fifth victory
for Jacky Ickx and Porsche,
it was also a good result for Le Mans*

By Ray Hutton and Nigel Fryatt

A RETURN to prominence for Le Mans, the world's most famous motor race? Well, yes and no. Yes, because the *Automobile Club de l'Ouest,* pursuing their independent policy of attracting the best machinery available, no matter which of the confusing array of sports car classes it was built for, have given a lead to the new and promising Group C regulations that will come into force next year. This year they had no less than seven categories and 12 classes, so that virtually anything with covered wheels and room for two seats could take part. The entry ranged from two ultra-sharp works Porsches, to the Rondeau Le Mans specials (winners in 1980) and the fairy tale comeback of the mighty Porsche 917. Yes, it was a good field.

And, yes, there was a story that was satisfying for popular press and enthusiasts alike: the return from retirement, for the second year running, of one of the greatest sports car drivers in racing history. Jacky Ickx had already won the race four times — an achievement matched only by his compatriot Olivier Gendebien. A fifth win would be sweet and much more than a line in the record books. In a time when established formula 1 drivers shun Le Mans, that, too, is good for the reputation of the classic 24 Hours.

While the achievement of Ickx and his British co-driver, Derek Bell, was impressive — starting from pole position, leading from the start and swapping first place during the early pits stops before establishing an unassailable lead in the fourth hour — their

Porsche was one of the very few cars that were able to run with any strategy in this year's race. An unusual amount of pit activity and car problems occured in the first few hours and there was an unwelcome, unlucky, return to Le Mans of serious accidents. The experienced Frenchman, Jean-Louis Lafosse, was killed when his Rondeau inexplicably crashed not far from the beginning of the Mulsanne Straight. Earlier, one of the Peugeot-engined WMs had crashed heavily at the "kink" two thirds of the way along the Straight, precisely at a marshal's post. One official was killed and two injured. Two more were injured in the Lafosse accident.

With new regulations introducing a pace car for the first time to slow the field in the case of a serious incident, the first couple of hours of the race were very disjointed. The pace car system had its teething troubles — not least with the radio links between the course cars stationed at three points on the circuit. There were cases of competitors overtaking the course cars and of a group, running in formation at about 50 mph, being caught up by another at full racing speed that had been

given the green light. Since the system was new, no penalties were imposed on drivers who did not comply with it fully. Accidents on the main straight are a big problem that require drastic measures; given better communications, the pace car idea could be a good development from the safety point-of-view.

Aerodynamic quirks apart, shunts on the Mulsanne are relatively rare. This year there were three, but there is no common bond between them. The WM of Thierry Boutsen seems to have had suspension failure or a sudden tyre deflation. Lafosse's car is reported to have hit the guard rail at the chicane a couple of laps before his accident and to have been progressing erratically thereafter. Another WM and the Gabbiani-Patrese Lancia Montecarlo crashed at the kink because the Lancia didn't move over for the faster car — or because the WM punted the Montecarlo up the rear; it depended on who you talked to.

A lot of the more experienced drivers complained about the speed differential and the standards of driving of some of the slower cars. Both are perennial Le Mans problems, but a number agreed that the situation was worse than ever this year and put down the large number of punctures to untidy driving. "It's like rallycross," said Rondeau team manager, Keith Greene, taping over stone chips on the windscreen of the Spice-Migault car.

The fastest cars, without question, were the Porsche 936s. With 620 bhp from 2.6 litre engines de-

Both Porsche 936/81s were sponsored by the French after-shave, Jules. Ickx and Bell's car had a trouble-free run to the record

Autocar Capri driver Gordon Spice and Francois Migault took the Otis lift sponsored Rondeau to third place, despite stripping fourth gear late in the race. The impressive Rondeau team also took second place with the French driving team of Jean-Louis Schlesser, Philippe Streiff and Jacky Hara...

Le Mans 24 hours

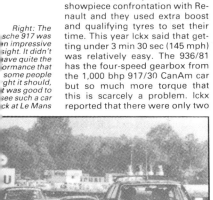

rived from those made for Porsche's stillborn Indianapolis project, there was no doubt that this classic long-tailed open Group 6 car was the fastest thing at Le Mans this year. It qualified 1.8 sec slower than Ickx had in 1978 but then they had been in a showpiece confrontation with Renault and they used extra boost and qualifying tyres to set their time. This year Ickx said that getting under 3 min 30 sec (145 mph) was relatively easy. The 936/81 has the four-speed gearbox from the 1,000 bhp 917/30 CanAm car but so much more torque that this is scarcely a problem. Ickx reported that there were only two

points on the circuit where he missed the use of the extra ratio in the earlier car's five-speed 'box. Otherwise the car was "perfect" — stronger brake calipers (the previous ones had flexed slightly) made the brake pedal more consistent. Ickx was clearly pleased to be there, back at Le Mans with the best car. "I gave up formula 1, retired, because I was tired of racing. But to come back to this; well it's like coming here 15 years ago." He had not driven a racing car for a year and, perhaps more significantly, Porsche had not run an endurance test with the 936 since the 1979 race. But the engineers at Weissach are thorough; and though it might be true, as Ickx joked, that they "took the car out of the museum," they did manage several hours' running with the new engine and transmission on a rolling road using a computer simulation of the Sarthe circuit.

Ickx's win was also Porsche's fifth. And Derek Bell's second, for they had shared the 1975 winning Gulf-Ford. The pairing of the two drivers that John Wyer has often praised as the best endurance drivers of the present generation

indicated Porsche's commitment to Ickx's ambition. The second 936/81 was entrusted to Jochen Mass, Vern Schuppan and Hurley Haywood. While the winning car was virtually trouble-free and ran around 3 min 40 sec throughout, day and night (Porsche wanted a more conservative target speed but Ickx said he wasn't sure he could go that slowly . . .), this second 936 was in trouble from the outset. It started the race on five cylinders and it took two time-consuming pit stops to diagnose a faulty sparking plug. Gradually it worked its way back through sheer speed to a supportive second place until the clutch failed a little after dawn and required an hour to replace. It pulled back up to fourth place before Schuppan was unlucky enough to have the fuel injection turn itself to full rich and the engine stop. Porsche's intercom system allowed him to receive instructions about adjustment and re-starting — and Aston Le Mans specialist Robin Hamilton happened to be there to give advice — but the whole episode with subsequent replacement of the fuel injection pump, took 1 hr 40 mins. The car could do no more than settle for 13th place at the end, though in the last hour it was lapping faster than anything on the circuit.

Hopes that an old Porsche 917, like that which set the still-extant distance record in 1971, would still be competitive were unfounded. Taking advantage of the free regulations, Erwin Dremer's team built a new 917 chassis and equipped it with a factory prepared 5-litre engine. Drivers Bob Wolleck, Xavier Lapeyre and Guy Chasseuil were enthusiastic but the car was not really quick

and retired at 9 pm with an engine oil line broken, never running higher than ninth.

By contrast, Reinhold Jost's 908/80 — the 936 "bitza" that he shared with Ickx for second place last year — led the race on the official results for the first and second hours. But it lasted only 4½ hours this time when Dale Whittington, younger brother of the 1979 winners, spun and damaged one side. He got it back to the pits, but by then a rear wheel was adrift and the team did

The Lola T600 started the race with high expectations and a lot of potential, but gearbox problems and oil leaks on the 3.3-litre DFL engine kept the car away from the leader board

not have the full range of parts needed for an inevitably lengthy rebuild.

Much had been made of a Porsche-versus-Ford confrontation but when the new Len Bailey-designed Ford C100 was withdrawn (the project started too late and the car was due to have its first test session, with Derek Bell driving, last Tuesday) it in the main became a Porsche-versus-Rondeau battle. And that is where tactics should have come into play, but didn't. Bucked by their win in 1980, and evidently financially much better supported, Rondeau presented an impressive five-car team of Cosworth-powered cars, based on the coupé design that first appeared as a Le Mans GTP in 1976. Two of this year's cars — for *Autocar* Capri driver Gordon Spice and Francois Miguault and French F3 drivers Jean-Louis Schlesser, Phillipe Streiff and veteran Jacky Haran — ran in the heavier GTP class and turned out to be the survivors. The ill-fated Lafosse-Ragnotti car was a regular 3-litre in Group 6 while the two others had the new DFL 3.3 litre version of the famous Grand Prix engine one of which was a

development Cosworth on loan from Ford. These were for three times winner Henri Pescarolo and Patrick Tambay and last year's victorious pairing, Jean-Pierre Jaussaud and Jean Rondeau. A variety of sponsors gave their names to these cars so that they were described as Otis (the lift people), Calberson (transport company), Oceanic *Le Figaro* and *L'Automobile* (the last two, magazines). Presiding over the whole complicated exercise was Gordon Spice's manager, Keith Greene — a tremendous compliment to the British saloon car team.

Ironically, the 530 bhp DFL versions were never strong contenders. Both had the mechanical high pressure fuel pump seize — the Jaussaud-Rondeau car on only its eighth lap — and this proved a particularly awkward thing to rectify. It was to put the Pescarolo-Tambay car out by 8 pm, for the pump failed again as Pescarolo came to the end of the Mulsanne Straight. He didn't get the supplementary electric pump switched on in time to stop the engine dying and the battery was weak so that it quickly flattened when he tried to re-start. Jaussaud and Rondeau retired shortly after midnight with an odd and disconcerting handling problem, the cause of which wasn't found, though they tried all the obvious corrections. In view of the uncertainty of the cause of the Lafosse accident, it was decided that they should retire.

Spice and Migault lay second from the seventh to the ninth hour, and third thereafter, being overtaken by their French teammates after a series of stops with a misfire. It took two sets of plugs and two ignition packs before they got it right, and after an uneventful night they stripped fourth gear. The Frenchman lost third soon after, so that both cars were being driven very gingerly and sounded worse than they were by holding on to unsuitably high gears through the twisting parts of the circuit. Nonetheless, to finish second and third in a race of so much mechanical trouble was creditable. Not much consolation for the loss of their teammate, of course, but compensation of a team of 120 who exist simply to compete at Le Mans.

Of the other Cosworth-engined contenders, the Guy Edwards Lola T600 had the most potential. There was to have been a second

was having a bad year in formula 1; driving for John Wyer at Le Mans was like racing in the 1960s again. There wasn't so much pressure, or money, at stake. For the only time that year it simply came down to doing a good, uncomplicated job.

1976? Ah, that was the Porsche 936 year, the year that showed that all things are possible. Their only problem in 1976 had been a broken exhaust pipe just before midday on Sunday. Otherwise, he and Gijs van Lennep had won easily. He had just driven sensibly, well within the limits of the car. Consequently, they had had no problems.

The King of Le Mans

JACKY ICKX is quiet, reflective in the Porsche garage, the 1981 Le Mans race before him. He has the best car, he has all the experience he needs. But so much can go wrong. All you can do is go through the motions and wait for the final result. Yes, there is a special way of driving — indeed, Ickx's Le Mans gearchanges have become something of a legend. Out of gear, find neutral, then select the next gear. But of a win there is no guarantee.

So what does Ickx think about as he watches his mechanics at work? Most likely, he thinks of what he did before in order to win. He thinks of 1969, the year he decided to have a little joke with Le Mans and walk to his car at the start. But the joke, of course, had been on them. He'd won, driving his JW Ford GT40 in the closing hours as if it was a Grand Prix, beating Hans Herrmann's Porsche by a length. So that was a lesson: the start at Le Mans matters not the slightest. It is your fitness at the finish that counts.

He thinks, then, of 1975, the "fuel consumption" year, when he had won with Derek Bell and the Gulf Mirage team. He'd driven the most part of his formula 1 career by then, and not won the World Championship. He'd beaten Jackie Stewart in an out-and-out fight at the Nurburgring and he'd won some classic Grands Prix. But the Championship had eluded him. In 1975 he

Then came the Renault challenge. That had improved Le Mans a lot. Ickx recalls the excitement at the Sarthe when Patrick Depailler put one of the French turbo cars on the pole. Again, though, sheer pace had not won the event. The engine of the Porsche 936 that Ickx shared with Henri Pescarolo had blown after three hours. He'd then been co-opted into the second 936 driven by Barth and Haywood. He remembers the hours of wet driving through the night. The wet! The only condition in which you can drive to some sort of limit at Le Mans. Ickx liked the wet. The following afternoon he'd gone on to win his fourth Le Mans.

What had happened since then? He'd driven the works formula 1 Ligier in the second half of 1979, but hadn't enjoyed it. There was that embarrassing moment when he spun on the warm-up lap of the French Grand Prix. Formula 1 had become too political, too commercial. Then he'd thought about retirement.

For the last two years he'd come out of retirement, just for Le Mans. Why not? It was still like racing in the era he enjoyed most — the late 1960s and early 1970s. There were motorhomes — but they were there for a purpose. And the event was still worth doing. Mulsanne at night. The atmosphere at the start. The record that had to be broken. He'd won four Le Mans. Why couldn't he make it five? □

Villota and Juan Fernandez, also had a 3.3 litre DFL. Lola chief Eric Broadley and Cosworth's Dick Scammell were on hand to watch progress of this first Lola contender for Le Mans victory in many years. But early difficulties with a new gearbox, a variety of oil leaks, including a particularly difficult one at the pipe that connects the scavenge pump to the block (requiring a hole to be cut in the venturi underbody), a series of broken oil coolers, a couple of spins and then more gearbox trouble meant that the car was never near the leader board; but when it was running well it was among the fastest.

The C100's no-show put Alain de Cadanèt back in his old car in the unfamiliar red and white colours of Belga cigarettes, for he had already "sold" the race to the Belgian saloon car specialists Jean-Michel and Philippe Martin, It ran well, as ever, and had climbed to fifth place by the 11th hour, but eventually it succumbed to engine trouble. The Dorset Racing Team's even older Lola-based De Cadanet that dates back to 1976 and had been part of the row about privateers' qualification last year, also put in a good performance but retired at 9 am with a leaking and overheating gearbox.

Ian Bracey's Ibec team spent a lot of their time rebuilding its gearbox, and, after a gallant try, Tony Trimmer and Tiff Needell had to retire early on Sunday morning with a cooked head gasket. Engine trouble also put paid to the Japanese Dome driven by Britons Chris Craft and Bob Evans which was competing in its second Le Mans and much better prepared than previously, while Andre Chevalley's DFV-engined ACR from Switzerland expired

with its clutch broken.

These DFV prototypes should be a force next year if the Group C regulations proposed go through with the currently anticipated fuel consumption requirements. Two cars were actually running to what are understood to be the 1982 rules this year. These were two of the WM coupes powered by the Peugeot-Renault-Volvo "co-op" 2.6 litre V6 engine with twin turbochargers and four-valves-per-cylinder heads. A little team made up in the main by engineers from the Peugeot research centre who build racing cars in their spare time, this year WM had a more professional look. They entered no less than four cars, two in the Le Mans GTP class and two new ones as "Group C". Although the two new cars were eliminated in accidents, and a third suffered engine failure and the last had a troubled run to 14th place, they were fast in the early stages. Now there are signs of more official support for WM from the increasingly sport-minded Peugeot group.

What is not so likely in the future is a resurgence of the big production-based Porsches, the very quick 750bhp twin turbo 935s. Porsche themselves don't enter them any more and although one won Le Mans as recently as 1979, it is clear that to repeat that now would require a great deal of good fortune. The current regulations give everyone the same fuel tank capacity regardless of class. Le Mans allows 120 litres (26.3gal) and restricts fuel delivery to 50 lit./min. so the thirsty 935s have to run very fast indeed to make up for the extra pit stops they require over the relatively economical Cosworths or the lighter Group 6 cars. Fastest of the 935s

Lola, entered by the American Cooke-Woods team for Brian Redman and Bobby Rahal, and with a 700 bhp Porsche 935 turbo engine instead of their usual 5.7 Chevrolet. But the car was very

new and had a fundamental design fault as during a few laps of practice the turbocharger could not be persuaded to boost properly. The Edwards Lola, with driving to be shared with Emileo

Le Mans 24 hours

An impressive [d]ut for the "944 [Le M]ans" 2.5 litre [...] 16 valve all-[alum]inium engine in the Jurgen Barth-Walter [R]ohrl Porsche [9]24. A steady [...] took the car [to] seventh place — its only pit stops were routine ones

in practice was the Kremer K3 of Ted Field and the 1979 winning Whittington Brothers, but the most consistent one in the race was the British-entered car of antique dealer Dudley Wood, a K3 run by Charles Ivey Racing and driven by John Cooper, Wood, and the experienced Belgian, Claude Bougoignie. It finished an excellent fourth overall behind the winning Porsche and the two Rondeaus, while the other Cooke-Woods racing entry, a K3 driven by patron Ralph Cooke, Bob Gar-

teams. Hans Stuck was good value, as ever, in the brightly-finished BASF-sponsored GS Tuning M1. BMW competitions manager Dieter. Stappert pasted a photograph on its instrument panel of Stuck's damaged car from 1980, reminding him how much time his impatience had cost in repairs but his car was again eliminated in an accident, though this time while co-driver Helmut Henzler was at the wheel. There were M1s in all sorts of classes from Group 5 to Group 4 and IMSA, all with the same 470 bhp engines but different in weight, bodywork, and wheel

[Fe]rrari had their [be]st Le Mans for [ma]ny years. This [Am]erican NART [51]2 BB was the [be]st Ferrari and [w]as running in [fif]th place until [ac]cident at the ["n]ew" White [Ho]use section of the circuit on [Sun]day morning. [Ab]ove right: A steady and [co]nsistent drive [b]y the Martini Lancia Montecarlos took them [to] a class win

[...]liar sight at [th]e end of the [...]e. The "thin [b]lue line" of [po]lice is soon [...]-run by the [enth]usiastic and [Pari]san French crowd

retson and Anne-Charlotte Verney was sixth, incidentally producing the best female Le Mans result in memory.

The Jean-Claude Andruet-Claude Ballot-Lena Ferrari Boxer snatched fifth place from the Cooke-Woods Porsche in the last hour and achieved the best Le Mans result for Maranello in eight years. Theirs was one of five of these impressive long-tailed 512s running in the IMSA class; armed with latest modifications from the factory, they performed relatively better than in previous years. Again a British entry — the Simon Phillips car driven by him with Mike Salmon and American Steve Earle — went well, while the NART car of Alain Cudini and John Morton was actually running in a regular fourth place on Saturday evening, but retired after an accident entering the "new" White House section of the circuit at 9 am on Sunday morning.

It wasn't the best of races for BMW, who had declined to bring their "Group C" IMSA car from America and gave only technical assistance to a number of private

sizes. The cars of Stuck-Jarier-Henzler and Surer-Quester-Deacon were pukka spaceframe specials but a design mistake meant that they had to run six-into-one exhaust systems which BMW knew from experience would break under a Le Mans pounding; they did. It seems that they also anticipated clutch trouble (which they also had) though all but one of the others retired with engine trouble, including the fast ex-Niki Lauda Procar converted to Group 5 and run by Michael Cane Racing for David Hobbs, Eddie Jordan and Pink Floyd manager, Steve O'Rourke. He flew in from a Saturday night rock concert only to find that the car was out by before 11 am.

And then there were the cars closer — a little closer — to the real world. Like the two Mazda RX7s with long tails brought from Japan and entered by a Tokyo dealer that had nothing but trouble. And the Lancia Montecarlo Turbos that were not fast in this company and didn't want to be — in fact, all the team wanted to do was to win the class on their

way to clinching the World Endurance Championship for the second year. The Cheever-Alboreto-Facetti car survived so well that it finished eighth overall and anyway their sole opposition, the Lundgarth-Plankenhorn-Wilds Porsche "Baby", with 1.4 litre turbo engine, failed early on with a broken piston.

For the second year, Porsche's factory effort embraced a team of 924 Carreras including a rather special one with a 2.5 litre 16-valve all-aluminium engine with "944 Le Mans" proudly cast on the cam cover — the prototype for a soon-to-be-announced road car engine. Though it ran way back in the early stages, a totally reliable run by Porsche test chief Jurgen Barth, and rally driver Walter Rohrl brought them seventh place overall while the more normal 2-litre version of Manfred Schurti and Andy Rouse had a repeat of 1980 troubles and ran on three cylinders for the last

six hours but nonetheless ended 12th.

In the 30th anniversary of their first Le Mans race, Porsche had good reason to be pleased. Dr Ferry Porsche was there in the pits, as was the firm's new chief executive, Peter Schutz. Porsche are experienced at winning; they even managed to avoid subjecting their car to the pressures of the excited, unruly crowd that broke down barriers to stand below the winner's balcony in the hope that some of the victory champagne would touch them. The size of that crowd, their enthusiasm and the man on the balcony who came back to become undisputed King of Le Mans tells you that even if 1981 was not a classic year, the significance of the world's oldest 24-hour race is undiminished. □

JEAN-LOUIS LAFOSSE, killed early in the Le Mans race when his works Rondeau snapped sideways on the Mulsanne Straight and ran head-on into a guardrail, was in many ways a victim of his era: had the French racing boom not produced so many other talented newcomers, he would have received even more recognition. As it was, Lafosse was a sort of French equivalent of Guy Edwards, one that could always be relied upon to obtain good sponsorship and to set up a neat, professional team. Born in 1941, he began racing with an old Lotus 18 in 1966. He did a season in *Formule France* in 1969 before progressing to formula 3 in 1971. Diversifying into sports car rac-

ing, he proved very quick in one of the 3-litre Jo Bonnier Lolas and, subsequently, in a 2-litre Lola backed by Gitanes.

It was at Le Mans, a race he enjoyed immensely, that Lafosse scored his biggest success. Driving a Gitanes Ligier, Lafosse finished second overall in 1975 — and he repeated the feat the following year with a Total-backed Mirage. He had recently proved successful at the wheel of a BMW in French production saloon car events, and with team-mate Jean Ragnotti was hoping for a good result at Le Mans this year. To his family and friends, *Autocar* extend their deepest sympathy.

PDW

Le Mans 24 Hours
13-14 June 1981

1 **Porsche 936/81 2.6 t/c**
(J. Ickx–D. Bell), 354 laps, 2998 miles, 124.9 mph *(Group 6)*
2 **Rondeau M379CL Ford 3.0**
(J. Haran–J-L. Schlesser–P. Streiff), 340 laps, 2878 miles *(GTP)*
3 **Rondeau M379CL Ford 3.0**
(G. Spice–F. Migault), 335 laps, 2835 miles *(GTP)*
4 **Porsche 935 K3 3.1 t/c**
(J. Cooper–C. Bourgoignie–D. Wood), 330 laps, 2793 miles *(Group 5)*
5 **Ferrari 512 BB 4.9**
(J. C. Andruet–C. Ballott Lena), 328 laps, 2776 miles *(IMSA)*
6 **Porsche 935 K3 3.1 t/c**
(A. C. Verney–R. Garretson–R. Cooke), 327 laps, 2768 miles *(IMSA)*
7 **Porsche 924 GTP 2.4 t/c**
(W. Rohrl–J. Barth), 323 laps, 2734 miles *(GTP)*
8 **Lancia Beta Montecarlo 1.9 t/c**
(E. Cheever–M. Alboreto–C. Facetti), 322 laps, 2725 miles *(Group 5)*
9 **Ferrari 512 BB 4.9**
(P. Dieudonne–J. Xhenceval–J-P. Libert), 320 laps, 2709 miles *(IMSA)*
10 **Porsche 935/2 3.0 t/c**
(D. Schornstein–H. Grohs–G. von Tschirnhaus), 320 laps, 2709 miles *(Group 5)*
11 **Porsche 935 K3 3.1 t/c**
(R. Akin–P. Miller–C. Siebert), 320 laps, 2709 miles *(IMSA)*
12 **Porsche 924 Carrera 1.9 t/c**
(M. Schurti–A. Rouse), 315 laps, 2666 miles *(IMSA)*
13 **Porsche 936/81 2.6 t/c**
(J. Mass–V. Schuppan–H. Haywood), 312 laps, 2641 miles *(Group 6)*
14 **WM P79/80 Peugeot 2.6 t/c**
(C. Mendez–D. Morin–M. Hathiot), 307 laps, 2599 miles *(GTP)*
15 **Lancia Beta Montecarlo 1.9 t/c**
(M. Finotto–G. Pianta–G. Schon), 292 laps, 2471 miles *(Group 5)*
16 **Lola T600 Ford 3.3**
(E. de Villota–G. Edwards–J. Fernandez), 287 laps, 2429 miles *(Group 6)*
17 **BMW M1 3.5**
(P. Alliot–B. Darniche–J. Cecotto), 277 laps, 2345 miles *(Group 5)*
18 **Porsche 934 Carurol 2.9 t/c**
(V. Bertapelle–T. Perrier–B. Salam), 274 laps, 2319 miles *(Group 4)*
19 **Lola T298 BMW 2.0**
(J-P. Grand–Y. Courage), 272 laps, 2302 miles *(Group 6)*
20 **Lola T298 BMW 2.0**
(P. Yver–M. Dubois–J. Heuclin), 203 laps, 1718 miles *(Group 6)*
21 **RD D31 ROC Chrysler 2.0**
(L. Descartes–J. Bayard–H. Preschey), 187 laps, 1583 miles *(Group 6)*
55 starters, 21 finishers.

LE MANS

FIRE AND RAIN

Bittersweet memories

BY BOB AKIN
PHOTOS BY JEFFREY R. ZWART

Last month, endurance racer Bob Akin shared his feelings of what it's like to drive a Porsche 935 K3 on the circuits of Silverstone and Nürburgring. The German race was stopped after only 17 laps of the scheduled 1000 km had been completed because of a fiery tragic accident involving the Porsche 908 of Herbert Müller and the Akin team's abandoned Porsche. Müller was killed; the Americans' car destroyed. Two weeks later, Akin and his co-drivers had a new car and, though badly shaken, they took on that most celebrated of long-distance runs: Les 24 Heures du Mans.

I WILL NEVER cease to be awed by the racing extravaganza. At least once each weekend, I stop to survey the display of opulence gathered in the paddock: dozens of tractor-trailers, custom transporters and motorhomes plus the exotic personal cars of the drivers and team owners. An assemblage of expensive toys that transmits the same feelings as the waterfront in Palm Beach or the lineup of executive jets at the Dallas Airport. A hobby for some that has become big business for everyone.

In the early days, I drove my Alfa Spider to the races, removed the bumpers, windshield and muffler, put on the Con-Tact Paper numbers and went racing. Later I graduated to flat-towing the racer behind an old Plymouth. Those

who brought their cars on trailers were considered big time. Gasoline, tolls, a motel room, and the $15 entry fee made a race weekend an expensive undertaking even if the car did not need work before or after. Wrestling the Alfa through the multiple turns and sprinting along the short straights at Lime Rock, it was hard to imagine a place where the straight was 3½ miles long, where the top speeds were twice that of the Alfa, where the spectators stood 10 deep all around the 8.4-mile course, keeping a vigil day and night as the combatants urged their 800-bhp contraptions on toward the ultimate of goals: Victory at Le Mans.

The new car needed to be completely disassembled and gone through before leaving for France. The crew worked at Kremer's shop, adding some of our touches and repainting it red to conform with our sponsor's wishes. Two weeks later in the sun-drenched city center of Le Mans, the car moved through the elaborate scrutineering process. Hoisted on the lift rack for inspection of the underbody, silhouetted against the sky and the medieval Le Mans Cathedral,

Akin's Porsche 936 (left) started in 30th place. Fellow American Ted Field (below) in his Porsche 935 K3 trails the Porsche 908/80 of Reinhold Jöst. Winners Jacky Ickx and Derek Bell celebrate with champagne.

FIRE AND RAIN

the car was magnificent and the horrors of Nürburgring were almost forgotten.

The first practice session began at 7:00 p.m. on Wednesday. Right off we were 10 seconds faster than last year and, while speeds on the straights were about the same, the braking was fantastic, cornering better and intake air temperature lower due to the larger intercooler. We posted a reasonable time to qualify midfield, then spent Thursday changing to the 3.0-liter engine. My co-drivers were Paul Miller and Craig Siebert, both thoroughly familiar with the 935. Paul had been with me last year when we went 19 hours before retiring with transmission problems; Craig drove with me at Daytona and Sebring but needed some time to learn the Le Mans circuit. The plan was to put a minimum of time on the car in the final practice. At this point, with the race engine in the car, every lap of practice was the same as an extra lap in the race.

Jacky Ickx had stormed around in the Porsche 936 in 3 minutes 29.44 seconds to win the pole over Jochen Mass in the other 936 team car at 3:32.61. This year's 936 is outwardly similar to those run in 1978 and 1979 and the 908/80 being campaigned by the Reinhold Jöst team this season. Inside, however, the new 936 uses the 2.6-liter engine originally developed for the aborted Indy project. Changes to the ignition and injection were necessary to convert from methanol to gasoline, but little more needed to be done. The unit produced 650 bhp with low boost settings and was certainly more reliable than the highly stressed 2.1-liter unit in the 908/80 and earlier 936s. Also this year's car used the sturdy 4-speed gearbox from the 917/30 Can-Am car, which had more than 1000 bhp. There was no question that this unit would

stand up to the test. Jöst put his 908/80 in 3rd spot with a 3:34.51 ahead of the two Rondeau-Cosworth DFLs of Henri Pescarolo/Patrick Tambay (3:35.16) and Jean-Pierre Jaussaud/Jean Rondeau (3:36.17). Surprisingly, the latest Kremer 935 K3 was 6th at 3:36.54. This car, in its rather alarming pink-and-white color scheme, was entered for Ted Field and Danny Ongais but Danny had his awful crash at Indy so Bill and Don Whittington were added to keep Ted company.

NASCAR champ Cale Yarborough managed to hurl his big IMSA Camaro around the 8.4 miles in 3:59.57 to qualify 39th. Cale was a perfect gentleman and kept a low profile but we couldn't help imagining what he would tell the good ole boys back home on the high banks.

Several potentially quick cars failed to live up to pre-race expectations. The Kremers had taken advantage of some loopholes in the rules to create a brand-new Porsche 917—complete with the fantastic 4.9-liter flat-12 used when the 917s dominated the Makes Championship in the early Seventies. The car had intake air problems in qualifying but still managed a 3:46.54. Brian Redman and Bobby Rahal were to drive a Lola T-600 prototype like the one Brian has used to terrorize the IMSA races lately; only instead of the Chevy engine (which everyone knows won't go 24 hours) Bob Garretson's shop had fitted a twin-turbo Porsche 935 unit. On paper this was the hot setup—on the asphalt it was a turkey. With no testing time before arriving at Le Mans, the crew encountered some problems with the rear axles and the turbos which could not be made to put out adequate boost in top gear. The axle problem was easily fixed and a new exhaust system was fabricated to solve the

boost problem. All for naught. The car failed to make a lap within the required maximum time and two of the world's best sports car drivers were relegated to the pit wall.

As race time approached the sun continued to shine. It was getting hot. No one believed that we would make it through without some rain. We just hoped it would not be like last year when a downpour at the start gave us some moments we will never forget. Race day was beautiful and the pre-race ceremonies were spectacular: hundreds of thousands of fans, 4000 police and marshals, flags, marching bands—and the national anthem of each participating driver.

The 55 cars are pushed silently to their starting positions. There are solemn handshakes between friends and other drivers before the helmets are pulled on. Orange gloves gripping the soiled hands of tense, exhausted crew members. Doors are closed and the final minutes before the start begin in solitude.

It's strangely quiet as you scan the dormant control panel, reviewing again the array of gauges, switches, levers and knobs: oil pressure, oil temperature, gearbox temperature, fuel pressure, intake air temperature, electric tach, mechanical tach, electric boost gauge, mechanical boost gauge, fuel reserve light, reserve switch, cooling fan light, oil pressure light, alternator light, brake bias knob, anti-roll bar adjustment lever, boost screw, shift lever, master switch, left and right ignition switches, fire extinguisher, defroster, radio talk button, headlights, auxiliary floodlights and hazard warning blinkers.

Outside, people are still milling about, waving and smiling, signaling with thumbs up. Crew members and old-time friends. Sponsors and rivals. Women you know and some you'd like to know. All traversing the oval slot in your helmet as the one-minute warning is given.

Gendarmes sweep through the grid, firmly guiding the last of the crews to the sidelines. The cars are lined on the vacant track as if in a deep canyon between the throngs that fill the towering grandstands. Finally the signal is given to start engines and in a moment the pace car moves off—to bring 30,000 horsepower around to the starting line exactly on the stroke of 3 o'clock.

Ickx was off to a big early lead as Mass pitted on the 1st lap to change a broken sparkplug. The Jöst 908/80 moved to 2nd and held comfortably behind Ickx in spite of his less powerful engine. Ted Field in the 935 K3 used his 3.2-liter engine to its fullest and stayed in the hunt along with several of the Rondeaus. Poor Cale lasted only till the 3rd hour before the big Camaro refused to stop for the sharp right-hander at Arnage, roaring down the escape road to collect the barriers and crunch the front end. Preston Henn's Porsche, second fastest qualifier of the 935s, stopped for good at Tetre Rouge with a broken injector pump belt.

As the early hours passed without incident, a wave of relief swept the pits and the crews began to settle in for the long ordeal. Pit stops began to scramble the standings and Ickx/Bell fell as far back as 5th before taking permanent possession of the lead in the 4th hour—never again to be threatened. "Jacky is the perfect teammate," explained Derek Bell. "He goes out and drives for 3 hours and I know he has never missed a shift, never overreved, never abused the car. I try to do the same. It's the only way in these races."

The Field/Whittington/Whittington Porsche with Bill at the controls made a brief appearance in the lead in the 3rd hour before the engine went south and Ted called in his helicopter to shuttle him to his hotel in Paris. Kremer's 917 replica was gone in the 7th hour after a brilliant drive by Bob Wollek took it to 9th spot. Co-driver Xavier Lapeyre put the slick yellow prototype well off the road, bending some important stuff in the rear, which led to its eventual retirement.

It was 3 hours before the first fatality. The Peugeot V-6 turbo-powered WM of Thierry Boutsen crashed at the fastest part on the Mulsanne Straight, the flat-out right-hand bend known as the "kink." At 230 mph the car broke something in the front suspension and hurtled into the guardrail, sending fragments in all directions. Miraculously Boutsen was unhurt but three course marshals were hit by debris and one died enroute to the hospital. An hour later another accident on the Mulsanne killed popular French driver Jean-Louis Lafosse as his Rondeau tore itself to pieces at more than 200 mph. Marc Surer, who had been following, said it was the worst crash he had ever seen. Not long after still another crash at the kink eliminated Jean-Daniel Raulet's WM and the Martini Lancia of Beppe Gabbiani. I was driving at the time and I thought the worst because the cars looked awful and there were several ambulances on the scene. Thankfully, this time no one was injured but a solemn curtain had descended as darkness replaced the colorful afternoon. Tragedy is the part of racing that we do not think about, yet when there is a fatality we are reminded that this really is not a game we are playing but a serious, threatening sport that can extract the ultimate price while it lures us with its promise of glory.

Paul Miller, Craig Siebert and I started in 30th position, way off the car's true potential. In the early going we moved up steadily—outbraking all but the 936s and outhandling even the nimble little 2-liter sports racers in the tight sections. But teething problems in the new car kept setting us back: fuel pressure, 2 laps lost; right side exhaust header, 5 laps lost; loose headlight fixture, 1 lap lost; left side exhaust header, 7 laps lost; loose ground wire, 1 lap lost; alternator, 4 laps lost. Each setback was followed by a dramatic charge—the car running perfectly between stops—flashing through the warm night and into the misty dawn.

In spite of Sunday's intense heat the fast pace continued. Usually some rain comes to slow things and save the engines, but not this year. Only Ickx and Bell cruised comfortably with a good lead. Everyone else was playing catch-up and the toll was high. By noon, with 3 hours to go, only 22 cars remained. Three of the four WM prototypes were out, the remaining car driven by Tampa real estate tycoon Charles Mendez was running 15th. The NART-entered Ferrari 512BB of Alan Cudini/John Morton/Philippe Gurdjian was gone after putting on a fine show and running for a while in 4th. The Jean-Claude Andruet/Claude Ballot-Lena 512 was still holding down 5th but having starting problems at each pit stop.

Ralph Cooke and Bob Garretson teamed with lady racer Anny-Charlotte Verney for a trouble-free run in Bob's 935 K3 finishing 6th overall, the best-ever finish for a woman at Le Mans. All week, it seemed, the Ralph Cooke/Roy Woods/Bob Garretson team was about to self-destruct. Confusion about plans for the balance of the season, frustration over the Lola/Porsche disaster and the clash of several strong egos led to ultimate collapse as Garretson and Cooke announced, after the race, that the team was splitting up, each claiming that the other could not make it on his own.

The Jochen Mass/Vern Schuppan/Hurley Haywood 936 had fought its way back from nearly last to 2nd in the 7th hour but a clutch problem lost them an hour and set the second works car back to 9th at dawn. With 4 hours remaining they were up to 4th, but then the injection pump quit and another 1½ hours were lost putting them 13th where they stayed until the finish.

Last year's winning Rondeau team saw their fortunes fall into the hands of their two backup cars, both with smaller 3.0-liter Cosworth engines. Running steadily they occupied 2nd and 3rd positions for the last 8 hours with no hope of catching the Ickx/Bell 936, which had compiled a 117-mile lead by the end.

Our last hours were trouble-free as we stormed up through the field with a decent finish still in sight. In the last hour with Paul Miller driving we were on the same lap as the 935 of Dieter Schornstein/Harald Grohs/Götz von Tschirnhaus in 10th spot and François Sicard's Ferrari 512 in 9th. Miller kept the pressure on till the last, turning laps at qualifying speeds, but we were not going to close the gap. With five minutes to go we were resigned to 11th—not bad, we agreed, in light of our problems. Miller passed the pits for the last time, seconds before the checker began to fall as the clock struck 3:00 p.m. The crowd broke through the lines of gendarmes and spilled onto the track to surround Derek Bell as he pulled the 936 slowly through the masses to take the flag. Champagne corks popped in our pit and someone was pouring the bubbly on Craig Siebert's head just as we heard the announcement that Miller had stopped out on the track—3 miles from the finish. We stared at each other—stunned silence in the midst of a celebrating throng. Out of fuel? No. Our calculations showed enough to finish. Could it be that we were to come all this way and not get credited with an official finish?

Out on the track Miller had just made the turn at the end of the Mulsanne Straight, acknowledged the cheers and waves from our signal pits and began to accelerate toward the Indianapolis turn when the cockpit filled with smoke and the power went off. Parked on the grass as the last finishers struggled past, Paul tried everything he knew to restart and complete the lap in the allowed 15 minutes after the checker. But it was no use. Our finish slipped away and we became the last entrant to retire in the 1981 24 Hours of Le Mans.

In the time that followed, each of us made his separate peace with the outcome and, in the main, we agreed we had come a long way from the disaster at Nürburgring two weeks before. The new car still needed some sorting but it was clearly better than the one we lost. It would be a good car to finish out the season. Our European tour had been a long ordeal and while we were gone the string of IMSA victories for the Porsche 935s had been ended. Three races had gone to the Lola T-600 prototype, one to the Zakspeed Ford. This summer and fall it would be increasingly hard to finish well with a 935. Evolution had turned to revolution in the sports car racing world.

What can be said at the end of an era? The 935s have carried me so many miles—delivered me safely from so many desperate moments. Now the great, cumbersome, rear-engine turbo car may be nearing the end of its long career. The new prototypes are real race cars—not based on street car chassis—lighter and swifter, with mid engines and ground effects. Less sturdy and more dangerous. Next year we may be forced to change but the 935 Porsche will always have a special meaning to me. In the solitude of the night at Le Mans, the chill of the dawn at Daytona, the triumph of victory at Sebring—the car and I were comrades and it's hard to turn away from a friend.

How I won Le Mans

DEREK BELL describes how he and Jacky Ickx took their Porsche 936/81 to victory in *Les Vingt-Quatre Heures du Mans*.

This year's Le Mans was a big occasion for me. Although Jacky Ickx was going for his fifth victory, it was my chance for a second win. Naturally I was anxious to repeat our success of 1975, and in the Porsche 936/81 we seemed to have the best possible car for the task. Needless to say, it all went like a dream, thanks to the car's faultless performance and Jacky's superb driving. AUTOSPORT has asked me to describe my race, so here is the story of how I won Le Mans for the second time . . .

It all worked out so well for me this year, right from the word go. First of all, Steve O'Rourke agreed to release me from driving his BMW M1 when Porsche asked me to drive — I later found out that Jacky had specifically asked that I should be his co-pilot — in their 50th anniversary year, and in the year of their 30th visit to Le Mans. The fact that Jacky was going for his fifth victory, and I for my second victory, meant that there was an immense burden on our shoulders. There was a lot of pressure to do well.

I hadn't seen the car until I went to scrutineering, which I nearly missed because I arrived late due to ferry strikes. I was very impressed: it looked superb. It was exhilarating the next day to see the mechanics pushing it up the road into the pits for practice. I had sat in it to have pictures taken earlier, but this was the moment when I would drive it.

I was very keyed up about driving it for the first time round a place like Le Mans, because I like to get to know a car on a slower circuit, like Paul Ricard or Silverstone. Jacky had been round before me in practice, so I knew the thing was safe, but what would it be like at 230mph?

Jacky, as I said, did a few laps, and then I went out. My fourth lap was a 3m 36.0s. I had never been that quickly round Le Mans before. The first two laps I took gently through the kink, but on the third lap I took it absolutely flat, so good was the car. It was just like sitting in an armchair.

The car had been fitted with the stronger four-speed CanAm gearbox to cope with the greater power of the 2.6-litre engine, so the gear-change was a little stiff as it had been designed to carry 1000bhp. It proved difficult to engage first in the pit lane, which in the race was very evident in our pit stops, as we lost a lot of time trying to select first. I wanted to slot it into first for Jacky just before I stopped to hand over, but I had to keep putting it into neutral so the Dunlop technician could spin the wheels with the car on its jacks. First gear is what one calls a road gear, because we were using it twice a lap and it was good for 80-90mph, so consequently it is very strong, and the selectors are heavy: unless the teeth were absolutely spot on when stationary, it wouldn't go into gear. When pulling away, you had to take second, get the car rolling and then engage first.

The one thing we were worried about — and Jacky mentioned this several times during the race — was the clutch. Obviously we didn't want to burn it out going up the pit road. The strange thing is that I did notice that the other 936's drivers, especially Hurley Haywood, used a lot of revs driving out of the pits. Not spinning the wheels, but slipping the

clutch more than us. That's why Jacky told me to watch the clutch when I went out for my second stint during the race. He had seen me drive out the first time, when I had slipped the clutch a little excessively. Obviously that was my first exit, which is likely to be a little harsh until you get used to the technique. Every effort you can make to save wear on the

> "The one thing we were worried about — and Jacky mentioned this several times during the race — was the clutch. The strange thing is that I did notice that the other 936's drivers used a lot of revs driving out of the pits . . . slipping the clutch more than us."

One of the night pit stops for the leading Porsche.

car helps over 24 hours. When I was getting anxious in the last hour, I worked out that I was doing only 21 changes a lap, and I never missed a gear.

Basically, however, the gearbox was perfect for the job. At the end of the race, it felt just as it had done at the start. On my last couple of laps on Sunday I took the engine up to 8,000rpm and gave the car stick through the corners, just to savour what a superb car it was. I've never treated a car like that before at the end, and it was probably a bit stupid, but I knew that I was never going to drive this car in the same form again, and wanted to make the most of it. I suppose it was a bit like having a lover, really the most beautiful lover in the world . . . perfection.

Throughout the race it felt very, very good. The temperatures were always low: oil temperature was running at 85, the water temperature was running at 78 on one bank and 82 on the other, the oil pressure was all the time at nine bars, and the gearbox was 100-105. And all this was in extreme heat. At Le Mans, where you are driving at around 230mph on the straight, you are bound to get the temperatures rising at sustained high speed, but on this car they never changed.

I wanted to give myself the thrill of driving it fast at the end, and on the quicker two laps I knocked 10secs off our normal race times, although I was still lifting on the straight. Jacky and I decided that, because of the turbochargers, we would lift occasionally on the Mulsanne. When I was driving for Renault in 1978, we burned the pistons

after 17 hours. I remember talking to Ralph Broad when I got back to England after that race: he asked me if I had lifted going down the straight, and of course I said that I hadn't. He explained that, at sustained high revs, the pressure from the turbo pushes the oil back from the tops of the pistons, and that a lift every now and then keeps everything properly lubricated.

Jacky and I discussed this very problem with Porsche this year, and they thought that lifting would do the engine no harm, and that in fact a quick off-and-on would drop the cylinder temperature by 30 degrees. Lifting obviously caused a loss in top speed, but it didn't really matter because the car cornered so well. At no stage did we dawdle through the corners. I remember when Jochen Mass was charging back up through the field after his first lap pit stop: I could stay with him all the way from Indianapolis through to Tertre Rouge, but then on the straight he was able to pull away easily.

In the last six hours, we were lifting off three times on the Mulsanne. We were using 7,800rpm in the gears and pulling 7,900 in top early in the race, but towards the end I was lifting off at 7,500 in top and letting it drop back to 7,000 before going back up to 7,500. That may seem like a very strange way to race, but I wanted to win. We had a big lead and it didn't really affect lap times significantly. We were lifting three times, but if it had been necessary we could have gone back to just one lift on the straight. I don't think this precaution cost any more than 5secs, at the outside, on lap times. Losing

3-400revs for half a mile really didn't matter. That was how we handled the engine.

Brakes are replaceable, whereas gearboxes are not. Coming down to Mulsanne Corner, for example, I was braking quite heavily at 350 metres, then coming off briefly for a second harder application while building the revs and slotting slowly from fourth into second, using that second gear right at the last moment. Rather than use first to slow the car, I would start to turn into the corner with one hand on the wheel and drop into first with the other hand, ready to put the power on. That technique put the minimum strain on the gearbox: anything you can do to save the car must be an advantage. I had to use first gear a couple of times, however, to slow down when someone got in my way.

The gearbox seemed to cope better with the race than those in the other cars I've driven at Le Mans. The Renault used a five-speed Hewland, and the change became a little sticky on that as the selectors gradually wore out . . . but, there again, I had to drive that car harder than the Porsche, particularly early in the race. The Porsche was so fast through the corners — the chassis was well-tuned from three previous Le Mans — that we could afford all this gentle treatment.

Throughout the race, the car was very comfortable: I didn't have any sores or any aches. In most cars, when you have driven for that long, you inevitably have weals on your back, or you have bruises where your elbows have knocked against something. The Porsche was so beautifully tailored that I felt fine after the race. The reason why I have felt tired all week after the race was because of the festivities, not the car! And Jacky, who must be two or three inches shorter than me, fitted into the car well with no changes to the seat. When we drove together in 1975 in the Mirage, the seat had to be altered slightly for him, but this time we put the seat in a compromise position, which was perhaps a pity. I would have liked to have sat just an inch further back, but then it would have been no good having Jacky so far back that he couldn't brake properly.

We had planned our driving schedule before the race. We decided to change drivers every two stints for the first session each, and then after that we would do three stints in a row before changing. Each lasted for nearly three hours, which did seem a long time. There was only one stint that I didn't enjoy: just before daylight I began to get rather fed up, wondering what the hell I was doing there, but it was glorious when the dawn came up. The darkness seems to go on and on, but at least daylight shows that the end is approaching. I know I said in my article before the race that I like driving at night, but it does drag.

When the second car had to have a new clutch, Jacky was even more worried that we should treat ours gently. He said that it was quite all right to use second gear through the chicane, to which I replied that I had been using it since the first lap. "Oh. I've been using first," he said. As it turned out, the car never missed a beat clutch-wise.

The other team car could have done just as well, because I'm sure that it was prepared identically. I think it is a disadvantage to run three drivers, as it must be harder on the car. I couldn't believe it when the car came in at the end of the first lap. My initial reaction was to feel desperately sorry for poor old Vern

How I won Le Mans

Schuppan, as he has had some very tough luck over the years . . . especially when we've been sharing a car. We don't seem to be very good for each other.

In fact, while I was driving, the car never faltered, apart from one little thing when I was out for my first stint. I had been flashing my lights occasionally in the dusk when coming up on other cars, using the flash switch attached to the steering column. Only bolted on with clamps, it ended up working its way off, until the whole lot came loose and jammed against my thigh. I was slightly worried that it might get trapped in a position to prevent me turning the wheel, but it was all right. I had to use the main light switch until I stopped, which meant driving at times with only one hand on the wheel on the Mulsanne.

That is the only thing I can recollect going wrong. Jacky did start to worry on one occasion. When I got in at 1.00pm, he was worrying about the turbo boost, wondering if there might be a crack in the head. Great. Two hours to go and he puts the fear of God in me! I watched the dials carefully, and the boost was lower than it had been, but I put that down to the fact that I had turned the boost down during the night because it rises in the cool temperature. I put it down to 1.25 instead of 1.3, which didn't seemed to affect top speed, so I left it there. As it got hotter on Sunday, the boost dropped to 1.2 or a fraction under, which I think was because the ambient temperature was so high. It's very easy to get carried away about things not being quite right, even if there is a perfectly logical reason for them.

I thought that this showed how much pressure Jacky felt to win for the fifth time. He was perhaps more tired than I was, but then he hadn't driven for a year. I know that I was the one who folded up at the end on the balcony, but I'm sure that was because I drunk all that beautiful champagne. I didn't sweat as much as him, which was probably because of his greater nervous tension.

It was the hottest Le Mans for some time, and many drivers were affected. I was sometimes a bit worried about overtaking because I saw a lot of silly mistakes. I think that the heat caused more errors than usual: the driving was appalling. For years I have returned from Le Mans saying how pleasantly surprised I have been about the driving standards, but this year there was some very poor driving. There were more fast cars than before, but a lot of the drivers shouldn't have been in the race.

I know very little about the accidents on the Mulsanne. I have heard two possible reasons for poor Lafosse's accident, one of which was that a tyre burst. One Goodyear man said that he had found nothing structurally wrong with the tyres which were holed during the crash, and Lafosse wasn't at high speed at that point, only 150mph. If there is any lesson to be learned from the accident, it is that the speed differential between the fastest and slowest cars is too great. That is the problem which must be solved. It would do no good at all to take the straight away, because it is an essential part of one of the greatest races in the world. And it makes the race easier for the driver, since it is not tiring to drive down the straight. The Daytona 24 Hours is more of a strain on a driver than Le Mans, because there is never an opportunity to cool off behind the wheel.

The accident in which one of the WMs ran up the back of Gabbiani's Lancia strikes me as completely stupid, but again I'm not surprised that it happened. On one lap during the night — driving on dipped headlights as it is unfair to cause too much dazzle — I was coming up on two cars on the Mulsanne, flashing the

Watch the clutch . . . Ickx eases away after a pit stop.

lights to show I was there. The faster car slotted back behind the slower car, so I thought that its driver had seen that I was behind, but he pulled out just as we were coming by and forced me right on to the dirt. Lunacy. There is no excuse, especially at night, for not seeing a car coming up behind.

Although I admire the little 2-litre sports cars that finished, some of them really were mobile death traps. I came across one going very slowly through Indianapolis, and, on a corner like that with a very quick approach, you are on top of a slower car in no time. The speed differential in that instance must have been 130mph, because this car was going very slowly just to reach the finish.

I was rather disappointed that I wasn't the first car over the line at 3.00pm on Sunday, but then it was nice to cross the line at all! I had the two Rondeau cars which finished for company and I didn't want to cross the line with them: why should they share in our glory? I dropped back from them — perhaps I should have gone ahead — and then found that I had to do another lap, since I crossed the line just 20secs before it was 3.00pm. The previous time round I had been able to see that the time was *around* five to three, but there is no point in slowing down enough to do a 5mins lap in a 936 — that really is *very* slow — so I thought I would probably have to do an extra lap.

That slowing down lap is amazing. I couldn't have had a race with anybody because all the marshals were out on the track waving flags. I was in fact trying to pass a very slow car: every time I moved out to go by, there was a whole pack of marshals in the way. It is a sight that no-one, except those in the race on that last lap, can appreciate. If you could film it, the pictures would be absolutely magnificent.

I never crossed the finishing line on that last lap as my car was besieged at the Ford chicane by a wall of photographers. All the time the gendarmes were telling me to ease forward, so I was slipping the clutch on my tired old car. In the end, the gendarmes whipped me out of the car so quickly that I left it with the engine still running. I found that rather sad. After living with the car for so long, it had become a good friend. I didn't see it again. Sentimental rubbish, isn't it?

I was carried all the way to the balcony. "I can manage all right on my own," I kept saying, but they told me that I was safe with them! I saw Jacky on the way, and we congratulated each other, but these characters with truncheons and guns still wouldn't put me down. Jacky was allowed to walk, but not me! When we got to the balcony, the noise was incredible. It was absolutely wonderful.

I drank quite a bit of that champagne just before I had to talk to Barrie Gill,

and as soon as he opened his mouth I went out cold! I've never ever done that before. I needed a drink after the race, and all there was was this champagne, which doesn't do a lot of good when you haven't eaten for 24 hours. The one thing you want after the race is water . . . I would have been very happy if someone had appeared with a champagne magnum full of water . . .

Somehow I ended up slumped over the rail. As I started to wake up I thought it was that dream again, that damned dream about winning Le Mans. I really do want to win it, and here I am dreaming about it again. It sounds corny, but that's what I thought!

I must have looked like death, especially as they threw cold water over me afterwards. All I wanted to do was to sit down, but I had to go first to the press room for some radio and television interviews, then to a *Moët et Chandon* do, and then to the ACO's prizegiving in the *Petit Welcome*. I met Monsieur Balestre for the first time . . .

After that we went to Les Hunaudières restaurant for M. Chandon's dinner for the winners. That was a splendid occasion, but it wasn't until about 11.00pm that I could finally get along to Teloché to see the mechanics, who by this time had got a terrific party going. We sang a few songs, drank more champagne and finally got to bed in La Châtre well into the early hours of the morning, only to have to get up at 7.00am to get to Cherbourg for the ferry!

It really is an amazing feeling of anti-climax when it's all over, knowing that you have achieved everything you set out to do after all that build-up over weeks and weeks. It's now six days since the race, and I've hardly relaxed at all. There have been so many things going on, like the Pink Floyd concert on Tuesday night, but tomorrow is Sunday, and I shall do sweet nothing . . . ∎

Only another eight hours to go . . . Bell rounds Arnage amid the long shadows of early morning.

LE MANS 1982

Much was expected of the 1982 Le Mans race but not all expectations were to be fulfiled. The new classification and the Group C regulations had attracted much interest - the hoped-for factory entries had materialised - and the accent was on fuel consumption as the regulations - restricted maximum tank capacity to 100 litres and the maximum number of fuel stops permitted during the race was 25. So even if there was no limit on engine capacity in Group C, the fuel consumption restriction would effectively keep down speed in the interests of economy.

Le Mans was open to the Group C cars, and also to the new production sports car category Group B - in the event there was only a single Group B entry, a Porsche 930 which failed to qualify for the race. But 1982 was an interim year, and the old categories were still permitted entry, including Groups 4 and 5 with their American equivalents, I.M.S.A. GT and I.M.S.A. GTX, and also Group 6 but only for cars of less than two litres' capacity. As the Group C regulations stated that the name of the engine manufacturer must be quoted before the name of the chassis constructor, the official entry list seemed to contain a lot of Fords; for Ford read Cosworth. But make no mistake about it, this was the year when Ford returned to Le Mans in their own right, with the promise of a Ford-Porsche duel as spectacular as the Ferrari-Ford-Porsche battles of the late 1960s.

Of 59 entries, 29 were in Group C, 11 in the I.M.S.A. GTX class, seven in Group 5, six in the I.M.S.A. GT class, four were two-litre cars in Group 6 and there was one entry each in Group B and Group 4. By the usual process of exclusion based on practice times this was brought down to the maximum permitted number of 55 starting cars; the unlucky ones were the Group B Porsche, a BMW M1 from Group 5, a BMW-engined R.D. two-litre in Group 6 and finally, the American-entered Ford-Cosworth engined Group C Mirage which was driven by the father and son team of Mario and Michael Andretti. This was not disqualified because it was too slow in practice - as it had returned the ninth best time; but with more than a touch of the sort of scandal that Le Mans is famous for, it was disqualified literally on the starting line because the gearbox oil cooler was mounted behind, rather than above the gearbox, thereby infringing one of the rules in the book. Some frantic re-designing took place in the paddock but the organisers had already allowed first reserve car to start instead. A modified and now legal Mirage was wheeled into the pit lane an hour after the start of the race, only to be parked in front of the marshals' box

where it sat forlornly for some time while team manager Harley Cluxton lodged an unsuccessful protest.

So of the 55 cars on the grid, 28 were Group C cars. Porsche had three of their new 956s, with monocoque bodywork and twin-turbo flat-six engines similar to the 'Indianapolis' engines of the previous year's 936s. There was also a single Porsche 936, modified so it conformed to Group C regulations and entered by Team Belga and Joest Racing whereas the three 956s were works entries by Porsche System, with Rothman as the main sponsor. These four cars were given start numbers 1 to 4 and three of them occupied the first three places on the grid - the 956s of Jacky Ickx/Derek Bell and Jochen Mass/Vern Schuppan, together with the Martin/Wollek/Martin 936, while the Haywood/Holbert/Barth 956 was further down the line.

No less than 16 cars in Group C relied on Ford-Cosworth power, with the newer DFL engine in 3.3 and 3.9 litre forms far outnumbering the old three-litre DFV. Ford's own pair of C.lOOs, entered by Ford and run by the German tuning firm Zakspeed, and driven by Surer/Ludwig and Winkelhock/Niedzwiedz, obviously caught the public fancy more than most other cars in the race. The French Rondeau marque defended its home territory with no less than six cars of which three were Otis-sponsored works entries, drivers apart from Jean Rondeau himself including French aces such as Pescarolo, Jaussaud, Migault and Ragnotti but also British driver Gordon Spice. In addition there were two Saubers from Germany, a Cougar from France and five British cars all with Ford engines: two Lola T610s, the De Cadenet-Lola, the Grid-Plaza and the Japanese sponsored Dome-Amada.

The remaining Group C entries used a wide variety of engines. The two WM-Peugeots were Le Mans regulars with their turbocharged 2.8 litre PRV-Peugeot V-6 engines but were in the running with a better chance than before, thanks to their straight line speed; besides, the Esso-sponsored cars were among the prettiest on the track. A U.R.D. had a 3.5 litre BMW straight six engine while the German Kremer company continued their association with Porsche by entering their own Group C car fitted with a Porsche engine. The biggest engines at Le Mans were the 5.8 litre Chevrolet V-8s fitted to the two March cars; although the Nimrods did not give them much away, with Aston Martin V-8s of 5,340 cc.

Nimrod's begetter Robin Hamilton normally runs an Aston Martin dealership in Burton-on-Trent but is no stranger to Le Mans, having run a specially prepared Aston Martin V-8 in the 24-hour race in 1977 and

1979. His desire to enter - and possibly win - Le Mans with a competitive, all-British car led to the formation of Nimrod Racing Automobiles in 1979, when Eric Broadley began the design of a chassis which would comply with the forthcoming Group C regulations and was to be fitted with the Aston Martin engine. The Aston Martin company supported the venture whole-heartedly, particularly after the enthusiastic and patriotic Victor Gauntlett of Pace Petroleum became Aston Martin Lagonda's chairman.

The Nimrod was first unveiled to the public at the end of 1981, attracting much attention from Fleet Street and other mass-media, while many motor racing insiders watched with no little scepticism - after all, the Nimrod was big and heavy and many wondered if the Aston engine really could develop enough power to make the car competitive in endurance racing, let alone down the Mulsanne straight. Nimrod's racing debut came in May 1982 in the Silverstone Six Hour Race; of two cars entered one retired but the other finished a creditable sixth. Two cars were again entered for Le Mans - the works car in silver and British racing green, driven by Geoff Lees, Bob Evans and Tiff Needell, and Viscount Downe's car sponsored by Pace Petroleum in the Pace colours of white, red and blue, driven by Simon Philips, Ray Mallock and Mike Salmon. The Pace-entered car was faster in practice and was twenty-third on the grid, the works car twenty-sixth.

Apart from the Group C cars, the other entry reck-oned to be in the race with a chance of winning were the two Lancia-Martini Group 6 cars with 1.4 litre Fiat-Abarth turbo-charged engines - just scraping in under the two-litre limit with the current 1.4 equalisation fac-tor for turbo engines. The team came fresh from wins at Silverstone and Nurburgring, where the low weight, nimbleness and good fuel economy of the Lancia had paid off, especially on a circuit like Silverstone which is scarcely fast enough for a big-engined Group C car to flex its muscles. The Lancias were among the few open cars in the race - as was the only other Group 6 entry, a Ford-Cosworth Chevron B36B. Group 5 held six cars - three Porsche 935s, a BMW M1 and two Lancia Beta Monte Carlos with engines similar to the Group 6 Lancias but bodywork like Lancia's most recent homolo-gation special rally car, with an ungainly high-lipped rainwater-retaining rear spoiler. The closely related I.M.S.A. GTX class was better supported, with four Porsche 935s, another BMW M1, four Ferrari Boxers for the traditionalists and two Mazda 254s - silhouette rac-ers based on the RX-7 road cars, with 2.7 litre rotary engines. In a spirit of Anglo-Japanese co-operation, they were entered by Tom Walkinshaw Racing and Mazdaspeed, with sponsorship by Nikon.

The relatively tamest cars in the race were those entered in the I.M.S.A. GT class, together with the sin-gle Group 4 car, a British entered Porsche 934. The I.M.S.A. GT cars were three Porsche 924 GTRs, with turbo-charged versions of the road-going 924's four cylinder two-litre engine; one of these had been the first reserve car, the Canon Camera-sponsored, GTI Engineering entered car driven by Richard Lloyd and Andy Rouse which had been permitted to start after the disqualification of the Andretti Mirage. The team was given rather less than ten minutes' notice that they were in the race and started from the pit lane rather than the grid itself. There was also a BMW M1 in the GT class, and finally a pair of Chevrolet Camaros entered by an American team. These had the distinction of being per-haps the noisiest cars in the race - no mean feat! - with a particularly earth-shaking rumble.

There were two practice sessions in the days before the race, on Wednesday and Thursday evenings; the second session was cut short by a brilliant thunderstorm whereupon the heavens opened. The weather on the Friday before the race was characterised by intermittent heavy showers; there had not been a wet Le Mans since 1979 but it began to look as if this was a distinct possi-bility. However, Saturday dawned dry, if windy and cloudy; the weather remained like this for the rest of the day, while Sunday turned out to be sunny and pleasantly warm.

The practice sessions put the Ickx/Bell Porsche in pole position, followed by two others of the same make, while the little Lancias confounded the sceptics by run-ning them a close fourth and fifth, ahead of the fastest Ford C.100. A mixed bunch of Group C cars followed - Sauber, Kremer, the Mirage which was subsequently dis-qualified and Guy Edwards' Lola which was timed at 220 mph through the speed-trap on the Mulsanne straight; only 1 mph slower than Ickx in the Porsche who was fastest of all. The second Ford was in eleventh position; followed by the two WM-Peugeots, the remaining Porsche 956, another Sauber, the first of the Rondeaus, the Grid-Plaza, the second Lola and then in nineteenth position, the first Group 5 car - a Porsche 935. Practice was interrupted by a spectacular accident in which German driver Harald Grohs suffered a blown-out tyre on his Porsche 935, doing 190 mph down Mulsanne; the car rolled and upon coming to rest caught fire. Amazingly, Grohs escaped unharmed - as the door was torn off the Porsche he was able to make a quick exit. In direct contrast to the strict rules of 1980 when engine changes from the start of the practice sessions to the end of the race were not permitted, such changes were by now commonplace, with even a few well-documented examples of cars qualifying on bigger engines than even-tually used in the race - exploiting an interesting loop-hole in the Group C unlimited capacity regulations.

In addition to the Wednesday and Thursday prac-tice sessions there was a 45-minute warming-up session Saturday morning, prior to the parades which precede the 24-hour race and help to pass the time for the spec-tators who have crowded into the grandstand and other public enclosures since 8 on Saturday morning. As 1982 was the fiftieth race the pre-race parade had a special historical content; not an historic race such as had been seen in earlier years but a dignified cavalcade of past Le Mans winners, from the Chenard et Walcker which won the first 24-hour race in 1923 to the Porsche which won in 1981. Bentleys and Jaguars featured strongly, with Victor Gauntlett enjoying life at the wheel of a Bentley Speed Six, but there were also examples of Alfa Romeo, Lagonda, Talbot, Aston Martin, Ferrari and Ford GT 40 - the latter disgraced itself and had to return on a lorry. As 1982 by coincidence saw not only the fiftieth Le Mans 24-hour race but also the fiftieth Monte Carlo Rally, there were also representatives of Monte Carlo Rally winners past and present in the cavalcade. These historic cars then went on display near the motor museum which is situated in the 'Village' behind the paddock area. A few modern cars such as the official Mercedes-Benz pace cars and examples of the new Bentley Mulsanne Turbo also took part in the pre-race parade.

The last hours before the start are spent in arranging the cars on the grid, and at six minutes to four the 55 cars start on the pace lap following the official car of the clerk of the course. At 4 pm exactly the pace car re-crosses the starting line and pulls in, and the race is under way.

The pattern which so often emerges at Le Mans is that the first few hours become almost a sprint race - a mad dash which provides a lot of the excitement in the race, for drivers and spectators alike. Perhaps there is an impish streak in even the most professional and mature driver which makes him put his foot down and join the fray like a schoolboy who rushes off the moment the bell goes at the end of a tedious lesson. However, some teams may coolly calculate and plan to send one car off as hare to the hounds, deliberately baiting other drivers who may then run out of fuel or blow their engines in the pursuit. Or other teams may, pessimistically, consider that they have little chance of getting through the twenty-four hours anyway, and decide to have their fun - and give the sponsor his money's worth by playing to the gallery for as long as they are in the race. It is during these hours between 4 pm and sunset that lap records are broken, and broken yet again; that the highest speeds are registered at Mulsanne; but it is also the time when the dangers of the race are greatest, with the majority of the cars still on the circuit, often moving at widely disparate speeds.

The Porsches had started the race at the head of the field and this was obviously where they intended to stay. Their main competitors were Rondeau and Ford, both launching determined challenges to Porsche's leadership but only succeeding in getting past temporarily whenever the Porsches stopped for fuel. The Porsche turbo engines turned out to be rather thirstier than the Ford-Cosworths, but with the aid of a computer in the pit, and flow meters with digital displays in the cars, the Porsche team had elevated the calculation of fuel con-

sumption to the state of a fine art. The other possible contenders, the Lancia 'Spiders', were dogged by a variety of electrical and mechanical problems - a succession of pit stops soon dropped them to the back of the field. The first retirement came within half an hour when the Grid-Plaza went out with piston failure, while the Dome and one of the Lolas both spent a very long time in the pits soon after the start.

As the afternoon turned into evening, the fastest lap of the race was put in by Jean Rondeau in the car bearing his own name - at 140.527 mph he failed to beat the 1981 lap record which is the record for the current circuit. Meanwhile a number of further retirements had taken place - many of the new Group C cars suffered mechanical breakdowns, while others had calculated their fuel consumption incorrectly or had simply driven with too heavy feet. Several retirements were due to cars running out of fuel on the track.

At 7.30 pm, hopes of an outstanding British performance were partly dashed when the works Nimrod crashed at Mulsanne, after having been driven from twenty-sixth into ninth position. It was believed to have been a slow puncture which developed into a blowout which caused the accident; the Nimrod began wagging its tail so furiously that Tiff Needell finally lost control and the car went backwards into the Armco, at a speed approaching 200 mph. Tiff was unhurt but the car was extensively damaged. After this, the most spectacular accident of the race, Nimrod's and Britain's hopes rested with the Pace Petroleum car.

With France on continental summer time but Le Mans nearly on the same longitude as London, Le Mans effectively enjoys double summer time and it is light until almost 11 pm, but as darkness finally descended, some cars were in trouble with electrical faults. Ironic that electrical gremlins should still strike after 50 versions of a 24-hour race which was originally arranged ostensibly to promote improvements to electrical systems and lighting. One car which had to retire with electrical faults was the Surer/Ludwig Ford C.100. Then within the hour, the sister car of Winkelhock /Niedzwiedz stopped on the track with engine failure. Before midnight, both Fords had retired, and one major challenge to Porsche supremacy had vanished. Meanwhile the Rondeaus were not faring much better; the three works cars had all retired by half-time, as had one of the privately-entered cars of this make.

After the retirements of the Fords and Rondeaus it must be admitted that some of the interest went out of the race as it seemed there was very little left by the way of competition for the Porsche team which was still intact. Ickx and Bell were leading, followed by Mass and Schuppan, with Martin/Wollek/Martin in the 936 in third place while the Haywood/Holbert/Barth 956 was fifth. In fourth place was the surviving Nimrod which despite its lack of straight line speed had steadily gained place by place on the lap chart due to its impressive regularity and reliability. But the rate of attrition meant that after the first twelve hours there were only 31 cars left in the race. Other retirements by this time included one of the Lancia-Martinis, and both the WM-Peugeots.

The Nimrod held on to its fourth place for some hours early on Sunday morning but with minor problems developing (brake discs, fuel pressure and finally oil consumption) it dropped back down the scoreboard, while fourth place was taken by a Ferrari Boxer, and several Porsche 935s were coming steadily up from behind as if ready to pounce should the leaders fail. At one stage the Haywood/Holbert/Barth Porsche dropped as low as ninth place after a door had blown off and a wheel bearing failed, but the car got under way again and had soon rejoined its team mates among the leaders. The Porsche team now showed their mastery of organisation by deliberately keeping speeds as low down as possible, saying ahead of any potential threat by a sufficient margin but not running the cars any faster than they had to. The performance of the team was in a way reminiscent of the Mercedes-Benz and Auto-Union Grand Prix teams of 45 years before, such was the effortless mastery with which Porsche by now held the race in their grasp though it would be wrong to assume that their control of the situation relied on disciplinary measures in the tradition of Rennleiter Neubauer, instead Porsche's performance must be ascribed to the utter professionalism with which they go racing. But in Derek Bell's quoted remark, 'It's just not very exciting is it?', perhaps one can detect a hint of regret.

It very nearly did get exciting though when Jacky Ickx had a puncture mid-morning but fortunately it happened at the Virage Ford immediately before the pits so he was able to drive straight home, instead of having to nurse the car round the entire circuit. And in the final two hours of the race, the Porsche works team went into formation establishing a 1-2-3 lead, in numerical order of starting numbers - with car number 4 in fourth place. As a demonstration of their supremacy it was effective, and Le Mans has not seen anything like it since the Ford 1-2-3 victory in 1966 but it was perhaps just a little bit naughty of Porsche. In fact with an hour to go the first six places were occupied by Porsches, and there were reasons for hoping that Stuttgart might equal Modena's all-time record from 1963 when the first six cars home were Ferraris. Alas, this achievement eluded the German make - within the last hour the Martin/Wollek/Martin Porsche 936 C blew its engine.

But the three works entered 956s crossed the line in 1-2-3 formation - or rather would have done so had not the crowds invaded the track as 4 pm approached on Sunday afternoon, when the marshals and the police finally abandon their twenty-four hour vigilance and permit themselves to be swept aside before the torrent of enthusiastic creators. This is something which happens at Le Mans every year but in 1982 it is perhaps a bit sooner than in the past and it is doubtful how many cars did in fact cross the actual finishing line! Ickx and Bell repeated their victories of 1981, and 1975, and Ickx's position in the record books became even more impregnable with six wins altogether; while for Porsche, it was their seventh victory. The winning distance was 3,044.140 miles at an average of 126.839 miles not of course anywhere near the 1971 records but with the exception of 1978 the fastest Le Mans of recent years. Jochen Mass and Vern Schuppan followed in second place, with Haywood, Holbert and Barth in third place. Fitzpatrick and Hobbs in a Porsche 935 were fourth and won the GTX class, while a similar car was fifth: so it was sixth place before another make featured - a Ferrari Boxer.

The Nimrod Aston Martin was seventh despite its troubles in the later stages of the race - to the delight of Victor Gauntlett (who immediately announced his intention to come back to Le Mans in 1983, 'God and cheque book willing') as well as the thousands of British spectators. The Nimrod also gained the award traditionally presented by Motor magazine to the best-placed British car. Cooper/Smith/Bourgognie's Group 5 - winning Porsche 935 followed, another Ferrari Boxer was ninth and the highest-placed of the surviving Rondeaus tenth. A Porsche 935 was eleventh, and a Lancia Monte Carlo twelfth, while the single Group 4 car, the Porsche 934 of Cleare, Dron and Jones finished thirteenth and automatically won its class. It was followed by one of the Mazdas, the second surviving Rondeau and in sixteenth place, the GT-class winning Porsche 924 GTR of Busby and Bundy. The two last cars home were a Chevrolet Camaro and a BMW M1 the other Chevrolet Camaro finished but had been going so slowly, with a race average of little more than 50 mph, that it did not classify.

Apart from filling the first five places, Porsche therefore won every single class or category, equalling their achievements in 1970 and 1971. The Porsche team was the only Group C team to finish intact only three other Group C cars did finish, the Nimrod and two Rondeaus, a fact not lost on commentators. This was perhaps to be expected, in the first year of a new formula with new and untried designs throughout; yet the Porsche 956 was as new as the rest, and it was remarkable that the vast majority of Ford-Cosworth engined cars should fall by the wayside. It is perhaps in the final analysis difficult to pinpoint any individual reason for Porsche's win in the 1982 race; though one is tempted to mention the fact that the competition was just not good enough, this is unfair to Porsche which would have stood an equally good chance of winning against much stronger opposition. The speed and reliability of the 956, coupled with the efficiency of the team organisation and the race planning, and the rare ability and experience of drivers such as Ickx and Bell - these factors all played their part.

C for change

Sports car racing has been in the doldrums. Now, with the classic 24 hour endurance race at Le Mans only a week away, prospects for this form of racing look better than they have for a long time. Nigel Fryatt looks at Group C endurance racing and explains the reasons for the optimism

GROUP C got off to a bad start. The first two rounds of the 1982 World Endurance Championship, at Brands Hatch and Mugello, had to be postponed. The rebirth of sports car racing, much heralded as the likely result of the new regulations, looked to be faltering. But when the flag drops for the Le Mans 24 hour classic next weekend, that situation will probably have resolved itself. With an entry list comprising of 39 Group C cars, the future of world endurance racing looks far more promising. But Le Mans has in the past been something of an enigma, an event that has somehow always managed to rise above the regulations and stage a race that teams wanted to enter and people wanted to watch, even when the sport itself was at a very low ebb. So, what is different this year? What are the prospects of the new formula?

The crux of the new Group C regulations is their ambitious attempt to entice the manufacturers back into sports car racing with fully-fledged "works"

teams. To this end, the regulations stipulate that there will be no limitation on engine size, configuration or make of engine — only that it is homologated. The equivalence factor for all the teams is controlled purely through fuel consumption. It is thought that dictating a certain fuel consumption will enforce a limitation of power, and produce closely matched cars. Fuel consumption is also a good "selling point" for the formula. With the 1980s being a very fuel-conscious era, it is good for the sport to be seen to follow that trend.

All Group C cars, therefore, carry 100 litre fuel tanks (22 gallons) and the fuel stops throughout a race are carefully monitored; in a six hour/1000 km race only five are allowed; for the 24 hours of Le Mans, 25 stops are permissable. The weight of the cars must not exceed 800kgs without fuel, the maximum rim width of the wheels must not exceed 16in. and in keeping with the policy of these being sports cars, each must have two seats.

The governing body of the sport was very slow in releasing exact details of the new rules, despite the enthusiasm of its president, M. Balestre. At the 1981 Le Mans he talked spiritedly about the "new world championship". But manufacturers could not build cars on enthusiasm; they needed to know and understand the rules and regulations. At the latter half of last year, a number of manufacturers tried to anticipate the new rules and built cars accordingly. The result brought one unfortunate consequence: BMW officially withdrew from long distance racing when the regulations were finally published. The Lola T600 was also built in anticipation of the new rules, but it did not comply with the regulations and constructor Eric Broadley has had to build a very different car, the T610, for this year's championship.

The delay in the regulations explains the postponement of the first two rounds of the 1982 championship. Teams were just not ready. For many, therefore,

next week's Le Mans really represents the start of the new era.

Probably *the* most important new recruit to Group C is Ford. Any success that Ford can achieve with their C100 is sure to make other manufacturers think more closely about the championship.

The Ford C100 first raced at the Flying Tigers 1000 at Brands Hatch at the end of last year. Complying with the then Group 6 regulations, it looked neat and tidy, won the pole — against admittedly limited opposition — and then led the race until forced to retire with gearbox problems. An inauspicious start, perhaps, but then everyone was waiting for 1982 and the start of Group C racing proper. The first round, at Monza in April, was really a disaster for Ford. The Len Bailey-designed C100 was overweight and uncompetitive. Drastic changes were called for, and they came in the form of Erich Zakowski and Tony Southgate. The plan had always been for the Cologne-based Zakspeed opera-

For sports car racing to return to its former prominence it needs the major manufacturers to return; it needs works cars like the Ford C100 (top) and the Porsche 956 (left)

C for change

tion to run the C100 programme, but even Erich Zakowski's determination to suceed was obviously not going to be enough. Ironically it was the FISA/FOCA dispute in formula 1 at Imola that came to Ford's rescue. The withdrawal of the FOCA teams from the San Marino GP meant that Arrows' designer Tony Southgate was free to work on the C100. Southgate's progress with the Ford C100 was shown at the Pace Six hours at Silverstone last month. The car, now with a honeycomb moncoque, revised rear suspension and steering geometry, was transformed from the machine that ran at Monza. No less than 40kg in weight had been shed, the car's performance now matching its looks.

Silverstone also saw the debut of the Group C Porsche 956. Porsche, the stalwarts of sports car racing while the formula was in the doldrums, are taking the new formula very seriously in-

Above: Showing a lot of promise: the Lola T610

deed. The 956 is the first true monocoque to come out of the Weisach racing department after many years of space-frame chassis design. The fuel consumption problem that so disappointed Porsche's drivers Jacky Ickx and Derek Bell at Silverstone is likely to be much improved for Le Mans. Five stops in six hours did not suit the flat six 2.6 litre turbocharged engine; 25 stops in 24 hours should suit it better. But even with the fuel restriction that forced the drivers to use only 4th and 5th gears, all the other Group C contenders will not need reminding that the Porsche 956 won the class and was beaten only by a Group 6 Lancia. The Rothmans-backed cars in the experienced hands of Ickx, Bell, Vern Schuppon and Jochen Mass, must start Le Mans as favourite.

Below: Turbocharged V6 Peugeot power from the French WM

ments.

The Lola T610 had a number of problems at Silverstone, but Eric Broadley's new car showed a lot of promise in this, its first appearance (it was disqualified at Monza). The Lola team is this year being run by ex-Williams' man Jeff Hazell, and before Le Mans the car is due to be tested in the Williams Grand Prix Engineering wind tunnel to improve its aerodynamics. Lola are an experienced team and they will have learnt a lot from last year's Le Mans and with the Guy Edwards-Rupert Keegan driver pairing, must be looking forward to this year's event with confidence.

The Cosworth DFL's problem may not be fuel consumption but vibration. The Swiss Sauber team have found that engine vibration broke engine mounts and damaged ancillaries like oil tanks and radiators. The Sauber SHS C6 is almost universally thought to be the best looking Group C car, but so far it is proving to be fast but fragile. For the Nürburgring 1000 kms one of the BSAF Saubers ran with a modified rear end — the Cosworth DFL is normally used as a stressed member for the chassis — in an attempt to cure the severe vibration. If it is decided that this is a better solution, both cars will be thus modified for Le Mans.

The French Rondeau team are proving to be much more than just Le Mans specialists. Monza this year was their first sortee away from Le Mans — and they

took first place. At Silverstone they tried out their new "wing car", the M482C, but it suffered a long list of new car problems. They have decided there is not enough time for development of the new car before Le Mans, but the team will race the Monza-winning "old" interim M382C. They, too, suffered vibration problems at Silverstone, but the professional team, again sponsored by Otis lifts and run by Englishman Keith Greene will be confident of success.

Group C's other important "catch" has been Aston Martin. The Nimrod team, started by the very British and the very enthu-

Two Group C newcomers seen at the Nürburgring 1000 kms. Above left: the Cougar C-01 lasted only one lap. Above: the German BMW-powered URD suffered a nasty accident in the hands of Harald Grohs and is not entered for Le Mans

Left: Built by Ian Dawson's GRID company — who used to run Hector Rebaque's formula 1 team — the Geoff Aldridge-designed GRID-Plaza is most distinctive

For the first time Jean Rondeau has been competing for honours outside Le Mans — and has had success with the "old" M382C car (below left). The new "wing car", the M482C (below) although striking, still needs development. Rondeau at present lead the manufacturers' championship.

siastic Victor Gauntlet and Aston Martin concessionaire Robin Hamilton, is exactly what Group C needs if it is to be a success. The Nimrod monocoque design was built for Robin Hamilton by Eric Broadley at Lola Cars, Huntingdon. Powered by a fuel-injected 5.3 litre Aston Martin V8 engine, Silverstone proved to be a good shakedown test. The "works" car ran for four of the six hours while a "private" entry by Viscount Downes and backed by Pace Petroleum, finished sixth. A little overweight, and lacking in straight-line speed, the Nimrod will be an important attraction, although they will need the gods very much on their side to realise their dream of winning Le Mans at the first attempt.

Another engine configuration essential to this new brand of sports racing car is the turbo-

charged V6 WM-Peugeot. A very individual design and very fast in a straight-line, the P82 looked distinctly out of sorts at Silverstone. It is to be hoped that the PSA board will see the possibilities of the WM-Peugeot and give the Gerald Weltier and Michel Meunir team more support. Group C needs these different cars.

There will be many other new machines for the 24 hour classic; longtime Le Mans competitor, Yves Courage, will drive his own Cougar C-01; two American Mirage M12s, one for Mario and Mike Andretti, one for Rick Mears; and notably there will be four March 82Gs, each powered by 5.7 litre Chevrolet V8s.

Le Mans will thus be a very big test for Group C. Le Mans itself seems to be big enough to survive on its own, but a good showing by the new cars will establish the new sports car championship's creditability and possibly entice other manufacturers into the series (Ferrari are said to be preparing a Group C car for 1983). There is still a long way to go before this form of racing reaches the prominance of the Golden Era of the 1950s when factory entries from Alfa Romeo, Aston Martin, Ferrari, Jaguar, Maserati and Mercedes-Benz held the limelight, but the signs are that it is getting off to a good, if stuttering, beginning. The C in Group C obviously stands for change; racing as a whole needs that change to be for the better. □

The fuel consumption equation has led the majority of teams to choose the evergreen Ford-Cosworth engine. In various forms, the "basic" 3.0 litre, the 3.3 litre or the 3.9 litre it is well able to meet the consumption require-

C:The details

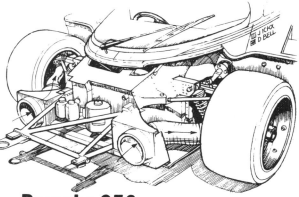

Porsche 956

Straightforward aluminium monocoque, with front bodywork supporting framework and brake cooling air pipes exposed. Turbochargers (hidden) pump air to intercoolers, then to each bank of inlet ram pipes. Engine is inclined upwards towards the rear to obtain maximum possible ground-to-underbody venturi effect

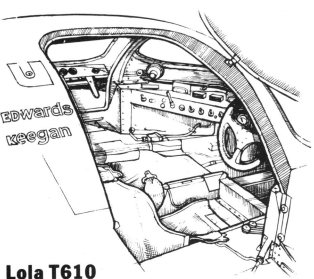

Sauber SHS C-6

Aircraft-like centre body section should maintain airflow to rear body and wing very efficiently. Upswept rear underside is beautifully clean

Lola T610

Group C regulations dictate at least a tolerable degree of cockpit space. Note relatively upright seating position

Drawings by Dick Ellis

Ford C100

Front end features twin cooling air pipes. Suspension is inboard with anti-roll bar working directly from top rocker arms. Rear rocker arms are attached (formula 1-like) to framework mounted on gearbox. Cooling for 3.9 litre Cosworth engine is via twin side mounted radiators

956: PORSCHE'S GROUP C WEAPON

Porsche take Group C very seriously. And the 956 is the first of a new generation of challengers. Paul Frère reports

THE 956 really starts a new generation of racing Porsches. Apart from the engine, which is almost identical with the 911-based 2.65-litre unit which won at Le Mans last year, virtually nothing has been retained from previous Porsche racing models. It is also the first-ever racing Porsche using a monocoque structure instead of the more usual tubular space frame which, in the last 12 years, was made of aluminium, except for three made in magnesium. And it is the first-ever Porsche designed as a ground effect car, this being the very reason why the tubular frame has been abandoned — very reluctantly, says Porsche's development boss Helmuth Bott, ''because building a tubular frame is so much easier than making a monocoque from sandwich material''.

The monocoque construction was used because it seemed too difficult to shape a ground effect car around a tubular space frame, and when I asked why Porsche had opted for aluminium sandwich panels, bonded and riveted together, rather than for a carbon fibre shell, the answer was that the Group C

rules effectively (if not specifically) exclude that sort of material because of the footwell safety regulations: a point for the FISA Technical Commission to watch, as this was certainly not its intention.

Open cars are not excluded from Group C, but the windscreen regulations are such that low drag virtually imposes a closed body, and the Porsche is no exception. Externally, it looks very much like a long-tail 917, but the central part of the front edge is raised to allow some air underneath the car and the bottom is quite different. Ahead of the driver's seat, the bottom of the monocoque is shaped to create some ground effect-induced downforce and on both sides of the central monocoque structure, the bottom of the car features inverted wells which become higher towards the rear of the body. How much depression can be created without using skirts is up to conjecture, but wind tunnel tests have indicated that with the aid of the large rear wing, the down force obtained for a drag coefficient of between 0.35 and 0.40 is noticeably higher than in the

936, and this is confirmed by the drivers who, first time out with the new car on the Paul Ricard circuit, lapped faster than any Porsche had before. Two different tail sizes will probably be used. Both are fairly long, but the longer one which uses up the maximum length of 4.80m allowed by the regulations will be used for Le Mans only. The full allowed width of 2m is also used up (with 1.5cm safety margin) in the interests of ground effect and the wheelbase of 2.65m is by far the longest ever used in any Porsche road or racing car (12 cm more than the latest 936 and 5cm longer than the 917/30 Can-Am cars, this also being a reflection on the regulations which limit the overhang in relation to the wheelbase.

The front suspension is quite straightforward and follows normal Porsche racing practice, but at the rear, the coil spring/damper units are operated by rockers and are mounted inclined, to meet their anchorage points above the gearbox, on a cross member of the rear tubular subframe carrying the entire power unit. This subframe is bolted to the monocoque structure which ends behind of the 100 litre fuel tank located between the cockpit and the engine compartment. The rear suspension itself is by transverse wishbones of which the lower ones are very flat to avoid disturbing the air flowing through the side channels, while the upper ones are located above the wells. The twin caliper brakes are outboard, inside the wheels, and Porsche's usual big titanium drive shafts have been replaced with high tensile steel shafts of much smaller diameter, to reduce air flow disturbance.

The side pods contain, arranged fairly symmetrically, the water radiators cooling the cylinder heads on either

side of the engine, the oil radiators and the intercoolers which are combined air/air and air/water units, the combination of air and water intercooling also being a novelty for Porsche, inspired from Renault. The two turbochargers are also located in the pods, out of the ground effect creating air stream.

The 600 bhp, 2.65 litre flat-six engine with air-cooled cylinders and water-cooled four-valve heads is virtually unchanged from last year's 936 and features Kugelfischer plunger pump fuel injection with an additional electronic control reducing the fuel output as the volumetric efficiency of the engine decreases with increasing rotational speed, this and a slight increase of the compression ratio to 7.0:1 being the main contributions to reducing the fuel consumption to the levels required by the Group C regulations. The belt-driven air cooling fan is mounted vertically and looks every bit like the production 911 part, but it is smaller, as it has only the cylinders, not the heads to cool. After it has done its job, the air escapes through louvres, cut far back in the central part of the car's bottom, so as not to fill the down force creating vacuum.

While the engine is almost old hat, a completely new gearbox had to be designed to replace last year's makeshift solution of bolting the beefy ''Can-Am'' four-speed gearbox to the 2.65 litre engine. For long distance racing, when it is limited to 8,500 rpm, the Porsche engine has a useful working range of only about 3,000 rpm and five speeds are really required, specially at Le Mans when the spread required between first gear for Mulsanne, Arnage and the Ford chicane and the long fifth required by the Hunaudières straight is too wide to be covered by four speeds only. As the

ve-speed box used in connection with he 2.1 litre engine was already the weakest part of the car, a completely new five-speed box was designed for the 956, still using Porsche-type synchromesh on all ratios.

The entire engine and gearbox unit is mounted sloping slightly forward in the car, to follow the shape of the car's bottom, dictated by air flow considerations.

When thinking of the transmission, one question immediately comes to mind: racing Porsches have been without a differential for the last ten years; will the 956 which produced more downforce than any of its predecessors be able to get away without one or not? Test runs have been made at the Paul Ricard Circuit both with solid drive and with a limited slip differential, and they seem to have been rather inconclusive.

The choice will probably depend on the particular circuits on which the car will be raced.

That, at least, was the situation when I visited Weissach in the first week of May and saw the car undergoing the routine test to which every new Porsche racing model is submitted: 1,000 kilometres on the destruction tracks of the Weissach proving ground: that ensures that no vital part of the car will break in at least 20,000 km of hard racing. The 936 has certainly proved it.

One thing is sure: Porsche take Group C very seriously. The best proof is that in this year's Le Mans race, they will concentrate on their Group C cars only — three of them — and will not run any modified production model, as they had done in the last two years. And they say, that is only part of their development programme: only next year will they seriously seek World Championship honours. . . .

Derek Bell: We have to take it easy on fuel

"It's going to be a handicap," says Bell.

Two-times Le Mans winner Derek Bell, hoping for a second consecutive 24-hour win alongside Jacky Ickx, is less concerned about the newness of the Porsche 956 than he is about its appetite for fuel. "We are going to have to be very careful at Le Mans, like everyone else," he says. "I don't expect the situation to be as bad as it was at Silverstone, but it's still going to be a handicap. The Porsche engineers have calculated that we will probably have to stop for fuel once every 45 minutes and with the new restrictions on the rate at which the tanks can be filled, it looks as though each stop will take around two minutes.

"When you add the time it takes to slow down and then get back on to the track that is going to lose us at least three minutes for each stop, maybe four. Personally, while I understand the need to stop anyone from bringing along a Chevvy-engined gas-guzzler, it's no way to go racing — to be running low revs and keeping in a high gear."

Bell is, understandably, much more en-

thusiastic about the work which has gone into the new car. "The only common point with the 936 tube-frame cars from last year is the engine" he points out. "Although this is the first monocoque that Porsche have ever built, and even the gearbox is new, there have been no serious problems in testing. We found at first that the engine intercoolers were not getting enough air flow so some ducts have been added. Perhaps the most impressive aspect of the project is that the Porsche insisted on running 1,000 Kms over the special bumpy section of the Weissach test track even though ten minutes of that at a time is enough for anyone, Herr Bott insists that there's nothing more important than safety . . . For a driver that's very reassuring."

There will be a long-tail body for Le Mans designed to generate less aerodynamic downforce in the interests of higher top speed. There is talk of 235 mph at Le Mans, which is 10 mph slower than Bell was doing at the Sarthe circuit ten years ago with a Porsche 917. Even so, he

The 956 will probably have to stop for fuel once every 45 minutes.

anticipates that the top speed will be appreciably less than would be possible with a flat-bottom car. To his relief, while the suspension has to be stiff enough to restrict the body movement which would upset the aerodynamics, the Porsche is much more comfortable to drive than the current breed of Formula 1 cars.

"At one stage Jacky was talking about having a third driver as a relief for Le Mans. I am glad to say that we have since decided that won't be necessary. Despite everything — the car's newness, the fuel consumption and so forth — I am feeling very confident that we can give the new Group C opposition a good run for its money."

MIKE DOODSON

Derek Bell took the flag in the winning Porsche 956-001 that he shared with Jacky Ickx to win Porsche's seventh Le Mans.

The Organisation

Ickx/Bell win again — Jacky's sixth, Derek's third — Works Porsches finish one-two-three — Rival Group C teams fail — British wins in four classes — Only 18 finishers — A largely processional Le Mans — Entry & Qualifying: QUENTIN SPURRING — Race: MARK HUGHES — Photography: JEFF BLOXHAM.

3.56 Saturday afternoon and it's all about to begin.

The Automobile Club de l'Ouest wanted something special to mark its 50th Le Mans 24 Hours race, and the club got it in the form of an amazing sixth victory by Jacky Ickx, the great driver who announced his retirement 2½ years ago. Last Sunday, the vast crowd also witnessed Derek Bell's third Le Mans win, and an outstanding one-two-three by the factory entered Group C Rothmans-Porsches.

Like the Ickx/Bell triumph last year, the victory was almost perfect, tarnished only by a puncture. The sister cars of Vern Schuppan/Jochen Mass and Hurley Haywood/Al Holbert/Jurgen Barth were briefly delayed, but no challenger remained to stop the trio of works Porsches from finishing the race in an impressive, humiliating line-astern.

Porsche System might have been struggling had the race been run at a fast pace, still marginal on fuel economy, but the anticipated rivalry from Ford, Rondeau and Lancia disappeared before half-distance. In a race of unusual attrition, which only 18 cars finished, there were no survivors either from Lola, Sauber, WM, March and the other C-car teams. IMSA GTX category Porsches backed up the works 956 cars with the next two places, with John Fitzpatrick/David Hobbs fourth overall.

It was a good 24 Hours for British drivers, who won four of the five classes which were represented at the end. Apart from Bell, Fitzpatrick and Hobbs, the class winners were John Cooper and Paul Smith (sharing their Porsche 935 with Claude Bourgoignie), who achieved a second successive Group 5 victory for Charles Ivey Racing, and Richard Cleare/Tony Dron/Richard Jones, the Group 4 winners with their Porsche 934. In fact, every category was won by a Porsche, for Jim Busby/Doc Bundy won IMSA GT with their 924 Carrera GTR. This was the first class victory for many years by a car fitted with road car tyres, the latest High-Tec radials from BF Goodrich.

In contrast with last year, there were few serious incidents, although a Porsche 935 was destroyed during qualifing, and the works Nimrod Aston Martin was wrecked after a rear end failure on the Mulsanne Straight. But there was good news for Nimrod, too: Viscount Downe's privately entered Pace entry claimed seventh position overall and was the best-placed stockblock Group C car.

Two of the private Rondeaus survived, protecting the French marque's World Endurance Championship lead, although Porsche are now challenging strongly.

NOTES ON THE CARS

Porsche

"For this year, Le Mans is our priority, not the World Championship." Porsche's competitions manager, Peter Falk, has been saying that for some months. Not until Le Mans week, though, did the full meaning really sink in. Porsche System have been accused of over-engineering their Group C cars. A moot point: but the fact remains that this is a superb motor racing team.

After its shakedown race at Silverstone, Rothmans-Porsche 956-001 completed a 24-hour Le Mans simulation test on the rolling road at Weissach so that the lessons learned could be incorporated into three sister cars. It then ran extended sessions at Paul Ricard to develop new bodywork front and rear, designed to reduce the ground-effect and therefore to improve straightline speed and fuel consumption. The engine was revised to take fuel injection systems further honed by the Bosch engineers. For qualifying, the 2.65-litre, twin-turbo flat-sixes were set at 1.2 bar boost pressure, producing 630bhp; for the race, a boost of 1.1 bar gave about 590bhp. The drivers had the benefit of a constant digital read out of petrol consumption, the cockpit gauge calibrated in litres per hour.

The immaculate professionalism of the factory Porsche team was, however, tarnished by the certainty that monocoque 956 cars would again be marginal on fuel during a fast Le Mans 24 Hours, and by the fact that all three of the new machines were still about 60 kilos overweight.

The purposeful works cars were backed by the Jöst-built Porsche 936C. The car, sponsored as usual by Belga cigarettes and Texas Instruments, was fitted here with the latest power plant to emerge from Reinhold's Absteinach factory, a flat-six of 2517cc, with two-valve cylinder heads and driving through a four-speed gearbox. The Martin brothers' team had also fitted longer rear bodywork and a revised nose section and, having discarded the 2.1-litre 936 engine in favour of this lower revving 2½, was looking for better fuel consumption and reliability. The tubular frame chassis needed substantial repairs after the 'Ring accident, and the car was still about 80 kilos (or 10%) overweight.

The Jöst-Porsche 936C is considered to be simply a Porsche for the purposes of the Makes Championship points. I wonder if the same will be the case for the new Kremer 'C82', which is now officially called the C-K5. Like the Jöst built car, the Kremer is a logical development of the familiar Porsche tubular frame sports-racing car, an all-enclosed flat-bottom coupé. The Cologne built C-K5, featuring a distinctive high 'spine' along the top of the rear body section and four 'snorkels' feeding cooling air into the engine compartment, was powered by a 2.8 Porsche 935 twin-turbo, and weighed almost precisely the same as the Jöst car at 877 kilos. Just like last year, the Kremer brothers had to rush to finish their Le Mans entry, and the car came to Le Mans untested.

These five represented Porsche's total Group C involvement, but it is easy to mistake Bob Akin's new 935 for a C-car at first glance. It does retain the roofline, door frame and rear window of the road car 911, but this is perhaps the most far-out variation yet on the IMSA GTX theme. It was designed by Akin's Atlanta team, the chassis was made in Georgia by Chuck Gaa, and Tony Cicale acted as design consultant on the aerodynamics. As well as Akin's own Hudson Wire livery, the red car carried the colours of his Red Lobster backed co-drivers. The team ran a 3.2 in qualifying, but the race engine started life as a 2.8, short-stroked by the Akin team to 2670cc, giving about 630bhp and good fuel consumption.

Vying with the Akin car for individuality was John Fitzpatrick Racing's latest acquisition, another Jöst built replica of the 'Moby Dick' Porsche 935-78. A spaceframe design, the Fitzpatrick car weighed in at 945 kilos, or almost 190 less than the monocoque Akin machine. Similar to Gianpiero Moretti's

The Fitzpatrick/Hobbs Porsche 935 struggled round on five cylinders to finish fourth.

replica, Fitz's was completed only just in time for scrutineering, and was sponsored here by John's regular Californian backer, J. David Dominelli, who runs a San Diego investment company. A 2.8-litre flat-six was again used for the first practice session before the Tim Schenken managed team switched to its race motor, one of Jöst's 2.6 units which differ from the works 956 power plants in that they have two-valve, rather than four-valve, cylinder heads. The other GTX Porsches were the old-stager K3 cars of the rival American teams run by Bob Garretson and Ralph Kent-Cooke, both running a 3.2 for qualifying and a 2.8 for the race. The Garretson car was backed by BP and Hertz, and the Cooke 935 by BP and Malardeau.

Only four Porsche 935s ran in Group 5, including the blue K3 of last year's category winners, Charles Ivey Racing, which featured additional sponsorship here from the weekend magazine *VSD*. The others were the 'works' Kremer K3-81 and Claude Haldi's K3, backed by Longines and UFO jeans, and Dieter Schornstein's Jöst built machine.

Richard Cleare gained a Le Mans entry with his rejuvenated Porsche 934, which picked up additional backing from Canon Cameras when it looked as though the company's regular billboard might not get a run. Richard Lloyd's IMSA GTO Porsche 924 GTR looked set for a good performance here thanks to its light weight (952 kilos) and slippery body shape, a much more competitive proposition than the two relatively standard 924 GTR cars entered by the American BF Goodrich tyre company.

Although fitted with a 3.3 engine, Raymond Touraul's virtually standard Porsche 911 Turbo was slow, another indication that no Group B car yet exists which can be a realistic Le Mans contender.

Ford

As expected, the Ford Motor Company, represented here once more by Zakspeed, ranged only two of the C100 cars against the Porsche factory team's C-cars. The Ludwig/Surer entry was an entirely new car, with minor body differences from the Silverstone/Nürburgring machine driven by Winkelhock/Niedzwiedz.

Apart from bodywork tuning, the cars running 'flatter' here, no major changes have been carried out, and no effort has been made to save weight, both the C100s still being around 70 kilos over the top. Contrary to rumour, Erich Zakowski used his 3.9 Cosworth DFL engines for both qualifying and the race.

Rondeau

Having run out of race-development time with the troublesome new M482C wing car, the Keith Greene managed Jean Rondeau team based its works effort on three of the flat-bottom interim M382C cars. Both the Otis lifts sponsored 382s driven by Pescarolo/Ragnotti and Jaussaud/Rondeau were completely new cars, hurriedly completed for Le Mans, and featuring the tall rear suspension and brakes from the 482 and the longer, lighter bodywork. The Spice/Migault/Lapeyre car, sponsored by Malardeau and *France Soir*, was the Monza winner, the car which has been run by the Champagné team all season and which put the marque into the lead of the Makes table before this race. All were fitted with 3.9 Ford DFL engines.

The works team was also assisting the privateer operation of Pierre Yver, running a 3-litre DFV in his Primagaz sponsored 382. Two more 382s were fielded by Jacky Haran (joined by Hertz and Air Florida backed Irishman Vivian Candy) and Christian Bussi, whose familiar car was repainted to promote a variety of new sponsors. Haran's was another 3-litre, but Bussi now had a 3.3.

Lola

For the first time, there were two of the new T610 cars. The Jeff Hazell managed factory team had continued to make effective improvements to its original chassis, sponsored here by Hawaiian Tropic as well as by Ultramar, *Newsweek* and Ventaire. A session in the Williams wind-tunnel at Didcot resulted in a number of aerodynamic changes, among them a completely new frontal treatment, the adjustable nose wing between the twin booms at the nose now replaced by a wide, flat panel. The team also continues to improve the brakes. Nick Faure was engaged as reserve driver.

Although its new car does not feature the frontal revisions, the Cooke Racing team has had the benefit of over three months of works development for its 610, which was built at the Huntingdon factory by the American team. There was just time to test this car at Snetterton and Donington before Le Mans. Sponsored by BP and Malardeau (like the CR team's Porsche), the yellow Lola was fitted with a brand new 3.9 DFL from Cosworth, similar to the unit in the works car.

For the first time in many years, no 2-litre Lola was in the field.

March

The Bicester team was represented by two of the new ground-effect 82G cars, due to make the type's long-awaited debut in the World Endurance Championship. The Gordon Horn managed works team fielded the car which was practised at Silverstone, sponsored here by Garvin Brown, Landmark Gil and Jensen Stereo, and fitted with a new Franz Weis 5.7-litre Chevrolet V8. Eight hours in scrutineering on the Tuesday did nothing for the morale of the hard-working March team . . .

The other March was Bob Garretson's Michelob backed 82G, which started life as an IMSA GTP entry and came to Le Mans after promising runs at Daytona and Sebring at the start of the season. The conversion to Group C rules was carried out in Bicester. For qualifying, the team ran a sprint Chevrolet V8 built by Russ Joseph, reverting to a Garretson developed 3.8 for race day. Additional backing came from Red Roof Inns.

Sauber

Both the Group C Sauber SHS C-6 cars appeared in the striped livery of BASF cassettes and featured heavily revised rear ends, evidence of the Domingos Piedade managed team's efforts to remove its persistent engine vibration problems. The Stuck C-6 had been sent to John Thompson's TC Prototypes company for chassis strengthening and a load-bearing engine subframe, and similar work (although actually slightly different in execution) had been carried out on the second car in the Peter Sauber factory in Geneva. The modifications have added about 20 kilos in weight to the Stuck machine (863 kilos) and about 10 to Walter Brun's car (855).

The vibration problems hopefully now overcome, both cars were fitted with 3.9 DFLs for qualifying, but Piedade took the precaution of fitting a 3.3 to Stuck's Sauber for the race.

Nimrod

After their strong runs at Silverstone, the two Aston Martin V8 powered Nimrods, the Robin Hamilton run works car and Viscount Downe's Pace Petroleum sponsored version, appeared at Le Mans but lightly modified. Both cars suffered badly at the hands of the scrutineers, the problem being the one which the teams foresaw, namely the heights of the windscreens. An ungainly protrusion appeared atop the screen of the works car, while the Pace team solved the problem by a smaller blimp and raised ground clearance. Although the 5.3-litre engines produce 580bhp, the Nimrod C2s are immensely heavy at about 1050 kilos.

WM

Gérard Weltier's Parisian team fielded two entirely new cars, better finished versions of

The Kremer Porsche CK5 went well on its debut race until let down by its engine.

the P82 we have seen in all the endurance races this season (and in fine new Esso livery) but to the same basic specification. The new P82 cars are significantly lighter than the original at around 825 kilos, and were expected to be competitive here. The latest version of the four-valve, twin-turbo PRV engine produces a useful 550bhp and, despite the light ground-effect built in to the 1982 WMs, very good straightline speed was anticipated.

Other C-cars

Harley Cluxton's Grand Touring Cars team managed to complete only one new Mirage M12 in time for Le Mans, the Phil Conte owned car sponsored by Pioneer hi-fi and Valvoline. The monocoque, powered by a 3.9 DFL, was designed by Howden Ganley to take ground-effect bodywork penned by John Horsman which was very reminiscent of the Lola T600, but plenty of testing Stateside (see last week's issue) had proved the car to be far better in a straight line. Power came from a 3.9 DFL.

For the first time, Ian Dawson's GRID team had a 3.9 installed in the Grid-Plaza S-1, although the big engine was used for qualifying only and the team reverted to its Alan Smith 3.3 for the race. Dawson switched from his regular Avons to Dunlops, favouring the latter's excellent Le Mans back-up and many years of experience here, even though the car is better suited to the Avon rubber. His new drivers brought additional backing from Carstensen, Levitan furniture and Hawaiian Tropic.

The Amada tools sponsored Dome RC82 came to Le Mans with a new braking system and other detail modifications, looking to be one of the best prospects for the Mulsanne Straight, despite the use of a 3.3 engine; the narrow track Dome was here to give Eliseo Salazar his first taste of 200mph plus motoring.

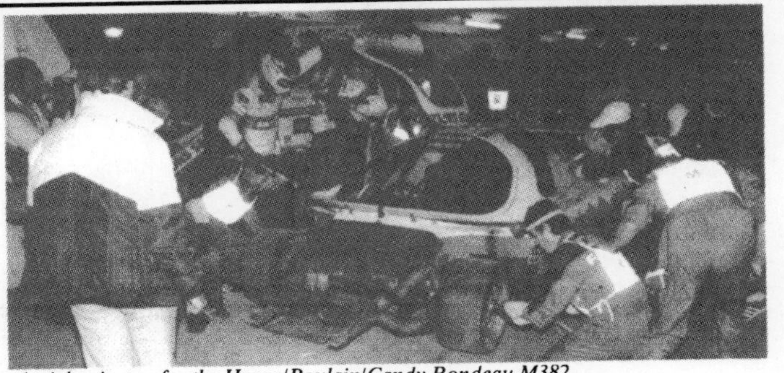

A night pit-stop for the Haran/Poulain/Candy Rondeau M382.

Yves Courage presented his nicely built Cougar C-01, backed by Primagaz. The car, now fitted with a 3.3 DFL, had successfully completed a six-hour test at the Bugatti circuit since its brief debut at the 'Ring.

One of the slots vacated by the 4-series Rondeaus was taken over by German constructor Ernst Ungar, who took the opportunity to run a works BMW-engined URD, with sponsorship from Wang and others. The car was brand new, and was powered by a 480bhp Schnitzer sprint motor for qualifying, replaced for race day by a 450bhp six from Weigel Renn Technik. Among the drivers was Michel Lateste, whose new March could not be completed in time.

François Duret's DRA entered, ADA built 'De Cadenet Lola' was equipped with better brakes and a revised frontal treatment in an effort to find more speed, with an adjustable central wing. At the last minute the John Goaté managed team received an offer of sponsorship from the local radio station Radio-Fil.

The ACC had no reason to be disappointed that only 29 C-cars arrived of the 35 which were originally entered.

Others

As ever, the Group C teams came to Le Mans looking over their shoulders for Lancia Martini, and anxious to know just how fast the Group 6 *barchettas* would go down the straight. On the weighbridge, the Lancias both indicated a little more than 700 kilos in Le Mans trim. Cesare Fiorio fielded only two of the open cars, fitted with long bodywork and, for the race, with low boost 24-hour 1.4 turbos. He did not leave in Turin, however, his qualifying motors . . .

The only other 2-litre G6 entry was Martin Birrane's Frox Clothing backed Chevron B36B.

Tony Garcia entered his untidy G4-type BMW M1 in the one-off IMSA GT class, and there were two G5-type BMWs, Roger Ennequin's wide-bodied car and Steve O'Rourke's Michael Cane Racing prepared machine, backed by EMKA Productions, Olympus and Crockford's, and running as a GTX entry.

Billy Hagan returned to Le Mans to show us the longevity of the Chevrolet Camaro, with two Dennis Frings built tubular frame cars. He was down to drive a new car, raced only at Daytona earlier this year, and powered by a 5.4-litre aluminium-head engine tuned for this race to provide about 575bhp to propel its 1109 kilos. The second Sea-Land Stratagraph entry was the car Yarborough drove last year, with a 5.8 power plant; this weighed 1142 kilos, on a par with a Porsche 935.

Tom Walkinshaw Racing was here again with a pair of GTX Mazdas, these the latest 254 cars with 320bhp rotaries. Each was based on a road shell, weighing about 970 kilos, and sponsorship came from Nikon.

Late entries were Team Vesuvio's ex-works 1.4 Group 5 Lancia Montecarlos, and the 58-car field was completed by the pleasingly inevitable Ferrari Boxers. Four of these beautiful cars arrived, variously modified and all superbly presented — particularly the US entered Prancing Horse Farm machine, the one driven by Pierre Dieudonné. Would-be Mirage driver John Morton got a run in the NART entry along with John Paul Snr, who was originally to have driven Preston Henn's T-bird Swapshop entry. The French importer Charles Pozzi entered a fourth Ferrari, in blue and sponsored by Pioneer.

Pos	No	Car	Engine	Class	Tyres	Drivers (Nat)				
1	1	Porsche 956	2.6 Porsche tc	GC	Dunlop	Jacky Ickx (B)	Derek Bell (GB)		**3:28.40**	3:37.77
2	2	Porsche 956	2.6 Porsche tc	GC	Dunlop	Jochen Mass (D)	Vern Schuppan (AUS)		**3:29.32**	3:37.91
3	4	Porsche 936C	2.5 Porsche tc	GC	Dunlop	Bob Wollek (F)	Philippe Martin (B)	Jean-Michel Martin (B)	3:38.96	**3:30.67**
4	51	Lancia Martini	1.4 Lancia tc	G6	Pirelli	Michele Alboreto (I)	Rolf Stommelen (D)	Teo Fabi (I)	3:43.42	**3:31.42**
5	50	Lancia Martini	1.4 Lancia tc	G6	Pirelli	Piercarlo Ghinzani (I)	Hans Heyer (D)	Riccardo Patrese (I)	**3:31.78**	6:02.53
6	6	Ford C100	3.9 Ford DFL	GC	Goodyear	Klaus Ludwig (D)	Marc Surer (CH)	Manfred Winkelhock (D)	3:38.16	**3:32.50**
7	20	Sauber SHS/C6	3.9 Ford DFL	GC	Dunlop	Hans-Joachim Stuck (D)	Jean-Louis Schlesser (F)	Dieter Quester (D)	3:36.18	**3:33.25**
8	5	Kremer C82	2.8 Porsche tc	GC	Goodyear	Danny Ongais (USA)	Dale Whittington (USA)	Ted Field (USA)	3:43.97	**3:37.01**
9	27	Mirage M12	3.9 Ford DFL	GC	Goodyear	Mario Andretti (USA)	Michael Andretti (USA)		3:41.79	**3:37.09**
10	16	Lola T610	3.9 Ford DFL	GC	Goodyear	Guy Edwards (GB)	Rupert Keegan (GB)	*Nick Faure (GB)*	**3:37.60**	3:41.12
11	7	Ford C100	3.9 Ford DFL	GC	Goodyear	Klaus Niedzwiedz (D)	Manfred Winkelhock (D)	Klaus Ludwig (D)	**3:38.02**	3:38.50
12	9	WM P82	2.8 Peugeot tc	GC	Michelin	Michel Pignard (F)	Jean-Daniel Raulet (F)	Didier Theys (B)	3:45.30	**3:38.06**
13	10	WM P82	2.8 Peugeot tc	GC	Michelin	Roger Dorchy (F)	Guy Frequelin (F)	Alain Couderc (F)	**3:39.58**	3:44.04
14	3	Porsche 956	2.6 Porsche tc	GC	Dunlop	Hurley Haywood (USA)	Al Holbert (USA)	Jurgen Barth (D)	**3:39.85**	3:45.22
15	19	Sauber SHS C6	3.9 Ford DFL	GC	Dunlop	*Hans-Joachim Stuck (D)*	Sigi Muller Jnr (CH)	Walter Brun (CH)	**3:40.57**	3:46.11
16	11	Rondeau M382	3.0 Ford DFV	GC	Dunlop	Gordon Spice (GB)	François Migault (F)	Xavier Lapeyre (F)	3:40.75	**3:40.71**
17	37	Grid-Plaza S-1	3.9 Ford DFL	GC	Dunlop	Emilio de Villota (E)	Desiré Wilson (ZA)	Alain de Cadenet (GB)	3:44.52	**3:42.77**
18	17	Lola T610	3.9 Ford DFL	GC	Goodyear	Jim Adams (USA)	Brian Redman (GB)	Ralph Kent-Cooke (USA)	3:48.89	**3:43.06**
19	64	Porsche 935 K3	3.0 Porsche tc	G5	Dunlop	Edgar Doren (D)	Antonio Contreras (MEX)	Billy Sprows (USA)	4:02.43	**3:44.05**
20	36	Dome Amada RC82	3.3 Ford DFL	GC	Dunlop	Chris Craft (GB)	Eliseo Salazar (RCH)		3:52.10	**3:44.12**
21	60	Porsche 935 K3	2.8 Porsche tc	G5	Dunlop	John Cooper (GB)	Paul Smith (GB)	Claude Bourgoignie (B)	**3:44.92**	4:04.92
22	24	Rondeau M382	3.9 Ford DFL	GC	Dunlop	Jean-Pierre Jaussaud (F)	Henri Pescarolo (F)	Philippe Alliot (F)*	3:50.26	**3:46.00**
23	32	Nimrod NRA C2	5.3 Aston Martin	GC	Avon	Ray Mallock (GB)	Mike Salmon (GB)	Simon Phillips (GB)	3:52.35	**3:46.34**
24	14	March 82G	5.7 Chevrolet	GC	Goodyear	Patrick Neve (B)	Jeff Wood (USA)	Eje Elgh (S)	3:49.58	**3:47.45**
25	30	URD C81	3.5 BMW	GC	Dunlop	Michel Lateste (F)	Hubert Striebig (A)	Jacques Heudin (F)	4:11.25	**3:47.62**
26	31	Nimrod NRA C2	5.3 Aston Martin	GC	Avon	Geoff Lees (GB)	Bob Evans (GB)	Tiff Needell (GB)	3:55.33	**3:48.17**
27	79	Porsche 935 K4	2.6 Porsche tc	GTX	Goodyear	John Fitzpatrick (GB)	David Hobbs (GB)		**3:48.50**	3:48.57
28	75	Porsche 935	2.8 Porsche tc	G5	Dunlop	Claude Haldi (CH)	François Hesnault (F)	Riccardo Teran (PAN)	**3:50.64**	4:01.13
29	35	Cougar CO1	3.3 Ford DFL	GC	Dunlop	Yves Courage (F)	Jean-Philippe Grand (F)	Michel Dubois (F)	**3:51.62**	3:53.85
30	29	March 82G	5.7 Chevrolet	GC	Goodyear	Bobby Rahal (USA)	Skeeter McKitterick (USA)		4:00.64	**3:51.70**
31	76	Porsche 935	2.8 Porsche tc	GTX	Goodyear	Bob Akin (USA)	David Cowart (USA)	Kenper Miller (USA)	3:54.46	**3:52.31**
32	26	Rondeau M382	3.0 Ford DFV	GC	Avon	Vivian Candy (IRL)	Jacky Haran (F)	Hervé Poulain (F)	**3:52.36**	4:00.35
33	81	Chevrolet Camaro	5.7 Chevrolet	GT	Goodyear	Gene Felton (USA)	Billy Hagan (USA)		4:07.52	**3:52.59**
34	78	Porsche 935 K3	2.8 Porsche tc	GTX	Goodyear	Dany Snobeck (F)	François Servanin (F)	René Metge (F)	**3:52.60**	3:52.90
35	25	Rondeau M382	3.0 Ford DFV	GC	Avon	Lucien Guitteny (F)	Pierre Yver (F)	Bruno Sotty (F)	3:53.49	**3:52.69**
36	38	Rondeau M382	3.0 Ford DFV	GC	Dunlop	Bernard de Dryver (B)	Christian Bussi (F)	Pascal Witmeur (B)	4:00.12	**3:52.90**
37	72	Ferrari 512BB	4.9 Ferrari	GTX	Michelin	Alain Cudini (F)	John Paul Snr (USA)	John Morton (USA)	**3:54.07**	4:03.90
38	12	Rondeau M482	3.9 Ford Cosworth DFL	GC	Dunlop	Henri Pescarolo (F)	Jean Ragnotti (F)		**3:54.81**	9:51.32
39	61	BMW M1	3.5 BMW	G5	Dunlop	Michel Gabriel (F)	Franco Gasparetti (I)	Roland Ennequin (F)	**3:55.40**	4:14.23
40	70	Ferrari 512BB	4.9 Ferrari	GTX	Michelin	Pierre Dieudonné (B)	Carson Baird (USA)	Jean-Paul Libert (B)	4:05.82	**3:56.52**
41	71	Ferrari 512BB	4.9 Ferrari	GTX	Michelin	Claude Ballot-Lena (F)	Hervé Regout (B)	*Jean-Paul Libert (B)*	3:58.02	**3:56.80**
42	86	Porsche 924 GTR	2.0 Porsche tc	GT	Goodrich	Manfred Schurti (D)	Patrick Bedard (USA)	Paul Miller (USA)	4:13.46	**3:58.65**
43	77	Porsche 935 K3	2.8 Porsche tc	GTX	Goodyear	Bob Garretson (USA)	Skeeter McKitterick (USA)	Anny-Charlotte Verney (F)...Ray Ratcliff (USA)	**3:58.84**	3:59.39
44	62	BMW M1	3.5 BMW	GTX	Dunlop	Steve O'Rourke (GB)	Richard Down (GB)	Nick Mason (GB)	**4:00.23**	4:01.70
45	39	de Cadenet Lola MM	3.0 Ford DFV	GC	Goodyear	Mike Wilds (GB)	Ian Harrower (GB)	François Duret (F)	**4:00.29**	4:00.33
46	80	Chevrolet Camaro	5.7 Chevrolet	GT	Goodyear	Dick Brooks (USA)	Herschel McGriff (USA)	Thomas Williams (USA)	4:09.54	**4:00.34**
47	66	Lancia Beta Monte Carlo	1.4 Lancia tc	G5	Goodyear	Max Cohen-Olivar (F)	Joe Castellano (I)	Jean-Marie LeMerle (F)	4:04.26	**4:02.58**
48	90	Porsche 934	3.3 Porsche tc	G4	Dunlop	Tony Dron (GB)	Richard Cleare (GB)	Richard Jones (GB)	4:11.74	**4:04.30**
49	55	Chevron B36B	2.0 Ford BDX	G6	Avon	John Sheldon (GB)	Martin Birrane (GB)	Neil Crang (GB)	4:09.22	**4:04.30**
50	82	Mazda 254	2.7 Mazda	GTX	Dunlop	Yojiro Terada (J)	Takashi Yorino (J)	Allan Moffat (AUS)	**4:04.74**	7:38.58
51	73	Ferrari 512BB	4.9 Ferrari	GTX	Goodyear	Preston Henn (USA)	Denis Morin (CH)	Randy Lanier (USA)	4:16.11	**4:07.32**
52	85	BMW M1	3.5 BMW	GT	Goodyear	Tony Garcia (USA)	Fred Stiff (USA)	Albert Naon (USA)	4:21.46	**4:10.02**
53	83	Mazda 254	2.7 Mazda	GTX	Dunlop	Chuck Nicholson (GB)	Tom Walkinshaw (GB)	*Peter Lovett (GB)*	4:18.18	**4:11.29**
54	65	Lancia Beta Monte Carlo	1.4 Lancia tc	G5	Goodyear	Bernard Salam (F)	Guilio Giudici (I)	Thierry Perrier (GB)	**4:12.79**	4:37.71
55	87	Porsche 924 GTR	2.0 Porsche tc	GT	Goodyear	Doc Bundy (USA)	Marcel Mignot (F)		**4:14.07**	43:37.92
56	95	Porsche 930	3.0 Porsche tc	GB	Michelin	Raymond Touroul (F)	Alain Gadal (F)	Jean-Yves Gadal (F)	5:06.76	**4:18.81**
57	84	Porsche 924 GTR	2.0 Porsche tc	GT	Dunlop	Richard Lloyd (GB)	Andy Rouse (GB)		**4:20.81**	5:29.17

Notes: Cars 95 and 84 did not qualify.
Drivers are listed in order of fastest qualifying times.

* Car 24 also qualified by Jean Rondeau.
Drivers in italics were not nominated to race.

QUALIFYING

As usual, the ACO laid on two four-hour qualifying sessions on the Wednesday and Thursday evenings, but a new departure was the provision of a 45-minute warm-up on race morning. The last half-hour of the second practice session was lost because of a spectacular electric storm which encircled the track for a while before unleashing a torrential downpour.

There was more than a touch of *déjà vu* about qualifying. Like last year, Jacky Ickx placed himself firmly on pole position early in the action. Like last year, a second factory Porsche joined the Ickx/Bell car at the front of the starting grid. Like last year, a Reinhold Jöst-built privately entered Porsche lined up third fastest.

Unlike last year, Ickx had no need of Dunlop's qualifying tyres to gain his pole, which was a shade over a second better than his time from 1981, set with the similarly engined flat-bottom 936-81 on soft rubber. All doubts about the Mulsanne potential of the new wing-car were quickly dispelled, and Jacky was timed at 221mph through the speed trap, the revised bodywork doing the job perfectly, and 956-001 absolutely stable. Apart from a puncture, the 'Jacky and Derek Show' ran trouble free, although there was a little concern after qualifying had ended when a check on the engine revealed a loss of compression in one cylinder. The pole was set at an average of 146.27mph.

In chassis 003, Vern Schuppan had a lurid moment on the Mulsanne Straight when a tyre blew, and the bodywork was savaged before Vern could bring the 956 to a halt. Nevertheless, Mass also took the car round under Ickx's qualifying record. The third Rothmans-Porsche, however, was plagued throughout by braking problems. The team found dirt in the master cylinder after the first session and thought that the trouble had been identified, but it persisted on Thursday, so an entirely new braking system had to be installed.

The works team never did see the need to resort to qualifying rubber and, of the leading drivers, only Bob Wollek used the soft tyres, lapping the Belga spaceframe car within 1.5 secs of Jochen's time.

Yes, the works Lancia Group 6 cars did pose a threat, even here. They qualified ahead of all the Ford powered C-cars, fourth and fifth overall, although not without the myriad little problems which seem to characterise the team's qualifying sessions.

Riccardo Patrese, delayed on a flight from Venice, arrived at the track only an hour before the end of the second session, so he only had half an hour of real opportunity with the car before the rain effectively ended activities. However, Riccardo, having qualified himself within the 125% rule with only two laps to spare stayed out in the heavy rain to run Pirelli's wet weather tyres.

His colleagues, who included Rolf Stommelen and Hans Heyer for this meeting, reaped the benefit of Pirelli's Q-tyres, which were given to the super-neat Michele Alboreto and the less smooth Piercarlo Ghinzani. At least the question was answered: the better Lancia went 201mph down Mulsanne.

The factory Ford C100s achieved a top speed of about 204mph down the straight on Wednesday, the cars achieving only 8400rpm. In the second session, the team flattened the cars and fitted longer gears, running up to 9000rpm. However, the drivers found the cars very nervous at speed, so the Zakspeed mechanics fitted

The privately-entered Nimrod Aston Martin, clearly showing the protrusion above the windscreen needed to pass scrutineering.

small 'Gurney flaps' at the rear edge of the wings. Klaus Ludwig was again the fastest Ford driver, the cars qualifying sixth and 11th, without using Q-types.

Hans Stuck qualified both the Saubers into their starting positions. His own lost some time late in the first session due to a faulty battery, and the sister car was delayed in the Thursday session with a split water pipe. A more serious worry for the team, though, was a persistent recurrance of the starter motor problem which afflicted the car at Silverstone, caused by engine vibration putting the bendix into contact with the flywheel. The team was at a loss with the problem, but hoped that the 3.3 race engine on the Stuck car would not produce the same symptoms. With the qualifying 3.9, Hans-Joachim managed 203mph down Mulsanne.

For a first-time-out car, the Kremer-Porsche C-K5 was impressive in qualifying, stable and reaching 207mph down

Mulsanne. The relatively well tested Mirage ran 212mph, and Mario Andretti qualified it only a mite slower than Danny Ongais. On Wednesday, his son Mike put the car into the mother of all spins which ended in no contact with the barriers, gyrating wildly on the fast approach to the Ford chicanes. He missed out altogether on Thursday, for a failed CV joint ended the team's practice just after his parent had set the time.

Right on the pace down the straight, but still a little disappointing in the turns, the works Lola achieved a remarkable 220mph but lined up only 10th. You might think that the ground-effect venturi had been eased off to reduce drag in achieving this speed, but there was an incident in practice which showed that this was far from the case. Indeed, so effective were the air tunnels that at one point the low pressure deformed the pre-pregnated, single-piece undertray to such an extent that it broke up, causing an

Porsche versus Ford: the crowd watch the battle that never really materialised.

alarming moment for Rupert Keegan. This apart, there was a tendency for the car to wander on the straight; aerodynamic improvements during Friday produced an improvement in straight-line stability in the race day warm-up.

The Esso WM-Peugeot cars enjoyed a circumspect and reliable practice on the whole, the faster of the two cars reaching almost 216mph down the straight. The only sign of stress was a burst oil line on the Frequelin car in the second session when, like almost all the other teams, WM were running fuel consumption testing in race trim.

But what of Rondeau? The French team came to Le Mans for the seventh time with the deserved reputation of having the most reliable cars in the game — a reputation strongly enhanced by events earlier this season. What a time for the cars to let the team down!

In qualifying, Rondeau's enclave at the bottom of the paddock was nothing less than a disaster area, with all three of the full works cars in trouble. The least afflicted was the red and blue Malardeau 382, but even this was halted out on the track on three occasions in the Thursday session, before a busted electrical master switch was diagnosed. The Pescarolo Otis entry was afflicted throughout by an incomprehensible fuel pressure problem, achieving 8500rpm at best. It was Friday evening before the team found that the engine fuel pick-up transducer was overheating.

And the second Otis 382 spent all of practice with a similar fuel difficulty. Again, it was Friday before it was found that there was an obscure installation fault with the fuel pickup on the end of the camshaft, after the car had spent almost as much time on tests on the nearby airfield runway as it did on the track. The best Mulsanne speed listed for a Rondeau, for the record, was 206mph for the Pescarolo car.

Things looked bleaker yet for triple winner Pescarolo, the 1982 Drivers series leader, when the fuel system problem on his car persisted in the race day warm-up, and Jean Rondeau ordered a new motor to be installed. The job, which normally takes up to five hours, was finished in three, just 10 mins before the deadline. The Grid-Plaza suffered the same starter motor problems as Sauber, with its 3.9, and also had a fuel feed problem, so the team had to switch to the combination mechanical/electrical pump set-up. In the second session, the team also had to set up the car again after adjustments to the wings had destroyed the aerodynamic balance.

The Cooke Racing Lola also had practice problems resulting from Ralph Kent-Cooke's excursion into the barriers at the Ford chicane, on his first flying lap in his new car. Damage was confined to the left side bodywork. Although worried about the chances at Le Mans of an all-new car, Brian Redman found the T610 to be lighter and easier to drive, although the yellow car was 10mph slower down the straight than the longer-nosed works entry. The CR machine would have been higher than 18th, but the team was set to send out Brian for a time when the rain fell.

As hoped, the Dome turned out to be one of the very fastest down Mulsanne, at 214mph, among the top six cars. In the first practice, however, the new braking system did not work well, and the John Macdonald team reverted to the original set-up, also changing the gear set back to the test specification. Time was lost in the Thursday session with the 'box jammed in first gear, and in the end Chris Craft was happy enough to have narrowly qualified under the 110% rule. There was a worry about the Japanese Dunlops, which had tended to chunk on the rear, and the team was still debating whether to run European Dunlops on the back when the worry became an alarming reality in the race morning warm-up. The left rear let go altogether as Salazar was tanking down Mulsanne, and the body and suspension was damaged before the shocked Chilean could bring the car to a standstill. Frantic work back in the paddock got the Dome onto the grid in the nick of time, albeit with a temporary repair.

The works Nimrod was set up for the straight, giving its drivers some white-knuckle work in the corners, and at 205mph went 16mph faster then the similar Pace entry. The latter, however, obviously found a better balance, and was almost 2secs quicker round the lap, much to the chagrin of the works team.

In contrast, although not without its practice imperfections, the works March 82G fared better than the private Michelob car, which got in very few laps. Having scrutineered on the Wednesday, the Garretson team arrived late for the session, and then lost out because of a leaking oil line. On Thursday, there was a gearbox lubrication problem, and Jim Trueman never got out. But an intervention by ACCUS persuaded the ACO to

let him run, on the grounds that he is theoretically 'graded', being a former 2-litre CanAm champion.

The URD ran reliably splitting the Nimrods and Marches. The Fitzpatrick 'Moby Dick' would have been much nearer the front, but the newly finished car had first session electrical fuel pump bothers, and the team opted to use Thursday for race spec testing.

At 201mph, the Cougar was on the pace for Mulsanne, although slower than the GTX Porsches of Fitzpatrick and Bob Akin. The event lost another of the potentially quick 935s when the unlucky Harald Grohs suffered his second massive accident in three weeks — and this time, he was very lucky to get out unhurt. Just after the kink on Mulsanne, at maybe 190mph, a tyre blew and sent the Vegla car into the barriers on both sides of the road, then into a series of rolls which took the helpless Grohs over the hump to the car's final resting place, 300 yards before Mulsanne Corner. Onlookers shuddered as the Porsche, its front end totally destroyed, caught fire, but there was great relief when, amazingly, Harald stepped out unharmed.

On this occasion, Billy Hagan's long wheelbase qualified 33rd, an outstanding performance for an AAGT entry.

At the back of the field, there was more

déjà vu, this time involving a disbelieving Richard Lloyd. In the first session, his normally reliable engine broke a piston. On Thursday morning, the team fitted another unit on loan from the factory, which had apparently done six hours on the bench. It blew a piston, too — and for the second year running, Lloyd was looking at a non-qualification. This was demonstrably unjust, since even with its dramas the Canon 924 (which was never driven by unlucky Jeff Allam) had qualified under both the 125% and 110% rules, unlike some entries among the fastest 55.

The BF Goodrich team's 924s were here to prove that a production road tyre (of the high-performance type which sell so well in the USA) could do a 24-hour race, but even so the team were compelled to use proper Dunlop competition rubber to get the cars into the race.

All the cars qualified under the 125% rule, but 12 of the 168 drivers here failed to do so. The ACO was persuaded to allow into the race Trueman, Alliot, Patrese, Ragnotti and ultimately (after an intervention from the RAC) Lovett, but among the unlucky ones were both Raymond Touroul's co-drivers and Richard Jones, who was the victim of a driveshaft failure in Richard Cleare's 934.

THE 24 HOURS

The 50th anniversary celebrations — including a historic car parade — and the fact that this was the first 24 hours to be run for the new C-cars gave an added sparkle to this great occasion, with glorious sunny weather helping to build the atmosphere of tension as the hands of the ACO's master clock edged towards 4.00pm.

As ever at Le Mans, there were losers even before the 55 car field had moved away on its warming-up lap. The longest face for the rest of Saturday was Mario Andretti's, for the Mirage had been spotted by a passing scrutineer to have its gearbox oil cooler illegally mounted behind the line of the gearbox. Mario was understandably livid, since the Harley Cluxton entered car had earlier passed scrutineering in exactly the same spec, but there was to be no arguing with the ACO: rules are rules, even if there had been an oversight. The Lloyd/Rouse Porsche 924 was allowed onto the back of the field to make up the 55 cars, while the Mirage had to stay put, even though the mechanics had hastily repositioned the offending oil cooler.

Rothmans Porsches in the hands of Ickx and Mass headed the field to take one of the gentlest starts seen at Le Mans, their side-by-side width preventing Alboreto's Lancia from finding a way through on the inside at the Dunlop Curve. Mass was in front at the end of the lap from Ickx, Wollek, Winkelhock, Ludwig, Pignard, Edwards, Field, Holbert, Migault, Stuck, Dorchy, Alboreto, Cooper, de Villota, Fitzpatrick and Rondeau. Alboreto's Lancia was clearly in trouble, but worse still for Cesare Fiorio's team was the news that Ghinzani had pulled off at Tertre Rouge, Lancia had won two of the three Group C races so far held, but their hopes for Le Mans could not have been bleaker. It turned out that both were suffering a problem with their electric fuel pumps: Ghinzani suffered first, but Alboreto also stopped on the following lap out on the circuit. Tinkering got both cars back to the pits where the electric pumps could be by-passed, but by the end of the first hour the two Martini cars were placed an undignified 53rd and 54th . . .

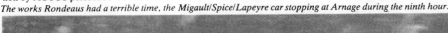
The Porsche 936C ran faultlessly until the last hour when it came to a halt out on the circuit, here passing the disappointing March 82G.

The works Rondeaus had a terrible time, the Migault/Spice/Lapeyre car stopping at Arnage during the ninth hour.

Also in trouble on that first lap were Brun's Sauber, suffering a recurrence of its jammed starter motor, and Craft's Dome, which had gingerly taken the start but spent the next two hours completing the extensive repairs to rectify damage from the morning's warm-up incident. Redman's Lola was also in the pits, having been wheeled off the grid. "For reasons that can't be explained, it just failed to start," said Brian.

The first 10 laps provided a feast of place changes among the top 20, turning the lap chart almost into a collection of random numbers. The only constant seemed to be that there was always a Rothmans Porsche at the front, Mass holding that position until passed by Ickx on lap 8. The Belgian was his usual circumspect self during the opening laps, his position on successive laps being second at the start, then fourth, sixth, fifth, fourth, and back to second as he disposed of the brief usurping attempts of Pignard, Winkelhock, Ludwig and Field.

The speed of the WM's was striking, Pignard holding his second place for four laps and Dorchy moving up from 12th on the first lap to seventh on lap 10. Edwards was settling into his stride effectively, recording a time that was to remain the fastest lap for several hours and rising to a challenging third place by lap 10, again finding the Lola's Mulsanne speed exceptionally good.

By the end of those 10 laps, then, the order stood with Ickx leading from Mass, Edwards, Holbert, Pignard, Winkelhock, Dorchy, Migault, Ludwig, Wollek, Stuck, Rondeau, Field (having lost five places after a spin at Ford chicane), Lees, Wood, Mallock and Cooper in the first of the Porsche 935s. A sad retirement after only seven laps was the Grid-Plaza, the victim of piston failure. "I looked in the mirrors at the Mulsanne corner," explained de Villota, "and saw blue smoke, so I took it slowly back to the pits even though all the gauges were showing their normal readings. I didn't feel anything to suggest that a piston had gone." One of the Rondeaus, the Pescarolo car which had qualified so disappointingly, was also in the pits from the seventh lap for a 40mins stay to trace an obscure electrical problem which could only be cured eventually by two new batteries, and an alternator.

The first fuel stops came after just 43mins, the two Nimrod Astons and Cooper's Porsche first to stop a lap before all three works Porsches and the two Lola T610s after 47mins. All these stops seemed well ahead of the approximate 1 hour target allowed by the rules, but by taking the pace lap and natural early race caution into account nobody seemed to have much to worry about. No team but Porsche could cope with all three cars on the same lap, but after they had all departed, virtually in line astern, team manager Peter Falk allowed himself a slight smile. His trio held first, second and fourth places, and he wasn't worried about their fuel consumption, the reduction to 1.1 bar of boost giving the cars long enough legs.

Positions at one hour showed that Cosworth engined cars drink less fuel, for Migault, Ludwig, Rondeau and Stuck were temporarily in the top four places, but their time came within five laps of the works Porsches, still split by the Lola until Keegan had to stop to have his door secured, losing three places.

WM's hopes had dived shortly before this when Dorchy collided with Bussi's private Rondeau, putting both cars in the pits for more than half an hour, Bussi to have damaged bodywork repaired and Dorchy, more seriously, to have burst oil and water radiators replaced. The sister WM, now in Raulet's hands, was holding

The Charles Ivey Porsche 935 of John Cooper/Paul Smith/Claude Bourgoignie finished well for the second year running.

sixth place behind the 1-2-3 Porsches, Spice (Rondeau) and Surer (Ford). A long way back but circulating quickly were the Redman Lola, twitchy on the straight but good in the corners, Rondeau's Rondeau and the two Lancias, both beginning to be affected by faltering electrics. Once again, the Italian team's Le Mans hopes seemed finished, but at least both cars were still on the track.

The new Group C fuel rules claimed their first victim just after the hour mark when Akin's 935 ran out of fuel — *Panne d'essence* would figure prominently on the retirements list — after a miscalculation by the team, while half an hour later Redman's Lola also stopped out on the circuit, out of gas after a storming recovery drive had consumed more than anticipated. C-cars falling by the wayside was to be expected, but not for such a simple reason. The Kremer Porsche was pushed away after an hour and a half with irrepairable damage to the cylinder head, but it had been a promising outing for this new car.

Ickx came in for his second fuel stop 51mins after the first to hand over to Bell, the Englishman given instructions to cool things a little as the team would now have to aim for 15-16 laps between stops. Team-mates Mass and Holbert came in a lap later to make life a little easier for the mechanics and handed over to Schuppan and Haywood respectively.

While this German demonstration continued, others sat in the pits and waited. An impatient Bobby Rahal watched his 'lobster-claw' March's fuel problems worsen until a diagnosed split fuel cell spelt retirement. The other

March 82G suffered clutch problems, and the British Lola slipped down to 32nd place after two separate starter motor problems caused long stops of 15mins apiece, but that fastest lap of 3m 37.4s still stood as some consolation.

The staggering of fuel stops again promoted the Spice Rondeau, the only one of the three cars under Keith Greene's care to be running without any electrical faults after two hours, and the two Fords into the top three places, but as they stopped in turn the two quicker Porsches took over, Schuppan holding the lead for a while through the third hour before Bell regained the front. They remained on the same lap until the fourth hour, when Mass/Schuppan lost 3mins having the rev-limiter changed to cure a high speed misfire. Quite how Mass discovered that misfire when driving increasingly economically is Porsche's business. . . .

Apart from British drivers in foreign teams, the patriotic fervour among the thousands of Britons who had trekked to Le Mans centred its loyalty on the Nimrod Astons, which had moved up reliably to nudge the top 10 thanks to faultless running and excellent speed on the straight. At 19.35, however, the green and silver works car struck disaster just before the Mulsanne kink Needell suffering terrifying backwards collision with the barrier at over 200mph. "I'm not sure what happened," said Tiff, "but it must have been a blown tyre at the back or a breakage in the rear suspension." As at Silverstone, Aston Martin would have to rely on the Viscount Downe car to pick up World Championship points. The

course car was brought out for the incident and stopped at the scene. The pit marshals mistook this for a pace car situation, causing an unnecessary 2-lap delay for Muller's Sauber, Stommelen's Lancia, Hobbs's 935 and the Cougar as they waited for the pit exit to be opened.

Positions at four hours: 1, Winkelhock/Niedzwiedz, 61 laps; 2, Haywood/Holbert/Barth, 61 laps; 3, Ickx/Bell, 60 laps; 4, Migault/Spice/Lapeyre, 60 laps; 5, Ludwig/Surer, 60 laps; 6, Raulet/Pignard/Theys, 60 laps; 7, Stuck/Schlesser/Quester, 60 laps; 8, Martin/Martin/Wollek, 60 laps; 9, Mass/Schuppan, 59 laps; 10, Mallock/Phillips/Salmon, 57 laps; etc.

Throughout the next four hours there was little to choose between the three Rothmans Porsches. Quicker pit stops and slightly more aggressive driving had brought the Haywood/Holbert/Barth car into the lead by a lap from Ickx/Bell, who were never more than a few minutes ahead of the Migault/Spice Rondeau which in turn was marginally ahead of the third works Porsche. It made for an interesting phase of the race, although the interest was more in anticipation of what might happen.

The only significant change among the leading 10 positions over the four hour spell was the quicker Sauber's slip down the order from fifth place after Schlesser came in to have the failing clutch bled, only to find that the starter motor had gone. The car was retired.

Theys's WM also lost five places with a stop to replace the alternator as darkness drew nearer, promoting the surviving Nimrod another place as it ran like clockwork to sixth place at the eight hour.

Porche versus Ford was how the race

Behind the phalanx of Porsches, Dieudonné/Baird/Libert guided their Ferrari 512BB into a fine sixth place.

had been billed, and for four hours there was little to choose between them. As darkness approached, however, both Fords hit troubles which would see them out of the race before seven hours were up. Shortly after one sixth distance, the clutch on Winkelhock's car started to give trouble. A stop to repair a broken input shaft dropped it down the order until the Cosworth finally blew, leaving the C100 stranded on the circuit. Surer's car, meanwhile, was in trouble with shaky electrics and within 40mins his car was also a retirement. The handsome Fords had performed well, but the Erich Zakowski run team, like Rondeau, is having problems with its 3.9-litre DFL engines.

There were some British disappointments as two private entries were forced out. The chubby De Cadenet of Wilds/Duret/Harrower had been suffering fuel pressure maladies for several hours and finally stopped by the Mulsanne signalling pits unable to pick up any more fuel, while the Birrane/Sheldon/Crang Chevron ended its race after less than five hours with a broken gearbox. Soon after, the Edwards/Keegan Lola, which had proved fast, was ultimately fragile, succumbing to a blown head gasket.

The Lancias, still at the back of the field, were having a dreadful time with constant stops, the Patrese/Heyer/Ghinzani car needing a new intercooler to cure a turbo leak and the sister car suffering continual electrical problems. The other disappointing works team was the Rondeau equipe. All the cars kept going, but the two blue Otis-backed cars were in and out of the pits with a succession of fuel and electrical problems; the Spice/Migault car in third place kept the French flag flying high. "We're having a miserable time," confessed Keith Greene, "but at least this car is running faultlessly." Its only problem was caused by the vibration common to all the DFL-engined cars, the Rellumit seal for the refuelling assembly having shaken itself apart. Rather than waste 20mins changing the whole coupling, a plastic plug was used to make good the seal, and only a few minutes were lost.

Positions at eight hours: 1, Haywood/Holbert/Barth, 121 laps; 2, Ickx/Bell, 120 laps; 3, Migault/Spice/Lapeyre, 120 laps; 4, Mass/Schuppan, 120 laps; 5, Martin/Wollek, 119 laps; 6, Mallock/Phillips/Salmon, 114 laps; 7, Cooper/Smith/Bourgoignie, 113 laps; 8, Rondeau/Ragnotti/Alliot, 112 laps; 9, Cudini/Morton/Paul, 112 laps; 10, Fitzpatrick/Hobbs, 111 laps; etc.

As half distance approached, the race moved into a significant new phase. The Porsche armoury showed a couple of hairline cracks but otherwise remained intact, while all the remaining serious rivals to the Rothmans equipe fell by the wayside. For Rondeau, the disappointments so far paled into insignificance as all three works cars had retired by half distance. By 4.00am the Rondeau pits were silent and the huge entourage of mechanics and drivers were on their way back to their farmhouse HQ to catch up on lost sleep.

The first to go, shortly after midnight, was the Pescarolo/Jaussaud car with a blown engine, due either to piston or oil pump failure. They didn't really care: it was almost a relief to be shot of the troublesome machine!

Shortly before 3.00am, Lapeyre parked the third-placed car at Arnage with distributor failure, only to be joined just 5mins later by the other Otis car, with Ragnotti driving. This was the car which had suffered the worst fuel system problems in practice, and after the Saturday morning engine change, evidently a fuel line had not been tightened home. It was this that had worked loose, leaving the car stranded and Rondeau's last hope dashed. Two private Rondeaus remained, but the Candy/Poulain/Haran car was very soon retired with engine failure after a valve had dropped. It was a sad end for the team carrying the hopes of all of France,

but one felt that it had been on the cards: the pressure of Porsche's opposition perhaps forcing the drivers to press on harder than in years past.

Porsche maintained their 1-2 throughout the night, Ickx/Bell pulling out a lap over Mass/Schuppan when the second car made an unscheduled stop to fix a temperamental fuel metering unit. The third Porsche slipped back to fifth place, but lost eventually 20 laps with two problems. First, the driver's door flew off, and then a rear wheel bearing broke, necessitating suspension repairs. When somebody fails to shut the door properly, there's not much that Porsche's fine engineering and superb team-work can do about it . . .

The Martin brothers and Wollek held a secure third place only four laps behind the leaders, the Jöst built Porsche having run with customary reliability. "We have no problems," explained the brilliant Bob, "apart from the factory cars. They are so much quicker on Mulsanne than we are."

Behind them the amazing private Nimrod Aston was beginning to look capable of great things. A totally reliable run had hauled it gradually up to sixth place, all three drivers keeping their fingers crossed that their good luck would continue.

Fitzpatrick's Porsche was also running cleanly to hold sixth and the IMSA GTX class lead ahead one of the two surviving Ferrari 512 BBs, that of Cudini/Morton/Paul. Morton was especially pleased to be doing so well, but like everyone else he was anxious about the dawn: "We musn't count our chickens before they're hatched." Further down the order, O'Rourke/Down/Mason had hauled their BMW M1 up to 11th despite a stop to change a crankshaft damper (a familiar M1 problem), while further weight from the British contingent came from the Walkinshaw/Lovett/Nicholson Mazda in 12th and the Cleare/Dron/Jones Porsche 934 in 18th, despite an alarming moment for Jones when first one and then the other headlight failed.

British retirements during this phase included the Dome, wheeled away with a chassis failure after a hopeless race, and the Lloyd/Rouse 924, which had done well to continue after running out of fuel on Saturday evening but finally suffered a broken driveshaft. Also out were both WMs, Frequelin/Dorchy/Couderc after another accident (the car caught fire) and Pignard/Theys/Raulet with a broken gearbox.

Positions at 12 hours: 1, Ickx/Bell, 180 laps; 2, Mass/Schuppan, 179 laps; 3, Martin/Martin/Wollek, 176 laps; 4, Mallock/Phillips/Salmon, 171 laps; 5, Haywood/Holbert/Barth, 169 laps; 6, Fitzpatrick/Hobbs, 169 laps; 7, Cudini/Morton/Paul, 168 laps; 8, Cooper/Smith/Bourgoignie, 167 laps, 9, Snobeck/Servanin/Metge, 164 laps; 10, Yver/Sotty/Guitteny, 159 laps; etc.

Redman's return to racing was not happy (above). The W M-Peugeots (below) again demonstrated their straight-line speed.

Porsche marched on. As dawn began to break, the situation was much the same as when the sun had set. The race's pattern was established, and there was no way that Ickx/Bell or Mass/Schuppan were going to break it. This was getting boring . . . and that was the drivers' view! All through the race the leading two cars had been lapping at more than 30secs off their practice pace, and with with no challengers in sight were more than capable of reaching the stringent fuel consumption requirement which had been a source of worry before the race. They were all happy to be doing so well, but as Bell said, "It's just not very exciting is it?" The leading car still continued without any delay, its only quirk being a shift in the mixture setting which had caused a slight misfire, but richening the fuel cured this.

The Jöst Porsche hung on in third, its drivers striving not to let the deficit to the works cars become too great, while the dependable Ferrari moved up to fourth place after a hiccough in the Aston's progress. The nip in the air at dawn had caused a front brake disc to crack as it heated up from cold under braking for Mulsanne Corner, and by the time the air had warmed up the team had again suffered the same problem, despite feathering the brakes well before that heavy braking zone to warm the dics gradually.

Still running like a dream, the Charles Ivey 935 was beginning to encourage hopes in the team that they might achieve a result as good as last year's fourth place, that position only three laps away from them. The Fitzpatrick car had been the only 935 ahead of it, but a blown cylinder head gasket stopped its progress just when it had hauled in the Ferrari for fourth place. The crew disconnected the injector from the offending cylinder, and Fitz carried on at a pace reduced by 15secs a lap.

The British BMW was beginning to show signs of clutch trouble, and several bleeds suggested that a change might soon be necessary, while the steady run of the Cleare Porsche was interrupted by two driveshaft breakages within two laps of each other while its owner was driving. And the British Mazda also began to falter, Lovett finally having to park on the Mulsanne when the engine went.

Positions at 16 hours: 1, Ickx/Bell, 240 laps; 2, Mass/Schuppan, 236 laps; 3, Martin/Martin/Wollek, 234 laps; 4, Cudini/Morton/Paul, 225 laps; 5, Mallock/Phillips/Salmon 223 laps; 6, Cooper/Smith/Bourgoignie, 222 laps; 7, Fitzpatrick/Hobbs, 222 laps; 8, Snobeck/Servanin/Metge, 220 laps; 9, Haywood/Holbert/Barth, 220 laps; 10, Yver/Scotty/Guitteny, 214 laps; etc.

After dropping down to ninth place, the third works Porsche driven by Haywood/Holbert/Barth began to work its way back up the order as the day brightened. By 11.00am it was back into fourth place, nine laps adrift of the Jöst Porsche in third place, but gaining appreciably. Shortly before this, however, at 10.40am, Ickx and Bell devotees held their breath as the Belgian limped round the circuit with a punctured tyre. He got to the pits for a replacement, losing three of his five laps lead over Mass/Schuppan. This was the only delay yet to break the regularity of the leading car's 15 lap stints between refuelling stops.

The optimism of the surviving Pace Nimrod team took a dive at 10.30am when Mallock brought their car in with a serious misfire, traced to a broken carbon bush in the distributor. This was the first hint of deeper problems as traces of blue smoke began to signal a suspected valve problem, but still the car kept going to the rapturous cheers of the Union Jack

waving Britons on the Dunlop Curve. Despite all the delays, Viscount Downe's car dropped only a few places to eighth by mid-day.

An unscheduled stop around the same time broke the rhythm of the Charles Ivey team, Cooper finding that the 935 would not pull properly on the straight. The loss of power was traced to a leak from the intercooler, but three stops later after the loss of 18 laps, they were back on the road with the help of borrowed bits for a replacement turbo unit.

The British disappointments did not end there, for the Mason/O'Rourke/Jones BMW's anticipated clutch change had to be carried out, the car losing nearly an hour but only one place on the road. Further traumas for BMW came with a long unscheduled halt for the Ennequin/Gabriel/Gasparetti car which defied all attempts to remove the transmission casing when the gearbox seized. The Perrier/Salam/Guidici Lancia Beta Montecarlo was also lost from the race through its exclusion because the team changed the gearbox, which the ACO does not allow.

Positions at 20 hours: 1, Ickx/Bell, 299 laps; 2, Mass/Schuppan, 296 laps; 3, Martin/Martin/Wollek, 288 laps; 4, Haywood/Holbert/Barth, 280 laps; 5, Cudini/Morton/Paul, 276 laps; 6, Fitzpatrick/Hobbs, 276 laps; 7, Snobeck/Servanin/Metge, 274 laps; 8, Mallock/Phillips/Salmon, 274 laps; 9, Yver/Sotty/Guitteny, 269 laps; 10, Dieudonné/Baird/Libert, 267 laps; etc.

The third of the Rothmans Porsches steadily made up ground on the third-placed Jöst car, which had had a steadily worsening misfire since dawn, but then the Belga backed Porsche stopped on the circuit with two hours remaining and it was left only for the might of Porsche System to maintain their 1-2-3 to the finish.

That they did with ease, the three blue and white Porsches forming up in numerical and race order with half an hour left. It was a mightily impressive display, taking the top three places with three brand new cars, and one which goes so show that the Porsche System works. And in 1982 it worked better than ever to give Porsche their most convincing victory in all their years of coming to Le Mans, bringing Jacky Ickx his sixth win in this classic race and Derek Bell his third.

Porsches, in fact, took the top five places. The Fitzpatrick 935 survived on five cylinders to finish fourth, four laps ahead of the reliable (but also on fewer than its usual six cylinders) 935 of Snobeck/Servanin/Metge. Ferrari took sixth place, Dieudonné/Baird/Libert moving up after the challenge of the rival Cudini/Morton/Paul Boxer faded in the closing hours.

The chances of the Nimrod Aston had looked perilous at times during the early afternoon, its misfire and oil smoke all the time looking ominous. On top of that, a fuel pressure problem had been growing for several hours, and at 1.30pm it came close to letting Mallock down. On the Mulsanne Straight, taking care to treat the car gently, he found that his fuel pressure was reading zero. "I stopped, fiddled about a bit and finally got enough pressure back to get back to the pits," explained Ray. They had to get that car to the finish, even if it meant "carrying it across the line". Despite the problems, seventh place was the result.

Next came the Ivey 935, the team pleased to make the finish after their turbo problems, while the Cleare/Dron/Jones 934 finished 13th despite losing first and third gears for the final hours.

The O'Rourke/Down/Mason BMW limped through past midday only to have a long stop for a new exhaust system. With two and a half hours to go, a sudden oil leak drained the engine, forcing poor O'Rourke to stop on the Mulsanne Straight.

That was a disappointing conclusion for one British team, but there were still British drivers in the first, fourth, seventh, and eighth cars.

The dangers of Le Mans: Harald Grohs crashed his 935 heavily during practice when a tyre blew (above). Cleare/Dron/Jones guided their 934 to a praise-worthy 13th (below). .

Most of the Group C cars suffered problems (apart from Porsche, of course). The Edwards/Keegan/Faure Lola leads Spice's Rondeau (above), while Brooks/McGriff/Williams soldiered to the end in their Camaro (below).

LES VINGT-QUATRE HEURES DU MANS

June 19/20, 24 hours over 8.467 mile circuit. **Organisers:** Automobile Club de l'Ouest. **Winning average speed:** 126.84mph. **Distance covered:** 3039.6 miles. **1981 winners:** Jacky Ickx/Derek Bell (Porsche 936/81), 354 laps at 124.93mph, 2997.3 miles.
Hourly classification of all starters showing final positions and retirements.

Grid	1	2	3	4	5	6	7	8	9	10	11	12	13	14	15	16	17	18	19	20	21	22	23	24
1	11	11	11	7	3	3	3	3	1	1	1	1	1	1	1	1	1	1	1	1	1	1	1	1
2	6	6	3	3	1	1	1	1	2	2	2	2	2	2	2	2	2	2	2	2	2	2	2	2
4	24	7	1	1	11	11	11	11	11	11	3	4	4	4	4	4	4	4	4	4	4	4	4	3
51	20	1	7	11	2	2	2	2	4	3	4	32	32	32	32	72	72	72	3	3	3	3	3	4
50	1	2	2	6	20	4	4	4	3	4	32	3	79	79	72	32	32	32	72	72	69	79	79	78
6	16	24	6	9	9	9	32	32	32	32	79	79	72	72	60	60	79	79	32	79	72	72	78	70
20	2	4	24	20	4	32	70	60	12	12	72	72	60	60	79	79	60	60	79	78	78	78	70	
5	3	3	9	4	32	60	60	12	60	79	60	60	78	78	78	78	78	3	78	32	32	32	72	32
16	9	20	20	2	60	79	24	72	79	60	11	78	3	3	3	3	78	78	60	25	70	70	32	60
7	7	9	4	32	79	24	79	79	72	72	78	25	70	70	70	25	25	25	25	70	60	60	60	72
9	4	31	31	60	72	72	12	9	9	78	26	62	25	25	25	70	70	70	70	60	25	25	25	25
10	5	16	32	72	26	62	9	78	78	26	62	83	62	62	62	62	62	62	62	77	62	77	77	77
3	10	26	79	26	62	78	62	62	62	62	25	70	83	82	77	77	77	77	77	77	62	66	66	66
19	35	22	72	71	24	12	78	26	26	25	12	65	65	65	82	82	82	61	66	66	66	62	90	19
11	79	79	60	79	70	26	26	70	38	82	82	77	82	65	82	82	65	66	61	90	90	90	82	82
37	31	17	71	31	78	70	70	25	25	70	70	82	77	83	66	61	61	82	40	61	82	82	38	38
17	30	14	30	24	6	82	82	38	82	65	83	90	90	90	90	61	66	65	82	82	38	38	87	
64	25	72	70	77	81	25	25	82	83	83	65	11	61	61	90	90	87	87	87	87	87	87	81	81
36	70	71	77	70	22	77	38	83	70	77	77	12	66	66	83	90	90	90	65	38	61	81	61	
60	71	25	62	62	12	38	83	24	77	38	90	66	87	87	87	38	38	38	38	81	81	61	80	
24	32	64	26	78	16	83	90	65	65	90	75	61	81	81	81	38	81	81	81	80	80	80	62	
32	76	30	78	81	77	65	65	77	90	9	61	87	38	38	81	50	50	80	80	65				
14	60	60	78	25	84	90	77	90	86	86	66	75	50	50	50	80	80	80	50					
30	14	62	16	14	83	84	86	86	24	75	87	81	86	86	86	80	83							
31	62	70	81	82	65	14	81	61	61	38	50	35	80	86										
79	64	77	75	55	14	20	51	61	75	81	86	38	80	35										
75	81	78	25	75	25	86	10	66	81	66	81	86	11											
35	26	81	64	84	19	75	61	87	75	50	35	12												
29	72	73	82	65	75	10	66	75	87	50	10	80	75											
76	78	39	55	83	38	81	87	10	10	85	35	26												
26	17	55	84	90	86	66	75	51	85	10	80	10												
81	38	82	39	16	7	16	14	85	51	35	35	9												
78	80	75	14	12	66	51	84	50	50	50	35	85												
25	84	84	83	86	18	61	50	14	36	80														
38	83	5	65	87	61	7	85	84	14	24														
72	73	86	86	85	51	50	36	36	84	51														
12	77	65	90	38	71	87	19	35	35	35														
61	82	83	85	50	55	6	35	80	80	14														
70	55	87	87	39	51	85	80	19																
71	87	90	38	66	39	55	20																	
86	86	85	66	61	87	39	16																	
77	39	61	12	30	19	19	7																	
62	75	66	50	10	50	36	6																	
39	90	38	61	73	73	35	71																	
80	19	80	19	51	64	80	55																	
66	61	29	10	19	36	29	39																	
90	65	12	17	64	35	64																		
55	29	19	29	29	29	29																		
82	85	50	51	36	18	73																		
73	66	35	5	18	31																			
85	12	76	80	35	30																			
83	37	10	35	17																				
65	50	51	76	5																				
87	51	36	36	76																				
84	36	37																						

No.	Class	Car	Drivers	Result
1	GC	Porsche 956	Ickx/Bell	1
2	GC	Porsche 956	Mass/Schuppan	2
3	GC	Porsche 956	Haywood/Holbert/Barth	3
79	GTX	Porsche 935	Fitzpatrick/Hobbs	4
78	GTX	Porsche 935 K3	Snobeck/Servanin/Metge	5
70	GTX	Ferrari 512BB	Dieudonne/Baird/Libert.	6
		Porsche 936C	Martin/Martin/Wollek	Engine
32	GC	Nimrod Aston Martin	Mallock/Phillips/Salmon	7
60	G5	Porsche 935 K3	Cooper/Smith/Bourgoignie	8
72	GTX	Ferrari 512BB	Cudini/Morton/Paul	9
25	GC	Ford Rondeau M379C	Yver/Sotty/Guitteny	10
77	GTX	Porsche 935 K3	Verney/Garretson/Ratcliff	11
66	G5	Lancia Beta MC	Lemerle/Cohen-Olivar/Castellano	12
19	G4	Porsche 934	Cleare/Dron/Jones	13
82	GTX	Mazda 254	Terada/Yorino/Moffat	14
38	GC	Ford Rondeau M382	Bussi/Witmeur/De Dryver	15
87	GT	Porsche 924 GTR	Busby/Bundy	16
81	GT	Chevrolet Camaro	Hagan/Felton	17
61	G5	BMW M1	Ennequin/Gabriel/Gasparetti	18
80	GT	Chevrolet Camaro	Williams/Brooks/McGriff	NC
	G5	BMW M1	O'Rourke/Down/Mason	Engine
	G5	Lancia Beta MC	Perrier/Salam/Guidici	DSQ
	G6	Lancia Martini	Patrese/Ghinzani/Heyer	Distributor
	GT	Mazda 254	Walkinshaw/Lovett/Nicholson	Engine
	GT	Porsche 924 GTR	Miller/Bedard/Schurti	Lost wheel
	GC	Ford Cougar CO1	Courage/Grand/Dubois	Chassis
	GC	Ford Rondeau M382	Spice/Migault/Lapeyre	Distributor
	GC	Ford Rondeau M382	Pescarolo/Ragnotti/Alliot	Engine
	GTX	Porsche 935T	Haldi/Teran/Hesnault	Differential
	GC	Ford Rondeau M379C	Haran/Poulain/Candy	Engine
	GC	Peugeot WMP82	Frequelin/Dorchy/Couderc	Accident
	GC	Peugeot WMP82	Raulet/Pignard/Theys	Gearbox
	GT	BMW M1	Garcia/Stiff/Naon	Engine
	GT	Porsche 924 GTR	Lloyd/Rouse	Driveshaft
	GC	Ford Rondeau M382	Jaussaud/Rondeau	Engine
	G6	Lancia Martini	Alboreto/Fabi/Stommelen	Engine
	GC	Ford Dome RC82	Craft/Salazar	Chassis
	GC	Chevrolet March 82G	Elgh/Wood/Neve	Electrics
	GC	Ford Sauber SHSC6	Brun/Muller	Starter motor
	GC	Ford Sauber SHSC6	Stuck/Schlesser/Quester	Engine mount
	GC	Ford Lola T610	Edwards/Keegan/Faure	Head gasket
	GC	Ford C100	Winkelhock/Ludwig	Engine
	GC	Ford C100	Surer/Niedzwiedz	Electrics
	GTX	Ferrari 512BB	Ballot-Lena/Andruet	Out of fuel
	G6	Chevron Ford B36	Birrane/Sheldon/Crang	Gearbox
	GC	Ford de Cadenet Lola MM	Wilds/Duret/Harrower	Out of fuel
	G5	Porsche 935 K3	Doren/Sprawls/Contreras	Engine
	GC	Chevrolet March 82G	Rahal/McKitterick/Trueman	Split fuel tank
	GTX	Ferrari 512BB	Henn/Lanier/Morin	Engine
	GC	Nimrod Aston Martin	Evans/Needell/Lees	Accident
	GC	BMW URD C81	Lateste/Heuclin/Strievit	Engine
	GC	Ford Lola T610	Cooke/Redman/Adams	Out of fuel
	GC	Porsche CK5	Field/Ongais/Whittington	Engine
	GTX	Porsche 935	Akin/Cowart/Miller	Out of fuel
	GC	Ford Grid Plaza S1	Villota/de Cadenet/Wilson	Engine

EVEN BEFORE THE start of the 1982 24 Hours of Le Mans I had a title for this story: "Andretti et Fils." It seemed an appropriate way to mix the subject of Mario Andretti and his son Michael co-driving a car in the classic French race. Perhaps I should have known better, as I once learned at Le Mans to never count your prize money until the checkered flag has dropped. And yet the prospects of the story seemed so perfect. John Lamm and I had spent time with Mario and Mike at Riverside International Raceway during the testing of the Mirage-Ford they would drive at Le Mans. Then again in France at dinner and during discussions before the race we'd talked with the father-son team that appeared to be such a natural combination. It would be a perfect story if the Andrettis won, but, hell, it was a damn good story once the Mirage had taken the green flag.

Then again, 1982 would be a very good Le Mans either way. The prospect of more than 30 of the new Group C cars—colorful, sleek and fast—was enough to raise our interest. There was also the possibility of the open-cockpit Lancia Group 6 cars spoiling the Cs' show. Then there were the 36 American drivers in the race, which is quite a proportion when you consider there were only 38 French drivers entered. And Luigi Chinetti, owner of the North American Racing Team and the Le Mans winner 50 years ago (see "Profile" in this issue), was to be honored in 1982. It had to be a good year.

All the possibilities were there when the cars were rolled out for their first practice session, which was Wednesday night from 7 o'clock until 11. Without a doubt the most impressive cars were the three Porsche 956s, one of which was for 5-time winner Jacky Ickx and Derek Bell. Another was assigned to Americans Al Holbert and Hurley Haywood, along with factory driver Jürgen Barth, whose father Eddie was not just an excellent race driver, but one of the genuine gentlemen of my racing era. The other Porsche-based C cars, the Joest 936C and the Kremer CK5, had the same well thought-out look as the 956s.

Then there were the two Ford C100s, said to be on the road to recovery after early development problems. Also Ford-powered

50ème 24 Heures du Mans

CLASSIQUE CONTRETEMPS

The Mirage is a mirage for the Andrettis

BY PHIL HILL
PHOTOS BY JOHN LAMM

Just before the start, the Mirage-Ford of Mario and Mike Andretti is pushed off the starting line.

Le Mans

were two Sauber SHS/C6s with their wonderful paint schemes: a pair of *Star Wars*-like Lola T610s; six Rondeaus of which five were M382s and one an M482; three new C cars, the Mirage, the GRID-Plaza S-1 and the Cougar C01; a Le Mans perennial, the Dome Amada RC82; and an ancient de Cadenet Lola MM. There were a duo of Chevrolet-powered March 82Gs, a somewhat scruffy-looking URD C81 with a 3.5-liter BMW engine, two of WM's very pretty P82s with turbo Peugeot V-6s and finally, but certainly not quietly, a pair of bellowing Aston Martin V-8 powered Nimrods.

The car we knew best, of course, was the Mirage M12. John Horsman of Harley Cluxton's Grand Touring Cars team had laid out the basic design of the car, along with the exterior shape. The chassis was built by Tiga cars in England. Unlike past years when the Mirages have been hampered by a lack of time or funds, 1982 was much more promising. There had been time in the Lockheed wind tunnel to check the aerodynamics, two test sessions at Riverside and then hours of high-speed running at Transportation Research Center in Ohio. With Mario at Indy, Mike did this testing and managed to get in hours of 210-plus mph top speed, 185-mph average speed driving during both day and night.

The point of all this driving was to shake down the car and give Mike Andretti plenty of time in what would be his first enclosed race car, all of his earlier experience being in go karts, Formula Fords and Super Vees. Horsman and Cluxton were very impressed with young Andretti's speed and, just as important, his attitude. When asked what he is able to teach Mike, Mario just replied, "I don't teach, I discuss." That approach obviously works.

During one of the test sessions at Riverside we'd had a chance to talk about Le Mans. Mario remembered the last time he'd raced there. It was 1967 and he was in a Ford Mark IV. In the early morning, while going into the esses the brakes on his Ford failed and in the aftermath three of the Ford team cars were written-off. Mario now laughs about the broken ribs and how he asked Roger McCluskey, who had been driving one of the other Fords, to convince the French ambulance drivers to take Mario to Ford's doctors. When McCluskey couldn't communicate with the French and they were about to drive Mario off to a local hospital, McCluskey took the keys from the Citroën ambu-

lance and threw them into the darkness. The French driver was furious as McCluskey helped Mario away.

I met Mario and Mike again at Le Mans and watched as they settled into the Mirage. In the two nights of practice Mario managed to qualify the car a comfortable 9th and did a very promising 212 mph on Mulsanne. And Mike got his first taste of Le Mans, suffering a spin near Arnage and a near-big moment at the kink on Mulsanne, but settling in very comfortably. It was easy to see the 19-year-old driver would have no trouble adapting to an endurance race. We talked again the day before the race about how one paces a long-distance event, avoiding dicing with other cars, treating the car gently. Everyone felt very good about the car's chances.

Though it's been 20 years since I last won at Le Mans and 15 years since I did my final 24-hour race there, I still find the place fascinating. The sheer size of the course, the number of people and the ambience are exciting, even if the Woodstock-cum-carnival commercialization is now a bit too much. There was a historic car parade again this year and Luigi Chinetti received the honors he deserved after so many years at Le Mans. In the early afternoon before the race he and I were taken on a tour of

the track in one of the Mercedes course cars. As we approached Les Hunaudieres Cafe, Chinetti suggested we stop for a small apertif, so we did, climbing over the Armco barrier. This was the place Chinetti had sometimes stayed when driving at Le Mans and the owner, who knew him well, joined us for a drink.

With a 4:00 p.m. starting time, the 24-hour race has a chance to really build momentum before the *depart*. Things get very noisy and hectic and exciting. You don't even get that momentary dead silence that used to happen when the drivers had to run to their cars before starting. Then the last 30 were quiet, followed by the sounds of the drivers sprinting across the road. Now the cars are rolled out to the track with a great deal of fanfare, the drivers chat with each other, pause to wish each other good luck (seen that at a Grand Prix recently?) and then slowly buckle into their cars.

Mario had already done this when, with only about 20 minutes to go before the race, the Le Mans officials ordered him out of the car and the Mirage pushed off the grid. There had already been quite a discussion between officials, Horsman and Cluxton, arguments that would go on for hours, but the disqualification would stand. As always at Le Mans these things aren't

Danny Ongais, Ted Field and Bill Whittington shared this Kremer Porsche CK5.

Another Porsche-based Group C car, the 936C.

Most colorful of the C cars was the Ford-powered Sauber SHS/C6.

The Ford C100s qualified 3rd and 7th, but looked to be a handful to drive quickly.

Even when the more sophisticated machinery broke, the pair of Chevrolet Camaros thundered on to the checkered flag.

Le Mans

simple, but here's basically what happened:

At about 10 minutes after 3:00 p.m., officials of the Automobile Club de l'Ouest told the Mirage team that their oil coolers were mounted 3 in. too far aft, being behind the transmission. They asked if the car could be altered to fit the rules before 4 o'clock and Horsman said no. Alternatives were thrown back and forth such as correcting the car in the pits before the start or running the car and ignoring the infraction. I was in on several of the hurried meetings and in my opinion the car was out of the event from the moment the Mirage team was told of the infraction.

While the race began on the track, behind the pits, Harley, his sponsors and other backers seethed, while the Mirage team went about replumbing the car and the coolant radiators were swapped for the oil radiators so the car would be legal. Fifty-six minutes later they pushed the car back to the pit lane, hoping for a chance to get the car in the race. Their pit had already been taken over by the first alternate car, a Porsche 924 GTS. Mario and Mike went to a Mirage trailer to wait for a decision.

There's no denying, of course, that the Mirage was illegal. Somewhere in the many months and details he went through before the race, John Horsman had gotten this one point incorrect. The new Lola 610s had suffered the same problem at Monza earlier in the season. And yet it seems terribly unfair to heap all the blame on Horsman. The Mirage had been through the technical inspection, two qualifying sessions and a warmup on Saturday morning. I could go on for pages about the affair, but it all comes down to the same thing: One has to blame Horsman for the technical error, but equal fault has to go the ACO for the messy and, in my opinion, very unfair manner in which it was handled. To make the ACO's actions even more ludicrous, Judy Stropus, whose reputation as a timer and scorer is well known, confirmed to us that seven Group C cars that did not qualify within 125 percent of the fastest car in their class were allowed to start the race. This regulation was added for safety reasons, as was the oil cooler rule, and is arguably even more important to running a safe race.

We talked with Mario and Mike as the team thrashed away at reworking the car. After his non-start at Indy, Mario was particularly and understandably upset. A racing driver steels himself against a great variety of troubles—a broken wheel on the first lap, a burned piston at half distance, even running out of fuel on the last lap—but not being able to take the green flag, and then for non-mechanical reasons, is something that's difficult for a driver to mentally prepare for. And Mario had just been deprived of taking the start in two of the world's top events in a matter of only three weeks. Oddly enough, I felt sorry for Mario. Generally one doesn't feel sorry for top-line race drivers, because it's almost an insult . . . empathize with them, curse their bad luck, but feeling sorry for them isn't part of the plan.

I remembered when I interviewed Mario for R&T after he'd won the World Driving Championship and I asked if he was ready to retire. Mario had a few specific things he wanted to do first, and one was to drive with Mike at Le Mans. Now in the trailer at Le Mans, thinking back to Indy, Mario said, "I'll tell you what I'm doing wrong, I'm in this business. . ."

As for Mike Andretti, well, he never had a chance to show his stuff . . . but he will.

By 6:00 p.m. the Mirage M12 had finally been pushed from the pits back to the paddock. Two hours later every trace of the Mirage team was gone from Le Mans.

Unfortunately, as the hours passed, a number of front-running American drivers dropped out. R&T contributor Bob Akin in his tube-frame, Group C-like Porsche 935 was eliminated early, a victim of foul handling and then fuel problems. By 1:30 a.m. there was little reason to stay longer and the next morning we breakfasted late with Bob, Ellen and Suzy Akin on a beautiful, warm morning.

When we returned to the track it was strangely quiet. It was noon and only 20 cars were still running, several of those with disabled cylinders. Now it was the survivors-only part of Le Mans, with Ickx and Bell well in command, the two other 956s making it an impressive 3-deep lead for the Porsche factory.

At 4:00 p.m. Sunday the three 956s were aligned for a victory parade. A dozen Americans remained in the race, Holbert and Haywood being the best. John Morton and John Paul Sr (with Alain Cudini) had gotten Luigi Chinetti's Ferrari Boxer as high as 5th before slipping back to 9th. Still racing and sounding quite healthy were the two Chevrolet Camaros entered by a NASCAR team and driven by Billy Hagan, Gene Felton, Dick Brooks, Herschel McGriff and Tom Williams. It would be nice to see the team get some serious Chevrolet backing for another attempt in 1983. And I took particular pleasure in seeing David Hobbs in 4th place in a Porsche 935T and Mike Salmon in 7th in one of the Aston Martin Nimrods. Why? Because they were racing at Le Mans when I won in 1962 . . . and both did better this year than 20 years ago.

A trio of Porsche 956s rolls on to a 1-2-3 victory.

PHOTO BY JOHN LAMM

PHOTO BY SPORT GRAPHICS

The impressive sight of Derek Bell leading the Porsche's home in their numerical order, which corresponded to their race order.

Porsche's third Le Mans

Britain's DEREK BELL gives a personal account of the preparation and the actual race that led to his third victory at Le Mans.

Five weeks after its auspicious competition debut in the Silverstone 6 Hours World Endurance Championship of Makes round, the Porsche 956 annihilated allcomers at Le Mans in probably the best regimented display of controlled speed and efficiency ever seen in a long-distance event. The works Rothmans-Porsche Group C coupés, bearing the numbers 1, 2 and 3, finished in their corresponding positions, way ahead of their opposition and bearing little evidence of the day's rigours. For the second year running, that inspired pairing of Belgian Jacky Ickx and Britain's own Derek Bell were the winners, marking Jacky's unprecendented sixth victory in the classic French race and a fine third triumph in eight years for Derek. Le Mans, however, is not won on individual performances but by a concerted and disciplined team effort, as Derek is eager to attest.

Derek Bell and the Belgian ace, Jacky Ickx, share a joke in the Le Mans pit.

Pre-Silverstone testing at Paul Ricard and Porsche's own facility at Weissach proved the 956 design to be very sound, and no more intensive circuit work was undertaken once the three chassis for Le Mans were completed. The engineers put in a great deal of work on the fuel system after Silverstone, to encourage the engine to give more miles per gallon, but I did nothing in the way of testing between events.

I went out to Weissach the Friday before Le Mans and drove my car and Jochen's car. Then they asked me to return on the Sunday to drive all three cars — literally on the Monday before the race. They really had not turned a wheel.

We had a minor problem, but this is where I find the people at Weissach so remarkable. In anything we do, there is never any shouting, any running — it's all done so efficiently. It just astounds me. It is the only team I have ever been with, ever, who work in this way. A small grease leak was found in a bearing, so Norbert Singer and Peter Falk got together with a couple of engineers in a corner of the workshop while I was

driving another car around. I brought it in, and there they were pouring over the problem. Within 20 minutes, they had left by car for the main factory, and a further 20 minutes later they returned with the modified components, stripped each car and fitted them. They were tested three hours later, and the trouble was solved!

What really amazed me is that Herr Singer — for whom I have probably greater admiration than for any engineer I have ever worked with — is so calm. Getting those cars to Le Mans was his baby. Both he and Peter Falk have a tremendous mental ability to cope with situations of stress and handle them. This is a major key to Porsche's success. Most people in similar positions would go round the twist, running the cars for the first time on the Monday before the 24 Hours, but Porsche have the confidence to know that nothing is going to go wrong. Incredible!

Prior to Le Mans, the only endurance testing done on the 956 was at Silverstone. At Ricard, we never did more than 10 laps at a time with the car, so we were not testing reliability until the first race. We knew that the engine had completed 24 hours trouble-free at Le Mans last year. In fact, as soon as the prototype car was brought back from Silverstone, the engineers put it on the rolling road and carried out a 24-hour test, which they didn't tell me about until I actually went to Weissach to try the Le Mans chassis.

I must say the results made me feel a lot happier, because I was very apprehensive for many reasons. Last year was a wonderful experience, particularly as Steve O'Rourke had released me from my contract to drive with Porsche. I had been second at Daytona, second at Silverstone, and then I won Le Mans. This season I was second at Daytona, second at Silverstone, and I was going to go to Le Mans with Porsche . . .

It was also my 13th Le Mans (I was apprehensive about that) and I was very conscious of the need to score a third win. Jacky had won it on five occasions and had three in a row — therefore it is not an impossibility to score three successive wins or even three in your career. It is so much to expect to go to Le Mans and win. I felt sure that one of our cars would do it, but I really did not believe that it would be he and I again.

Each set of drivers was allotted its car a week before

Porsche's third Le Mans

the race — all being to precisely the same specification — and the first batch of engines was installed. The interesting thing was that a lot of people thought, as I know Jochen did, that we had the best engine. Maybe ours was a little better than the others in qualifying, but we never put qualifying tyres on — we ran it purely on Dunlop's race tyres. Everybody was saying, 'We could have got down to your time', but the fact was that we didn't have the time to put the soft rubber on — everyone else did!

We had a problem with the car initially, when I tested it at Weissach. I said to Herr Singer that it seemed to pull; the steering was very heavy on right-handers. We talked about it briefly but I then had to drive another car. We arrived at Le Mans, and it was very difficult to turn in to right-hand corners again and the steering was heavy here and light when turning the other way. This was a bit tricky, so Jacky came in during qualifying to adjust it. I then got in the car and suggested that we should alter the castor, which we did, and this improved the problem. But by this time it was dark on the first night and we had lost a little time.

They put the race engines in after practice — so we had three more engines for the 24 Hours and they were all very similar. During practice we found the rev limiter wasn't working, even though we were not taking it right up there, so they asked me to give the car a run to check it — in the rain on slicks. They sorted it out. I brought it back in again, and parked it.

The next morning they were checking all the engines only to find a problem with ours. They said the only answer was to change the engine again. So by this time the mechanics had put an engine in each car for qualifying; replaced them with the race units; and now found another engine change to be necessary. We therefore had what was probably the seventh best unit in for the race, but then of course it worked well and we won in the end. We had no major dramas whatsoever. Amazing.

The fuel consumption was obviously going to be the greatest problem from the outset — if we were under any kind of pressure. Had anyone been able to push us hard we would have been in all sorts of problems. We had probably enough fuel for another 20 minutes at the end, which is not too great a margin — it would only have been five laps. If we had had to go any faster, or made one fewer fuel stop during the race, we would have been in plenty of trouble.

As it was, we were lapping, I would say, 10 seconds off the 956's ultimate pace in the interest of fuel economy, and at times about 15 seconds down towards the end. Then we dropped our laps to 3m 50s, whereas during the night we were doing consistent 3m 42s and 43s. At Holbert, Hurley Haywood and Jurgen Barth were going very fast but weren't really going under 3m 40s, so I don't think realistically that we could have gone much quicker than 3m 37s with all the traffic and the fuel constraints. I say that, but had we been able to turn the boost up, faster laps were possible. But naturally nobody wanted to stress their car.

> "It was also my 13th Le Mans (I was apprehensive about that) and I was very conscious of the need to score a third win . . . It is so much to go to Le mans and win."

We agreed tactically that we should run faster at the start than we would later on — to show that we were not prepared to sit around as we had at Silverstone — so we went out and the team cars lay in the first three places for most of the way. We really wanted to give the public something to look at, certainly for a few laps, but Jacky's early pace meant that he was only getting 12 or 13 laps to a tank of petrol at that stage: only about 45-50 minutes between stops, and clearly a pace which we could not afford to maintain. When I got in, my task was to establish a pattern of refuelling every 15 laps or so to get back on schedule.

Having got back on to our 57½ minute stops we could then run a bit quicker again. We had turned the boost right down and were running fewer revs, but it was fine to do that because, unfortunately, our competition just did not materialise. It was rather disappointing in that respect.

I was very disappointed in the other major teams. It is not as though you could say we murdered them — I feel we absolutely annihilated the opposition, but the reliability of many of the cars was appalling. Somebody with a good 3-litre or 3.3-litre Ford engine, well put together, should have been well in

> "As Jochen said to me afterwards, what we did right and the other crews did wrong was to keep going steadily. The other cars pitted whenever their drivers wished to report the slightest problem — consequently losing precious minutes to the leading car."

I was very disappointed in the other major teams. It is not as though you could say we murdered them — I feel we absolutely annihilated the opposition, but the reliability of many of the cars was appalling. Somebody with a good 3-litre or 3.3-litre Ford engine, well put together, should have been well in contention. Ford have won Le Mans on numerous occasions, and a well-equipped, well-planned outfit could have been up there. There is no reason at all why not — except that people think they are entering a sprint race . . .

A lot of the Group C cars look very dramatic and appear to be beautifully built, but what is the point if they fall to pieces just as quickly as they went together?

It was a pity for the spectators that they did not get more of a race out of Le Mans. I think they deserved a greater race (as at Silverstone) but it is not our fault that these events ran as they did. If we (Porsche) had fallen out at Le Mans, it would have been a complete disaster. At least Porsche made it a unique race with cars 1-2-3 finishing 1-2-3. That was marvellous for the company as a whole and great for their reputation of reliability, but I think it was very bad for Group C.

Derek Bell in typical pose, concentrating hard.

I know that manufacturers now have a year in which to develop the new cars for the future, and they may now know exactly what has to be done. And it can be done. The Ford, for instance, is already very fast, whereas I don't think our car can become that much quicker. The engineers cannot do much to the Porsche engine other than make it more economical. They are limited to such a degree by the regulations. They might lose a little power to aid fuel consumption for another year, and obviously they will continue to develop the chassis, as everyone does.

I do think that other teams take things much more on a race-to-race basis, rather than realising that Le Mans is the most important event of the year. You must not forget the other races, but you must keep bearing the 24 Hours in mind during a car's development. Will the latest tweak work for Le Mans? If you don't think so, don't bother to do it.

The fuel consumption is the uppermost worry with the new regulations. We were waiting for the fuel light to come on before we stopped. If it lit less than a kilometre from the pits, we'd press the reserve tank and do one more lap. If it came on shortly after them, we had to stop at the end of the lap, but we could drive quite quickly on it. The pick-up worked down to the last cupful of fuel — we tested it.

We had the one engine which had never been run in the car — only on the dyno — and when Jacky went out in the warm-up he found it was not running that well, and they found a fault in the mixture meter. It turned out eventually to be a fault in the little carbon-monoxide gauge we have to set it up. After Jacky's opening stint, they leaned the mixture right off. At night, this adjustment proved far too much and a misfire — our only trouble in the race — set in. Jacky handed the car to me as the air was getting colder, saying that the engine was misfiring like mad, especially down the straight and in the high power range. What we didn't notice was that the oil and intercooler gauges were right down to zero, and that the engine was running very cold. Neither of us mentioned it to the team (so that ducts could be taped) so they treated it purely as a mixture problem. Then they talked about changing the injection pump, a half-hour job. We thought that was it. So I said not to change it unless we were doing desperately bad times.

Of course, all the time the engine is running lean, it is vulnerable to internal damage. Often in such cases the temperature rises but, anyway, when dawn came and the sun came up the temperature rose, and the misfire cleared. By that time we had probably taken the edge off the engine with prolonged running in that condition. It did not stop me having a dice with Al Holbert during the night, though, to maintain the lead which we had held since the 10-hour mark!

As Jochen said to me afterwards, what we did right and the other crews did wrong was to keep going steadily. The other cars pitted whenever their drivers wished to report the slightest problem — consequently losing precious minutes to the leading car.

Le Mans in 1983? It would be unbelievable to pull off a hat-trick and certainly I think it is possible with such a wonderful team. I do have the confidence now. This year, I didn't have the confidence, with a lot of people saying, 'You and Jacky are the favourites again'. Now somehow the pressure is not as strong.

Obviously, I'm very flattered to be paired with Jacky and for some reason we do have this rapport together within the car. Whenever I climbed in to the car after him it was exactly as I had left it three hours earlier — just immaculate, which is as it should be. I've driven with other great drivers, of course, and I am not criticising any of them.

I think Jacky has always been a very lucky driver. I've not always been that lucky — although one can't say three wins at Le Mans is being unlucky.! But the past two years I've had such a good car and such a good team-mate, and we are suited to driving that sort of race. Again, Jacky and I had an extraordinarily good technical team behind us, and our victory is as much a tribute to their skill and efficiency as it is to the Porsche's on-track performance.

A 100 per cent team effort.
Derek Bell was talking to Marcus Pye.

RESULTS

The following tables are not a complete list of results but list the most important results of each race, as follows: first three cars finishing; all class and category wins; subsidiary awards, such as Biennial Cup and Index wins. The tables are in nine columns as follows:

Column 1:
Overall placing.
Colum 2:
Make and nationality of car; nationalities: B Belgium, CS Czechoslovakia, D Germany, F France, GB Great Britain, I Italy, US U.S.A.
Column 3:
Number of cylinders; where appropriate arrangement of engine if other than in-line as follows: F Flat (horizontally opposed), V V, t/s two-stroke.
Column 4:
Capacity of engine in cc.
Column 5:
Names of drivers; quotation marks indicate pseudonym.
Column 6:
Distance covered, in miles.
Column 7:
Average speed, in miles per hour.
Column 8:
Class-winners only: indicates which capacity class won. Note changes in capacity class structure in 1960. NB: Not listed from 1975 onwards.

Column 9:
Category wins – particularly important from 1975 onwards – and subsidiary awards. Abbreviations used: Bi-cup, Biennial Cup; Tri-cup, Triennial Cup; Ind. Perf, Index of Performance; Index T.E., Index of Thermal Efficiency. Categories: 1959: Sport-prototype and Grand Tourisme; 1960–61: Sports Cars and Grand Tourisme; 1962: Experimental Cars and Grand Tourisme (with subsidiary category for under-2,000 cc GT); 1963–65: as 1962 but Prototypes replace Experimental Cars; 1966: as 1963–65 but with added Sports Car category; 1967: as 1966 but under-2,000 cc GT deleted, and under-1,300 cc Sports Car category added; 1968–71: Sports Car, Sports Prototype and Grand Tourisme – last category is called GT Special 1970–71; 1972–74: Group 5 sports cars, Group 4 GT special, Group 2 special touring; 1975: Group 6 sports-prototypes (with subsidiary two-litre class), and GTX – experimental GT cars – in addition to 1972–74 categories; 1976–81: Group 6, Group 5 and Group 4 as in 1975, GTX now unhomologated production GT cars, new class for GTP – Le Mans prototypes, and categories for I.M.S.A and N.A.S.C.A.R cars. Group 2 category deleted. N.A.S.C.A.R category only in 1976. 1981: Group C cars first admitted.
Note: There have not been entrants, or finishers, in all categories and classes every year.

All results listed in the Appendix have as far as possible been checked against official Automobile Club de l'Ouest figures and have been converted from kilometres to miles using 1.60935 kilometres equals 1 mile.

1	2	3	4	5	6	7	8	9
43rd race—1975, 14–15 June. Circuit: 8.475 miles.								
55 cars starting, 30 cars finishing. Fastest lap: C. Craft (De Cadenet-Lola T.380), 130.504 mph								
1	Gulf-Mirage DFV (GB)	V-8	2,986 cc	J. Ickx/D. Bell	2,855.548	118.981		Sports, over two-litres
2	Ligier JS.2 (F)	V-8	2,983 cc	J-F. Lafosse/G. Chasseuil	2,841.770	118.407		
3	Gulf-Mirage DFV (GB)	V-8	2,986 cc	V. Schuppan/J-P. Jaussaud	2,799.193	116.633		
5	Porsche Carrera (D)	F-6	2,992 cc	J. Fitzpatrick/G. van Lennep	2,676.846	111.535		GT Special
10	Porsche Carrera (D)	F-6	2,992 cc	Maurer/Beez/Straehl	2,508.538	104.522		GT Production
15	Porsche Carrera (D)	F-6	2,142 cc	Beguin/Zbinden/Haldi	2,464.490	102.687		GT Experimental
21	Moynet-Simca (F)	4 cyl	1,994 cc	Hoepfner/Mouton/Dacremont	2,286.263	95.261		Sports, under two-litres
27	BMW 2002 (D)	4 cyl	1,990 cc	Brillat/Gagliardi/Degoumois	2,131.774	88.824		Touring Special
44th race—1976, 12–13 June. Circuit: 8.475 miles.								
55 cars starting, 26 cars finishing. Fastest lap: J-P. Jabouille (Alpine-Renault A 442), 136.824 mph								
1	Porsche 936 (D)	F-6	2,142 cc	J. Ickx/G. van Lennep	2,963.882	123.495		Group 6 over two-litres
2	Mirage-DFV GR.8 (GB)	V-8	2,986 cc	J-L. Lafosse/F. Migault	2,871.218	119.634		
3	Lola-DFV T.380 (GB)	V-8	2,996 cc	C. Craft/A. de Cadenet	2,860.715	119.196		
4	Porsche 935 (D)	F-6	2,808 cc	R. Stommelen/M. Schurti	2,809.390	117.058		Group 5
8	Inaltera-DFV (F)	V-8	2,993 cc	H. Pescarolo/J-P. Beltoise	2,587.559	107.815		GT Prototype
12	Porsche Carrera (D)	F-6	2,992 cc	'Segolen'/Ouviere/Gadal	2,477.977	103.249		Group 4
14	Porsche Carrera (D)	F-6	2,992 cc	Laffeach/Rullon Miller/Vaugh	2,402.533	100.106		IMSA
15	Lola-Cosworth T292 (GB)	4 cyl	1,998 cc	F. Trisconi/G. Morand/A. Chevalley	2,370.524	98.772		Group 6 under two-litres
24	BMW CSL (D)	6 cyl	3,003 cc	J-L. Ravenel/J-M. Detrin/J. Ravenel	2,003.017	83.459		Group 2
45th race—1977, 11–12 June. Circuit: 8.475 miles.								
55 cars starting, 20 cars finishing. Fastest lap: J. Ickx (Porsche 936), 140.736 mph								
1	Porsche 936 (D)	F-6	2,142 cc	J. Ickx/H. Haywood/J. Barth	2,902.805	120.950		Group 6 over two-litres
2	Mirage-Renault (GB/F)	V-6	1,999 cc	V. Schuppan/J-P. Jarier	2,808.457	117.019		
3	Porsche 935 (D)	F-6	2,856 cc	C. Ballot-Lena/P. Gregg	2,676.565	111.524		Group 5
4	Inaltera-DFV (F)	V-8	2,993 cc	J. Ragnotti/J. Rondeau	2,675.248	111.469		GT Prototype
6	Chevron-ROC (GB)	4 cyl	1,996 cc	M. Pignard/J. Henry/A. Dufrene	2,575.002	107.292		Group 6 under two-litres & Index T.E.
7	Porsche 934 (D)	F-6	2,991 cc	B. Wollek/P. Gudjian/'Steve'	2,526.529	105.272		Group 4
8	BMW CSL (D)	6 cyl	3,152 cc	J. Xhenceval/P. Dieudonne/S. Dini	2,473.415	103.059		IMSA
46th race—1978, 10–11 June. Circuit: 8.475 miles.								
55 cars starting, 17 cars finishing. Fastest lap: J-P. Jabouille (Renault-Alpine A 443), 142.445 mph								
1	Renault-Alpine A442 (F)	V-6	1,997 cc	D. Pironi/J-P. Jaussaud	3,134.514	130.605		Group 6, over two-litres
2	Porsche 936/78 (D)	F-6	2,140 cc	B. Wollek/J. Barth/J. Ickx	3,087.035	128.626		Index T.E.
3	Porsche 936/77 (D)	F-6	2,140 cc	H. Haywood/P. Gregg/R. Joest	3,070.016	127.917		
5	Porsche 935/77A (D)	F-6	3,000 cc	B. Redman/D. Barbour/J. Paul	2,862.907	119.288		I.M.S.A.
6	Porsche 935/77A (D)	F-6	3,000 cc	J. Busby/C. Cord/R. Knoop	2,853.929	118.914		Group 5
9	Rondeau-DFV M 378 (F)	V-8	2,989 cc	B. Darniche/J. Rondeau/J. Haran	2,497.294	104.054		GT Prototype
11	Chevron-Chrysler B36 (GB)	4 cyl	1,996 cc	M. Pignard/L. Rossiaud/L. Ferrier	2,409.799	100.408		Group 6, under two-litres
12	Porsche Carrera (D)	F-6	2,994 cc	A-C. Verney/X. Lapeyre/F. Servanin	2,372.337	98.847		Group 4
47th race—1979, 9–10 June. Circuit: 8.467 miles.								
55 cars starting, 22 cars finishing. Fastest lap: J. Ickx (Porsche 936), 141.053 mph								
1	Porsche 935 (D)	F-6	2,993 cc	Ludwig/Whittington/Whittington	2,593.556	108.065		Group 5
2	Porsche 935 (D)	F-6	2,993 cc	D. Barbour/P. Newman/R. Stommelen	2,540.041	105.835		I.M.S.A.
3	Porsche 935 (D)	F-6	2,993 cc	L. Ferrier/F. Servanin/F. Trisconi	2,478.177	103.257		
4	Porsche 934 (D)	F-6	2,991 cc	A. Pallavicini/H. Müller/M. Vanoli	2,468.541	102.856		Group 4
5	Rondeau M 379 (F)	V-8	3,000 cc	B. Darniche/J. Ragnotti	2,433.837	101.410		Group 6, over two-litres
14	W.M. P 79 (F)	V-6	2,661 cc	J-D. Raulet/M. Mamers	2,263.994	94.333		GT Prototype
17	Chevron-Ford B 36 (GB)	4 cyl	1,998 cc	A. Charnell/R. Smith/R. Jones	2,189.790	91.241		Group 6, under two-litres

1	2	3	4	5	6	7	8	9

48th race—1980, 14–15 June. Circuit: 8.467 miles.
55 cars starting, 25 cars finishing. Fastest lap: J. Ickx (Porsche 908/80), 138.176 mph

1	Rondeau M 379 B (F)	V-8	2,993 cc	J. Rondeau/J-P. Jaussaud	2,863.280	119.303		Group 6, over two-litres & Index T.E.
2	Porsche 908/80 (D)	F-6	2,140 cc	J. Ickx/R. Joest	2,847.924	118.663		GT Prototype
3	Rondeau M 379 B (F)	V-8	2,998 cc	G. Spice/J-M. Martin/P. Martin	2,789.873	116.244		
5	Porsche 935 K.3 (D)	F-6	3,164 cc	J. Fitzpatrick/B. Redman/R. Barbour	2,688.700	112.029		I.M.S.A
8	Porsche 935 (D)	F-6	2,991 cc	Schornstein/Grohs/von Tschirnhaus	2,652.220	110.509		Group 5
16	Porsche 911 SC (D)	F-6	2,994 cc	T. Perrier/R. Carmillet	2,374.629	98.942		Group 4
17	Chevron-ROC B 36 (GB)	4 cyl	1,994 cc	P. Hesnault/B. Sotty/Laurent	2,342.897	92.620		Group 6, under two-litres

49th race—1981, 13–14 June. Circuit: 8.467 miles.
55 cars starting, 18 cars finishing. Fastest lap: J. Mass (Porsche 936/81), 142.437 mph

1	Porsche 936/81 (D)	F-6	2,649 cc	J. Ickx/D. Bell/J. Barth	2,998.321	124.930		Group 6, over two-litres
2	Rondeau M 379 CL (F)	V-8	2,998 cc	J. Haran/J-L. Schlesser/P. Streiff	2,882.731	120.114		GT Prototype
3	Rondeau M 379 CL (F)	V-8	2,998 cc	G. Spice/F. Migault	2,840.405	118.350		
4	Porsche 935 K 3 (D)	F-6	3,122 cc	J. Cooper/C. Bourgoignie/D. Wood	2,800.833	116.701		Group 5
5	Ferrari BB-512 (I)	F-12	4,942 cc	J-C. Andruet/C. Ballot-Lena	2,777.167	115.715		I.M.S.A GTX
11	Porsche 924 Carrera (D)	4 cyl	1,983 cc	Schurti/A. Rouse	2,673.724	111.355		I.M.S.A. GTO
17	Porsche 934 (D)	F-6	2,943 cc	V. Bertapelle/T. Perrier/B. Salam	2,322.328	96.763		Group 4
18	Lola-BMW T.298 (GB)	4 cyl	1,998 cc	J-P. Grand/Y. Courage	2,308.226	96.175		Group 6, under two-litres & Index T.E.

50th race—1982, 19–20 June. Circuit: 8.467 miles.
55 cars starting, 18 cars finishing. Fastest lap: J. Rondeau (Rondeau M.382), 140.527 mph

1	Porsche 956 (D)	F-6	2,649 cc	J. Ickx/D. Bell	3,044.140	126.839		Group C
2	Porsche 956 (D)	F-6	2,649 cc	J. Mass/V. Schuppan	3,018.696	125.779		
3	Porsche 956 (D)	F-6	2,649 cc	H. Haywood/A. Holbert/J. Barth	2,883.216	120.134		
4	Porsche 935 (D)	F-6	2,676 cc	J. Fitzpatrick/D. Hobbs	2,788.810	116.200		I.M.S.A. GTX
8	Porsche 935 K.3 (D)	F-6	3,121 cc	J. Couper/P. Smith/C. Bourgoignie	2,676.430	111.518		Group 5
13	Porsche 934 (D)	F-6	2,994 cc	R. Cleare/T. Dron/R. Jones	2,466.970	102.790		Group 4
16	Porsche 924 GTR (D)	4 cyl	2,008 cc	J. Busby/H. Bundy	2,307.880	96.162		I.M.S.A. GT